HANDBOOK ON
JAPANESE
MILITARY FORCES

HANDBOOK ON
JAPANESE
MILITARY FORCES

U.S. War Department

With a new Introduction by David Isby
and
Afterword by Jeffrey Ethell

Louisiana State University Press
Baton Rouge and London

Library of Congress Cataloging-in-Publication Data
Handbook on Japanese military forces / by US War Department:
with a new introduction by David C. Isby and afterword by
Jeffrey Ethell.
p.   cm.
ISBN 0-8071-2013-8 (pbk. : alk paper)
1. Japan – Armed Forces – Handbooks, manuals, etc.
2. Japan – Armed Forces – History – World War, 1939–1945.
I. United States. War Dept.
UA847.H36   1991   91-20930
355'.00952'09044 – dc20   CIP

INTRODUCTION

"Fear is the beginning of understanding," said General William Tecumseh Sherman, the man credited with saying 'war is hell', who marched to the sea to cut the Confederacy in two during the American Civil War and who obviously knew what he was talking about. TM–E 30–480 *Handbook on Japanese Military Forces*, 1 October, 1944, is an example of understanding that started in fear. It represents the culmination and distillation of years of combined efforts by Allied intelligence to understand the ground and air forces of the Empire of Japan as they existed in the course of the Second World War.

For those who look to go beyond broad generalizations in their understanding of how the Japanese land and air forces made war in the Pacific, this edition of the *Handbook on Japanese Military Forces* is the most accurate and accessible English-language source. No valid military force is static. They are all forces in the course of change and *Handbook on Japanese Military Forces* shows, in its late-war analysis, how the Japanese forces had evolved under the harsh Darwinism of the battlefield, first in China and then against the Allies.

Handbook on Japanese Military Forces is a fascinating and important book because it serves two purposes. First, it is a thorough and accurate guide to Japanese land and air power. It sets out the organizations, weapons, equipment and tactics in use at each level of command, from the national command authority on down. To show how these different elements were integrated together, it details the chain of command, from the highest national level to the rifle squads on the firing line. These elements are the heart of any military force, historical or current, and determine whether or not it will be successful on the battlefield.

Second, *Handbook on Japanese Military Forces* is evidence of how the Allied perception of the Japanese way of war had evolved in the course of the war. The disdain of the pre-war years – the popular images of thick-spectacled buck-tooth pilots in obsolete aircraft – was matched at higher levels by a lack of understanding not only of Japanese strategic objectives, but of the capabilities of the military forces that were to be used to attain many of those objectives. In the six months following Pearl Harbor, the cost of this lack of understanding was brought home to the Allies. Then, fear-driven threat inflation started to give way to understanding as the modern and far-reaching intelligence and analytical capabilities of the Allies were first created and then focussed on Japan.

The first editions of *Handbook on Japanese Military Forces* appeared in 1942 to meet real and immediate needs, being carried ashore with U.S. Marine units on Guadalcanal. The need for haste often precluded thorough analysis. The public also wanted to know about their new enemy and how they had achieved their remarkable successes of 1941–2. Penguin, for example, published an original 'special', *How the Jap Army Fights* in 1942, which presented a mix of insight and ignorance. This made it little different from its confidential official counterparts.

Understanding of the Japanese military was hindered by the fact that military analysis in general, and that of Japan in particular, had been too often lacking before 1942. The systematic study of actual or potential enemies, the dissemination of the results of this analysis, the need to guide the thinking and direct the training of those who would be doing the fighting and providing data on current and future threats that research and development must counter are among the daily work of armed forces and defense ministries throughout the developed world today. Before 1942 these needs were often not met, especially in the English-speaking world. Neglect of defense in the 1920s and 30s had included a neglect of military intelligence. Failures in intelligence and analysis fueled further failures of statecraft and grand strategy, of tactics, and in the development and procurement of weapons and equipment.

The failures and limitations of pre-war intelligence and analysis were especially significant in dealing with Japan. The Japanese military, despite its lengthy war in China, had been much more of a closed book to the Allies than had been the forces of their European enemies. The high-level intelligence failures that led to the whole chain of Allied strategic decisions culminating in the surprise of Pearl Harbor had their counterparts in other elements of intelligence. For example, the performance of the Japanese Navy's Mitsubishi A6M2 Type Zero fighter came as a surprise that left Allied aircraft burning across Asia and the Pacific. Yet reports of the Zero's development and subsequent combat in China had been received by Allied intelligence for over a year before Pearl Harbor and were by no means ignored. But they were not put to effective use. A few energetic combat leaders used this intelligence input and set to work, on their own initiative rather than responding to high-level concern, devising effective anti-Zero tactics. Overall, however, not only did Allied intelligence organizations fail to fully analyze information, but those holding command in the field failed to effectively act as a result of receiving this analysis.

The results of these two-sided intelligence failures – intelligence organizations not analyzing and understanding, and the commanders in the field not acting – were repeated at both high and low level in the opening stages of the Pacific War. The publication of successive editions of *Handbook on Japanese Military Forces* was intended to help prevent such failures and their cost in battles and lives from being repeated.

By 1944, the Japanese defeat had started in both the Pacific and Burma. Allied fighting men had learned that the Japanese – though not the demonic figures of 1942 capable of incredible combat feats as well as off-battlefield brutality – had strengths to match their emerging weakness. Fear in 1942 had led to understanding in 1944. That understanding is represented by this edition of *Handbook on Japanese Military Forces*.

The strengths of the Japanese military led to it fighting hard until the order to surrender was given. Its weakness – and the weakness of the national strategy that directed it and the national economy that attempted to sustain it – guaranteed that surrender was an order that would, inevitably, have to be given, either as a result of invasion or, as it turned out, of bombardment and blockade.

These strengths and weakness, at both high and low level, in organization, tactics, weapons and equipment, are detailed in *Handbook on Japanese Military Forces* which is, for a wartime product, both accurate and impartial. It was the definitive edition of this publication. Dated October 1944, it was to be kept as current as possible, which accounts for its original looseleaf format with chapters paginated independently to facilitate easy replacement with updated information.

Issue of this edition largely took place in early 1945. One former Marine intelligence officer recalls receiving his copy of *Handbook on Japanese Military Forces* when he signed for his maps of Iwo Jima as he embarked on an assault transport. It was a book studied with intense interest on the voyage northwest, and used, along with more specific intelligence reports, to prepare briefings for the officers and NCOs who would be leading the Marines ashore into one of the fierce battles of the Pacific war.

Accuracy in a book such as *Handbook on Japanese Military Forces* was more than a scholarly goal. It was literally a matter of life and death on the battlefield. It is accurate because, by 1944, the Allies had not only encountered a broad range of Japanese forces in battle but had the benefit of the full range of wartime intelligence gathering and analysis, including captured individuals and documents. It is impartial because, as a wartime publication intended for those doing the fighting, there was no larger political or bureaucratic agenda being served other than the obvious one of winning the war. The authors were not seeking to secure larger budgets for the armed forces or alert an indifferent public to the Japanese threat.

Handbook on Japanese Military Forces was compiled by a Washington-based committee of military officers, integrating the results of other teams each responsible for different sections. While a U.S. Army publication, it included substantial input from the Marines as well as British and Australian intelligence, as is obvious from the contents. This committee-style compilation, together with the wide range of institutions involved in updating this edition from earlier ones, makes it unlikely that any one view would dominate.

The circumstances of writing *Handbook on Japanese Military Forces* were such that its intended users could rely on it in combat. Fifty years after Pearl Harbor, others interested in the Japanese military can rely on it as well. *Handbook on Japanese Military Forces* still represents the best single reference source on the wartime Japanese military available in the English language. There has been no fully revised postwar edition, incorporating declassified Allied and Japanese holdings, of *How the Jap Army Fights* or scores of more worthwhile publications, including *Handbook on Japanese Military Forces*.

It may seem strange that perhaps the most valuable single English-language reference source on Japanese military forces is dated 1944. However, despite the rivers of ink that have flowed as a result of the Second World War and despite the existence of some excellent books, the war against Japan has not received its share of writing in comparison with other subjects. The trans-Pacific nature of the fighting has led to much of the research concentrating on naval and air topics, which also has the advantage of focussing on interesting hardware in the form of warships and combat aircraft. But for information on ground forces in general, and on organization and tactics in particular, the researcher is left with *Handbook on Japanese Military Forces*.

That this is the case is not surprising. Part of the reason for both the slow and painful process of the Allies moving from fear to understanding in 1942–4 and for researchers to move beyond these efforts in post-war writing has been language. In 1942, there were simply not enough Japanese-speakers to understand or use the intelligence that was coming in. The teams that put together *Handbook on Japanese Military Forces* had in large part, been taught their Japanese by their respective military forces in the preceding months. Today, researchers who may have the knowledge of military forces and history to put the information in context still often do not have the necessary command of Japanese to use post-war histories or the surviving original documents in Japanese archives (although copies of some, and translations of others, are held in the U.S.).

Even for those who have the language skills, Japanese sources are difficult to locate or consult outside Japan. Their size, while offering scope for wide-focus historical research, makes ready reference more difficult. There are over 125,000 surviving original documents in the Japanese archives. The 'Series of Military History of World War II', the Japanese official history, was originally published as a 96-volume project in 1966–76 and has since been expanded. These volumes stress narrative more than military analysis. Again, the organization, tactics, and capabilities of the Japanese military as detailed in *Handbook on Japanese Military Forces* have value, even to supplement research based on thorough use of Japanese-language literature.

The teams of intelligence analysts that the Allied war effort applied to understanding the Japanese military synthesized the material available to them down to one volume that can be carried in the field. It is hard to imagine how comparable levels of effort on the subject could be marshalled today, even by the most perceptive and devoted researcher. *Handbook on Japanese Military Forces* has errors of detail and missing weapons systems. But the basic thrust of the book as a study of the wartime Japanese military remains valid, which is an impressive achievement for the 'temporary professionals' who produced it.

'Mirror imaging' is a besetting sin of much military analysis, and the experienced researcher will always look for it when using a source that examines other peoples' forces or systems. *Handbook on Japanese Military Forces* has avoided much 'mirror imaging', and has shown that the forces it described were a uniquely Japanese response to Japanese conditions. The forces proved, in the end, to be an inadequate response, but given the basically insoluble nature of the Japanese Empire's strategic and economic problems – which are outside the scope of the current volume but which have been documented elsewhere – it is unlikely that they could have been otherwise. US military intelligence personnel, writing to inform US military officers about their enemy, would be remiss if they did implicitly or explicitly make reference to US practices and capabilities, simply because that is what both would be familiar with, but this is different from seeing the Japanese military as but the US military in different uniforms and with different equipment.

One area of divergence that is seen implicitly in looking at the force that appears in *Handbook on Japanese Military Forces* in comparison with the US and Allied forces that defeated them is the relative neglect of service support functions in the Japanese forces. Where the Allies expended prodigious resources and accomplished great feats of engineering and organization to make it possible to operate modern military forces in remote places, *Handbook on Japanese Military Forces* shows forces that existed through make-do and improvisation. This approach paid off spectacularly well in 1941–2, but when this edition of *Handbook on Japanese Military Forces* appeared, the Japanese were paying the price for their neglect of logistics, communications, and much that made the Second World War a modern conflict. Part of the reason was the mindset of many Japanese commanders, especially in the army. They saw themselves as warriors, conquerors and samurai. The job of getting men their food and equipment was not what a warrior did. The fact that the economy could never produce enough food or materiel certainly discouraged them from looking to these elements as deliverance from their strategic and tactical problems.

These deficiencies underline the uneasy mix of bamboo spear and modern technology that characterized so much of the Japanese war effort. The weapons and equipment detailed in *Handbook on Japanese Military Forces* also show this same divergence. At a theoretical or prototype level, much of what the Japanese considered was comparable with anything in the world. Japan had done research on developing the atomic bomb (before resource short-ages and a laboratory explosion curtailed the project), heat-seeking anti-shipping guided missiles, and jet and rocket powered fighter aircraft (using German technology). Yet their fighting forces – especially on the ground – were forced to rely on improvisation and bravery rather than applied technology. The inability to design, produce, and deploy sufficient effective weapons led to tactics such as the well-known practice, in Burma, of substituting, in place of unavailable anti-tank mines, soldiers stationed in spider holes armed with an aircraft bomb and a rock with which they were to strike the fuze as a tank rolled over them. The Allied forces that fought the Japanese in the last year of the Second World War encountered many such tactical adaptations, but less technical innovation.

However, the ability to extract results from limited resources in terms of both manpower and materiel that characterized the Japanese war effort is evident in this volume. The Japanese war economy partially compensated for its weakness by a high degree of mobilization. The Japanese also squeezed all they could from their manpower pool. As a result, Japan organized more divisions than did the United States. But while the number of divisions may have been impressive, the ability to equip them with adequate weapons and sustain them on distant battlefields was absent. Looking at numbers – of divisions, of weapons, of personnel – is never an adequate substitute for thorough analysis. *Handbook on Japanese Military Forces* aims to show the substance behind the numbers. Doing the same for today's armed forces – friends and opponents alike – is a never-ending yet vital task.

It is significant that this reprint edition is appearing in 1991, a year that not only saw the 50th anniversary of the start of the Pacific War but also the conclusion of the Gulf War. There, once again, General Sherman was proven right. The Iraqi military seemed formidable when it rolled into Kuwait the year before – a half-million of the victors of the long war with Iran armed from the arsenals of the world – was revealed, after six weeks of airstrikes, to be a collection of ragged and hungry men and boys commanded by absent bunglers. Unlike the Japanese who opposed the grandfathers of those fighting in the Gulf, the Iraqis made no speciality of desperate resistance. But as they did when facing the Japanese, the Allies, once again starting in fear, ended in understanding their enemy.

David C. Isby
Washington, D.C., 1991

CONTENTS

NEW INTRODUCTION by David C. Isby
AFTERWORD by Jeffrey L. Ethell

FOREWORD

1. This handbook on Japanese Military Forces (TM–E 30–480) has been prepared by the United States War Department, with the assistance and cooperation of representatives from the following headquarters:

> British War Office.
> General Headquarters, Southwest Pacific Area.
> Southeast Asia Command, and General Headquarters, India.
> Headquarters, United States Army Forces in South Pacific Area.
> Headquarters, United States Army Forces in Central Pacific Area.
> Allied Land Headquarters, Australia.

In general, it represents the agreed views of these headquarters at the time this hand book was written.

For the most part, the material contained in this handbook is based on information obtained in operations to 30 June 1944. This has been supplemented by study of Japanese Army manuals and other official and unofficial documents published by the Japanese before and after the beginning of hostilities, and by reports and observations of American and British military attachés and observers.

2. PURPOSE AND SCOPE. The purpose of this handbook, which constitutes a revision of TM 30–480, 21 September 1942, is to give in a single publication the broad outlines as well as pertinent details of the organization, equipment, and training of the Japanese Army. In addition, Japanese tactical doctrines and techniques, as set forth in their manuals and observed in action, are discussed. The handbook is not intended to be complete or final; detailed information on particular subjects may be found in the special publications already available or in preparation by the various agencies and commands concerned.

3. LANGUAGE DIFFICULTIES. In cases where confusion might result, Romaji or the romanized form of the Japanese terms is given, together with the translation. A Japanese-English and English-Japanese glossary of the more important items is also included.

Because of differences in American, British, and Japanese terminology for certain army units, a translation of the Japanese terms has been used throughout. Thus units of all arms and services are called regiments, battalions, companies, platoons, and squads (sections). For American readers the change in terminology should cause no particular confusion except that some Japanese regimental organizations, especially in the Cavalry and the Engineers, correspond more closely to battalions in that they contain only three or four companies.

Since the handbook is intended for use by both American and British forces, commonly accepted or understood military terms of both nations have been used. Where no common term exists, both British and American terms appear, the British in parentheses.

4. REVISIONS. It is intended to keep the handbook up to date with necessary revisions and corrections as further information becomes available. In order that this may be facilitated, it is requested that all suggestions for changes or additions be communicated to the Military Intelligence Division, War Department, Washington 25, D. C.

WAR DEPARTMENT TECHNICAL MANUAL

TM-E 30-480

This manual supersedes TM 30-480, 21 September 1942.

HANDBOOK ON

JAPANESE MILITARY

FORCES

WAR DEPARTMENT • 1 OCTOBER 1944

United States Government Printing Office

Washington : 1944

Figure 1. Japanese infantry soldier.

CHAPTER I

RECRUITMENT AND TRAINING

Section I. GENERAL

1. ARMS AND SERVICES. The personnel of the Japanese Army is classified as follows:

a. Line branch (Heika). The various arms—Infantry, Cavalry, Artillery, Engineers, Air Service, and Transport—since 1940 have been grouped under the generic term of Line Branch. This change permits the easy shifting of personnel from one arm to another, but it has not changed the basic functions of the component arms. The personnel is listed without specific designation—that is, Army captain instead of Army Infantry captain.

b. Services (Kakubu). These include the Medical, Veterinary, Intendance, Technical, Judicial, and Military Band departments. Personnel is listed by service—for example, Army veterinary captain or Army technician corporal.

c. Military police branch (Kempei). Formerly listed with the arms, the Military Police branch continues to use a specific designation for personnel—for example, Army Military Police major.

d. Categories for assignment. The following table shows the official categories (Heishu) used for assignments in the Japanese Army. It will be noted that the categories differ slightly for officers and enlisted men—for example, privates are not assigned to chemical warfare, meteorological, and special motor transport, but are detached from other units for such service.

Officers	Warrant and noncommissioned officers	Privates
Arms		
Infantry	In the Line Branch they are classified according to the type of unit in which they serve.	Infantry.
Chemical warfare		Tank.
Mechanized (including cavalry)		Cavalry.
Field and mountain (light) artillery		Field (light) artillery.
		Mountain (light) artillery.
		Horse (light) artillery.
		Intelligence.
Medium artillery		Medium artillery.
Heavy artillery		Heavy artillery.
Antiaircraft defense		Antiaircraft defense.
Balloon		Balloon.
Engineers		Engineers.
Air (Kōkū)		Air (Hikō).
Meteorological.		
Railway		Railway.
Signal (Denshin)		Signal (Tsūshin).
Transport		Transport.
Special motor transport.		
Infantry mortar		Infantry mortar.
Services		
Technical department:	Technical department:	Technical department:
Technician	Technician	Technician.
Air technician	Air technician	Air technician
Intendance department:	Intendance department:	
Finance	Finance.	
	Construction technician.	
	Intendance technician.	
Medical department:	Medical Department:	Medical department:
Surgeon.		
Pharmacy.		
Sanitary.	Sanitary	Sanitary.
Dental	Ward master.	
Veterinary department:	Veterinary department:	
Veterinary.		
Veterinary duties	Veterinary duties.	
Judicial department.		
Military Band	Military Band.	

2. RANKS. Below is a tabulation of the various grades in the Japanese Army, their Japanese names, and their normal command. It should be noted that the Japanese have no brigadier-general rank. It also will be noted that one new grade has been added for enlisted men, a rank corresponding to lance corporal but listed among privates (*Hei*) rather than among noncommissioned officers (*Kashikan*). The rank of field marshal (*Gensui*) is not included in the list, since it is an honorary rank granted by the Emperor to generals.

Grade	Name	Normal command
General	Taishō	Army commander.
Lieutenant general	Chūjo	Division commander.
Major general	Shōshō	Infantry group or brigade commander.
Colonel	Taisa	Regimental commander.
Lieutenant colonel	Chūsa	Second-in-command of regiment.
Major	Shōsa	Battalion commander.
Captain	Tai-i	Company commander.
First lieutenant	Chū-i	Platoon commander.
Second lieutenant	Shō-i	Platoon commander.
Warrant officer	Jun-i	Command and administrative duties.
Sergeant major	Sōchō	First sergeant.
Sergeant	Gunsō	Squad (section) leader.
Corporal	Gochō	Squad (section) leader.
Lance corporal (leading private).	Heichō	
Superior private	Jōtōhei	
First-class private	Ittōhei	
Second-class private	Nitōhei	

Section II. CONSCRIPTION SYSTEM

1. GENERAL. a. In peacetime all male Japanese subjects between the ages of 17 and 40 are subject to service in the Armed Forces. Some may postpone their service, but only those seriously disabled and certain criminals are exempted by law. Since all Japanese are obliged by law to attend primary school for 6 years, this is the minimum educational standard for the Army. The 20-year-olds were examined yearly and classified according to fitness for service. From those fit for active service, the desired number was inducted into the Army and given 2 years' training. All others were put into a reserve designed for furnishing replacements and

given a small amount of training. Those classified as fit for limited service were given no training but were put into the 2d National Army, where they, as well as the boys between 17 and 20 years of age, were liable to call in case of emergency.

b. Under the stress of war, many modifications have occurred. The term of enlistment has been prolonged to 3 years and more, depending upon the circumstances. Reservists of various categories have been called up as needed to form new units or to furnish replacements for units in the field. The extent to which men assigned to the 2d National Army have been used is not clear. The recruits continue to be called up, but the training given them usually takes the form of 3 months in Japan proper and as much more in Japan or occupied areas as circumstances require. (See fig. 2.)

2. CONSCRIPTION SYSTEM AS OF 1941. a. Conscription classes. Every Japanese male is subject to military service. If a youth's twentieth birthday occurs before 2 December, he reports and is examined for service in the 16 April–31 July period preceding his birthday. If his twentieth birthday occurs after 2 December, he reports and is examined in the 16 April–31 July period following his birthday. He is given physical and mental examinations and classified according to his fitness for military service in the following manner:

Class A—Not less than 1.52 meters (5 ft.) in height, and in good physical condition. *Available for active service.*
Class B–1. Taller than 1.5 meters (4 ft. 11 in.) but under the standard of Class A. *Available for active service.*
Class B–2—Same as B–1, but with poorer hearing and eyesight. *Available for 1st Conscript Reserve.*
Class B–3—Same as B–2, but with poorer eyesight and general physical condition. *Available for 2d Conscript Reserve.*
Class C—(a) Same height as B–3, but in poorer physical condition. (b) Of 1.45 meters (4 ft. 9 in.) to 1.5 meters (4 ft. 11 in.) in height, and not suffering from a disabling ailment. *Available for service in the National Army; assigned to 2d National Army.*
Class D—(a) Less than 1.45 meters in height. (b) Suffering from certain specific ailments which are not readily improved by treatment. *Rejected as unfit for service.*
Class F—Suffering from a temporary ailment. *Reëxamined yearly.*

Enough men from Classes A and B–1 are chosen to fill the requirements of the Armed Forces, and the others are put in the Conscript Reserve, along with men from Classes B–2 and B–3. All men of Class C automatically go into the 2d National Army, along with those between 17 and 20 who are not in the Armed Forces.

b. Active service conscripts (Genekihei). Those men who are assigned to active service in a given year are called to the colors for a period of 2 years as of 1 December of that year. They have already been classified according to physical condition, aptitude, and training, and allotted accordingly to the various arms and services, while certain promising individuals have been earmarked as officer material. Training begins on various dates from 1 December and lasts until November of the second year. Upon completion of 2 years of active service, trainees are assigned to the First Reserve (Yobieki) for 15 years 4 months. During that time they may be called for training for five periods up to 35 days each, or for fewer periods

are subject to an annual inspection muster, they, too, enter the 1st National Army until they reach the age of 40. The Conscript Reserve is divided into the 1st Conscript Reserve and the 2d Conscript Reserve, the distinction between the two being based purely on the physical qualifications of the men.

d. National Army conscripts (Kokumin-hei). The 1st National Army is composed of men between the ages of 37 and 40 years who have served in the First Reserve and the Conscript Reserve and who are therefore either fully or partly trained. The 2d National Army is composed

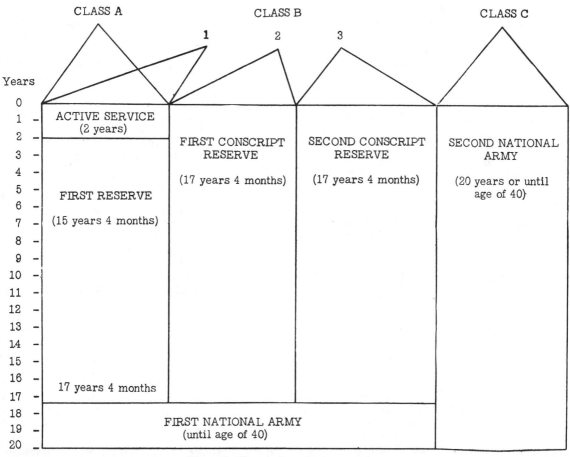

Figure 2. Classes of service in peacetime.

if any tour of duty is prolonged as much as 50 days. While in reserve they are also subject to the annual inspection muster. After this service in the First Reserve, they go into the 1st National Army until they reach the age of 40.

c. Conscript, or replacement, reservists (Hojuhei). These are made up of men from Classes B–2 and B–3, and from those in Classes A and B–1 who are not needed to fill the yearly quota of the standing army. They may be summoned for a period of training not to exceed 180 days, and after 17 years 4 months, during which time they

mainly of men who have been classified as fit only for limited service (Class C). They are given no training but are subject to call in emergency. Men between 17 and 20 years of age who are not in the Armed Forces are, automatically, also a part of the 2d National Army.

e. Exemption and deferment. No exemption is allowed by law except for criminals and the permanently disabled. Japanese living abroad, except those in Manchuria and China, may request postponement of examination annually for a period of 1 year, and unless they return to Japan for more than 90 days at a time they will be excused from military service upon reaching the age of 37 years. When a man's enlistment will work a hardship on his family, his service may be deferred for 2 years, and if the distress lasts until he is 37 years of age, he is excused from service. Students who have not finished their education may postpone their service up to various ages, depending upon the school they attend, but in no instance beyond 26 years of age.

f. Reduction and extension. Graduates of normal schools may have their terms of service shortened by not more than 60 days, and graduates of youth schools (sec. IV, par. 1a) by an indefinite period. The terms of all conscripts may be lengthened in cases of necessity.

g. Volunteers. Two kinds of volunteers are recognized by law: males between the ages of 17 and 20 years, over 1.60 meters (5 feet 2.8 inches) in height, and in Class A or B–1 as to physical condition; and conscripts who volunteer for immediate service without waiting to be selected. A special Army volunteer system was established for Koreans in 1938 and for Formosans in 1942. There is also an extensive apprentice system which trains youthful volunteers for technical work in both Army and Navy.

3. RECENT CHANGES IN THE CONSCRIPTION SYSTEM. a. Age limits. The military age has been lowered to 19, and the liability for service extended to 31 March of the year in which the subject becomes 45.

b. Deferment. Deferment has been cancelled for all students except those in specified types of study, mainly technical or scientific; and for Japanese in the southern regions occupied by the Japanese Army, where, as formerly for Japanese in Manchuria and China, examinations are conducted at nearby military headquarters or consulates.

c. Conscription of Koreans. Military conscription of Koreans has been decreed, to begin in 1944, and of Formosans, to begin in 1945. Koreans and Formosans have been recruited in increasing numbers during the past few years as civilian laborers under the direct supervision of the Army and the Navy. These laborers, who receive no military training, are used in construction corps.

d. Exemption of specialists and technicians. It is reported that exemption from military service now is granted to specialist and skilled technicians, especially in airplane industries, arsenals, and munition factories.

e. Term of service. The nominal term of service is now 3 years.

Section III. PROCUREMENT OF OFFICERS

1. COMMISSIONED OFFICERS. a. General. (1) There are two general classifications of officer personnel in the Japanese Army: Regular

Army officers and reserve officers. There are three distinct types of officers, depending upon their background and education.

(*a*) Those who have graduated through the full course at the Japanese Military Academy.

(*b*) Those who have obtained commissions either through the reserve officer candidate courses after serving in the ranks or direct from technical institutions.

(*c*) Former warrant and noncommissioned officers who have risen from the ranks.

(2) All candidates for commission serve as probational officers with their assigned units for a period of 2 to 6 months after completion of training.

b. Regular Army officers. These may be further classified according to their training as follows:

(1) Graduates of the Military Academy and the Air Academy as officers of the line branch.

(2) Graduates of technical and scientific institutions and of the Intendance School as officers of the services. Most of these are selected while still in school and are educated at government expense in specified universities and colleges which offer stipulated curricula. University graduates receive their commissions as first lieutenant.

(3) Selected warrant and noncommissioned officers in the active service under 38 years of age who became candidates for commission (Shōi Kōhosha) and received 1-year courses at the Military Academy, the Air Academy, the Military Police school, or other Army schools. In peacetime they do not usually advance beyond the grade of captain because of retirement for age.

c. Reserve officers. (1) These are made up chiefly of Class A reserve officer candidates (Kōshu Kambu Kōhosei) who have passed the necessary course. They are drawn from regular conscripts who have certain educational qualifications (formerly the equivalent of 2 years at high school, now lower). After 3 months of training in their unit, they become candidates, and after a further 3 months they are classified by examination into "A" candidates, those suitable for officers, and "B" candidates, those suitable for noncommissioned officers. The "A" candidates then are sent to one of the regular courses for reserve officer candidates. (Sec. IV, par. 3). Upon receiving a commission, in time of peace, they usually pass into the reserve from which they may be called to active duty in time of war. These reserve officers recalled to active duty (Shōshu Shōkō) comprise a large proportion of Japanese officers in the present war.

(2) There are recent announcements of a new system for training special reserve officer candidates by which boys between 15 and 20 years of age, with educations equivalent to the third year of middle school, may become noncommissioned officers at the end of 1½ years' training. Then they become eligible for selection for training to become reserve officers or, by special examination, Regular Army officers. The branches open to the candi-

dates are air, shipping troops, signal troops, technicians, and air technicians.

d. Special volunteer officers (Tokubetsu Shigan Shōkō). Until recently these were taken from field and company officers in the reserve who were allowed to volunteer for active service for a period of 2 years, and for additional periods of 1 year until they attained specified age limits. According to recent information, this designation appears now to be given regularly to young reserve officer candidates after they have served a probationary period with troops. Special volunteer officers may qualify by examination for a 1-year course at the Military Academy, after which they become special volunteer regular officers and may rise to be majors.

2. WARRANT AND NONCOMMISSIONED OFFICERS.
Warrant officers (Junshikan) are usually selected by the promotion of noncommissioned officers and are treated as officers. There are only three ranks of noncommissioned officer (Kashikan): sergeant major; sergeant; and corporal. In addition to those obtained by regular promotion and those who are recalled to duty from the reserve, noncommissioned officers are recruited mainly from the following sources:

a. Noncommissioned officer schools. Conscripts who after about 3 months' active service in the Army volunteer to become noncommissioned officers and after 9 additional months in special training with troops are selected to become noncommissioned officer candidates (Kashikan Kōhosha). They are then given a period of training, formerly 1 year but now shortened, at one of the noncommissioned officer schools (Kyōdō Gakkō) or at one of the Army branch schools or service schools.

b. Class "B" reserve officer candidates.

c. Apprentices. Apprentices in the various units open to Army Youth Soldiers (Rikugun Shōnenhei)—see section IV, par. 1.

Section IV. TRAINING

1. PRECONSCRIPTIONAL TRAINING. a.
In schools. In Japan military indoctrination begins from infancy. Formal regimentation and training begin at about the age of 8 years, when, beginning with the third year of primary school, all boys are given semimilitary training by their teachers. Those going on to middle school, higher school, college, or university receive military training under Regular Army officers. In peacetime this amounts to 2 or more hours per week with 4 to 6 days of annual maneuvers, but recently the amount of time devoted to military subjects has been greatly increased. Those who take up employment after finishing primary school receive considerable military training at youth schools (Seinen Gakko) set up for their particular benefit by the Government. Aviation training in schools, particularly in the use of gliders,

has recently received much emphasis. Numerous courses of purely military nature are being added to the curriculum in order to turn the middle schools into a training camp for cadets, and the universities and higher schools into military academies for reserves.

b. In Army apprentice units. An Army apprentice system to procure trained noncommissioned officers in technical fields at ages below the conscription minimum has grown rapidly in recent years, especially in aviation. The Japanese Navy and Merchant Marine have also developed extensive training of a similar nature. The Army apprentices, called Army Youth Soldiers (Rikugun Shōnenhei), are primary school graduates who begin their apprentice training at the age of 14 or 15 years (lowered from 15 or 16 years in 1943). At some point in their training they are inducted into the Army as youth soldiers with the rank of superior private, serve as lance corporals (leading private) for a probationary period of 6 months after graduation, and then become corporals. These apprentices take one of the following courses:

(1) *Aviation (Shōnen Hikōhei).* The usual course lasts 3 years. After a first year at a general aviation school at Tokyo or Otsu, all students are divided into three groups. Pilots go to Utsunomiya or Kumagai, signalmen to Air Signal School, and mechanics to Tokorozawa or Gifu. They spend 2 years at one of these special schools, the last year as youth soldiers in the Army. Those with special qualifications may omit the first year and go directly to flying school at Tachiarai or maintenance school at Gifu.

(2) *Signal (Shōnen Tsūshinhei).* Two years at the Army Youth Signal School.

(3) *Tank (Shōnen Senshahei).* Two years at Army Youth Tank School near Mt. Fuji.

(4) *Artillery (Shōnen Hōhei).* Two years at the Army Field Artillery School, the Army Heavy Artillery School, or the Army Air Defense School.

(5) *Ordnance.* There is a 2-year course at the Army Ordnance School similar to the apprentice courses described above.

2. CONSCRIPT TRAINING (see sec. II).
a. In peacetime the training of men assigned to active service (Classes A and B–1) covers a period of 2 years. The first year for the infantry is usually divided into four periods as follows:

January to May.	Recruit training. This includes general instruction, squad (section) training, bayonet training, and target practice. In February a march of 5 days, with bivouacking at night, is held to train men in endurance of cold.
June and July.	Target practice, field works, platoon and company training, and bayonet training. Marching 20 miles a day.

| August. | Company and battalion training, field work, combat firing, swimming, and bayonet fighting. Marching 25 miles a day. |
| October and November. | Battalion and regimental training. Combat firing. Autumn maneuvers. |

b. It will be noted from the above program how the infantry training progresses from the smallest unit, the squad (section), to platoon, company, battalion, and regimental training, and culminates in combined maneuvers at the end of the year. In the second year, the periods of training are similar, but more time is allotted to specialist training in the respective branches.

c. Throughout the course of training, special attention is given to the inculcation of "morale" or spiritual instruction. The "Imperial Rescript to Soldiers," issued by the Emperor Meiji on 4 January 1882, is frequently read to the men, and the five principles of military ethics contained therein— loyalty, courtesy, courage, truthfulness, and frugality—are much emphasized.

d. First and Second Conscript reserves have to undergo a 6 months' period of training. The training is not so intensive as that given to active service men, but nevertheless endeavors to cover, in a comparatively shorter time, all that the active service men have learned in their 2-year course.

e. In peacetime, men who have served the compulsory 2 years of active service with the Army and subsequently been relegated to the First Reserve must undergo further military training from time to time during their period of liability (see sec. II). It is known that under stress of wartime conditions, the minimum periods of training prescribed in peacetime have not been continued.

f. Conscripts may often receive the bulk of their training in operational areas. The Japanese are known to have used the Chinese Theater for training purposes, where men perform garrison duties and sometimes get actual combat experience during their period of training.

g. Japanese infantry training is a gradual toughening-up process that grows in intensity, until, finally, long marches with full equipment and stiff endurance tests are used to produce ability to withstand hunger and fatigue for long periods.

3. TRAINING OF OFFICERS AND NONCOMMISSIONED OFFICERS. a. General.

The thorough training of Japanese troops is attributable in turn to the thorough training of the officers and noncommissioned officers, who are largely the products of the Army schools. The school training, though somewhat narrow, arbitrary, and inflexible in its system of indoctrination, is progressive, thorough, and modern. However, its rigidity often has inhibited originality of thought and action.

b. General training of regular line officers. Most regular line officers who reach field grade are graduates of the Military Academy (Rikugun Shikan Gakkō). Candidates are rigidly selected from graduates of 3-year courses at one of the military preparatory school (Rikugun Yōnen Gakkō) at Tokyo, Osaka, Nagoya, Hiroshima, Sendai, and Kumamoto, and from other applicants who possess the proper physical and educational qualifications. These applicants may be enlisted men in the active service—noncommissioned officers under 25 years of age and privates under 22, or applicants-at-large between 16 and 18 years of age. In peacetime, cadet training consisted of 2 years at the Junior Military Academy (Rikugun Yoka Shikan Gakkō) at Asaka in Saitama-Ken; 8 months duty with troops in a designated branch of service; and 1 year 8 months at the Military Academy at Zama in Kanagawa-Ken, or, in the case of air officers, at the Air Academy in Tokyo. After graduation candidates spend 4 months on probation in the grade of sergeant major before receiving a commission. Instruction at the Military Academy is confined almost entirely to general military subjects and practical work in the branch to which the cadet is assigned. There are also 1-year courses for special volunteer officers and for enlisted candidates for commissions (Shōi Kōhosha).

c. Staff training of regular line officers. Courses at the General Staff College (Rikugun Daigakkō) in Tokyo are open ordinarily to company officers who have had not more than 8 years of commissioned service and at least 1 year with troops, but in wartime they have been opened to officers of units in fighting zones, irrespective of age or grade. In peacetime, a regular 3-year course in command and staff work, a 1-year version of the regular course, and a 4-month special course for aviation general staff work are offered.

d. Training reserve officers (sec. III, par. 1c). Class A reserve officer candidates, after completing at least 6 months of training with units, take various courses specially designed for them. They are trained in reserve officer schools at Morioka, Toyohashi, Kurume, Maebashi, Kumamoto, Sendai, and Mukden for infantry; at Toyohashi for artillery; at Kurume for transport; and at special reserve officer candidate courses in schools for cavalry, engineers, signal, medical, veterinary, intendance, and certain phases of artillery. The instruction, normally lasting 11 months but reduced in some instances to 6, covers, principally, training regulations and tactical textbooks, accompanied by practical training which, although somewhat elementary, is carried out realistically and thoroughly. Upon graduation, the candidates serve with units on probation for about 4 months before receiving their commissions.

e. Training of noncommissioned officers. Except for apprentices (sec. IV, par. 1b and class B reserve officer candidates (sec. III, par. 1c), noncommissioned officer candidates are trained at one of the noncommissioned officer schools at Sendai, Kumamoto, Toyohashi, and Kungchuling (Manchuria). These schools are devoted almost entirely to infantry, except for some artillery and cavalry training at Toyohashi. Candidates in artillery, cavalry, engineers, signal, veterinary, intendance, and ordnance are trained at the respective Army branch and services schools. Special courses, usually technical, for noncommissioned officers are also given in these schools, as well as in the Tank School, the Military Police School, the various air schools, the Medical School, and the Mechanized Equipment Maintenance School.

f. Training in Army branch schools. The following schools offer special courses for officers and conduct research in the technical aspects of the branch concerned:

> Infantry School near Chiba City.
> Field Artillery School near Chiba City.
> Heavy Artillery School at Uraga, Kanagawa-ken.
> Air Defense School in Chiba City.
> Cavalry School in Chiba-ken (horse and mechanized).
> Engineer School at Matsudo, Chiba-ken.
> Tank schools at Chiba in Japan, and at Kungchuling and Ssuping (Kai) in Manchuria.
> Signal School at Onomura, Kanagawa-ken.
> Transport School at Tokyo.
> Military Police School at Tokyo.
> Air schools (See par. 10 h).

g. Training in Army services schools. The Army obtains its officers for the services by granting commissions to graduates of higher institutions after they have served 2 months with troops as probational officers. Most of them have been chosen beforehand and had their technical education paid for by the Army. The Army services schools are designed to supplement the technical training obtained in civilian institutions and to adapt that knowledge to military purposes. The Intendance School has also a cadet course for intendance officers similar to that for line officers at the Military Academy. Recent changes point to an effort to keep pace with increased mechanization and the use of highly technical equipment in the Army. The following may be classed as Army services schools:

> Medical School at Tokyo.
> Veterinary School at Tokyo.
> Intendance School at Tokyo.
> Science School (formerly Artillery and Engineer School) at Tokyo.
> Ordnance School (formerly Artificer School) at Onomura, Kanagawa-ken.
> Narashino School in Chiba-ken (chemical warfare).
> Toyama School at Tokyo (physical training, military music).
> Mechanized Equipment Maintenance School at Tokyo.

h. Air training. (1) In addition to "spiritual training" and inculcation of the martial spirit, increasing efforts have been directed toward making Japanese youth air-minded. As far as information is available, pilots are drawn from the following sources:

> Youth air schools.
> Universities, higher, and middle schools.
> Civilian training centers.

In order to encourage volunteers for the air branch of the Army, elementary instruction in air mechanics is given from primary school upward. Construction of model airplanes is taught, and some schools have gliders for training purposes. By means of such encouragement, more pupils are drawn into the youth air schools, after finishing the primary school course at the age of 14 years. (See sec. IV, par. 1b.)

(2) Prospective pilots for the Army Air Service are sent to special training schools, where initial army air training is given. Six such schools in Japan, and one each in Korea and Manchuria, have been reported. The course at these schools formerly lasted 10 months but now has been reduced to 3 months. More time is given to theoretical training than to actual flying. After this initial training, candidates are separated into bomber, fighter, and reconnaissance pilots; gunners; and technicians. Those found unfit for flight duties are relegated to ground assignments.

(3) Those selected for advanced training are sent to Army training schools, which are reported as follows:

> Fighter pilots—3 in Japan—1 in Formosa.
> Bomber pilots—4 in Japan—1 in Manchuria.
> Reconnaissance pilots—2 in Japan.
> Gunners—5 in Japan.
> Technicians—5 in Japan, 1 in Manchuria.

(4) Operational training is the function of the regular establishment; 1 training division, 4 independent training brigades, 10 training regiments and 13 training units have been identified and appear to be charged with this responsibility.

Section V. PROMOTION, PAY, AND AWARDS

1. PROMOTION. a. A recruit entering the Army is given the rank of 2nd-class private and, as a rule, is automatically promoted to 1st-class private after 6 months. According to regulations, the minimum time in which promotion may be made from 1st-class private to superior private is one year, and from superior private to lance corporal 6 months; nevertheless, qualified 1st-class privates have been promoted to the superior grade within 6 months.

b. Enlisted men can be promoted to the various ranks of noncommissioned and warrant officers without taking the course at a noncommissioned officers' school, provided they have the necessary qualifications. Minimum time limits within which promotion can be made to a higher rank, after assumption of the preceding lower rank, have been laid down, by Imperial Ordinance as follows:

> To corporal, after 1 year as lance corporal (leading private).
> To sergeant, after 1 year as corporal.
> To sergeant major, after 2 years as sergeant.
> To warrant officer, after 4 years as sergeant major.

c. All noncommissioned officer promotions are subject to recommendation and selection, and in time of war the process of promotion is considerably accelerated in accordance with the demands of the situation. Men who have taken courses at noncommissioned officers' schools may gain promotion more rapidly than those who have not done so.

d. Minimum periods of service in any one rank before promotion can be attained have also been laid down for officers. However, according to an Imperial Ordinance promulgated in March 1941, both officers and enlisted men can be advanced by as much as two grades at a time for particularly meritorious service in the field, distinguished service in military affairs, retirement from service because of wounds or illness, or, posthumously, if killed in battle. As a rule company officers must serve 3 years with troops before promotion to field officers, and field officers 2 years before promotion to general officers, but in wartime exceptions to this rule are made. General officers are appointed by the Emperor from lists of eligible officers submitted by the Minister of War. Other officers are appointed by the Minister of War with the Emperor's approval. Commanders of independent units, in appropriate cases, may be especially entrusted with the power to determine promotion.

2. PAY. a. The basic rates of pay of Japanese officers and men would be considered low, judged by American and European standards. Japanese standards of living are lower, but in recognition of rising living costs in Japan and the resultant need to safeguard the livelihood of the soldier's dependents, additional pay is now allowed to all ranks. These payments range from 80 percent to a little more than 100 percent of basic pay, according to the country or area in which the soldier is called upon to serve. Overseas pay was also formerly given for service in Formosa, Manchuria, and Korea, but the rates of pay listed below are believed to represent those now in force.

b. Extra pay is also granted to technicians and bandsmen; warrant and noncommissioned officers in the Military police; and personnel employed as interpreters. Pay to both officers and enlisted personnel varies according to the length of service within each grade. Officers are usually paid in the last 10 days of each month, and other ranks every 10 days. Before going into the field 10 days' pay or more may be advanced. Japanese Army pay books, which have thin khaki covers, are usually carried on the person; in them the owner's name and the name or code number of his unit will normally be found.

c. The following table shows the basic rates of pay in the Japanese Army (figures in Japanese Yen per month).

General	550. 00	
Lieutenant general	483. 33	
Major general	416. 66	
Colonel	310. 00–370. 00	(Three pay classes.)
Lieutenant colonel	220. 00–310. 00	(Four pay classes.)
Major	170. 00–220. 00	(Four pay classes.)
Captain	122. 00–155. 00	(Three pay classes.)
First lieutenant	85. 00– 94. 16	(Two pay classes.)
Second lieutenant	70. 83	
Probational officer	25. 00– 40. 00	
Warrant officer	80. 00–110. 00	(Four pay classes.)
Sergeant major	32. 00– 75. 00	(Four pay classes.)
Sergeant	23. 00– 30. 00	(Three pay classes.)
Corporal	20. 00	
Lance corporal (leading private)	13. 50	
Superior private	10. 50	
First-class private	9. 00	
Second-class private	6. 00– 9. 00	(For grades B and A respectively.)

Prior to 7 December 1941, one yen was approximately equivalent to 23 cents (U. S.) and 1ˢ/2ᵈ (British).

3. DECORATIONS AND AWARDS. The granting of medals, decorations, and citations for valor, distinguished and meritorious service, good conduct, and long service figures prominently in the Japanese military system. In peace, decorations are awarded by boards assembled at the War Ministry or important military stations, on the recommendation of divisional commanders. In the field, Army commanders may award up to and including the fifth class of the Order of the Golden Kite. All awards are finally approved by the War Ministry Boards, and decorations are issued, with a certificate from the Emperor, to the commanders of units concerned. They are distributed to officers by the divisional commander and to enlisted men by the unit commander. Decorations are returned to the War Ministry on the death of the recipient. All soldiers who have served with good conduct in a campaign receive a decoration or medal of some kind. A list of the principal decorations awarded in the Japanese Army will be found under Chapter XI.

Section VI. MORALE, DISCIPLINE, AND EFFICIENCY

1. MORALE. a. The individual Japanese soldier's whole outlook and attitude to life are naturally influenced by his home life, his schooling, his particular social environment with its innumerable repressing conventions, and his military training.

b. In the Japanese social system, individualism has no place. Children are taught that, as members of the family, they must obey their parents implicitly and, forgetting their own selfish desires, help each and every one of the family at all times. This system of obedience and loyalty is extended to the community and Japanese life as a whole; it permeates upward from the family unit through neighborhood associations, schools, factories, and other larger organizations, till finally the whole Japanese nation is imbued with the spirit of self-sacrifice, obedience, and loyalty to the Emperor himself.

c. Superimposed on this community structure is the indoctrination of ancestor worship and of the divine origin of the Emperor and the Japanese race. Since the restoration of the Imperial rule in 1868 the Japanese Government has laid much stress on the divine origin of the race and its titular head, and has amplified this teaching by describing Japan's warlike ventures as "divine missions." Famous examples of heroism and military feats in Japan's history are extolled on stage and screen, in literature, and on the radio; hero worship is encouraged. Regimentation of the Japanese national life by government authorities, with their numerous and all-embracing regulations, has been a feature for many centuries.

d. Throughout his military training the Japanese soldier is not allowed to forget all he has been taught in the home, school, or factory. It is drummed into him again and again while his military training proceeds by repeated lectures from unit commanders, given under the guise of "spiritual training" (Seishin Kyoiku). The object of all this concentrated spiritual training is to imbue the Japanese soldier with a spirit which can endure and even be spurred on to further endeavors when the hardships of warfare are encountered. But even though his officers appear to have an ardor which might be called fanaticism, the private soldier is characterized more by blind and unquestioning subservience to authority. The determination of the Japanese soldier to fight to the last or commit suicide rather than be taken prisoner, displayed in the early stages of the war, may be prompted partly by fear of the treatment he may receive at the hands of his captors. More likely it is motivated by the disgrace which he realizes would be brought on his family should he fall into the enemy's hands.

2. DISCIPLINE. a. Because of his training and background the Japanese soldier is generally well disciplined and very amenable to law and order. With firm leadership, the discipline to which he has been accustomed in Japan can be, and usually is, maintained in the field and in territories under Japanese occupation.

b. Elated with success in war and imbued with the idea of Japanese racial superiority, the Japanese soldier is apt to adopt a superior attitude towards conquered people and to forget the strict instructions given him during military training. Numerous instances of breaches of the military laws have occurred, and evidence shows that crimes of rape, plundering, drunkenness, and robbery have been committed. Cases of soldiers deserting their posts, or mutilating themselves in order to avoid taking part in combat, are not unknown, and a few cases of insubordination and desertion also have been reported.

3. EFFICIENCY. It already has been shown (par. 1) that the Japanese soldier in civilian life is a subservient unit in the Japanese family system, and that individualism is discouraged. In the army his position is similar. Army training and the Japanese social system place emphasis on teamwork rather than on individual enterprise. As a member of a squad (section), platoon, or company, the Japanese soldier meticulously performs duties allotted to him; he is an efficient cog in the machine and will carry out instructions to the letter.

CHAPTER II

JAPANESE MILITARY SYSTEM

Section I. THE JAPANESE HIGH COMMAND

1. THE EMPEROR. The Japanese Constitution provides that the Emperor is Commander-in-Chief of the Army and Navy; that he determines their organization; and that he declares war, makes peace, and concludes treaties. He is advised by two military councils: the Board of Marshals and Admirals and the Supreme Military Council.

2. IMPERIAL HEADQUARTERS. In wartime or in case of grave emergency an Imperial Headquarters is established, under the supervision of the Emperor, to assist in the exercise of supreme command. It consists of the Chiefs of the Army and Navy General Staffs, the Ministers of War and of Navy, and a staff of specially selected officers (see fig. 3).

3. ARMY HEADS (Corresponds to U. S. War Department). Subordinate to the Emperor and Imperial Headquarters, the direction of the Army is in the hands of four principal agencies. These are (see next column)—

The General Staff (Sambō Hombu).
The Ministry of War.
The Inspectorate General of Military Training.
The Inspectorate General of Aviation.

4. THE GENERAL STAFF. The General Staff comprises five bureaus: General Affairs, Operations, Intelligence, Transport, and Historical. It is charged with the preparation of war plans; the training and employment of combined arms; the direction of large maneuvers; the movement of troops; the compilation of field service regulations, maps, and military histories; and with supervision of the General Staff College and the Land Survey Department. The Chief of the General Staff is appointed by the Emperor. The General Staff is organized as shown in figure 4.

5. THE MINISTRY OF WAR. a. Functions. The Ministry of War is the administrative, supply, and mobilization agency of the Army. Its chief, the Minister of War, is a member of the Cabinet and provides liaison between the Army and the

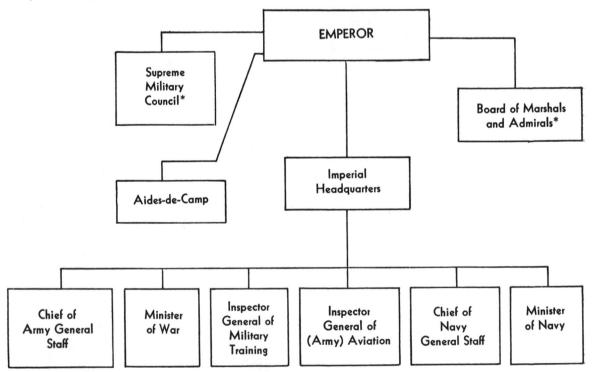

Figure 3. The Japanese High Command.

*The Supreme Military Council and the Board of Marshals and Admirals act in an advisory capacity.

Diet. He must be a general or lieutenant general on the active list, and he is directly responsible to the Emperor. The Ministry of War is subdivided into the Secretariat and eight bureaus (see fig. 5).

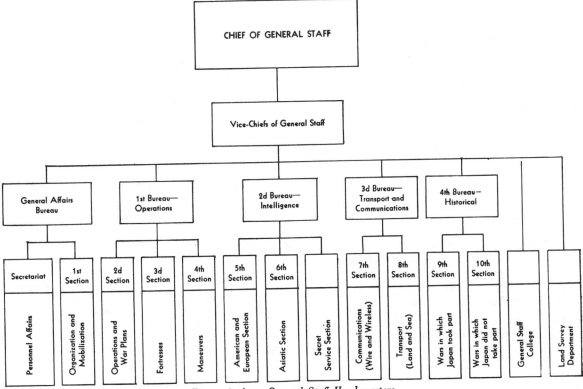

Figure 4. Army General Staff Headquarters.

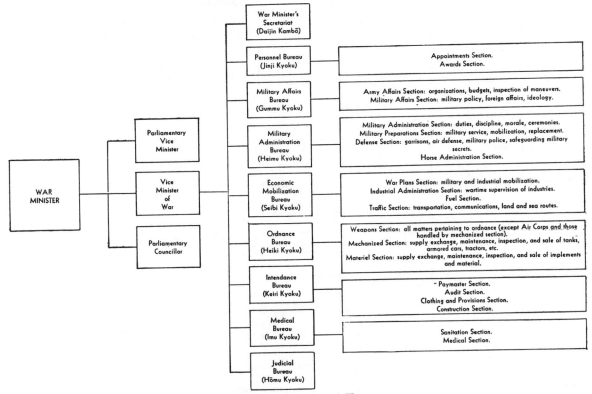

Figure 5. Ministry of War.

b. Other duties. In addition to the duties shown in figure 5, the Minister of War supervises the following:

>Technical Headquarters, including Scientific Research Institute.
>Provost Marshal General.
>Remount Depot.
>Fortifications Department.
>Transportation Department.
>Fuel Depot.
>Army Supply Depot (military supplies other than ordnance).
>Mechanized Headquarters, believed to include training and development of mechanized units.
>Military Police School.
>Ordnance School.
>Intendance School.
>Medical School.
>Veterinary School.
>Research Laboratories.
>Medical and Veterinary Supply Depots.
>Provisions and Clothing Depots.

c. Other supervisory duties. He also supervises the activities of the following agencies:

(1) *Aviation Headquarters.*
>Air technical research laboratory.
>Flight test department.

>Air depots.
>Air arsenals.

(2) *Ordnance Depot.*
>Ordnance Administrative Headquarters.
>Ordnance supply depots.
>Arsenals.

6. THE INSPECTORATE GENERAL OF MILITARY TRAINING. The Inspectorate General of Military Training consists of a general affairs bureau, a so-called 2nd Bureau (Dai Ni Bu), and several inspectorates. It is responsible for technical and tactical training of the separate arms, except the Air Service and of other services not under the War Ministry. (See fig. 6.)

7. THE INSPECTORATE GENERAL OF AVIATION. This agency was created by an ordinance issued 7 December 1938 to supervise Air Corps training. It comprises a General Affairs Department and a Training Department and is headed by a general or lieutenant general. In aviation training matters, only, is it directly responsible to the Emperor; in other respects, the Inspector General of Aviation is subordinate to the "Big Three" (Chief of General Staff, War Minister, and Inspector General of Military Training). The Inspector General of Aviation may be said to rank with, but after, the "Big Three."

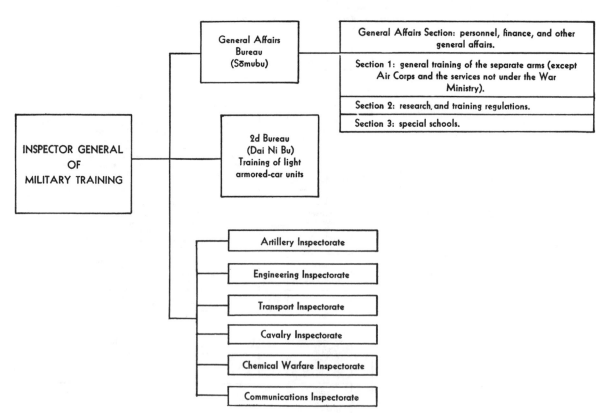

Figure 6. Inspectorate General of Military Training.

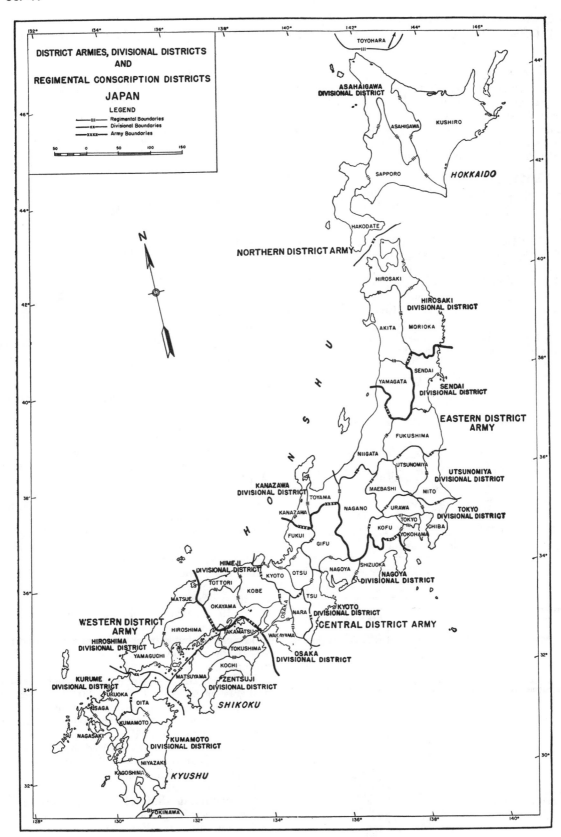

Figure 7. Conscription Districts of Japan.

Section II. TERRITORIAL ORGANIZATIONS, INCLUDING DEPOT DIVISIONS

1. TERRITORIAL ORGANIZATIONS. a. Japan Defense Army. The territorial army organizations of Japan proper, Korea, and Formosa are under command of the General Defense Headquarters (Boei Soshireibu) which was created in 1941 and is responsible, through the Imperial General Headquarters, to the Emperor.

2. ARMY DISTRICTS. Japan proper is divided geographically into four army districts; Eastern, Central, Western, and Northern. (See fig. 7.)

3. DIVISIONAL AND REGIMENTAL DISTRICTS (Shikan, Rentaiku). The army districts are split into divisional districts. These, in turn, are divided into regimental districts which raise recruits for all arms and services. The geographical distribution of these districts is shown in the following table. Numbers following in brackets show the original division raised in the district and perhaps do not represent the division now stationed there.

Army	Head-quarters	Divisional districts
Northern District Army.	Sapporo	Asahigawa (7), Hirosaki (8).
Eastern District Army.	Tokyo	Tokyo (1) (Guards)*, Sendai (2), Kanazawa (9), Utsunomiya (14).
Central District Army.	Osaka	Nagoya (3), Osaka (4), Himeji (10), Kyoto (16).
Western District Army.	Fukuoka	Hiroshima (5), Kumamoto (6), Zentsuji (11), Kurume (12).

*Guards Divisional District Headquarters is located in Tokyo, but recruits are drawn from all over Japan.

4. REGIMENTAL DISTRICTS. The infantry regiment districts are located as follows:

Army	Divisional district	Regimental districts and military affairs district
Northern District Army (headquarters Sapporo).	Asahigawa (7th).	Sapporo. Hakedate. Kushiro. Asahigawa. Toyohara (Karafuto).
	Hirosaki (8th).	Aomori. Morioka. Akita. Yamagata.
Eastern District Army (headquarters Tokyo).	Tokyo (1st).	(Tokyo). Kofu. Urawa. Yokohama. Chiba.
	Utsunomiya (14th).	Mito. Utsunomiya. Maebashi.
	Sendai (2d).	Sendai. Fukushima. Niigata.
	Kanazawa (9th).	Kanazawa. Toyama. Nagano.
Central District Army (headquarters Osaka).	Nagoya (3d).	Nagoya. Gifu. Shizuoka.
	Kyoto (16th).	Kyoto. Tsu. Otsu. Fukui.

Army	Divisional district	Regimental districts and military affairs district
Central District Army (headquarters Osaka.)	Osaka (4th).	Osaka. Nara. Wakayama.
	Himeji (10th).	Kobe. Tottori. Okayama.
Western District Army (headquarters Fukuoka)	Hiroshima (5th).	Hiroshima. Matsue. Yamaguchi.
	Zentsuji (11th).	Takamatsu. Matsuyama. Tokushima. Kochi.
	Kumamoto (6th).	Kumamoto. Oita. Miyazaki. Okinawa. Kagoshima.
	Kurume (12th).	Fukuoka. Saga. Nagasaki.
Korea (Chosen) (headquarters Keijo).	Ranan (19th).	Ranan. Kanko.
	Keijo (20th).	Keijo. Heijo. Taikyu. Koshu.
Formosa (Taiwan) (headquarters Taihoku).		Taihoku. Tainan. Karenko.

5. DEPOT DIVISIONS. a. Functions. A depot division (Rusu Shidan) is primarily a training division. In peacetime, the depot division was engaged mainly in the training of the usual yearly class of conscripts, called up as described in paragraphs b and c, section II, chapter I. Its functions now include also:—

(1) Equipping and providing refresher training for recalled reservists. Small detachments of the depot division are assigned these duties.

(2) Organizing and equipping new divisional units.

(3) Providing loss replacements for divisions and other active units, furnished by the divisional district in which the depot division is stationed.

(4) (a) Other functions are: recruiting and training nondivisional units located in the divisional district; supervising men transferred to the reserve and military training in the district's schools; and arranging for the return to Japan of casualties and the ashes of the dead.

(b) In some cases, a field division, which originally was raised in one of the divisional districts, will return to that district to rest and refit, and may absorb or take over the functions of the depot division.

b. Strength. The strength of depot divisions probably varies from 10,000 to 20,000, depending upon the number of conscripts and reservists being trained. Since depot divisions generally are organized to engage in field exercise and other forms of combined training, it is believed that after a brief period of field preparation, the units should be capable of engaging in combat, especially in defense of their homes areas.

c. Recruiting districts. Japan proper has 14 divisional recruiting districts (Shikan) divided into regimental districts (Rentaiku). Korea has two divisional recruiting districts, Ranan and Keijo, divided into military affairs districts (Heijiku). Formosa possibly has one divisional recruiting district, likewise divided into military affairs districts. While the exact functions of these military affairs districts are not established, it is believed that their principal duty is the recruitment of resident Japanese and natives.

d. Dispatch of troops to field. In war each divisional district dispatches to theaters of operations, or other assignments, several divisions and other units, including, for example, independent mixed brigades. This is accomplished by one or two methods.

(1) The method used in an emergency is to send to the field the bulk of the depot division, raising it to full strength with first reservists (Yobihei) and conscript reservists (Hojuhei), and retaining in the divisional district a small cadre for each unit of the depot division. The division sent to the field retains the number of the depot division. The depot division then is rebuilt by calling other conscripts and reservists to the colors.

(2) A second method is to form the new division from a small nucleus of each unit of the depot division by adding to this cadre a large number of reservists. Under this method the new division usually is mobilized in billets or camps in the vicinity of depot divisions, but it does not actually occupy peacetime barracks. Such a division is given a new numerical designation. It is likely that both methods, as well as variations of these methods, have been employed.

e. Names of depot divisions. Depot divisions are designated by the names of their home stations, as well as numerically, such as Nagoya or 3rd Depot Division. All depot divisions have been triangularized to accord with the general triangularization of field divisions. The Infantry Regiments left over when the depot divisions were triangularized are under the control of the District Army under whose jurisdiction they fall. They probably are used for the activation of new infantry units and possibly for furnishing replacements. A depot division at present, therefore, will probably be organized as follows:

> Depot Division Headquarters.
> Division Staff.
> Military Affairs Department (Heimubu).
> 3 Infantry Regiments (Replacement Units (Hojutai)).
> 1 Artillery Regiment (Replacement Unit).
> 1 Cavalry or Reconnaissance Regiment (Replacement Unit).

> 1 Engineer Regiment (Replacement Unit).
> 1 Transport Regiment (Replacement Unit).
> 1 Medical Unit (Replacement Unit).
> 1 Signal Unit (Replacement Unit).
> 1 Hospital.
> 1 Supply and Repair Depot.
> 1 Horse Training Center.

Section III. FIELD REPLACEMENT SYSTEM

1. GENERAL. The complements of Japanese field units are usually sufficiently high to provide for what are ordinarily considered first replacements. When these supernumeraries have been exhausted, two methods of reinforcement are normally employed.

2. METHODS OF REPLACEMENT. a. Direct call on depot division. The first is for the unit to call directly upon the depot division, or the active division occupying its divisional district. The replacements consist of officers and enlisted men of such rank and degree of training as specified by the field commander. This method is the one preferred by the Japanese, for it preserves their system of having all men in a unit come from a particular divisional district. It has the obvious disadvantage of being time-consuming.

b. Field replacement units. In order that a unit in the field, which has suffered heavy casualties, may receive replacements quickly, the Japanese have devised a second replacement system. Under this, they have placed in the theater of operations a unit known as a Field Replacement Unit which normally consists of two infantry battalions plus auxiliary troops. Men in a Field Replacement Unit do not come necessarily from the same divisional district as the combat units it serves. They may be in various stages of training, ranging from veterans to those who just have finished basic training. Replacements are provided over a wide area, probably a particular theater of operations.

c. Divisions as replacement. There is also evidence that after a campaign a division, which has been assigned a station in a relatively quiet area overseas (such as the rear areas in China), may perform the functions of replacement for other units not necessarily from the same divisional district. This is done by sending newly raised troops from Japan to the division for a final period of intensive training with experienced troops. After the new recruits have completed this training they are forwarded as replacements for other units.

CHAPTER III

FIELD ORGANIZATION

Section I. MAJOR ORGANIZATIONS

NOTE. In some cases in this chapter, sufficiently definite and comprehensive information has not been available to enable representatives of the participating headquarters to reach fully agreed figures. Therefore, although the main structure of the Japanese organization is considered to be well established, some of the details are likely to need amendment in the light of future experience.

1. FIELD COMMAND. The Japanese Army in the field is organized into groups of armies, area armies, armies, and forces with special missions which initially do not come under command of any army. The Chief of Staff of the Japanese Army is responsible for the general direction of the army forces in the field.

2. GROUPS OF ARMIES. A group of armies, such as the Kwantung Army, might be considered the equivalent of the command of a theater of operations.

3. AREA ARMIES. An area army, such as the 8th Area Army, may be considered the equivalent of an American or British Army.

4. ARMIES. A Japanese Army should be considered the equivalent of an American or British Corps. It is composed of a headquarters, a variable number of infantry divisions, and army troops. Such a force normally comprises from 50,000 to 150,000 officers and enlisted men. The 18th Army in the

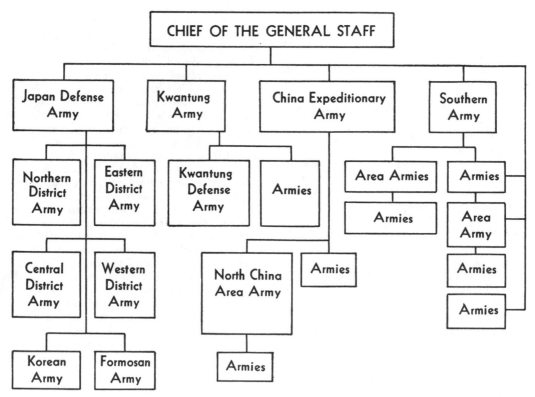

Figure 8. Field command.

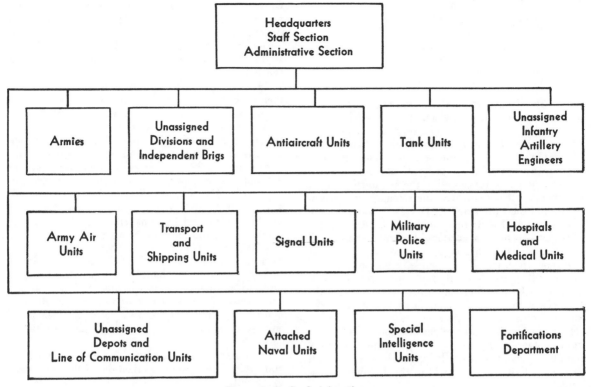

Figure 9. Staff administration.

Southwest Pacific area during April 1943 had a nominal strength of about 130,000, but its actual strength was always greatly below this figure because of attrition en route, casualties, and detachments.   It included the following units:

3 Divisions—plus small elements of a fourth.
1 Independent mixed brigade.
2 Infantry mortar battalions.
4 Independent field antiaircraft artillery companies.
6 Independent field searchlight companies.
6 Field antiaircraft artillery battalions.
2 Field machine cannon companies.
1 Independent antitank gun battalion.
1 Engineer group.
7 Independent engineer regiments.
1 Independent engineer company.
2 Field road construction units.
1 Field airfield construction unit.
3 Field duty units.
3 Shipping engineer regiments.
1 Field motor transport depot.
2 Field transport commands.
1 Independent transport regiment.
3 Independent motor transport battalions.
6 Independent motor transport companies.
1 Signal unit.
2 Fixed radio units.
5 Line of communication hospitals.

1 Water purifying unit.
2 Debarkation units.
2 Anchorages.
2 Construction duty companies.
3 Land duty companies.
5 Sea duty companies.
1 Water transport unit.
5 Airfield battalions.
3 Airfield companies.
2 Base forces (Naval troops).
1 Field freight depot.
1 Field ordnance depot.
4 Line-of-communication garrison (sector) units.

5. ARMY CORPS. Japanese military terminology does not include the term army corps (see par. 4).

6. INFANTRY DIVISION. a. General. In its basic form the Japanese infantry division is composed as follows:

Division headquarters.
Division signal unit.
Infantry group headquarters and 3 infantry regiments.
Artillery regiment.
Cavalry regiment or reconnaissance regiment.

Engineer regiment.
Medical unit.
Field hospitals.
Water-purification unit.
Transport regiment.
Ordnance unit.
Veterinary unit.

b. Classification and strength. Organic units of the Japanese division exhibit various differences in organization and strength, because they are organized for different roles and varying types of terrain. The Japanese themselves classify these organic units into three general categories: A, or the strongest; B, representing the standard; and C, the special. Consequently, the strength and classification of their divisions are largely dependent upon organization of their organic units. However, this does not constitute a hard-and-fast rule whereby all Japanese divisions are composed exclusively of any one type of units. For example, a basically standard, or "B" type, division often may have "A" type artillery. In addition, there are also strength differences within the division units themselves. In an "A" type infantry regiment, the regimental infantry gun unit could be either one company of four guns or two companies of four guns under a small battalion headquarters. In general, however, all Japanese divisions come within the following classifications:

(1) *The standard division.* This type of division has been encountered most frequently in present operational areas. It is composed of organic elements listed in paragraph a above.

(2) *The strengthened division.* This division is composed of "A" type units (augmented personnel and firepower) and may include an artillery group, consisting of a group headquarters, a field or mountain artillery regiment, and other artillery units; an organic tank unit; and a chemical or decontamination unit for gas control. This type of division so far has not been encountered in its entirety in the field.

(3) *The strengthened division (modified).* Elements of this type of division were known to exist during the early stages of the war, and the division may have been a fore-runner of the strengthened type described above. It includes an artillery group, but has no organic tank element or gas decontamination unit. The infantry rifle companies are found without the heavy weapons platoons of the strengthened type division, decreasing the rifle company strength from 262 to 205. In such case the heavy machine guns and antitank rifles are found in the machine gun and antitank companies.

(4) *The special division.* This is a lighter type of division composed of two brigades, each of four independent infantry battalions supported by small units of auxiliary troops (mainly "C" type units). The future operational role of this type of division is difficult to forecast, but to date it has been found employed in garrison and antiguerilla activities in China.

c. Charts and tables. The following charts and tables depict the organization of the four types of infantry divisions listed above. However, in view of the many possible combinations of types of units within a division, these charts and tables cannot be taken as exact models for all divisions. Following the charts and tables are presented detailed analyses of organization and strength. Where known, variants are included. Emphasis has been placed, however, upon the standard division.

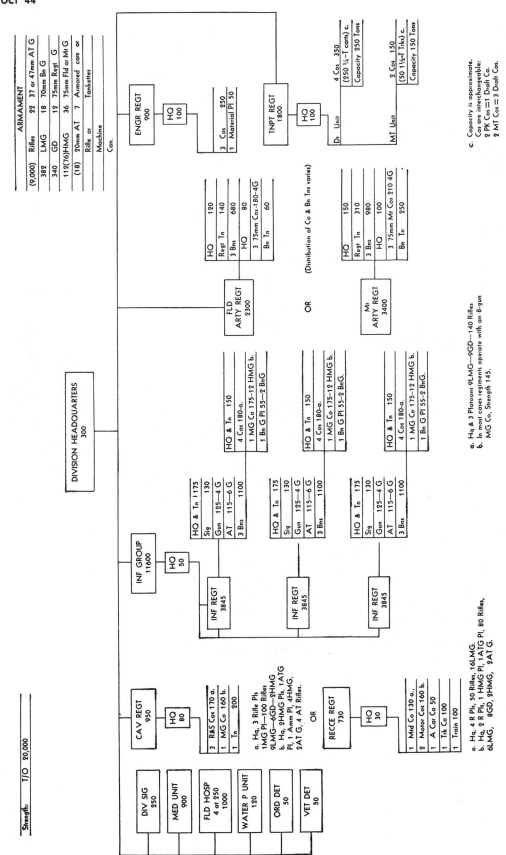

ARMAMENT		
(9,000)	Rifles	22 37 or 47mm AT G
382	LMG	18 70mm Bn G
340	GD	12 75mm Regt G
112(76)HMG		36 75mm Fld or Mt G
(18)	20mm AT	7 Armored cars or
	Machine	Tankettes
	Can.	

c. Capacity is approximate.
Cos are interchangeable:
2 PK Cos = 1 Draft Co.
2 MT Cos = 3 Draft Cos.

This division has been generally encountered during the course of present operations. Figures are to nearest "5".

a. Hq & 3 Platoons 9LMG—140 Rifles.
b. In most cases regiments operate with an 8-gun MG Co, Strength 145.

a. Hq, 3 Rifle Pls
1MG Pl—100 Rifles
9LMG—6GD—2HMG
b. Hq, 2HMG Pls, 1ATG
Pl, 1 Amm Pl, 4HMG,
2AT G, 4 AT Rifles.

a. Hq, 4 R Pls, 50 Rifles, 16LMG.
b. Hq, 2 R Pls, 1 HMG Pl, 1ATG Pl, 80 Rifles,
6LMG, 8GD, 2HMG, 2AT G.

Strength: T/O 20,000

Figure 10. Japanese "Standard" Triangular Infantry Division.

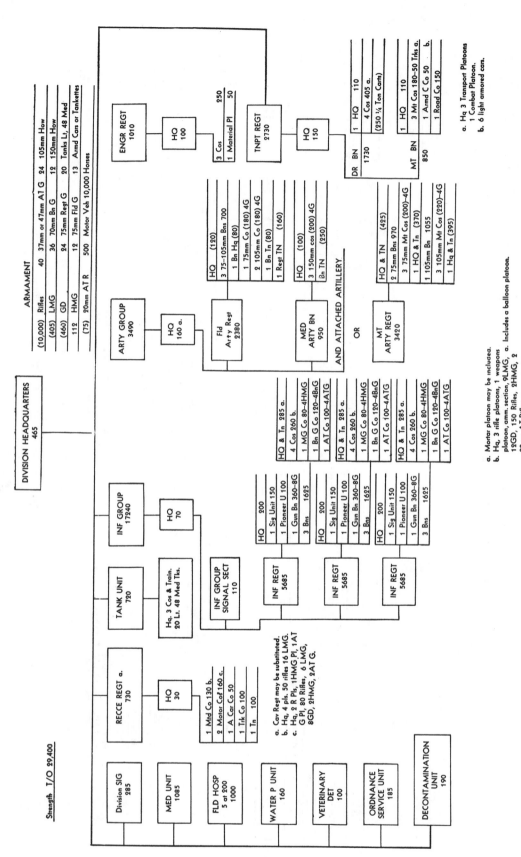

Figure 11. Japanese "Strengthened" Triangular Infantry Division.

PLATE I.—ARMY UNIFORMS: OFFICERS

M1938 FIELD DRESS

M1930 FIELD DRESS

OVERCOAT

SERVICE DRESS

CAPE

RAINCAPE

PLATE II.—ARMY UNIFORMS: NONCOMMISSIONED OFFICERS AND ENLISTED MEN

M1938 FIELD DRESS, FRONT (EM)

M1938 FIELD DRESS, REAR (EM)

M1938 OVERCOAT

M1938 SERVICE DRESS

M1930 SERVICE DRESS

TYPICAL FATIGUE DRESS

PLATE III.—WINTER AND TROPICAL ARMY UNIFORMS

OLD STYLE WINTER COAT

WINTER FATIGUE COVERALL

WINTER COAT

OFFICER'S TROPICAL COAT

EM'S TROPICAL COAT

TROPICAL DRESS

PLATE IV.—MISCELLANEOUS ARMY UNIFORMS

RAINCOAT

COTTON FATIGUES

TANK COVERALL

FLYING SUIT

ANTIGAS SUIT

GUARD'S OVERCOAT

From J. A. N. No. 1

PLATE V.—NAVY UNIFORMS: OFFICERS AND PETTY OFFICERS

OFFICER (BLUES)

OFFICER (WHITES)

SP LANDING FORCE OFFICER

PO (BLUES)

PO'S CAP INSIGNIA

ADVANCED
SPECIAL TRAINING

ELEMENTARY
SPECIAL TRAINING

PO (WHITES)

From J. A. N. No. 1

PLATE VI.—NAVY UNIFORMS AND INSIGNIA: PETTY OFFICERS AND SEAMEN

SEAMAN'S CAP

SEAMAN'S CAP BAND

SEAMAN (WHITES)

SEAMAN (SP LANDING FORCE)

SP LANDING FORCE CAP

FIGHTER PILOT

BOMBER PILOT

SEAMAN (BLUES)

EXCELLENT CONDUCT

GOOD CONDUCT

PO'S BUTTON

SEAMAN'S BUTTON

From J. A. N No. 1

PLATE VII.—INSIGNIA OF RANK

ARMY OFFICERS

GENERAL	LT GENERAL	MAJOR GENERAL	COLONEL	LT COLONEL	MAJOR

CAPTAIN	1ST LIEUTENANT	2D LIEUTENANT	WARRANT OFFICER

ARMY NONCOMMISSIONED OFFICERS AND ENLISTED MEN

	SERGEANT MAJOR	SERGEANT	CORPORAL	LEADING PVT	

ACTING NCO	SUPERIOR PVT	1ST CLASS PVT	2D CLASS PVT	ACTING SUP PVT

NAVY OFFICERS

ADMIRAL	VICE ADMIRAL	REAR ADMIRAL	CAPTAIN	COMMANDER

LT COMMANDER	LIEUTENANT	LIEUTENANT (JG)	ENSIGN	WARRANT OFFICER

NAVY PETTY OFFICERS AND SEAMEN

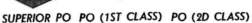

SUPERIOR PO	PO (1ST CLASS)	PO (2D CLASS)	LEADING SEAMAN	SUPERIOR SEAMAN	SEAMAN (1ST CLASS)	SEAMAN (2D CLASS)

PLATE VIII.—INSIGNIA OF ARM WORN ON BREAST OF M1938 COAT

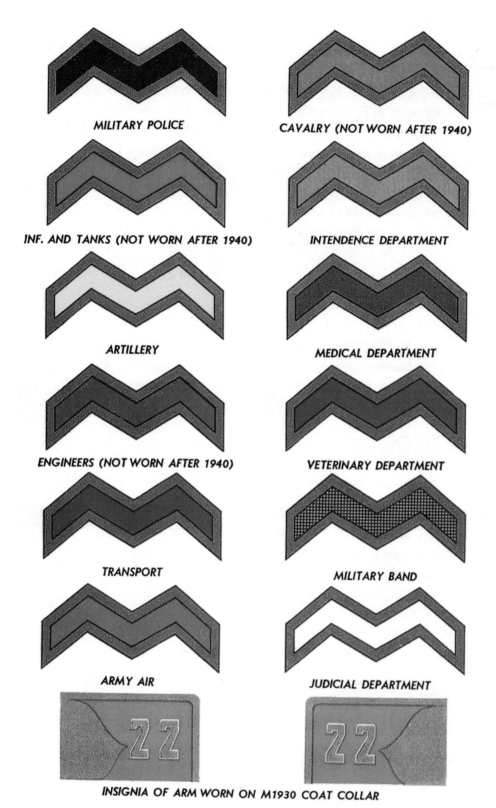

MILITARY POLICE

CAVALRY (NOT WORN AFTER 1940)

INF. AND TANKS (NOT WORN AFTER 1940)

INTENDENCE DEPARTMENT

ARTILLERY

MEDICAL DEPARTMENT

ENGINEERS (NOT WORN AFTER 1940)

VETERINARY DEPARTMENT

TRANSPORT

MILITARY BAND

ARMY AIR

JUDICIAL DEPARTMENT

INSIGNIA OF ARM WORN ON M1930 COAT COLLAR

From J. A. N. No. 1

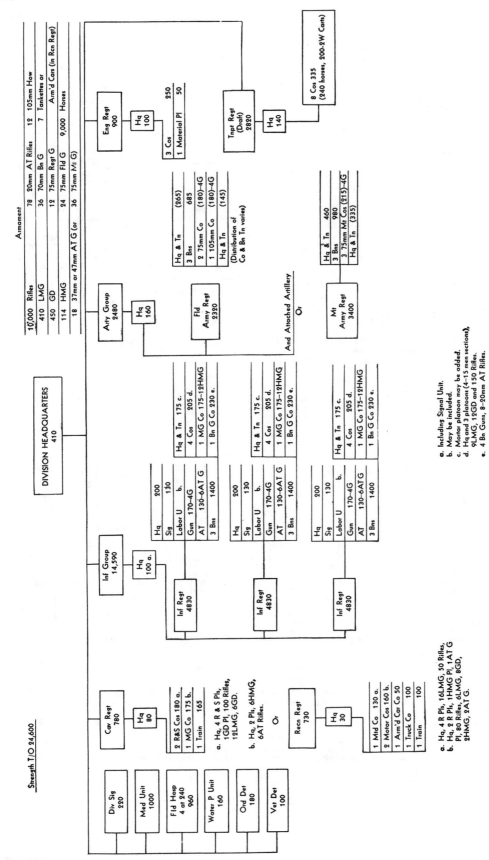

Figure 12. Japanese "Strengthened" (Modified) Triangular Division.

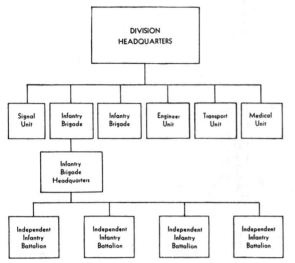

Figure 13. *Japanese "Special" Division. This type of division has been identified in China engaged in garrison and antiguerilla activities.*

Units	Personnel	Horses	Rifles	Light machine gun	Heavy machine gun	Grenade discharger	Light mortars	70-mm battalion gun
Division headquarters	250	160	180	4				
2 Infantry brigades	9,500	1,000	5,600	100	32	100	16	8
Each	4,750	500	2,800	50	16	50	8	4
Signal unit	200	30	70					
Engineer unit	600	100	500	6		12		
Transport unit	1,800	1,290	500					
Medical unit	650	80	100					
Total	13,000	2,660	6,950	110	32	112	16	8

Figure 14. *Strength and weapons of special division (all figures are estmates).*

Units	Personnel T/O	Personnel Operational	Horses	Rifles	Light machine gun	Grenade discharger	Heavy machine gun	Machine cannon or 20-mm antitank rifle	37-mm or 47-mm antitank gun	70-mm battalion gun	75-mm regimental gun	75-mm field or mountain gun	Tankette or armored car
Division headquarters	300	300	(160)	(180)	(4)	( )							
Division signal unit	250	220	40	(100)		( )							
Infantry group headquarters	71	70	18	( )	( )								
3 infantry regiments, each 3,843	11,529	9,000	2,130	6,393	(336)	324	108(72)		18	18	12		
Division field artillery regiment	2,300	2,000	2,000	(450)	(1)							36	
Division reconnaissance regiment	730	650	(188)	(260)	28	16	4		4				7
Division engineer regiment	900	750	(150)	(700)	(9)								
Division medical unit	900	750	(110)	( )	( )								
4 Field hospitals (Operational 3)	1,000	690	( )	( )	( )								
Division water purification unit	120	90	( )	( )	( )								
Division transport regiment	1,800	1,400	(1300)	( )	( )								
Division ordnance unit	50	40	( )	( )	( )								
Division veterinary unit	50	40	( )	( )									
Total	20,000	16,000	(7,500)	(9,000)	(382)	(340)	112(76)		22	18	12	36	7
Alternatives:													
Division mountain artillery regiment	3,400		(1,400)	(450)	(1)							36	
Division cavalry regiment	950	900	(1,100)	(500)	28	18	10	4	2				
Infantry group tankette unit	100		( )	( )	( )	( )							10–17

NOTES

1. Figures in parentheses are interpolations.
2. Parentheses only indicate presence but insufficient evidence is available to estimate a figure.
3. The figure of 72 heavy machine guns shown in brackets for the three infantry regiments assumes the presence of the 8-gun company.

Figure 15. *Strength and weapons of standard division.*

Units	Personnel	Horses	Motor Vehicles	Rifles	Light machine gun	Grenade discharger	Heavy machine gun	Machine cannon or 20-mm antitank rifle	37-mm or 47-mm antitank gun	70-mm battalion gun	75-mm regimental gun	75-mm field or mountain gun	105-mm Howitzer	150-mm Howitzer	Light tanks	Medium tanks	Tankette or armored car
Division headquarters	465	66	23	( )	( )												
Division signal unit	287	48	( )	(120)	( )												
Infantry group headquarters	69	18	3	( )	( )												
Infantry group signal unit	114	24		( )	( )												
3 Infantry regiments, each 5,687	17,061	3,249	----	7,110	345	441	108	72	36	36	24						
Artillery group headquarters	159	99	6	( )	( )												
Field artillery regiment	2,379	2,463	49	( )	( )							12	24				
Medium artillery battalion	951	769		( )	( )									12			
Division reconnaissance regiment	730	188	61	260	28	16	4	( )	4								7
Division tank unit	717		81	( )	( )										20	48	
Division engineer regiment	1,012	116	12	(800)	(9)												
Division medical unit	1,083	1,468	----														
5 field hospitals	1,009	145	22	( )	( )												
Division water purification unit	163		19	( )	( )												
Division transport regiment	2,729	1,222	176	( )	(21)												6
Division ordnance unit	185		14	( )	( )												
Division veterinary unit	105	32	6	( )	( )												
Chemical (decontamination) unit	190		30	( )	( )												
Total	29,408	9,906	502	(10000)	(405)	(457)	112	72	40	36	24	12	24	12	20	48	13
Alternatives:																	
Division mountain artillery regiment	3,420	1,835	----	( )	( )							24	12				
Division cavalry regiment	950	1,100	----	(500)	28	18	10		4	2							
Infantry group tankette unit	100	----		( )	( )	( )	( )	( )									10–17

NOTES

1. Figures in parentheses are interpolations.
2. Parentheses only indicate presence but insufficient evidence is available to estimate a figure.
3. This division is described as from Japanese sources.

Figure 16. Strength and weapons of "strengthened" division.

Units	Personnel	Horses	Motor Vehicles	Rifles	Light machine guns	Grenade dischargers	Heavy machine guns	Machine cannon or 20-mm antitank rifle	37-mm or 47-mm antitank gun	70-mm battalion gun	75-mm regimental gun	75-mm field or mountain gun	105-mm howitzer	Tankette or armored car
Division headquarters	415	217	(20)	( )	( )									
Division signal unit	220	38	(20)	(100)	(4)									
Infantry group headquarters	48	11	(5)	( )	(3)									
Infantry group signal unit	52	12		( )										
3 infantry regiments	14,493	2,268	----	(7,110)	(345)	441	108	72	18	36	12			
Artillery group headquarters	160	94	(10)	( )	( )									
Field artillery regiment	2,315	1,834	(30)	(400)	( )							24	12	
Division cavalry regiment	783	831		(300)	25	12	6	6						
Division engineer regiment	899	150	(15)	(700)	(9)									
Division medical unit	995	117	(15)	( )										
4 Field hospitals	948	304	( )	( )										
Division water purification unit	163		(19)	( )										
Division transport regiment	2,819	2,025	(135)	(930)	(24)									(6)
Division ordnance unit	185		(15)	( )										
Division veterinary unit	105	30	( )	( )										
Total	24,600	7,930	(284)	(10,000)	(411)	453	114	78	18	36	12	24	12	(6)
Alternatives:														
Mountain Artillery Regiment	3,441	1,822	----										36	

NOTES

1. Figures in parentheses are interpolations.
2. Parentheses only indicate presence but insufficient evidence is available to estimate a figure.
3. This division is described as from Japanese sources.

Figure 17. Strength and weapons of "strengthened" (modified) division.

d. Identified Japanese divisions and their principal components. (1) The following chart shows the identified divisions of the Japanese Army, their component units, the districts from which they are conscripted, and the location of the depots from which they are supplied. Division signal and medical units, although included in the divisions, are not shown on the chart.

(2) The area from which an identified regiment is conscripted is the regimental conscription district. When the location of its depot differs from the headquarters of the conscription district, the depot location is shown in parentheses. The supporting units are conscripted from the whole divisional district. When the location of the depot differs from the headquarters of the divisional district, the depot location also is shown in parentheses.

[As of May 1944]

Divisions	Regimental conscription district and/or location of depot	Div inf regt	Div cav or recn unit	Div tank unit	Div arty regt	Div arty grp	Div engr regt	Div tnpt regt
1 Gds		1 Gds 2 Gds 6 or 7 Gds	1 Gds Cav (Tokyo).		1 Gds FA		1 Gds	1 Gds.
2 Gds Tokyo	(Tokyo) (Tokyo) (Tokyo)	3 Gds 4 Gds 5 Gds	2 Gd Recn (Tokyo).		2 Gds FA of the Arty grp (Tokyo).	Gds	2 Gds (Tokyo)	2 Gds (Tokyo).
1 Tokyo	Tokyo Kofu Chiba (Sakura)	1 49 57	1 Recn Tokyo	1	1 FA of the Arty grp Tokyo.	1	1 Tokyo	1 Tokyo.
2 Sendai	Sendai Niigata (Shibata) Fukushima (Wakamatsu).	4 16 29	2 Recn Sendai		2 FA of the arty grp Sendai.	2	2 Sendai	2 Sendai.
3 Nagoya	Nagoya Shizuoka Gifu	6 34 68	3 Cav Nagoya		3 FA of the Arty grp Nagoya.	3	3 Nagoya (Toyohashi).	3 Nagoya.
4 Osaka	Osaka Osaka (Sakai) Wakayama	8 37 61	4 Recn Osaka		4 FA Osaka (Shinoda-yama).		4 Osaka (Takatsuki).	4 Osaka.
5 Hiroshima	Hiroshima Matsue (Hamada) Yamaguchi	11 21 42	5 Recn Hiroshima		5 FA Hiroshima		5 Hiroshima	5 Hiroshima.
6 Kumamoto	Kumamoto Miyazaki (Miyakonojo). Kagoshima	13 23 45	6 Cav Kumamoto		6 FA Kumamoto		6 Kumamoto	6 Kumamoto.
7 Asahigawa	Hakodate (Asahigawa) Kushiro (Asahigawa) Asahigawa	26 27 28	7 Recn Asahigawa		7 Mtn Asahigawa		7 Asahigawa	7 Asahigawa.
8 Hirosaki	Aomori Akita Aomori (Hirosaki)	5 17 31	8 Recn Hirosaki	8 (Co)	8 FA of the Arty Grp Hirosaki.	8	8 Hirosaki (Morioka).	8 Hirosaki.
9 Kanazawa	Kanazawa Nagano ? (Matsumoto). Toyama	7 19 35	9 Cav Kanazawa		9 Mtn of the Arty Grp Kanazawa.	9	9 Kanazawa	9 Kanazawa.
10 Himeji	Okayama Kobe (Himeji)	10 39 63	10 Recn Himeji		10 FA of the Arty Grp Himeji.	10	10 Himeji (Okayama).	10 Himeji
11 Zentsuji	Takamatsu (Marugame). Tokushima Kochi	12 43 44	11 Cav Zentsuji		11 Mtn of the Arty Grp Zentsuji	11	11 Zentsuji	11 Zentsuji.
12 Kurume	Fukuoka Nagasaki (Omura) Fukuoka (Kurume)	24 46 48	12 Recn Kurume	12	24 FA of the Arty Grp Kurume.	12	18 Kurume	18 Kurume.
13 Sendai	Niigata (Shibata) Fukushima (Wakamatsu). Sendai	116 65 104	13 Div Cav unit (Sendai)		19 Mtn Sendai (Takata).		13 Sendai	13 Sendai.
14 Utsunomiya	Mito Maebashi (Takasaki) Utsunomiya	2 15 59	14 Recn Utsu		20 FA Utsu		14 Utsu (Mito)	14 Utsu.
15 Nagoya?, Kyoto	Tsu	51 60 67		15	21 FA		15	15.
16 Kyoto	Kyoto Kyoto (Fukuchiyama) Tsu	9 20 33	16 Recn Kyoto		22 FA Kyoto		16 Kyoto (Fushimi).	16 Kyoto.
17 Himeji	Tottori Okayama Kobe (Himeji)	53 54 81	17 Inf Grp Tkette Co.		23 FA Himeji		17 Himeji (Okayama).	17 Himeji.
18 Kurume	Nagasaki (Omura) Fukuoka (Kurume) Fukuoka (Kokura)	55 56 114	22 Cav Bn?		18 Mtn Kurume		12 Kurume	12 Kurume.
19 Ranan	(Ranan) (Kainei) (Ranan)	73 75 76	19 Recn		25 Mtn of the Arty Grp (Ranan)	19	19 (Kainei)	19 (Ranan).
20 Keijo	(Ryuzan) (Ryuzan) (Taikyu)	78 79 80	20 Recn (Ryuzan)		26 FA of the Arty Grp (Ryuzan).	20	20 (Ryuzan)	20 (Ryuzan).
21 Kanazawa		62 82 83	21 Div Tkette Co		51 Mtn		21	21.
22 Utsunomiya Kanazawa?	Mito Maebashi (Takasaki) Nagano (Matsumoto).	84 85 86	22 Inf Grp Tkette Co Utsu.		52 Mtn Utsu		22 Mito?	22 Utsu?
23		64 71 72	23 Recn	23	13 FA of the Arty Grp	23	23	23.
24 Zentsuji, Hirosaki.	Matsuyama Yamagata	22 32 89	24 Recn		42 FA of the Arty Grp	24	24	24.
25 Osaka, Himeji, Kurume.	Fukuoka (Kokura) Tottori Wakayama?	14 40 70	75 Cav		15 Mtn of the Arty Grp.	25	25	25.
26 Nagoya?	Nagoya Gifu? Shizuoka?	11 Ind 12 Ind 13 Ind	26 Recn		11 Ind FA Nagoya?		26	26.

Divisions	Regimental conscription district and/or location of depot	Div inf regt	Div cav or recn unit	Div tank unit	Div arty regt	Div arty grp	Div engr regt	Div tnpt regt
27 All Japan?	(Tokyo) (Tokyo)	1 China 2 China 3 China	27 Recn		27 Mtn (Tokyo)?		27	27 (Tokyo)?
28 Tokyo, Sendai, Kyoto.	Tokyo Niigata (Takata) Fukui (Sabae)	3 30 36	28 Cav		28 Mtn of the Arty Grp.	28	28	28.
29 Nagoya, Kanazawa, Osaka.	Nagoya (Toyohashi) Nara Nagano (Matsumoto)	18 38 50	29 Cav		29 Mtn		29	29.
30 Ranan, Heijo	(Kanko) (Heijo)	74 77	30 Recn		30 FA		30	30.
31 Sendai, Osaka, Kurume.	Niigata (Shibata) Fukuoka Nara	58 124 138			31 Mtn		31	31.
32	Tokyo ?	210 211 212	32 Inf Grp Tkette Co.		32 FA		32	32.
33 Sendai ?	Niigata (Shibata) ? Fukushima (Wakamatsu) ?.	213 214 215			33 Mtn		33	33.
34 Osaka	Osaka Osaka (Sakai) Wakayama	216 217 218	34 Recn Osaka		34 FA Osaka (Shinodayama).		34 Osaka (Takatsuki).	34 Osaka.
35		219 220 221	35 Inf Grp Tkette Co.		35 FA		35	35.
36 Hirosaki	Aomori (Hirosaki) Akita Yamagata	222 223 224	36 Inf Grp Tkette Co.		36 Mtn Hirosaki?		36 Hirosaki (Morioka).	36 Hirosaki.
37		225 226 227	37 Inf Grp Tkette Co.		37 Mtn		37	37.
38 Nagoya	Nagoya Gifu Shizuoka	228 229 230	38 Inf Grp Tkette Co. Nagoya.		38 Mtn Nagoya		38 Nagoya (Toyohashi).	38 Nagoya.
39 Hiroshima	Matsue (Hamada) Yamaguchi	231 232 233 234	39 Recn Hiroshima?		39 FA Hiroshima?		39 Hiroshima?	39 Hiroshima?.
40 Zentsuji	Takamatsu (Marugame)? Tokushima Kochi	235 236	40 Cav Zentsuji		40 Mtn Zentsuji		40 Zentsuji	40 Zentsuji.
41 Utsunomiya?	Mito? Maebashi (Takasaki) Utsunomiya	237 238 239			41 Mtn Utsunomiya		41 Utsu (Mito)	41 Utsu.
42 Sendai	Fukushima (Wakamatsu). Sendai Niigata (Shibata)	129 130 158	42 Recn Sendai		12 FA Sendai		42 Sendai	42 Sendai.
43 Nagoya	Shizuoka Nagoya Gifu	118 135 136	43 Recn Nagoya		43 FA Nagoya		43 Nagoya (Toyohashi).	43 Nagoya.
46 Kumamoto	Kumamoto Kagoshima Miyazaki (Miyakonojo).	123 145 147	46 Recn Kumamoto.		46 FA Kumamoto		46 Kumamoto	46 Kumamoto.
47 Hirosaki	Yamagata Akita Aomori (Hirosaki)	91 105 131	47 Cav. Hirosaki		47 Mtn Hirosaki		47 Hirosaki (Morioka).	47 Hirosaki.
48 Formosa	(Taihoku) (Tainan)	1 Form. 2 Form. 47	48 Recn		48 Mtn		48	48
51 Utsunomiya	Utsunomiya Mito Maebashi (Takasaki)	66 102 115	51 Recn Utsunomiya.		14 FA of the arty grp Utsunomiya	51	51 Utsunomiya (Mito).	51 Utsunomiya.
52 Kanazawa	Toyama Kanazawa Nagano (Matsumoto)	69 107 150	52 Cav Kanazawa		16 Mtn Kanazawa		52 Kanazawa	52 Kanazawa.
53 Kyoto	Fukui (Tsuruga) Kyoto Tsu	119 128 151	53 Recn Kyoto		53 FA Kyoto		53 Kyoto (Fushimi).	53 Kyoto.
54 Himeji	Kobe (Himeji) Tottori Okayama	111 121 154	54 Recn Himeji		54 FA Himeji		54 Himeji (Okayama).	54 Himeji.
55 Zentsuji	Takamatsu (Marugame). Tokushima Kochi	112 143 144	55 Cav Zentsuji		55 Mtn Zentsuji		55 Zentsuji	55 Zentsuji.
56 Kurume	Fukuoka Nagasaki (Omura) Fukuoka	113 146 148	56 Recn and 56 Inf Grp Tkette Co Kurume.		56 FA Kurume		56 Kurume	56 Kurume.
57 Hirosaki	Aomori (Hirosaki) Akita Yamagata	52 117 132	57 Recn Hirosaki		57 FA of the Arty Grp Hirosaki.	57	57 Hirosaki (Morioka).	57 Hirosaki.
58 Kumamoto?		[1] 92 [1] 93 [1] 94 [1] 95 [1] 96 [1] 106 [1] 107 [1] 108					58 Div Engr Unit Kumamoto	58 Div Tnpt Unit Kumamoto.

[1] I. I. Bn.

Divisions	Regimental conscription district and/or location of depot	Div inf regt	Div cav or recn unit	Div tank unit	Div arty regt	Div arty grp	Div engr regt	Div tnpt regt
59		¹41 ¹42 ¹43 ¹44 ¹45 ¹109 ¹110 ¹111					59 Div Engr Unit	59 Div Tnpt Unit.
60 Japan?	(Tokyo) (Tokyo) (Tokyo)	¹46 ¹47 ¹48 ¹49 ¹50 ¹112 ¹113 ¹114					60 Div Engr Unit	60 Div Tnpt Unit.
61 Tokyo	Tokyo? Kofu? Chiba (Sakura)	101 149 157					61 Div Engr Unit	61 Div Tnpt Unit.
62	Fukui (Tsuruga)? Kyoto? Tsu?	¹11 ¹12 ¹13 ¹14 ¹15 ¹80 ¹81 ¹137					62 Div Engr Unit?	62 Div Tnpt Unit?
63		¹21 ¹22 ¹23 ¹24 ¹25 ¹77 ¹78 ¹79					63 Div Engr Unit?	63 Div Tnpt Unit?
64	Matsue (Hamada)? Yamaguchi?	¹51 ²52 53 54 55 131 132 133					64 Div Engr Unit?	64 Div Tnpt Unit?
64 Ind Inf Group, Osaka.	Nara Kobe (Sasayama)	106 153 168						
65	Shizuoka	¹56 57 58 59 60 134 135 136					65 Div Engr Unit?	65 Div Tnpt Unit?
65 Brigade, Zentsuji, Hiroshima.	Hiroshima (Fukuyama).	141					65 Brig Engr Unit	
68		¹61 62 63 64 65 115 116 117					68 Div Engr Unit	68 Div Tnpt Unit.
69 Hirosaki	Akita? Yamagata? Yamagata? Aomori (Hirosaki) Akita Yamagata	¹82 ¹83 ¹84 ¹85 ¹86 ¹118 ¹119 ¹120					69 Div Engr Unit Hirosaki (Morioka).	69 Div Tnpt Unit
70 Hiroshima	Hiroshima Matsue (Hamada) Matsue (Hamada) Yamaguchi Hiroshima Yamaguchi	¹102 ¹103 ¹104 ¹105 ¹121 ¹122 ¹123 ¹124					70 Div Engr Unit	70 Div Tnpt Unit.
71	Tottori	87 88 140	71 Cav		71 Mtn		71	71.
104 Osaka	Osaka Osaka (Sakai) Wakayama	108 137 161	104 Cav Bn		104 FA Osaka (Shinodayama).		104 Osaka (Takatsuki).	104 Osaka.
110 Himeji	Okayama Kobe (Himeji)	110 139 163	110 Cav Bn		110 FA Himeji		110 Himeji (Okayama.)	110 Himeji.
116 Kyoto	Kyoto Kyoto (Fukuchiyama) Tsu	109 120 133	120 Cav Bn?		122 FA Kyoto		116 Kyoto (Fushimi).	116 Kyoto.

¹ I. I. Bn.
² Bn.

7. DIVISION HEADQUARTERS. a. General.

A division is commanded by a lieutenant general, with a colonel of the General Staff as Chief of Staff. The staff is in two sections—the General Staff section and the administrative section. To the staff are attached five departmental sections (see d below) and an ordnance, a signal, and a veterinary detachment. In all, there are about 300 officers and enlisted men.

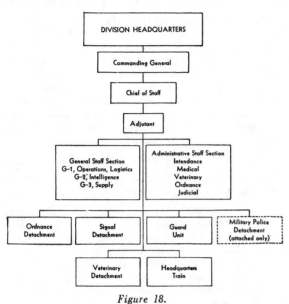

Figure 18.

b. General Staff section. (1) The General Staff section is composed of about 75 officers and enlisted men. The Chief of Staff supervises and coordinates the work of the General and Administrative Staffs. He acts as the link between the division commander and the unit commanders, heads of departments, and the civil authorities. All questions are referred to the Chief of Staff before submission to the division commander either by heads of departments or by the group or regimental commanders.

(2) G–1 is a lieutenant colonel who deals with operations, communications, and training. He has a signal officer, a code officer, a gas officer, and an ordnance officer as assistants.

(3) G–2 is a major who deals primarily with intelligence, maps, censorship, and mobilization.

(4) G–3 is a captain who deals with rear services, supplies, and line-of-communications matters.

(5) The adjutant is a lieutenant colonel who is assisted by a captain and a lieutenant.

c. Administrative staff section. This section, together with the departmental sections, is composed of about 175 officers and enlisted men. The head of the section is a lieutenant colonel who deals with all reports, except those relating to operations, and exercises general supervision of administrative work. The section includes a captain or lieutenant in charge of promotions, appointments,

personal records of officers and noncommissioned officers, personnel, and administrative details of mobilization; a captain or lieutenant in charge of all affairs connected with the departmental services, and who is responsible for administrative orders; and a captain or lieutenant in charge of documents and the secretarial work of the division.

d. Departmental sections. The number of officers employed in each special staff section varies with divisions. The services represented are as follows:

(1) *Intendance.* A colonel, three field officers, and seven or more captains or lieutenants.

(2) *Medical.* A colonel and two or three other medical officers.

(3) *Veterinary.* A lieutenant colonel and one or two other veterinary officers.

(4) *Ordnance.* One field officer and two or more captains or lieutenants from the technical service.

(5) *Judicial* (*legal*). Several officers.

e. Detachments. The ordnance, signal, veterinary, and guard detachments, together with the drivers of vehicles used to transport the division staff and part of its equipment, make up the rest of the headquarters.

8. DIVISION SIGNAL UNIT. a. General.

The division signal unit, commanded by a captain, is composed of a headquarters, two wire (line or L/T) platoons, one radio (wireless or W/T) platoon, and a material (equipment) platoon. Its strength is about 250 officers and enlisted men.

b. Organization.

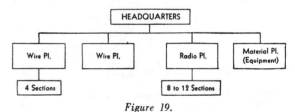

Figure 19.

(1) Variations in the strengths of this unit as shown in the different divisions may be explained by the varying number of radio sections. In all signal units it is common practice to add or decrease the number of radios as required.

(2) The company headquarters consists of a command section composed of the captain in command and about 20 noncommissioned officers and enlisted men. A runner or liaison section may be included.

(3) Each wire (line or L/T) platoon is divided into four sections. Total strength of the platoon is about 50 officers and enlisted men. A first or second lieutenant is in command. The radio (wireless or W/T) platoon is divided into sections each with one set. The number of sections varies from about 8 to 12. Total strength is about 100 to 125 men. A first or second lieutenant is in command.

The material (equipment) platoon is divided into two equipment sections. Total strength is about 35.

c. Equipment. The approximate total of signal equipment in the unit is 32 telephones, 30 miles of insulated wire, 2 radio sets (ground to air), and 8 to 10 other radios. The unit also utilizes pigeons, dogs, helio lamps, semaphores, and ground panels, as well as plane pickups. Some personnel are armed with rifles.

9. THE INFANTRY GROUP. a. General.

The infantry group is commanded by a major general and consists of a headquarters, an infantry group signal unit (only in the strengthened division), and three infantry regiments. In some instances, tankette companies, of 80 to 120 men with 10 to 17 tankettes, have been assigned to the infantry group.

b. Infantry group headquarters. The headquarters, composed of 70 to 100 officers and men, is divided into an administrative staff, a headquarters guard (equipped with automatic weapons), and a small field (baggage) section. In the standard division a small signal unit may be furnished from the division signal unit.

c. Infantry group signal unit. Found only in the strengthened divisions, this unit usually is commanded by a captain and is divided into a company headquarters, a wire (line or L/T) platoon, and a radio (wireless or W/T) platoon. The strength is about 115 officers and enlisted men.

Strength analysis.
   Unit Commander—Captain_____ 1
   Unit Headquarters_____ 17
   Line (L/T) Platoon_____ 57
   Radio (or W/T) Platoon_____ 40

Infantry group signal unit—Total____ 115
   Equipment includes an estimated 12 telephones, 5 light radio sets, 2 switchboards, 11 miles of insulated wire and 24 horses.

d. Infantry group tankette company. These units have been identified in a few divisions. They are believed to be organized into three or four platoons and a company train, with a total of from 80 to 120 personnel. They are believed to have 10 to 17 tankettes and trailers. They probably are used for reconnaissance purposes, since divisions in which they are found normally do not have cavalry or reconnaissance regiments. They also may be used for front-line transport.

10. THE INFANTRY REGIMENT. a. General.

The regiment is commanded by a colonel and its components are, in general:

   Regimental headquarters (including regimental train).
   Regimental signal company.
   Regimental infantry gun unit.
   Regimental antitank gun company.
   3 infantry battalions.
   A pioneer or labor unit may be added.

b. Tabular strength and equipment tables.

Units	Personnel	Horses	Rifles	Light machine gun	Grenade discharger	Heavy machine gun	37-mm or 47-mm antitank gun	70-mm battalion gun	75-mm regimental gun
Regimental headquarters (with train)	176	107	(30)	1					
Regimental Signal Co	132	23	(30)						
Regimental Infantry Gun Co	122	37	(20)						4
Regimental Antitank Co	116	23	(20)				6		
3 Infantry Battalions	3,297	483	(2,031)	111	108	36		6	
Each	1,099	161	(677)	37	36	12		2	
Battalion Headquarters and train	147	96	(50)	1					
4 rifle Cos (each)	181		139	9	9				
1 machine gun Co	174	45	(50)			12			
1 Battalion gun platoon	55	20	(20)					2	
Total, Regimental	3,843	(710)	(2,130)	112	108	36	6	6	4

Usually regiments operate in the field with only 24 heavy machine guns.
Figures in parentheses are estimates.

Figure 20. Standard regiment.

The following tables illustrate the two types of the strengthened regiment, as described by the Japanese. The first table illustrates a substantially stronger infantry regiment in which a heavy weapons platoon has been added to the rifle companies and more infantry guns have been added to the regiment.

Units	Personnel	Horses	Rifles	Light machine gun	Grenade discharger	Heavy machine gun	20-mm anti-tank rifle	37- or 47-mm anti-tank gun	70-mm battalion gun	75-mm infantry gun
Regt Hq (with train)	(195)	(140)	(50)	4	( )					
Regt Sig Co	(150)	(25)	(35)	( )	( )					
Regt Inf Gun Bn	(364)	(55)	(45)	( )	( )					8
Regt Pioneer Unit	(100)	(15)	(50)	( )	( )					
3 Inf Bns	4,878	(846)	2,190	111	147	36	24	12	12	
Each	1,626	(282)	730	37	49	12	8	4	4	
Bn Hq and Train	(282)	(159)	50	1	1					
4 Rifle Cos (each)	262	(17)	150	9	12	2	2			
1 MG Co (4 guns)	(73)	(12)	( )			4				
1 AT Co	(100)	(18)	( )					4		
1 Bn Gun Co	(122)	(24)	( )						4	
Total, Regimental	5,687	1,083	(2,370)	(115)	(147)	36	24	12	12	8

Figure 21. Strengthened regiment.

Units	Personnel	Horses	Rifles	Light machine gun	Grenade discharger	Heavy machine gun	20-mm anti-tank rifle	37- or 47-mm anti-tank gun	70-mm battalion gun	75-mm infantry gun
Regt Hq (with train)	(198)	(125)	(50)	(4)	( )					
Regt Sig co	(130)	(23)	(30)	( )	( )					
Regt Inf Gun co	(170)	(42)	(20)	( )	( )					4
Regt AT co	(130)	(23)	(20)	( )	( )			6		
3 Inf Bns and Train	4,203	543	(2,250)	111	147	36	24		12	
Each	1,401	181	(750)	37	49	12	8		4	
Bn Hq and Train	(177)	96	(50)	(1)	(1)					
4 Rifle cos (each)	205		150	9	12					
1 MG co (12 guns)	(174)	(45)	( )			12				
1 Bn Gun co	(230)	(40)	( )				8		4	
Total, Regimental	4,831	756	2,370	(115)	(147)	36	24	6	12	4

Figures in parentheses are interpolations.
( ) indicates presence believed.

Figure 22. Strengthened—modified—regiment.

c. Infantry regimental headquarters. (1) *General.* The infantry regimental headquarters normally is composed of about 55 officers and enlisted men. It consists of a staff, made up of administration, code and intelligence, ordnance, and intendance sections. In addition there is an antiaircraft section, or headquarters guard, and a color guard. Total strength of headquarters with train is about 176 officers and enlisted men.

(2) *Strength analysis.* (a) *Officer personnel.*

Regimental commander—colonel	1
Operations and training officer—major	1
Adjutant—major or captain	1
Color bearer—lieutenant	1
Code and intelligence officer	1
Gas (or smoke) officer	1
Ordnance officer	1
Intendance officer	1
Medical officers	2
Veterinary officer	1
Total	11

(Additional officers may be attached.)

(b) *Administration section.*

Sergeant major in charge of personnel records	1
Sergeant major in charge of supply	1
Sergeant major in charge of arms and equipment	1
Sergeant major in charge of orders (liaison)	1
Runners and orderlies	6
Medical orderlies	2
Veterinary orderlies	2
Total	14

(c) *Code and Intelligence section.* Two noncommissioned officers and eight men.

(d) *Ordnance section.* One ordnance noncommissioned officer and six technical noncommissioned officers.

(e) *Intendance section.* Three men, including pay noncommissioned officer.

(f) *Antiaircraft section or headquarters guard* (1 light machine gun). One noncommissioned officer and four men.

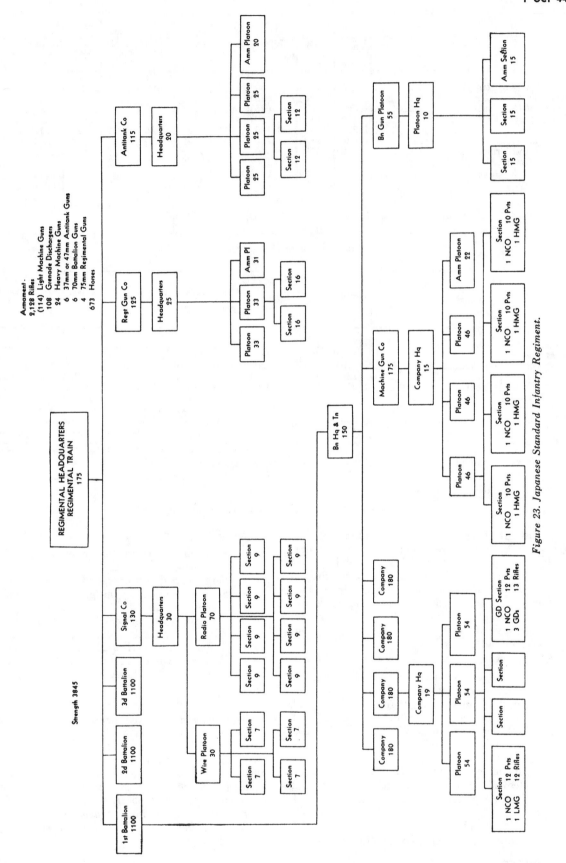

Figure 23. Japanese Standard Infantry Regiment.

(g) *Color guard.* Five men.

(3) *Regimental train.* (a) *General.* The regimental train is divided into a field (baggage) section and an ammunition section. The baggage section usually includes about 30 one-horse, two-wheeled transportation carts, or about 40 pack horses. It carries the regimental baggage as well as one day's rations for regimental units not included in battalions. Kitchen equipment normally is carried in the division train, but it may be attached to regiments. Frequently all trains of all regimental units are grouped in one body. The ammunition train, equipped with horses and two-wheeled transport carts, carries a day's unit of fire for the regiment.

(b) *Strength analysis.*

1. *Field (baggage) section.* One noncommissioned officer and 39 men.
2. *Ammunition section.* One noncommissioned officer and 80 men.
3. *Regimental train.* 121 men.

(c) Size of the regimental train will vary. If motorized, the train will be reduced in most cases.

d. Regimental pioneer (labor) unit. The type "A" organization definitely includes in its establishment a regimental pioneer unit of set composition. This consists of a commander, 6 sections, and a material section. It numbers from 100 to 200 men, and its duties consist of general construction work. When "B" class divisions are moved into areas where personnel are required for demolition work, road construction, etc., a labor unit, consisting of four or five sections, can be drawn from the infantry companies and augmented by a few engineers. While a regimental labor company, with a strength as high as 250, may be found in any division, this does not necessarily involve any increase in the strength of the regiments.

e. Regimental signal company. (1) *General.* The signal company consists of a headquarters, one wire (line or L/T) platoon, and one radio (wireless or W/T) platoon, with a total of about 132 officers and men.

(2) *Organization.*

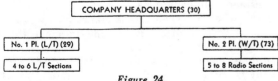

Figure 24.

The number of radio sets used in comparison with the number L/T sets will depend on the type of operations involved.

(3) *Strength analysis.* (a) *Company commander*—captain or first lieutenant.

(b) *Company headquarters (command section).* Twenty-nine men.

1. *Administration section.*

Sergeant major in charge of personnel records	1
Noncommissioned officer in charge of supply	1
Noncommissioned officer in charge of arms and equipment	1
Orderlies	5
Medical orderlies	2

2. *Runner (liaison) section.* Warrant officer in charge and 18 men.

(c) *No. 1 Platoon (Wire or L/T).* Twenty-nine men.

Platoon commander—lieutenant.
4 wire sections (noncommissioned officer and 6 men per section).

(d) *No. 2 Platoon (radio or W/T).* Seventy-three officers and men.

Platoon commander—lieutenant.
8 Radio sections (noncommissioned officer and 8 men per section).

(4) *Equipment.* The approximate signal equipment in the company is 12 to 20 telephone sets, 11 to 30 miles of insulated wire, 3 to 5 light radio sets, 2 to 3 ground to air sets, ground to air panels, dog sections, pigeons sections, heliograph, and other usual signal equipment.

f. Regimental infantry gun company. (1) *General.* The company consists of a headquarters, a firing unit of 2 platoons (total of 4 guns), and an ammunition platoon. The total strength is 122 officers and enlisted men.

(2) *Organization.*

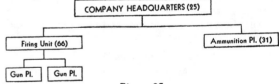

Figure 25.

(3) *Strength analysis.* (a) *Company commander.* Captain.

(b) *Ordnance officer.* Captain.

(c) *Company headquarters (command section).* Twenty-three men.

1. *Administration section.*

Sergeant major in charge of personnel records	1
Noncommissioned officer in charge of supply	1
Noncommissioned officer in charge of weapons and equipment	1
Runners and orderlies	6
Medical orderlies	2

2. *Signal section.* Noncommissioned officer and six men.

3. *Observation section.* Noncommissioned officer and four men.

(d) *Firing unit (two gun platoons, each thirty-three)*. Nos. 1 and 2 gun platoons.

> Platoon commander—lieutenant.
> 2 gun sections (noncommissioned officer and 15 men per section).

(e) *Ammunition platoon*, 31 men.

(f) *Regimental infantry gun company*. Total—122 men.

(5) The armament of the regimental gun company often has been found to consist of two regimental guns and two antitank guns, instead of the standard four 75-mm regimental infantry guns. At times mortars (probably the short barreled 81-mm) may be substituted or included.

g. Regimental infantry gun battalion. (1) *General.* The battalion consists of a small headquarters group of 24 officers and enlisted men and 2 "A" type gun companies. The company comprises a firing unit of 2 platoons (total of four guns) and an ammunition platoon. The strength of the company is 170, and the total strength of the battalion is 364 officers and enlisted men.

(2) *Organization.*

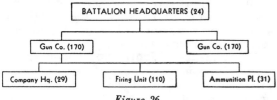

Figure 26.

(3) *Strength analysis of "A" type gun company.* (a) *Company commander.* Major or captain.

(b) *Ordnance officer.* Captain.

(c) *Company Headquarters (command section).* Twenty-seven men.

> 1. *Administration section.*
>
> | | |
> |---|---|
> | Warrant officer in charge of personnel | 1 |
> | Sergeant major in charge of personnel records | 1 |
> | Noncommissioned officer in charge of supply | 1 |
> | Noncommissioned officer in charge of weapons and equipment | 1 |
> | Runners and orderlies (1 Mounted) | 3 |
> | Medical orderlies | 2 |
>
> 2. *Signal section.* Noncommissioned officer and six men.
>
> 3. *Observation section.* Noncommissioned officer and 10 men.

(d) *Firing unit (two gun platoons, each fifty-five)*. Nos. 1 and 2 gun platoons.

> | | |
> |---|---|
> | Platoon commander—lieutenant | 1 |
> | 2 gun sections (noncommissioned officer and 26 men) | 54 |

(e) *Ammunition platoon.* 31 men.

(4) *Equipment.* Four 75-mm regimental infantry guns.

h. Regimental antitank company. (1) *General.* The regimental antitank company consists of a headquarters, a firing unit of three platoons, and an ammunition platoon. The total strength is about 115 officers and enlisted men equipped with six antitank guns.

(2) *Organization.*

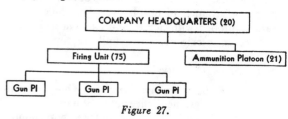

Figure 27.

(3) *Strength analysis.* (a) *Company commander*—Captain.

(b) *Company headquarters (command section).* Nineteen men.

> 1. *Administration section.*
>
> | | |
> |---|---|
> | Sergeant major in charge of personnel | 1 |
> | Noncommissioned officer in charge of supply | 1 |
> | Noncommissioned officer in charge of arms and equipment | 1 |
> | Runners and orderlies | 7 |
> | Medical orderlies | 2 |
>
> 2. *Observation section.* Noncommissioned officer and six men.

(c) *Firing unit (three gun platoons, each 25)*. No. 1 gun platoon (Nos. 2 and 3 platoons the same).

> | | |
> |---|---|
> | Platoon commander—lieutenant | 1 |
> | 2 gun sections (noncommissioned officer and 11 men) | 24 |

(d) *Ammunition platoon.* 21 men.

(4) *Equipment.* Six 37-mm antitank guns.

(5) A common variant is for this unit to be merged with the regimental infantry gun unit, the armament of which then consists of 2 regimental guns and 2 antitank guns.

(6) The "A" type antitank gun company has increased strength of about 130 officers and enlisted men and is equipped with six 37-mm antitank guns. In the strengthened type division the antitank company is not a regimental unit, but there are 3 antitank companies, one in each infantry battalion, and each company usually is equipped with 4 antitank guns. The strength of this 4-gun company is approximately 100 officers and enlisted men.

i. Infantry battalion (standard). (1) *General.* The infantry battalion normally is commanded by a major and consists of a headquarters and train, 4 rifle companies, and machine gun company, and a battalion gun platoon. Its total strength is 1,100 officers and enlisted men.

(2) *Organization.*

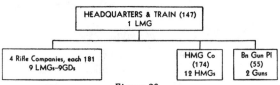

Figure 28.

(3) *Equipment.* There are approximately 677 rifles, 36 grenade dischargers, 37 light machine guns, 12 (8) heavy machine guns (7.7-mm), 2 battalion 70-mm guns.

j. Infantry battalion (strengthened). (1) *General.* This infantry battalion normally is commanded by a major and consists of a headquarters and train, 4 rifle companies, a machine gun company, a battalion gun company, and a battalion antitank company. Its total strength is 1,626 officers and enlisted men.

(2) *Organization.*

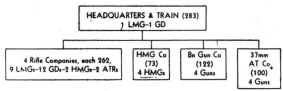

Figure 29.

(3) *Equipment.* There are approximately 730 rifles, 37 light machine guns, 49 grenade dischargers, 4 heavy machine guns (7.7-mm), eight 20-mm antitank rifles, four 37-mm antitank guns, 4 battalion 70-mm guns.

k. Infantry battalion (strengthened, modified). (1) *General.* This infantry battalion normally is commanded by a major and consists of a headquarters and train, 4 rifle companies, a machine-gun company, and a battalion-gun company. Its total strength is 1,401 officers and enlisted men.

(2) *Organization.*

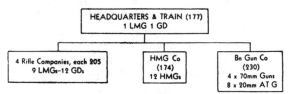

Figure 30.

(3) *Equipment.* There are approximately 750 rifles, 37 light machine guns, 49 grenade dischargers, 12 heavy machine guns (7.7-mm), eight 20-mm antitank rifles, and four 70-mm battalion guns.

l. Battalion headquarters. (1) *General.* The battalion headquarters normally consists of about 37 officers and enlisted men, divided into administration, ordnance and intendance, liaison, code and

intelligence, and an antiaircraft. or headquarters guard, sections. In addition there is a battalion train. Total strength of battalion headquarters and train is 147 officers and enlisted men.

(2) *Strength analysis.*

(a) *Officer personnel.* 8 men.

Battalion commander—major_____	1
Adjutant—captain or lieutenant_____	1
Ordnance officer_____	1
Intendance officer_____	1
Medical officers_____	3
Veterinary officer_____	1

(Additional officers may be attached.)

(b) *Administration section.* 14 men.

Sergeant major in charge of personnel__	1
Sergeant major in charge of supplies___	1
Sergeant major in charge of arms and equipment_____	1
Sergeant major in charge of orders (liaison) _____	1
Runners and orderlies_____	5
Medical orderlies_____	4
Veterinary orderly_____	1

(c) *Ordnance and intendance section.* Two noncommissioned officers and one technician.

(d) *Liaison section.* 4 men.

(e) *Code and intelligence section.* One noncommissioned officer and two men.

(f) *AA section or headquarters guard (1 LMG).* 5 men.

(3) *Battalion train.* The battalion train is generally similar in equipment and function to the regimental train.

(a) *Field (baggage) section.* Noncommissioned officer and 49 men.

(b) *Ammunition section.* Noncommissioned officer and 59 men.

(c) *Battalion train.* 110 men.

Note. Strength of the battalion train may vary. If motor transport is used it will normally be reduced.

m. Infantry rifle company ("B") type. (1) *General.* The company consists of a company commander, usually a captain, a company headquarters, and three rifle platoons. Total strength is 181 officers and enlisted men.

(2) *Organization.*

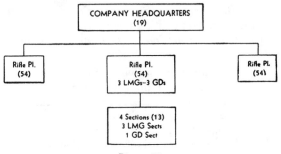

Figure 31.

(3) *Strength analysis.* (a) *C o m p a n y com-mander.* Captain.

(b) *Company headquarters (command section).*

Warrant officer in charge of personnel___	1
Sergeant major in charge of personnel records_____	1
Noncommissioned officer in charge of supply _____	1
Noncommissioned officer in charge of arms and equipment_____	1
Runners and o r d e r l i e s (including buglers) _____	10
Medical orderlies _____	4
Total_____	18

(c) *3 Rifle platoons (each 54).* 162 officers and men.

1. No. 1 platoon.

Platoon commander—lieutenant_	1
Liaison noncommissioned officer_	1
3 rifle-Light machine gun sections (noncommissioned officer and 12 men)_____	39
1 grenade discharger section____	13

2. No. 2 and No. 3 platoons. Same as No. 1.

(4) *Equipment.* There are in the company 139 rifles, nine light machine guns, and nine grenade dischargers.

n. Infantry rifle company ("A" type without heavy weapons platoon). (1) *General.* The company consists of a company commander, usually a captain, a company headquarters, and 3 rifle platoons. Total strength is 205 officers and enlisted men.

(2) *Organization.*

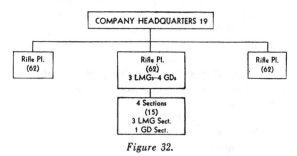

Figure 32.

(3) *Strength analysis.* (a) *Company commander.* Captain or First Lieutenant.

(b) *Company headquarters (command section).* 18 men.

Warrant officer in charge of personnel__	1
Sergeant major in charge of personnel records _____	1
Noncommissioned officer in charge of supply_____	1
Noncommissioned officer in charge of arms and equipment_____	1

Runners and orderlies (including buglers) _____	10
Medical orderlies_____	4

(c) *3 Rifle platoons (each 62).* 186 officers and men.

1. No. 1 Rifle platoon.

Platoon commander_____	1
Liaison noncommissioned officer_____	1
3 rifle-light machine gun sections (noncommissioned officer and 14 men) _____	45
1 grenade discharge section (noncommissioned officer and 14 men) _____	15

2. No. 2 and No. 3 rifle platoons. Same as No. 1.

(4) *Equipment.* There are in the company 150 rifles, 9 light machine guns, and 12 grenade dischargers.

o. Infantry rifle company ("A" type with heavy weapons platoon). (1) *General.* The company consists of a company commander, usually a captain, a company headquarters, 3 rifle platoons, a heavy weapons platoon, and an ammunition platoon. Total strength is 262.

(2) *Organization.*

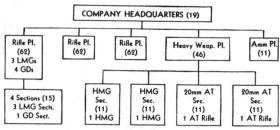

Figure 33.

(3) *Strength analysis.* (a) *Company headquarters and 3 rifle platoons.* 205 officers and men.

(b) *Heavy weapons platoon.* 46 officers and men.

Platoon commander_____	1
Liaison noncommissioned officer_____	1
2 heavy machine gun sections (noncommissioned officer and 10 men)_____ (2 7.7-mm heavy machine guns)	22
2 antitank rifle sections (noncommissioned officer and 10 men)_____ (2 20-mm antitank rifles)	22

(c) *Ammunition platoon.* Eleven men.

(4) *Equipment.* There are in the company 150 rifles, 9 light machine guns, 12 grenade dischargers, 2 heavy machine guns, two 20-mm antitank rifles.

p. Battalion machine-gun company (12-gun company). (1) *General.* This machine-gun company consists of a headquarters, a firing unit of 3 platoons (each having 4 heavy machine guns), and an ammunition platoon. The total strength is 174 officers and enlisted men.

(2) *Organization.*

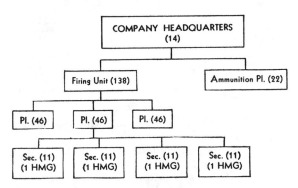

Figure 34.

(3) *Strength analysis.* (*a*) *Company commander.* Captain or First Lieutenant.

(*b*) *Company headquarters* (**command section**). 13 men.

Warrant officer in charge of personnel__	1
Sergeant major in charge of personnel records_____	1
Noncommissioned officer in charge of supply_____	1
Noncommissioned officer in charge of arms and equipment_____	1
Runners and orderlies (including buglers)_____	6
Medical orderlies_____	3

(*c*) *Firing unit* (*3 platoons, each 46*).

1. No. 1 machine gun platoon.

Platoon commander, first or second lieutenant_____	1
Liaison noncommissioned officer_	1
4 gun sections (noncommissioned officer and 10 men)_____	44

2. No. 2 and No. 3 machine gun platoons. Same as No. 1.

(*d*) *Ammunition platoon.* 22 men.
Noncommissioned officer in charge.
3 sections of 7.

(4) *Equipment.* The company has twelve 7.7 heavy machine guns.

q. Battalion machine-gun company (8-gun company). (1) *General.* The eight machine-gun company consists of a headquarters, a firing unit of 4 platoons (each having 2 heavy machine guns), and an ammunition platoon. The total strength is 144. It is this company which has been met most commonly in recent operations.

(2) *Organization.*

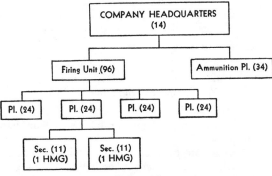

Figure 35.

r. Battalion machine-gun company (4-gun company). (1) *General.* This company has only 4 machine guns; the other 8 of the normal battalion complement of 12 guns usually have been allocated to the rifle companies and are shown in the rifle companies' strengths. The company consists of a headquarters, 2 gun platoons, and a small ammunition platoon. The total strength is 73.

(2) *Organization.*

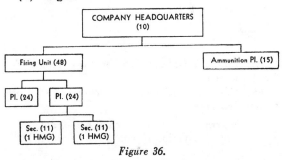

Figure 36.

s. Battalion gun platoon. (1) *General.* The battalion gun platoon consists of a headquarters, a firing unit of 2 gun sections, and an ammunition section. Its total strength is 55 officers and enlisted men. It is equipped with two 70-mm battalion guns.

(2) *Organization.*

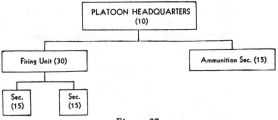

Figure 37.

(3) *Strength analysis.* (*a*) *Platoon commander.* First or Second Lieutenant.

(*b*) *Platoon headquarters* (*command section*). Nine men.

Sergeant major in charge of personnel records_____	1
Noncommissioned officer in charge of arms and equipment_____	1

Noncommissioned officer in charge of the observers_____ 1
Runners and orderlies_____ 5
Medical orderly_____ 1

(c) *Firing unit.* 30 men.

    1. *No. 1 gun section.* Noncommissioned officer, two observers, 12 gunners.
    2. *No. 2 gun section.* Same as No. 1.

(d) *Ammunition section.* 15 men.

(4) *Equipment.* The platoon has two 70-mm battalion guns.

t. Battalion gun company (without antitank rifles). (1) *General.* The battalion gun company consists of a headquarters, a firing unit of 2 gun platoons, and an ammunition platoon. Its total strength is 122.

(2) *Organization.*

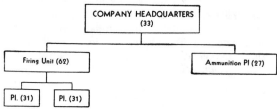

Figure 38.

(3) *Strength analysis.* (a) *Company commander.* First Lieutenant.

(b) *Company headquarters (command section).* Thirty-two men.

Warrant officer in charge of personnel__ 1
Sergeant major in charge of personnel records_____ 1
Noncommissioned officer in charge of supply_____ 1
Noncommissioned officer in charge of arms and equipment_____ 1
Noncommissioned officer in charge of liaison_____ 1
Signal section (noncommissioned officer and 8 men)_____ 9
Runners and orderlies_____ 5
Medical orderlies_____ 2
Observation section (noncommissioned officer and 10 men)_____ 11

(c) *Firing unit (two gun platoons, each 31)*_ 62

Platoon commander—First or Second Lieutenant_____ 1
2 gun sections (noncommissioned officer and 14 men)_____ 30

(4) *Equipment.* The company has four 70-mm battalion guns.

u. Battalion gun company (with antitank rifle). (1) *General.* The battalion gun company consists of a headquarters, a firing unit of 2 gun platoons armed with 70-mm battalion howitzers, 4 platoons of 20-mm antitank rifles, and an ammunition platoon. Its total strength is about 230.

(2) *Organization.*

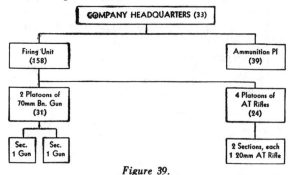

Figure 39.

(3) *Strength analysis.* (a) *Company commander.* Captain or First Lieutenant.

(b) *Company headquarters.* 32 men.

(c) *Firing unit.* 158 men.
    2 70-mm gun platoons (each 31)_____ 62
    4 20-mm rifle platoons (each 24)_____ 96

(d) *Ammunition platoon.* 39 men.

(4) *Equipment.* The company has four 70-mm battalion guns and eight 20-mm antitank rifles.

11. DIVISION ARTILLERY. a. General. The normal artillery component of a standard division is a 36-gun regiment of 75-mm field or mountain artillery which may be motorized, horse-drawn, or pack.

b. Field artillery regiment (horse-drawn). (1) *General.* The regular field artillery regiment consists of a regimental headquarters, three battalions of 75-mm guns (each battalion having a battalion headquarters, three gun companies, and a train), and a regimental train. Total strength is about 2,300 officers and enlisted men. Normal armament is thirty-six 75-mm guns.

(2) *Organization.*

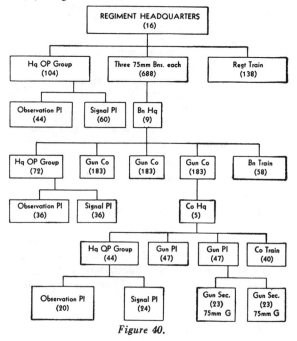

Figure 40.

(3) *The regimental headquarters.* The regimental headquarters consists of a colonel or lieutenant colonel in command, an adjutant, and a staff of about 14 noncommissioned officers and enlisted men. There is a headquarters operational group composed of an observation platoon, and a signal platoon consisting of one wire (line or L/T) section and one radio section. The total strength of the headquarters, including the headquarters operational group, is about 120 officers and enlisted men.

(4) The regimental train is commanded by a captain or a lieutenant and is divided into the 3 ammunition platoons and a field (baggage) platoon. The total strength is about 140 officers and enlisted men.

(5) A battalion consists of a headquarters, 3 companies, and a train. The strength is about 680 to 700 officers and enlisted men.

(6) Battalion headquarters, commanded by a major, is composed of a battalion staff and a headquarters operational group. The latter is divided into an observation platoon and a signal platoon. A machine-gun section for defense also is reported. The total strength of the headquarters, including the headquarters operational group, is about 80 officers and enlisted men.

(7) The battalion train is commanded by a captain or lieutenant and consists of 3 ammunition sections and a field (or baggage) section. The total strength is about 60 officers and enlisted men.

(8) Companies, commanded by captains, are composed of a company staff, a headquarters operational group, 2 gun platoons (each of 2 sections of about 20 men each), and a company train. The total strength is about 180 officers and enlisted men, with four 75-mm field guns.

(9) *Regimental equipment.* There is a total of thirty-six 75-mm field guns. It is estimated that there are 450 rifles (138 per battalion and 34 per company) and approximately 2,000 horses to the regiment.

(10) Should the artillery regiment be fully motorized the following estimates are likely:

Regimental headquarters___	124 personnel
Regimental train _____	107 personnel
Three battalions (each 563)_	1689 personnel
Total regimental strength__	1920 personnel

c. Mountain artillery (pack). (1) *General.* Mountain artillery regiments are similar to field artillery regiments, except that all equipment is carried on pack animals, and the companies are armed with 75-mm mountain guns instead of 75-mm field pieces. Strengths are increased so that the regimental totals are about 3000 to 3400 officers and men with thirty-six 75-mm mountain guns. Some mountain artillery regiments may include a battalion of 105-mm pack (mountain) howitzers. Existence of such a weapon has been reported but not confirmed.

(2) *Organization.*

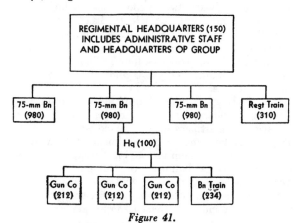

Figure 41.

(3) *Strength analysis* (estimate only).
(a) *Regimental Headquarters.* 150 men.
   1. *Administrative Section.* 15 men.
   2. *Headquarters operational group.* 135 men.

Observation platoon _____	60
Wire (L/T) section_____	50
Radio (W/T) section_____	25

(b) *Regimental train.* 310 men.
(c) *Three battalions* (*each 980*). 2,940 men.
   1. *Battalion headquarters.* 100 men.

Administrative section_____	10
Headquarters operational group_	90

   2. *Battalion train.* 234 men.
   3. *Three gun companies* (*each 218*).

Company headquarters_____	60
Company train_____	42
2 gun platoons (each 55) _____	110

(4) *Regimental equipment.* There is a total of thirty-six 75-mm mountain guns.

d. Mixed field artillery regiment. (1) *General.* The field artillery regiment normally consists of a headquarters and train and 3 battalions of 75-mm field guns or 105-mm howitzers. When horse-drawn, the regiment numbers approximately 2,380 officers and enlisted men. This figure will decrease with the degree of motorization.

(2) *Organization.*

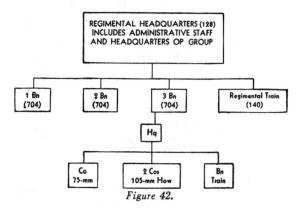

Figure 42.

(3) *Equipment.* There is a total of twelve 75-mm field guns and twenty-four 105-mm howitzers.

e. The medium artillery battalion. This battalion consists of a headquarters (divided into an administrative staff and a headquarters operational group) and 3 companies of four 150-mm howitzers. Its total personnel strength is about 950, and there are 769 horses.

f. Artillery in the strengthened divisions. (1) The artillery element in strengthened divisions consists of an artillery group, composed of the artillery group headquarters, a regiment of field artillery containing 75-mm and 105-mm weapons, and a medium artillery battalion of 150-mm howitzers. Other independent artillery and antiaircraft units may be assigned or attached. The artillery group is under command of either a major general or a colonel.

(2) *Artillery group headquarters.* An artillery group headquarters consists of approximately 160 officers and enlisted men. It includes a staff, a small guard, and a train, and an observation-balloon platoon also may be included. The functions of the group headquarters are to command the organic artillery of the division and unify control of attached artillery.

12. DIVISION CAVALRY. a. General. Each infantry division normally contains either one cavalry or one reconnaissance regiment or unit. Within both the standard and the strengthened divisions, the regimental cavalry is organized basically along the same lines. However, within the modified strengthened division there is a marked difference of organization; accordingly, a separate detailed organization has been shown for the modified cavalry regiment. Also within this division, unlike the other two, there does not appear to be a reconnaissance regiment as an alternative for the cavalry regiment.

b. The cavalry regiment. (1) *General.* The division cavalry regiment consists of a headquarters and train, 3 rifle and saber companies, and a machine gun company. The total strength is 950 officers and enlisted men.

(2) *Organization.*

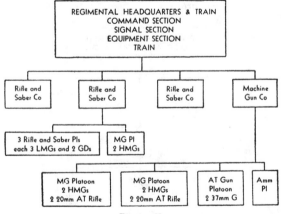

Figure 43.

(3) *Equipment (estimate only).*

	Regimental Headquarters	Rifle and Saber Company	Machine Gun Company	Regimental totals
Rifles or carbines	200	100		500
LMGs	1	9		28
GDs		6		18
HMGs (7.7-mm)		2	4	10
20-mm AT Rifle			4	4
37-mm AT Gun			2	2
Horses	380	180	180	1,100

Figure 44.

(4) *Strength analysis.* (a) *Regimental headquarters.* Eighty-two men.

Command section _____ 20
Signal section (mainly radio) _____ 50
Equipment section _____ 12

(b) *Regimental train.* Two hundred men.

(c) *Three rifle and saber companies (each 170).* Total 510.

Company commander _____ 1
Company headquarters _____ 16

(d) *Three rifle and saber platoons (each 43).* Total 129.

Platoon commander.
Liaison noncommissioned officer.
3 light machine gun sections (noncommissioned officer and 10 men).
1 grenade discharger section (noncommissioned officer and 7 men).
2 grenade dischargers.

(e) *One machine gun platoon.* Twenty-four men.

Platoon commander.
Liaison noncommissioned officer.
Two machine gun sections (noncommissioned officer and 10 men).

(f) *Machine gun company.* One hundred fifty-eight men.

Company commander _____ 1
Company headquarters _____ 13

1. Two machine gun platoons (each 46).

Platoon commander.
Liaison noncommissioned officer.
2 machine gun sections (noncommissioned officer and 10 men).
Two 20-mm antitank rifle sections (noncommissioned officer and 10 men).

2. One antitank gun platoon (37-mm). Twenty-seven men.

Platoon commander.
Observer section.
Two gun sections (noncommissioned officers and 10 men).

3. Ammunition platoon. Twenty-five men.

Platoon commander.
3 sections of 8 men.

c. Cavalry regiment (modified organization). (1) *General.* The cavalry regiment consists of a headquarters, 2 rifle and saber companies, and a machine-gun company. Total strength is about 785 officers and men.

(2) *Organization.*

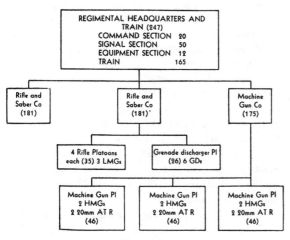

Figure 45.

(3) *Equipment (estimates only).*

	Regimental Headquarters	Rifle and Saber Company	Machine Gun Company	Regimental totals
Rifles and carbines	100	100	------	300
LMGs	1	12	------	25
GDs	------	6	------	12
HMGs (7.7-mm)	------	------	6	6
20-mm AT Rifles	------	------	6	6
Horses	349	191	200	831

Figure 46.

d. Reconnaissance regiment. (1) *General.* Reconnaissance units are divisional cavalry troops and may be used as an alternative to a cavalry regiment. The reconnaissance regiment consists of a headquarters, 1 cavalry company, 2 motorborne companies, 1 armored car (or tankette) company, and 1 motor-truck company. The total strength is about 730 officers and enlisted men.

(2) *Organization.*

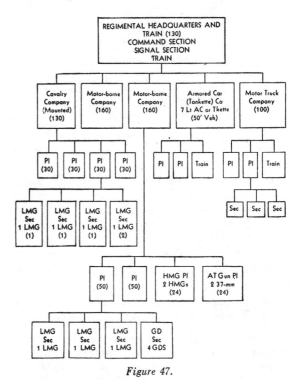

Figure 47.

(3) *Equipment (estimates only).*

	Totals
Rifles or carbines	260
Light machine guns	28
Heavy machine guns	4
37-mm or 47-mm antitank guns	4
Grenade dischargers	16
Light armored cars or tankettes	7
Other vehicles	61
Horses	188

13. DIVISION TANK UNIT. a. General. Only the strengthened divisions contain an organic tank unit equipped with light and medium tanks. The majority of Japanese divisions, however, will be found to have tankettes, either in the infantry group tankette company or in the reconnaissance regiment. Division tank units are believed to have about 20 light tanks and 48 medium tanks, with some of these held in reserve within the combat train. The unit consists of a headquarters, one light-tank company, two medium-tank companies, and a combat train. There are about 80 trucks included in the train.

b. Organization.

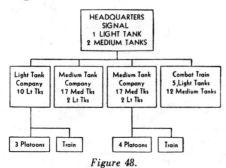

Figure 48.

c. Strength analysis.

	Totals
Headquarters	100
Light tank company	86
2 medium tank companies (each 141)	282
Combat train	250
Tank unit—total	718

d. Equipment.

Light tanks	20
Medium tanks	48
Trucks	80

14. ENGINEERS. a. The three-company regiment. (1) *General.* The engineer regiment of a division is normally composed of a headquarters, three companies, and a regimental material platoon. The total strength is 900 to 1,000 men. Division engineers include among their personnel men trained in tank trap construction, demolition work, and small river crossing operations. The 3 companies of the regiment do not specialize in one particular aspect of engineering, but are designed for sub-allotment, one to each infantry regiment, to fulfill their ordinary engineer requirement. If extensive engineer tasks, such as large scale bridging operations, have to be carried out, specialized engineer units are attached for the purpose.

(2) *Organization.*

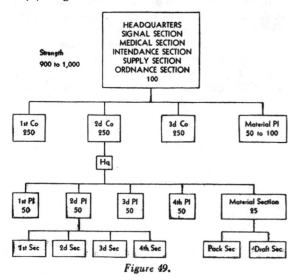

Figure 49.

(3) Regimental headquarters consists of a colonel or lieutenant colonel in command and 4 to 6 other officers; it has a total of approximately 100 officers and enlisted men. It is divided into various sections charged with signal, medical, intendance, ordnance, and supply duties. The men are armed with rifles, and it is estimated that the armament of the regiment includes 6 each of light machine guns, grenade dischargers, mortars, and flame throwers.

(4) Companies are commanded by captains or first lieutenants and are composed of company headquarters, 4 platoons, and a material section. The headquarters is believed to total about 25 men. Platoons usually are commanded by second lieutenants and are divided into 4 sections each. A platoon consists of about 50 men. The material section carries tools and other equipment, with pack and draft sections; its strength is about 25 men. The total company strength is about 250 men.

(5) The regimental material platoon comprises a headquarters and 2 sections, with a total of 50 to 100 men. Equipment may include 15 motor trucks and various construction implements.

b. Two-company regiments. Some divisions may have two-company engineer regiments. The company consists of a headquarters, 4 platoons, and a material section; its total strength is about 240 men with 20 horses. Included as well, is a regimental headquarters and a material platoon, bringing the strength of the regiment to about 600 men.

c. Engineer units. These are few in number; they sometimes appear as components of the small-sized, special type divisions. The commanding officer is a captain. Little information has been received to indicate the numerical strength and composition of such units, but it has been reported to consist of a headquarters and 3 platoons of 4 sections each.

15. MEDICAL. a. General. The Japanese division medical service is an extensive one and includes a medical unit, 3 to 5 field hospitals, and a water purification unit. In addition, other components of the division include a number of medically trained personnel. A reason for this extensive organization is probably the Japanese principle of keeping their casualties as far forward as possible in order to facilitate their quick return to fighting units. Another factor which the Japanese may consider a compensation for the size of their medical organization is that a large proportion of the personnel in medical units are reported to be armed, and instances of their employment as fighting troops are known.

b. Organization.

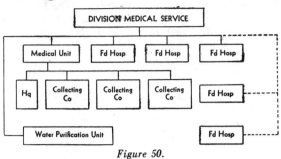

Figure 50.

c. Medical unit. The medical unit consists of a headquarters and train and 3 collecting companies of 3 stretcher platoons and 1 ambulance platoon each. The medical unit, with a personnel strength of 700 to 1,000, is equipped with about 180 litters and 45 ambulances. The collecting companies each have about 20 litters and 15 ambulances. Headquarters train has additional carts for loading medical supplies and patients' clothing, as well as for chemical warfare decontamination material.

d. Field hospitals. (1) *General.* Each field hospital, with its required train, has a personnel of about 250 and is organized to accommodate 500 patients. It may be motorized, pack, or draft. The medical personnel of the field hospitals is under direction of the chief medical officer of the division. Although divisions are known to have 4, and sometimes 5, field hospitals in their organization, only 3 are usually identified as active in combat zones. The fourth, sometimes called the field reserve hospital, has been identified functioning as a convalescent and evacuation station on the line of communications.

(2) *Organization.*

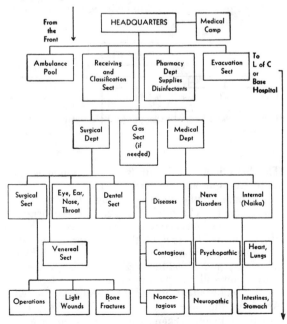

Figure 51.

e. Water purification unit. These units normally have a personnel strength of 50 to 150. They are equipped with material for supply and purification of water for the division, and are charged with prevention of infectious diseases.

f. Medical personnel in division units. Medical officers are attached to units of all arms on the approximate scale of three per battalion or equivalent unit. In addition, the battalion medical officer usually is assisted by two medical service noncommissioned officers, while medical service orderlies are attached to subunits on an average of one to a platoon.

16. TRANSPORT. a. General. The transport regiment has two battalions which may be draft, pack, or motorized. Regimental strength varies between 1,800 and 2,800. About one-third of the personnel may be equipped with rifles.

b. Organization. (1) A standard division transport regiment is believed to be composed of a headquarters, one motor battalion, and one draft battalion. The draft battalion will be made up of three or four companies, with each company divided into three transport platoons, each of which in turn is divided into three sections. The motor battalion is believed to be made up of a headquarters and two or three truck companies, each of three platoons, with each platoon divided into three sections.

(2) Each truck company is estimated at 150 men. Some motor battalions may include a road maintenance company of 125, and an armored car transport company of 50 men. These units are in addition to the truck companies. The truck company has about 50 vehicles. Truck capacity is about 1½ tons. The draft company has 250 single-horse, 2-wheeled, transportation carts, each with a capacity of 400 to 500 pounds.

(3) Evidence is available that a division transport regiment also could be composed of a headquarters, 8 draft companies, and a veterinary detachment. Each of the draft companies approximates 350 officers and enlisted men and is divided into 3 transport platoons and a combat platoon. Two pack-horse companies may be substituted for one draft company. A pack horse company, consisting of approximately 450 officers and men, is similar in organization to the draft company. It has about 300 pack-horses, each with an average loading capacity of 200 pounds.

(4) In an eight-company draft regiment, typical supply columns are loaded as follows:

I Small arms ammunition,
    1 company and 1 platoon
II Artillery ammunition,
    2 companies and 1 platoon
III Chemical warfare_____ 1 platoon
IV Rations and forage_____ 4 companies

17. VETERINARY UNIT. Each division has as part of its organization a veterinary unit of from 50 to 100 officers and enlisted men. It probably consists of a veterinary hospital staff with individual sections assigned during combat to the various divisional units.

18. ORDNANCE UNIT. Divisions also have ordnance personnel assigned from the technical service. The unit consists of 50 to 200 officers and enlisted men depending on the size of the division.

19. CHEMICAL WARFARE UNIT. a. Available evidence indicates that only the strongest divisions have an organic decontamination unit. Such a unit is divided into three platoons, each of three sections, and a unit train. The first two platoons, which are apparently similar in organization, have a number of armored transport vehicles and trailers for decontaminated roads and other areas. The third platoon has decontamination cars for handling contaminated clothing and equipment, while the three-section wagon train carries the necessary equipment and reserve clothing.

b. The decontamination unit may be either motorized or pack; basic organizations of each type are similar. If motorized, the unit's total strength approximates 150; a pack unit will have a personnel of about 250.

c. No gas or decontamination units are known to exist in other type divisions. However, picked personnel in all units have been designated as "gas personnel" and are responsible for decontamination in addition to their regular duties. This personnel also can be formed into special "smoke" companies for the laying of smoke screens, and it is probable that in some cases they are capable of handling chemical warfare agents as well.

20. TANK GROUPS (ARMORED DIVISIONS). a. General. A number of reports have been received of the existence of tank groups (Senshadan). These are believed to consist of 3 or 4 tank regiments plus a signal and engineer unit. (For the organization of a tank regiment, see sec. II, par. 3a (1).) Other evidence indicates that the Japanese may have formed armored divisions, of which the tank groups may be the nucleus.

b. Organization. Organization of such an armored division has been described as follows:

	Strengths	
	Personnel	Vehicles
Headquarters	200	30
Infantry unit, motorized	3,800	475
3 tank regiments (about 250 tanks)	2,550	640
Artillery unit	650	100
Eight 105-mm guns.		
Four 155-mm howitzers.		
Antitank unit (eighteen 47-mm A/T)	500	70
Antiaircraft unit (four 75-mm)	175	25
A/A Machine-gun unit (sixteen 20-mm)	300	50
Engineer unit	500	60
Transport unit	1,500	350
Medical unit	285	50
Total	10,500	1,850

21. GROUPS, BRIGADES, AND OTHER ORGANIZATIONS. a. General. The Japanese have several varieties of organizations, all of which have been designed to fit particular operational conditions and requirements.

b. Cavalry groups and cavalry brigades. (1) *General.* Japanese cavalry groups consist of two cavalry brigades, signal units, and trains.

(2) *Organization of cavalry brigade.*

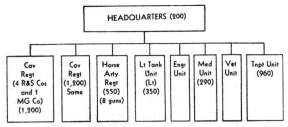

Figure 52.

(3) Antiaircraft and antitank units have also been reported as forming part of these brigades. The total strength of the cavalry brigade has been reported to be about 5,000 to 6,000.

c. Independent infantry groups. The normal infantry group is sometimes found to be independent—that is, it has three infantry regiments without supporting arms and services.

d. Independent infantry brigades. In addition to the infantry brigades assigned to the "special" division (see fig. 14) the Japanese have a number of independent infantry brigades. These brigades consist of four independent infantry battalions and a signal unit. Their estimated strength is 4,900.

e. Independent mixed brigades. (1) *General.* The Japanese independent mixed brigades, as they were formed in China in 1937–38 for garrison and antiguerrilla duties, are believed to be organized as follows:

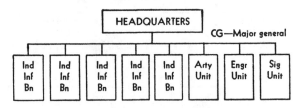

Figure 53.

The battalions consist of 3 or 4 companies, and their strength has been reported to be about 700 to 900 men. Other units are thought to be comparatively small. The total strength of these brigades has been variously reported at between 6,000 to 10,000 men. Several of these independent mixed brigades recently have been converted into infantry divisions, and it is believed that this process of conversion still may be in operation.

(2) *Independent mixed brigades (motorized).* At about the time of the outbreak of the present war the Japanese began to form independent mixed

brigades for a different purpose from those which existed in China. These brigades were shock troops and included tanks, antiaircraft guns, and medium artillery. The infantry element was an infantry regiment of three battalions each of four companies. At least one of these brigades is known to have been motorized. Its organization follows:

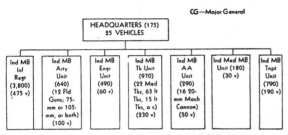

Figure 54.

f. Amphibious brigades. (1) *General.* A new type of unit has recently made its appearance. It is composed of a headquarters and 3 battalions and its strength is about 3,200. A battalion described by the Japanese follows:

(2) *Organization.*

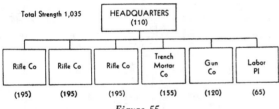

Figure 55.

The rifle companies were composed of three rifle platoons, of five sections each, a trench mortar platoon, and a heavy weapons platoon. The trench mortar company consisted of three platoons of four sections each, while the gun company had three mountain and two antitank guns. The 1st Amphibious Brigade had supporting artillery tank, engineer, machine cannon, and signal units directly under brigade headquarters, bringing total personnel strength to about 4,000. The brigade was commanded by a major general.

22. BORDER AND INDEPENDENT GARRISON UNITS. a. Border garrisons. Border garrisons are commanded either by major generals or colonels and vary in size. No. 1 Border Garrison, for example, is divided into four sectors, each under the command of a colonel. Each sector contains an infantry unit, an artillery unit, and an engineer unit. Most of the other border garrisons are not subdivided into sectors and contain only the three units, the infantry and artillery units being commanded by lieutenant colonels, and the engineer units by captains. It may be assumed that these infantry units are roughly equivalent to battalions. At present all the border garrisons are located in Manchuria.

b. Independent garrisons. Independent garrison units usually are commanded by major generals, although one or two are commanded by colonels. They contain three or four infantry battalions, but apparently no supporting arms or services. They are employed in rear areas.

23. FORTRESSES. a. General. The coastal defense fortresses in the Japanese Empire are to be found in Japan Proper, Korea, Formosa, the Bonin Islands, the Ryukyu Islands, the Pescadores, and Manchuria. These fortresses are commanded by officers ranging from lieutenant general to colonel, according to importance of the fortress. The fortress commander is responsible either to the commander of the army district or to the army commander in the area concerned. Fortification construction comes under the Fortifications Directorate which is responsible to the Chief of Staff.

b. Organization. The normal organization of fortresses is believed to be—

Headquarters:
One heavy artillery regiment or battalion.
One or more infantry battalions.
Construction and port engineers.
Signal units.
AA units.

Armament includes coastal guns ranging from 4.7-inch to 12-inch caliber. It is probable that there are also 14- and 16-inch guns in some units

c. The following are Japanese fortified zones:

Name of fortress	Area	Rank of commanding officer	Division or army command
Amami Oshima	Ryukyus	Colonel	Western Dist. Army.
Chichijima	Bonins	Major general	Eastern Dist. Army.
Chinkai Bay	Korea	Major general	Korean Army.
Eiko Bay	Korea	Colonel	Western Dist. Army.
Funauke	Ryukyus	Colonel	Western Dist. Army.
Hoyo	Japan		Western Dist. Army.
Iki	Japan	Major general	Western Dist. Army.
Keelung	Formosa	Major general	Formosan Army.
Maizuru	Japan	Colonel	Central Dist. Army.
Nagasaki	Japan	Major general	Western Dist. Army.
Nakagusuku Bay	Ryukyus	Colonel	Western Dist. Army.
North Kuriles	Japan	Colonel	Northern Area Army.
Pescadores	Off Formosa	Major general	
Port Arthur	Manchuria	Lt. general	Kwantung Army.

Name of fortress	Area	Rank of commanding officer	Division or army command
Rashin	Korea	Major general	Korean Army.
Reisui	Korea	Colonel	Korean Army.
Shimonoseki	Japan	Lt. general	Western Dist. Army.
Soya	Hokkaido	Lt. colonel	Northern Area Army.
Takao	Formosa		Formosan Army.
Tokyo Bay	Japan	Lt. general	Eastern Dist. Army.
Tsugaru-Hakodate	Japan	Major general	Northern Area Army.
Tsushima	Japan		Western Dist. Army.
Yura	Japan	Colonel	Central Dist. Army.

Section II. ARMS (NONDIVISIONAL)

1. INFANTRY. a. Independent infantry regiments and battalions. (1) The independent infantry regiment or battalion basically will be the same unit as that shown under divisional infantry, modified to perform such special duties as may be required.

(2) *Independent mixed regiments.* A few units known as independent mixed regiments exist. It is believed that they are independent infantry regiments into which small elements of artillery, engineers, etc., have been incorporated.

b. Independent infantry mortar units. (1) There are two types of mortar units, the infantry mortar units (Hakugeki tai), and the artillery mortar unit (Kyuhō tai). The former, commanded by infantry officers, are mobile units; the latter, commanded by artillery officers, are probably siege, or heavy, semifixed, defense units. It is possible that the independent infantry mortar regiment is largely an administrative or training unit, for only independent battalions so far have been encountered in the field.

(2) *Organization.* The independent infantry mortar battalion is organized as follows:

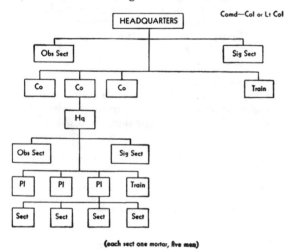

Figure 56.

The total strength of the battalion is approximately 900 men, and its armament 36 mortars.

2. CAVALRY. a. The cavalry regiment. The nondivisional cavalry regiment is believed to consist of a headquarters with a signal section, ammunition train and transport, four rifle and saber companies, and a machine-gun company. The organization of rifle and saber companies is identical with that of the division cavalry regiment. The machine-gun company has four platoons, of two machine guns each, and a fifth platoon with eight antitank guns. This type of regiment is found in the independent cavalry brigades.

b. Organization.

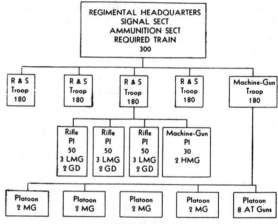

Figure 57.

3. TANKS. a. Tank regiment. These units have been reported to have a headquarters, 3 or 4 companies, a regimental ammunition train, and a total strength of 800 to 850 men equipped with 85 to 95 light and medium tanks.

(1) *Organization.*

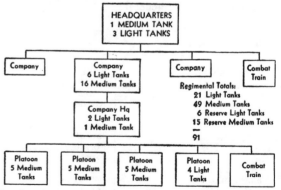

Sometimes the light tanks in the above organization are assembled in one company making a fourth, or light tank, company.

Figure 58.

(2) *Variant.* There are indications that a different organization for the regiment exists, consisting of a headquarters, 1 light-tank company (10 light tanks), 2 medium-tank companies (each with 10 medium tanks and 2 light tanks), and a regimental train. The total strength is estimated at 700 officers and enlisted men with approximately 60 tanks.

b. Cavalry-brigade tank unit. Cavalry-brigade tank units are reported to consist of a headquarters, 2 companies of light tanks, and a unit train. The companies are of 3 platoons each and include 10 light tanks and a company ammunition train. The unit ammunition train carries chemical warfare material and has 6 reserve light tanks. The total personnel strength of the unit is about 350 officers and enlisted men equipped with 30 tanks. There are about 80 trucks included in the trains.

c. Independent mixed-brigade tank unit. The organization of this type unit is believed to include a headquarters, 3 light-tank companies, 1 medium-tank company, 1 light-armored-car company, and a combat train. It is reported to have a total of about 20 medium and 65 light tanks, 25 armored cars, and a personnel strength of about 970 men.

d. Independent tank companies. Reports have been received of independent tank companies. These may be tank companies, either light or medium, detached from a tank regiment for temporarily independent operations.

e. Independent light-armored-car (tankette) companies. These independent companies are divided into two categories by the Japanese, one type being listed as Sokosha (armored vehicle) companies and the second as Keisokosha (light armored vehicle) companies. It is possible that both types are equipped with armored cars, but it is believed that tankettes have been substituted for those vehicles. In either case the company is believed to number approximately 130 officers and enlisted men, divided into a headquarters, four platoons, and a company train, with 17 tankettes or armored cars.

4. ARTILLERY. a. Field artillery. A few independent field artillery regiments and battalions have been identified. Their organization is believed to be similar to that of the field artillery regiment or battalion in the standard divisions, except that the regiment may have only two battalions.

b. Mountain artillery. These units are organized into independent regiments and battalions.

(1) *The regiment.* The regiment is commanded by a colonel or lieutenant colonel. It consists of a headquarters, a regimental train, 2 battalions (each with three companies), and a battalion train. The regimental strength is approximately 2,500 officers and enlisted men. A regiment seen in action operated approximately 1,500 strong, although it had left most of its horses and large parts of its train in rear areas. Units were as follows:

(*a*) Regimental headquarters and field train originally consisted of about 750 officers and enlisted men; battalion headquarters, of approximately 230 officers and enlisted men.

(*b*) Each company had approximately 185 officers and enlisted men, divided into 2 gun platoons and an ammunition platoon. The first gun platoon had 2 guns while the second had only 1 gun and a pioneer squad. (Normal armament is believed to be four guns to a company.)

(*c*) The battalion field train had about 140 officers and enlisted men. (Overstrength in headquarters was presumably attributable to the necessity of manhandling the equipment.)

(2) *The battalion.* The independent mountain artillery battalion is believed to be identical with the battalion of the independent regiment. It has a total strength of some 925 officers and enlisted men. In operations the strength has fallen as low as 500.

c. Medium artillery. (1) *The regiment.* There are several types of medium artillery regiments in the Japanese Army. One type of unit encountered was organized into a regimental headquarters; a regimental train; and 2 battalions, each of 3 firing companies and a train. The regiment was equipped with 24 tractor-drawn Type "96" 150-mm howitzers and numbered approximately 1,500 officers and enlisted men.

(2) *Organization.*

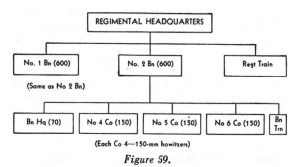

Figure 59.

(3) *Variants.* It is likely that other regiments are equipped throughout with 105-mm guns, or are mixed and have one battalion of guns and one of howitzers. The 105-mm gun battalion has been reported to have only two companies of four guns each.

(4) Figures of strength for medium artillery regiments equipped with the older horse-drawn 150-mm howitzer would necessarily be higher than those quoted above and might be expected to approximate 2,300 officers and enlisted men.

(5) *The battalion.* Medium artillery also is organized into independent battalions. The organization and armament of such units probably approximates that of the battalion of the regiment.

d. Heavy artillery. (1) *General.* Japanese heavy artillery units fall into two categories, mobile and fixed. Some fixed heavy artillery units were designed originally to fulfill a coast defense role for the Japanese Empire. Some, however, also are located to protect strategic centers farther afield.

(2) *Organization.* The following four types of heavy artillery regiment organization have been reported, but the details are not confirmed.

(*a*) Headquarters and train.
   2 battalions.
   2 companies, four 240-mm howitzers.
   Total regiment 1,533 men, sixteen 240-mm howitzers, 95 motor vehicles.

(*b*) Headquarters.
   2 companies, four 240-mm howitzers, tractor-drawn.
   Regimental ammunition train.
   Total regiment 789 men, eight 240-mm howitzers, tractor-drawn, 167 motor vehicles (includes 52 tractors).

(*c*) Headquarters.
   2 companies, two 300-mm mortars.
   Total regiment 623 men, four 300-mm mortars, 40 vehicles.

(*d*) Headquarters.
   Regimental train.
   2 companies, four 150-mm guns.
   Total regiment, 637 men, eight 150-mm guns, tractor-drawn, 115 vehicles.

e. Antiaircraft artillery. (1) *General.* Japanese antiaircraft artillery is organized into brigades, regiments, battalions, and companies. In addition there are searchlight and other miscellaneous units.

(2) *The brigade.* These are apparently assigned one to each district army. They are commanded by general officers and composed of two or more antiaircraft regiments.

(3) *The regiment.* The regiment is believed to consist of two battalions, a company of light antiaircraft and a searchlight battalion.

(4) *The battalion.* The antiaircraft battalion has alternative organizations; one giving it a main armament of eighteen 75-mm guns, and the other twelve 75-mm guns. (It is believed that some units may be equipped with larger caliber antiaircraft guns.)

(*a*) *The 18-gun battalion.*

   1. This battalion consists of a headquarters, 3 firing companies and a battalion train. Tabular strength of the unit is approximately 575 officers and enlisted men, with eighteen 75-mm antiaircraft guns and 6 to 9 machine guns.

2. Organization.

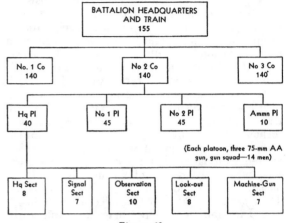

Figure 60.

3. The battalion is commanded by a lieutenant colonel; headquarters and train number some 155 officers and enlisted men. It has been found, however, that these units may enter operations overstrength, the reason for this addition being apparently the inclusion of an extra number of antiaircraft machine guns. Thus one battalion headquarters and train operated with 210 officers and enlisted men equipped with 16 machine guns.

4. Strength for the company is approximately 140 with an armament of six 75-mm antiaircraft guns and 2 machine guns. These units also have been seen in operations well overstrength and with additional machine guns.

(*b*) *The 12-gun battalion.* The organization of this unit is similar to that outlined above, except that each platoon has only two 75-mm guns, thereby reducing the battalion armament to 12 guns. Its total strength is estimated at 400 officers and men.

(5) *The independent (heavy) antiaircraft company.* These companies are similar in organization to those of the battalions. They may have either four or six 75-mm guns and include a train.

(6) *The machine cannon company.* (*a*) *General.* The machine cannon company normally consists of a headquarters, 3 platoons, and a train. Its strength, when motorized, is 160 men, and it has six 20-mm machine cannon and six 13-mm machine guns. The unit also may be horse-drawn or pack, in which cases the strength would be appropriately increased.

(b) *Organization.*

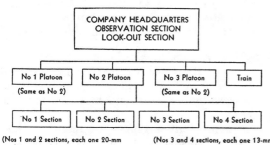

Figure 61.

(c) *Variants.* There are variants of the above organization. The company may consist of 4 platoons with 2 machine cannons in each of the first 3 platoons, and 6 machine guns in the fourth platoon. Alternatively, the armament of the unit may be increased from 12 to 16 weapons and the strength to 200.

(7) *Field searchlight battalion.* The battalion is composed of a headquarters and 2 searchlight companies each of which is divided into a company headquarters and 2 platoons. The platoons are divided into 3 sections each equipped with a searchlight and a sound locator. All equipment is carried on trucks. The total strength is about 450 men, 12 searchlights, 12 sound locators, 50 motor vehicles.

(8) *Independent searchlight companies.* These units are organized similarly to the company of the battalion.

(9) *Other antiaircraft units.* Antiaircraft observation units and barrage balloon units are known to exist, but details of their organization are not available. Certain units are listed as field air defense units. They appear to be in the nature of group or higher organization headquarters, controlling all antiaircraft defense in a selected area, and have under their command antiaircraft battalions or companies, machine cannon units, searchlight units, and possibly barrage balloon or antiaircraft observation units. Their size will depend entirely upon the situation and the guns and equipment available. The larger units are commanded by major generals or colonels.

(10) *Independent mortar regiments and battalions (artillery).* In addition to the independent "infantry" mortar regiments and battalions described in paragraph 1 b, there are other independent mortar regiments and battalions which are commanded by artillerymen and probably are artillery units. The regiments may be composed of a headquarters and 2 or more battalions. The battalions are commanded by majors or captains and probably are divided into 3 companies.

(11) *Shipping artillery.* Japanese shipping artillery regiments are designed to afford transports and other shipping protection from attack by air-

craft or submarines. The regiment normally is composed of a headquarters and 12 companies, but the 2 regiments encountered have included 6 or more additional companies. Tabular organization calls for about 2,300 men to the regiment and about 190 men per company; operating strengths have been about 150 men per company. Companies include antiaircraft gun companies (six 75-mm AA guns each), 75-mm field artillery companies (four 75-mm field guns each), and machine cannon companies (six 20-mm machine cannons). They are organized into headquarters, including observation and signal squads, gun platoons, and gun squads. Units usually are broken up to operate in small detachments. Two field artillery gun sections and two machine cannon sections frequently are assigned as the complement of small army transports.

(12) *Artillery intelligence units (sound and flash).* (a) *Artillery intelligence regiments.*

1. *General.* The regiment is commanded by a lieutenant colonel and is divided into a headquarters group, a survey unit, a plotting unit, and a sound detector unit. When horse-drawn, it is believed to number approximately 675 officers and men.

2. *Organization.*

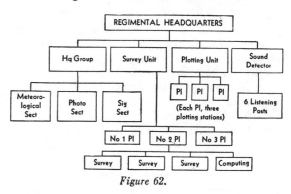

Figure 62.

(b) *Observation balloon regiments and companies.* The Japanese are known to have balloon regiments and companies, and such units were employed to give artillery observation during the final assault on Singapore. A motorized balloon company is reported to have a strength of approximately 145 personnel, 23 motor vehicles, and 1 observation balloon.

5. ANTITANK UNITS. a. General. Apart from the antitank gun units included in infantry organizations, there are a number of independent antitank gun battalions and companies as well as cavalry brigade antitank units. Antiaircraft units, especially machine cannon companies, are designed to fulfill a dual-purpose role.

b. Independent antitank battalion. (1) *General.* The battalion is an 18-gun unit, with a strength of about 500 officers and men. It has been seen to operate with as few as 350. It may be motorized, horse-drawn, or pack.

(2) *Organization (motorized).*

Battalion

Commanding officer__	
Headquarters_____	55 officers—45 men.
Headquarters section_	4 officers — 21 men.
Transport section____	24 men.
3 Independent anti-tank companies.	5 officers—121 men, six 37- or 47-mm AT guns, 15 vehicles.
Headquarters section_	1 officer — 20 men.
3 gun platoons_____	1 officer — 24 men, two 37- or 47-mm AT guns.
2 gun squads_____	11 men, one 37- or 47-mm AT gun.
1 ammunition platoon.	10 officers—29 men.
1 Battalion ammunition train.	1 officer — 61 men.

(3) Its total strength is 490 men and it has eighteen 37- or 47-mm AT guns, and 67 motor vehicles. The above personnel figure should be increased for horse-drawn or pack units.

c. Independent antitank company. The independent company is 6- or 8-gun unit, and, as in the case of the battalion, it may be motorized, horse-drawn, or pack. The organization of the 8-gun unit is shown below.

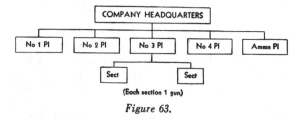

Figure 63.

(1) *As a pack unit*, the company has 250 men, eight 37-mm guns, 2 light machine guns, 5 riding horses and 76 pack horses. As a horse-drawn unit, the armament would be similar, but the exact strength figure is unknown.

(2) *As a motorized unit*, the company might number 180 to 200 and be armed with eight 37-mm or 47-mm guns.

(3) *Six-gun units* are generally similar, with strength decreased proportionally.

d. Cavalry brigade antitank unit. The antitank unit of the cavalry brigade consists of three firing platoons, each of two 37-mm or 47-mm guns, and an ammunition platoon. The total strength is about 140 officers and men with six 37-mm or 47-mm guns.

6. ENGINEERS. a. Engineer groups. These are administrative units commanded by a general officer. They supervise engineer activity and control independent engineer units in a theater of operations.

b. Independent engineer regiments. These units are often attached to divisions in the field. They are divided into the following six different types according to the principal function they fulfill:

Type	*Function*
'A' KO_____	Open warfare.
'B' OTSU___	Position warfare.
'C' HEI____	Heavy bridge building.
'D' BO_____	Shipping-landing operations.
'E' TEI_____	River crossing.
'F' KI_____	Attacking pillboxes and special firing positions.

They are similar in general organization, consisting of a regimental headquarters, 3 companies, and a material platoon. The tabular strength of each is approximately 1,000 men. The commanding officer is a colonel or lieutenant colonel. Companies are composed of 4 platoons of 4 or more squads each and average 250 to 300 men. The number of motor trucks varies. Personnel carry rifles and probably some light machine guns. It has been noted that regiments are prepared to undertake special duties other than those for which they are designated.

c. Independent engineer battalions. These are known to exist. They are commanded by lieutenant colonels or majors.

d. Independent engineer companies. These units consist of a headquarters and 2 platoons of 3 or 4 sections each. One unit had an operational strength of approximately 165 officers and men.

e. Field road construction units. These are engineer troops organized into a unit of a headquarters and 2 or 3 companies. Duties are general construction, particularly of roads and airfields. Units are commanded by lieutenant colonels and majors; companies are estimated to have about 125 officers and enlisted men.

f. Bridge-building and river-crossing material companies. These units consist of personnel and equipment for bridge building and river crossings. Strengths vary from 250 to 600, depending upon whether they are draft or motorized.

g. Construction-duty companies. (See shipping units, anchorages, sec. III, par 2 *c.*, p. 50.)

7. CHEMICAL WARFARE. a. The Japanese are known to have a chemical warfare service and organized chemical warfare units. The division units previously have been discussed (see p. 1/m). Besides these, gas battalions and independent gas companies are known to exist. The Japanese have used sternutatory or suffocating gas in China. They have established factories for poison gas manufacture, developed antigas measures, and issued an efficient gas mask to their services. They, therefore, should be considered capable of gas warfare.

b. Picked personnel from all Japanese units are trained in decontamination and antigas work. Although normally acting as regular troops, such personnel are specially equipped to carry out chemical warfare duties; upon occasion they may be formed into temporary smoke (gas) units for the conduct of offensive chemical warfare. It is estimated that there are about 250 such men in an infantry regiment or its equivalent.

8. AIRBORNE UNITS. a. General. The Japanese Army raid-training department has experimented with airborne units, and it is probable that in addition to known parachute units some airborne troops are available for service. The Japanese have referred to an airborne force composed of a glider force and parachute force but give no details.

b. Parachute force. The parachute force has been described as composed of a headquarters, two parachute battalions, and an artillery unit. Total strength is estimated to be about 1,750.

c. Parachute battalion. The battalion is composed of a headquarters and 3 companies with a small nonflying supply section. Companies are of 3 platoons, each of 2 rifle sections and 1 heavy-weapons section. A rifle section has 6 riflemen and an antitank group. The heavy-weapons section has a heavy machine gun section of 9 men, and a cannon section of 5 men. The total strength is estimated to be about 600 to 700.

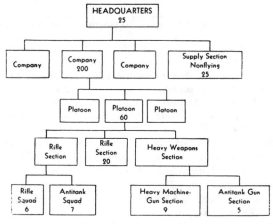

Figure 64. Organization.

Section III. SERVICES (NON-DIVISIONAL)

1. GENERAL. The services of the Japanese Army are:

> Intendance.
> Technical, including ordnance.
> Medical.
> Veterinary.
> Judicial (legal).
> Military band.

All services listed above are under control of the Ministry of War with lieutenant generals in command. Although the Japanese consider transport and signal communications as line branches, they are grouped here with the services for convenience of discussion.

2. TRANSPORT. Transport is divided into road (animal and mountain), railway, and water units.
  a. Road transport units. (1) *General.* Transport regiments of depot divisions form the source of personnel for division and independent transport regiments as well as for other units requiring transport personnel.
  (2) *Field transport commands.* (Yasen Yusobu). These are usually commanded by major generals. They are administrative organizations probably controlling all independent transport units under an army command.
  (3) *Field motor transport depots* (Yasen Jidoshasho). These are usually under command of a colonel or lieutenant colonel, except in the larger theaters of operations (Asiatic Mainland) where a major general commands. They are believed to be administrative units responsible for storage, maintenance, and control of motor transport in a given operational area.
  (4) *Independent transport regiments* (horse). These are estimated to number about 3,000 officers and men. Commanded by a colonel or lieutenant colonel, they are composed of a headquarters and from 4 to 8 draft or pack transport companies.
  (5) *Motor transport regiments.* These consist of about 1,500 officers and men with 300 vehicles. They are commanded by a colonel or lieutenant colonel.
  (6) *Independent transport battalions* (horse). These are estimated at about 1,700 officers and enlisted men and usually are commanded by majors. They are composed of a headquarters and 3 to 4 draft or pack transport companies.
  (7) *Independent motor transport battalions.* These are estimated at about 800 officers and enlisted men divided into a headquarters and three companies. Usually commanded by majors, they are believed to be equipped with about 150 one and one-half ton trucks.
  (8) *Independent transport companies* (horse). These are estimated at about 350 officers and enlisted men, and commanded by captains or first lieu-

tenants. They usually are equipped with about 200 to 250 single-horse, 2-wheel, transportation carts (¼-ton).

(9) *Independent motor transport companies.* Estimated at about 175 officers and men and about 50 trucks, these units are commanded by a captain or first lieutenant. They are divided into 3 platoons and a maintenance section, with the platoons consisting of 4 or 5 sections each.

(10) *Provisional transport units.* Such units, formed by assigning combat or service elements other than transport to provisionally formed transport units, will be found operating behind the lines. Their size, organization, and equipment will vary depending upon their mission; after its completion they return to normal duties.

(11) *Line of communication transport supervision detachments.* These consist of military and civilian personnel, whose duties are to supervise and control locally commandeered transport.

b. Railway units. (1) *Railway commands (Tetsudo Bu), field railways (Yasen Tetsudo), special railways (Tokusetsu Tetsudo), and railway transport (Tetsudo Yuso).* These units are believed to maintain, control, and coordinate rail traffic in the larger theaters. They are composed of a headquarters, one or more railway regiments, supply depots, and construction and operation units. They are commanded by general officers.

(2) *Railway regiments.* The railway regiment consists of a headquarters, 4 battalions (2 companies of 4 platoons), and a supply depot. Strength is approximately 2,500 officers and enlisted men, commanded by a colonel or lieutenant colonel. Such regiments are designed to operate and guard railways.

(3) *Armored train units.* These are reported to consist of about 500 officers and enlisted men (infantry, artillery, and engineers) and to operate armored trains.

c. Water (shipping) units. Water (shipping) units are headed by a sea transport headquarters in Japan.

(1) Branch offices, termed shipping groups, are situated at the principal base ports in theaters of operations. They control a variable number of shipping engineer regiments and debarkation units.

(2) *Shipping engineer regiments.* These units are the barge operators in the Japanese Army. They are equipped with the necessary landing craft and equipment for amphibious operations and movement of supplies and men. Organizational strength approximates 1,200 officers and enlisted men, divided into a headquarters and 3 companies of several sections each. A lieutenant colonel normally commands. The regiment is equipped with 150 to 200 landing craft of all types.

(3) *Debarkation units.* These include necessary personnel and equipment for the loading and unloading of transports at the more forward bases or during landing operations. Strength is estimated at 1,000 officers and enlisted men.

(4) *Shipping transport commands (headquarters).* These, like shipping groups, are situated at the principal base ports, where they are responsible for the shipping installations at these bases. They also fuel vessels, store cargoes and, in conjunction with the Navy, plan and route sea transport in a given area. Size of the unit depends on the volume of shipping in the theater.

(5) *Shipping transport area units.* These are variable sized units responsible for the armament and defense of vessels operating in a particular area. They control shipping ordnance, shipping antiaircraft artillery, and shipping signal units, detachments of which are assigned for the defense of intercommunication between vessels and convoys.

(6) *Anchorage units.* These are believed composed of a headquarters and variable number of land duty, water duty, and construction duty companies. Respectively, these companies are probably a stevedore company of approximately 350 officers and enlisted men, a barge and lighter operations company of the same strength, and a general construction engineer company probably also of the same strength.

(7) *Shipping transport battalions.* The existence of these units is known, but details of their organization are lacking. They are believed to operate small sailing and motor craft.

3. INTENDANCE. a. General. Intendance service is responsible for clothing, rations, forage, contracts, pay, and the upkeep of army buildings. It is a separate organization combining functions of the U. S. Army Quartermaster Corps and Finance Department. It is under the control of the Intendance Bureau of the War Ministry. Intendance personnel are assigned to armies, divisions, and lower units, they also are found at various depots, factories, and other places requiring accounting and quartermaster services.

b. Field freight depots. They are to be found functioning as units or split into branches along the lines of communication of armies. Each depot is responsible for the supply of several divisions. They store and supply rations, clothing, and other supplies.

4. ORDNANCE (TECHNICAL SERVICE).
a. General. Prior to organization of the technical service (Gijutsu Bu) in 1941, ordnance duties in the Japanese Army were performed by personnel detailed from various branches, usually artillery and engineers, who functioned under general supervision of the ordnance bureau of the War Ministry. At present, however, ordnance personnel belong to the technical service. As the name implies, this service includes the various types of technicians in the army, such as gunsmiths, mechanics, electricians, saddlers, etc., all of whom may be attached or assigned to units as required.

b. Functions. Ordnance personnel are responsible for providing arms, ammunition, engineer stores, and supplies not furnished by the intendance service.

Ordnance functions are discharged in the field by field ordnance depots, stationed at principal rear bases. Size of these depots will vary according to the theater of operations, and branches will be found along the lines of communications.

5. MEDICAL. a. General. The medical service is a separate service functioning under the medical bureau of the War Ministry. In addition to divisional medical service, the following units are known to exist:

b. Casualty clearing stations. These are unassigned medical units with a strength of approximately 100 officers and enlisted men. They evacuate casualties from the division field hospitals to line of communication hospitals.

c. Line of communication hospitals. These, with a strength of about 250 officers and enlisted men, can accommodate 500 to 1,000 patients. They consist of 2 sections and are usually found at rear bases or along the lines of communication.

d. Army hospitals. These are larger hospitals of varying size generally situated well behind forward base areas.

e. Base hospitals. In each home divisional district, there are hospitals to meet the requirements of the various units in peacetime. These, as well as private and other Government hospitals, are utilized as base hospitals during wartime.

6. VETERINARY. This is a separate service which functions under the horse administration section, military administration bureau, of the War Ministry. A veterinary department or section is attached to the staff of armies, area armies, divisions, and other oversea commands, while detachments operate with all units containing animals. Veterinary hospitals, with a staff of about 150 capable of handling 700 sick horses, and veterinary quarantine hospitals are found along the lines of communication or at bases.

7. SIGNAL. a. General. Before the war the functions of the signal corps were performed by communication units of the corps of engineers. In 1941, however, an Inspectorate of Communications was set up directly subordinate to the War Department General Staff. This was tantamount to the establishment of a separate signal corps. Troops are classified as signal communication men.

b. The signal regiment (army signal unit). (1) The regiment is composed of a headquarters, several wire companies (motor, draft, or pack), several radio platoons (motor, draft, or pack), a fixed radio unit, a radio intercept unit, and a field pigeon unit.

(2) The headquarters consists of about 120 officers and enlisted men, and includes a transport section, a repair section, and an air-ground radio section.

(3) The wire companies' approximate strengths are 260 men draft, 320 pack, and 300 motor. They are believed to be equipped with 36 telephones and 8 telegraph instruments. The draft and pack companies carry about 35 miles of wire, while the motor companies carry 70 miles. Companies include a signal platoon, 3 maintenance platoons, and a transport platoon.

(4) Radio platoons operate 1 radio station. They include draft, pack, or motor transportation, and are of 35 to 45 men in strength.

(5) The fixed radio unit has a strength of about 25 officers and enlisted men and operates a long distance radio station.

(6) The radio intercept unit is divided into a headquarters with train, an intercept unit equipped with 6 receivers, and a direction-finder unit equipped with 4 direction finders. Its strength is approximately 290 officers and enlisted men.

(7) The pigeon unit has a headquarters of some 20 officers and men, including a train, as well as several pigeon platoons. A platoon has about 50 men and is divided into 3 sections, each equipped with 40 carrier pigeons.

(8) Although complete signal regiments as outlined above are likely to be found operating with the larger headquarters, it will be more usual to find their individual components operating as independent units on the line of communication or with smaller organizations in the field to supplement their signal networks.

c. Shipping signal units are composed of a headquarters and 2 companies. Personnel is assigned to maintain radio liaison between transports and shipping establishments. Companies have a strength of about 300, while the regiment totals 635 officers and men.

d. The air signal unit is a company of about 320 officers and enlisted men. It is divided into 3 platoons and is employed chiefly in maintaining communciations within an air brigade. The unit probably also operates direction-finder apparatus.

8. ARMY POSTAL SERVICE. The Japanese Army's postal system operates through networks of central, field, and branch post offices set up in forward and rear areas. APO numbers evidently are assigned to localities, rather than to units, and remain fixed. In certain instances field post offices may act as paying agencies for the army, in addition to accepting and delivering military mail and handling postal money orders and military postal savings. A free air-mail service for army personnel is reported in operation.

9. JUDICIAL. The judicial (legal) service of the Japanese Army formerly was entirely in the hands of civilians attached to various units. In 1941 these civilians were commissioned in the Army, where they continue to perform their usual legal duties.

10. MILITARY BAND. This service furnishes the personnel for the Japanese army bands. These bands do not appear to have any secondary duties.

Section IV. MILITARY INTELLIGENCE

1. GENERAL. Military intelligence is a function of the 2nd Bureau, Army General Staff, headed by a major general. Intelligence of a more general nature flows to the High Command through a complex organization, at the top of which is the Intelligence Department of the Imperial General Headquarters. In a subordinate position, there is also the Central Commission for Intelligence, a coordinating body which maintains contact with all government departments and disseminates information. Intelligence received from armed forces in the field is routed through the usual military channels to the 2nd bureau of the General Staff. This purely military function resembles the system employed by other armies.

2. COMBAT INTELLIGENCE. Intelligence officers are assigned to army, division, and regimental staffs. While they appear to have no permanently organized units for collecting combat intelligence, geographic areas are assigned to various regular units which are made responsible for the usual items of information sought in combat intelligence. It is noteworthy that the Japanese recently have been stressing the amount of military information that can be gathered from prisoners of war and from captured documents.

3. THE TOKUMU KIKAN (SPECIAL SERVICE AGENCY). This agency is believed to be directly under orders of the Imperial General Headquarters and organized into units which are assigned only to armies or geographic areas. Espionage, counterespionage, propaganda, and fifth column activities, together with a measure of undercover supervision over occupied territories, appear to be principal duties of personnel of this agency. A major general was declared to be in command of the Tokumu Kikan organization at Canton in 1942. Close cooperation between the Tokumu Kikan and military police apparently can be effected when required, inasmuch as counterespionage is included among the duties of the latter. (For details of the Japanese military police service, see chapter 6.)

Section V. REORGANIZATION

GENERAL.—Many indications show that the Japanese Army is in the process of reorganizing and modernizing various units. Some of this modernization program has been accomplished and it must be expected that there will be continued progress. On the other hand there are definite limitations to the speed with which equipment can be obtained and distributed, and personnel indoctrinated and trained. It is believed, therefore, that while there will be a gradual increase in the number of the stronger and more modern units the bulk of the army will continue to be composed, as it is at present, largely of average organizations such as have been described.

CHAPTER IV

JAPANESE AIR SERVICE

Section I. GENERAL

GENERAL. Japan does not have an independent Air Service. The Japanese Army Air Service is an integral part of the Army, while the Japanese Naval Air Service is organized independently as an integral part of the Navy. The Emperor, through Imperial Headquarters, controls the Japanese Army Air Service. Such control involves three agencies: The Army General Staff, The War Ministry, and the Inspector General of Aviation. The Japanese Navy Air Service also is controlled by the Emperor through Imperial Headquarters and involves three agencies: The Navy General Staff, The Navy Ministry, and Naval Aviation Headquarters. This chapter will cover the Japanese Army Air Service organization only.

Section II. ORGANIZATION OF THE JAPANESE ARMY AIR SERVICE

1. ORGANIZATION OF THE JAPANESE HIGH COMMAND. a. Inspector General of Aviation (Rikugun Koku Sokambu). The

Inspector General of Aviation is directly responsible to the Emperor for matters pertaining to air training, while in other respects he is subordinate to the "Big Three" (Chief of General Staff, Minister of War, and Inspector General of Military Training). (See chart in fig. 65.) The War Minister holds the Inspector General of Aviation responsible in matters pertaining to personnel and military administration, and the Inspector General of Aviation is responsible for operations to the Chief of the General Staff.

b. Aviation headquarters (Koku Hombu). The office of Chief of Aviation Headquarters antedates the Inspector General of Aviation by 3 years. This post is a subordinate agency under the Minister of War. The principal functions of the Aviation Headquarters agency would appear to be largely procurement and supply.

2. LOWER ECHELON ORGANIZATION OF THE JAPANESE ARMY AIR SERVICE. Air Army (Kokugun.) The Japanese Army Air Service is organized into five known Air Armies, each having clearly defined areas, and func-

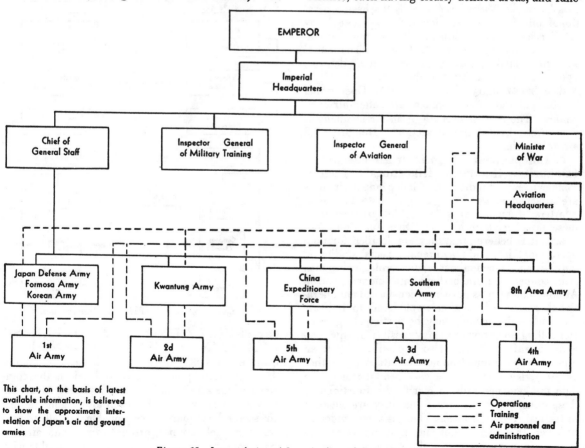

This chart, on the basis of latest available information, is believed to show the approximate inter-relation of Japan's air and ground armies

Figure 65. Inter-relation of Japan's Air and Ground Armies.

tioning as an administrative headquarters for its tactical units. The tactical organization in an Air Army is explained in paragraph 3. Coordination between air and ground forces is obtained by placing the Air Army under the command of the theater commander. This enables him to control operationally both air and ground forces.

3. TACTICAL ORGANIZATION.

a. Air division (Hikoshidan). The largest tactical organization in the chain of command in the Japanese Army Air Service is known as an air division. Such a division exercises both operational and administrative control over lower air units in its command.

b. Air brigade (Hikodan). Subordinate to the air division is a tactical force known as the air brigade. There are normally two or more air brigades under the command of an air division. The air brigade is a very mobile operational organization and is flexible in its composition. It has a small headquarters, the officers of which are concerned principally with tactical operations. The usual combat strength consists of 3 or 4 air regiments with each regiment almost invariably equipped with one type of aircraft, such as fighters, light bombers, or medium bombers.

c. Air regiments (Hikōsentai). The next lower unit of an air brigade is called an air regiment, three or four of which compose the strength of a brigade. The air regiment is the basic operational unit in the organization of the Japanese Army Air Service. It is composed of three or more squadrons. A squadron is called a Chūtai. The actual strength or striking force in an air regiment depends upon the type of aircraft in the unit.

d. Air company (Hikō Chūtai). Operational combat units in an air regiment are called air companies. The normal strength of an air company is 9 aircraft, divided into 3 sections (Hentai) of 3 aircraft each.

e. Independent air units or air companies (Dokuritsu Hikotai or Hikochutai). There is some evidence to indicate that independent air units are attached either to air armies or to the headquarters of an air division. Although several of these units have been identified, their function is not clear. It is believed that they are detailed for nonoperational duty and may prepare special studies on long distance reconnaissance, meteorological flights, army cooperation, and perhaps antisubmarine patrol. Although these units have been considered nonoperational, recent information would tend to indicate that such units actually may be participating in or controlling operations and may possibly be equipped with aircraft. There is also a possibility that an independent air squadron may be attached to either an air division or to air brigade headquarters. To date the evidence fails to clarify the functions of these units, but it is assumed that they are engaged in tactical reconnaissance. There is some evidence, however, that such a unit may function as ground support in cooperation with the Army, indicating a possibility that in some cases it may be an Army cooperation unit. It is assumed that the normal strength of an independent air squadron is 9 aircraft, with the possibility that these may be fighter, light bomber, medium bomber, or reconnaissance types.

f. Direct-cooperation air units (Chokkyo Hikotai). Information so far obtained fails to disclose the function of a direct-cooperation air unit, but it is assumed that these units operate either in support of ground forces or as liaison. Some of these units have been named for the district army to which they are attached.

g. Air intelligence regiment or unit (Koku Joho Rentai or Tai). Intelligence organizations have been identified: namely, the air intelligence regiment, and air intelligence units, but little is known of their functions. It is assumed that the air intelligence regiment is attached to an air division, with detachments of air intelligence units in the forward areas, and that all these units are engaged in collecting, evaluating, and disseminating intelligence as well as reporting on weather.

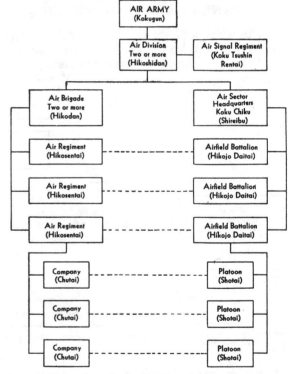

Figure 66. Lower Echelon Organization.

4. SERVICE UNITS IN JAPANESE ARMY AIR FORCES.

a. Air sector headquarters (Kōkū Chiku Shireibu). Presumably this organization is the highest level in the command of the service units in the Japanese Army Air Forces. It is assumed that each air brigade has an air sector headquarters responsible for all administration, fuel supplies, ground stores, and aircraft maintenance. This organization is comparable with the Air Service Command in the United States Army Air Forces.

b. Airfield battalion (Hikojo Daitai). This unit is a component and subsidiary unit of the air sector headquarters. Its function is to perform ground duties for an air regiment. The organization is three-fold; an aircraft maintenance unit, a guards section, and a supply section. The maintenance section's chief function is aircraft maintenance, while the supply section is responsible for maintaining supplies and transporting them from dumps to the airfields. The purpose of the guard section is to relieve the infantry troops from the duty of protecting airfields.

c. Airfield companies (Hikojo Chutai). These units are subordinate to the air sector headquarters and perform the same function as an airfield battalion, but on a smaller scale.

d. Field airfield construction units (Yasen Hikōjō Setteitai). It is known that these units do exist, but little is known of their function or organization. It is assumed that as the name implies, their principal function would be airfield construction.

e. Field air repair depots (Yasen Koku Shurisho). It is assumed that these units are organized to do third or fourth echelon aircraft repair work. Information indicates that this organization has several units or branches which make minor aircraft repairs in the forward areas.

f. Air signal regiments or units (Koku Tsushin Rentai or Tai). Signal requirements of the operational units are handled presumably by air signal regiments, air signal units, or air signal companies. Although these units exist, little information relative to their organization is known.

g. Navigational aid regiments (Kosūku Rentai). These are believed to operate control beacons, direction-finding stations, etc., and are believed to be attached to the air sector headquarters.

h. Mobile air repair section (Ido Koku Shurihan). Some of these units are known to exist, and it is assumed that they are equipped with mobile machine shops to make repairs to damaged aircraft.

5. SUPPLY. Some separate units appear to be charged with the delivery of aircraft, bombs, ammunition, etc., in bulk to operational theaters and with the repair of damaged aircraft. Practically no organizational data concerning them have been found. They are listed below in the approximate order of their importance:

Air main depot___ (Kōkū Honshō).
Air branch depot_____ (Kōkū Shishō).
Air subdepot____ (Kōkū Bunshō).
Field air depot___ (Yasen Kokusho).
Field air supply depot_____ (Yasen Kōkū Hokyusho).

Field air replacement unit_____ (Yasen Hojū Hikotai).
Field airfield construction unit_ (Yasen Hikōjō Setteitai).
Mobile air repair section_____ (Idō Kōku Shūrihan).
Shipping air depot_____ (Sempaku Kokusho).

6. UNIT DESIGATIONS, AND EQUIVALENTS.

Romanized form	Translation	Abbreviation	Closest United States equivalent (by function)
Hentai	Air Section		Flight.
Hikō Chutai	Air Company		Squadron.
Hikō Sentai	Air Regiment	FR	Group.
Hikōdan	Air Brigade	FB	Wing or division.
Hikō Shidan	Air Division	FD	Numbered air force.
Kōkūgun	Air Army	FA	Theater or allied air force (strategic and tactical).

Section III. STRATEGIC DOCTRINE

1. GENERAL. Strategic doctrines are based upon the national policy. The strategic function of all arms is to implement the national mission by maintenance of control of all territory within the Japanese sphere of conquest. The Japanese Air Forces have been assigned a role of greatest importance in attaining these objectives.

a. Naval Air Service. The Japanese Naval Air Service was organized originally as a highly effective striking weapon, with light maneuverable aircraft of high performance characteristics that were well adapted to support swift thrusts by amphibious forces. The function of the air force in these operations was to provide cover for the task forces involved, and, by swift surprise attacks, to destroy the opposing enemy air force on the ground or in the air, thereby clearing the way for landing operations. The Naval Air Service was equipped to operate either from carriers or from land bases and frequently has undertaken the permanent defense of land areas.

b. Army Air Force. The Army Air Force has been assigned the function of providing support for the ground troops and conducting counter-air-force operations.

c. Disposition. With the completion of Japan's planned conquests in mid-1942, the Army and Naval Air Services were disposed for the strategic defense of the vast areas under her control. As the threat of war with the Soviet Union diminished, strength was reduced in Manchuria and in Japan, and distributed along the perimeter of the newly acquired Empire, apparently in accord with relatively fixed predetermined commitments. These commitments were maintained fairly consistently until early 1944, when heavy Allied pressure, brought to bear simultaneously on several fronts, forced a realignment.

d. Mobility. The Japanese have achieved great mobility for their Air Forces by the construction of many new airfields throughout their sphere of conquest. Strength can be shifted quickly from one area to another on interior lines and, because of the availability of facilities in depth, can readily be withdrawn from sustained combat as occasion demands.

e. Strategy. It may be assumed that the ultimate strategic objective of the Japanese Air Force will be to defend Japan itself and the inner zone. Meanwhile, until the vital parts of the Empire are threatened, both Army and Navy Air Services will give support to troops and naval forces only in defensive or offensive-defensive operations up to the point where their overall strength is not seriously impaired.

f. Abandonment of perimeter defense. Consistent with this doctrine of strategic defense, the Japanese Air Forces have curtailed or abandoned the air support of ground troops at outlying points along the perimeter whenever the cost of such support has become excessive.

Section IV. JAPANESE AIR TACTICS

1. BOMBING TACTICS. a. Formations. Japanese bombing tactics exemplify certain of their natural traits; courage, indifference to losses, and adherence to preconceived plans. Bombers usually have flown in multiples of 9 in a V of V's, although occasionally attacks have been made in line abreast, with fighters weaving about in loose escort formations. The formations encountered until the close of 1943 were 6 separate flat V's, occasionally with one or two vacancies and often with 1 plane at the rear of the apex of the V; a V of three 9-plane V's, with the leading V 50 or 100 feet above the others, changing to a slightly staggered formation of 1 V when 7 or 10 miles from the bomb release point; 3 flights of 9 bombers, successively stepped up 250 feet from port to starboard, and in line with fighters weaving about the formation; two 9-plane V of V's, with the leading echelon highest and the left echelon next highest.

b. Characteristics. Attacks were characterized by a long approach in close formation, held persistently regardless of antiaircraft fire and/or fighter opposition. Bombs usually were dropped on a signal from the leader at altitudes ranging from 7,000 to 26,000 feet, depending upon the nature of the target and the opposition. Generally, the formation was well maintained until bombs were dropped, when it was loosened up somewhat. The flights then engaged in a series of surges up and down, losing and gaining about 500 feet in altitude.

c. Reconnaissance. The Japanese usually precede long-distance bombing missions by ample air reconnaissance. Scouting aircraft communicate with the home base by radio. Before the main bombing force leaves its base, alternative objectives are designated. Airfields are given high target priority.

d. Evasion. Evasive tactics against antiaircraft fire are taken by maintaining altitude above the effective range of such fire, by occasional changes in altitude, and by weaving in formation.

e. Escort. Fighter escort on bomber missions varies according to the opposition expected and the number of fighters available. The position and escort technique of fighters protecting bomber formations constantly change. Frequently bombers are escorted by fighters above and behind the bomber formation.

f. Follow-up. Bomber operations against important targets have been characterized by repeated attacks and "follow-up" missions. Many of these attacks appear to have been made along the same route and at the same time each day, although not necessarily by the same type of formation.

g. Tactical changes. By the close of 1943 the Japanese, finding themselves on the defensive in many theaters, were obliged to change their bombing tactics. This resulted in:

(1) Virtual abandonment of *daylight* horizontal bombing attacks on Allied land bases or convoy with air cover.

(2) Adoption of dawn and dusk bombing by fighters, and night bombing by medium, torpedo, and dive bombers.

(3) Improved efficiency and coordination in *night* torpedo and bombing attacks against Allied shipping en route and at anchor in advanced bases.

2. DIVE BOMBING. a. General. Japanese dive-bombing attacks, most frequent and effective in the early months of the war, are largely directed against shipping and equipment on beachheads. The accuracy of Japanese dive bombing is not outstanding and has been affected by Allied antiaircraft fire and fighter interception. Numerous reports make it clear that damaged planes, particularly dive bombers, attempt to crash on their targets as a last resort.

b. Formations. (1) The usual Japanese dive-bombing formations are in multiples of 3 as follows: 3-plane Vs in line astern; in 6- or 9-plane Vs; in Vs of Vs. The number of dive bombers employed varies with the nature of the target; for example, larger formations are employed against naval vessels than against merchant ships. Efforts are made to saturate enemy defenses by increasing the density of attacking planes. Of late, because of Allied fighter opposition, the approach to the target has been generally at altitudes of from 12,000 to 18,000 feet. Immediately before the initial dive, which is approximately one of from 35° to almost vertical (more often dives approximating 45°), the Japanese change their formations to one of loose echelon or string. Upon this change-over, the individual dives commence in rapid succession, usually from up-sun, from areas of restricted visibility, or from coordinates exposing them to minimum antiaircraft fire. The bomb release point varies from 500 feet to as high as 3,000 feet. This release point, it is believed, is governed by the pull-out point of the lead plane or the intensity of antiaircraft fire. It also has been noted that the bomb-release point is generally higher during dives approaching the vertical where greater speeds have been attained.

(2) When larger formations have been employed, Japanese dive bombers frequently divide their strength into smaller forces and attack a given target simultaneously from different directions.

3. GLIDE BOMBING. a.
While occasional reports of dive-bombing attacks at angles of 70 to 80° have been received, the majority of attacks have been made by a powered glide at an angle of 45 to 50°.

b. Bombers begin the dive at a height of 3,000 to 5,000 feet and follow each other down until near the target before releasing their bombs. Subsequently, the planes employ their machine guns against ground installations. Retirements are effected at high speed, with evasive action usually limited to short climbs and dips. Attacks are well coordinated and usually are made out of the sun.

4. TORPEDO BOMBING. a. Daylight.
Daylight torpedo bombing approaches are usually made in close formation at medium altitude. Attacks may be made in a wedge or loose diamond formation, or in small groups which separate to attack individual objectives from different directions. Glides are made at an angle of 40 to 45°, and torpedoes are dropped from an altitude of 200 to 300 feet at a range from 500 to 1,200 yards from the target. Approaches are planned from the direction where the least concentration of antiaircraft fire may be expected. Full advantage is taken of the position of the sun and cloud formations.

b. Night. Night torpedo attacks (including dawn and dusk) were greatly developed by the Japanese in 1943 and followed a nearly uniform pattern. Reconnaissance planes drop variously colored flares to reveal the course of the convoy and to identify targets by types. Torpedo planes then attack singly, with the bulk of the force coming from one direction, while a few attempt to approach from another course. The attackers skim the surface of the water; drop their torpedoes at less than 1,000 yards; and perform S curves, dips, and rises for evasion on the way out.

5. FIGHTER TACTICS. a. General.
Japanese fighter tactics against Allied fighters and bombers necessarily vary both with the number and type of aircraft encountered, the conditions under which attacks are executed, and the skill and ability of the Japanese pilots.

b. Formations. (1) The Japanese fighter tactical unit is normally a squadron of nine planes, subdivided into three flights in either V or echelon formation. Formerly, a V of three fighter aircraft was employed, flanked by echelons of two fighters. Fighter formations usually fly at altitudes of 15,000 to 20,000 feet, but are believed to operate effectively at altitudes of 27,000 feet or higher.

(2) The last months of 1943 showed a trend towards Japanese adoption of the standard United States Air Force basic fighter formations, consisting of two-plane sections and four-plane flights. Considerable coordination between planes and sections is evident, with sections fighting in pairs and alternating in attack.

c. Characteristics of fighter tactics. (1) The Japanese fighter pilots usually work with, and believe in, high cover. Their flights frequently take off about ½ hour apart, so that when one flight has exhausted its fuel a second flight can take over.

(2) Individual Japanese pilots seldom engage Allied formations or even single aircraft; usually they require numerical superiority before they will attack.

d. Deception. Deceptive tactics of various kinds have been extensively employed by Japanese fighters in efforts to lure Allied aircraft out of formations. Fake "dogfights" have been staged, and decoy tactics have been employed with one plane at a low altitude protected by others flying as high cover.

e. Avoidance of head-on attacks. Head-on attacks against Allied fighters generally were avoided until after increased armor was installed in Japanese fighters. Frequently attacks against Allied fighters have been made from above and the side, and, if possible, out of the sun. Evasive tactics were characterized by abrupt and violent skids, turns, and rolls. Japanese fighter pilots attempted to draw their opponent up into a steep climb and into stalling position, after which they would do a quick wingover or snap-loop back on their opponent's tail. By late 1943, the favorite evasive maneuver of Japanese fighters was a Split "S." This is a downward half snap-roll followed by a pull-out to normal flight, thus obtaining a 180° change in direction with loss of altitude.

f. Attack on bombers. According to reports Japanese fighter attacks against Allied heavy bombers come from all directions, with a decreasing trend in frontal attacks. They have attacked Allied bombers from 10 to 2 o'clock and at both 9 and 3 o'clock positions. Frequently these attacks have been coordinated by two fighters on each side; one comes in above the wing and one passes below, each peeling off to rake the fuselage of Allied aircraft.

g. Characteristics of attacks on bombers. (1) The degree of coordination achieved by Japanese fighters varies greatly. In many cases attacks are not coordinated, and at other times a high degree of coordination has been attained. Reports from the Southwest Pacific Area indicate a trend towards greater coordination in frontal and waist attacks.

(2) The Japanese rely to a great extent on the maneuverability of their planes, and while their tendency towards acrobatics has steadily diminished, the variety of the types of attacks employed has commensurately increased.

(3) Japanese fighters are particularly observant of any damage inflicted on Allied bombers and are quick to take all possible advantage of it. Stragglers

are a favorite target for concentrated attacks, and, when a tight formation is maintained by Allied bombers, attacks are usually concentrated on the leader. However, Japanese fighter pilots are not consistent in the degree to which their attacks are pressed home.

6. JAPANESE NIGHT FIGHTERS. a. During 1943 Allied heavy bombers, operating at night over enemy bases in New Britain and the Upper Solomons, encountered increased fighter opposition as the Japanese concentrated greated efforts on night interceptions in order to oppose these bombardment missions. Generally, Japanese night fighters have been sighted at 10,000 feet or above that level.

b. The trend of employment of Japanese night fighters suggests a continued interest in this phase of interception and may indicate an increasing development of techique.

7. AIR ATTACKS ON AIRFIELDS. a. An analysis of Japanese attacks on Allied airfields shows distinct changes in the methods employed. It is believed that these changes do not result from the development of improved tactics but were forced on the enemy by the increased strength of Allied air interception and ground defenses.

b. During the early period of Japanese occupation and expansion, full advantage was taken of the weakness of Allied air and ground defenses. Japanese carrier-borne aircraft operated in conjunction with land-based medium bombers. Dive bombers attacked antiaircraft positions and ground installations, with fighters strafing grounded aircraft from low level.

c. Later, as ground and fighter defenses became more formidable, the Japanese were forced to conduct their bombing operations from higher altitudes. By 1943, their characteristic attack was by night, with single aircraft or small to medium formations of medium bombers. There have been occasions when the Japanese have reverted to daylight attacks, as in their attacks on aircraft based on forward strips in support of Allied ground forces in New Guinea.

8. AIR-TO-AIR BOMBING. a. The use of small air-to-air bombs against Allied bomber planes was first reported in May 1942 in the Southwest Pacific Area. Since that time there have been an increasing number of reports of the use of air-to-air bombs against Allied heavy-bombing formations.

b. Air-to-air bombs dropped by the Japanese are reported to be accurately-timed high explosives combined with some incendiaries. They have been released both singly and in pattern arrangement. The majority of these bombs appear to weigh about 50 pounds each, and the explosion, based upon its blast effect on Allied planes, is estimated to be about the same as that of a heavy antiaircraft shell.

c. The presence of a Japanese "spotter" plane flying at the level of the formation to be attacked is a frequently observed characteristic of Japanese air-to-air bombing.

Section V. EQUIPMENT

1. GENERAL. a. Aircraft. (1) *Basic design principles.* Japanese aircraft have been built largely for the purpose of attaining great maneuverability, thereby sacrificing protection, firepower, and sturdiness. However, armorplate now is found on an increasing number of aircraft, as is also light leak-proofing for the fuel tanks. These belated attempts to provide more protection for their aircraft may mean that the Japanese are becoming aware of the importance of crew protection.

(2) *New developments.* A few recent improvements have been noted in Japanese aircraft, and further innovations may be expected. Greater attention to streamlining, and the use of larger, more powerful, and differently designed engines appear to be the two outstanding lines of development. The streamlining of the cockpit of type 99 Dive Bomber VAL Mk 2, and the use for the first time in a modern Japanese fighter of a liquid-cooled, inline engine in type 3 Fighter TONY are examples of these trends. The standard fighter armament is two 7.7-mm and two 20-mm guns; however, a 37-mm gun has been found on the twin-engine fighter NICK.

2. ARMAMENT. a. General. The Japanese show very little originality in their aircraft armament, except in modifying foreign designs, such as those of Great Britain, United States, Switzerland, and Germany. The only weapon that might be called truly Japanese is the Model 89, Nambu type, magazine-fed, aircraft machine gun which was converted from the Nambu ground machine gun. However, even this is a modified Hotchkiss design. It appears that a great variety of noninterchangeable types of ammunition exist for aircraft guns of the same caliber.

b. Guns. The Japanese employ aircraft guns with calibers ranging from 7.7-mm to 37-mm. Details of each type are shown in figure 67.

3. OTHER EQUIPMENT. a. Radio. See chapter 10.

b. Oxygen apparatus. (1) The designs of Japanese oxygen systems and their parts are good, although the basic principles used are not considered the best. The high pressure system has been generally disregarded in favor of a low pressure one, in view of the vulnerability of the former. The Japanese system usually consists of the following parts; high pressure oxygen bottle, pressure reducing regulator, pressure gauges, automatic regulator, and masks or tubes.

(2) There are two types of bottles. The first is a forged cylinder; the second a drawn and welded bottle. Neither of these containers has been found

Model	Caliber (mm.)	Weight, pounds	Length, inches	Type of operation	Rate of fire rounds/ minute	Type of feed	Ammunition Quantity rounds	Type	Remarks
89 Mk. II	7.7	27	40.75	Recoil	700–900	Belt		Ball, A. P., T., I., H. E.	Vickers type—fixed. Muzzle Velocity (with British .303″ MK VII ball) 2,450 ft/sec. Used on ZEKE.
89 Mk. II	7.7	20	39	Gas	750–850	Drum or clips	{70 90}	}Ball. A. P., T., I.	Flexible.
89	7.7		35.5	Gas	600	Drum	97	Ball, T., A. P., I.	Lewis type, flexible, single or twin.
89	7.7	21.25	42	Gas		Magazine	About 70		Flexible. Used on SALLY.
Twin 89 (Spec.)	7.7	50	45	Gas		Magazine	90 each [1]		
92	7.7		39	Gas		Drum	47		Flexible, Lewis type. Used on JAKE.
96	7.7	[2]24	40–42	Recoil	[1]700–800	Magazine	73		Flexible, automatic only. Used on SALLY.
(Twin) I	7.7			Gas				A. P., T., H. E.	Used on SALLY.
98	7.92	15.5	42.5	Recoil	1000–1100	Saddle drum	75	A. P., I.	Flexible. Copy of German MG 15. Used on LILY.
Twin 00	7.92	36	37.5	Gas	[1]400–600	Saddle drum	100	A. P., I.	Range 820–1150 ft. Flexible. Used on LILY.
89	12.7	52	48	Recoil	983	Disintegrating link.		A. P., T., H. E., I.	H. E. range good. M. V.—2515 ft/sec. Operations assisted by muzzle-recoil booster.
99	20	57.5	55	Recoil	450	Drum	60	Ball, I., A. P., H. E.	Oerlikon type used on ZEKE.
High velocity	20			Gas		Saddle Drum	60	H. E., A. P.	Aircraft version of Model 97 anti-tank gun used on HELEN.
98 (tank gun)	37								Used on NICK.

[1] Estimated.
[2] Approximately.

Figure 67. Japanese aircraft guns.

with protective measures, such as armor or wire wrappings, to prevent shattering.

(3) There is an automatic regulator of good design. The flow of oxygen is shut off until 10,000 feet is reached, at which altitude an aneroid lifts the metering needle allowing oxygen to pass through the outlet.

(4) On a few Japanese operational aircraft, an emergency chemical oxygen generator has been found.

c. Navigation equipment. (1) The Japanese seem to have good navigation equipment, for the few navigational instruments that have been captured in good condition have been of simple but effective design, indicating much copying from other countries. An octant taken from a Japanese reconnaissance airplane was found to be fairly accurate, easy to use, and painstakingly manufactured. A navigation calculator, consisting of a simple, but neatly made, celluloid disc is used.

(2) A Japanese drift sight operating on a bubble gimbal system was found easy to use, for it reduces the effect of roll and pitch. The optical system is arranged so that the apparent motion of the image of the bubble is in the same direction as the motion of the sight. The treatment of various parts of the sight to prevent corrosion is of good quality. The compasses that have been examined are of conventional design, and their workmanship is good as a general rule. An automatic pilot that was examined was found to be so similar to a type manufactured in the United States that parts in some instances were interchangeable. The case and some of the internal parts were heavier than that used by United States manufacturers, but the workmanship was good.

d. Instruments. Japanese instruments on the whole are more or less copies of instruments used in this country several years ago. Mass production methods were used on some of them, while on others, much hand finishing was in evidence. A more or less conventional design was followed in the case of engine instruments, about the only deviation being in the manifold pressure gauge which had new type of markings on its face. Boost pressure was shown in red on the right-hand side of the dial, and negative pressure in black on the left-hand side; zero mark, or atmospheric pressure, was the dividing line between the two colors.

e. Night-fighting equipment. Night-flying equipment on the aircraft examined to date shows very little improvement over that used in the United States Air Force several years ago. No individually lighted instruments, except the pilot's compass, have been found. Cockpits are lighted by small dashboard type lamps; some of the lamps are controlled by rheostats, while others have no control at all, but simply are turned on by a toggle type switch. Recent night fighter activities of the Japanese in the South Pacific area have shown an improvement in effectiveness which may indicate an advancement in technical aspects of their equipment as well as improved tactics.

f. Parachutes. (1) The Japanese use a quickly attachable seat type parachute for their bomber and transport crews. Another seat type parachute is used by pilots of fighters and other smaller aircraft. There have been reports that the Japanese use a chest type chute, but to date no information is available in regard to the type of aircraft with which it is used. The construction is of circular type. Four red-colored lines, attached to four of the main risers extending inside the canopy to the apex (top vent), are used for "spilling" the chute.

(2) The material in the canopy and shrouds is a good quality silk, and harness and pack are made of an equally good quality cotton. Although the harness is finely woven, it is not as strong as those manufactured in the United States. In general, except for the advantageous four red shrouds mentioned above, this type parachute is inferior to those made in the United States. As for the chest type parachute, there is not an adequate amount of data available to date, except that the Japanese silk webbing of the harness is much less bulky than American cotton but not as strong.

g. Photographic equipment. To date very little is known about the advanced designs of Japanese photographic equipment. All of it in good enough condition to test has been copied from equipment manufactured in the United States several years ago. Only a few minor changes had been made, namely, the handle grip sight and in the film magazine. Workmanship on the camera was excellent and indicated adherence to conventional practice. On a later-model camera that was recovered, the cone and part of the body were made of heavy cardboard. This specimen may have been an experimental camera, for no other models have been found. The film used had a nitrate base, and the emulsion was a little slower than that used by United States forces.

h. Flotation gear. Flotation gear has been found in some of the Zekes and Hamps; in both types of planes it was placed in the rear of the fuselage. This equipment consists of a rubberized cloth bag which is held in place by 8 pieces of woven cotton reinforcing tape attached to each corner. The gear is inflated by a CO_2 cylinder which is located behind the pilot's seat. Evidence of flotation gear in dive and torpedo bombers shows that it is installed in the top of the wings near the fuselage. This type air equipment is used mostly in training and on routine flights.

i. Fuel tank protection. There are three main types of Japanese fuel tank protection. The first, and least effective, is called "leak absorbing;" it consists of four layers of natural rubber joined together and totaling 3.1-mm ($\frac{1}{8}$ in.) in thickness. This is covered by a kapok matting which in turn is covered by a silvered fabric resembling balloon silk. The second type, termed "leak-proofing," is 12-mm (0.47 in.) thick. It is composed mostly of heavy crude rubber in 2 layers. The third type, referred to as "self-sealing," is 28.6-mm ($1\frac{1}{8}$ in.) thick; it is made up of 6 rubber layers reinforced by an inner silken mesh and an outer galvanized iron mesh. The self-sealing properties of this type appear to be good, at least on the outer surface. A jettisonable fuel tank made of wood has been examined, the length of which is 5 feet 2 inches, the diameter $15\frac{1}{4}$ inches,

and the capacity approximately 35 United States gallons. The construction is of plywood panels 7/64 inch thick.

j. Fuels and lubricants. From the samples of fuels and lubricants that have been obtained, it has been found that the Japanese fuels are good, although some contain a rather high amount of aromatics. The lubricants tested, although similar to those used in the United States, do not have some of the cold properties of the latter. Samples of greases in wheels and propellers also were found to be similar to American products.

k. Bombsights. Examination of a damaged bombsight revealed that it operated on the same principle as the French bombsights manufactured at the beginning of the present war. Stabilization of this sight is obtained by means of a level bubble in the optical field which is maintained in a stabilized position by hand. This sight worked on a timing principle and did not have electric bomb release. Another bombsight used by the Japanese was essentially a $3\frac{1}{2}$-foot telescope with no stabilizing or levelling aids. The eyepiece had no adjustment, but the sight incorporated range rate correction, deflection rate correction, and focusing.

l. Bombs and torpedoes. (1) Japanese bombs in general are made of steel and usually are not streamlined. Except for the armor-piercing and semiarmor-piercing bombs, they are of three-piece construction, consisting of nose, body, and tail. The nose and tail units are screwed in, welded, spot welded (the point of welding is the weakest part of the bomb), or riveted to the body of the bomb. The tail cones of some general-purpose bombs are filled with explosives; in these bombs, the body and tail units are filled in separate operations and subsequently attached. Either nose and/or tail fuses are used which are all mechanically operated. Long delay fuses, operated by a solvent dissolving a celluloid screw, also have been employed, while others are operated by a slight pyrotechnic delay.

(2) Some of the more common type bombs are the antipersonnel bombs ranging from 1 to 15 kilograms (2.2 to 33 pounds); incendiaries from 1 to 250 kilograms (2.2 to 550 pounds); and high explosives from 50 to 800 kilograms (110 to 1760 pounds). A gas bomb of 50 kilograms (110 pounds) also has been employed. For night tactics there is a 33 kilogram (72.6 pounds) illuminating flare.

(3) The Japanese make use of 5 types of torpedoes which differ in weight, length, diameter, speed, and explosive charge. Most standard models measure 17 feet long with a diameter of 17.7 inches. These torpedoes weigh 1,800 pounds and have an approximate speed of 42 knots. There exists one model which weighs 3,245 pounds, and is 22 feet long, with a diameter of 21 inches and a speed of 45 knots.

m. Sea rescue equipment. A limited amount of Japanese sea rescue equipment has been made available for examination. A 5-man, pneumatic, rubber life raft, measuring 12 feet long by 3 feet 10 inches wide, was found to be below current standards. The principal fault was the fact that the floor consists of meshed tarred cord which does not protect the occupants from the effects of salt water. As to sea rescue equipment for one man, a kapok life belt was examined and found to be identical with the Navy kapok jacket. A horseshoe-shaped, pneumatically inflated life preserver also is known to be used by the Japanese. This preserver, of single-ply construction, is weaker, but considerably lighter, than any equivalent preserver made in the United States. It has a good rubber coating, but is not designed to fit the individual. The ropes attached to the side indicate that the user hangs on to the preserver instead of wearing it.

n. Clothing. (1) The Japanese Air Force receives a good grade of clothing. Their flying suits, made of good silk and cotton, are well tailored and are similar in design to flying suits used by the United States Army Air Forces. All items of flight clothing recovered were sewed by skilled operators on standard machines, and the materials had received water- and flame-proofing treatment.

(2) The Japanese also have an efficient, electrically heated flying suit, which, when worn as an outer garment, compares favorably with United States electric suits. This suit, when tested, showed no hot spot when worn as an outer suit, but it did heat up too much around the shoulders when worn under other clothes. It also had cold spots on the back of the legs and on the inside of the arms. The fabric used is chocolate colored, and is of good quality.

4. CHARACTERISTICS OF OPERATIONAL JAPANESE AIRCRAFT. a. Markings. Japanese aircraft markings usually consist of a large red disc on the top and bottom of the outer section of each wing and on each side of the fuselage. The side marking is omitted on Army aircraft, but is retained on Navy aircraft. Occasionally the red disc is surrounded by a narrow white line. On biplanes wing markings appear only on the top of the upper wing and the bottom of the lower wing.

b. Designation of types. Tables in this chapter present the main characteristics of operational Japanese aircraft. It will be noted that both a type number and an identification or eode name are given for each airplane. Under the Japanese system of airplane designation, the type number indicates the year in which the aircraft was adopted. Type 97 corresponds to the Japanese year 2597 (our year 1937) and type O (Zero) to 2600 (our year 1940). For this reason, various categories of aircraft—fighters, bombers, reconnaissance, and others—all may be designated, for example, as Type O.

c. Identification or code names. In order to eliminate the confusion regarding the designations of Japanese aircraft, a code name was assigned each airplane by the Allied Air Forces in the Southwest Pacific in September 1942. The fighters and floatplanes were given masculine names, such as Zeke and Pete, whereas the bombers, land-based reconnaissance, and flying boats were given feminine names, such as Betty, Dinah, and Emily. Transports were assigned names beginning with the letter "T." When the existence of a new type is confirmed, a new code name is assigned to the aircraft.

NOTE—CHANGES IN AIRCRAFT CODE NAMES

The standard system of nomenclature for types of Japanese aircraft was revised while this handbook was on the press, making it impossible to correct the old code names in the text. The new code names, given below, should be substituted for those found in tables, and under silhouettes and photographs, on the following pages.

Old code name	New code name	Old code name	New code name	Old code name	New code name
Alf	Alf	Jake	Jake 11	Sally Mark 3	Sally 3
Babs Mark 3	Babs 11	Judy	Judy 12	Slim	Slim 11
Eetty	Betty 11	Kate	Kate 12	Sonia	Sonia 1
Cherry	Cherry 11	Lily Mark 1	Lily 1	Tess	Tess 11
Claude	Claude 14	Mavis	Mavis 22	Thelma	Thelma 1
Dave	Dave	Nate	Nate 1	Tojo	Tojo 2
Dinah	Dinah 2	Nell	Nell 23	Tony	Tony 1
Emily	Emily 22	Nick	Nick 1	Topsy	Topsy 1
Glen	Glen 11	Oscar Mark 2	Oscar 2	Val Mark 2	Val 22
Helen	Helen 2	Pete	Pete 11	Zeke	Zeke 11
Ida	Ida 1	Rufe	Rufe 11		

ZEKE Mk2

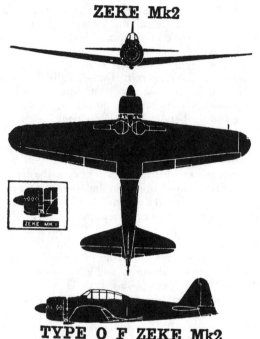

TYPE 0 F ZEKE Mk2
Span 39' 5"   Length 29' 9"
(Mk1: Span 39' 5''; Length 29' 7'')

HAMP

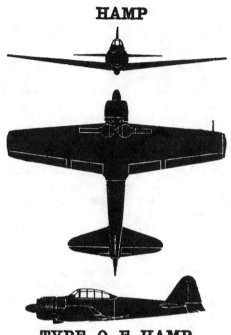

TYPE 0 F HAMP
Span 36' 2"   Length 29' 9"

OSCAR Mk2

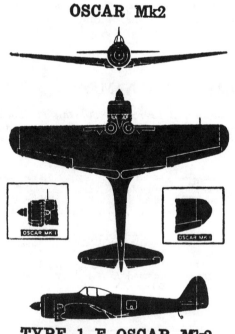

TYPE 1 F OSCAR Mk2
Span 35' 7"   Length 29' 3"
(Mk1: Span 37' 6''; Length 29' 1½'')

TOJO

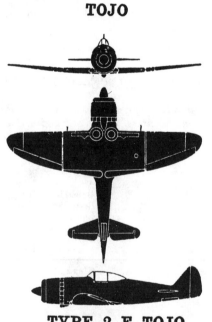

TYPE 2 F TOJO
Span 31' 0"   Length 29' 2½"

Figure 68.

TONY

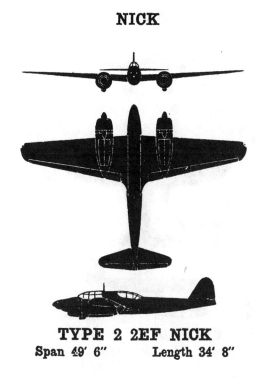

TYPE 3 F TONY
Span 39′ 4″   Length 28′ 9″

NICK

TYPE 2 2EF NICK
Span 49′ 6″   Length 34′ 8″

RUFE

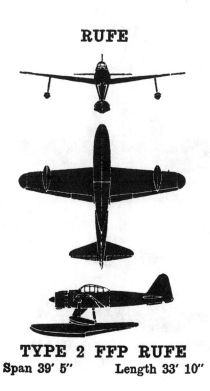

TYPE 2 FFP RUFE
Span 39′ 5″   Length 33′ 10″

PETE

TYPE 0 FP PETE
Span 36′ 2″   Length 30′ 6″

Figure 68—Continued.

JAKE

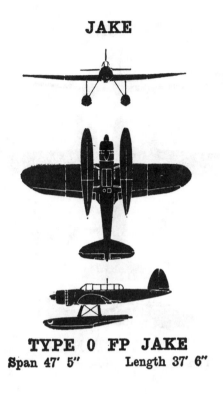

TYPE 0 FP JAKE
Span 47′ 5″   Length 37′ 6″

SONIA

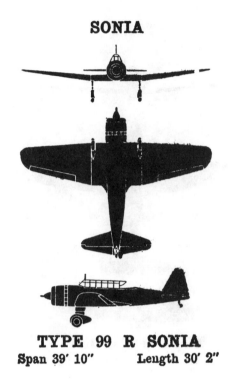

TYPE 99 R SONIA
Span 39′ 10″   Length 30′ 2″

JUDY

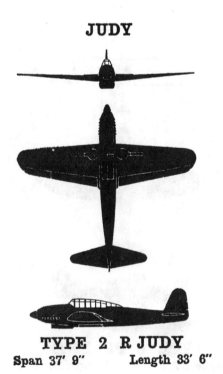

TYPE 2 R JUDY
Span 37′ 9″   Length 33′ 6″

DINAH

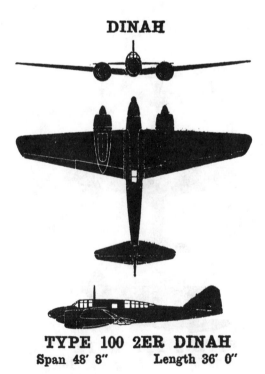

TYPE 100 2ER DINAH
Span 48′ 8″   Length 36′ 0″

Figure 68—Continued.

VAL Mk2

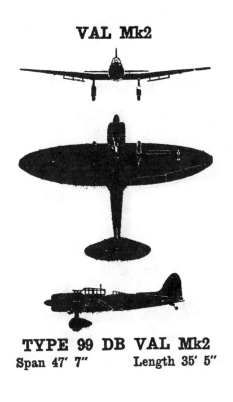

TYPE 99 DB VAL Mk2
Span 47′ 7″   Length 35′ 5″

KATE

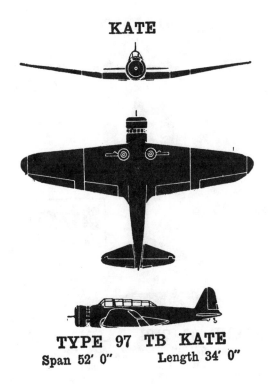

TYPE 97 TB KATE
Span 52′ 0″   Length 34′ 0″

LILY

TYPE 99 2EB LILY
Span 58′ 0″   Length 42′ 0″

NELL Mk 2

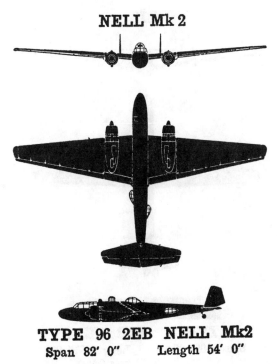

TYPE 96 2EB NELL Mk2
Span 82′ 0″   Length 54′ 0″

Figure 68—Continued.

SALLY Mk3

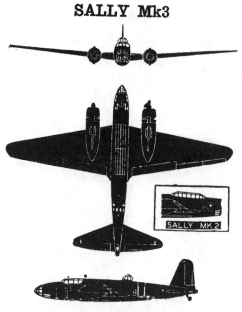

TYPE 97 2EB SALLY Mk3
Span 74' 8"   Length 52' 0"
(Mk2 Dimensions Same)

BETTY

TYPE 1 2EB BETTY
Span 81' 8"   Length 65' 7"

LIZ

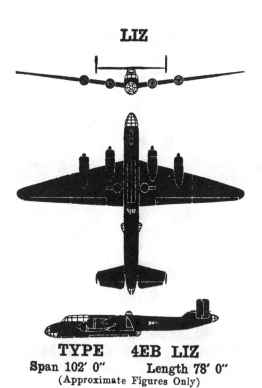

TYPE 4EB LIZ
Span 102' 0"   Length 78' 0"
(Approximate Figures Only)

HELEN

TYPE 100 2EB HELEN
Span 68' 0"   Length 54' 0"
(Approximate Figures Only)

Figure 68—Continued.

MAVIS

EMILY

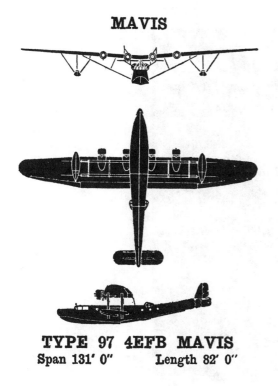

TYPE 97 4EFB MAVIS
Span 131′ 0″   Length 82′ 0″

TYPE 2 4EFB EMILY
Span 124′ 0″   Length 98′ 0″

CHERRY

TYPE 99 2EFB CHERRY
Span 85′ 0″   Length 55′ 6″
(Approximate Figures Only)

Figure 68—Continued.

*Figure 69. Model 99 (1939)   63 Kilogram   General Purpose
H. E. Bomb.*

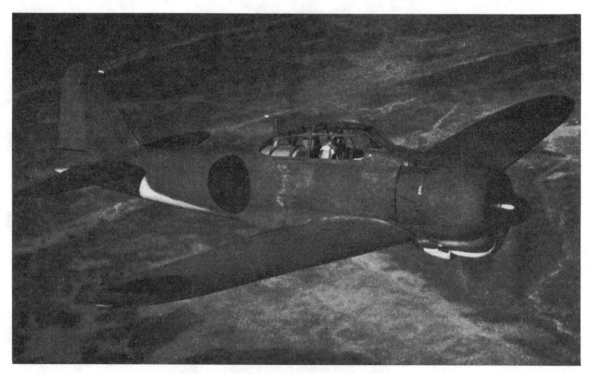

Figure 70–A. Type O Fighter "Zeke" Mark 1.

Figure 70–B. Type O Fighter "Hamp".

Figure 71–A. Type 3 Fighter "Tony".

Figure 71-B. Type 1 Fighter "Oscar" Mark 1.

Figure 72-A. Type 2 Fighter "Tojo".

Figure 72–B. Type 2 Twine engine Two seat Fighter "Nick".

Figure 73–A. Type 1 Medium bomber "Betty".

Figure 73–B. Type 100 Medium bomber "Helen".

Figure 74–A. Type 97 Medium bomber "Sally" Mark 3.

Figure 74–B. Type 99 Dive bomber "Val" Mark 2.

Figure 75–A. Type 100 Reconnaissance "Dinah".

Figure 75–B. Type O Float plane "Pete".

Characteristics of Operational Japanese Aircraft.

FIGHTERS

Type	Code name	Description	Span (Ft.)	Span (In.)	Length (Ft.)	Length (In.)	Height (Ft.)	Height (In.)	Wing area (gross) (Sq. ft.)	Weight Landing (Lbs.)	Weight Normal load (Lbs.)	Weight Maximum load (Lbs.)	Fuel load Normal (U.S. gal.)	Fuel load Maximum (U.S. gal.)	Armament	Bomb load (lbs.) (normal) (maximum)
96	Claude	Single-engine low-wing monoplane. Wings elliptical. Open cockpit. Fixed landing gear.	36		24	7	9	10	[1] 180	3,700	4,400	4,700	96	135	2 x 7.7 mm	[1] 132
97	Nate	Single-engine, low-wing monoplane. Tapered wings. Open or closed cockpit. Fixed landing gear.	35	10	24	4	8	0	200	3,854	4,643	5,200	96	156	2 x 7.7 mm	
0 (Mk. 1)	Zeke	Single-engine, low-wing monoplane. Tapered wings, rounded tips. High-set cockpit inclosure. Retractable landing gear.	39	5	30	3	9	2	248	3,918	5,247	6,136	144	231	2 x 7.7 mm and 2 x 20 mm.	265
0 (Mk. 2)	Hamp	Single-engine, low-wing monoplane. Tapered wings, square tips. High-set cockpit inclosure. Retractable landing gear.	36	4	29	9	9	2	232.4	4,113	5,650	6,331	134	221	2 x 7.7 mm + 2 x 20 mm.	265
1 (Mk. 2)	Oscar, Mk. 2	Single-engine, low-wing monoplane. Straight leading edges; tapered trailing edges. Full-length rudder. Retractable landing gear; fixed tailwheel.	37	7	29		9	0	240	4,370	5,500	6,096	149	257	2 x 12.7 mm	
2 (floatplane)	Rufe	Single-engine, single-float, low-wing monoplane. Similar to ZEKE, except for full-length rudder and floats.	39	5	29	5	14		248	4,345	5,920	6,436	141	227	2 x 7.7 mm + 2 x 20 mm	May carry small bomb under each wing.
2	Nick	Twin-engine, low-wing, single-seat fighter. Wings, stabilizer, and elevators tapered. Pointed nose. Long, slender fuselage. Tail fin and rudder.	49	5	34	6									2 x 12.7 mm + 1 x 37 mm + 1 x 7.9 mm.	1 bomb rack under each wing.
2	Tojo	Single-engine, low-wing monoplane. Tapered leading, elliptical edges. Retractable landing gear.	31		27	3	9	6	161.4	[1] 5,000	6,095	6,611	128	197	2 x 12.7 mm + 2 x 7.7/12.7 mm.	
3	Tony	Single, inline engine, low-wing monoplane. Cockpit fairs into fuselage. Large air-scoop under fuselage. Resembles Hurricane.	39	6	29	6	9		210	5,200	6,700	7,400	199	299	2 x 12.7 mm + 2 x 7.7/12.7 mm.	1,000

MEDIUM BOMBERS

Type	Code name	Description	Span (Ft.)	Span (In.)	Length (Ft.)	Length (In.)	Height (Ft.)	Height (In.)	Wing area (gross) (Sq. ft.)	Weight Landing (Lbs.)	Weight Normal load (Lbs.)	Weight Maximum load (Lbs.)	Fuel load Normal (U.S. gal.)	Fuel load Maximum (U.S. gal.)	Armament	Bomb load (lbs.) (normal) (maximum)
96 (Mk. 3)	Nell	Twin-engine, mid-wing monoplane. Sharply tapered wings, Junkers-type flaps and ailerons. Twin fins and rudders.	82		54	3	12	7	860	13,925	22,300	23,500	940	1,372	3 x 7.7 mm 1 x 12.7/20 mm	1,538 / 2,660
97 (Mk. 3)	Sally (Mk. 3)	Twin-engine, mid-wing monoplane. Tapered wings. Front cockpit rear dorsal turret. Single fin and rudder.	72		52	5	12		675	14,225	21,500	22,000	684	953	4 x 7.7 mm + 1 x 12.7 mm	2,200 / 4,400
100	Helen	Twin-engine, mid-wing monoplane. Fowler-type flaps and frise ailerons fitted. Has rear tail turret.	66	7	53						[1] 28,500		1,157		4 x 7 mm + 1 x 79 mm + 1 x 20 mm.	2,300
1	Betty	Twin-engine, mid-wing monoplane. Cigar-shaped fuselage. Transparent nose and tail.	82		65	7	19	8	838	16,700	26,975	27,015	1,300	1,554	7.7 mm + 1 x 20 mm.	1,554 / 3,300

TORPEDO, DIVE AND LIGHT BOMBERS

Type	Code name	Description	Span (Ft.)	Span (In.)	Length (Ft.)	Length (In.)	Height (Ft.)	Height (In.)	Wing area (gross) (Sq. ft.)	Weight Landing (Lbs.)	Weight Normal load (Lbs.)	Weight Maximum load (Lbs.)	Fuel load Normal (U.S. gal.)	Fuel load Maximum (U.S. gal.)	Armament	Bomb load (lbs.) (normal) (maximum)
97	Kate (Torpedo Bomber)	Single-engine, low-wing monoplane. Long transparent cockpit inclosure.	52		34	3	10	7 3/4	415	6,039	8,379	8,940	290	331.5	3 x 7.7 mm	1,760
99 (Mk. 2)	Val Mk. 2 (Dive Bomber)	Single-engine, low-wing monoplane. Elliptical wings. Dive-brakes. Long fin fairing on fuselage. Fixed landing gear.	47	3	35	5	13		370.5	5,800	8,379	9,000	286	373	3 x 7.7 mm	814 / 2,200
99 (Mk. 1)	Lily Mk. 1 (Light Bomber)	Twin-engine, mid-wing monoplane. Resembles U. S. Martin "Baltimore" with abruptly-narrowing rear fuselage.	56	11	47	3	14	9	465	10,600	15,500		420	492	2 x 7.9 mm + 2 x 7.9 mm or 1 x 12.7 mm	1,650

	Name	Description	Span	Length	Height							Armament	
94 (Mk. 2)	Alf (float-plane)	Single-engine, twinfloat biplane. Equispan wings, slightly staggered. Single fin and rudder.	46 10½	32 5	15 10	682	4,920	6,540		145	216	2 x 7.7 mm	---/500
95	Dave (float-plane)	Single engine, single float biplane.	Top 35 8 Lower 34 6	28 4	13 2	302	4,280	5,800		145	145	2 x 7.7 mm	265
96	Slim (float-plane)	Probably a very small single-engine, single-float biplane, designed to be carried by and launched from a submarine.						13,060				Probably 1 x 7.7 mm	
0	Pete (float-plane)	Single-engine, single-float biplane. Staggered wings are tapered with single interplane strut.	Upper 36 1 Lower 35 10	32 4	15	365	4,890	5,623	6,471	169	169	3 x 7.7 mm	440
0	Glen (float-plane)	Probably a small, single engine, single-float biplane designed to be carried by and launched from a submarine.						3,320				Probably 1 x7.7 mm	Probably ---/300
0	Jake (float-plane)	Single-engine, low-wing, twin float monoplane. Elliptical wings. Long cockpit inclosure.	46 9½	34 4	14 8¾	[1]385	6,468	9,223	9,603	388	368	1 x 7.7 mm	530
100	Dinah	Twin-engine, low-wing monoplane. Sharply tapered wings. Fore and aft cockpits.	48¾	38		375	9,165	11,925		400		1 x 7.7 mm	
2	Judy	Single-engine, low-wing monoplane. Tapered wings pointed nose. Landing gear retracks.	47 9	33 6		254	5,818	8,055		275	448	3 x 7.7 mm	Small bomb bay
98	Babs Mk. 3	Single-engine, low wing monoplane. Tapered wings. Transparent cockpit inclosure merges into the fin inclosure. Fixed landing gear.	[1]40	[1]28	9 4	[1]220	4,350	5,750		120	217	3 x 7.7 mm	660/1,000
98	Ida	Single-engine, low-wing monoplane. Long cockpit inclosure merges into fuselage. Fixed landing gear.	47 9	34	11 10	290	6,045	7,800	9,800	84	168	3 x 7.7 mm	660/1,000
99	Sonia	Single-engine, low-mid-wing monoplane. Tapered wings. Long transparent cockpit inclosure.	39 10	30 2	11 6	220	5,100	6,500		204	204	3 x 7.7 mm	550/1,000

	Name	Description	Span	Length	Height							Armament	
97	Mavis	Four-engine, parasol-wing monoplane. Single 2-step hull. Twin braced fins and rudders.	131	84 6	20 7	1,776	27,607	43,156	50,546	1690	3510	4 x 7.7 mm + 1 x 20 mm	3,300/3,528
99	Cherry	Twin-engine, high-wing monoplane. Wing braced to hull. Twin fins and rudders.	108	[1]86	8 2	750	14,200	18,000		360	600	(Possibly) 2 x 7.7 mm + 1 x 20 mm	1,600
2	Emily	Four-engine, high-wing monoplane. Single fin and rudder.	124	95			38,347	54,022		5120		4 x 7.7 mm + 3 x 20 mm	1,584/3,440

	Name	Description	Span	Length	Height								
Mc 20	Topsy	Twin-engine, low-wing monoplane. Sharply tapered wings.	74	52 8	16	755	12,705	18,300	19,750	45-3	68-1		2,360 (freight)
Lockheed	Thelma	Twin-engine, low-midwing. Wings taper sharply. Twin fins and rudders.	65 6	49 10	11 10		11,000	15,500	17,500	644			4,400 / 10 Pass.
DC-2	Tess	Twin-engine, low-wing monoplane. Single fin and rudder.	85	64 5	16 11		12,800	18,500	19,000	822			---/6,000

1 Estimated

FIGHTERS

Type	Code name	Armor	Power plant — Engine	Horse-power	Altitude (Ft.)	Speeds (m.p.h.) — Maximum	Normal cruising	Economical cruising	Ranges — Normal (Miles)	Maximum (Miles)	Climb to altitude (ft./min.)	Service ceiling (normal load) (Ft.)	Crew	Remarks
98	Claude	None	(1) Nakajima "Kotobuki," 41 9-cyl., air-cooled radial.	645	S.L.	250 at 9,000.	205 at 13,000.	125 at 13,000.	650	980	15,000/6.25	33,000	1	An obsolescent carrier borne fighter.
97	Nate	None. Wing root fuel tanks protected.	(1) Nakajima "Hikari," 9-cyl., air-cooled radial.	915	12,000	284 at 13,500.	196 at 11,500.	143 at 11,500.	489	962	10,000/3.4	35,100	1	Is obsolescent and only in occasional use.
0 (Mk. 1)	Zeke	None	(1) Nakajima "Sakae" 12, 14-cyl., twin-row, air-cooled radial. Mk.2 has Sakae 21.	955	14,500	328 at 16,000.	240 at 14,500.	171 at 14,500.	806	1,590	20,000/7.9	38,600	1	Still remains one of Japan's best single-seat fighters.
0 (Mk. 2)	Hamp	None	(1) Nakajima "Sakae" 21, 14-cyl., twin-row, air-cooled radial.	1,020	6,400	328 at 16,600.	257 at 18,600.	189 at 18,600.	725	1,510	10,000/3.3	35,000	1	One of Japan's best fighters.
1 (Mk. 2)	Oscar, Mk. 2	Pilot protected. Self-sealing fuel tanks.	(1) Nakajima type 2, 14-cyl., twin-row, air-cooled radial, similar to Sakae 12.	1,130	8,000	342 at 17,500.	252 at 15,600.	178 at 15,600.	792	1,710	20,000/6.5	38,400	1	Oscar Mk. 1, with improved engine, performance and armament.
2 (floatplane)	Rufe	None	(1) Nakajima "Sakae" 12, 14-cyl., twin-row, air-cooled radial.	955	14,500	278 at 16,000.	204 at 14,000.	153 at 14,000.	640	1,280	10,000/4.6	35,400	1	A widely used operational floatplane fighter.
2	Nick	Pilot protected. self-sealing fuel tank.	(1) type 2, 14-cyl., twin-row air-cooled radial.	1,050	8,000	1 350							2	Operational twin-engine fighter.
2	Tojo	Pilot protected, fuel tanks protected.	Nakajima type 2, 14-cyl., twin-row, air-cooled radial.	1,415	11,000	376 at 17,000.	313 at 17,000.	270 at 9,840.	650	1,310	17,000/5.25	35,000	1	Newest operational Japanese fighter.
3	Tony	Pilot's seat protected from rear. Self-sealing fuel tanks.	(1) Kawasaki type 2, 12-cyl., liquid-cooled, 60°, inverted "V."	1,100	13,000	363 at 17,000.	262 at 15,000.	191 at 15,000.	1,014	1,812	10,000/3.8	35,700	1	Is the first modern Japanese fighter to have in-line engine and armor plate.

MEDIUM BOMBERS

Type	Code name	Armor	Power plant — Engine	Horse-power	Altitude (Ft.)	Speeds (m.p.h.) — Maximum	Normal cruising	Economical cruising	Ranges — Normal (Miles)	Maximum (Miles)	Climb to altitude (ft./min.)	Service ceiling (normal load) (Ft.)	Crew	Remarks
96 (Mk. 3)	Nell	None.	(2) Mitsubishi "Kinsei," 62, 14-cylinder, twin-row, air-cooled radial.	1,175	3,500	1 240 at 7,700	180 at 6,500	140 at 6,600	1,760	3,130	10,000/8.3	24,000	4 to 7	An older type bomber still in operation but becoming obsolescent.
97 (Mk. 3)	Sally (Mk. 3)	Pilot dorsal turret protected. Self sealing fuel tanks.	(2) Mitsubishi Type 100, 14-cylinder, twin-row, air-cooled radial.	1,480	7,200	285 at 15,000	210 at 7,200	148 at 7,200	1,120	1,960	10,000/5	29,800	7	Operational bomber. Mk. 1, dorsal rear cock pit, no tail gun, Mk. 2, same but with tail gun.
100	Helen	Pilot, co-pilot, fuel tanks protected.	(2) Nakajima Type 2, 14-cylinder, twin-row, air-cooled radial.	1,415	11,000	270 at 12,000	225 at 10,000	170 at 10,000	1,750	1,950		35,000	5 to 7	The newest type bomber identified in service.
1	Betty	2 x 3/16 in. thick tail-plates. Self sealing fuel tanks.	(2) Mitsubishi "Kinsei" 15, 14-cylinder, twin-row, air-cooled radial.	1,475	10,000	276 at 15,000	205 at 7,200	151 at 7,200	2,110	3,220	10,000/6.7	28,800	7 to 9	One of the most widely used medium bombers.

TORPEDO, DIVE AND LIGHT BOMBERS

Type	Code name	Armor	Power plant — Engine	Horse-power	Altitude (Ft.)	Speeds (m.p.h.) — Maximum	Normal cruising	Economical cruising	Ranges — Normal (Miles)	Maximum (Miles)	Climb to altitude (ft./min.)	Service ceiling (normal load) (Ft.)	Crew	Remarks
97	Kate (Torpedo Bomber).	None.	(1) Nakajima "Sakae" 11, 14-cylinder, twin-row, air-cooled radial.	985	7,500	222 at 8,500	166 at 7,500	131 at 7,500	1,060	1,600	10,000/8.8	23,800	2 to 3	{The standard, single-engine torpedo bomber.
99 (Mk. 2)	Val Mk. 2 (Dive Bomber).	None.	(1) Mitsubishi "Kinsei" 54, 14-cylinder, twin row, air-cooled radial.	1,175	3,500	254 at 13,000	190 at 12,000	145 at 12,000	1,050	2,000	10,000/5.6	29,800	2	{Improved modification of Val Mk. I which it probably is intended to supersede.
99 (Mk. 1)	Lily Mk. 1 (Light Bomber).	4 of 6 fuel tanks protected.	(2) Kawasaki Type 99, 14-cylinder, twin-row, air-cooled radial.	955	9,000	278 at 10,000	206 at 9,000	157 at 9,000	980	1,490	10,000/5.9	28,200	3 or 4	Operational light bomber Mk. 2 has Kawasaki Type 2 engine rated at 1,130 horsepower at 8,000'.

No.	Name	Engine(s)	Protection			High speed	Cruising	Landing				Ceiling	Crew	Remarks
94 (Mk. 2)	Alf (float-plane)	(1) Mitsubishi Zuisei 11, 14 cyl., twin-row, air-cooled radial.	None	780	7,000	147 at 7,000	125 at 7,000	90 at 7,000	390	420	7,000/7.5	22,000	3	Obsolescent biplane float-plane, probably being replaced by Jake.
95	Dave (float-plane)	(1) Nakajima Kotobiki 3, 9-cyl., air-cooled radial.	None	650	7,000	185 at 11,000	140 at 11,000	115 at 11,000	770	863	10,000/9.9	20,500	2	Obsolescent biplane float-plane encountered occasionally.
96	Slim (float-plane)	(1) Assumed "Amakaze" 12, 9-cyl., air-cooled radial.	None	285[1]	S. L.	170[1] at 11,000	132[1]	92	500[1]		10,000/11[1]	16,000[1]	2	Probably obsolescent submarine-borne float-plane believed to be in service. 17 min. launching time.
0	Pete (float-plane)	(1) Mitsubishi "Zuisei" 13, 14-cyl., twin-row, air-cooled radial.	None	940	13,100	238 at 14,000	171 at 13,100	130 at 13,100	627	832	10,000/4.5	33,100	2	Latest type biplane float-plane in operation.
0	Glen (float-plane)	(1) Assumed "Amakaze" 12, 9-cyl., air-cooled radial.	None	285[1]	S. L.	220[1]	140/160	115[1]	500[1]	700[1]			2	Newest model submarine float-plane reported in service. May be small version of Jake. 15 min. launching time.
0	Jake (float-plane)	(1) Kinsei 43, 14 cylinder, twin-row, air-cooled radial.	None	1,060	6,500	216 at 7,500	157 at 6,500	122 at 6,500	1,205	1,520	10,000/6.8	24,400	3	A currently-operational floatplane.
100	Dinah	(2) Mitsubishi Type 1, 14-cylinder, twin-row, air-cooled radial.	Pilot protected	1,050	8,000	343 at 13,000	251 at 10,800	180 at 10,800	1,105	1,435	10,000/3.8	34,700	2	A widely-used aircraft.
2	Judy	Aichi 12 cylinder, liquid-cooled inverted "v".	None	1,270	16,250	350[1] at 17,000							2	Newest reconnaissance aircraft.
98	Babs Mk. 3	(1) Mitsubishi "Kinsei" 44, 14-cylinder, twin-row, air-cooled radial.	None	1,050	6,600	270[1] at 15,000	235[1] at 15,000	160[1] at 15,000	1,450[1]	1,240[1]		30,000	2	Operational reconnaissance bomber.
98	Ida	(1) Mitsubishi 14 cylinder, twin-row, air-cooled radial.	None	900	9,000	260 at 13,000	225 at 13,000	200 at 13,000	500	790	13,000/10.75	27,000	2 or 3	An obsolescent light reconnaissance bomber still reported in service.
99	Sonia	(1) Mitsubishi type 99, 14-cylinder, twin-row, air-cooled radial.	Pilot protected 4 of 7 fuel tanks protected.	900	S. L.	270 at 8,000	220 at 10,000	130 at 10,000	420	600	10,000/5	16,000	2	An operational reconnaissance bomber.
FLYING BOATS														
97	Mavis	(4) Mitsubishi Kinsei 46, 14 cyl., twin-row, air-cooled radial.	None	1,060	13,800	237 at 15,000	176 at 13,800	127 at 13,800	1,650	4,400	10,000/8.6	27,700	8 to 10	Flying boat in operation.
99	Cherry	(2) Nakajima Shinten 21, 14 cyl., twin-row, air-cooled radial.	None	1,010	S. L.	175 at 7,000	160 at 7,000	100 at 7,000	460	1,080	7,000/6	24,000	6	Flying boat in occasional use.
2	Emily	(4) Mitsubishi Kasei 22, 14 cyl., air-cooled radial.	Installed	1,440[1]		230[1]	150	150	1,500				8 to 10[1]	Newest type flying boat in operation—a possible successor to Mavis.
TRANSPORTS														
Mc 20	Topsy	(2) Mitsubishi Kinsei 43 two-row, air-cooled radial.	None	985	9,200	266 at 10,500	197 at 9,200	144 at 9,200	1,020	1,890	10,000/6.6	23,000	4	An operational transport.
Lockheed	Thelma	(2) Air-cooled radials.	None	900[1]	S. L.	230	185 at 10,000	150 at 10,000	970		10,000/11.5	25,000	2 to 3[1]	An operational transport, originally of Lockheed 14 design.
DC-2	Tess	(2) Mitsubishi Kinsei 43, 14 cyl., twin-row, air-cooled radial.		1,060	6,500	212	150		1,100			22,000	2 to 3[1]	Douglas-designed transport in operation.

[1] Estimated

Figure 77. Characteristics of Operational Japanese Aircraft.

Figure 76–A. Type 97 Flying boat "Mavis".

Figure 76–B. Type 2 Flying boat "Emily".

CHAPTER V

SPECIAL FORCES

Section I. NAVAL LAND FORCES

1. ROLE AND CHARACTER. Until several years after World War I, Japan had no separate permanent naval landing organization corresponding to the U. S. Marine Corps. Instead, naval landing parties were organized temporarily from fleet personnel for a particular mission and were returned to their ships at its conclusion. This practice was made possible by the fact that every naval recruit was given training in land warfare concurrently with training in seamanship. The results of such training, together with any special skills such as machine gunner, truck driver, etc., were noted on the seaman's service record to serve as a basis for his inclusion in a landing party. Normally, the fleet commander designated certain ships to furnish personnel for the landing party. This practice, however, depleted their crews and lowered their efficiency for naval action. Therefore, in the late 1920's Japan began to experiment with more permanent units known as Special Naval Landing Forces (Rikusentai). Those units were formed at the four major Japanese naval bases: Sasebo, Kure, Maizuru, and Yokosuka, and were given numerical designations as formed; for example, there is a Sasebo 2nd Special Naval Landing Force and a Kure 2nd Special Naval Landing Force. They are composed entirely of naval personnel with a naval officer, usually a commander, in charge. These forces, first used against China and later against the Allies, have gone through several stages of evolution as the general war situation has changed. As the present war progressed, and the Japanese Navy became more involved in the seizure and defense of Pacific islands, other naval land organizations came into existence. Examples of these are: the Base Force (Tokubetsu Konkyochitai), the Guard Force (Keibitai), the Pioneers (Setsueitai) and the Naval Civil Engineering and Construction Units (Kaigun Kenchiku Shisetsu Butai).

2. SPECIAL NAVAL LANDING FORCES.
a. Use in China. Special naval landing forces were used extensively in landing operations on the China coast beginning with 1932, and often performed garrison duty upon capturing their objective. Their performance was excellent when unopposed, but when determined resistance was encountered they exhibited a surprising lack of ability in infantry combat. These early special naval landing forces were organized as battalions, each estimated to comprise about 2,000 men divided into 4 companies. Three companies each consisted of 6 rifle platoons and 1 heavy machine gun platoon; the fourth company, of 3 rifle platoons and a heavy-weapons platoon of four 3-inch naval guns, or two 75-mm regimental guns and two 70-mm battalion guns. Tank and armored car units were employed in garrison duty and, where the terrain and situation favored their use, in assault operations.

b. Offensive use in World War II. When the present war began, special naval landing forces at first were used to occupy a chain of Pacific island bases. Wake Island was taken by one such force, while another seized the Gilbert Islands. Later they were used to spearhead landing operations against Java, Ambon, and Rabaul, where the bulk of the attack forces consisted of army personnel. During this period the special naval landing forces, although heavily armed, were used as mobile striking units. They consisted of two rifle companies (each having a machine-gun platoon), and one or two companies of heavy weapons (antitank guns, sometimes antiaircraft guns, and tanks), a total of 1,200 to 1,500 men. A small number of special troops (engineer, ordnance, signal, transport and medical) was also included. Figure 78 illustrates the composition of this type of unit, and also the change to heavier fire power as compared with the organization of the earlier types of naval landing forces used in China from 1932 to 1937.

c. Special naval landing forces in defense. Special naval landing forces, or similar organizations, are occupying a number of outlying bases, because the Army has been reluctant to take over the defenses of these outposts. Since Japan has lost the initiative in the Pacific, these forces have been given defensive missions, and the Japanese Navy has changed their organization accordingly. This point is strikingly illustrated by a comparison of the organization of the Yokosuka 7th Special Naval Landing Force (fig. 79), encountered on New Georgia, with that of the Maizuru 2nd (fig. 78). The Yokosuka 7th has a larger amount of artillery, and its guns are mainly pedestal-mounted naval pieces. As first organized, the Yokosuka 7th was deficient in infantry troops and infantry weapons for defense, but later it was reinforced by a second rifle company. This new company consisted of 3 rifle platoons of 1 officer and 48 enlisted men each (3 light-machine-gun squads and 1 grenade-discharger squad), and a heavy-machine-gun platoon of 1 officer, 58 enlisted men, and 8 heavy machine guns.

Other special naval landing forces probably started with an organization similar to that of the Maizuru 2nd, but their gun strengths and organizations most

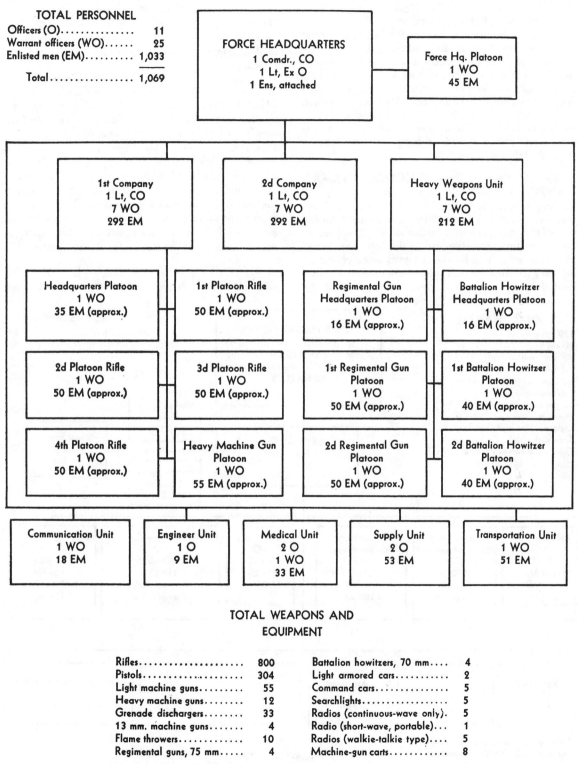

TOTAL PERSONNEL

Officers (O)..............	11
Warrant officers (WO)......	25
Enlisted men (EM).........	1,033
Total...............	1,069

FORCE HEADQUARTERS
1 Comdr., CO
1 Lt, Ex O
1 Ens, attached

Force Hq. Platoon
1 WO
45 EM

1st Company
1 Lt, CO
7 WO
292 EM

2d Company
1 Lt, CO
7 WO
292 EM

Heavy Weapons Unit
1 Lt, CO
7 WO
212 EM

Headquarters Platoon
1 WO
35 EM (approx.)

1st Platoon Rifle
1 WO
50 EM (approx.)

Regimental Gun
Headquarters Platoon
1 WO
16 EM (approx.)

Battalion Howitzer
Headquarters Platoon
1 WO
16 EM (approx.)

2d Platoon Rifle
1 WO
50 EM (approx.)

3d Platoon Rifle
1 WO
50 EM (approx.)

1st Regimental Gun
Platoon
1 WO
50 EM (approx.)

1st Battalion Howitzer
Platoon
1 WO
40 EM (approx.)

4th Platoon Rifle
1 WO
50 EM (approx.)

Heavy Machine Gun
Platoon
1 WO
55 EM (approx.)

2d Regimental Gun
Platoon
1 WO
50 EM (approx.)

2d Battalion Howitzer
Platoon
1 WO
40 EM (approx.)

Communication Unit
1 WO
18 EM

Engineer Unit
1 O
9 EM

Medical Unit
2 O
1 WO
33 EM

Supply Unit
2 O
53 EM

Transportation Unit
1 WO
51 EM

TOTAL WEAPONS AND
EQUIPMENT

Rifles....................	800	Battalion howitzers, 70 mm....	4
Pistols....................	304	Light armored cars...........	2
Light machine guns........	55	Command cars..............	5
Heavy machine guns.......	12	Searchlights.................	5
Grenade dischargers........	33	Radios (continuous-wave only).	5
13 mm. machine guns.......	4	Radio (short-wave, portable)...	1
Flame throwers............	10	Radios (walkie-talkie type)....	5
Regimental guns, 75 mm.....	4	Machine-gun carts...........	8

Figure 78. Maizuru No. 2 Special Landing Force: organization as of 19 November 1941.

probably have veered toward that of the Yokosuka 7th. This process was found to have occurred in the Gilberts and Marshalls. Under Allied pressure Japan has found it necessary to increase the defenses of some islands by reinforcing the special naval landing force, or by combining two or more special naval landing forces into a new organization known as a Combined Special Naval Landing Force. In New Georgia the Kure 6th, the Yokosuka 7th, and portions of the Maizuru 4th were combined into the 8th Combined Special Naval Landing Force. In the Gilberts a special naval landing force was combined with a guard or base force to form a Special Defense Force.

3. TRAINING OF SPECIAL NAVAL LANDING FORCE.
The earlier special naval landing forces received extensive training in landing operations and beach defense, but their training in infantry weapons and tactics does not appear to have been up to the standard of the Japanese Army. More recently there has been a greater emphasis on infantry training for units already in existence. Tactical doctrine for land warfare follows that of the

Army, with certain changes based on lessons learned during the current war. The platoon is the basic tactical unit, rather than the company. The Japanese Navy has not hesitated to cut across company lines in assigning missions within the landing force and in detailing portions of a landing force to detached missions.

4. UNIFORMS AND PERSONAL EQUIPMENT.
Small arms and personal equipment are similar to that used by the Army. Dress uniform consists of navy blues with canvas leggings. The Japanese characters for "Special Naval Landing Force" appear on the naval cap in the manner in which the words "U. S. Navy" appear on the caps of U. S. enlisted men. Field uniforms are similar to the Army in cut and color, although the color is sometimes more green. The typical Army cloth cap and steel helmet are used, but the insignia is an anchor instead of the star of the Army (see ch. XI).

5. MISCELLANEOUS NAVAL ORGANIZATIONS.
a. Base force or special base

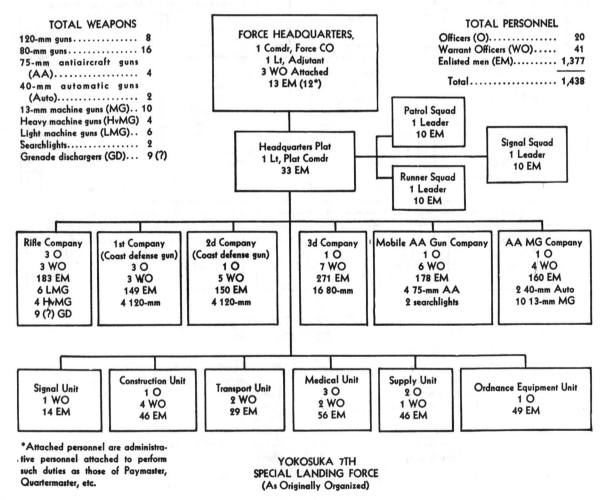

TOTAL WEAPONS
120-mm guns.............. 8
80-mm guns.............. 16
75-mm antiaircraft guns (AA)................. 4
40-mm automatic guns (Auto)................. 2
13-mm machine guns (MG).. 10
Heavy machine guns (HvMG) 4
Light machine guns (LMG).. 6
Searchlights.............. 2
Grenade dischargers (GD)... 9 (?)

FORCE HEADQUARTERS,
1 Comdr, Force CO
1 Lt, Adjutant
3 WO Attached
13 EM (12*)

TOTAL PERSONNEL
Officers (O)............... 20
Warrant Officers (WO)..... 41
Enlisted men (EM).......... 1,377
Total................... 1,438

Patrol Squad
1 Leader
10 EM

Signal Squad
1 Leader
10 EM

Headquarters Plat
1 Lt, Plat Comdr
33 EM

Runner Squad
1 Leader
10 EM

Rifle Company
3 O
3 WO
183 EM
6 LMG
4 HvMG
9 (?) GD

1st Company
(Coast defense gun)
3 O
3 WO
149 EM
4 120-mm

2d Company
(Coast defense gun)
1 O
5 WO
150 EM
4 120-mm

3d Company
1 O
7 WO
271 EM
16 80-mm

Mobile AA Gun Company
1 O
6 WO
178 EM
4 75-mm AA
2 searchlights

AA MG Company
1 O
4 WO
160 EM
2 40-mm Auto
10 13-mm MG

Signal Unit
1 WO
14 EM

Construction Unit
1 O
4 WO
46 EM

Transport Unit
2 WO
29 EM

Medical Unit
3 O
2 WO
56 EM

Supply Unit
2 O
1 WO
46 EM

Ordnance Equipment Unit
1 O
49 EM

*Attached personnel are administrative personnel attached to perform such duties as those of Paymaster, Quartermaster, etc.

YOKOSUKA 7TH
SPECIAL LANDING FORCE
(As Originally Organized)

Figure 79.

TOTAL PERSONNEL

Officers (O)............... 26
Warrant officers (WO)...... 44
Enlisted men (EM)......... 1,750

Total.................... 1,820

TOTAL WEAPONS

120-mm guns............. 8
80-mm guns.............. 16
75-mm antiaircraft guns
(AA)............... 4
40-mm automatic guns
(Auto)................ 2
Antitank guns (37-mm)..... 2
13-mm machine guns (MG).. 10
Heavy machine guns (HMG) 12
Light machine guns (LMG).. 24
Light trench mortars......... 4
Searchlights............... 2
Grenade dischargers (GD)... 41 (?)

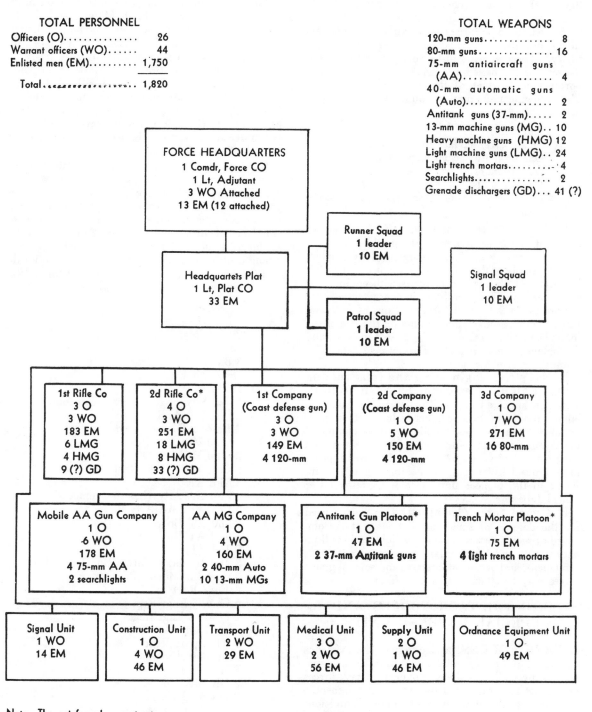

FORCE HEADQUARTERS
1 Comdr, Force CO
1 Lt, Adjutant
3 WO Attached
13 EM (12 attached)

Runner Squad
1 leader
10 EM

Headquarters Plat
1 Lt, Plat CO
33 EM

Signal Squad
1 leader
10 EM

Patrol Squad
1 leader
10 EM

1st Rifle Co
3 O
3 WO
183 EM
6 LMG
4 HMG
9 (?) GD

2d Rifle Co*
4 O
3 WO
251 EM
18 LMG
8 HMG
33 (?) GD

1st Company
(Coast defense gun)
3 O
3 WO
149 EM
4 120-mm

2d Company
(Coast defense gun)
1 O
5 WO
150 EM
4 120-mm

3d Company
1 O
7 WO
271 EM
16 80-mm

Mobile AA Gun Company
1 O
6 WO
178 EM
4 75-mm AA
2 searchlights

AA MG Company
1 O
4 WO
160 EM
2 40-mm Auto
10 13-mm MGs

Antitank Gun Platoon*
1 O
47 EM
2 37-mm Antitank guns

Trench Mortar Platoon*
1 O
75 EM
4 light trench mortars

Signal Unit
1 WO
14 EM

Construction Unit
1 O
4 WO
46 EM

Transport Unit
2 WO
29 EM

Medical Unit
3 O
2 WO
56 EM

Supply Unit
2 O
1 WO
46 EM

Ordnance Equipment Unit
1 O
49 EM

Note: The reinforced organization consists of the unit as originally organized, plus the units marked with an asterisk (*).

YOKOSUKA 7TH
SPECIAL LANDING FORCE
(As Reinforced)

Figure 79—Continued.

force (Tokubetsu Konkyochitai). This unit is the Naval Command echelon for the defense forces of a prescribed area. In addition to headquarters personnel, the base force has certain heavy coast artillery and also heavy and medium antiaircraft artillery. There appears to be no fixed organization, the size of the base force depending upon the importance and extent of the area to be defended. The following units may be found attached to base forces:

> Aircraft.
> Small naval surface units (patrol boats).
> One or more special naval landing forces.
> One or more guard forces.
> Pioneer units.
> Navy civil engineering and construction units.

b. Pioneers (Setsueitai). The function of this unit is the construction of airfields, fortifications, barracks, etc. It is commanded by a naval officer, usually of the rank of captain or commander, has attached officers and civilians with engineering experience, and is semimilitary in character. There appear to be 2 types of organization, of 800 and 1,300 men respectively, depending on the size of the job. The unit contains from $\frac{1}{4}$ to $\frac{1}{3}$ Japanese, and the balance are Koreans or Formosans. The 15th Pioneers was such a unit.

c. Navy civil engineering and construction unit (Kaigun Kenchiku Shisetsu Butai). This unit appears to be used primarily for common labor, and is of little combat value. It is commanded by a Japanese civilian and is composed mainly of Koreans, with about 10 percent armed Japanese to serve as overseers. Its size appears to be around 1,000 men. In combat value, it is inferior to the pioneer unit since it contains fewer armed Japanese.

d. Guard force (Keibitai). This unit is used for the defense of small installations. It is composed of naval personnel, and has light and medium antiaircraft and heavy infantry weapons. Its size, armament, and organization vary, and several guard forces may be attached to a base force.

Section II. TASK FORCES AND SPECIAL DEFENSE UNITS

1. TASK FORCES. a. General. The existence of a large number of independent units in the Japanese Army facilitates the employment of task forces or combat teams temporarily organized for specific missions. Rather than attempt to equip all divisions with heavy components of antitank guns, artillery, tanks, etc., the Japanese have segregated these weapons into independent units for assignment to divisions or task forces as needed. They do not hesitate to divide and/or combine units to form special forces for particular missions. Task forces or combat teams of widely varying strength and degree of combined training have been encountered in the theaters of operations. In the early part of the war well-trained combat teams were instrumental in the rapid advance down through Malaya and the Indies to New Guinea and the Solomons. Lately, facing greater odds and reversed circumstances, the Japanese have shown evidences of more hasty assembling and organization of their task forces, which frequently are thrown into action without the benefit of combined training. In one instance the 6th Independent Antitank Battalion was rushed from Manchuria to Guadalcanal in 23 days to bolster the task force organized late in 1942 to attempt to retake Henderson field.

b. Organization. While there is no uniform type of task force, the organizations of two such forces encountered in the Southwest Pacific will serve to illustrate general characteristics with adaptations for specific missions. A task force on Guadalcanal, organized with the 2nd Infantry Division as a nucleus, comprised a total personnel strength of about 25,000. It was charged with the mission of recapturing the airfield in October 1942 and was found to be organized as follows:

> 2 Division
> 16 Inf Regt
> 29 Inf Regt
> 230 Inf Regt
> 3 Bn of 124 Inf Regt
> Det 4 Inf Regt
> 17 Army Arty Gp HQ
> 2 Fd Arty Regt (less detachments)
> 2 Co 75 F. A. Regt
> 2 Bn of 2 Fd Arty Regt
> 10 Ind Mtn Arty Regt
> 20 Ind Mtn Arty
> 2 Co 20 Med Arty Regt
> 38 Fd AA Arty Bn
> 45 Fd AA Arty (less detachments)
> 3 Co 47 Fd AA Arty Bn
> 2 Ind AT Bn
> 6 Ind AT Bn
> 9 Ind AT Co
> 3 Ind Infantry Mortar Bn (less 3 Co)
> 3 Co 1 Ind Mortar Regt
> 2 Engr Regt
> 1 Co of 7 Engr Regt
> 1 Pl of 15 Engr Regt
> Engr Unit
> 2 Transport Regt
> Transport Unit
> Kitao Force
> 2 Div Sig Unit
> 2 Div Med Unit
> 2 Fd Hospital
> 2 Div Water Purifying Unit
> One part of 24 Water Pur Unit
> 76 L of C Hospital
> One part of 67 L of C Hospital
> Motorcycle Unit

c. Nankai Task Force. While the above task force was heavily armed with artillery for its particular mission, a contrasting type in that respect was the Nankai Task Force, organized in Rabaul in May 1942 for an overland campaign against Port Moresby. This force was to operate over very rough jungle and mountain terrain where practically all roads were no better than trails. It consisted of elements of the 55th Division with the 41st Infantry Regiment from the 5th Division and supporting troops and was comparatively weak in artillery. It was organized as follows:

55 Division Infantry HQ
    144 Inf Regt
    41st Inf Regt (from 5th Div)
    3rd Co with one AT Gun Section attached, of the 55th Cav Regt
    1st Bn 55 Mtn Arty Regt
    1st Co and part of Material Platoon, 55 Engr Regt
    2nd Co 55 Transport Regt
    55 Div Medical Unit (part)
    1st Field Hosp 55th Div
Attached Troops:
    11th Pioneer Unit
    15th Ind Engr Regt
    14th Ind Engr Regt
    4th Ind Engr Co
    47th Field AA Bn (less 1 Co)
    55th Construction Co
    61st Construction Co
    1st Bridge Construction Co of 9th Div
    88th Wire Comm Co (1 platoon)
    24th Signal Regt (1 Wire Co)
    Two Ind Radio Platoons
    One Fixed Radio Unit
    10th Evacuation Hosp Unit
    53rd and 54th Casualty Collecting Stations
    67th L of C Hosp Unit (less 1 part)
    38th Ind Auto Bn
    212th Ind Auto Co
    3rd Field Transport Command (part)
    55th Veterinary Depot (part)
    16th Veterinary Depot (less 1 part)
    17th Water Purification Unit
    24th Water Purification Unit
    55th Water Purification Unit

d. Raiding forces (Teishintai). (1) *General.* These forces in general are formed for the purpose of delivering attacks on some particular objective independently of the main force. Selected from infantry and other units, they may return to their original organizations after completion of their mission.

(2) The raiding units (teishintai) employed in the Southwest Pacific appear to have been developed from the special forces (betsudōtai) originally encountered in China. During the fighting in the Buna, Gona, and Salamaua areas in 1943, the Japanese on occasion sought to destroy enemy artillery by direct assault, and raiding units were organized for such purposes. The strength of such units depended upon the number of guns in the objective and whether a surprise assault or storming attack was planned. The Oba Teishintai was formed at Salamaua in August 1943 by order of the 51st Division commander. It was composed of one company of infantry and one of engineers, together with one section of a signal unit. The unit was ordered to destroy an enemy artillery ammunition dump. For attacking and destroying four enemy guns, the basic strength of a Teishintai was found to be about as follows:

Hq group, 1 O, 1 liaison NCO and 1 orderly.
Demolition section and Assault section, about 15 men.
Support section, about 12 men.
Reserve section, about 12 men.

Similar specialized raiding units included small groups organized for raids into enemy territory to destroy bridges and lines of communication; assault (special fire point) units for attacking pillboxes and fortified positions; close-combat forces, a suicide squad to protect some definite point to the last man; demolition forces to remove obstacles such as wire entanglements; and tank-fighting units for direct assault on tanks. All of these may be combined into a special assault group, or used in various combinations depending upon the objective.

(3) *The Betsudōtai.* These raiding units, or flying columns, were found in China where open country gave them great mobility. They comprised infantry and cavalry elements in varying strength, and in some cases it appeared that armored cars, tanks, light artillery, engineers, signal, and medical units might be included. Organizational data are meager and highly varied, but the general purpose of the flying columns was to deliver attacks at a considerable distance from the main force in order to disrupt or destroy enemy lines of communication. One source specifies the duties of a Betsudōtai as follows:

(*a*) To threaten the enemy flanks and their rear.
(*b*) To harass and disrupt enemy rear communications by destroying roads, railway bridges, etc.
(*c*) To occupy important and advanced positions prior to the movement of the main force.
(*d*) To carry out surprise attacks in and on unexpected localities.
(*e*) To ambush.
(*f*) To assist the main force when it is in a dangerous position.
(*g*) To carry out reconnaissance and other duties.

2. SPECIAL DEFENSE UNITS. a. General. Temporary defense of a locality occupied by assault forces may be assigned initially to a garrison unit (Shubitai). If a more permanent defense is required for the area the Shubitai is changed to a Keibitai. The Shubitai is usually established by making the infantry commander of the troops occupying the locality the defense commander in addition to his other duties. He is assigned certain Army and, in special cases, Navy units for defense of the area. For the Keibitai a special defense commander is designated and furnished with service troops and a small number of garrison troops for the nucleus of the defense force. Various Army and Navy troops in the area may be attached temporarily to complete the defense force. An Army or Navy officer may command the Shubitai or the Keibitai.

b. Organization. (1) *Kavieng Keibitai.* This unit at one time consisted of the following:

	Warrant officers and above	Non-commissioned officers and men	Total
Det 8th SNLF Base Garrison Unit	1	58	59
1 SNLF Platoon	3	75	78
AA Gun Unit	1	29	30
	5	162	167

Main weapons: 2 AA guns, 2 Mtn guns, 2 HMG, 4 LMG.

(2) In the Southwest Pacific, the Merkus Shubitai in December 1943 was found to consist of:

1st Co. (temp) of 115th Inf	152
2nd Co. (temp) of 14th Fd Arty	151
3rd Fd Hosp of 51st Div	27
One Ind Wireless Sec	8
MPs	3

Naval Coastal AA Unit (1 element)	48
(1 element)	13
Total	402

This garrison covered a coastal area of approximately 10 miles from Cape Merkus to the Pulie River, in New Britain.

c. Line-of-communication garrison (sector) units. These Keibi or permanent defense units are found on the line of communications between a base and forward areas. Their duties embrace a wide variety of activities, including guard, assistance in moving personnel and supplies, cooperation with shipping-engineer units, inspection of native areas, observation, and labor. Some of the line-of-communication units have been commanded by colonels or lieutenant colonels and have included 4 or more companies in addition to temporarily attached troops. One line-of-communication garrison company was listed as having 5 officers and 165 enlisted men.

d. Observation posts (coast-watching stations). In areas they have occupied, the Japanese have established a system of observation posts intended to give advance warnings of Allied air attacks and landing operations. These posts supplement normal air and surface reconnaissance; their size, spacing, and density naturally vary with the strategic value of the areas and installations. Most of these posts are equipped with radio (WT) sets and in some cases with radar.

CHAPTER VI

JAPANESE MILITARY POLICE

1. ADMINISTRATION. a. The military police (Kempei) form a branch of the Army under the Provost Marshal General who is responsible to the Minister of War. They are sometimes erroneously referred to as gendarmerie. Under Acts of 1898 and 1929 the headquarters is divided into two sections:

> General Affairs Section.
> Service Section.

The General Affairs Section concerns itself with policy, personnel, discipline, records, and the control of thought in the Armed Forces. The Service Section has three main functions: the supply, organization, and training of police units; security; and counterespionage.

b. The military police take orders from different authorities according to the areas in which they are stationed. For example, in Japan during peacetime, they were responsible to the Minister of War for their normal military duties, to the Minister of Home Affairs insofar as they assisted the civil police, and to the Minister of Justice for duties connected with law administration. In fortress zones they come under the command of the fortress commanders. In Manchuria, Korea, and Formosa, although they are primarily responsible to the commanders-in-chief, they also may be called upon to assist the local civilian authorities. In all areas their broad duties are the surveillance of military discipline, the enforcement of security, the protection of vital military zones, the execution of conscription laws, and the detection of crime among soldiers. In combat areas and occupied areas additional duties have been allotted to them (see par. 7).

2. RECRUITING. The Military Police consists of officers, non-commissioned officers, and superior privates only; lower ranks are attached from other services when needed. Officers are obtained by transfer from other branches of the Army and are permanently assigned to the military police. In peacetime men are recruited voluntarily; they are supposed to be of good character and of a high physical standard. In time of war such additional police as are necessary are drawn from all branches of the service. Both officers and enlisted men undergo training either in military-police schools or training units, as well as in their unit barracks. The principal schools are in Tokyo and Keijo (Korea). The duration of these courses in wartime is not known, but in peacetime a noncommissioned officer's course would last 6 months and an officer's course 1 year.

3. UNIFORM AND EQUIPMENT. On normal duty the military police wear the usual uniform of the mounted services, with heavy boots of undressed leather. They are equipped with a cavalry saber and a pistol. A white band bearing two characters reading Kempei is worn on the left arm. The color of the insignia is black. In combat areas the military police usually will be armed as infantry, but while on special duties they may wear civilian clothes.

4. STRENGTH. In 1937 there were believed to be 315 officers and over 6,000 men in the Japanese Military Police. In 1942 the evidence suggests that there were a minimum of 601 regular officers in military-police units. In 1942, these officers are believed to have been distributed as follows:

Japan and Karafuto	142
Manchuria	114
Korea	23
Formosa	24
North China	100
Central China	97
South China	16
Southern Area (including Field Units)	85

No information is available about reserve officers who have been recalled to the colors to perform military-police duty since the outbreak of the present war. A number of military-police units which are known to have existed in 1941 have not been reported since. However, they must be assumed still to exist, for otherwise a number of important prefectures in Japan would be without military police. Therefore this list of military-police officers is incomplete and the total strength of the forces cannot be estimated accurately.

5. UNITS. According to a report from China dated March, 1940, the basic military-police unit consisted of a section of 40 men under a captain or lieutenant. These sections were grouped in detachments and distributed throughout China. It is clear, however, that detachments vary in size and composition according to the areas in which they operate and the nature of their duties. No recent confirmation has been received of evidence that the section of 40 is the basic organization.

6. DISTRIBUTION ACCORDING TO AREAS. a. Military police are divided into three main categories:

(1) Regional organizations which come under the command of area army headquarters and per-

form duties in the homeland, or in static or base areas such as Manchuria, Korea, and North China.

(2) Numbered field units (Yasen Kempei Tai) which provide parties or sections to operate in the fighting or forward operational areas.

(3) Military police auxiliaries.

b. Regional organizations. Regional organizations are to be found in the military police districts of Japan proper under the direct command of military police headquarters at Tokyo, and in the Kwantung Army (Manchuria), the Korean Army, the Taiwan Army (Formosa), the North China Area Army, and the Southern Expeditionary Force under regional headquarters.

(1) *Japan and Karafuto.* In peacetime the military police in Japan were organized into units to correspond with the 14 divisional districts and their headquarters were at the headquarters of the depot division concerned. A small section would form part of the staff of the depot division. In wartime, however, military police districts do not necessarily correspond with the divisional areas. They are in fact designated by the Minister of War according to the density of the population and the strategic or industrial importance of the area. For example, Kobe, strategically a part of the Hanshin industrial belt, which comes in the Himeji divisional area, is assigned to the Osaka Military Police District. There undoubtedly have been several important changes in organization since 1941, notably the establishment of new units at Kure and Yokosuka, the naval bases.

(2) *Korea and Formosa.* The military police in Korea and Formosa are both commanded by major generals. Detachments are to be found in all the main towns.

(3) *Manchuria.* The Kwantung Military Police are commanded by a lieutenant general with headquarters at Hsinking. Under him come a number of units and detachments allocated to industrial and strategic areas.

(4) *China.* In North and Central China the military police are under a major general; in South China under a colonel.

(5) *Southern Area.* A Southern Expeditionary Force Military Police Training Unit was established in August 1942, presumably at Singapore, probably for the training of natives. It is thought that the military-police work throughout the whole of the Southern Area, at present occupied by the Japanese Army, comes under the charge of the Field Military Police Units.

c. Numbered field military-police units. Numbered field military-police units have been identified. These units probably are based at important headquarters (one has been identified at Rabaul, the headquarters of the area army in charge of operations in the Solomons-Bismarcks area) and are responsible for specified geographic sections. It seems likely that these units provide sections not only for duty with divisions and other field units but also for the enforcement of discipline in the base areas. Small military-police sections normally appear to accompany divisions operating in the field.

d. Military-police auxiliaries. Laws dated 1919 and 1937 established volunteer native auxiliaries to the military police in Korea and Manchuria. They may hold ranks up to the equivalent of sergeant major, and presumably come under the orders of the Japanese military-police units in the areas concerned. No information is available about their strength. Natives also have been employed in the Pacific areas as police and espionage agents.

7. MILITARY POLICE DUTIES IN THE FIELD. In addition to the normal military and field security police duties, such as the issue of travel permits, the detection and arrest of fifth columnists, and the scotching of subversive rumors, field military-police sections are assigned various duties connected with the natives in the occupied areas and may also engage in combat. In the Pacific area they are responsible for pacifying hostile natives and for settling disputes between the natives and Japanese soldiers, as well as for requisitioning native foods and supplies. They also are charged with the recruitment of native labor and the organization of native espionage nets operating in and behind Allied lines. According to reports, the military police were given charge of a native force in New Guinea both for reconnaissance purposes and in order to harass the enemy. An order to the Lae military-police commander directed him, in addition to continuing his present duties, to "complete the training of the native 'army' and form a roving defense of the left bank of the Markham river. He will send the native 'army' forward in the right bank section and will be responsible for directing the harassing of the enemy's rear."

8. MORALE AND VALUE FOR WAR OF MILITARY POLICE. Testimony varies as to the qualities of the Japanese military policeman. There is little question but that in peacetime they were picked and well-trained men who carried out their duties efficiently. Like all persons in authority in wartime they are frequently disliked and feared, and complaints have been made by the ordinary line soldiers about their strictness and abuse of power. But it seems likely that, as in other armies, they are first-class troops who carry out their many and varied duties competently.

CHAPTER VII

TACTICS OF THE JAPANESE ARMY

INTRODUCTION

The basic tactical principles of the Japanese Army have been carefully developed from studies of foreign army techniques and its own valuable experiences gained in combat under varying conditions. Japanese forces have fought against regular military organizations of several first-class nations and have had considerable experience in combating the constant harassing action of guerrillas on supply lines and rear areas.

They have engaged in tank actions on the plains of Manchuria and in mountain battles in Central and Southern China; they have conducted landing operations under varying conditions of terrain and climate. They have been highly successful in their earlier jungle operations, on terrain where good roads and railroads are practically unknown, and where every type of natural obstacle exists. They are not merely jungle fighters, however, for much of their success has been on terrain where principles of open warfare have been applied effectively. By studying the areas over which they expected to operate they effectively organized, trained, and equipped their forces and evolved techniques designed in each case to fit the terrain and meet the logistical requirements peculiar to their own army.

The Japanese lay great stress on offensive actions, surprise, and rapidity of movement, with all commanders and staffs operating well forward in order to keep themselves constantly informed of the situation. Their tactical doctrine is based on the principle that a simple plan, carried through with power and determination, coupled with speed of maneuver, will so disrupt the plans of hostile forces that success will ensue. Combat orders, in both attack and defense, from the highest to the lowest unit, generally carry the admonition that the "enemy forces will be annihilated." Surprise is an ever present element, while the envelopment is the preferred form of attack. Thorough reconnaissance also is taught, and the practice of infiltration is greatly stressed. The Japanese willingness to attack a position with forces which other nations would consider insufficient for the task, is based on the assumption of their so-called military superiority. An explanation of this assumption calls for an analysis of Japanese psychology, national vanity, and past military successes, which is beyond the scope of this study. To the Japanese officer, considerations of "face" and "toughness" are most important, and they are therefore prone to indulgence in "paper" heroics. They have evinced boldness against poorly equipped troops; however, against first-class, well-equipped forces, it may be expected that they will adopt more circumspect methods.

Despite the opportunities presented during 6 years of active combat, the Japanese have continued to violate certain fundamental principles of accepted tactics and technique. Their tendency to persist in such violations is based primarily upon their failure to credit the enemy with good judgment and equal military efficiency. Whether or not they have profited by recent experiences remains to be seen.

PART I

GENERAL TACTICAL DOCTRINE

Section I. GENERAL

1. GENERAL. The part on the General Tactical Doctrine of the Japanese Army is based on actual observation of their field maneuvers, and map problems, their operations against Russia and China, and a study of their field manuals. It is believed that their tactical principles, taught and studied for years, will not change materially. The tactical methods described here are primarily those which the Japanese consider appropriate for fighting in open country such as North Asia. They have had ample opportunity to test their tactics and to observe those employed by other Armies. Any study of their

teachings must be approached with the knowledge that the Japanese are quick to copy and may even improve on the tactics of their enemies. Technique, or application of tactical principles, will vary, and is limited only by the imagination and initiative of individual commanders.

Section II. OFFENSIVE

1. DOCTRINE. Japanese tactical doctrine insists vigorously on the inherent superiority of the offense, and Field Service Regulations state that the offensive should be resolutely taken. The object of all maneuver is to close quickly with the enemy so that the assumed Japanese superiority in close combat can be realized to the utmost. Even when the enemy strength is markedly superior, or when the Japanese commander has been placed temporarily on the defensive, he is supposed to use every effort to regain the offensive and take the initiative. The Japanese seem to feel that there is some mystic virtue in the attack and defensive combat is looked upon as a negative form of action to be adopted only when confronted with a markedly superior enemy. Even in defense, the offensive principle is strongly emphasized. Both as a result of this training and because of faith in the offensive doctrine, Japanese officers often reach attack decisions where, by all orthodox tactics, the situation patently requires some form of defensive action. Their teachings have been found to place very little emphasis on time and space factors, with the result that concentration of effort and the cooperation of all arms are frequently neglected. The division used for illustrative purposes in this section is the Japanese triangular division. It should be borne in mind, however, that while all Japanese divisions are not identically organized, tactics will not materially differ, although there will be differences in composition of columns and grouping of units.

2. FORMS OF ATTACK. a. Envelopment.

(1) The Japanese consider the envelopment as the preferred offensive maneuver. Envelopment will be accompanied by a determined frontal pressure, while the main force attacks a flank. In ascending order of effectiveness, the envelopment may be single, double, or a complete encirclement (kanzen hoi). Contrary to generally accepted tactical principles, the Japanese are willing to try a double envelopment without any considerable numerical superiority and regard it as possible, sometimes, even by an inferior force which relies on surprise and deception. The Japanese commander may seek to obtain envelopment in one of several ways.

(a) The force advances in two or more parallel columns, with one or more columns directed toward the enemy flank and rear during the advance to contact.

(b) The force advances with certain units in the rear which can later be deployed to execute a flank envelopment.

(c) After the force has encountered the enemy and partially deployed, some units may be moved laterally for envelopment if natural cover, darkness, fog, or smoke are available.

(2) The procedure of (1) (a) above is considered the normal one for units of the size of a division; (1) (b) is especially applicable to small units, but (1) (c) is considered feasible only under most favorable conditions. Those units of a division executing the frontal holding attack often will make a close-in envelopment in performing their mission. Units of this force, such as squads and platoons, seek to obtain the effect of flanking fire (shageki hōi).

(3) The question of which flank to envelop is decided by weighing normal factors such as terrain, location of hostile reserves and heavy weapons, etc.

(4) To increase the effectiveness of the envelopment the Japanese often send a small force around to attack the enemy rear. When such a movement (ukai) is employed, the force sent around by a division in attack is relatively weak, comprising about a battalion reinforced by light artillery and a squad of engineers. The mission of such a turning force is often similar to that of a pursuit detachment; in fact this force may become a pursuit detachment if the main attack succeeds.

b. Frontal attack. (1) Japanese regulations contain the usual admonitions against a frontal attack. Situations which may give rise to a frontal attack are those to which Allied armies are accustomed. In observed practice, however, the time element, or the fear of allowing the enemy leisure to improve his position, often is allowed to justify a questionable decision to make a frontal attack.

(2) The main effort of a frontal attack is made against a "soft spot" in the line, leading in a decisive direction into the enemy rear areas. Effort will be made to penetrate deeply and swiftly at the first attempt by keeping narrow the battle fronts of units in the area of the main attack, making dispositions in depth, and coordinating employment of artillery. Tanks, if available, may participate. In general the Japanese are weak in artillery support and depend heavily on extensive employment of their infantry guns and infiltration practices.

c. Comments. The impressions gained from a study of Japanese teachings on the forms of attack and their application in practice show that:

(1) The Japanese will attack in many cases where the orthodox decision would call for less positive action. The attack may be rash and costly but will never lack vigor and determination.

(2) The frontal attack, often with inadequate supporting arms, is not uncommon.

3. MEETING ENGAGEMENT (ENCOUNTER). a. Doctrine.

The meeting engagement is the foundation of Japanese combat training, with official regulations giving more space to it than to any other form of combat. Japanese military writings define the meeting engagement as the collision of two hostile forces in motion, or the meeting of a force in motion with one which has halted but has not had time to organize a detailed position. Training strongly emphasizes this form of combat as allowing the optimum development of the alleged Japanese aptitude for swift and decisive offensive action.

b. Artillery seems to be assigned missions in excess of its capabilities. Aircraft are expected to conduct constant reconnaissance of the situation of enemy and friendly troops as well as to cooperate with the artillery. Tanks may be used independently or in direct support of the infantry; when they are sent on distant raids. other mobile units, if available, may accompany them.

c. The rules governing the Japanese in the meeting engagement may be summarized as follows:

(1) The seizure and retention of the initiative.

(2) Bold, independent action by subordinate commanders.

(3) Prompt occupation of important terrain features.

(4) Energetic leadership during combat.

d. In the words of a Japanese writer, "The Imperial Army seeks to wage a short war to a quick and decisive conclusion. The meeting engagement conforms to this spirit and is to be sought whenever possible."

4. ADVANCE. a. General. The formations in the advance in day or night movements are similar to those used by other Armies and are governed by the same considerations. Parallel columns, each self-contained. are usual, unless precluded by the road net. When the enemy is strong in aviation and mechanized units, long columns are broken up into short serials containing antiaircraft and antitank weapons. Each main column is preceded by an advance guard, while the division cavalry, if present, usually acts as a reconnaissance screen in front of the advance guards. When the division is to advance at night, the division commander often sends forward in daylight a reconnaissance detachment and motorized infantry to seize important terrain features and to cover the night movement. As a meeting engagement becomes likely, the division commander modifies the formation, as needed, to facilitate the entry of the division into action with a view to enveloping one or both flanks of the enemy.

b. Advance in two columns. (1) A study of Japanese tactical problems illustrates the division advancing in one, two, and three columns, with the two-column formation being the most favored. In the two-column formation the essential components of the division are disposed as follows:

Reconnaissance Detachment

1st Cavalry
(Less detachment)

Left column	*Right column* *Advance guard*
1st Infantry Regt. (less 3d Bn)	2d Infantry Regt (less 3d Bn)
1st Co 1st Ind Antitank Bn	2d Co 1st Ind Antitank Bn
1st Bn 1st FA Regt	2d Bn 1st FA Regt
1st Co 1st Engr Regt	1st Engineers (less 1st Co)
⅓ Decontamination Unit	⅓ Decontamination Unit
⅓ Casualty Clearing Unit	⅓ Casualty Clearing Unit
	Main Body
	Division Headquarters
	Infantry Group Headquarters
	1st Troop (Company) 1st Cavalry Regt
	3d Bn 2d Infantry Regt
	1st FA Regt (less 1st and 2d Bns)
	1st Ind Antitank Bn (less 1st and 2d Cos)

Left column	*Right column*
	1st Bn 1st Med FA Regt (150 mm Howitzer)
	3d Infantry Regt
	3d Bn 1st Infantry Regt
	Advance Section, 1st Transport Regt
	Division Trains
	1st Transport Regt (less detachment)
	⅓ Decontamination Unit
	⅓ Casualty Clearing Unit

With the above formation, the division commander expects, if anticipatory plans have been correct, to execute an envelopment of the hostile left flank.

Figure 80.

(2) The composition of the march column illustrated above is covered in the division field order. It is noteworthy that an advance guard is designated by the division commander for the right column only; the left column merely receives an indication of the units composing it. This march formation is the result of the curious system of command which the Japanese employ. The division commander concurrently commands the division and the right column. In the latter capacity, he prescribes the detailed organization of the right column. The detailed organization of the left column falls to the senior commander of that column who designates an advance guard for its protection. Thus the advance guard of the left column is not an instrumentality for the protection of the division as a whole and is not directly under the control of the division commander. Therefore, as a meeting engagement becomes imminent, the immediate subordinates to whom the division commander issues orders directly are the colonel of the 1st Cavalry Regiment (commanding the reconnaissance detachment), advance guard commander (right column), commanders of the major components of the right column, and the commander of the left column. It is not clear how the division commander plans to coordinate the action of his right column advance guard with that of the left column. The term "advance guard" as subsequently used applies only to that which is controlled directly by the division commander.

(3) In the above formation, the infantry strength in the advance guards of the 2 columns is about one-third of the division's infantry. When there is a greater number of columns employed, the combined infantry strength of the advance guards sometimes reaches half that of the division. *Strong advance guards are characteristic of the Japanese Army in approaching a meeting engagement.*

c. Advance in other than two columns. An advance in one column is avoided because of the delay incident to developing the division for an attack. Therefore whenever that formation is adopted it is imposed by limitations of the road net. An advance in 3 columns was undertaken by a Japanese infantry division at Rangoon in March 1942, as follows:

Left	Center	Right
One Bn Inf (less one Co). One Co Engrs (less one Pl) with collapsible boats.	One Inf Regt (less one Bn—less one Co). One Co FA (Pack) with Ind Tpt Unit. One Co Engrs (less one Pl). One Ind A/Tk Co (37 mm). Detch Div Med Unit. Detch Water Purif Unit. One Co Ind Tpt Unit. One Section Div Sig Unit.	Inf Regt. One Bn FA (Pack) (less one Co). Tpt Unit (less detch). One Pl Engr. Div Med Unit (less detch). Water Pur Unit (less detch). One Co Army Sig Troops. Two Sections Div Sig Unit.

Figure 81.

The whereabouts of the remainder of the division is not known. The above illustration is taken from a British source which states that the initial advance of the division was made by 2 regiments, i. e., 6 battalions, spread over a frontage of 40 miles. The 3 columns were divided with approximately a 20-mile space between each. In this case the left column hardly could be considered as self contained. Use was made of roads, trails, and waterways wherever possible. In advance in 3 columns, the division commander remains the commander of the strongest column. More than 3 columns may be found, but such employment will be exceptional.

d. Transport and trains. The division transport and trains normally follow the main columns of the division under division control in the following order: advance section transport regiment, unit trains, and the remainder of the transport regiment. Distances between these units are normally from 1 to 2.5 miles. The massed trains are under a commander, who is designated by the division commander. The advance section of the transport regiment consists of an infantry ammunition section, 2 artillery ammunition sections, and a veterinary section. Two field hospitals may be attached to the advance section of the transport regiment.

e. Attachments. Units of light and medium artillery, antiaircraft artillery, observation aviation, antitank units and other supports frequently are attached to a division in the advance.

f. Antiaircraft protection on march. For the advance, each front-line division may have attached an antiaircraft organization. This unit, often motorized, moves by leapfrogging from critical point to critical point along the axis of the division's advance. The guns go into position during the noonday halt, while passing defiles, while in bivouac, etc. If possible, antiaircraft units move forward by roads not used by the other elements of the division. The effective radius of action of one company of 75-mm antiaircraft artillery is considered to be 6,800 yards.

g. Antitank protection on the march. In areas where there is a threat of enemy tank action against a column, the Japanese usually hold some tanks in readiness for employment against hostile tank forces. Active reconnaissance by both air and cavalry units warns the division commander of impending hostile tank action. Antiaircraft artillery may at times be employed to supplement normal antitank protection measures.

h. Advance detachments. (1) There is a notable tendency for the division commander to send forward a mobile detachment in advance of the division for one of the following purposes:

(*a*) To cover a night march to the probable battlefield where the division expects to be committed to action shortly after daylight.

(*b*) To secure a vital terrain feature on the front of the division.

(*c*) To execute demolitions of the road net and hamper the movement of the enemy.

(*d*) To execute surprise attacks while the enemy is in march formation.

(2) These detachments generally consist of the division cavalry, some infantry and engineers in trucks, and a company of light artillery. The infantry strength ordinarily will not exceed a regiment, except where the division plans an active defense. In this latter case, as much as half of the division may be pushed forward by forced marches to occupy a defensive position, while the remainder of the division follows more slowly with the intention of launching a counteroffensive against an enemy flank.

5. ACTIONS OF THE DIVISION COMMANDER IN APPROACHING A MEETING ENGAGEMENT. a. Reconnaissance. The formation of the advancing division contains in it the germ of the maneuver which the division commander expects to adopt if he encounters the enemy on the march. When the hostile force is reported approaching from a considerable distance, the division commander estimates where the battle will occur and communicates to his subordinates the general plan of maneuver which he expects to adopt, taking into consideration the use of terrain which the enemy considers generally impassable. He indicates time and place for the delivery of reports and designates a message dropping ground for the air service. His artillery and engineer commanders receive technical information from their own patrols marching with the advance guard and reconnaissance detachment. As contact becomes imminent the division commander, hitherto marching at the head of the main body of the principal column, moves forward on personal reconnaissance accompanied by appropriate staff officers. An advance message center may be designated behind the advance guard, one of the important functions of which is to facilitate collection and dissemination of enemy information.

b. Orders. From his personal reconnaissance and the reports of his reconnaissance agencies, the division commander determines the area in which the division will make its decisive effort, the plan of maneuver, and the location of the division command post. He then issues fragmentary operational orders to initiate deployment of the division. Japanese Combat Regulations warn against waiting for overdetailed information before reaching a decision, and this injunction seems to authorize a very short reconnaissance phase at this point.

6. DEPLOYMENT OF DIVISION. a. Advance guard.

(1) (a) The advance guard in the meeting engagement performs the following functions: it secures enemy and terrain information needed to form the basis of the decision of the division commander; it protects the deployment of the main body; and secures important terrain features to facilitate the subsequent attack.

(b) The advance guard commander, bearing in mind these general functions, is expected to exercise initiative and boldness of action in specific cases. He obtains the necessary information by vigorous patrolling and, if necessary, by a small-scale attack. He protects the deployment of the division, either by offensive or defensive methods, and attacks when necessary to obtain important geographical points. Left to his own devices, however, the advance-guard commander usually elects to drive headlong into the advancing enemy, unless specifically restrained by division order.

(2) As the advance guard closes to contact, its artillery prepares to furnish continuous support by leapfrogging from position to position in rear of the infantry. Normal artillery missions are to interdict (harass) the movement of enemy columns, to support the action of the advance guard infantry, and to perform limited counter-battery missions. Extreme ranges for interdiction by the 75's are 7,500 to 9,000 yards, but in practice missions are seldom fired at over 5,500 yards. Positions are chosen with a view to supporting the attack of the main body without change of position. The advance-guard artillery reverts to the control of the artillery commander at the time of the attack of the main body.

(3) It must be borne in mind that the advance guard discussed is that of the column directly commanded by the division commander. The security detachments in advance of other columns are for their local protection only.

b. Main body. (1) Deployment (a) In his basic decision for the deployment of his division, the division commander determines whether it will be coordinated or piecemeal. The basis for this decision is found in the Japanese Combat Regulations, a translation of which reads:

"The division commander, in order to profit by or to extend an advantage won by the advance guard, may have to commit to combat each march column and each element of the main body successively upon arrival. However, if the situation permits, the division commander should seek the coordinated entry into action of his units, in which case he orders the deployment of each unit, establishes close

cooperation between infantry and artillery, and coordinates the time of the infantry attack."

(b) The question of whether to make a piecemeal attack thus appears to be decided largely by the success of the advance guard action. In map problems studied, the piecemeal engagement of all or part of a force often is justified by the necessity of seizing some prominent terrain feature or by the desire to get out of a defile. The object of the piecemeal attack is to take advantage of a sudden opportunity, while the coordinated attack aims at securing effective use of the combined arms at the expense of time.

(2) Coordinated deployment. (a) As indicated above, the Japanese prefer a coordinated development "if the situation permits." The measures taken by the division commander to secure this coordination are: the assignment of a line of departure (tenkaisen) behind which the major units of his command are to deploy for the attack; detailed arrangements to assure coordination between the artillery and the infantry; and announcement of an hour of crossing the line of departure. The line of departure is usually an extension of the line held by the advance guard. If the enemy has secured the advantage of priority in deployment, the main body of the division may endeavor to escape a threatened envelopment or premature engagement with superior numbers by deployment along a line behind the advance guard or to the flank and rear thereof. In the event the deployment is to the flank and rear, the advance guard supported by all the division artillery covers the deployment and delays the advance of the enemy.

(b) If the enemy, in anticipation of a collision with the Japanese troops, assumes the defensive, the deployment is modified to resemble the relatively cautious procedure of the attack of a position. In this case also the division commander tries to develop and attack in the same day to avoid giving the enemy time to improve his position.

(c) The phase of the passage from march column to complete deployment is indicated by the following nomenclature used in Japanese regulations: (It must be realized that the following definitions are the translation of the Japanese and do not necessarily bear the same connotations in the Allied terminology.)

1. *Bunshin.* Breaking from march column into small ones out of hostile artillery range at the beginning of the approach march.
2. *Tenkai.* Deployment along a line of departure (tenkaisen) with a view to performing an assigned combat mission.
3. *Sokai.* Advance from the tenkaisen in small (squad or section) columns.
4. *Sankai.* Final deployment of front-line units to permit firing during the last few hundred yards of the assault.

These phases are shown diagrammatically in figure 82

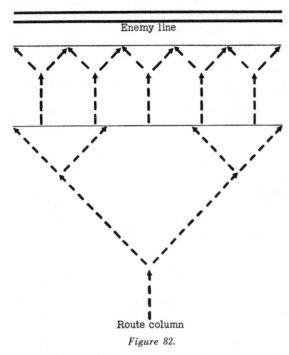

Route column

Figure 82.

(*d*) It is important to note that the coordinated attack from the Japanese point of view does not imply passing into assembly areas. However, this passage into assembly areas, called "kaishin" usually is observed in the attack of a position. If a coordinated attack follows the meeting engagement, columns deploy directly behind the line of departure (tenkaisen) without halting prior to arriving on it. No special time is allotted for ammunition issue and final reconnaissance.

(3) *Piecemeal attack.* (*a*) In the piecemeal attack the troops are committed to action in order of their arrival on the field. The division commander, decentralizing control to his column commanders, limits himself to a designation of routes of advance with a view to subsequent attack in the desired directions. No division "tenkaisen," no common hour of attack, and no detailed plans for coordination between the various arms are stipulated.

(*b*) Despite the lip service rendered in regulations to the coordinated deployment and attack, the piecemeal method is very common on the map, on the maneuver ground, and in observed operations. Often this is the result of the precipitate action of the advance guard commander who gets himself seriously engaged on his own initiative. In such a case, a sort of hybrid deployment sometimes is executed, with a part of the main body going in piecemeal to help the advance guard, while the remainder makes an orderly deployment. Occasionally, a column commander has been known to stage a piecemeal attack all of his own in a situation where the prompt seizure of a terrain feature on his front

seemed essential to the subsequent success of the division. Such action was taken without waiting for orders or authorization from the division commander.

(*c*) The rate of march of the infantry as it enters the zone of effective hostile artillery fire is reduced. In this zone the artillery moves forward by bounds of battalions while furnishing continuous support to the infantry. The theoretical rate of movement forward for this artillery is 2.5 miles per hour, although this may be increased to about 5 miles per hour if a battalion is allotted a road for its exclusive use. As the range limit is reached the battalion prepares to move forward.

(*d*) *Unit trains.* When contact becomes imminent the transport regiment and the unit trains are halted in a sheltered location. The advance section of the transport regiment will often be as close as 2.5 miles to the anticipated contact, while the trains are normally about 5 to 6 miles in the rear of this line. The remainder of the transport regiment will be behind the trains.

7. DIVISION ATTACK ORDER. a. Deployment. The division deployment order gives a combat mission to the advance guard and march directions to the several columns with a view to executing a preconceived maneuver. While the elements of his command are carrying out these orders, the division commander watches the development of the advance-guard action and, with a minimum of delay, issues a verbal attack order to his principal subordinates.

b. Attack order. The division attack order generally is issued in fragmentary form to the commanders concerned.

c. Orders to infantry. In the organization of the infantry for combat, the advance-guard infantry becomes one wing and executes the holding attack. The second regiment executes the main attack, and it may deploy as the other wing along a line of departure (tenkaisen), generally in prolongation of the advance guard position. About one regiment of infantry is held in division reserve. This attack order is issued when the enemy is fixed in a given area where contact is expected, but often prior to making actual contact and before the advance guard has developed the situation. The order assigns to the infantry wing(s) specific objectives or a very general attack mission, depending upon the degree of clarity of the situation. Specific objectives would be such as "to attack the hostile forces on X ridge and seize the X position," while a general attack mission might be something like "to advance in the direction of Y and locate and attack the enemy's right flank." This latter type of objective is appropriate in an obscure situation when the plan of maneuver is predicated largely on a study of the terrain. In this case the attack direction given is one which is certain to take in flank any formation or position which the enemy may reasonably assume. A study of Japanese attack orders reveals that in an extreme case an order was issued 7.4 miles from the expected point of contact of the advance guards.

d. Orders to artillery. (1) The artillery order indicates the location of the positions in general terms, and detailed reconnaissance is made by artillery commanders to determine the exact locations. Attachment of artillery to infantry is considered to be justified when:

(*a*) The front of attack is very wide.

(*b*) Liaison with the infantry is difficult.

(*c*) Combat begins unexpectedly.

(*d*) The terrain is broken and wooded.

(2) In the normal case the division retains control of the artillery and coordinates its action. Typical missions during the successive phases of the combat are as follows:

(*a*) *Phase I.* During the approach march and deployment.

> 1. *Objectives (targets) in order of importance.* Hostile artillery and machine guns firing at extreme ranges.
> 2. *Purpose.* To cover the deployment of the infantry.

(*b*) *Phase II.* During the attack.

> 1. *Objectives (targets) in order of importance.* Hostile infantry, artillery, and reserves.
> 2. *Purpose.* Close support of infantry.

(*c*) *Phase III.* During final assault.

> 1. *Objectives (targets) in order of importance.* The area of the decisive attack; the enemy reserves.
> 2. *Purpose.* Neutralization and interdiction (harassing) of movement of reinforcements.

e. Orders for piecemeal attack. The division attack order described in the foregoing applies to the coordinated attack. In the piecemeal engagement columns are organized into wings and receive attack directions and the attachment of the proper auxiliary arms. There is no coordinated deployment of any unit larger than a battalion. The artillery, less detachments, is kept under division control. The maneuver takes the form of a frontal collision without any effort to coordinate direction of the various columns to obtain the effect of envelopment.

8. FRONTAGES AND DISTANCES. a. Frontages. The following frontages are averages derived from studies of several problems:

Battalion as a covering force_____	1,600 yards.
Regiment in a holding attack_____	3,000 to 4,400 yards.
Regiment in the decisive attack_____	1,600 to 2,200 yards.

b. Distances. Distances from the line of departure.

Division command post_____	2,200 to 3,300 yards.
Artillery positions__	600 to 1,500 yards.
Division reserve____	1,200 to 2,800 yards.
Advance echelon, division transport___	4,500 to 6,500 yards.
Unit trains_____	8,800 to 11,000 yards.
Remainder of division transport____	11,000 to 13,000 yards.

c. Assault. Attacking units do not try to retain alignment, and where the going is easy they press ahead. When gassed areas may be encountered the leading wave includes decontamination squads. A gassed area is avoided when possible; if it must be traversed, the local gas squads use their light decontaminating equipment to neutralize it. When such equipment is insufficient or absent, the troops are taught to cross the gassed area resolutely at an increased gait. The artillery advances by bounds close behind the infantry, while its forward observers advance with the infantry. As the attacking infantry approach the enemy positions, infantry and artillery fire is increased, and reserve units are brought up. The cavalry closes in on the enemy flank and rear, and victory is won by closing with the bayonet. The division reserve is used to extend and exploit an advantage gained, to meet a counterattack, or to extend the flank of the enveloping forces. If darkness interrupts the attack, it will be continued at night or renewed at dawn.

9. COMMENTS. a. Meeting engagement. In the Japanese meeting engagement all elements of the division show boldness and vigor. Speed in decision and execution is stressed in regulations and carried out in application. A commander encountering a Japanese division may expect to receive a quick and energetic attack, and, unless his covering forces are solidly deployed on their position, the Japanese attack is likely to upset his own plans for a coordinated attack.

b. Piecemeal action. In practice the Japanese have shown an excessive willingness to engage in piecemeal action; Allied combat regulations, on the other hand, strongly favor the coordinated attack. Generally, according to Allied doctrine, the piecemeal attack is considered justifiable only if time is pressing, if there is a limited objective, and if combat superiority is on the attacker's side. If these criteria are applied to the situations in which the Japanese commander has decided to make a piecemeal attack, it will be found that time is pressing, and there is usually a limited objective, but not necessarily superiority. In fact, in the problems studied, the enemy was always superior, and in at least an equal state of readiness for combat. (In one map problem, the Japanese division was marching in one column while the enemy was in two). The only combat superiority was in the mind of the Japanese commander. Such a doctrine tends to make wasteful, piecemeal action the rule rather than the exception and develops a dangerous over-confidence, unjustified when faced by first-class troops.

c. March formation. The march formation in which the division commander is also a column commander is awkward, for it needlessly burdens the division commander with the details of organizing and commanding a column. It complicates the handling of the advance guards which are usually not coordinated under division control. In fact, the advance guards of columns adjacent to the one commanded by the division commander generally are ignored in the division plan of maneuver. As a result the division does not appear to develop behind solidly organized covering forces which can assure an uninterrupted deployment through coordinated defensive action, even though the numerical infantry strength of the advance guards is usually large, averaging from a third to a half of the infantry of the division.

d. Faults. The frequent use of the advance guard reinforced to make a holding attack and generally deployed on a wide front, renders control difficult and the organization of an effective attack even more difficult. The close-in envelopment so often chosen arises from a desire to get the attack off quickly and from the weakness of the organic artillery of the division. The Japanese teachings are to keep the artillery in a central location so that fire can be maneuvered over most of the front of both holding and enveloping attacks. If done this would restrict the scope of the possible attack directions.

e. Reconnaissance. Map problems and terrain exercises which have been studied show that an insufficient time is allocated for reconnaissance and organization of the attack. In one map problem only 1½ hours elapsed between the decision of the division commander and the jump-off of the so-called coordinated attack. While this is an extreme case, the impression of insufficiency of time for preparation is general.

f. Summary. In summary, the characteristics of the Japanese division in the meeting engagement are:

(1) Rapid, aggressive offensive action by all elements.
(2) A tendency to uncoordinated piecemeal action.
(3) Development behind weakly linked covering forces.
(4) Frontal attack or restricted close-in envelopments.
(5) Inadequate artillery support.
(6) Sacrifice of proper reconnaissance and organization to obtain speed in attack.
(7) Attack through terrain generally considered to be impossible.

10. ATTACK OF POSITION. a. General. When the enemy has had time to occupy and organize a position, the Japanese commander endeavors to fight the decisive action outside of the organized area by turning the position. This is often attempted by an approach over terrain said to be impassible or under adverse weather conditions. The intention in both cases is to achieve surprise in the direction and time of attack. However, the presence of other Japanese units on the flanks often may limit the possible maneuver area. The technique of such an attack resembles that of the coordinated meeting engagement in the use of the approach march and the development of the situation by the advance elements; it differs in the amount of time necessary for reconnaissance and attack preparations. However, the need for carefully executed attack preparations, according to the Japanese, must not be made the excuse for allowing the enemy undue time to improve his position. As shown in map problems, when a commander encounters a position which has been strengthened during a period of several days, he ordinarily drives in the covering forces and reconnoiters during all or part of one day and launches his main attack the following morning. He appears quite capable of attempting all of this in one day if time is pressing.

b. Development. (1) The hostile position normally will be covered by outposts which will vary in strength from patrols to a relatively strong force supported by artillery and deployed as an outpost line of resistance. As the Japanese advance guards approach contact with the covering forces, and before the main body comes under long-range artillery fire, the division commander usually orders his column into assembly areas.

(2) It should be noted that going into assembly areas is a phase of the attack of a position not ordinarily present in the meeting engagement. In problems studied these areas are from 2,200 to 4,400 yards from a hostile outpost line and thus 4,000 to 6,000 yards from the hostile artillery. In the typical case of the division advancing in two columns three assembly areas are designated, one for the main attack force, one for the force making the secondary effort, and one for the division reserve. The assembly is covered from positions about 1,100 to 1,600 yards in advance.

11. DRIVING IN COVERING FORCES. a. Procedure. In order to obtain adequate information about the main defensive position, the Japanese division ordinarily first drives in the hostile covering forces and then executes the necessary reconnaissance for the main attack. If these covering forces are weak and do not form a continuous front, the advance guard commander drives them in on his own intiative; otherwise, the division commander organizes the operation under cover of strong artillery support. In the typical case, this attack takes place in the afternoon of one day, and is followed by attack of the main position at daylight the next day or shortly thereafter. When the opposing forces occupy positions very close together, two nights may be necessary to get the attacking forces and matériel into position.

b. Continuous attack. This procedure of successive attacks, while designated as orthodox in Japanese Combat Regulations, often is replaced in practice by a continuous attack on both outpost and main position. It is not clear when this variation is considered justified, but apparently the deciding factors are whether the artillery can support the attack through both positions without displacement (moving) and whether the time element is pressing. When the continuous attack is made, that on the outpost line becomes a phase of the main attack, and the attacking infantry usually pauses briefly on the captured position, and then continues the assault. In about half of the map problems studied the continuous method was adopted, although there was no apparent need for especial haste in launching the attack.

12. ATTACK ORDER. While the infantry is deploying in assembly area (kaishin haichi) and the advance guard is driving in the covering forces, the division commander, after completion of his plan of attack based on reconnaissance reports, issues his order for the final deployment of the division and the subsequent attack. The order includes familiar elements, except that the infantry in the assault is divided into right and left wings (occasionally into a right wing, left wing, and center) in accordance with the scheme of maneuver.

13. TECHNIQUE OF ATTACK. a. Infantry. (1) The typical disposition of the units in the assault is into wings, with the preponderance of strength in one wing assigned to make the main effort, while the other wing makes the secondary attack. The infantry units, in accordance with the plan of deployment, advance from the assembly areas to their assigned positions along the line of departure, where they make final attack preparations. When the attack is to jump-off about dawn (first light), the advance to the line of departure is made under cover of darkness; if made in daylight, all means are utilized to conceal and protect this movement. In problems, the lines of departure vary from 550 to 2,000 yards from the enemy main position, and the line is chosen so as to be protected from effective small-arms fire. When the attack on the main line of resistance and the outpost line of resistance is continuous, a pause and a realignment may take place along the rear edge of the outpost position which then becomes a phase line in the course of the attack. Attack objectives (terrain features) or attack directions are given the front-line infantry units according to the known details of the enemy position. Normally, the line to be reached by the attack is deep in the zone of the hostile artillery. The hour of attack is usually about 1 or 2 hours after dawn, as the Japanese have little

confidence in the ability of their artillery to adjust and fire a preparation at night. In case of an attack entirely in daylight, a minimum of 4 hours is allowed between the time of the attack order and the assault to provide for distribution of the order and for artillery preparation.

(2) In the decisive effort the average frontages of attack are:

	Yards
Company	225
Battalion	400 to 600
Regiment	1, 100

Frontages are 20 to 25 per cent greater for units making the secondary attack.

(3) The division reserve is assembled under cover in the zone of the main effort approximately 1½ to 2 miles from the line of departure.

b. Tanks. When available, tanks are brought up with great secrecy to assault positions. Here they are attached to front-line battalions and jump off at the same time as the front-line infantry. The infantry is warned not to stop if the tanks are destroyed but to continue the advance. Tank missions are the breaching of enemy wire and destruction or neutralization of hostile elements.

c. Artillery. (1) The division artillery frequently is reinforced with light and medium battalions. Its combat organization usually provides for a direct support group of from one to two battalions for each wing without any artillery being held in general support. If a fourth battalion is attached it may be employed as a counter-battery group in a relation similar to general support. Fire missions are varied according to the phases of the proposed action, a typical assignment where there is no reinforcing artillery being the following:

(*a*) *Phase I.* Attack of the outpost position. Missions: counter battery by one battalion, direct support fire by two battalions, with special attention given to the troops of the main effort.

(*b*) *Phase II.* From the occupation of the outpost line of resistance to the opening of the artillery preparation. Missions: counter battery, harassing, and interdiction fires.

(*c*) *Phase III.* The artillery preparation.

    1. Duration one to two hours.
    2. Subdivisions (approximate).
        ½ hour of fire for adjustment (ranging) in daylight.
        ½ hour for wire-cutting accompanied by slight counterbattery.
        ½ hour of fire on infantry position.

(*d*) *Phase IV.* The attack. Mission: direct support fires with particular attention to the main effort.

(2) All the division artillery deploys for the attack of the outpost line of resistance. The artillery positions are pushed forward to within 500 to 800 yards of the infantry line of departure so as to be able to support the attack of the main position without moving. At the time of the attack on the main

position, 1 or 2 artillery companies often are attached to the main effort as accompanying artillery.

(3) The ammunition allowance for the light artillery in an attack of a position is usually 3 to 3½ days of fire (1 day of fire 75-mm equals 300 rounds).

(4) Two to three airplanes normally are attached to the artillery for observation and command purposes.

(5) Implied gunnery methods seem to be elementary, with main reliance on axial ground observation and with observation posts generally close to the guns. The Japanese Combat Regulations imply, however, that the artillery is capable of registering at night and of opening fire promptly at dawn.

d. Antiaircraft artillery. The usual attachment of antiaircraft artillery to a division appears to be a battalion, consisting of three gun companies (and sometimes a searchlight company). Such machine guns as are in this battalion are for its own local defense. In the attack of a position, the gun companies are placed in the zone of the main effort, in initial positions about 2,700 to 3,300 yards from the line of departure of the infantry.

e. Cavalry or reconnaissance. About one platoon is normally attached to each wing for duty as messengers and orderlies. The remainder is divided for flank protection with the bulk on the decisive flank. As the strength of the division cavalry regiment is light, the combat value is not as great as might be expected.

f. Engineers. Engineer missions in the typical case are: maintenance of communications; assistance to the artillery and tanks; wire cutting; and the removal of obstacles.

g. Command posts. The average distances of command posts from the line of departure for the attack of the main positions are:

	Yards
Infantry regiment	1,100
Artillery regiment	2,700
Division	2,700

h. Destruction of obstacles. The Japanese normally assume there is some wire in front of the hostile position. An attack order therefore includes provisions for cutting the wire in one of the following ways:

(1) By detailed destruction fires by the artillery.

(2) By artillery fire in the most important places, supplemented elsewhere by hand cutting by infantry, tanks, and engineers.

(3) By the artillery cutting the wire imperfectly at all points, with the cutting to be completed in detail by infantry, tanks, and engineers. Where there are several bands of wire, it is normal to make the destruction of the first band the exclusive duty of the infantry and engineers.

i. Medical troops. About one-third of the medical troops are assigned to support each wing; the remainder are in reserve. These detachments set up and operate division collecting (dressing) stations located behind the regimental dressing stations. Locations are from 1,600 to 2,200 yards behind the line of departure. Two field hospitals are set up about 2,500 to 4,000 yards from the line of departure; the division is capable of setting up one additional hospital held initially in reserve.

j. Ammunition supply. The advance section of the transport regiment (senshin shicho) ordinarily opens an infantry ammunition distributing point in rear of each wing as well as one artillery distributing point.

14. ASSAULT. There is little in tactical problems which bears specifically on the conduct of the assault. While the infantry pushes ahead boldly without regard to alignment, and with bayonets fixed, the division commander influences the action by the fire of his artillery and by the division reserve. This reserve may be used to meet a counterattack, to exploit a success, or to cover the flank of a penetrating unit. The division reaches its objective prepared to pass to the pursuit in accordance with plans previously made by the division commander.

15. COMMENTS. a. Characteristics. In their concept of the attack of a position the Japanese show complete disregard of casualties in pressing it to a successful conclusion. Their campaigns initially met with a great measure of success in tropical countries because they had trained extensively in jungle terrain and adapted their technique to capitalize on what their enemies considered hindrances and handicaps. The following characteristics were common to their campaigns:

(1) Careful, meticulous staff work in the detailed planning of the operation, training and equipping of the forces to be used, and in coordinating and carrying out the action.

(2) Great boldnesses, both in the conception of the operation and in execution of its details.

(3) Fearlessness of the enemy and the ground weapons he had at his disposal.

(4) Disregard of casualties in attaining an objective.

(5) Use of surprise and deception.

(6) Refrainment from advancing to the attack before interdiction of all nearby enemy airfields and attainment of air superiority in the area of the attack.

(7) Great speed in infiltration, envelopment, and pursuit.

(8) Willingness to attack through terrain normally considered impassable and in adverse weather conditions.

b. Criticisms. (1) The willingness with which the Japanese commander will order an attack on an outpost simultaneously with the attack on the main position has already been mentioned; this is done in spite of the prescription in Combat Regulations which indicates that effective reconnaissance can only be obtained after the outposts have been driven in. His shortening of the time allowed for reconnaissance and preparation has in many cases reduced the already slender chances of reaching the final objective.

(2) The deployment of the division is generally along orthodox lines, excepting that the assembly areas are invariably within effective enemy light artillery range.

(3) The plan of maneuver offers nothing of special advantage for the direction of the attack, as it usually culminates in a parallel, frontal, or semifrontal push executed by the two wings of the division, with one wing—the decisive one—somewhat stronger in infantry and artillery. However, if this form of maneuver is accepted, there is still a weakness in the absence of a decisive massing of force on a decisive point.

(4) Japanese use of artillery is subject to much criticism. The fundamental fault is that there is generally not enough of it. This weakness in artillery may be the result of a lack of appreciation of the need for adequate fire support, or of a feeling that past experience has not demonstrated the need for stronger artillery. The period of daylight fire for adjustment prior to the fire for effect reduces tactical surprise and diminishes the moral effect of the preparation. This unwillingness to fire the preparation unobserved at night would suggest low gunnery efficiency. Also the absence of general support artillery reduces the flexibility of the artillery fires and limits the ability of the division commander to intervene promptly in the action by the use of his artillery. From the picture drawn in the tactical problems, one can feel reasonably sure that the Japanese infantry will jump off, even though their extensive preparations have neither destroyed hostile wire nor neutralized the enemy artillery and machine guns. The detailed workings of the direct support fires are not described in the problems studied; hence, no estimate of their effectiveness can be made other than that implied by the absence of detailed plans for infantry-artillery liaison.

(5) While the detailed administrative plan of the attack does not appear in the problems studied, such establishments as are located on the situation maps are considerably closer to the front line than is considered standard. Lack of depth is characteristic of both the tactical and administrative dispositions of the Japanese division and has its origin in their lack of appreciation of the effect of modern fire power, particularly that of the hostile artillery. A period of contact with a well-equipped enemy may furnish correctives for this tendency.

(6) In general, although the adverse criticisms are numerous. it is not to be assumed that the Japanese will persist long in these errors. if errors they prove to be on the battlefield. The Japanese gifts

for adaptation and improvisation can be counted upon to remedy quickly many of the faults in their doctrine.

17b. PURSUIT. a. General. Japanese regulations and tactical doctrines place the normal emphasis on the need for pursuit to reap the full fruits of victory. They also recognize the existence of many deterring elements, such as fatigue of the troops, disorganization, and depletion of supplies. In spite of these, the Japanese commander is urged to pursue relentlessly to avoid the need for another battle against a reorganized and possibly reinforced enemy.

b. Preparation for pursuit. The Japanese commander throughout an engagement plans constantly for the pursuit. The enemy is observed carefully, especially at night, for signs of an intention to withdraw. To determine this intention, the Japanese use ground reconnaissance patrols and spies. and they may use observation aviation if it is available. When these means are inadequate, the commander is urged unhesitatingly to stage a local attack to gain the required information. While he is pushing this reconnaissance, he makes preparation for a possible pursuit. These preparations take the form of alerting certain units for immediate pursuit. of assembling sufficient ammunition for the operation, and of outlining a tentative administrative plan.

c. Types of pursuit. While the quick destruction of the defeated enemy is the object of all pursuit, this cannot always be effected immediately by a single simple maneuver. In seeking to destroy his opponent, the pursuer usually will try to fix him by direct pressure while enveloping or turning one or both flanks. If this maneuver fails, he may try to push the retiring enemy off his line of retreat or into a disadvantageous position where he can be attacked more effectively. In recognition of these differing situations, Japanese writers treat the operation under two types: Type 1, where the enemy is destroyed near the field of battle where he sustained his initial defeat; and Type 2. where the enemy has partially succeeded in extricating himself, and the pursuer must take distant objectives deep in the enemy's rear after resuming semimarch dispositions. In both types, the destruction of the enemy is accomplished by fixing him with direct pressure, while mobile pursuit detachments, moving around the flanks, occupy the critical points along his line of retreat and fall upon his rear.

d. Technique of pursuit. (1) (a) *Type (1)*. This form of pursuit finds its type example in the case of the daylight withdrawal of a hardpressed enemy. The withdrawal is observed by the attacker, who immediately redoubles the frontal pressure, while available reserves are quickly formed into pursuit detachments which turn the enemy's flank and fall upon his rear. Boundaries between front-line units are readjusted as needed. The destruction of the enemy thus is accomplished in or near the original field of battle. The detailed action of the separate arms is essentially the same as in type (2), except that distant marches, with a reforming of march columns by the frontal pressure force of the infantry, are not required.

(*b*) *Type* (2). This form of pursuit is regarded as the usual one by the Japanese. Most problems studied were of this type, wherein the enemy succeeds wholly or partially in disengaging himself and beginning a withdrawal. The initial withdrawal usually is accomplished under cover of darkness and may not be discovered at once. When the Japanese front line unit commanders find out what is occurring, they renew the attack individually and upon their own initiative in an effort to push through or around the hostile covering forces. As these Japanese units push through the enemy position, reserve units, formed into pursuit detachments, are started around the flanks with objectives deep in the enemy rear. When the Japanese front line infantry units have passed through the zone of resistance of the covering forces, the division commander halts them, organizes and sends forward additional pursuit detachments, and causes the remainder to form march columns to follow in the trace of the pursuit detachments. As this form of pursuit is considered to be usual, the subsequent remarks on the missions of the various arms apply specifically to this type, although they are also applicable with slight modification to Type (1).

(2) *Front-line infantry.* All units are individually responsible for discovering the hostile intention to withdraw. After such discovery, they drive into the enemy covering forces on their own initiative. In order to get through the enemy covering forces the Japanese prefer to turn the organized localities by maneuver or by infiltration through the gaps. When neither is possible, a quickly organized attack on a narrow front is indicated. As the action of front-line units is decentralized, most of the division artillery is attached to front-line infantry regiments. Tanks are sent in to block the enemy's retreat and to attack his artillery and command posts. To avoid a serious loss of control, the division commander usually indicates a line in rear of the probable enemy covering positions where the troops halt and reform for further pursuit. A part of the front-line infantry is then organized with previously formed pursuit detachments. The bulk of the division reforms into march columns and follows after the pursuit detachments.

(3) *Artillery.* When the enemy is discovered to be withdrawing, the artillery endeavors to disrupt the enemy's retreat by interdicting (harassing) the important defiles and bottlenecks in the road net. As the front-line infantry penetrates into the covering position, the artillery, attached to infantry units, follows by bounds close behind the advancing troops and concentrates its fire on the resisting enemy infantry. Some artillery is attached to pursuit detachments.

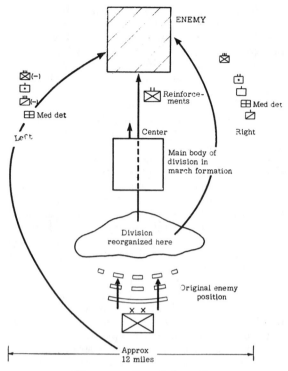

Figure 83. Pursuit formation.

e. Comments. The Japanese pursuit in theory offers little variation from standard practice. Japanese regulations urge the utilization of all available transport, but, in the absence of especially attached motor transport, the division has been incapable of giving the required mobility to the pursuit detachments. The well-known marching power of the Japanese infantry can be counted upon to compensate in a measure for this deficiency in motor transport. The pursuit is a form of operation thoroughly in line with the offensive spirit of the Japanese Army, and the war in China has shown that the Japanese pursue just as vigorously and unhesitatingly as their regulations prescribe. The North China campaign was particularly rich in examples of rapid pursuit. In the advance down the Pinghan and Tsinpu Railways, the Japanese put their pursuit detachments on freight cars and sent them far into Chinese territory, while the main body of the divisions followed partly by rail and partly by marching. Where rail transportation was not available, the Japanese organized special motorized units (kaisoku butai) to give rapidity to their pursuit.

17. RIVER CROSSING. a. General. (1) Japanese river crossing methods are essentially those of other Armies. Success is sought through surprising the defense by concealment of preparations and rapidity of action after the crossing starts. Normal attachments to a division contemplating a river crossing include units of antiaircraft, observation aviation, engineers, artillery, and armored cars.

(2) The advance to the river is made on a broad front and is preceded by advance detachments to drive back enemy patrols from the near bank and to seize existing bridges, bridging materials, and boats. The aviation reconnoiters both banks of the river, while the Engineers conduct a detailed reconnaissance for possible ferry and bridge sites, and for local engineer supplies.

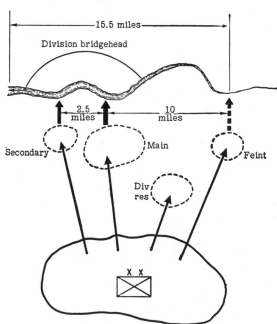

...Positions occupied night June 2-3
Preparations complete 9 PM, June 3
Time of feint, midnight June 3-4
Time of crossing, 1 AM, June 4

Figure 84. Typical river crossing.

b. Comments. The river crossing methods described are in general so orthodox as to occasion little comment. However, the pooling of all the Engineers into a unit in general support of the crossing is a deviation from the usual method of attaching Engineers to the crossing commanders. The weakness of the division artillery makes extremely difficult the support of an operation on a wide front such as a river crossing. It becomes difficult to allot any artillery to the distant feint, without which there cannot be much deception. The use of the reserve to create false activity, and the strict measures taken to control spies among the civilian population, are further examples of the emphasis placed on secrecy and deception in all Japanese operations.

18. NIGHT ATTACK. a. General. The Japanese Army has a strong partiality for the night attack. This form of combat favors the bayonet fighting stressed in infantry training and tends to cover the weaknesses in artillery and cooperation of the combined arms which have characterized the Japa-

nese Army. The Japanese are further encouraged in their faith in night attacks by successful experiences in the Russo-Japanese War and subsequent operations in China and during the early part of the present war. The night attack sometimes is referred to as "a specialty of the Japanese Army" and as "a traditional Japanese method."

b. Advantages and disadvantages. The advantages attributed to the night attack are avoidance of losses, concealment of movement, and rapidity in closing with the enemy. Disadvantages conceded are loss of cooperation between units, loss of unified direction, a greater chance of mistakes, and confusion. The Japanese believe trained troops can overcome these disadvantages and succeed even when opposed by superior numbers. Thus, in justifying a night attack, there is a tendency to reason, "The enemy is too strongly organized or too numerous for us to hope to defeat him in daylight; only by a night attack have we any possible chance to defeat him and accomplish our mission."

c. Occasions for night attacks. (1) Night attacks are considered appropriate for units varying in size from company to division. Orthodox situations calling for night attacks are the following:

(*a*) A large unit (division) wishing to extend or complete a success during a daylight engagement may continue the attack at night.

(*b*) Large units (divisions) may use a part of their force to seize by surprise points needed to assist the attack of the following day.

(*c*) Local night attacks may be used to distract or mislead the enemy and to conceal Japanese activity elsewhere (for example, a night withdrawal).

(2) These three occasions mentioned above are referred to as orthodox since they are the ones described in Japanese Combat Regulations. In practice the night attack has been used in the following additional situations:

(*a*) By a large unit to prevent a hostile night withdrawal or to complete the defeat of the enemy before he could be reinforced.

(*b*) When superior fire power of the enemy prevented the reaching of attack objective in daylight.

d. Hour of attack. Combat Regulations indicate that the period just after dark and just before daylight are desirable hours of attack. In 4 peacetime exercises the hours were, dusk, 2400, 0030, and 0200. The considerations involved in choosing these hours were that the engineers need at least 2 hours to cut paths in the hostile wire prior to the attack and that the objectives should be reached shortly before dawn to allow a coordinated renewal of the attack from the new line of departure a little after daylight.

e. Reconnaissance. Regulations insist on the importance of a thorough knowledge of the terrain on the part of all commanders involved in night attacks. Japanese commentators stress the need of detailed information as to the location of enemy strong points. machine guns. obstacles, searchlights, etc. In observed peacetime practice, however, the time allotted for reconnaissance was usually quite short. Concrete examples noted were:

(1) A regimental commander, hard pressed in a meeting engagement, decided at 1530 on a night attack at dusk, less than 4 hours later.

(2) In two separate map situations, two brigade commanders decided at 1600 and 1700, respectively, while in the course of attacking a prepared position, to make a night attack shortly after dusk of the same day. These decisions are believed to have been made at such time and under such conditions as would preclude much real reconnaissance.

f. Objectives. (1) "The objectives of a night attack are limited and are shallow in comparison to those of daylight attacks." (Japanese Combat Regulations.) Each subordinate unit receives terrain objectives as clearly defined as possible. Villages are avoided, since they are difficult to attack at night.

(2) Objectives assigned are often ambitious. The boundaries of tactical localities assigned frequently are not clearly defined features which guarantee against errors in the dark. The final objective is usually the rear edge of a position about 1,100 yards deep. Apparently about half of this is believed enough for the first bound. It will be seen in the discussion of attack dispositions that this depth of objective requires a night passage of lines on the first objective. Advance infiltration units usually precede the main attack to neutralize the enemy.

g. Conduct of attack. (1) *Infantry.* (*a*) The infantry of a night attack usually is disposed in two assault echelons and a reserve. If the objective is shallow, one assault echelon may suffice. In the normal situation, however, a first wave rushes forward and seizes the line which constitutes the first objective; the second wave passes through the first and moves on to the second objective. This second wave also has the missions of repulsing counterattacks and destroying enemy searchlights. The relative strengths of the first and second waves depend on the relative strengths of the first and second positions. In general, a force of from one or two platoons, commanded by an officer, is given the mission of attacking and occupying a definite enemy strongpoint. A battalion generally attacks in a 450 to 550 yard sector, with 2 rifle companies in the first wave, 2 companies less a platoon in the second wave, and a platoon in battalion reserve. The battalion is expected to reach and occupy 2 objectives, the more distant being some 1,100 yards from the jump-off line. Where the rear objective is more distant than this, or the going is more difficult, 2 battalions may attack in column, the rear battalion being responsible for the taking of the second objective. The following is a schematic representation of a typical attack formation.

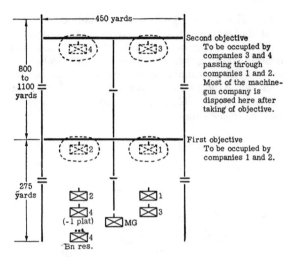

Figure 85. Battalion in night attack.

(*b*) In the foregoing dispositions, companies 1 and 2 are in a line of platoons, each platoon being in a line of squad columns; companies 3 and 4 are about 100 yards behind the leading companies in a line of platoons, each platoon in a column of squads. Exact intervals between platoons are not known, but the frontage of a company is relatively narrow, about 100 to 175 yards. The battalion reserve follows the preceding company at about 50 yards. While the Japanese recognize that this dense formation is highly vulnerable to fire, they consider it justified by ease of control and effectiveness of shock action.

(*c*) The infantry assault is with the bayonet without firing. Battalion guns may be used against searchlights and obstacles, and machine guns will participate in protective fires.

(2) *Wire-cutting, gas, and smoke.* Engineers are attached to the assault battalions for cutting lanes through the enemy wire. This cutting starts secretly after dark, about 1½ to 3 hours before the attack. About 3 lanes per battalion apparently are considered sufficient. If gassed areas are to be encountered decontaminating detachments precede the assault; chemical detachments for laying smoke screens also may be pushed forward if the enemy searchlights are troublesome.

(3) *Artillery.* (*a*) Night attacks are classified as "kishu" and "kyoshu." The first is translated as "attack by surprise" and the second "attack by force." Attack by surprise (kishu) is characterized by an infantry rush with bayonet, but without a preparation or accompanying fires by the artillery or infantry weapons. Attack by force (kyoshu) implies coordinated accompanying fires and possibly a preparation. The attack of the first objective is an attack by surprise (kishu), unless the enemy is thought to be expecting a night attack; the attack of the second objective is an attack by force (kyoshu).

(*b*) A battalion of artillery normally supports an infantry regiment. The artillery commander, after conference with the commanding officer of the infantry, prepares fires to be available on call during the attack. The usual method of call is by rocket. In preparing fires, special consideration is given to possible enemy counterattacks. The artillery may be required to cut wire, but this is costly in ammunition.

(4) *Maintenance of direction.* Maintenance of direction at night, being difficult, requires special measures. Devices used are—

(a) Compass bearing.

(b) Road markers, such as white stakes, strips of paper, lines of chalk or flour, and ropes.

(c) Flares.

(d) Searchlights.

(e) Shells fired for direction of artillery.

(f) Rear lights giving direction by alignment.

(g) Company commanders wearing two crossed strips of white cloth on their backs; lieutenants, a single strip.

(5) *Comments.* (1) An enemy facing the Japanese Army may expect to receive frequent attacks at night, at least until this form of combat proves definitely unprofitable. Factors favoring the success of such attacks are:

(a) Detailed training in night marches, maneuvers, and attack.

(b) Special emphasis placed on use of the bayonet and hand-to-hand fighting.

(c) Emphasis placed on the element of surprise in the execution of night attacks.

(d) Constant use of infiltration, outflanking movements, and attacks from the rear in country where cover is dense.

(2) It is believed that the following defects will militate against the success of the Japanese night attacks in the face of an alert enemy:

(a) An overreadiness to attack at night in the hope of retrieving a check received in daylight fighting.

(b) Insufficiency of time allowed for reconnaissance, planning, and distribution of orders.

(c) Over-ambitious objectives.

(d) Mass attack formations highly vulnerable to enemy fire.

(e) Reserve units following on the heels of assault waves where they would soon be lost to control of the commander.

(f) Inadequacy of artillery support to neutralize enemy automatic weapons and to cover the operation with protective fires.

(g) An attempt to execute a night passage of lines in the course of an attack.

(3) Against an enemy who has not been determined to hold at all cost, the night attack has had and may be expected to have many successful applications. However, against a vigilant enemy, strong in automatic weapons, it has proved costly to the Japanese.

Section III. DEFENSIVE

1. GENERAL. a. Japanese attitude. The defensive form of combat generally has been distasteful to the Japanese, and they have been very reluctant to admit that the Imperial Army would ever be forced to engage in this form of combat. So pronounced has been their dislike for the defensive that tactical problems illustrating this type of combat are extremely rare.

b. Object. The object of the defensive is to inflict on the superior hostile forces such losses by fire power, disposed appropriately on the terrain and behind man-made defensive works, that the initial disparity of forces becomes equalized to the point of authorizing a passage eventually to the offensive.

c. Doctrine. The old Combat Regulations (Sento Koyo), superseded in November, 1938, based discussion of the defensive on the active defense. The newer regulation (Sakusen Yomurei) takes the passive defense, assumed in the presence of overwhelmingly superior forces, as the typical case, of which the active defense is a variant calling for special discussion. This latter viewpoint is definitely contrary to former practice where a return to the offensive is always present in the plans for the defense, even though the initial dispositions are not those of an active defense in the true tactical sense of the word. This indicates a change in official emphasis, but probably means no real change in the practice of the defense, since in actual combat and in illustrative problems there is always present the characteristics of active defense.

2. DEFENSE OF A POSITION. a. Selection of the position. The qualities sought for the main battle position (observation, protected flanks, fields of fire, covered lines of communications, obstacles, etc.) are those standard in all schools of military doctrine. In accordance with the current trend, the Japanese emphasize the importance of antitank obstacles across the front and flanks of their position. In the presence of an enemy who may use gas, the main line of resistance will avoid depressions where it is likely to accumulate. The importance of cover and concealment is fully recognized. Reconnaissance for the position is made by the division commander, assisted by his artillery and engineer commanders as well as other appropriate staff officers.

b. Occupation of the position. (1) When the general outline of the position has been determined, the division commander directs the subordinate elements of his command to their respective defense areas where they deploy directly upon the position which they are to occupy. The division commander directs his cavalry (often reinforced by some infantry) to cover the deployment and organization of the position. This force takes position far enough in advance of the area to be organized to keep hostile artillery fire off the main line of resistance. The division commander's reconnaissance must include:

(a) Determination of the probable direction of hostile attack.

(*b*) The probable direction of a division counter-attack or counteroffensive.

(*c*) Antitank measures.

(*d*) The assignment of troops within the defensive area.

(*e*) The use of artillery including antiaircraft.

(*f*) The composition and location of the division reserve.

(*g*) The use of tanks.

(*h*) Communications and liaison.

(*i*) Supply.

The completeness of the reconnaissance is dependent on the time available. He then issues his defense order.

c. Organization of the position. (1) The defense is based on a main position (shujinchitai) which is held to the last extremity. The division commander normally divides the defensive position into right and left sectors (chiku) the defense of which he assigns to his two senior infantry commanders. In cases where the front is unusually broad, or a counter-offensive is planned, he may add a center sector. The Infantry is disposed along the main line of resistance by units of battalions, with frontages determined by the terrain and mission. When a broad defense is adopted, battalion centers of resistance are organized for an all-round, independent defense, in which the lateral intervals can only be partially covered by fire. In this form of defense, reserve units, kept as large as possible, are held mobile to attack hostile elements which filter through. Battalion frontages in the broad defense along the main line of resistance may approach 3,000 yards, while the normal defense frontages average from 800 to 2,000 yards.

(2) Support and local reserve units are deployed behind the front line infantry to give the position a depth of 700 to 1,500 yards. Throughout this zone automatic and antitank weapons are echeloned in depth. Usually heavy machine guns are found deployed along the support position, from which they attempt to cover the front with interlocking fires (criss-cross fires).

3. THE OUTPOST POSITION. a. The outpost position (Keikai Jinchi) is indicated by the division defense order and is garrisoned by troops dispatched by the sector commanders. The order may specify the strength of the garrison, its mission, and manner of withdrawal. Troops on the outpost line of resistance normally pass to division reserve when relieved. The outpost line of resistance is generally from 1,500 to 3,000 yards in front of the main line of resistance, so as to be within supporting range of light artillery. Combat Regulations tend to recommend the shorter distance so as to obtain the fire support of machine guns from the main line of resistance. However, in observed practice, the Japanese seem to attach little importance to the uncertain support of long-range machine gun fire.

b. The normal missions of the outpost line of resistance are (1) to obtain enemy information by observation and patrolling, (2) to cover the main line of resistance and prevent its surprise, (3) to delay the hostile attack on the main line of resistance, and (4) to act as an advance defensive position (Zenshin Jinchi). Missions (1) and (2) are the minimum case, where the outpost line of resistance is not much more than a line for observation and reconnaissance with little defense strength. Missions (3) and (4), frequently present in observed practice, imply a considerable increase in defensive means approaching that of a true advanced defensive position.

c. The troops assigned to garrison the outpost line of resistance, while variable in strength with the mission assigned, are kept to a minimum. For the front of a division, 1 to 2 battalions of infantry were normal in the problems consulted. Comments on these problems indicate that about 2,000 yards for the infantry company is considered the absolute maximum extension consonant with the retention of any sort of control by the unit commander. With the usual weak allotment of troops, it is impossible to hold the line continuously. Instead, important points are occupied in some strength, while the intervals are covered by observation and fire as far as possible. The Japanese do not expect to be able to organize a continuous system of infantry and artillery fires in front of the outpost line of resistance. With the help of attached engineers, the infantry strengthens the outpost position by defensive works to the extent permitted in the time available. In the case of the defense on a very wide front the outpost line of resistance is reduced to a line of observers, or may even be dispensed with entirely.

4. ADVANCED DEFENSIVE POSITION.

a. The division commander at times may order the occupation and organization of an advanced defensive position (Zenshin Jinchi) in the zone between the outpost line of resistance and the main battle position. The purpose of such a position is to prevent as long as possible the occupation of critical points of terrain by hostile forces near the main defensive zone, to delay the enemy preparations for the attack, and to induce the enemy to launch his attack in a false direction which will expose his flank. The organization of a formal advance defensive position is not standard Japanese practice, although the assignment of such a mission to the outpost position is not uncommon. Typical cases where the advanced positions have been organized are: (1) where in order to obtain observation the outpost line of resistance has been pushed well forward, leaving an important ridge in the foreground of the main battle position ungarrisoned; and (2) where an oblique position is organized between the outpost position and the main battle position, with one flank resting on the outpost line of resistance while the other rests on the main line of resistance, thus inducing the enemy to expose a flank.

b. The garrison of the advance position may come from the troops assigned to the outpost position or from those of the main battle position, reinforced by machine guns and antitank weapons. Artillery elements may be assigned support missions. The delicacy of withdrawing this force is fully appreciated by the Japanese, and the division commander is cautioned to issue clear and simple missions to this force and to specify the time and manner of withdrawal.

c. In cases where the division commander elects not to organize an advance position, the zone between the outpost position and the main battle position is covered by observers sent forward by the front line infantry battalions. These troops patrol the foreground, cooperate with those of the outpost line of resistance, and execute local reconnaissance.

5. RESERVES. a. Reserves are held out by all units from the company upward for the purpose of executing counterattacks. The division reserve generally varies in size from 1 to 3 battalions. Its position is initially from 5,500 to 6,500 yards in rear of the main line of resistance, in a sheltered position conveniently situated with respect to the probable counterattack of the division. Tanks often will be attached to this force.

Motor transportation generally is not attached to the reserve because of the paucity of organic motor transport in the division.

b. When the division commander has planned an active defense, the general reserve as a rule will not exceed a third of the infantry strength, since front line units themselves are expected to return to the offensive at the earliest opportunity.

6. ARTILLERY. The artillery is disposed in depth behind the main line of resistance so as to be able to mass its fire in support of the main position in the area of the hostile probable main effort. One or two artillery companies may be initially in forward positions to support the outpost positions or an advanced defensive position. Artillery positions generally are echeloned through a zone about 2,500 yards in depth, extending to the rear from a line about 1,700 to 2,200 yards behind the main line of resistance. Ground observation is not considered effective under normal conditions for ranges over 5,500 yards.

7. COMMAND POSTS. a. General. Command posts generally are established in well sheltered positions in rear of the main line of resistance; that of the division is usually located at a distance of about 5,500 yards, that of the infantry group at about 2,700 yards, and that of the infantry regiment at about 1,300 yards in rear of the main line of resistance.

b. Organization of the ground. (1) In the early phases of the reconnaissance of the position, the division commander gives initial instructions to his engineer regarding the supplying of entrenching tools, material, and equipment. The defense order indicates the priority of work, a typical one being the following:

(*a*) Principal points on the main line of resistance.

(*b*) Fields of fire and observation posts of the main line of resistance.

(*c*) Obstacles in front of the main line of resistance.

(*d*) Communications, trenches, and personnel shelters.

(2) In tactical problems it is seldom assumed that there is time available for elaborate field works. The division usually has from about 3 hours to a half day to complete its organization of the ground. Three hours is considered the minimum required to organize a rudimentary system of trenches and obstacles along the main line of resistance. The time-work unit in engineering calculations is the 12-man squad which is considered capable of digging about 25 yards of standing fire trench in a little over 3 hours. In situations in which the use of gas by the enemy is expected, the division commander will order the distribution of protective materials at suitable points throughout the area. Stress is laid on camouflage and the construction of dummy field works, the completeness of which is dependent upon the time available. A typical plan followed by the Japanese in the construction of the field works of a company position on the main line of resistance is illustrated in figures 86, 87, and 88.

c. Conduct of the defense. (*a*) *Advanced elements.* As the enemy approaches the position, he will encounter first the advanced elements of the defense (the outpost line of resistance or advanced defensive position). These forward elements conduct themselves in accordance with their mission which normally directs their withdrawal into division reserve before becoming seriously engaged. Artillery companies in forward positions delay the hostile advance, cover the withdrawal of the infantry, and then fall back to prepared positions in the artillery zone where they revert to the control of their organic commander. The cavalry which has withdrawn to the flank, while maintaining contact with the advance positions, will carry out its normal missions.

(*b*) *Defense of the main line of resistance.* As the hostile infantry forms up for the attack on the main line of resistance, the defensive artillery brings down its counter preparation fires. Tanks may be sent forward, covered by artillery, to upset the preparations of the enemy. As the hostile attack enters the zone of infantry fires, the sector commanders conduct the defense of their sectors, first by fire, then by the bayonet in front of their entrenchments. Commanders of all units counterattack unhesitatingly as the integrity of their positions becomes threatened by the hostile attack. The artillery assists the close-in defense by standing barrages and concentrations brought down within the defensive position.

(*c*) *The counterattack or counteroffensive.* The division commander is constantly on the alert to determine the proper time for the division counterattack or counteroffensive. The favorable moment will generally be at the time the hostile attack has been stalled; when the enemy has blundered into an unfavorable position; when a favorable opportunity has been created by a successful local counterattack; and when the enemy pauses to reorganize or consolidate his position. The plan for a return to the offensive will be made tentatively well in advance of the occurrence of the opportunity. The direction of the counterattack generally will be aimed at an envelopment; however, at times, the situation may compel a purely frontal attack. The mass of artillery, and tanks if present, will support the counter-

attack or counteroffensive. The division commander may directly control the counteroffensive, or he may delegate control to a sector commander.

8. COMMENTS. a. Aggressive character. Since the defensive in Japanese regulations and military writings is branded as a negative form of combat, un-Japanese in essence and spirit, it has been very difficult to write a tactical problem for which officers were willing to advocate a defensive solution. In problems studied, the basic decision to defend already had been made by the division commander, a school device to control the offensive elan of the student officers. Even when thus forced on

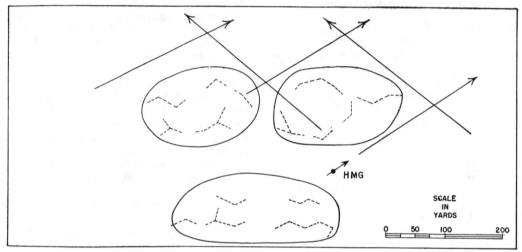

Figure 86. A company position after approximately 2 hours of work.

NOTE. After approximately 6 hours of work the individual firing trenches within a squad position will be connected, forming a single line.

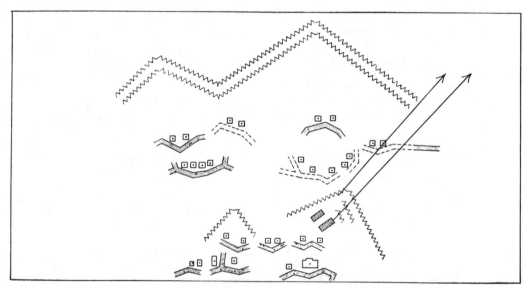

Figure 87. The company position after approximately a week of construction time (56 hours).

NOTE. Squad positions will be enlarged standing trenches. The communication trenches will be deep enough for crawling, and the shelters will be of light construction, accommodating 6 men. Only the machine gun shelters will be built to resist 150-mm howitzer fire. The wire entanglements beyond the front-lines will be 8 meters in depth.

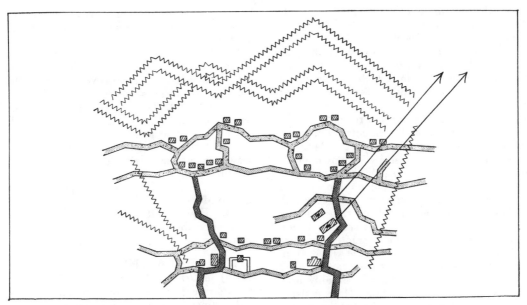

Figure 88. A company position after approximately 4 weeks of construction time.

the defensive. Japanese officers have the return to the offensive always uppermost in their minds and are quick to launch counterattacks, large and small, coordinated and uncoordinated, on the slightest provocation. On the maneuver ground, troops are always ready to abandon their prearranged system of infantry fires to meet the attacker with the bayonet in front of their trenches. The defects of a defense so conducted are glaring to the occidental student of tactics, but its positive and aggressive character has virtues which will, on occasions, upset a careless or overconfident attacker.

b. Other characteristics. In spite of the usual instructions issued relative to the need of echelonment in depth of the defense, there is an apparent tendency to concentrate a disproportionate strength in the front lines. This is especially true of the special weapons (machine guns, battalion guns, etc.). The appearance of the "broad defense" in Combat Regulations appears to be a recognition of the increased strength of frontal resistance of modern infantry, as well as an official corrective to the often remarked Japanese tendency to a shoulder-to-shoulder disposition of units both on the attack and defense.

Section IV. RETROGRADE MOVEMENTS

1. THE WITHDRAWAL. a. General. There is little military literature obtainable to elaborate on the bare substance of the provisions of the Japanese Regulations governing the withdrawal. In general, the method of withdrawal appears to be standard. It is notable, however, the usual strong insistence on the dangers of a daylight withdrawal is not in regulations. No information has been obtained as to when the Japanese commander considers a

withdrawal required or justified since, in the cases studied, the withdrawal was executed on army order and was not considered as imposed by the enemy.

b. Preparations for the withdrawal. The division commander, in anticipation of a withdrawal, first attempts to clear his rear area of supply troops and installations, improves the roads which he expects to use, and orders preparations for demolitions to delay the enemy follow-up. All preparations are made with the utmost secrecy while preserving a bold front.

c. Daylight conduct of the withdrawal. (1) *Local covering forces.* The breaking of contact of the front line infantry is done under the protection of local covering forces, disposed from 1,500 to 2,000 yards behind the firing line. These troops are obtained from battalion, regiment, or other reserves not committed to the front line fighting. The position occupied is, when possible, to the flank of the line of retreat on commanding ground permitting overhead fire in support of the retiring troops. The local covering forces give support by fire and, on occasion, may execute local counterattacks to aid in disengaging the front line infantry. About the equivalent of one regimental sector in open warfare appears to be an average strength for the local covering forces in the problems consulted.

(2) *General covering force (Shuyo Jinchitai).* In addition to these local detachments, the division commander organizes a general covering force behind which he reforms the major elements of his command. The division reserve is usually the principal component of this covering force which, in principle, is made up of the freshest troops at the disposal of the commander. The bulk of the division artillery withdraws and deploys behind this covering position to protect the withdrawal. The Japanese

try to place the covering position at an oblique angle to the axis of retreat and from 3,000 to 5,000 yards in rear of the front line. The division command post is set up behind the covering position for the purpose of controlling the withdrawal and organizing the subsequent retirement for which the troops on the covering position eventually become the rear guard.

(3) *Execution of withdrawal.* Protected by the covering forces, the front line infantry withdraws straight to the rear assisted by support units in the second echelon. The Japanese feel that it is desirable for all front line units to pull back simultaneously, but often some must hold on longer than others. The division artillery, the bulk of which already has retired to the general covering position, supports the withdrawal. In some sectors, a sudden local counterattack may be warranted in order to create a favorable situation for the withdrawal. Retreating units reform progressively, arriving by many small columns in the general assembly area behind the general covering position. Here, division march columns are formed and directed toward the final terrain objective of the withdrawal. The engineers execute demolitions to retard the enemy, while columns move off covered by a rear guard. The cavalry and aviation reconnoiter for turning movements around the flanks by pursuit detachments. The aviation may be called upon to attack ground troops which are endangering the success of the withdrawal.

d. Night conduct of withdrawal. (1) *General.* The night withdrawal differs from that in daylight in the following important respects:

a. The local covering mission is performed by a "shell" of small detachments left in position on the front line throughout most of the hours of darkness.

b. Retiring units reassemble and form march columns nearer the front line than is the case in daylight.

c. A general covering position is ordinarily not organized. Detailed preparation in daylight is necessary prior to a night withdrawal. This includes a designation and marking of roads to be used by retiring units, as well as the usual clearing of the rear area. Secrecy is essential throughout to conceal the intention to withdraw.

(2) "*Shell.*" The breaking of contact by the front line infantry is done under the cover of a thin line of infantry detachments, strong in machine guns and supported by a small amount of artillery. This "shell" simulates the usual sector activity throughout the night to deceive the enemy and, if attacked, sacrifices itself in place to protect the retirement. Its time of withdrawal, usually about daylight, is set by the division commander. The mission of the "shell" may be facilitated by local attacks executed early in the night by front line detachments prior to their withdrawal. Normally no general covering force is needed to supplement the "shell." An exception is the case where the "shell", left in place until dawn, requires protection to get away without undue losses.

In such a case, a small general covering force, strong in cavalry and mobile troops, may be organized for the benefit of the "shell."

(3) *Execution of withdrawal.* The behavior of the front line units is essentially the same as in daylight. They reform progressively as they retire, assembly areas being somewhat nearer the front line than in daylight. One or two companies of artillery remain until nearly dawn to support the "shell" and carry out normal activity.

e. Comment. Japanese procedure in the withdrawal is generally orthodox. The absence of the customary injunctions against the daylight withdrawal is symptomatic of the Japanese under-estimation of the effects of modern fire power and aerial attack. However, it is unwarranted to assume that, in practice, they will not try to avoid daylight withdrawals when the situation permits.

2. THE DELAYING ACTION. (JIKYU-SEN). *a. General characteristics.* (1) The Japanese do not recognize the delaying action as a separate and distinct form of military operation but include it in the broader term, "jikyusen" (holding-out-combat). The expression is used to cover, in addition to pure delay, a number of types of operations characterized by a desire to avoid a fight to a finish, but in which the idea of delay is somewhat remote. Thus, in addition to the typical delay situations, such as the action of rear guards and covering forces, the Japanese treat under "jikyusen" demonstrations, reconnaissances in force, and night attacks designed to cover a withdrawal. In the subsequent discussion, an effort is made to disregard the elements not bearing directly on delay which the Japanese inject into the treatment of "jikyusen."

(2) The usual purpose of delaying action is to gain time to contain or to divert a superior enemy while avoiding decisive combat. "Although these ends are frequently achieved by defensive action, there are occasions when the mission can be accomplished only by offensive action." The proceeding sentence is a literal translation from the Sakusen Yomurei. Elsewhere, the same regulation urges that even when defensive measures are initially better adapted to the situation, the commander must always be ready to take advantage of an opportunity for offensive action. However, when offensive action is indicated, in order to avoid becoming deeply engaged, the division commander designates limited objectives and rigidly controls the number of troops committed to action. In comparison to the meeting engagement, fronts of deployment are wide in such an offensive action.

(3) Mobile troops, well equipped with automatic weapons and artillery, are best adapted to delaying actions. The infantry fire fight generally takes place at long ranges as the engagement is broken off when the enemy draws near. Frontages are wide, and the breadth is obtained by increasing the intervals between occupied key positions. Reserves are kept large to cover withdrawals, to give continuity to

the resistance of the delaying force, and to provide troops for such limited offensive actions as the commander may undertake.

b. Choice of a delaying position. While the situation may force the commander to seek the required delay on a single position, such a disposition creates a danger of becoming involved in a fight to the finish or in a costly withdrawal at close range from the enemy. It is thus preferable to delay on successive positions separated by about two to three miles. A delaying position is chosen for its observation, distant fields of fire, and covered routes of withdrawal.

c. Conduct of the delaying action. (1) When the decision has been reached to delay an advancing enemy, the division commander sends out his cavalry to establish and maintain contact and initiate the delaying action within limits of its combat capacity. He then selects the position or positions upon which he expects to gain the required time for the accomplishment of his mission. He often will send forward an infantry detachment of from 2 companies to a battalion to occupy an advanced position ahead of the first delaying position. Such an advanced position is located within range of artillery support from the delaying position in accordance with the principles for choosing an outpost line of resistance. These forward troops assist the cavalry, as the latter falls back to the flanks of the delaying position, and impose some loss of time on the advancing enemy.

(2) The enemy is taken under fire by the division artillery at extreme ranges. Artillery positions are close behind the infantry, and are grouped together for ease in fire direction in the belief that there is little to fear initially from the hostile counterbattery. Eventually, the infantry machine guns join in the fire fight as the enemy comes within range.

(3) The division commander makes every effort to hold out a large reserve. In cases noted, this amounted to from a third to a half of his infantry and a battalion of artillery. The main purpose of this large reserve is not to counterattack (although some of it on occasion may engage in local offensive action) but to reconnoiter, prepare, and occupy the next delaying position from which it covers the withdrawal of the troops of the first position. The Japanese thus contemplate, in effect, delay on successive positions occupied simultaneously, although this form of action is implied rather than clearly defined.

(4) The engineers of the division find their principal missions in road maintenance, route marking, and the preparation and execution of demolitions. The last are carefully planned to cover the flanks and routes of direct approach to the delaying positions.

(5) As in other forms of combat, the Japanese count heavily on measures of deception to assist in accomplishing the delaying mission. Devices used to create this deception are: dummy engineer works; demonstrations; economy of force in wooded and covered areas while strength is displayed in open terrain; roving artillery; proclamations; propaganda. All these measures aim to create an impression of strength which will cause the enemy to adopt a cautious attitude toward the delaying force. In spite of the fact that such measures impose fatigue on the troops and, in extreme cases may lead to a serious dispersion of effort, the Japanese feel that their use is justified.

d. Withdrawal. The troops on the delaying position retire on order of the division commander while the enemy is still at a distance, unless the mission specifically required a long delay on a single position. When the hostile infantry gets within 1,000 yards of the position it is considered time to go, and the troops on the next delaying position cover the withdrawal. Detachments left in the zone between the positions effect intermediate delay. When it has not been possible to prepare and man a second position, the division commander tries to put off his withdrawal until nightfall.

e. Comments. (1) As a defensive form of combat the delaying action does not appeal to the Japanese soldier who thinks first and last of fixing bayonets and moving forward. Influenced by the strength and weakness of this psychology, the Japanese commander often will choose offensive action when the defensive is better suited to the immediate situation. It has been noted that a little fresh encouragement has been given in the new Combat Regulations to the use of offensive action to obtain delay, an encouragement of which Japanese commanders can be expected to take full advantage in order to seek delay through attack. It is felt that this over-aggressiveness may ill serve the usual purposes of delay.

(2) The injunction to hold out a large reserve does not agree with the usual teachings on delay. A reserve suggests the intention to counterattack, whereas a delaying position usually is abandoned before the enemy has come within counterattacking range. In the practice of map problems, this large reserve was always used to occupy a rear delaying position, so that the operation became, in effect, a delay on successive positions simultaneously occupied. Thus, the requirement of holding out a large reserve, in spite of its apparent contradiction, becomes reconciled with tactical orthodoxy.

(3) The Japanese dislike for using their light artillery at long ranges tends to keep successive delaying positions relatively close together (3,000–4,000 yards). It is generally considered that 5,500 yards is the extreme limit of effective terrestrial observation, and it is rare to assign missions beyond that range. Japanese artillery has had little experience in fire with air observation.

(4) It is reasonable to suppose that the Japanese have learned the latest methods of withdrawal as employed by modern armies which place great emphasis on the use of tanks, mobile artillery, motorized infantry, mines, tank traps, aircraft, and a new concept of distance.

Section V. EMPLOYMENT OF TANKS AND MECHANIZED UNITS

1. GENERAL. a. Background. As a result of experiences in the Manchurian Incident, the war in China, and the clash with the Russians at Changkufeng, the Japanese Army has acquired a lively appreciation of the value of mechanization. Much thought was given to the proper use of this new weapon in the light of the experiences of the Japanese and German Armies. A distinguishing feature was the early modification, extension, and detailed expatiation on the paragraphs devoted to the use of tanks and mechanized units in combat regulations. However, the new changes in regulations, while giving additional space to mechanization, treat the subject with broad generalities which leave considerable doubt as to whether the Japanese have worked out many of the practical details of such highly involved questions as infantry-tank-artillery liaison, control by higher commanders, and logistics of mechanized forces.

b. Estimated strength. (1) At the outbreak of the present war, the known mechanized strength of the Japanese Army consisted of at least 4 tank regiments. While the wartime expansion of tank units is not definitely known, it is believed that there are now additional tank regiments. The reliance on cooperation with the infantry may explain the large number of "Independent" armored units, which can be attached to other formations as and when required. The lack, or failure, to identify artillery, infantry, etc., with the Tank Group also may be explained by this policy, and this formation may, in fact, be more of the Army Tank Brigade type than of the armored division. This view again is borne out to some extent by Japanese teaching, and it is thought that the Tank Group may be employed in conjunction with infantry formations, working in close cooperation with infantry divisions, rather than fulfilling the role of an armored division, which would be to destroy enemy armored formations. It is believed, however, that there are at least 2 armored divisions in Manchuria at the present time.

(2) Weight for weight, the speeds of Japanese tanks do not compare unfavorably with those of other Armies, but it is considered that these speeds drop rather more appreciably across country than do those of Allied tanks. The Japanese tanks are bulkier for their weight since their armor basis is smaller. This can be accounted for by the fact that the Japanese regard their tanks as infantry support weapons, and therefore they rely on the infantry to neutralize the enemy anti-tank weapons.

c. Tactics. Our very limited experience with Japanese tank tactics in Burma and the South West Pacific Area leads to the conclusion that the Japanese regard the tank primarily as a close support weapon for the infantry. Only on one occasion did a small tank versus tank action develop; even then the Japanese tanks are believed to have been surprised during a reconnaissance, and not to have been

seeking the armored battle in which they were so badly out-fought. There is little doubt, however, that the Japanese have carefully studied the tactical trends of tank warfare in Europe, and, while industrial limitations make the general employment by the Japanese of large tank organizations unlikely, should they fight in suitable terrain, they reasonably may be expected to employ armor at least as a spearhead to infantry enveloping attacks. Should the nature of the ground permit, the Japanese have, in the tank, an ideal weapon for exploiting their favorite maneuver of a wide and rapid encircling movement which cuts the enemy's lines of communication and generally disorganizes his rear areas. With the Battle of France before them, it is unlikely that they would neglect the advantages gained by the use of armor in this, their favorite offensive maneuver.

2. TRAINING. Japanese tank troops are highly trained in night fighting, and in fighting under extremes of weather. They are obsessed with the value of the attack, and crews will not hesitate to leave their tanks to fight on foot when pressed or in coming up against manned obstacles. Japanese tank training stresses the need for: (1) rapid decisions; (2) rapid mobility; (3) rapid concentration of fire; (4) concealment of intentions; and (5) supply and repair. Frequent practice is given in maneuvers over varied ground; in developing close cooperation within the tank between driver and gunner; and in bringing accurate fire to bear in the shortest possible time. In combat training successive stages are the advance, deployment, attack, mopping-up, and pursuit.

3. TANKS WITH THE DIVISION. a. Offensive. (1) The tanks with a division are normally used as accompanying tanks attached to the infantry units making the principal attack. Prior to the attack such tanks are brought up secretly to assembly positions about 3 miles behind the line of departure. Here final reconnaissance and attack preparations are completed. Tank commanders confer with the infantry regimental and battalion commanders to whom they are to be attached as well as with the artillery which is to support the attack: Topics for conference and decision are: tank objectives and the hour of attack; tank jump-off positions, routes to the jump-off position and the subsequent zone of advance; type of artillery support desired and its coordination with the advance of the tanks; plan for meeting a counterattack by hostile tanks; signal communications between infantry, tanks, and artillery. On the night preceding the attack, the tanks move to jump-off positions under cover of the noise of artillery firing and low-flying airplanes. Attack formations aim at obtaining the effect of mass by disposing the tanks in several waves across the front of the infantry unit to which they are attached. The tanks move forward, followed closely by the infantry and supported by the artillery which neutralizes enemy antitank weapons by fire and smoke. Tank objectives are: obstacles blocking the advance of the infantry; the enemy automatic weapons left unneutralized by the artillery; and eventually, the hostile artillery and command system. The infantry must stick close to the tanks; if the latter get too far ahead, they may have to turn around and rejoin the infantry.

(2) The foregoing discussion applies particularly to the attack of a position where the need for tanks is especially acute. In the meeting engagement, the tactics of the tanks are in general the same, except that preparations and liaison arrangements are not so detailed, and the attack moves more rapidly. Also, in a favorable situation, the division commander, prior to the main attack, may send out all or part of his tanks ahead of the advance guard to upset the hostile deployment and derange the command system of the opposing force. In such a case, the tanks are given a rendezvous point where they assemble and return to the main body in time for use with the principal attack.

(3) The peculiar local conditions of the war in North and Central China caused certain additional uses to be made of accompanying tanks. In the case of the attack of a walled town, the tanks moved out ahead of the infantry and cleaned up the outer defenses of the town gates. Then, while the infantry closed in to assaulting range, the tanks stood by close to the wall and neutralized the defenders of the rampart by the fire of their machine guns. After the infantry entered the town, the tanks again led the way and assisted in mopping up hostile elements that continued to resist. Such use of tanks is possible only against an enemy weak in antitank weapons.

(4) *Leading tanks.* It is doubtful whether the Japanese have had actual experience in the use of leading tanks, although the new Combat Regulations contemplate their use in cases where tanks are available in plentiful numbers. The Japanese first satisfy the requirements for accompanying tanks; those in excess of this requirement are organized into a leading tank detachment under division control. Several minutes ahead of the main attack, they rush deep into the zone of the hostile artillery and command system. They are given a zone of action, a rallying point, and a mission type of order that includes the subsequent course of action. Artillery support is planned carefully to cover the tanks through the forward area of hostile antitank weapons. Long range artillery coordinates its fire with the movement of the tanks so as not to interfere with their progress.

(5) *Miscellaneous uses of tanks.* The following miscellaneous use of tanks have been noted:

(a) Tanks were used to break through the defenses at the mouth of a defile, reconnoiter the inner defenses, and return.

(b) Tanks executed local battlefield liaison and reconnaissance missions as well as transported essential supplies in the areas beaten by small arms fire.

(c) Tanks were used as the main force in a frontal

holding attack, while the remainder of the division enveloped a flank.

(d) Tanks were used to block the escape of retreating forces through the rear gates of walled towns.

(e) In November, 1937, three Japanese tanks formed a stationary battery while infantry were crossing the Suchow Canal. In February, 1938, 40 tanks were similarly employed at the crossing of the River Hwai. A few months later, tanks were used as pursuit troops driving along both sides of the Yangtze at the same time. In 1938, during the attack on Suchowfu, tanks made a wide circling move and cut the railway lines nearly 40 miles from the city.

(f) Against road blocks the Japanese used their tanks to pin down the troops covering the block, while the infantry tried to infiltrate and attack from the rear and flanks. In Malaya, whenever the infantry was held up, the Japanese brought up tanks to support the attack, overcoming any obstacles caused by demolitions, or ferrying tanks over fast-flowing rivers. Normally, they attempted to force the tanks through frontally, and, when successful, broke in among the troops on both sides of the road. When the tanks were held up frontally, they were brought in on the flanks. At the battle of Slim, Malaya (1942), the Japanese attacked with 30 tanks. These moved parallel to the main highway for several miles through roads of the adjacent rubber plantations and then cut in to the main road, moving straight down it to a depth of 20 miles.

(g) At Milne Bay a few light tanks were used as were about 12 on Guadalcanal. On each occasion their use was restricted by the terrain, but on neither was there any outstanding tactical employment.

b. Defensive. On the defense, the division commander usually holds his tanks initially in division reserve, under cover from artillery fire and attack from the air. Eventually they are attached to the infantry making the division counterattack. They are considered particularly valuable in stopping a hostile mechanized force, for the defensive tanks can defeat a superior number of the enemy's if the latter have run away from their artillery support or have become dispersed. Occasionally, the defending commander may use his tanks in a raid on the hostile assembly areas before the enemy attacks. In all cases, tank actions must be supported by carefully arranged artillery fire to neutralize the hostile antitank guns.

4. MECHANIZED UNITS. a. Organization. In China the Japanese have used provisional mechanized units, varying in size and composition according to the material at hand and the mission to be accomplished. In general, these units have a strong nucleus of tanks, supported by motorized infantry, engineers, field and antiaircraft artillery, antigas, and signal detachments. The whole force is supplied by a truck train formed from line of communication (heitan) supply units. Observation aviation is usually attached.

b. Tactics. (1) *Offensive.* (*a*) A mechanized force normally receives an offensive mission whereby advantage can be taken of its high mobility and capacity for independent action. In general, its tactics are about the same as those of a large cavalry force. By secrecy and rapid movement (usually at night) it surprises the enemy force in a terrain suitable for the tanks which form the backbone of the combat strength of the command. The commander, keeping his tanks under central control, masses them for a quick blow in a vital attack direction. The motorized infantry receives any or all of the following missions: (1) It covers the tanks and facilitates their action. (2) It holds the ground won by the tanks. (3) It occasionally takes over a front in a holding attack or makes an attack to create a diversion either by day or night. The infantry always fights dismounted but stays in its carriers as long as possible. The artillery performs normal support missions with special attention to enemy antitank guns.

(*b*) As a mechanized force draws near the enemy, the commander prepares tentative plans to meet varying hypotheses as the situation is susceptible to sudden changes in this fast-moving type of combat. He activates reconnaissance and security agencies, meanwhile gradually reducing the depth of his dispositions. As the enemy situation clears somewhat, he chooses an assembly area in conformance with his tentative scheme of maneuver. This area is as close to the enemy as is consonant with safety. If there is danger of a sudden collision with the enemy, the commander may traverse the final distance between himself and the enemy by bounds from one terrain line to another.

(*c*) A bold envelopment or turning movement is the maneuver best suited to a mechanized force. Such a force often will march at night, assembled in darkness, and attack at dawn. In the assembly area, reconnaissance is made, order is restored, and missions are assigned for the subsequent attack. When the enemy situation is vague, the usual objective is a terrain feature the possession of which is

essential to the enemy. In the final deployment troops remain in vehicles until the danger of hostile fire forces them to dismount. When this has occurred, empty vehicles are parked under cover from air and ground observation. The unit reserve is usually infantry but on occasion may include some tanks. The detailed conduct of the attack follows the tactics of a large cavalry force.

(*d*) Mechanized units are particularly well adapted to pursuit and exploitation. The objectives assigned to them are those suitable to any pursuit force, but their range of action permits a deeper penetration into the hostile areas. It is in this form of action that the Japanese mechanized forces have found their chief employment in China. Examples abound in which such units have cut the roads and railroads behind a Chinese front on the verge of collapse and have assailed the hostile rear. The broad plateaus of Suiyuan and Chahar have afforded a terrain particularly favorable to such armored tactics.

(2) *Defensive.* Since the defensive nullifies the mobility of a mechanized force, it is a form of combat to be avoided. However, it may be imposed by the situation. In such a case, the commander usually disposes his dismounted infantry in a discontinuous line of strong points, with most or all of the tanks held in reserve. The defense is conducted along customary lines, with the principal concern of the commanders being the engagement of his tanks in a counterattack. In the usual defensive situation the enemy will be superior in tanks; hence, the commander must endeavor to stage the decisive tank action out of range of the hostile artillery but within the range of his own antitank guns. Under such conditions, his inferiority in tanks is compensated for by the supporting fires of his artillery. When the hostile tanks are defeated the crisis is passed and the counter-offensive often is justified.

5. COMMENTS. The value of mechanization is fully appreciated by the Japanese Army, and its armored tactics should not be taken lightly. It has acquired considerable battlefield experience in small scale tank actions and in the use of improvised mechanized forces. Such units as have been encountered do not have the striking power of the elaborated mechanized forces of Western powers.

PART II
APPLICATION OF TACTICS

Section VI. ANTIAIRCRAFT

1. GENERAL CLASSIFICATION OF JAPANESE ANTIAIRCRAFT MEASURES. a.

Passive. Passive antiaircraft measures consist of concealment, camouflage, and dummy works. By these means, an attempt is made to hide the defended object from air observation. to make it look like either a natural part of the terrain or a non-mili-

tary objective, or to construct dummy works so that they will draw the fire of attacking aircraft. Frequently combinations of these methods are used. On the whole, camouflage in the field and of small installations has been excellent, while attempts at camouflage of large installations so far covered have not been particularly successful. Manuals place considerable emphasis on the use of both large and small-scale smoke screens, but this has not so far been observed in practice.

b. Active. Active measures in general are as follows:

(1) Antiaircraft guns of calibers ranging from 7.7-mm to 127-mm are known to be in use. These are high velocity weapons with effective ranges up to altitudes of 25,000 feet. They are used for direct action against attacking planes, to shoot them down and to break up their bomb runs. Ammunition ranges from incendiary to high explosive fragmentation projectiles with time fuses.

(2) Barrage balloons are used for protection against dive bombers. These are usually camouflaged a greenish blue when defending objects on the water, and are difficult to see. They offer no protection against high level bombing, because their maximum elevation is not great enough—usually being about 1,000 feet.

(3) Night fighter planes, equipped with radar or operating in conjunction with ground searchlights, are used to seek out and destroy hostile planes.

2. ORGANIZATION. a. Areas to be defended. Areas to be defended are: (1) important points, such as bridges, beachheads or docks, anchorages, isolated military stores, and movement of troop columns thru defiles; (2) important towns or cities; (3) airfields. No definite priority can be placed on these areas, for it depends on their relative importance which is subject to change.

b. Home defense. For active defense, the Japanese homeland is divided into antiaircraft defense areas. The organization of defense measures is usually entrusted to the senior Army officer in the district who coordinates the efforts of military, naval, and civilian units. The Army units include the fortress artillery of fortified zones, individual units of field antiaircraft artillery, and army aircraft.

3. SEARCHLIGHTS, FIRE CONTROL INSTRUMENTS, AND WARNING METHODS. a. Searchlight tactics. (1) At the end of 1943, Japanese searchlight operation was still ragged and inefficient compared with Allied standards. However, they were rapidly improving their methods. There were indications that some type of radio direction finder for searchlights was coming into use by the Japanese in certain areas. Reports state that some Allied aircraft have been picked up as soon as the searchlights were turned on and illuminated for as long as three minutes, even when evasive action was taken.

(2) It is believed, however, that the majority of Japanese searchlights are directed by sound locators.

(3) Lights apparently are controlled centrally, as they are frequently illuminated simultaneously, searching in the same direction.

(4) Cooperation between searchlights and night fighters has improved. Searchlights have frequently been seen waving vertically or scissoring, especially when about to focus on a plane. Searchlights have been waved together vertically on one side or the other of hostile aircraft, presumably to give direction to a night fighter.

(5) Emplacements are generally circular and from 15 feet to 35 feet in diameter, with most being of the larger size. Searchlights are generally emplaced in an oval pattern with the defended area in the center.

b. Fire-control instruments. (1) Japanese fire control instruments examined to date show no new improvement, and in general, they are obsolete judged by modern standards. The standard heavy antiaircraft (75 mm.) guns recovered in the Aleutians, the Solomons, and New Guinea were all manually operated from data transmitted by voice to the gun crew members from the operators of off-carriage instruments. No directors have been used in conjunction with the 40 mm, 25 mm, or 20 mm automatic cannons. However, reports indicate that Allied flyers have experienced heavy accurate antiaircraft fire over Japanese bases, even through cloud cover, which would seem to indicate that fire-control equipment of more advanced design is in use.

(2) It is a common practice for single Japanese planes to fly at the same altitude as enemy bombers although well out of range. These planes make no effort at interception; their evident purpose is to transmit to the guns data as to the elevation and speed of the target, for when these "spotter" planes are present, the corrections of antiaircraft fire have been rapid.

c. Warning methods. Three warning methods are in general use by the Japanese:

(1) Sound locators of the trumpet type are still used, although they are not very effective against modern high speed planes.

(2) Radar is in use in many important defenses, but its range appears to be rather limited. Development by the Japanese in this field has lagged behind that of Allied nations. The number of occasions when Allied planes have reached their objective undetected would indicate that the use of radar is limited.

(3) Visual observers are extensively used to give warning. Outposts with the mission of reporting the movement of hostile planes are placed in advantageous positions. These outposts attempt to get as close as possible to points from which they can observe the movement of enemy planes from airfields. It must be expected that some of these groups will actually be within the enemy lines. Other observers are posted on high terrain features and on ships. They work in short tours of observation with frequent relief, and report plane movements by radio. Their equipment for observation is usually limited to binoculars. There are instances where the only

warning system employed consisted of the gun crew itself, acting as observers.

4. POSITIONS. a. Location. (1) Japanese antiaircraft companies observed are usually situated within a 1-mile radius around the area to be defended, with the greatest concentration of guns between the defended areas and the sea approaches thereto, along shore lines, and in the direction of enemy territory. Guns are mounted both in single positions and in batteries of from 2 to 12 guns. The distance between guns in both heavy and medium companies varies from 40 to 250 feet, with the majority of revetments between 50 and 110 feet apart. Machine guns usually are placed either within the group or a short distance from the group for protection against low flying aircraft.

(2) The only distinction between the locations of medium and heavy antiaircraft companies is that medium companies are rarely placed outside the 1-mile radius except along beaches. while some heavy companies may be as far as 4 miles from the defended area.

b. Arrangement. In general the arrangement of the positions is dependent on the number of guns involved and the terrain. When 3 guns are used, the position is usually in the form of a triangle, with 1 gun at each corner and the command post in the center. In the case of 4 guns, the shape of the position is usually rectangular. If more than 4 guns are employed, the position is normally in the shape of a shallow arc. Small caliber, automatic guns are normally employed nearby for close in protection from low flying planes. Where the terrain permits, some gun positions may be located on commanding ground, thus providing for all around traverse. Command posts vary in both number and location relative to the gun positions. They are usually located inside and near the mid-point of the battery pattern.

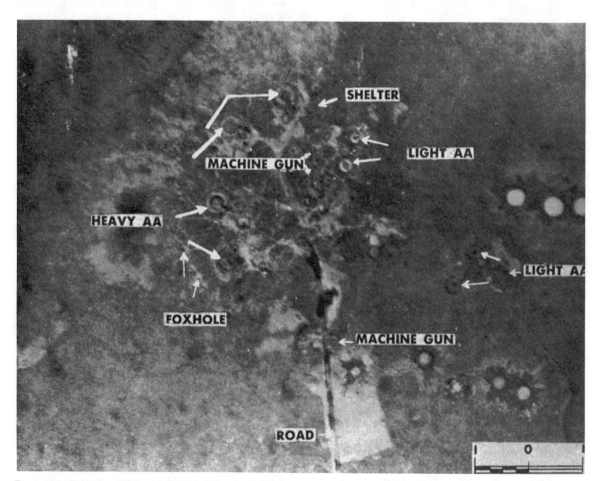

Figure 89. Four Gun Heavy Antiaircraft Battery (Emplacements Empty). Emplacements are built of earth over which grass has grown. Pattern is a shallow arc with fire control installations in center. A three-gun light antiaircraft and a two-gun light antiaircraft are also present. The large emplacements could house 75-mm or 105-mm guns. The small emplacements are probably for heavy machine gun or 13-mm antiaircraft.

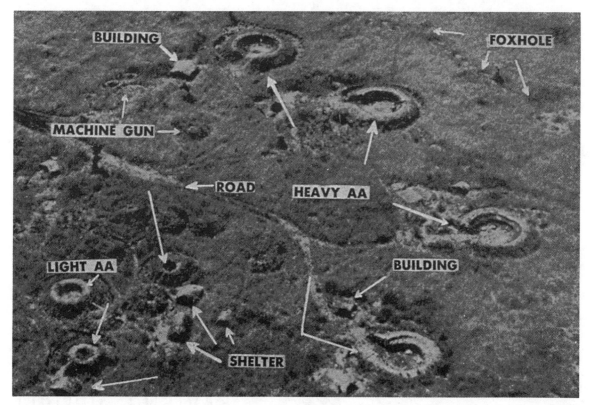

Figure 89. Continued.

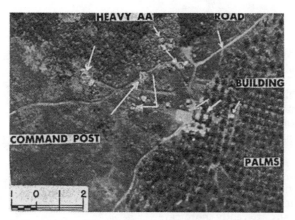

Figures 90, 91. Note the Rough Trapezoidal Pattern of this Four-Gun Heavy 75-mm Antiaircraft Battery. The command post is centrally located. This pattern is used most often at permanent, strongly established Japanese bases. The emplacements are shallow excavations with thick, strong revetments.

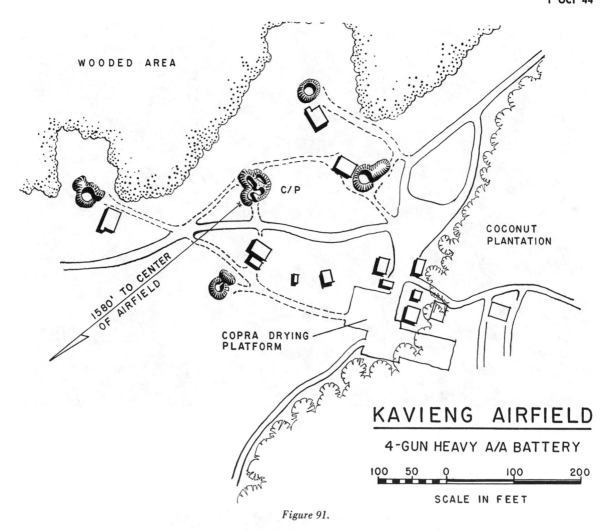

KAVIENG AIRFIELD

4-GUN HEAVY A/A BATTERY

100 50 0   100   200

SCALE IN FEET

Figure 91.

5. GUN EMPLACEMENTS. a. Standard type. The standard type of gun emplacement used almost exclusively is of circular or semi-circular construction, either level with the surface of the ground or slightly dug in. It is surrounded by a revetment built up of logs, coral, sand bags, and other materials to protect the gun and its crew. The opening usually is protected by a blast wall. A variation of this type of emplacement is constructed with two concentric circular revetments. (This type is commonly called the "doughnut.") The almost rigid adherence to these types of emplacements makes them readily identified from the air. Recently more care has been taken to conceal them by decreasing the slope of the revetment and planting it with natural growth so that shadows will not be so apparent.

b. Sizes. The caliber of the gun can be determined roughly from the size of the emplacement. Approximate sizes of emplacements for certain guns are listed below:

105-mm _____ Normally 25 feet in diameter.

75-mm mobile _____ Normally 20 feet in diameter.
75-mm static _____ Normally 15 feet in diameter.
Machine cannon _____ Normally 13–15 feet in diameter.
13-mm machine guns_ Normally 8 feet in diameter.

c. Camouflage. Little or no effort is made to camouflage or conceal the guns, but extensive use is made of dummy and alternate positions, even to the extent of constructing dummy guns.

6. EMPLOYMENT OF ANTIAIRCRAFT. a. General. It is normal to attach antiaircraft units to divisions. Their missions are the same as those assigned in Allied armies, but the division commander is given direct control over them.

b. All antiaircraft guns are dual purpose, most being capable of a minus depression; however, there is no evidence of armor-piercing ammunition for the larger caliber guns.

Figure 92.

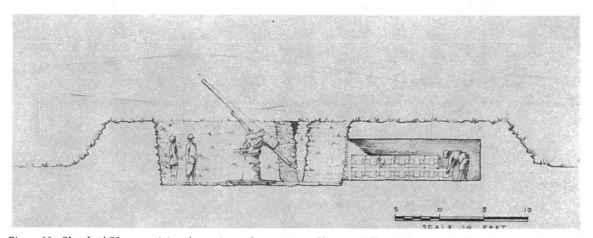

Figure 93. Sketch of 75-mm antiaircraft gun in earth revetment. Note partially excavated type of emplacement with high revetment and built-in Ready Magazine. Note also zigzag entrance trench.

c. Methods of fire. (1) All guns in a position frequently concentrate their fire on the leading plane of a formation and fire on succeeding planes if time permits.

(2) Colored spotting rounds often are used.

(3) Instances of accurate fire above the overcast indicate the probability of radio direction equipment.

(4) In areas where the ground is often blanketed with clouds, such as in the Aleutians, all guns direct their fire at the opening in the clouds where the enemy planes may normally be expected to appear.

(5) Barrage fire has been employed.

(6) In jungle country, the Japanese have shown an increased tendency to attack with light machine gun and rifle-fire against low flying aircraft. Such fire is encountered particularly along lines of communication, and its effectiveness should not be discounted.

Section VII. ANTITANK DEFENSE

1. GENERAL. a. Background. (1) The antitank methods adopted by the Japanese Army in antitank measures follow normal modern practice, except that the army as a whole is weak in antitank weapons. More thought, however, is given to the simpler forms of antitank defense, such as the use of antitank mines, incendiary grenades, gas grenades, obstacles, and the employment of special infantry assault squads (tank fighters).

(2) Experience in fighting Russian tanks at Nomonhan, Manchuria, in 1939 gave the Japanese Army an initial warning that more definite provisions must be made in its tactical organization for handling enemy tanks. As a result of much consideration of this problem, which was stimulated by the successful use of tanks by the Germany Army in the early days of the present war, a definite plan for resisting tank attacks was adopted. There is every indication that the Japanese have been studying and applying modern principles of antitank defense with the same careful attention which they devote to other tactical problems.

b. Exploitation of tank disadvantages. The Japanese envisage the inherent disadvantages of tank operations to be as given below, and their antitank instruction stresses taking every advantage of these conditions.

(1) Natural and artificial obstacles.

(2) Long tank columns which are difficult to camouflage.

(3) Adverse weather conditions which may prevail.

(4) Unfavorable working conditions and difficult observation which lower efficiency of crews.

c. Tank-hunting. Since the Japanese Army teachings lay a pronounced emphasis on coming into close contact with enemy tanks, it is well to draw attention to the fact that tank-hunting tactics are likely to be employed to a greater extent by the Japanese than by other armies. The reason for this is

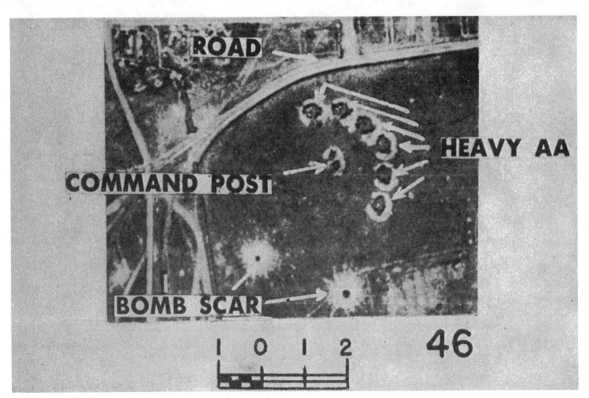

Figure 94. Six-Gun Heavy (105-mm) Antiaircraft Battery. Note shallow arc pattern with command post in center.

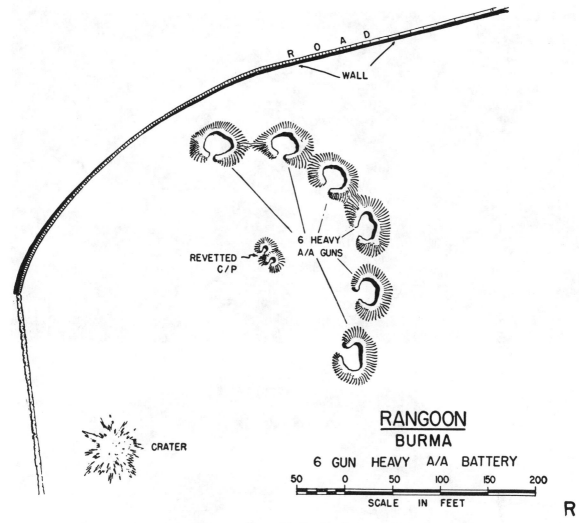

Figure 94. Continued.

three-fold: (1) it is another manifestation of the Japanese spirit of the bayonet—the hand-to-hand encounter, in which the individual is expected to triumph over material, even if armed only with grenades; (2) the Japanese appear to be short of modern anti-tank guns, and only by denying one front do they produce reasonably strong concentrations on another; and (3) most of the ground over which they have been fighting lends itself to a close assault.

2. ANTITANK WEAPONS AND ANTI-TANK UNITS. a. Weapons.
The Japanese Army generally has disliked single-purpose weapons. However, this dislike was abandoned from necessity, and early steps were taken to produce a 20-mm automatic antitank rifle which has been found with units in the field. It is carried by 4 men in combat, and transported on a cart or packed on 1 horse if not carried by hand. While the 37-mm gun is still retained in service and is used as a dual-purpose weapon, the 20-mm automatic antitank rifle is be-

lieved to be primarily used for antitank purposes. Other field and antiaircraft artillery weapons are considered suitable for use against tanks. A modern 47-mm gun, equipped with a high speed mount, has recently made its appearance. This weapon should have an effective antitank performance, while its low silhouette will aid in its concealment.

b. Nondivisional units. Nondivisional antitank units did not exist in the Japanese Army before the Nomonhan incident, but as a result of experiences in fighting Russian tanks, these independent antitank units were formed for attachment to divisions when necessary.

3. PASSIVE DEFENSE MEASURES.
Concealment, camouflage, obstacles, reconnaissance, and warning nets are considered essential.

4. ACTIVE MEASURES.
These include—
a. Action by antitank guns, accompanying guns, and mortars.

Figure 95. New Type Double Revetment (Nusa Island battery across Wavieng channel), showing detail of construction.

b. Bullet splash from machine guns and rifles at a short range (at least one squad firing at each tank).

c. Mines.

d. Tank fighters. These comprise men with special training and equipment for direct assault on tanks.

e. Tanks.

5. ANTITANK TACTICS. a. Mines. A cheap method of passive defense against tanks is by the use of tank mines. In an exercise involving an infantry division, 12,000 mines were laid by all units of the division. Where enemy units are known to have tanks, the laying of tank mines is considered the most essential duty of the division engineer regiment. The mines are placed in a conventional manner covering the logical routes' of tank approach. Bridges in defensive areas are habitually mined, and any bridge which has been in Japanese hands must be carefully examined for the presence of contact mines before a tank unit is allowed to cross. Tank barricades have all possible detours heavily mined, and it is common practice to lay a few mines under temporary barricades with the idea that if the enemy removes the barricade, he will not suspect that mines have been laid in the ground underneath.

b. Tactics. A Japanese military term applying to antitank defense is "dansei bogyo," which is translated as "an elastic defense" and is highly descriptive of their entire theory of antitank defense. Briefly, this method of combat does not provide for strong resistance to tank attacks along front lines. Not more than 20% of available heavy infantry weapons are employed against a tank attack from front-line positions. On the approach of a tank attack all units, with the exception of one squad per platoon, fall back to positions from 800 to 1500 yards in the rear. The squad from each front-line platoon left in position scatters widely and, under cover of smoke laid down by the use of the grenade discharger, attacks the tanks with incendiary grenades as they come through the smoke. It is contemplated that this initial stage of the fight will scatter the enemy tanks, reduce control, and cause some casualties. If the tanks overcome the resistance of the front-line detachments they come under fire from the main strength of all available weapons of the infantry. While this and the front-line combat have been going on, some of the division artillery moves forward to positions from which it can fire with direct laying. If the heavy weapons of the infantry are unable to stop the attack, the main infantry strength, using smoke and incendiary grenades, makes a direct attack, relying on the artillery to their immediate rear to handle any tanks that get through. The main feature of this defense, as stated by provisional regulations, is that once an attack is stopped the enemy is pinched off, and by the operation of scattered units can be destroyed with grenades or any available weapons; and the infantry, although scattered, still can offer successful opposition to enemy infantry attempting to exploit the advance of the tank units.

c. Estimate. While it may appear that the Japanese Army will offer but weak resistance against a tank attack because of the nonavailability of modern weapons in sufficient numbers, this assumption should not lead to the belief that strong and suicidal resistance by individuals will not be offered.

6. DETAILED METHODS OF ATTACKING A TANK. a. Choice of ground.
When employing tank-fighters, it is desirable to choose ground where tanks must travel slowly and where the attack does not interfere with the action of antitank guns.

b. Special troops. Each rifle company (sometimes machine-gun and heavy-weapon companies organize similar detachments) trains certain individuals as tank-fighters, and these are specially equipped for such action. Each man is armed with antitank mines and smoke hand grenades.

c. Methods. Three ways of attacking tanks are:
(1) The tank-fighter crawls toward the tank under cover, until he is within the dead space of the tank weapons. Next, he throws the mine, attached to a long string, about 15 feet in front of the tank and, by means of the string, pulls it directly under the tank.

(2) Several pairs of tank fighters move forward under cover and place a number of mines in front of the tank in such a manner that the tank must drive over one of them.

(3) A number of mines are fastened, 1 foot apart, to a 150-foot line. Two men conceal themselves with this chain of mines and draw the mines across the path of the tank as it approaches.

The tank-fighter is also taught to attack the tank by jumping on top, usually from the rear, and damaging the guns or rotating mechanism of the turret with picks. The pistol may be used to fire on the crew through openings in the tank. Another method is to blind the tank crew by throwing a shelter-half over the turret, covering the slits with mud, or "smoking it out." Naturally, all these forms of assault are feasible only if the friendly infantry can neutralize the hostile infantry accompanying the tanks. Tanks have been delayed, and finally stopped, by driving 3-inch wooden poles or 1- to 1½-inch rods between the spokes of its wheels. Magnetized armor-piercing mines are also used at times.

7. EMPLOYMENT OF ANTITANK WEAPONS. a. Allotment.
In country that is suitable for the operation of tanks a company of Japanese infantry may be found to be supported by from 2 to 6 antitank guns (37-mm or 47-mm). The infantry regimental antitank guns either may be allotted to forward battalions or, on rare occasions, held in reserve under regimental control. The 20-mm antitank, automatic rifle is described by the Japanese Infantry as "delivering antitank fire at short range and engaging the enemy's foremost heavy weapons." If there is any danger of a night attack by tanks, the 20-mm weapon may be posted forward of the main line of resistance and supported by tank hunting detachments.

b. Siting. The bulk of the antitank guns allotted to a position are sited as far forward as possible. Great stress is laid on siting guns in concealed positions and camouflaging them. To quote from Japanese regulations, "positions are to be selected at well covered points near the front line." Experience has shown that once dug in, these weapons are difficult to locate. It is likely that an antitank gun will sometimes be sited in very thick cover, with a small fire-tunnel cut out to enable it to cover a trail or other likely area for tank approach. The Japanese have sited machine guns in this way, and the practice well may be applied to antitank guns. Guns also may be sited on steep ridges or rocky slopes, from which positions they can fire at hostile tanks while themselves remaining inaccessible. Alternative positions are prepared, the regulations stressing that "it is advisable to move the gun from place to place thus avoiding casualties from enemy fire." In action the fire unit is generally the individual gun (a section), and the gun commander chooses suitable targets and directs fire upon them. While most of the guns are sited in foremost defended localities, a few are held in the depth of the position with the apparent task of dealing with penetration of enemy tanks. In the event of such penetration, infantry regimental guns, as well as field artillery weapons, also will engage the hostile armored vehicles. The fire plan of the infantry weapons is coordinated with that of the antitank unit. Except for reserves—if any—all guns are sited to cover the most likely lines of approach of enemy tanks. They are also sited to cover obstacles. An infantry platoon often is disposed on the route of approach in advance of the main position, but within range of artillery support from it. This platoon may have an antitank gun attached to it.

8. EXAMPLES OF POSITIONS. a. Natural and artificial obstacles combined. The position illustrated in figure 96 was prepared by the Japanese near Akyab, Burma. It provides an interesting example of an all-round tank obstacle, partly natural and partly constructed. A ditch, approximately 14 feet wide and 7 feet deep was dug as shown. Dirt, thrown out on both sides formed a small parapet, while water filled the ditch. The trench system dug near the ditch included 7 covered positions, each measuring 45 by 30 feet.

b. A plan for antitank defense. In figure 97 there is shown a Japanese plan for antitank defense of an area in Burma. The following troops and guns were allotted to the position:

(1) *Area No. 1* was to be garrisoned by 1 company of infantry, reinforced with half a company of heavy machine guns (4 guns), 2 antitank guns, and 4 infantry (mtn) guns (75-mm).

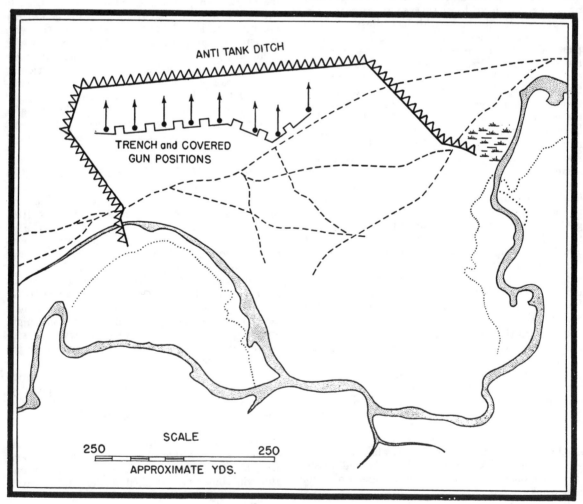

Figure 96. Antitank defense position.

(2) *Area No. 2* was allotted 1 infantry company with half a company of heavy machine guns (4 guns), 5 antitank guns and 4 infantry (mtn) guns (75-mm).

(3) *Area No. 3* was assigned 1 company of infantry, and 2 Mountain (inf) guns (75-mm).

(4) *Area No. 4* was defended by 1 company of infantry, one half of a heavy machine gun company

(4 guns), 4 antitank guns and 2 Mountain (inf) guns (75-mm).

(5) *Area No. 5* was allocated 1 platoon of infantry and 1 heavy machine gun platoon (2 guns).

(6) *Area No. 6* was assigned 1 platoon of infantry and 4 antitank guns.

c. Obstacles. At Butaritari Island, Makin Atoll, the Japanese dug deep antitank ditches outside of

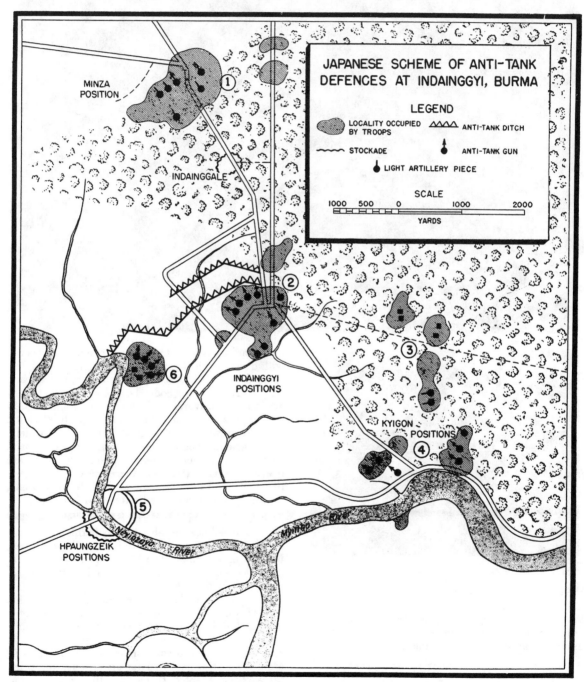

Figure 97. Japanese Plan for Antitank Defense.

Figures 98, 99. Antitank obstacles.

their main defenses at the tank traps, with winding narrow roads leading into the outer edges. (Fig. 98.) The crossings were covered from antitank gun pits and machine gun nests. Palm logs served as a tank barricade near one tank trap. (Fig. 99.)

Section VIII. JUNGLE WARFARE
A. GENERAL

1. TERRAIN. Jungle warfare, as referred to in this manual, is warfare in the larger island and mainland areas which to a great extent are covered with dense tropical jungle. These jungles are interspersed with open, grass (kunai) covered areas, and frequently, along the coast, large coconut plantations are under cultivation. Swamps are numerous in the lower areas, and streams rise rapidly after the heavy tropical rains. The terrain differs widely, but in general it is rugged, except along the coastal strips. The principal means of communication are over native trails (tracks) ; there are very few roads that will stand up under the load of military traffic. Visibility in the jungle is limited to a few yards.

2. EARLY JAPANESE SUCCESSES. The tactical principles and illustrations in this section are based on operations in the Solomons, New Guinea, Malaya, and Burma. The Japanese enjoyed remarkable success during the Malaya and Burma operations and during the early phase of the New Guinea campaign. They had trained extensively for this type of warfare; their known lack of modern motor transport did not hinder them, and their reliance on commandeered local supplies and equipment materially helped to solve their supply problems in Malaya and Burma. In later operations, the Allied forces have adapted themselves to jungle combat from the standpoint of organization, training, and equipment, and have shattered the myth of the invincibility of the Japanese in this type of warfare.

The principle that the advantage lies with the side which holds the initiative applies in jungle warfare as well as in other types.

B. OFFENSIVE

1. GENERAL CONSIDERATIONS OF OFFENSIVE COMBAT. a. Reconnaissance. Reconnaissance is recognized as essential, and great stress is placed on it. Preliminary map reconnaissance and study of aerial photographs are normal, and the employment of advance agents and fifth columnists is standard practice. Reconnaissance patrols are used extensively; they are well trained in sketching, and their composition and equipment are planned in considerable detail. A variety of ruses is employed in accomplishing their reconnaissance mission. They frequently engage in small-scale combat and purposely expose themselves to determine the location of hostile automatic weapons.

b. Security. Security in the advance is accomplished through the normal use of advance guards, rearguards, and flank patrols. In the jungle, the activities of flank patrols are of course limited. The Japanese are not especially security-minded, particularly in bivouac areas, and leave their lines of communication and headquarters installations relatively unprotected. Their theory is that by pressing a vigorous offensive the enemy will be kept on the defensive and have little opportunity to do much damage on the flanks and rear.

c. Surprise. Surprise is a cardinal principle of all Japanese action. It is accomplished through rapidity of advance, deception of all kinds, and infiltration and demonstrations in the enemy rear; in short, all means available are utilized, and speed is greatly emphasized.

d. Fire and movement. The standard principles of fire and movement are observed. The fire generally is placed in the area of the holding attack, while the main effort maneuvers silently. Preparatory fires seldom are used; the common method of attack is to attempt to approach within assaulting distance of the objective unseen by the enemy.

e. Mutual support. Mutual support by and contact between adjacent units are poor by accepted standards. Advance guards of parallel columns are not coordinated and generally do not maintain contact with each other. Frequently, in attack orders, each unit is given an objective and a direction, but the details of lateral communication and coordination are not covered. This is especially true in the case of infiltration, where units, and even individuals, work their way through hostile lines and rendezvous at some predetermined point.

f. Tenacity. The Japanese will hold tenaciously to the advantages gained through offensive action. They teach that the assault must immediately be followed up by pursuit, but in the later phases of their offensive campaigns this doctrine has not always been carried out. If their attack is retarded, they will hold what they have gained and will use

other units, which they have kept in reserve, to maneuver and put pressure on the flank or rear of the enemy.

g. Pattern of offensive. Japanese offensive action seems to follow a definite pattern, and in many instances is drill-like in its execution. Orders are brief and to the point. Supply and administrative details are almost ignored. Simplicity is gained at the expense of general coordination, emphasizing the Japanese belief that the infantry can gain its objective solely by vigorous offensive action.

h. Faults. There is a notable tendency toward disorganization when a commander becomes a casualty, although recently emphasis has been placed on correcting this deficiency. Unity of command tends to break down in larger attacks because of lack of coordination between units.

i. Reserves. Japanese units of all sizes habitually hold reserves. These vary in strength, depending on the situation and the mission, but in general they approximate one third of the infantry strength.

j. Maintenance of direction. Maintenance of direction in the jungle is extremely difficult. Roads are practically non-existent, and trails seldom run in the right direction. Also, since visibility is limited, it is impossible to march on terrain features. Reliance therefore is placed on the compass, and advance and guide parties habitually are equipped with this instrument. Routes are selected by these parties, and marking is accomplished by blazing trees or stringing long vines. For night marches, luminous wood is used.

2. FORMS OF ATTACK. a. Tactical forms of attack. The main attack is normally an envelopment of one or both flanks, or a penetration. Frontal attacks are not recommended and, when they are made, the aim is generally a point penetration, which may be followed by an envelopment on one or both sides of the breach. The secondary attack is normal and usually frontal. Generally it takes the form of a demonstration, accompanied by obvious movements and noise, and is used to cover the movements of the main effort.

b. Envelopment. Envelopment is the most usual form of Japanese attack. It has been said by the Japanese that the perfect solution to a tactical problem is a neatly performed stratagem, followed by an encirclement or a flanking attack pushed home with the bayonet. The envelopment may be of one or both flanks, and although the wide envelopment is taught, in general practice the close-in envelopment is customary.

c. Point pentration. The point penetration frequently is employed. It invariably is directed against a soft spot that has been discovered by patrol activity and reconnaissance, or created by night action against heavy weapons that have disclosed their location by premature firing as a result of Japanese deceptive measures. Since their tactical doctrine states that once an advantage has been gained, it must be exploited to the fullest, it can be expected that the main strength of the Japanese attack will be directed against this point.

3. DEVELOPMENT OF OFFENSIVE COMBAT.

The advance and approach march differ from that in open warfare because of the close nature of the terrain, where troops more often are restricted to one route of advance. In dense jungle it is not feasible to break down into small columns and extend in width because separate tracks would have to be cut for each column—a slow and tiring process. The usual formation is an advance in one column, with elements in the rear echelon available for maneuver to either flank. Rapidity in the advance is essential and is limited only by the rate of march of the heavy weapons elements.

4. CONDUCT OF THE ATTACK.

a. Meeting engagements. There have been few clear-cut examples of meeting engagements except in the early stages of the war, and then in fairly open jungle. The advance guard, upon contacting the enemy, promptly notifies the elements in rear and attempts to knock out the opposition. If this does not seem readily possible, the advance guard, by use of ruses, attempts to make it appear as though it is deploying for battle. At that point it seeks out the flanks of the enemy and attempts to locate his heavy weapons. In the meantime, the main body moves to one or both flanks and advances as rapidly as possible with the intention of striking deep in flank or rear. If the hostile force presses the attack against the advance guard, it disperses to the flank and joins the main body.

b. Against deployed defense. Two methods of attack commonly are used against a deployed defense. First, an attempt is made by maneuver to strike the enemy in flank or rear; the actions are similar to those described for meeting engagements. That is, a demonstration is made on the front, using much noise, movement, and promiscuous firing to simulate strength, while the main force moves silently to a flank to make the envelopment. The second method is to feel out the front for soft spots. By use of ruses and deceptive tactics an attempt is made to locate automatic-weapons positions. When these are located, a heavy concentration of mortar fire is brought down so that troops may reach assaulting distance without being discovered. The assault is made, usually on a narrow front, and if the objective is not attained at once, succeeding waves follow through in an effort to overwhelm the enemy. The objective generally is set deep in enemy territory, and the assault attempts to carry straight through to it, leaving for succeeding elements the job of mopping up and, if necessary, consolidating. Intermediate objectives seldom are designated in the case of daylight attack.

c. Against position (static) defense. Tactical principles employed in an attack against a position defense in the jungle do not materially differ from those already discussed in open warfare.

The difficulties of supply, communication, and control are great, and as a result there have been few successful coordinated attacks. Attempts frequently are made to attack a position at several points simultaneously, but most of these have resulted in piecemeal attacks. The Japanese belief in the inherent superiority of their infantry often leads them to attack without adequate artillery support, although their tactical doctrine calls for the neutralization of hostile artillery fire before attacking a position. This has seldom been accomplished, and, against the fire power of modern weapons, such an attack is usually disastrous. As in other types of attack, extensive use is made of demonstrations and other ruses to mislead the enemy into committing his reserves, as well as to discover the location of automatic-weapons and security detachments. If the position is entered, the leading elements will continue on through, not waiting to consolidate their gains until they have reached their objective or until they have been definitely stopped. Attacks on important positions often are rehearsed beforehand.

5. PLANS OF ATTACK.

The plan of attack is thought out carefully by the commander and his staff, but many details, normally considered necessary by other armies, are omitted when the actual order is issued. The disposition of troops is not covered in detail, and boundaries are seldom given, for commanders depend on the training of their subordinates for the detailed conduct of the attack. By accepted standards, the directions issued to the artillery and other supporting arms are generally vague. Supply and administrative details as well as signal communication instructions are covered superficially. Emphasis is placed on the utilization of captured supplies and weapons, and a study of enemy weapons is included in Japanese training. Rapidity of the advance and vigorous attack are counted upon to overwhelm the enemy, and reliance is placed on the ability of the Japanese soldier to live off the land, fight with the bayonet, and withstand hardship until the objective is taken. It is evident that the Japanese Army is expected to be so well trained that detailed orders are unnecessary.

6. SUPPORTING FIRES OF INFANTRY WEAPONS.

a. Machine guns. Machine guns normally are employed in pairs and are placed well forward to support front-line infantry. They go into position under cover, and advance preparations are made so that, by opening fire accurately and with surprise effect, fire superiority over the enemy may be quickly gained. Positions are selected with a view to advancing as the attack progresses. Forward movement to new positions may be by individual gun, or by pairs, depending on the terrain and the situation, but preference is shown for the latter. It is normal for the guns of the platoon to fire on the same target. Emphasis is placed on close cooperation with front-line infantry, but the guns are not used as a base of fire to the extent practiced by the U. S. Army.

b. Antitank guns. Antitank guns have a primary antitank mission, but in the absence of tank targets they fire on infantry. They are placed in position well to the front and go forward with the advance of front-line infantry.

c. Battalion and regimental guns. Battalion and regimental guns are assigned the primary mission of neutralizing the enemy's heavy guns and machine guns. They are located well forward and are prepared to move ahead to new positions with the infantry. They, too, are put in position under cover and seek surprise in opening fire. They are prepared to carry out indirect fire in missions, and, as in the case of antitank guns and machine guns, are directed to give close support to the front-line infantry.

d. Long-range fire. Although long-range fire of heavy infantry weapons is discussed in training manuals, it is seldom practiced. The bulk of the supporting weapons are placed well forward, and depend for the accomplishment of their mission on a heavy volume of fire accurately delivered with surprise effect.

7. SPECIAL OFFENSIVE OPERATIONS.

a. Raids. Raids are extensively carried out for the purpose of harassing the enemy rear, striking at command posts, destroying artillery units, and penetrating defenses. The parties making these raids are highly organized and trained. Their composition and equipment depend on the mission. (See Chap. V.) Frequently the mission is a suicidal one and these parties will go to extremes in accomplishing it.

b. Night operations. The Japanese favor the night attack. Such attack is generally made on a narrow front and has a limited, well-defined objective. Where possible the Japanese attack uphill. This prevents their being silhouetted on the skyline, and the hill itself helps them to maintain direction. Night attacks are often accompanied by excessive use of signal flares, and, usually, a demonstration is carried out at some distance from the actual point of attack. An effort is made silently to destroy known heavy weapons positions just prior to the assault. The advance to the assault often is made with great secrecy and stealth. All supporting weapons may be used in the night attack.

C. DEFENSIVE

1. GENERAL.
The Japanese dislike of the defensive is evident throughout all of their teachings. It is regarded as a negative form of combat and one to be especially avoided in view of the heavy fire power it permits a modern army to build up against them. Their system of defense therefore is based on surprise, maneuver, and counterattack.

2. SELECTION AND OCCUPATION OF POSITION. a. General.
The Japanese concept of selection and occupation of positions is normal.

They defend high ground generally, although in view of the advantages of concealment in the valleys, on occasion they have strongly organized these low areas for defense. There is no such thing as a normal frontage for units in the jungle; generally the terrain is so close that small units can defend the limited avenues of approach. The Japanese habitually establish an outpost line of resistance, but this frequently consists of only a few snipers and observers, well forward on the trail in front of the position. The mission of this personnel is to warn its main position of the approach of the enemy, and to slow their approach by harassing tactics. The snipers may withdraw when the pressure becomes great, but it is not unusual for them to let forward elements of the enemy pass through and then to accomplish their mission by firing on his rear and by disrupting lines of communication.

b. Artillery. (1) There has not been sufficient use of artillery in the defense to enable conclusions to be drawn as to its normal method of employment. However, certain comments made by Japanese officers may be helpful in this connection. It was recommended that they site their guns on the flanks of the infantry, thus permitting fire to be brought to within a few yards of their own front lines without endangering their own troops. This method of siting also would help to overcome the difficulty of knowing just where the front lines were.

(*a*) Deceptive measures were stressed for the purpose of drawing hostile fire. Two methods mentioned were the construction of dummy positions and the lighting of fires, both at a distance from the positions actually occupied.

(*b*) It also was recommended that artillery fire be withheld until the enemy comes within close range, since this will result in more effective fire and will not disclose the artillery positions prematurely.

(2) Considerable emphasis is placed on the infantry guns, but these have been effective only for harassing missions.

(3) Small raiding parties have been used successfully to raid and destroy artillery positions. It is believed that the Japanese may regard this as a substitute for counter-battery.

3. ORGANIZATION OF THE GROUND.
a. General. Defensive organization of the ground is very thorough. It consists of a series of strong points, organized in depth and mutually supporting, each one covered from the flanks and rear by riflemen in fox holes and in trees. The position normally is organized for all-around defense. Once the position or area to be defended has been selected, the commander plans his "fire-net" or locates the positions and sectors of fire for his automatic weapons. Riflemen are disposed around these weapons, and the preparation of earthworks is commenced without delay. When the terrain permits, caves are utilized for the location of both automatic weapons and riflemen. Machine guns are recognized as the backbone of the defense and are sited both singly

and in groups. Normally, they are given only a final protective mission; their sectors of fire are extremely limited and generally close in front of the position. Lanes of fire for these guns are cut by tunneling through the underbrush, thus making it extremely difficult to locate them, but at the same time restricting their field of fire. Long range machine gun fire is not practical in the jungle. The guns are usually sited for cross fire. They may also be sited in ravines to deny this route of approach to the enemy, and on reverse slopes to catch troops as they come over the crest. Extensive use is made of alternate and dummy positions, and weapons are frequently moved from one position to another. Training publications indicate a knowledge of the use of barbed wire, but very little employment of it has been made in the jungle. This may be due to the difficulties of supply, since instances have been recorded of the use of thorny vines, interlaced to hinder the advance of the enemy.

b. Progressive improvement of position. Organization of the ground is progressive and continuous, and the longer a position is occupied, the better it will be dug in. Starting with only "fox holes," (rifle pits), the position ultimately will have a pillbox or "bunker" for the heavy weapons, constructed out of earth, palm logs and coral, or other local materials. These fortifications are improved as time permits until they are safe from practically anything except a direct hit by a large delayed-action shell or bomb. They are provided with several firing ports, and the earth is so arranged around them as to minimize dead space. Where the height of the water table will not permit these earthworks to be dug well into the ground, they are built up, sometimes to a height of six feet. Separate bomb-proof shelters are constructed as living quarters for personnel. Fox holes of supporting riflemen and alternate positions are connected by shallow communication trenches. No concrete or steel has been used to date in the construction of jungle pillboxes, reliance being well placed on local materials. Palm logs and coral do not splinter and will absorb a lot of punishment. Pillboxes and personnel shelters usually are constructed with a blast wall, or with the entrance at an angle to the main structure, so that grenades or shell bursts nearby will not affect the occupants. (See Defense Structures Sec. X.)

c. Concealment. Excellent fire discipline and lack of movement within the position, combined with good camouflage, are so effective that there is often doubt that the position is even occupied. Use has been made of dummy positions manned by dummy personnel in an effort to draw attackers' fire. The Japanese have made full use of the lush and rapid growth of jungle plants to conceal positions. When bunkers are used, the earth is built up with a slight gradient so as to avoid shadow and to present a natural appearance.

4. CONDUCT OF THE DEFENSE. a. Action of outposts. Individual snipers and small groups of infantry well to the front alert the main position upon the approach of hostile forces. Then they may either withdraw or remain concealed to harass the enemy during his approach. As reconnaissance or small advance parties approach the position, they are taken under fire by individual riflemen located on the flanks and in trees. Should the enemy scouts approach too closely to any of the pillboxes, they are fired upon by the covering riflemen. The automatic weapons do not fire at this early stage, and extreme care is taken not to disclose their location.

b. Action at main position. Surprise in the defense is regarded as vitally important and is achieved by withholding fire until the enemy is close on the position. A training manual states, "make preparations to be able to fire effectively, but it is important not to suffer losses by firing too quickly and exposing your position." Often fire is not opened until the enemy has approached to within ten yards of the position, and his mortar and artillery fire has lifted. If the position is attacked by a large force, the firing must begin at least when it is outside of grenade throwing distance (i. e. approximately 50 yards). Not until the enemy in force enters the lanes of fire do the automatic weapons open up, and when they do, their mission is to annihilate the enemy before he enters the position. A heavy volume of fire is delivered at close range, and this is supplemented by the use of grenade dischargers and mortars from positions located in rear of the front line. Frequently, certain gun positions that are not threatened remain silent during this initial phase, only to open fire later with surprise effect. In dense jungle, observers in trees may be used to signal the automatic gunners when to open fire, since the concealment of the pillboxes limits visibility. Even though one or more pillboxes are neutralized, remaining automatic weapons will maintain their fire to assist counterattacking troops. Garrisons are imbued with the idea that they must fight to the last man; consequently, pillboxes can be expected to hold out as long as there is an armed man left to defend them.

c. Counterattack. Counterattack is a vital part of Japanese defense. It is an offensive action, and in the mind of the soldier makes up for the "inglorious" defense he has been forced to adopt. Every unit has a counterattacking force. The counterattack is violent, and timed to strike before the enemy has had an opportunity to reorganize or consolidate. It frequently is preceded by a heavy concentration of mortar fire and is always supported by all available riflemen and automatic weapons. It differs from the normal in that it is seldom coordinated with other units, and the possibility of its failure is not considered. Since units of all sizes counterattack, the force often consists of as few as 8 or 10 men led by an officer or a noncommissioned officer. However, as the attack progresses through the position, larger counterattacks may be expected from the reserves of higher units. Because of the difficulties of movement through the jungle, these counterattacks are usually local. As a variation of the counterattack, mortar and artillery concentrations are plotted on the positions and can be promptly laid down if the enemy occupies them or attempts to reorganize near them. These concentrations have been known to make a captured position untenable by fire alone. In the case of positions that have been well built, mortar fire may safely be brought down on the position even though Japanese troops still occupy it.

5. AMBUSHES AND ROAD BLOCKS. a. Ambushes. The jungle offers many ideal opportunities for ambush which the Japanese have exploited, and they have been trained well in this type of operation. The size, composition, and armament of the force depend on the mission. No new principles are involved.

b. Road blocks. Due to the paucity of roads, road blocks are especially effective in slowing up the movement of road-bound equipment. One method is to place a block across the road, just around a bend. The party defending the block is disposed on either side of the road, and an antitank gun, or a larger caliber weapon is located in prolongation of the road, before the bend. These weapons are emplaced close to the block and are fired at point blank range. (See fig. 100.)

The Japanese have established road blocks in rear of the enemy, along his route of withdrawal. An enveloping force or raiding party is generally charged with this mission, which is very effective in disrupting the movements of the enemy at a critical time.

6. ANTITANK DEFENSE. a. General. The employment of tanks in the jungle has been rather limited, and the standard methods of defense, such as tank ditches and mine fields covered by antitank guns, are used. Antitank mines are sometimes augmented by an additional charge of explosive. Small antitank mine fields were laid in Guadalcanal in defiles to retard the American advance, but were not very effective. Anti-mines also were employed on roads in New Guinea.

b. Methods. The close nature of jungle terrain permits close-quarter attack. Special antitank defense parties are organized within lower units and

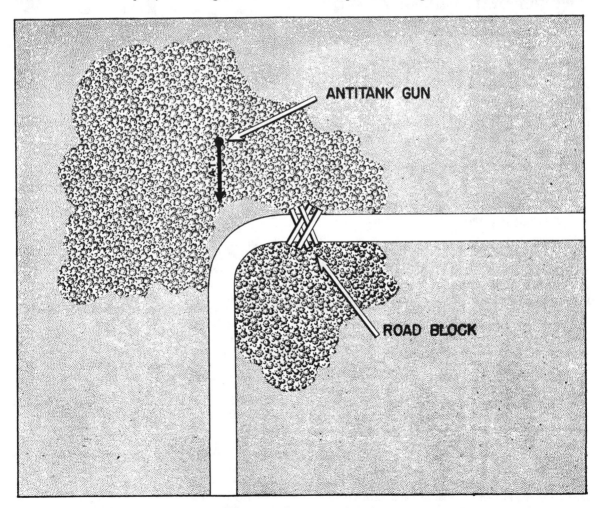

Figure 100. Japanese road block.

trained in the technique of destroying hostile tanks. Some of their methods are as follows:

(1) When the advance of tanks is canalized, or can be anticipated, antitank mines are fastened to a long cord or vine. Two men conceal themselves on opposite sides of the route to be taken by the tank. As the tank passes between them, they quickly draw the antitank mine in front of the vehicle. Following the explosion, they attack the tank with Molotov Cocktails and small-arms fire directed at the ports.

(2) Different methods are employed to blind the tank, such as throwing paper bags of mud and lime at the ports or covering them with a blanket or shelter-half. When the tank is blinded, explosive charges are applied.

(3) Grenades or other explosive charges, fastened to a pole, are pushed into the tracks or under the treads.

(4) Magnetic mines are placed on the body of the tank where armor is most vulnerable.

7. ANTIAIRCRAFT DEFENSE. (See sec. VI.)

8. WITHDRAWAL.
Withdrawal, like defense, is contrary to the Japanese concept of war. Little attention is devoted to it in their texts and training, and reference to it is made as "retreat combat." Lack of medium artillery properly to cover a withdrawal, and the difficulties of long range machine gun fire in the jungle, often result in the sacrifice of the covering force. A training manual states: "During retreat, machine guns do not think of loss, but sacrifice themselves for the army by firing fiercely against strong pressure of the enemy or against the enemy which is of greatest danger to the first-line infantry. They must make the withdrawal of friendly troops easy. Allow no enemy advantage." Mines and booby traps are used to a limited extent. In the case of night withdrawals, snipers are left behind to harass and delay the enemy.

D. MISCELLANEOUS

1. EMPLOYMENT OF TANKS AND MECHANIZED UNITS.
Tanks and mechanized units have been employed to such a limited extent that no new tactical principles have been observed. Successful use of medium tanks in jungle terrain by Allied forces undoubtedly will point the way toward their use by the Japanese.

2. EMPLOYMENT OF AIRCRAFT.
The density of the jungle makes it difficult for air observers to see small troop movements and installations that are properly dispersed. Air observation is used, however, to locate new tracks being prepared for large troop movements. Close support of ground troops by air is difficult, because ground troops generally cannot accurately indicate their location. The Japanese have used aircraft to bomb rear areas and known installations and have supplied ground units by parachute drop.

3. COMMENTS.
The Japanese have made certain comments on Allied combat methods, some of which are reproduced because they indicate their trend of thought in improving their technique:

a. The Australians and Americans are better trained and equipped than their "former enemies."

b. When making frontal attacks, it is essential to neutralize Allied fire power.

c. The enemy (Allies) have great fire power. On defense they try to annihilate us before we enter their position. Sometimes they withdraw gradually and then bring heavy concentrations of artillery and mortar fire on us. It is essential to keep close on their heels; breaking through the heavy concentration of fire in front of the enemy's position is difficult, but once through it the attack becomes unexpectedly easy.

d. Plan to split the Allied advance through the use of artillery and machine guns, and counterattack to destroy the divided groups.

e. Allied artillery is accurate. Positions constructed of coconut logs will stand up under mortar and light artillery fire, but will be destroyed by delay-fused shells and "rapid fire guns."

f. Allied troops make good use of the correct approach and do not open the attack except at extremely short range. Therefore, the Japanese should clear lanes of fire for about 50 yards in front of their position.

g. The Allied troops take limited objectives then halt to reorganize before continuing the attack.

h. The Japanese are cautioned against replying to the fire of patrols as this discloses their gun positions.

i. The Allies attempt to hold frontally and envelope; the Japanese are advised to "envelope the envelopment."

j. Infiltration is regarded as easy, because Allied outposts are not located at regular intervals and are often far apart.

k. Allied outposts can be located by searching out the wire communications leading into them.

l. Australians are excellent guerrilla fighters.

m. When two patrols meet unexpectedly, the Japanese think that a few rifle shots or bursts from a light machine gun will rout the enemy.

n. Troops are instructed to concentrate on the personnel carrying automatic weapons as these are regarded as leaders.

o. Dawn and dusk, especially during rain, are considered by the Japanese as the best times for launching attacks because the enemy have tents over their trenches and are not alert.

4. RUSES. a. Description.
The employment of ruses of all kinds by the Japanese cannot be overemphasized as these play a very important part in their operations. The variety of ruses that may be used is limited only by the imagination of the Japanese commanders. A few of those encountered to date are described below:

(1) Lighted cigarettes, firecrackers, moving vehicles, and barking dogs were used opposite one of

the beaches on Singapore Island to lead the defenders to believe that the main attack would be made at that point.

(2) English speaking Japanese have called out commands in English in order to confuse their enemies.

(3) They have listened for the names of certain individuals and later called out to them by name. When the person addressed showed himself he was shot.

(4) Booby traps have been fastened to dead soldiers, fused to detonate when the body is moved.

(5) They have placed a dead Allied soldier in a conspicuous place and sited an automatic weapon to cover it. Thus, when Allied troops attempted to remove the body, they were shot.

(6) Even when badly wounded, or apparently dead, they have produced hand grenades from their clothing and attempted to kill medical personnel who would aid them.

(7) They have used the white flag of truce to get close to their enemy for combat purposes.

(8) They use firecrackers to simulate machine gun fire.

(9) They will expose themselves deliberately in an attempt to get their enemy to fire and thus disclose the location of his positions.

(10) In one case, a wave of Japanese skirmishers turned and fled. The Allied troops pursued and suddenly the retreating Japanese threw themselves on the ground. At this moment, heavy machine gun fire opened up on the Allied troops from the Japanese rear.

(11) They shake the bushes by ropes or other means in order to draw hostile fire and so locate gun positions.

E. COMMENTS

1. Tactical principles in the jungle do not differ materially from those employed in open warfare. The technique or application of these principles, however, does vary, and the Japanese have taken advantage of this.

2. The Japanese use deceptive measures extensively and may be depended on to use ruses of all types to harass and deceive their enemy.

3. They stress the principle of surprise and employ it in the defense as well as in the offense. They do not disclose the location of their heavy weapons prematurely.

4. There is no such thing as impassable terrain, even in the jungle.

5. Japanese operations thus far have been characterized by inadequate artillery support, except in Malaya and the Philippines.

6. Speed is another cardinal tactical principle of the Japanese. They attempt to achieve surprise through rapidity of movement.

7. They take full advantage of natural cover and concealment, and thoroughly understand the importance of camouflage.

8. They believe strongly in the inherent advantages of vigorous offensive action, and often attack prematurely.

9. They have not made full use of supporting artillery.

10. Their organization of the ground and field fortifications are uniformly good.

11. On the defense their automatic weapons have very limited fields of fire, usually close in front of their position.

12. They will counterattack promptly when their position has been overrun, either by fire and movement or by fire alone.

13. They are hard fanatical fighters. On the defense they will often hold out to the last man. In the attack, once a plan of action has been decided upon, they will follow it through, even to a disastrous conclusion, since apparently they are unable or unwilling to readjust their plan.

14. They place a low value on human life and do not count the cost in taking an objective. Despite their extensive training and inborn confidence in the bayonet, they have not been outstanding in close combat.

15. The final conclusion to be drawn is: now that the Japanese have come up against forces in great numbers and units with unlimited resources of heavy equipment, their originally successful concept of jungle warfare, with their tactics based on surprise, mobility, and light equipment, has been shattered.

Section IX. SMALL ISLAND DEFENSE

1. GENERAL. The information in the following section has been obtained mainly from observations made before and during operations against Japanese island bases in the Central Pacific Area and also from detailed studies of these bases after capture by Allied Forces. Studies of the Japanese island bases, made before their occupation by Allied Forces, checked very closely with the defenses as found on the ground. The defenses of these islands are probably typical of those of other Japanese island bases in the Pacific.

2. TYPES OF SMALL ISLANDS. a. General. The small islands of the Pacific fall into two main classes: the coral atolls and the volcanic islands. Japan has established bases on islands of both of these types. The particular type of base set up has been dictated by terrain considerations, geographical location, and strategical necessity. Thus, not all of the Japanese bases in the Pacific are large ones and not all of them can be considered as supply and command centers.

b. Coral atolls. Coral atolls are small low-lying, generally oval-shaped rings of islets inclosing a lagoon which may run from about 2 to 65 miles in diameter. (See figure 101.) These islets may extend from a few yards to a mile in width and from a few yards to several miles in length. The total land area of an atoll may range from a few hundred square yards to 6 square miles as in the case of Kwajalein, the largest known one. Atolls are rarely more than 25 feet above sea level, and, with few exceptions, are covered by dense growths of coconut palm, pandanus, and salt marsh. The water table is usually only a few feet below the surface of the ground, and, as a result of this, deep entrenchments and fortifications cannot be dug. A bomb crater generally fills up with water in a few hours. This limitation on excavations on coral atolls forces the defenders to build their fortifications above the ground in most cases and has resulted in the adoption of the bunker and pillbox type of fortification for atoll defense. The one exception to the above mentioned limitation is the antitank ditch. When these are constructed in low lying places they sometimes fill up with water and become a better obstacle. Some atolls have excellent large vessel anchorages in the lagoon (Kwajalein and Wotje), while others have no channel into the lagoon and only provide offshore anchorage, such as Uterik and Namorik.

and there is room on these islands for air-bases. The terrain is rugged and mountainous and is similar to some of the Hawaiian islands.

3. DEFENSE OF VOLCANIC ISLANDS.
The defense of volcanic islands consists of beach positions, heavy naval guns up to 12-inch size, and mobile reserves. Beach defenses consist of observation posts, strong points, and obstacles, but these are not to be considered a perimeter defense. Large-sized units are held as reserves and are employed in counterattacking at threatened points. The defenders have the advantage of dominant observation, knowledge of the terrain, and large amounts of supplies. In addition to this, they have maneuver room, and if driven into the hills are quite capable of carrying out harrassing operations for long periods. Airstrips are located on the volcanic island bases, and both landbased and naval aircraft are used in the defense. Antiaircraft artillery is used in the defense of harbors and landing

Figure 101. Coral atoll.

c. Volcanic and raised coral islands. The Marshalls and Gilberts, and all but five of the Carolines, are coral islands. The exceptions are volcanic, or volcanic and coral. Some of the coral islands, such as Nauru and Ocean, are not atolls and contain no lagoons. These islands are large, circular, raised land masses and have been developed into bases by the Japanese. In common with the atolls they are surrounded by coral reefs.

d. Volcanic Islands. The volcanic islands of the Central Pacific have been developed into major bases by the Japanese. These run in a line from East to West as follows: Kusaie, Ponape, Truk, Yap and Palau. (See fig. 102.) These volcanic islands are much larger in size than the atolls and can support considerable garrisons. Most of the volcanoes are extinct, but some in the northern Marianas are active. Some, like Truk, are groups of islands. Truk is completely surrounded by a coral barrier reef located some distance off shore; and it contains a fine harbor and considerable anchorage space. Fresh water supplies are generally ample,

fields. Army troops, as well as Special Naval Landing Forces, are likely to be encountered on these bases.

4. TYPES OF ATOLL ISLAND BASES.
Some of the atolls have been developed into large airfields, while others are not large enough to contain an airstrip, and are used as seaplane bases where the aircraft use the lagoon as an anchorage and landing area. Others are not suitable for either of the above types of base and are used as weather stations and radio relay points.

5. LIMITATIONS ON SIZE OF GARRISONS.
There is a physical limitation on the number of men that can be placed on an atoll in view of the limited space and the difficulties of fresh water supply. On most atolls, evaporators must be used to supplement the rainwater cisterns and the brackish water wells. The problem of supply and storage area also limits the size of garrisons. Natural food supplies on an atoll are very scanty, with

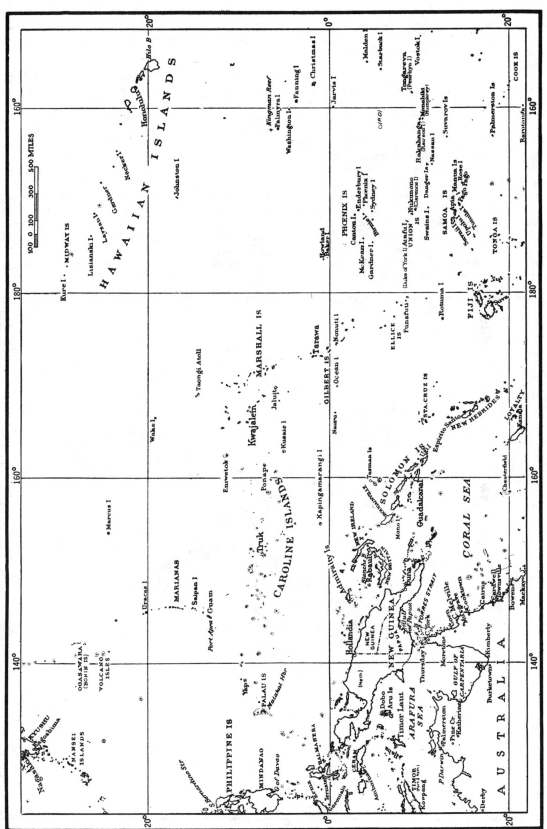

Figure 102. Map of Pacific.

the exception of fish, and since this is a staple of Japanese diet it is used a great deal to supplement the rations shipped in. Refrigeration is also a problem as foodstuffs spoil rapidly in tropical climates.

6. CORAL REEFS. All coral atolls are surrounded by reefs on both the ocean and lagoon sides of the islets. This is a great natural obstacle in favor of the defenders. In the Makin and Tarawa operations, certain landing craft could not negotiate the reef, and the landings therefore had to be made in amphibious tractors or by wading ashore several hundred yards in chest deep water. These reefs may extend from shore for a few yards or as much as a half mile. During high tide the reef is submerged below a few feet of water, while at low tide it may be completely exposed and above water. At low tide the reef makes a perfectly flat cleared field of fire for the defenders. As a rule no reef is found opposite the mouth of a river.

7. TYPES OF ATOLL DEFENSES. Two major types of defense are encountered on coral atolls: the perimeter defense and the fortified central area with outposts.

a. Perimeter defense. The perimeter defense is the one almost always used by the Japanese and is usually encountered on small islets in the atoll ring which are generally large enough only for an airbase. The landing field covers most of the islet, and the remainder of the installations are located around the field. Defensive works are a continuous band around the islet and are not generally in great depth. Practically all men are committed to the perimeter at the outset of a fight with few troops held in reserve. All types of weapons are on the perimeter, from 6.5-mm rifles to 8-inch naval turret guns. Trenches, pillboxes, barbed wire, mine fields, and antitank ditches are used in the defense. An example of the perimeter defense is shown in figure 103.

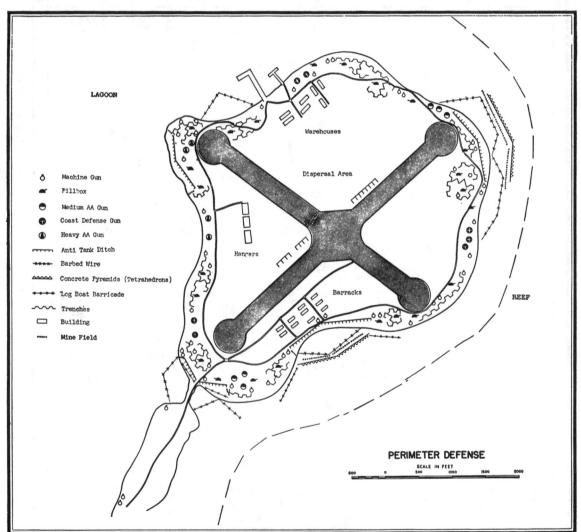

Figure 103. Perimeter defense.

b. Fortified central area. Another type of defense is used on islets which are long and narrow, or which are too long for the use of a perimeter defense with the amount of troops available at the time. The Japanese do not fortify the entire perimeter, but generally group their installations in a central area, build tank traps at the ends of the area, and install their defensive works behind the tank traps facing out. Small outposts are placed on the remainder of the islet, but there is no continuous line of defenses outside of those in the fortified area. The tank ditch apparently plays the most important role in the defense plan, since a great part of the defenses are arranged to keep attackers from penetrating that line, and the majority of the pillboxes are located there. The heavier guns are placed near the shores between the tank ditches, since most of them are fixed guns and could not be used for close-in defense. The outposts generally consist of antiaircraft batteries and machine gun posts located at the extremities of the islets. A typical central fortified area is shown in figure 104.

8. DETAILS OF ATOLL DEFENSES. a. Antiaircraft defenses. (1) *Early warning measures.* The first evidence of Japanese radar in the Central Pacific was encountered early in 1943. While the performance of this equipment has not been up to accepted standards, improvement can be expected in the future. The extreme range of Japanese radar noted to date is 60–70 miles. The Japanese also make use of watchers as well as radio and weather stations on small undefended atolls as a means of passing early warning back to their defended bases.

(2) *Antiaircraft weapons.* In small islands encountered so far the only heavy antiaircraft guns definitely identified are the 75-mm (7-cm) antiaircraft gun and the twin-mount 127-mm dual purpose gun. These weapons are generally in two or three gun batteries and seldom in large groups. All weapons are well emplaced in heavily constructed revetments. The Japanese also have 20-mm and 25-mm antiaircraft automatic weapons. In the Gilberts 13.2-mm machine guns in single and twin-mounts were used. Automatic 7.7-mm and 6.5-mm guns are also used as antiaircraft weapons.

(3) *Passive defensive measures.* The Japanese have constructed heavy air raid shelters of palm logs, sandbags, and loose sand. On Makin and Tarawa these were extensively used during the bombardment by the Japanese troops, civilian laborers, and natives. Fox holes (weapon pits) and heavily revetted buildings also were encountered. Storage buildings and planes were dispersed as widely as the size of the islets permitted.

(4) *Camouflage.* Where used, camouflage is excellent, but is confined mostly to small weapons emplacements, antiaircraft guns, and alternate positions. Some buildings are dazzle painted. Great use is made of dummy installations in island defense and the Japanese take great pains in this. Most camouflage is obtained by the use of natural materials. (See figs. 105, 106, and 107.)

b. Antilanding measures. (1) *Obstacles and mine fields.* The greatest obstacle in the attack of a small island is the coral reef which surrounds it. The reefs are found on *both lagoon and ocean sides* of the atolls and on the ocean side of other islands. However, there may be small stretches of beach on the lagoon side of the islets which are free of reefs and small stretches of reef-free beaches on the windward face of the ocean side of the islets. The Japanese have strengthened this natural obstacle by placing concrete pyramids (tetrahedrons), horned scullies, coral cairns, barbed wire, and log boat barricades on the reef. (See figs. 108, 109, 110.)

Interspersed with these is a mine field of waterproof mines containing a heavy charge of explosives detonated by a chemical-electric fuse. The detonating nipples of the mines are connected by wire to the obstacles and some also by wire to the shore. They can then be detonated by three methods: by direct contact, by hitting a trip wire, or by a pull wire from shore. Antitank mine fields also are placed on the beaches on both flanks of the antitank ditches. The reef is hard and will support medium tanks with ease.

(2) *Pattern of fire and defensive weapons.* (a) The defense of the beach is built around the machine gun and a final protective line. The beach defense usually consists of a shallow line of strong points, with a secondary line of lesser density located slightly to the rear. Because of the small size of the islands, depth of the defense is limited. The strong points consist of a group of bunkers and pillboxes connected by trenches and are covered by fire from riflemen in fox holes all around the installation. These fox holes are connected by communication trenches. The pillboxes and bunkers within the strong point are mutually supporting. Each rifleman protecting the pillbox generally has several alternate positions. He runs from one to another, and during combat this practice sometimes leads to an over-estimation of the strength of the defenders. The Japanese make extensive use of hand grenades in the defense of small islands, and flame throwers were present on Tarawa and Kiska.

(b) The Japanese defense of small islands is based on breaking up an attack before it reaches the shore, and all coast defense guns up to the 8-inch are sited so that they can be employed against small boats and landing vehicles. Batteries have local fire director control, generally 2 or 3 guns with observation towers at the gun position. Flat trajectory weapons predominate, with howitzer type weapons in the minority. These weapons are placed well forward on the beach where direct laying can be used against landing craft. Their grouping is shallow, all weapons being sited so that they can be used to repel a sea-borne invasion. This also applies to antiaircraft guns, the secondary mission of which is to repel surface craft and landing vehicles. To date coast defense guns found on these islands have

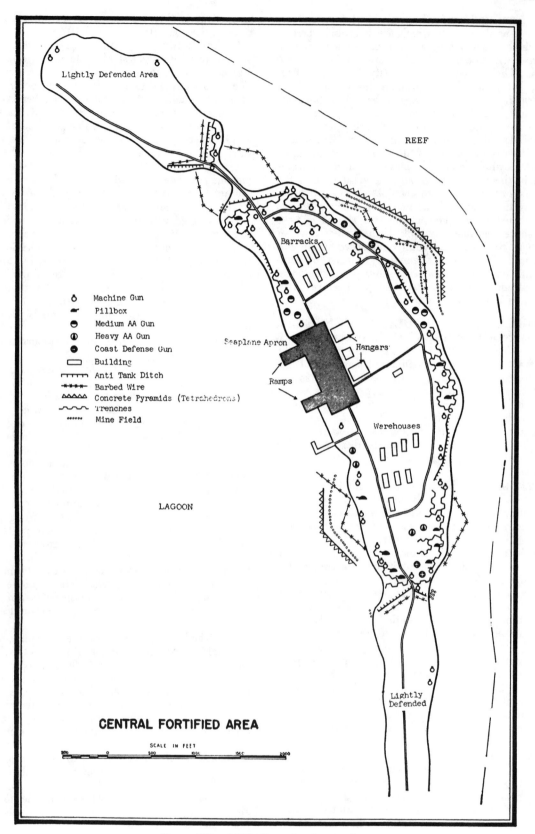

Figures 105 and 106. Examples of camouflage.

Figures 105 and 106, Examples of camouflage.

Figure 107. Example of camouflage.

Figure 108. Japanese beach obstacles.

Figure 109. Beach obstacles.

Figure 110. Beach obstacles.

ranged from 3 to 8 inches. The 8-inch guns were in turrets, while the 6- and 5-inch had shields. All were well emplaced in heavy revetments, with ammunition storage in covered emplacements close to the guns.

(c) All machine guns are sited to fire outward around the perimeter. Most of them are sited for cross-fire and cover the beach obstacles with enfilading fire. A few are also sited to fire to the rear of their positions. Some machine guns are in open emplacements, while others are set up in pillboxes. Those in open emplacements are generally dual purpose and have wide fields of fire; those in pillboxes have narrow fields of fire and are sited to fire only in one direction. All emplacements are protected by riflemen in foxholes and trenches around the installations. Some infantry regimental guns and battalion howitzers are used. Small use was made of trench mortars at Makin and Tarawa; however, this probably was so because of the limited number of such weapons in the Special Naval Landing Forces. Small arms used are both 7.7-mm and 6.5-mm caliber.

(3) *Field fortifications.* The Japanese defense of small islands is characterized by the extensive use of field fortifications. The bunkers and pillbox emplaced machine guns are the backbone of defensive fire. These fortifications have been developed from small installations, composed of a single layer of palm logs and sand bags and large enough for only a few men, into massive structures 6 to 8 feet thick, housing more than a squad. Palm logs are giving way to reinforced concrete and completely enclosed steel structures. These bunkers are relatively safe from damage by anything less than a direct hit by a 155-mm shell or larger. (See figs. 111–112.) The Japanese defend these to the last man, and some have been known to remain in these positions for days amid rotting corpses subsequently to come out fighting during mopping-up operations. (This was true at Tarawa and Makin.) A typical "bunker" and pillbox strong point protecting a coast defense battery is shown in figure 113.

c. Antitank defense. (1) *Obstacles.* To date the Japanese have constructed tank barriers only on the islets where there are airstrips and seaplane bases. These, generally, are antitank ditches and lines of obstacles. The ditches run from 4 to 8 feet in depth and from 10 to 20 feet in width. (See fig. 114.) They extend completely across the islet in the case of the central fortified zone and usually are protected by mine fields on the flanks. At communication points along these ditches the Japanese construct bridges guarded by palm log barricades filled with rocks. In the perimeter defense these ditches are found at the ends of airstrips and backing up critical landing beaches. Low palm log hurdles are placed in front of the ditches in order to slow up tanks approaching the trap. Concrete pyramids

Figure 111. Japanese field fortifications.

Figure 112. Field fortifications.

Figure 113. A typical coastal defense strongpoint.

Figure 114. Antitank ditch.

(tetrahedrons) and horned scullies are used on the reef as continuous barriers. Only very recently have the Japanese begun to use mines in defense of islands. On Tarawa a thick mine field was laid on the reef in the space between the tetrahedrons. On Kiska thin mine fields were found. On Makin several hundred mines were found in a warehouse, but none had been laid. Indications point to greater use of mines in the future.

(2) *Antitank weapons.* Although they possess more modern guns the Japanese so far have employed 37-mm rapid-fire guns in island defense. These guns are employed behind the tank barricades and ditches and are usually in open emplacements. Alternate positions are prepared for these guns, since the Japanese tactics are to keep antitank weapons mobile. Light tanks were included in the defense of Japanese bases recently captured, and the Japanese doctrine was to employ them against tanks landed by the attackers. All Japanese small arms are assigned the mission of firing against tanks and have done so in Pacific operations. Another antitank weapon is the magnetic mine which has been in use in all Pacific theaters.

d. Supply installations. (1) Japanese supply installations on small islands closely follow the prin-cipal of dispersion. Supplies are placed in small dumps, in many cases in shallow excavations, as a protection against bombing. Perishables and food are generally in warehouses, and refrigeration is used on some bases. With the increase in the size of island garrisons which has been apparent since the latter half of 1943, the Japanese have been plac-ing a large part of their supplies on islets adjoining those on which their major defenses are sited. In the case of ammunition, the warehouses are con-nected by a narrow gauge railway. Causeways have been built between the islets to make communication easier.

(2) The Japanese also secrete small arms and ammunition in caches at various points on the islets, as at Makin, so that in case of a withdrawal from their fortifications they can fall back along their supply line. Canteen supplies, beer, and sake were plentiful, and there was no shortage of food. Sup-ply vessels called at regular intervals. From most data available a level of supplies of about 6 months seems to have been maintained at all out-lying bases. Clothing supply was good. The Japanese in the Gilberts and Marshalls were all well supplied with food and clothing and were in excellent physical condition.

(3) The policy of reinforcing the island bases has been that each ship calling at a base drops off a few more guns and additional ammunition. The caliber varies, but each type of weapon is incorporated in the defense according to its capabilities. Ships bring supplies from central island bases or direct from the Japanese mainland.

9. AIRFIELDS AND SEAPLANE BASES.
a. Types of airstrips. The type of airstrip used on the Japanese bases depends on the shape and size of the islet. On the circular islets the field is made up of two crossed strips. On crescent-shaped islets a triangular-shaped pattern is used. On narrow islets a single strip is laid. These patterns are fairly regular. Runways are surfaced with coral and have large turn-arounds at each end. The layout of the runways takes advantage of prevailing winds. Aircraft revetments are the palm log type, covered with sand. A new development has been the use of small railway cars loaded with logs and sandbags which, during an air raid, are rolled in place in front of revetments to serve as blast walls. Hangars are located on the service aprons and are of conventional design. The presence of underground hangars has been indicated on some bases. Seaplane bases are uniform in design, and generally consist of two concrete ramps extending into the lagoon, with a concrete apron on the shore bordered by hangars and machine shops. As a rule these seaplane bases are in the center of a fortified area.

b. Type of planes used. The types of planes encountered on small islands have been: four-engined flying boats; twin-engined medium bombers; land based pursuit; and single-engined float planes. The four-engined flying boat is used for long-range patrol work and now carries the brunt of aerial reconnaissance. Japanese interception tactics are normal.

10. SUCCESSIVE STAGES IN CONSTRUCTION OF BASES.
Since the Allied offensive in the Central Pacific began, construction of air bases on most atolls long enough to support an airstrip has been noted. The first stage in construction of a base is building the airstrip. The antiaircraft defenses are next set up followed by emplacement of coast defense guns. Tank barriers and ditches come later, and pillboxes and bunkers last. The Japanese have used considerable numbers of civilian laborers in the construction of their bases. These laborers are not permitted to work on the defenses but only on the airstrips, barracks, and docks. They are carefully segregated from the Japanese military personnel and are not permitted access to the fortified zone. During the defense of some bases, they were given arms by the Japanese and were told to fight. Many did, while others merely hid in air raid shelters and then surrendered.

11. HISTORICAL EXAMPLE OF JAPANESE DEFENSE AGAINST AN AMPHIBIOUS ATTACK ON A CORAL

ATOLL. a. Defense of Makin Atoll. (1) *During assault phase.* The Japanese used air attacks in order to break up the Allied assault before it reached the island. As the transport groups moved in for the landings the Japanese opened fire with every weapon available. During the initial landing small arms and automatic weapons opened up when the attacking forces came within range. They did not wait until troops got close in. Practically all of the defending troops were in the defensive works, and very few were held in reserve. They were unable to destroy or break up the assault or to prevent the establishment of beachheads. In the early stages Japanese defense was mainly by fire and very little by movement. Many remained in their bunkers and pillboxes until killed. During the first night the Japanese tried to infiltrate into the attackers' lines to reoccupy positions lost during the day's fighting.

(2) *During mopping up phase.* When their line of bunkers and pillboxes was breached, the remaining Japanese broke up into small groups and withdrew into covered areas, where they re-formed and then counterattacked. When these counterattacks were broken up, they formed into small groups to take refuge in bunkers, air raid shelters, and the salt marsh jungle. Japanese suicides were frequent during the mopping-up phase. Some remnants of their forces hid out for days after the fighting ceased, subsisting on coconuts and stolen rations, while others tried to escape out to sea. Probably because of the speed of Allied operations and the rapidity with which their positions were overrun, the Japanese were unable to destroy equipment and stores.

(3) *Conclusions.* Since the Japanese were unable to break up the Allied assault before it hit the beach and prevent landings, their beach strong points were overrun rapidly, and their defense plan was nullified. In order to counterattack they had to withdraw men from their prepared positions and thus lost the advantage of their fortifications. Their prompt counterattack was entirely in keeping with their normal tactical doctrine.

Section X. JAPANESE COASTAL DEFENSE

1. GENERAL. a. Scarcity of information.
(1) Coast defense, as referred to in this section, is generally the method of defense adopted for large island and mainland areas, where defended localities are placed in strategic positions.

(2) The information on Japanese permanent or fixed coastal defense methods is very meager. However, thorough study of their training regulations, aerial photographs, and defensive measures carried out in the North and Southwest Pacific Areas as well as in Burma, present a fairly clear pattern of their methods for semi-permanent installations. As yet it is impossible to give a complete analysis of this subject, since it is only comparatively recently

that it has been possible to draw on active combat experience. Furthermore, it is to be expected that Japanese technique is not as yet fully developed, and changes will no doubt ensue. It is believed, however, that the general methods and defensive layouts described and illustrated herein will be of value in estimating the form coastal defense may take in the future.

b. Doctrine. (1) It must be borne in mind that the Japanese conception of defense is essentially offensive, consequently they do not envisage coast defense as a passive process of merely resisting a hostile attack, but rather one offensive in nature, where-

2. PERMANENT FORTIFICATIONS. a. General. The fixed fortifications of Japan proper are primarily coast defenses. Although very little information as to age or character of gun complement has been obtained, there are indications that some modern guns as large as 16-inch caliber are emplaced in some areas. Antiaircraft guns are included in the plan of defense.

b. Mission. The coast defense system is the second line of defense, designed to insure the security of the Empire, independently of the fleet. Defense zones are located throughout the main islands to guard strategic areas. Army and Navy aircraft act

Figure 115. A coast defense position.

by the enemy forces must be attacked and destroyed before landing or as close thereafter as possible.

(2) A natural corollary of this offensive attitude is the determination not to surrender, but to fight on to the last man and the last round. An excellent example both of this characteristic and of the offensive spirit was given by the Japanese defenders of Attu in the Aleutians. Here, after stubborn fighting, the defenders were ejected from their prepared positions, and those that remained were driven back and thrown into an obviously hopeless situation. However, rather than surrender, all of the able and wounded alike joined in a final desperate charge which was only stopped as the last of them was killed. This tenacity of the Japanese in defense must always be reckoned with when calculating the resistance to be expected from a coast defense position.

in concert in coast defense, although the primary responsibility is recognized to be that of the Navy.

c. Mines. Great reliance is placed on mining operations which are a function of the Navy. The Japanese envisage the extensive use of mines to cover the entrances of all approaches along their coast and to block entrances to the narrow seas between Japan and the Asiatic mainland. This inner edge of the mined area is to be patrolled by surface craft and aircraft from nearby fields to prevent mine sweeping operations. Inner mine barrages will be laid covering strategic points, and these will be covered by shore batteries.

3. ATTU ISLAND DEFENSE PLAN. a. Figure 116 shows that portion of Attu Island over which fighting took place during its recapture by

United States forces in the spring of 1943, and it also gives some idea of the mountainous nature of the terrain.

The Japanese defense plan for Attu Island seems to have been based entirely on the assumption that any Allied attack would take the form of a landing in the main bays and subsequent advance up the valley beds. The guns and positions covering the main northern bays were so sited and concentrated that landing craft would find it extremely difficult to reach shore while one gun still remained to fire. All positions were well emplaced, and the guns were secure against everything except a direct hit. In addition, in order to meet the contingencies that hostile naval fire and air bombardment might knock out the dual purpose guns, and a beach landing might be made, the Japanese had prepared almost innumerable positions flanking the Holtz Bay beaches and facing inward and even to the rear. Behind the

most inviting landing beaches they apparently had prepared 4 successive lines of resistance, with a final defensive line at the valley head. The setting for their plan was completed by the defense layout in Massacre Valley, where the lower positions flanking the valley were hidden by excellent camouflage, while those higher up were shrouded by the prevailing mist and clouds.

b. From the evidence of the siting of these positions, it is reasonable to assume that the Japanese appreciation of the course of the battle for Attu was that either a direct frontal assault would be made on the Holtz Bay beaches, or a back-door approach would be attempted via Sarana or Massacre Bays, the latter seemed more probable, for the exit from Sarana is blocked by Lake Nicholas. Their plan for Holtz Bay was designed chiefly to annihilate the attacking forces on the water or on the beaches and then to exterminate the few that might penetrate

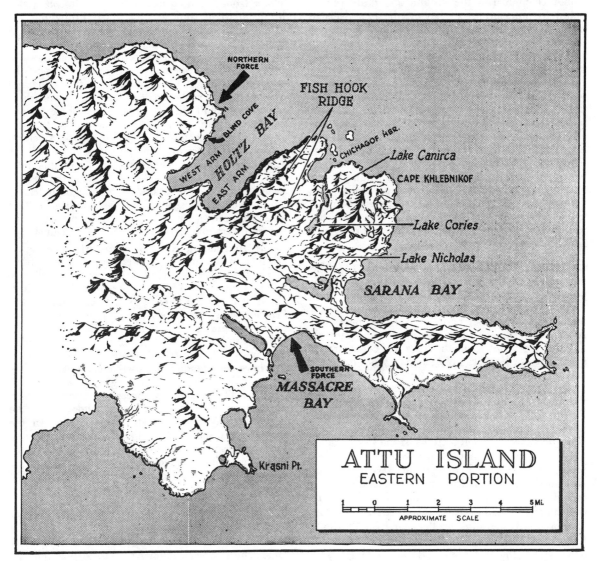

Figure 116. Map of Attu Island.

into the valleys by concentrated enfilade fire. On the other hand, the apparent intention for Massacre Bay was to meet attack by more subtle means. Because of good camouflage and cloud cover, few positions in that area were likely to be located by previous reconnaissance, and the few visible tents, trails, and fox holes would suggest that the valley was only thinly out-posted. The few scattered soldiers who fled the beach at the approach of the attacking force may well have been a decoy to invite an advance up the bed of Massacre Valley. Against that march the enemy probably only intended to use enough frontal resistance to ensure the building up of a powerful force. When that force was pocketed in the valley, all the flanking machine guns and mortars would open fire, grenade discharger and rifle fire would plunge down from above, and finally the artillery at the head of the valley would complete the process of annihilation. The Allied Forces thus would be pinned to the ground and destroyed in detail by inferior forces having the two decisive advantages of concealment and absolute command of terrain.

c. The plan of defense for Attu failed, as do so many Japanese plans, because it made no provision for the unexpected. The direction of the attack of the Northern Force (shown on the map) took them by surprise and out-flanked their carefully prepared Holtz Bay positions which lacked adequate all-round defense. The direction of attack of the Southern Force from Massacre Bay had been anticipated correctly, but not the nature of its execution which involved the quick movement to high ground outflanking and dominating Japanese positions. The defense plan met some slight initial success, but was frustrated completely when Allied troops took the initiative by fire and movement tactics and promptly seized dominating terrain features.

4. KISKA DEFENSES. a. General. (1) The garrison at Kiska was composed of Army and Navy personnel in about equal numbers. Although a few Naval personnel were found at Attu, the garrison was composed almost entirely of Army men, and consequently the barracks, weapons, etc., were all of Army type. At Kiska the Navy was concentrated around Kiska Harbor, while the Army occupied the area around Gertrude Cove. Barracks and weapons of the Navy differed in some respect from those of the Army. In the future, particularly in the North Pacific Area, it is reasonable to expect installations similar to those on Kiska, where both the Army and Navy occupied different sections of the same island.

(2) The Japanese development of Kiska was much more extensive than had been the development of Attu. Almost all beaches possessed some defenses including barbed wire and mines. In addition to the gun types found at Attu (75-mm and 20-mm AA, 75-mm and 37-mm Mtn. artillery, and small arms), Kiska ordnance included 6-inch, 4.7-inch, and 76-mm naval CD guns, 25-mm and 13-mm (single and twin mount) antiaircraft guns, and 3 light tanks.

Heavy machine guns in a few cases were mounted in concrete pill boxes. Passive defenses included a radar installation, two 150-cm searchlights, and two 98-cm searchlights. Medical facilities were housed in well equipped underground hospitals.

(3) In contrast to undeveloped Attu, Kiska defensive areas were linked by a fairly well developed road net. Nearly 60 trucks, 8 sedans, 20 motor-cycles, and 6 bantam-sized autos operated over this system. Two small bulldozers, tractors, and rollers were available for work on the airfield. The submarine base, the seaplane base, 2 machine shops, a foundry, and a saw mill complete the list of Kiska's special installations.

(4) Water and power systems were well established at Kiska in contrast to rather primitive systems employed at Attu. Power was provided mainly by 3 large power houses, but many additional smaller units supplied special buildings and outlying areas. Water from half a dozen small reservoirs was piped to installations and fire hydrants throughout the Main Camp area. Three complete radio stations, a radio-type navigation aid, and a well installed telephone system made up the communication network.

b. Beach defenses. (1) For the most part the Kiska shoreline is lined by steep cliffs, with sand or gravel strips at the heads of the many coves which indent its bluff line. Exits from these gravel beaches are provided by steep stream valleys that rise abruptly between towering hills to the high central ridges of the interior. In emplacing his beach defenses the Japanese made excellent use of this naturally rugged terrain. Nearly all of the usable beaches at Kiska possessed at least light defenses, and in the island's strategic mid-section beaches that gave access to the built-up areas around Kiska Harbor and Gertrude Cove were strongly defended.

(2) In general, Kiska beaches, which were accessible to landing craft, were mined; tank traps blocked possible overland exits; and barbed wire barriers were strung between breaks in the bluff line. From high ground at each of their extremities most beaches were completely covered by well camouflaged machine gun dugouts and rifle pits. In the hills behind these beaches other covered machine gun positions and trench systems with numerous fire bays commanded all possible exits along valley routes. At a few of the strategic coves single 75-mm and 37-mm artillery pieces were established in covered emplacements that commanded both the beach landing and its water approaches. In the more thickly settled areas like the Main Camp and the Sub Base the shoreline was honeycombed with dug-in machine gun positions, and in a few cases defenses were bolstered by reinforced concrete pill boxes.

5. THE DEFENSE OF A PROMONTORY.
a. General. (1) The Japanese positions, shown in Fig. 117, have been located by aerial photography alone, therefore it cannot be assumed that the picture is complete in all respects. Sufficient informa-

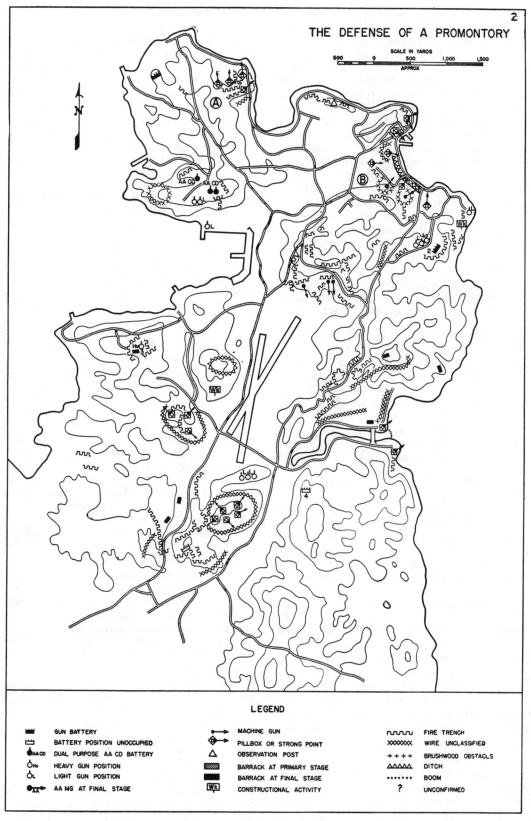

Figure 117. The defense of a promontory.

tion seems to be available, however, to make clear the general pattern of defense, namely, the concentration of positions on the high ground so as to provide for coast defense, by means of fire power directed from well constructed positions on dominant ground, and to afford direct defense for the two landing strips. The exception to this principle is the siting of defense positions (Position B) close to the water line in the bay on the North-east of the promontory; this, however, can be explained by the relatively low-lying ground inland in this area, which necessitates the more forward placing of positions. It can be expected that many, if not all, the antiaircraft guns shown have been sited with a view to use in a dual-purpose capacity.

(2) There seems to be a similarity in the general defense layout between this system and that of Attu Island, except in the important point of camouflage. That little effort at concealment has been made in the present instance is clear from the amount that aerial photography has been able to reveal, whereas on Attu Island close attention was paid to camouflage and a good degree of concealment was achieved.

b. Development Area A. (1) Figure 118 illustrates the various stages in the construction of a defense position sited on a spur of high ground giving good fields of fire over the neighboring beaches. The locality is that shown at position (A) overlooking the main bay from the East at the north end of the promontory shown in figure 117.

(2) The earliest constructional activity consisted only of ground clearance, the marking out of the trench system, and a little preliminary digging. A month later the position was already fairly well advanced, for by then the trench system, up to a length of some 700 yards, had been completed, and 3 strong points had been incorporated in the general layout. The developments in the position which were seen to have taken place several months later are indicated as Stage 3. As can be seen, its defenses have been improved by additional trench digging, while a fourth strong point has been added, and wire defenses also have been erected. In addition, the communications have been improved by the making of a new trail into the position. In its final form, the locality can be deemed to be of good intrinsic strength, well sited, and designed to cover the beaches to the North and East.

c. Development Area B. (fig. 119). (1) Shows the development of the position (B) as illustrated in figure 117. In its early stages the only really significant forward defenses were the pillboxes covering the length of the sea-front. Further back, a start had been made with the construction of defenses on the rising ground.

(2) At Stage 2, the position has taken its proper shape. It can be seen that the locality is sited in 2 'lines,' the first covering the sea-wall and its immediate sea approaches, while the second is set some distance back on rising ground having a good field of fire over the flat terrain intervening between it and the sea-wall.

(3) Another interesting feature which has appeared at this stage is the extensive ditch, presumably designed as an antitank obstacle, which has been dug behind the sea-wall. This ditch is 15 to 20 feet wide and some 600 yards long. It should also be noticed that the most southerly defenses, which first appeared only as a ring of wire with a few isolated weapon-pits, have developed into an extensive light antiaircraft position, with ground defenses incorporated. This position is almost certainly sited to fulfill a dual-purpose role.

6. THE DEFENSE OF A BEACH-LINE. a. General. (1) The system of siting defense positions as shown in fig. 120 of a coastal area in Burma is in evident contrast to that detailed in paragraphs 3 and 5. In this case, obvious emphasis has been laid upon siting defenses as far forward as possible. The frontal wire obstacles in places have been laid actually below the high water line, and the proximity of all the positions to this line is a very noticeable feature.

(2) Another interesting point of comparison between this layout and that of Attu Island is the extensive use made of wire obstacles and antitank ditches. In view of this, it is not unreasonable to presume that antitank mines have also been much more freely employed, probably both on the beaches and to cover the likely lines of approach of armored vehicles within the area.

(3) The relatively large number of strongpoints included within each defensive position is noteworthy. The majority of these are probably designed as fire positions for heavy and light machine guns, but some of the larger emplacements are designed to take heavier weapons, in particular the 37-mm antitank gun. This is a versatile weapon which has been freely used by the Japanese to fire against both landing craft and personnel, as well as in its original role.

(4) The siting of the central position, set back so as to enable it to cover by fire the rear of the forward positions, is of interest. It is presumably in this position, conveniently and centrally placed, that the local reserves would be held. Note also the similarity of this defense with the central fortified area described in Small Island Defense, Section IX.

b. Development of Area A. (1) The position shown in figure 121 is that marked as position (A) on the map of the beach defense layout (fig. 120). It is noteworthy for its speed of construction, since it reached the first stage shown in something under 3 weeks. During that time an extensive trench system was completed, 2 strongpoints were incorporated, and a long, forward zig-zag line of wire was erected. About a month later the locality had reached its final stage. By then, 4 new strongpoints had been constructed, a short length of communicating trench dug, and the wire defenses increased and brought round to link up with the creek

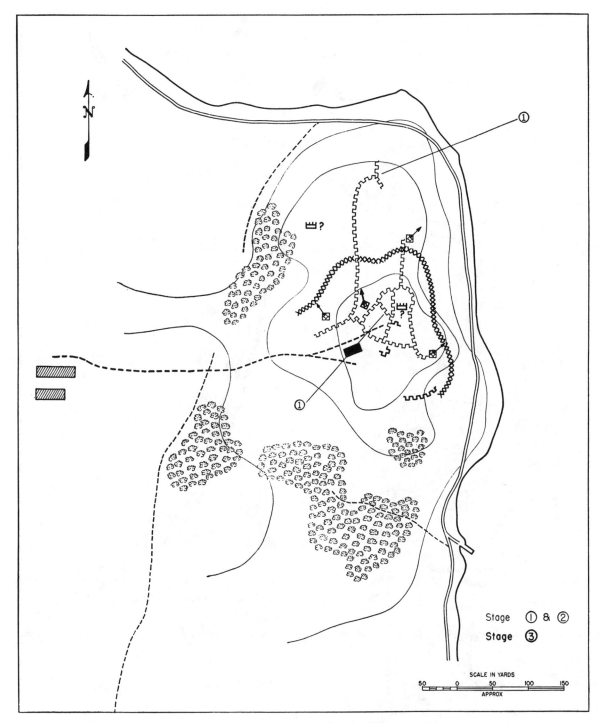

Figure 118. Stages in the construction of a defense position.

on to which the position backs. A short forward length of brushwood also had been staked down in one sector.

(2) In general, this position may be said to be a typical example of the Japanese siting of a position for all around defense.

c. Development of Area B. (1) The defended locality illustrated in figure 122 (position (B) in the beach defense figure 120) was already at a fairly advanced stage of development when first photographed. Its chief interest lies in the number of strongpoints, eventually incorporated in it—no less

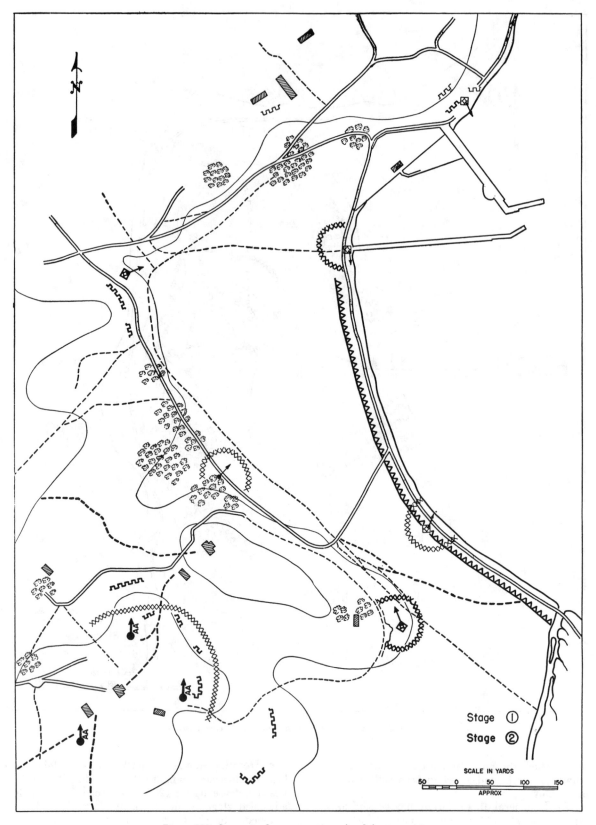

Figure 119. Stages in the construction of a defense position.

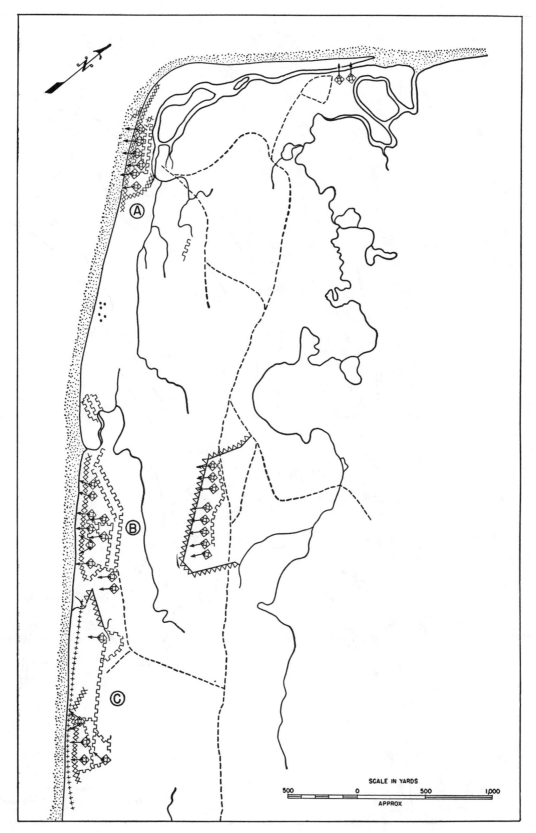

Figure 120. A beach defense layout.

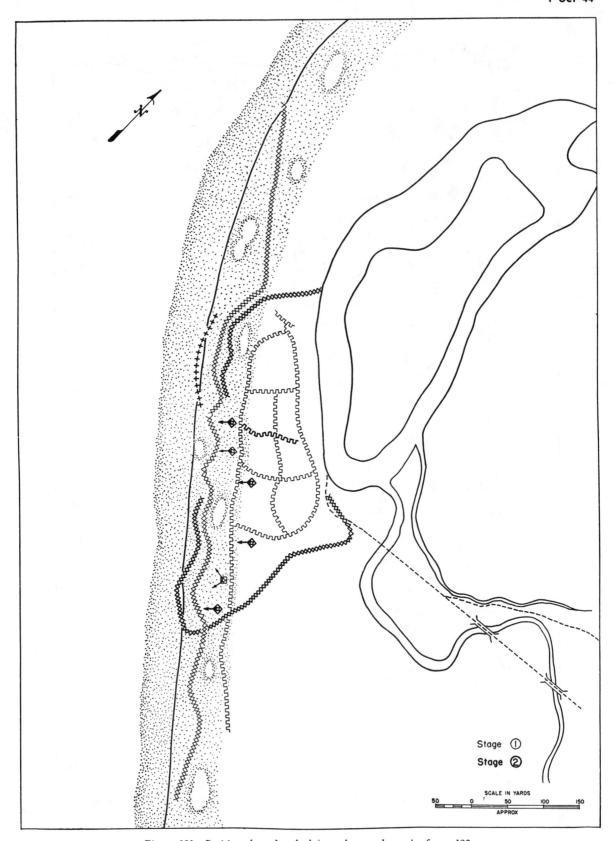

Figure 121. Position A on beach defense layout shown in figure 120.

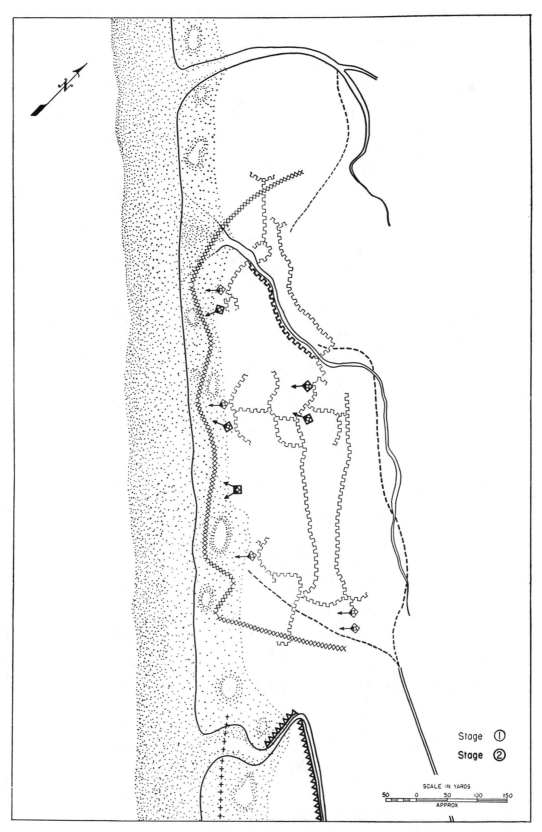

Figure 122. Position B of beach defense layout shown in figure 120.

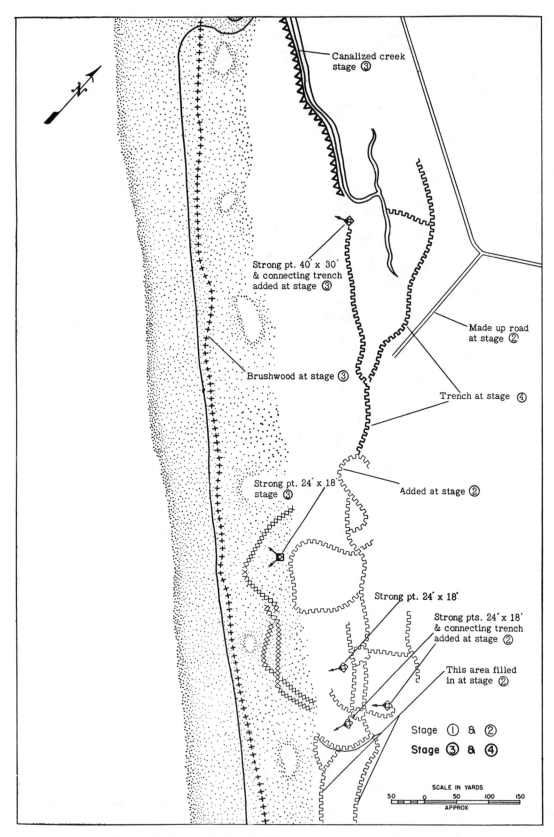

Figure 123. Position C of beach defense layout as shown in figure 120.

than ten in a position with a total frontage of under half a mile. One of these strongpoints, added at a later stage as can be seen from the sketch, is noteworthy both for its exceptional size and for the fact that it is set right forward and not apparently connected with the general trench system.

(2) In general, the position seems to be one of particular strength, and it is to be noted that, in addition to being covered on one flank by the antitank ditch and brushwood obstacle of the adjacent position described below, it is also covered on the other flank by a creek.

d. Development of Area C. (1) The locality here given in detail in figure 123 is that shown as Position (C) in figure 120.

(2) When first photographed, the defended locality consisted of a fairly extensive trench system with numerous firing bays and one covered strongpoint together with a forward zig-zag line of wire. It can be seen that during the second stage of development the position was extensively altered by the filling-in of a large portion of the trench system and by the adding of 2 further strongpoints and a short length of trench. In addition, a road was brought in to the north of the position.

(3) During the final constructional stages the locality underwent even more radical changes, one of the most interesting of which was the addition of an antitank ditch formed by canalizing a small creek. For a distance of about 400 yards, its banks were dug vertical, thus making an antitank position.

A considerable trench system was also added at one of the later stages, which, as annotated in the sketch, is remarkable for the size of the strongpoint incorporated in it as compared with those in the rest of the locality. This particular strongpoint is of the double-bay type, in contrast to the more common single-bay variety. The defenses of the position also were strengthened by the addition of another obstacle in the form of a staked-down line of bushes sited well forward on the beach. This obstacle extends for nearly a mile, covers the whole front of the position, and links up with the adjacent defended locality described above.

7. TYPICAL SMALL BEACH DEFENSE POSITION. In figure 124 there is illustrated in detail a beach defensive position which the Japanese constructed in Burma. The zig-zag trench system, within wire defenses, consisted of 5 groups, inclosing irregular areas, separated by a tidal creek. The trenches were approximately 5 feet wide at the top, with firing bays projecting outwards, thus affording an all round field of fire. Approximately 66 bays, equally divided between the two areas, were constructed in the system at intervals, varying between 23 and 70 feet. A pillbox, about 10 feet square, was located within the northern trench system covering the stream. Both double and single lines of wire, set on posts at approximately 10-foot intervals, furnished obstacle protection to the area.

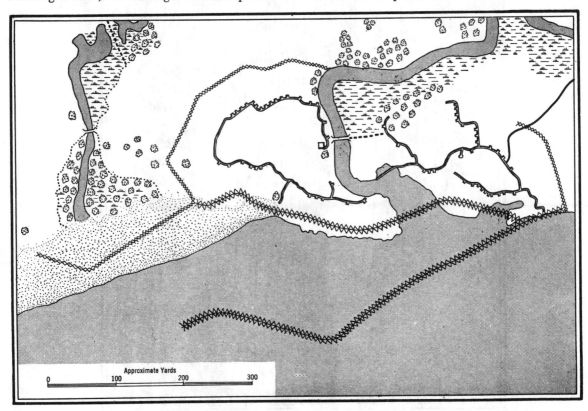

Figure 124. A typical beach defense position in Burma.

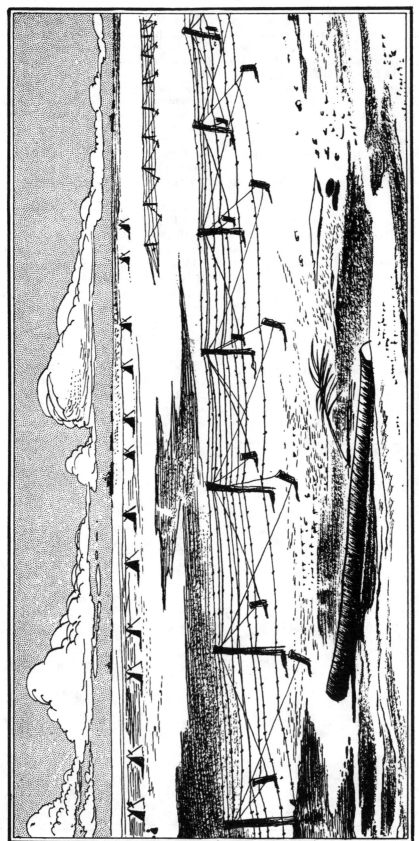

Figure 125. Use of artificial obstacles in beach defense.

8. DEFENSE INSTALLATIONS. a. General.

(1) Japanese defense positions, both inland and coastal, generally include strong, mutually-supporting emplacements of a permanent or semi-permanent nature. The use of artificial obstacles has not been a universal feature. In various combat areas, however, there are indications that fairly widespread use is made of artificial obstacles for coast defense. This tendency can be expected to be intensified the more the Japanese Army is driven back on the defensive.

(2) Construction details illustrating obstacles have been taken from Japanese manuals and training

(b) The double-apron type illustrated in figure 127 was found at Betio Island in the Central Pacific. Lanes sometimes are left between the lines of this type so that movable obstacles may be utilized. Here, again, both barbed and smooth wire are utilized.

(c) Passageways through wire entanglements are illustrated in figure 128.

(d) In New Georgia the Japanese used a prickly vine in lieu of barbed wire to form obstacles around defensive positions.

(2) *Movable barriers.* The Japanese feel that movable obstacles are not very effective, but realize

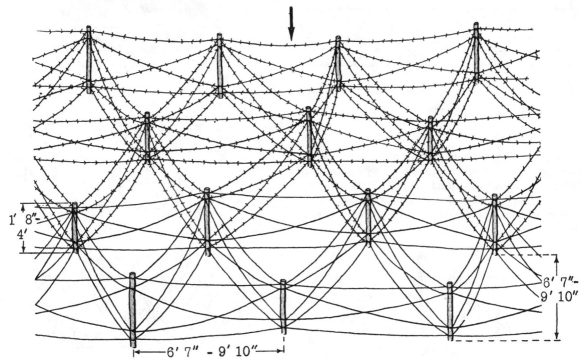

Figure 126. A barbed-wire entanglement.

instructions and may reasonably be expected to represent their current practice.

b. Obstacles. According to Japanese teaching, "obstacles are built to obstruct the enemy's advance and, combined with firepower, to destroy or hinder his movements, or to prevent surprise attack." They further state that wire entanglements and movable obstacles, combined with mines, abatis, and snares, normally are used. For antitank defense, ditches, mines, and obstacles for separating the infantry from their accompanying tanks are employed. The following details of their methods are given:

(1) *Wire entanglements.* (a) In figure 126 there is illustrated the net-type wire entanglement. Note that both barbed and smooth wires are used in the construction. Except for the lower horizontal line, the Japanese stipulate that the wires need not be tight, but they stress that the efficiency of the obstacle is increased by stretching wires between the main wires to thicken the net.

that they are easy to transport, set up, and conceal. They are used when an obstacle is needed to surprise opposing forces, when concealment of positions is necessary, when closing up a passageway in an ob-

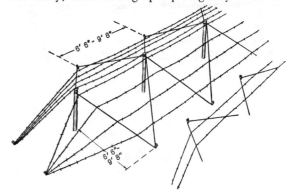

Figure 127. A double-apron type of barbed-wire entanglement

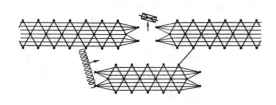

Figure 128. Passage-ways through barbed-wire entanglements.

stacle, to block roads, and where it is difficult to drive posts in rocky or frozen ground. The length and height are varied according to the tactical requirements and the convenience of transportation. The following three figures illustrate the type commonly used:

(a) *Movable wire barriers.*

Figure 129.

(b) *Cheval-de-frise (knife-rest) barrier.*

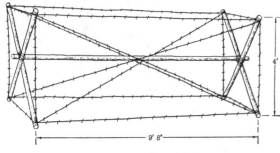

Figure 130.

(c) *Spiral (concertina) barriers.*

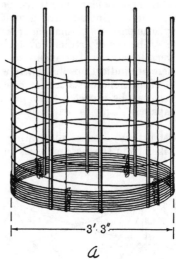

a

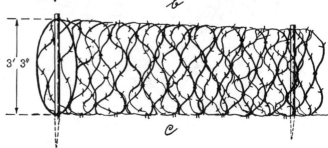

b

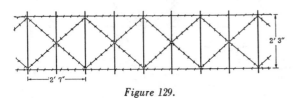

c

Figure 131.

(3) *Other types of barriers.* (a) *Abatis.* The Japanese recognize that abatis are easy to destroy, but they frequently use them in areas where trees are plentiful. Figure 132 shows a type made by

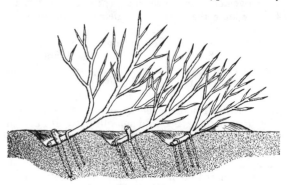

Figure 132.

cutting away the smaller branches of tree limbs, sharpening the ends of those remaining. The Japanese sometimes construct abatis by feeling trees at a height of 2 to 3 feet from the ground; the trees, not completely cut loose from their stumps, are felled in the direction of opposing forces, and their limbs are prepared much in the same manner shown above.

(b) *Folding screen.* The frames are made separately and then connected as illustrated in figure 133. These may be used in rows.

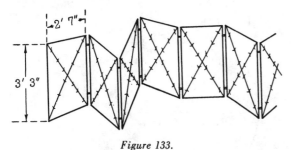

Figure 133.

(c) *Wire snares.* These may be of three types, illustrated in the following figures. It appears that either plain or barbed wire may be used, with the latter the most effective.

It is evident that snares are laid in "fields" at times on the principle of a mine field. In coast defense, they logically might be employed below the high water level, where they might well be expected to take attacking troops wading ashore by surprise.

(d) *Example of the use of barbed wire.* Barbed-wire defenses at Kiska were of four types:

> Double apron (2½–3 feet high at center and 10 feet wide).
> Four strand fence (2½–3 feet high—crisscrossed strands).
> Low entanglements 1–1½ feet off the beach designed merely to stall advancing troops momentarily.
> Specially designed entanglements.

(1) Double apron fence predominated and was used principally to block the mouths of the stream valleys which at most beaches provide ingress to the interior. Usually, this fence was found erected along the slopes of grassy dunes just inland from the beach. In only a few cases was the wire established upon the beach itself. Pegs and posts used in stringing wire were of wood—apparently odds and ends left from building materials, etc.

(2) Four strand fence defenses were cleverly located at the crests of steep beach bluffs, where the barbs would retard the attacker after his energy had been spent in climbing. Heavy machine gun positions usually commanded the full length of these barriers.

(3) Low entanglements were stretched upon pegs just off the rocks of a few of the lesser beaches. In most of these cases the wire blended so well with rocks and sand that the observer could not see the barrier until he was within a few feet of it.

(4) (a) At Reynard Cove a unique wire defense was set up in which the barbed strands were strung from the top of a 15 foot bluff behind the beach to pegs driven in the beach itself. This arrangement created a thorny maze of wire through which attacking troops would have had to climb in order to reach the high ground behind the bluff.

(b) Barbed-wire defenses at Kiska were not set up in depth, however, and probably would not have hindered the attackers greatly. Except at 1 beach where 2 fences existed, no more than 1 wire barrier stood between the sea and the island's interior. At many of the beaches unused coils of barbed wire observed in storage piles may indicate that further defenses were planned.

c. Defense structures. (1) *General.* (a) Japanese defense structures have not followed a set pattern to date, but have been made to conform as nearly as possible to the surrounding terrain and to meet the immediate tactical requirements. With some exceptions, these structures have been relatively

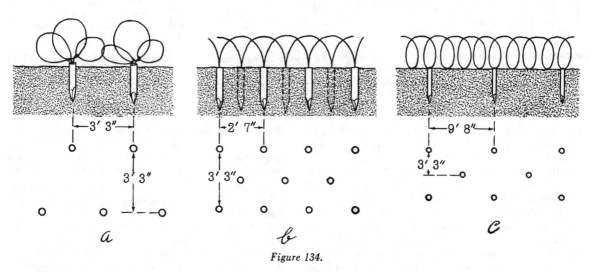

Figure 134.

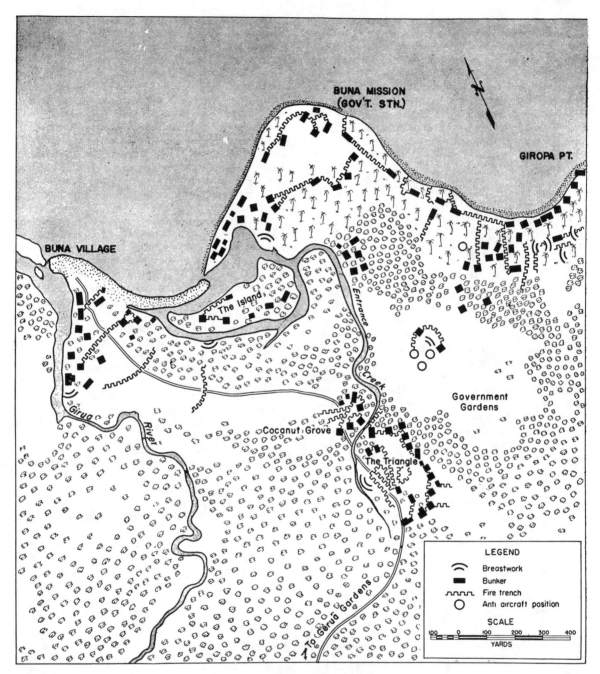

Figure 135. Japanese defenses at Buna.

flat, extending 3 to 5 feet above the ground level, or irregularly shaped positions built around the bases of trees. A Japanese manual on field fortifications states that "it is most important not to adhere blindly to set forms in construction work, but to adapt such work to fit the tactical situation."

(*b*) When forced to take up an active defense, the Japanese apparently follow the theory that construction of defensive positions involves a continual process of development. First, the positions merely constitute a series of foxholes; subsequently, if time

and circumstances permit, these are linked together to form a coordinated defense system. The third stage involves construction of strong points, bunker and pillbox types of earthworks, and log positions.

(*c*) Japanese positions have included bunkers, pillboxes, dugouts, shelters, blockhouses, rifle and machine-gun emplacements, fox holes, trenches, and antiaircraft emplacements and revetments. The terms "bunker," "pillbox," and "dugout" have been used fairly loosely, and it is sometimes difficult to do more than roughly differentiate between them.

(*d*) *New Guinea.* In New Guinea the Japanese terrain utilization between Buna Village and the coconut plantation at Cape Endaiadere was an excellent example of a complete defensive system. With the sea to their rear, they anchored their right flank on Buna Village where the unfordable Girua River and Entrance Creek enter the sea (figures 135, 136 and 137), and their left flank on the sea below Cape Endaiadere. They built a system of bunkers with connecting trenches on all the high ground; this forced the attacking force to advance frontally along rather narrow corridors of dry ground or through impassable swamps.

(2) *Bunkers.* (*a*) Generally speaking, bunkers may be said to differ from pillboxes by their size, shape, and shallow foundations. Usually they have been found on a large scale only in those areas where high-water levels preclude the digging of deep trenches, and in more or less open terrain (for example, in coconut groves and on the edges of airfields.)

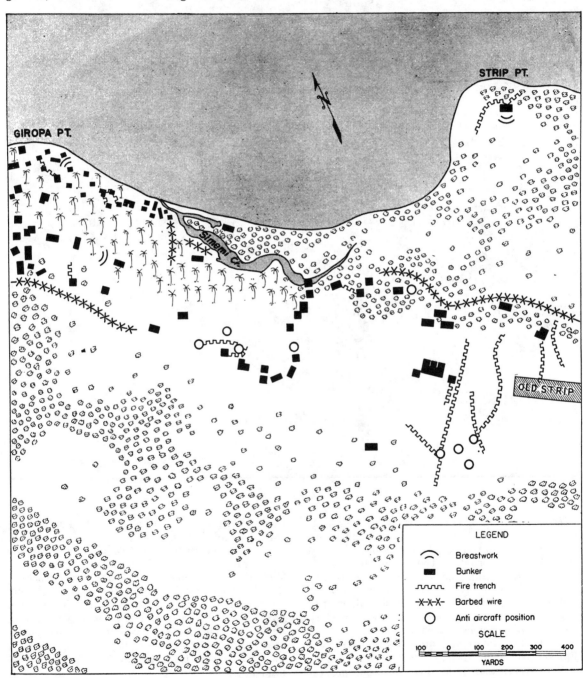

Figure 136. Japanese defenses at Buna.

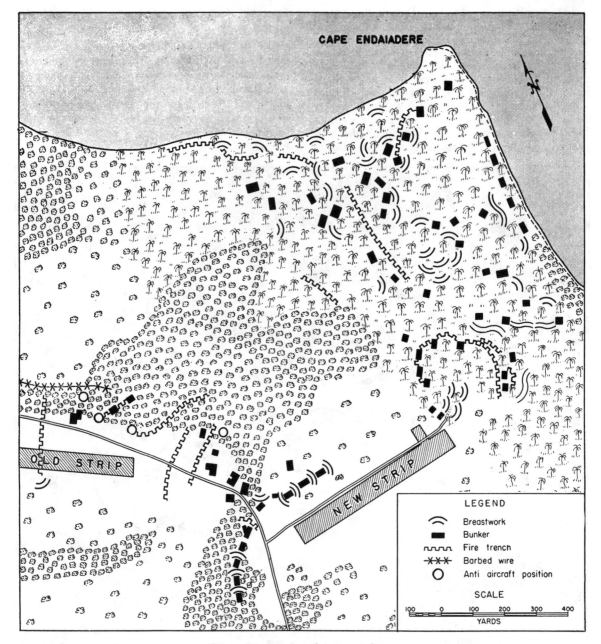

Figure 137. Japanese defenses at Buna.

(*b*) Figure 138 illustrates typical bunker construction. The finished interior of bunkers varies from 4 to 6 feet in height, 6 to 10 feet in width, and 12 to 30 feet in length. The larger bunkers are found sometimes with 2 bays, or compartments, separated by a large solid block of earth. Each bunker has 1 or more narrow firing slits, difficult to hit even at close ranges. These slits are covered by some form of camouflage when not in use.

(*c*) In the Buna-Gona area, the bunkers and pillboxes (the latter have also been referred to as small bunkers) were built along the same general lines. With a shallow trench as a foundation, log columns and beams were erected, log revetment walls were constructed, and a ceiling then was made of several layers of logs, laid laterally to the trench. With the completion of this basic superstructure, the revetment walls were reinforced by such materials as sheets of iron, oil drums and ammunition boxes filled with sand, and additional piles of logs. Lastly, the outside was covered with dirt, rocks, coconuts, and short pieces of logs. For camouflage, the surface was planted with fast growing vegetation.

Figure 138. A typical Japanese bunker.

Figure 139. Close-up of typical Japanese bunker.

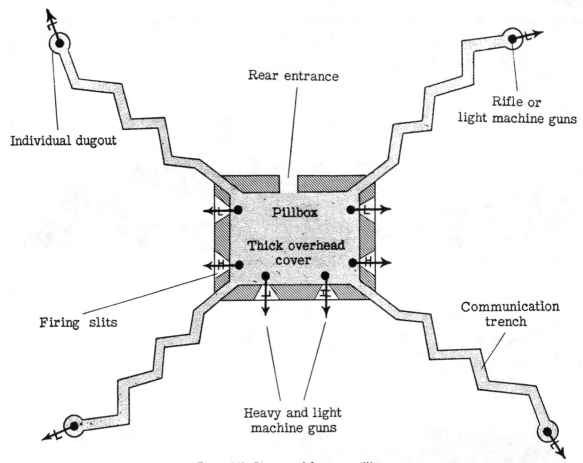

Figure 140. Diagram of Japanese pillbox.

(*d*) Different types of entrances were used. Some had direct openings from fire trenches, while others had tunnels from the rear. With very few exceptions, all openings were constructed in such a way that the explosion of a grenade inside the entrance would not injure personnel inside the bunker.

(*e*) A few bunkers were used to shelter accompanying weapons such as antitank guns and therefore had large direct openings.

(3) *Pillboxes.* Usually Japanese pillboxes are constructed over, or near, dugouts, to which the enemy can flee for protection while being shelled or bombed. Some have been described as having front and rear compartments—the front part for firing and the rear for protection, storage of supplies, and rest or sleep. Some of the dugouts are 10 feet deep or more. Figure 141 is a front view of a typical pillbox. Note the narrow firing slit, cut at an angle to permit a wide field of fire, and the iron fasteners. Figure 142 shows how the inside of a large pillbox or shelter usually is constructed.

(*a*) *Buna area.* In the Buna area some of the pillboxes were made as follows: sand-filled oil or gasoline drums were placed at intervals in front of the trenches—enough interval was left to permit firing by automatic weapons and by rifles. Heavy palm logs were piled 3 to 5 feet in front of the

Figure 141. Front view of a pillbox.

drums, in such a way that they did not block the loopholes for firing. The structure then was covered with sod and otherwise camouflaged by shrubs and saplings, which were planted in a realistic manner.

(*b*) *New Georgia.* (1) Many of the pillboxes on New Georgia consisted of two decks, which permitted personnel to drop through a connecting door during heavy shelling. All were described as mutually supporting and very well concealed. The pillboxes usually housed heavy weapons, while communication trenches leading out on the flanks generally concealed light machine guns.

(2) Coral rock, better than ordinary rock because it is more resilient, formed part of the protective covering on many of the New Georgia pillboxes (see fig. 144). It was used in conjunction with coconut logs, earth, and miscellaneous materials at hand. A large number of the pillbox tops had as many as four layers of coconut logs which were topped with dirt and coral rock. Ferns and growing shrubs were planted in the chinks to round out a well-camouflaged appearance.

(*c*) *Betio.* Pillboxes—along with blockhouses, open and covered trenches, individual rifle emplacements, and open revetments—formed the main defensive system on Betio. They were situated within 100 feet of the high tide mark. The pillboxes were constructed mainly of reinforced concrete (several of these were 16 inches thick), coconut palm logs, and sand. Hexagonal (6-sided) steel pillboxes used as command posts, roughly in pyramidal shape, were found on all the beaches (see fig. 145). Apparently they had recently been installed, and were designed to be reinforced with concrete (concrete had already been placed around 2 of them). They had not been camouflaged, and were badly damaged, since most of them had not been reinforced by sandbags or coconut logs.

These pillboxes, apparently prefabricated, are designed to serve as command and observation posts. They have a double wall, between which sand and other material is placed for added protection. Apparently most of the beach-defense guns on Betio were emplaced in dugouts with overhead protection. Many of the dugouts were made of reinforced concrete. Figure 146 illustrates the concrete pillbox.

Figure 142. Inside view of Japanese pillbox.

Figure 143. Exterior view of pillbox.

Figure 144. A New Georgia pillbox.

Figure 145. A hexagonal steel pillbox.

Figure 146. A concrete pillbox.

Ammunition and supply dumps were scattered about the island in bomb-proof dugouts.

(*d*) *Burma.* (1) In general, the Japanese pillboxes in the jungle country of Burma were found to be similar to those in the South Pacific. The two types of structures for bunkers commonly identified in coast defense positions in this area are shown in figure 147.

The details of construction are as follows:

(2) The Double Bay type is built in 2 sizes, 25 feet by 15 feet and 60 feet by 40 feet. They consist of mounds of earth from 5 feet to 12 feet in height, with a rear entrance well recessed into the mound. Forward, a central, apparently solid, block projects to form 2 bays. These bays vary in size.

(3) The Single Bay type consists of a roughly circular mound of earth about 25 feet in diameter and 5 feet high, with an entrance at the rear opening into a crawl trench or the main trench system. In front is a firing-slit; on, or slightly above, ground level, it is from 6 to 8 feet long and about 1 foot 6 inches to 2 feet high.

(4) The structures are designed for use by any of the weapons of the Japanese Infantry Regiment, but probably are best adapted for use by 37-mm antitank guns or heavy machine guns.

9. CONCLUSIONS. a. Pattern and principles.
The tentative pattern and principles of coast defense which seem to emerge from study of the

problems are: the Japanese may set their positions back from the coast line on high ground, with the intention of gaining complete control of ground and covering the beaches by fire alone, or if neighboring high ground is not available, their positions will be sited right at the water's edge with the intention of engaging any landing troops in direct combat at the moment most difficult for them. The selected localities will be well laid out and positions carefully constructed, while they will include a number of of strong points with interrelated fields of fire. In comparison with inland defense positions, greater use is likely to be made of both anti-personnel and anti-vehicle obstacles, which may be of a variety of different types. Any artillery in the position will be boldly employed and sited, while its use in a dual-purpose role definitely is to be anticipated.

b. Tenacity. The Japanese conduct of the defense is characterized by tenacity and a determination to fight to the last man and the last round. As a corollary, any attacking force which gains a foothold in a Japanese coastal defense position must expect to meet concentrated and accurate fire from flanking strong points and must be ready to withstand an immediate and determined counterattack.

c. Weaknesses. The main weakness shown by the Japanese has been an inability to adapt themselves to the unexpected, and their coast defense positions have been found particularly vulnerable to surprise either in the nature or direction of attack. The Japanese also have shown themselves partic-

THE DOUBLE BAY "BUNKER"

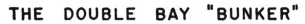
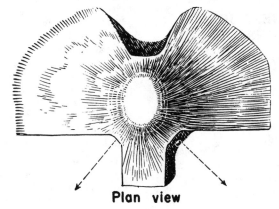

Plan view

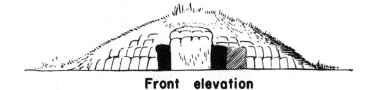

Front elevation

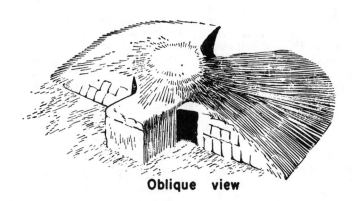

Oblique view

THE SINGLE BAY "BUNKER"

Front elevation

Plan view

Oblique view

Figure 147. Types of bunkers.

ularly susceptible to attack coming from ground higher than that on which their own positions were sited. Both these weaknesses were successfully exploited by the attacking forces on Attu Island.

Section XI. JAPANESE JOINT OPERATIONS

1. GENERAL. a. Definition. Joint operations as discussed in this chapter are operations involving both Army and Naval forces, including air; transportation by sea and a landing on hostile shores are entailed.

(1) *Troop commander* is the officer commanding all the forces which are to land.

(2) *Convoy commander* is the naval officer in charge of the movement by sea to the debarkation point. When there is an escort accompanying the convoy, the Escort commander is superior to the Convoy commander.

(3) *Transport officer* commands the special troops whose duty is to embark and debark the landing force. It is believed that this title is synonymous with that of Debarkation commander.

b. Purpose. Joint operations usually are employed for the purposes of seizing an island, establishing a beachhead as a prelude to future operations, or enveloping a hostile flank by sea. The principles of planning are essentially the same regardless of the purpose. Joint operations are usually large scale undertakings, although it is interesting to note the increased employment of the envelopment by sea, which may be attempted with a relatively small force.

c. Composition of forces. The size and composition of the force depend on the anticipated enemy strength, the terrain to be encountered, knowledge of defensive installations, and the scope of the operations. The force will include such special troops and equipment which are considered necessary to overcome anticipated difficulties. In some instances, a Special Naval Landing Party has been included to cover the landing of the Army troops.

d. Doctrine. Complete cooperation between Army and Navy is essential, the Army commander being given more responsibility in the operation than is awarded the naval commander. Secrecy, careful preparation, quick action, and deception also are prerequisites of success. Since landing operations are made under relatively unknown conditions, control and communications are difficult, and therefore all commanders should be ready to display initiative and to make individual decisions when instructions are lacking. Confusion can be expected with resultant demoralization. In view of this fact, troops must execute landing operations forcefully and with initiative in spite of bad weather, rough seas, persistent attacks by hostile planes and submarines, or strong enemy resistance.

2. RECONNAISSANCE AND PLANS. a. Reconnaissance. (1) Prior reconnaissance may result in loss of the element of surprise; nevertheless it is essential.

(2) Air reconnaissance of the proposed landing points must be made by competent officers who will participate in the landing. Aerial photographs showing the landing points both at high and low tides must be studied by all units.

(3) Reconnaissance from the sea must be carried out with secrecy. Submarines may be used, but their activities are limited by the depth of their draft and the limited view through their periscopes. Speed boats may be used, but care must be taken lest they disclose the plan.

(4) Although the method of reconnaissance will vary according to the mission, the time of day, and the equipment available, the following information should be gained at the earliest opportunity:

(*a*) General topography.

(*b*) Enemy dispositions.

(*c*) Hydrography.

(*d*) Topography, width, nature, and facilities of the beach.

(*e*) Condition of surf at high and low tides.

(*f*) Objectives and routes of advance.

(*g*) Existence of airfields.

(*h*) Correctness of existing maps.

b. Plans. (1) Based on the reconnaissance, the troop and convoy commanders select the anchorage and landing beach. Wherever possible, the beach selected should be one where enemy fortifications are weak. It should be so located that the plan of attack can be easily carried out, and it must be suitable for the landing of equipment. Alternate landing points should be selected in case the enemy situation or condition of the surf should dictate a change. When landings are to be made at more than one point, excessive dispersion must be avoided.

(2) The landing plan must have a margin of flexibility and must provide for delegation of authority so that rapidly developing situations can be met promptly.

(3) Plans must be worked out in every detail and all personnel be thoroughly familiar with them.

3. EMBARKATION AND REHEARSAL. a. Embarkation. The transport officer assigned to the convoy must carefully consider the troop commander's plan for landing. Based on this plan, he allocates space aboard the ships and prepares the order of loading. Extreme care must be exercised in loading the first wave so that its debarkation will be expedited. All matériel to be used by troops must be so loaded that it goes ashore in the correct sequence and at the time it is needed. If tanks are to be used with the first wave, they must be loaded on the same transport as the troops of that wave. Matériel should be so divided among the several ships of the convoy that the loss of any one will not seriously affect the success of the operation. If cranes will carry the load, boats and barges should be put over the side fully loaded.

b. Rehearsal. A transport which has completed loading will normally proceed either singly or in formation to the assembly point where it joins the convoy. Rehearsals of the landing will be undertaken at the assembly point as a continuation of previous training. Since the time for this is limited, emphasis must be placed on the more important aspects of the landing. During the trip from the assembly area to the anchorage or debarkation point, all final arrangements will be made and instructions issued.

4. ACTIONS BEFORE LANDING.
a. Transport commander's orders. At the assembly point, or immediately after leaving it, the transport commander will issue orders pertaining to the debarkation of the various units. These orders generally will cover the following points:

(1) Time for completion of landing preparations.
(2) Order of landing.
(3) Assignment of boats and barges.
(4) Hour of debarkation.
(5) Formation of ship to shore movement.
(6) Antisubmarine, antiaircraft, and antigas measures.
(7) Time for recall of boats.
(8) Communications between transports and beach.
(9) Rescue measures.

b. Responsibility of the convoy commander.
(1) Formation of the convoy.
(2) Communication between transports.
(3) Use of weapons for protection of the convoy.
(4) Care of casualties aboard transports while en route.
(5) Protection of the landing force. (This, it is believed, refers to naval gun fire covering the landing.)
(6) Formation of ships in the anchorage. They should be anchored parallel to the beach, and in single or multiple columns.

c. Other requirements. Landing units and debarkation units must complete all preparations for the landing the evening prior to arrival at the debarkation area. Commanders of all grades must be familiar with all details of the operation.

5. ACTION DURING LANDING.
a. Timing. The landing should be timed so that the first wave will reach the shore just before dawn. If attack from the air, or an advance up a long defile is expected after landing, it may be necessary to start landing about midnight so that most of the personnel will be ashore by dawn. If the landing cannot be made at night or under cover of fog, a daylight landing may be necessary. In this case the landing should be covered by smoke, laid by the use of floating smoke candles. Transports may also fire smoke shells on important enemy positions such as observation posts and searchlights. (Fig. 148.)

b. Formation of landing waves. Generally all boats of each wave get under way at the same time. If the anchorage is at a considerable distance from shore, the landing barges may come shorewards in columns for ease of control and direction. In this formation, a certain amount of maneuver is possible so as to deceive the enemy as to the exact landing point. As the column approaches the beach it deploys and continues to the shore, regardless of hostile resistance.

c. Functions of work units. Work units from the debarkation troops are charged with the removal of under water obstacles, marking the route for succeeding waves, construction of landing installations, rescue of men in the sea, salvage of damaged barges and when the occasion requires, they also act as combat troops.

d. Protection. The movement of landing craft from ship to shore should be protected against flank attack by the employment of armed barges, patrolling on the flanks.

e. Liaison, communication, and supply. (1) Liaison must be established between combat and debarkation units.
(2) Communication is maintained by the use of high-speed armored boats, radio, carrier pigeons, flag and lamp signals, and, when the anchorage is close inshore, by the use of submarine cables.
(3) Since the landing of supplies frequently is delayed, landing troops must carry extra food and ammunition. Supply dumps will be established near the shore as soon as possible.

6. ACTION AFTER LANDING.
a. The first wave. The crucial time of the landing is when the boats reach the beach and troops disembark. The first units to land will deploy at once and immediately attack in full force to rout the immediate enemy and push inland. The first wave will secure the beach, and if necessary, dig in and hold till reinforcements land, at which time the offensive will be resumed. Bicycles and motor vehicles must be assigned to those units leading the advance or to reserves who will be used to exploit success.

b. Assault detachments. Each company commander should organize and have trained special assault detachments designed to neutralize fortifications and reduce centers of resistance by attacking them from the rear. Personnel of such detachments should land as a unit in one boat.

c. Feints. Feints may be used with success at appropriate times. These may be made through the employment of mine sweepers, aerial reconnaissance, bombing, ship's gun fire, by the routing of a transport to a false landing point, and even by making a temporary landing.

d. Supplementary landings. It is possible to assist the main landing by putting a unit ashore on a headland or difficult beach where the enemy is not expecting a landing. This unit can work around in rear of the enemy, attack his flank, and cut his lines of communication.

e. Artillery. (1) When naval gun fire is used to cover landings, care must be taken so as not to disclose the plans prematurely. The troop commander issues the orders for opening fire.

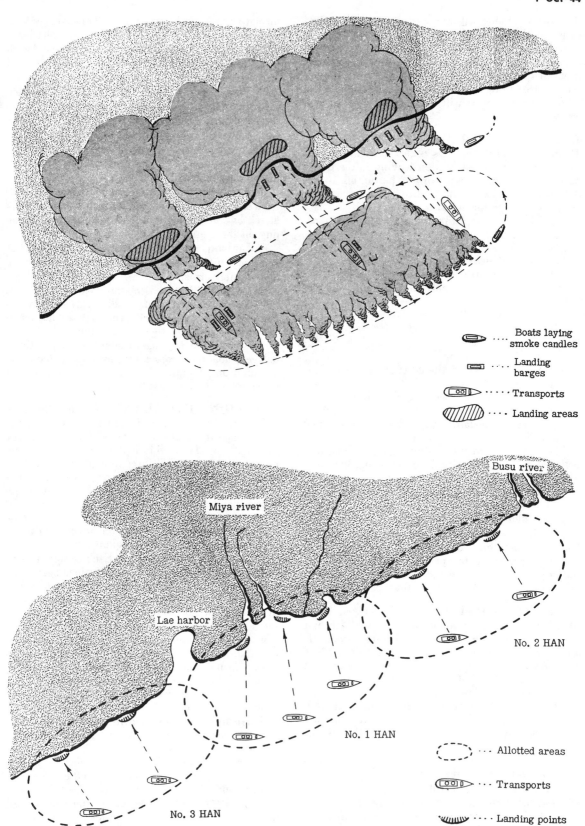

Figures 148 and 149. Smoke action during landing operations in eastern New Guinea.

(2) Part of the field artillery should be landed early to give direct support to the infantry near the water's edge. It is assigned the mission of neutralizing fire from fortifications and weapons protecting hostile flanks. Liaison must be maintained among artillery units so that fire may be coordinated. Positions for artillery should be chosen near the landing point but away from distinctive terrain features; they should be concealed from the air and inaccessible to hostile tanks. Infantry commanders give the accompanying artillery units assistance in changing positions or in moving forward.

f. Tanks. If tanks are used in the landing operations, they may be attached to front line battalions for employment at the water's edge, or retained for use in the attack at a later stage. If the situation dictates, the battalion commander must not hesitate to sub-allot tanks to companies.

7. NAVAL SUPPORT. a. General. In most landings that have been observed, naval units have escorted the troop transports to the point of debarkation and have supported the landing. During the earlier operations, naval vessels showed a marked tendency to leave the point of debarkation as quickly as possible, undoubtedly because of fear of hostile air attacks.

b. Naval gun fire. Naval gun fire in most instances has not been employed far in advance of the actual landing; the general practice has been to open fire on shore installations just prior to the hour of debarkation. At Kota Bharu, the naval gun fire did not commence until the troops had transferred from transports to landing craft. Fire was well placed and controlled.

c. Air support. In all Japanese landings first consideration has been given to neutralizing hostile air strength. Such effort has been highly successful in most cases, but at Kota Bharu the plan to destroy British planes on the ground failed, and, as a result, severe casualties were suffered. Japanese air has cooperated closely with ground units and has supported them well in the advance after the landing.

8. NOTES ON LANDING OPERATIONS. a. The Philippines. The principles of surprise and deception are well illustrated in the Japanese landings on the Philippines. A surprise air attack gave the Japanese quick control of the air. After this was secured, landings were made at opposite ends of the island of Luzon, the forces in each case comprising a special naval landing party and a reinforced brigade. Both landings were unopposed, and the forces at once began to establish beachheads, apparently to provide for the main landings which were yet to come. Each had naval escort and air support, and the landings were carried out rapidly and without confusion. When the main landings did occur, they were made on opposite sides of the cen-

tral (narrow) part of the island, and although they were opposed, forces from the initial landings were able to put sufficient pressure on the defender's flanks to cause him to withdraw.

b. Kota Bharu. The landing at Kota Bahru in northern Malaya was made in 2 echelons. The first echelon, consisting of engineers, infantry, tanks, 37-mm guns, and mortars was to land and cover the debarkation of the remainder of the division. Under cover of darkness it entered the anchorage, supported by a squadron of heavy cruisers and 2 aircraft carriers. The Japanese knew that the beach was organized for defense and that their landing would be opposed. When the initial landing wave had been transferred to landing craft, the guns of the naval escort opened fire on shore installations, the first indication that a landing was being attempted. The first wave proceeded rapidly toward the beach and suffered heavy casualties, both from fire and from under water obstacles. Naval gun fire was well directed and finally concentrated on one portion of the beach where a few of the defensive guns had been put out of action. A channel was cleared through the obstacles to this beach, and succeeding waves, proceeding slowly and guided by the engineers, landed with few casualties. The Japanese reserves were used up in this landing, and their position would have been critical had not the main force arrived in the anchorage at that time and rushed reinforcements ashore. Planes from the carriers were assigned the mission of destroying British planes on the airfield, but, as a result of faulty timing, arrived over the target after the British had taken to the air. Japanese fear of hostile air was well founded in this case, as the few British planes caused heavy damage to the transports.

c. Both landing operations described here had been well rehearsed beforehand.

9. COMMENTS. a. The Japanese plan their landing operations carefully and issue orders complete in every detail.

b. Reconnaissance is thorough, and even small units are given maps and aerial photographs.

c. The army troop commander has more authority in the planning than the naval commander.

d. Landings are always escorted by naval vessels and supported by air.

e. Control of the air is regarded as necessary to a successful landing, and the Japanese have attempted to neutralize hostile aircraft in every instance.

f. The principle of surprise generally is employed in landing operations, either by concealing the time of landing or its exact location.

g. Deception, as in all Japanese tactics, is frequently used to conceal the location of the main landing or to land smaller forces at an unexpected point to assist the main landing.

Section XII. JAPANESE PARACHUTE TROOPS

1. GENERAL. Only small forces of parachute troops have been used by the Japanese in their operations during the current war. They have made only very modest claims for their achievements and early realized that considerably more thought must be given to the training and organization of these forces.

2. EMPLOYMENT TACTICS. a. Palembang. At Palembang, Sumatra, in February 1942, Japanese parachute troops were assigned a two-fold mission; to gain control of the airfield at Palembang; and to seize the 2 large oil refineries there before they could be put out of commission by the opposing forces. The airfield and the 2 refineries were so widely separated that the battalion (about 700 men) was divided into 3 combat teams, each of which had to operate independently and out of support distance of the units attacking the other 2 objectives. The force used appears to have been too small to accomplish the missions properly. However, even though the parachute force was practically destroyed, and the entire operation was characterized by the utmost confusion, the effort served the Japanese well as a training maneuver. It also served as an effective diversion (possibly unintentional) while the Japanese were moving in from the sea to take Palembang.

b. Timor. On Timor Island, in June 1942, parachute troops were employed by the Japanese on two successive days, during sea borne landings, to cut the communication lines of the defending forces. The operation is described as follows: Twenty to 25 troop carriers came in supported by bombers and fighters. The bombers operated in groups of 9, in arrow formation. It was estimated that each carrier contained from 15 to 25 troops, which were dropped in groups of 6 to 8. There was no wind when the operation took place at 0830, in bright sunlight. The objective on each occasion was a position astride the hostile line of communication. The area chosen was fairly level, but timbered with high palm trees from 15 to 20 feet apart over certain portions, with thick undergrowth in the adjoining areas. There was no air opposition, and the objectives were from a mile and a quarter to a mile and three quarters from the nearest company outpost area and about

5 miles from the main defenses. Japanese paratroops landed from a low altitude, estimated to be 300 feet. During descent automatic weapons were fired, and considerable noise was made. While the landings were being made, the escorting planes bombed and machined gunned the defending positions. The paratroops, upon landing, quickly took up ambush positions; some climbed trees from which they acted as snipers. Forward positions were marked with Japanese flags, to facilitate their quick location by aircraft, and alternative positions were used extensively as soon as each squad was fired upon or outflanked. It was the use of these troops which prevented the withdrawal of the relatively small defending garrison which was opposing a landing of a large Japanese force in the Koepang area, since the paratroops had cut off the line of retreat.

c. Central China. In November 1943, in the Tungting Lake Campaign, in Central China, it was reported that the Japanese used parachute troops in the attack on Taoyuan, Hunan. Previous to this attack the Japanese carried out a thorough air reconnaissance of the area and subjected it to heavy strafing before dropping the troops. During the landing of the troops, made on elevated ground, the Chinese positions were kept under constant bombing and strafing attack from low flying planes. It was estimated that approximately 60 men were dropped, all landing near their objective. The leader of the force fired a flare which was apparently a signal for plain clothes men in the city to aid the attack. The parachute troops collected their equipment, which had been dropped first, and organized for the ground attack in approximately thirty minutes after landing.

3. CONCLUSION. The Japanese Army no doubt has acquired the practical appreciation of the value of parachute troops and the proper methods for their employment, although they have used them only in a limited capacity. The Japanese must also realize that the successful employment of these forces is contingent upon air superiority and absence of ground troops in the areas in which they are used. This assumption, however, should not be given too much weight when gauging expected Japanese action, even though they might lack air superiority. It must be borne in mind that this type of troop employment is in keeping with Japanese principles of surprise and their spirit of sacrifice, and it is reasonable to assume that a parachute troop attack may be attempted by them even though air superiority is not established.

CHAPTER VIII

SUPPLY, MOVEMENTS AND EVACUATION

Section I. SUPPLY

1. OUTLINE OF SYSTEM OF SUPPLY.

a. General. (1) The executive control required for maintaining a force in the field is provided by the services, under the supervision and direction of both the Administrative Staff and the Transportation Section (or Department) of the General Staff. The Chief of the General Staff is responsible for planning and policies, and the Transportation and Communications Bureau of the General Staff is responsible for the technical details of both land and sea transportation to implement the Chief of the General Staff's plans.

(2) The services—intendance, ordnance, medical, and veterinary—each have their respective bureaus (Directorates) in the Ministry of War, and are represented by their staffs on the lines of communication, army, division, and unit headquarters.

(3) In the Japanese Army, the Intendance Bureau in the Ministry of War is responsible for the supply and maintenance of provisions (rations and forage), equipment (clothing etc.), and pay; the Ordnance Bureau, for the supply and maintenance of arms, ammunition, engineer and transport equipment. The transportation of supplies, except within the forward units, is controlled by the Transportation Section of the General Staff. The transport of supplies within the forward units themselves is undertaken by the transport regiments and the various trains, such as the regimental and battalion trains.

(4) Variety in means of transportation is a characteristic of the Japanese Army; animal transport is largely used, and the most commonly employed vehicle is a 2-wheeled cart with a carrying capacity of 400 to 500 pounds. In mountainous country or places where roads are absent, pack horses are frequently used. In jungle terrain, the use of porters is common. Throughout the island areas of the Southwest Pacific barges and small craft are extensively employed. Motor transport is found where roads are available, though its exclusive use anywhere is exceptional.

b. Functions of lines-of-communications units. (1) The line-of-communications units establish and maintain a series of supply and evacuation centers along a main supply line (road, rail or waterway) extending from the communication zone, (or from the base ports of an oversea force), forward into the areas of the front-line divisions. Their general functions are—

(a) To establish depots, where required, for the handling of all classes of supplies.

(b) To receive, stage, ration, and forward men and animal replacements.

(c) To receive, store, and forward supplies.

(d) To evacuate casualties, prisoners of war, surplus supplies, salvage, and captured equipment.

(e) To provide medical and veterinary service for transients.

(f) To assess local supply resources and to requisition them as required.

(g) To provide local defense of line-of-communications establishments.

(2) The layout of a line-of-communications system is shown in figure 150. It will be noted that supplies may be passed direct from the base to the field-maintenance center (sea, road or rail-head), or an advanced base may be interposed when the line of communications is long and liable to interruption; also that the introduction of supply relay points is dependent upon the necessity for changing the type or method of transportation between various delivery centers.

c. Line-of-communications headquarters, depots and units. (For more detailed organization see chapter III.)

(1) *Line-of-communications headquarters.* The headquarters administers the line of communications and its branches as ordered by the army line-of-communications command. It is able to provide up to 14 line-of-communications branches (garrison or sector units).

(2) *Line-of-communications garrison (or sector) units.* Branches are formed in order to decentralize the administration on a long line of communications. The number required will depend on the distance from the base of the force being supplied. Each branch will be given its own headquarters and signal communications and includes a combat defense force.

(3) *Line-of-communications signal units.* Usually there are two or more companies, the personnel of which are allotted to the line-of-communications headquarters and branches.

(4) *Combat units in reserve.* Used to provide local protection and escorts as required along the line of communications.

(5) *Transportation units.* (a) *Line-of-communications transport units—land.*

1. *Line-of-communications transport headquarters,* also referred to as field Transport Headquarters or commands, administer several transport regiments and several transport supervision detachments.

2. *Independent transport companies (draft horse transport).* Each company has a carrying capacity of about 60 tons and a strength of about 350 men. They are attached on the approximate scale of 4 per division with a variable number for army troops.

3. *Independent transport companies (motor transport).* Each company has approximately the same carrying capacity as a wagon company and a strength of about 200 men. They are attached on the scale of 1 per division with a variable number for army troops.

4. *Independent transport companies (pack horse transport).* When necessitated by the terrain, pack-horse companies are employed. The carrying capacity of two pack-horse companies equals that of one wagon company.

5. *Provisional transport units.* These are engaged in transporting food, supplies, and ammunition to line-of-communications dumps but may be attached to armies or divisions. In the Southwest Pacific Area many of these units are formed as required and often have to operate without motor transport or horses. Each unit contains from 200 to 800 men.

6. *Line-of-communications transport-supervision detachment* (transport escort—unit). Provides personnel necessary to organize and command locally commandeered transport facilities. A transport-supervision detachment, with a strength of about 200, may operate 6 or 7 locally-formed transport companies.

7. *Railway units (railway commands, railway regiments, armored train units, etc.)*

8. *Tractor units.*

(b) *Line-of-communications transport units (sea).*

1. *Shipping headquarters.* All water transport is under the Shipping Headquarters, a branch of the Transport Section of the General Staff. The headquarters is located at Ujina, a port near Hiroshima in Japan, and allocates, as well as commands the various units necessary for the preparation of transport vessels and the actual operation of sea transportation. The following units are under its command:

Shipping groups.
Shipping transport headquarters (or commands).
Shipping transport area headquarters.
Anchorage units.
Shipping transport battalions.

2. *Shipping groups.* These branch offices, established by the Shipping-Transport Headquarters, are located at the principal base ports—Singapore, Manila, and Rabaul—in theaters of operations. They control a variable number of Shipping engineer regiments and debarkation units.

(a) *Shipping Engineer regiments.* These units are used for getting troops and supplies ashore, particularly in landing operations. They operate barges, speed boats, armored craft, etc., and man the craft on coastal and inter-island runs. Strength is approximately 1,100 men with about 150 assorted small crafts.

(b) *Debarkation units.* The functions of these units are vague. They would appear to be responsible for the actual unloading and landing of troops and supplies on and from the transports to the small craft operated by the shipping engineers, when no anchorage unit is present as in the case of landing operations. Strength is approximately 1,000 men.

3. *Shipping transport headquarters (or command).* These are directly responsible to the shipping headquarters at Ujina. Shipping transport headquarters are located at the principal base ports where they are responsible for the required installations such as wharves and warehouses, the fueling and provisioning of ships, the storage of cargoes (exclusive of unit equipment), and the planning and writing of sea transport in conjunction with the Navy. They also supervise the embarkation of troops.

4. *Shipping transport area units.* These units control shipping ordnance, antiaircraft artillery, and signal troops detachments of which are assigned for the defence and armament of shipping and for intercommunication within and from convoys on transports.

5. *Anchorage.* These units are port administrative organizations. They are located at the principal base ports as well as at the smaller bases. In addition, they may establish branches at small subsidiary bases. Anchorages are composed of a variable number of so-called Land Duty, Sea Duty and Construction Duty Companies.

(a) *Land duty companies.* These are stevedore companies of approximately 350 men.

(b) *Sea duty companies.* These are barge and lighter operating units of approximately the same strength as the Land Duty Company.

(c) *Construction duty companies.* These are used for general construction work, such as roads, warehouses, etc.

(d) As there might appear some confusion between the duties of Debarkation Units and Anchorages, it is well to remember that the former are responsible for getting troops ashore in actual landing operations where port facilities may be non-existent, whereas the latter function in established areas.

6. *Shipping transport battalions.* It is assumed that these units are responsible for the operation of small craft, other than those operated by the shipping engineers.

(6) *Ordnance units.* (a) *Field ordnance depots.* These depots stock, issue, and repair ordnance equipment and supplies other than ammunition, motor transport, and air stores, and collect and dispose of ordnance salvage. A depot is able to provide 2 branch depots and 4 advanced sections, and may have 4 mobile repair sections attached. Branch depots are installed at field maintenance centers (sea, road, or rail-heads) and at advanced bases during temporary maintenance stage. On a line of communications for a single division, a field ordnance depot combines the functions of the field ordnance depot and the field ammunition depot. In this case it is able to provide one advanced section and one mobile repair section.

(b) *Field ammunition depots.* These depots stock, issue and repair all types of ammunition, chemical warfare equipment, and salvage. A depot is able to provide 2 branch depots and 4 advanced sections. Branch depots are installed similarly to the Field Ordnance Branch Depots.

(c) *Field motor-transport depots.* Furnishes and maintains motor transport.

(d) *Field shipping ordnance depots.* See under "Shipping Transport Area Units."

(7) *Intendance units.* (a) *Field freight (supply) depots.* Also known as Field Clothing and Ration Depots, they stock and issue rations, forage, canteen supplies, clothing, etc., and make, repair, and sterilize clothing. They collect and dispose of the same type of salvage. A depot is able to provide two branch depots and four advanced sections and may have 4 mobile clothing repair sections attached. Branch depots are installed similarly to the field ordnance branch depots. On a line of communica-

tions for a single division a field supply depot includes the functions of a field medical supply depot. It is able to provide one advanced section, and may have one mobile clothing repair section attached.

(b) *Pay.* The Intendance Service is responsible for the pay and accounts of the Army.

(8) *Engineer units.*
Engineer stores depot.
Field road construction unit.
Field construction units.
Field fortification units.
Field water supply units.

(9) *Personnel.*
Labor and carrier units.
Field military police units.
Personnel for staging camps.
Personnel for labor camps.

(10) *Army Air Force.*
Field air depot.
Field air repair depot.

(11) *Remount.*
Horse purchasing depot.
Field remount depot.

(12) *Medical and Veterinary.* (a) *Line-of-communications Hospitals and field reserve hospitals.* These have a capacity for 500–1,000 patients each. If necessary each type of hospitals can be divided into two hospitals.

(b) *Line-of-communications Veterinary Depots.* These have a capacity for 700 horses.

(c) *Field Medical Supply Depots.* These stores, issue and repair medical supplies, patients' clothing, veterinary supplies and horse shoes. A depot is able to provide two branch depots and four advanced sections. The branch depots are usually installed similarly to the Field Supply Branch Depots. On a line of communications for a single division, the field supply depot may combine the functions of the field supply depot and the field medical supply depot.

(d) *Casualty Clearing Stations.*

(e) *Ambulance Transport Units.*

(f) *Field quarantine department.*

(g) *Veterinary quarantine hospital.*

d. Maintenance of line of communications (see fig. 150). (1) *General.* The supply columns of a line of communications are organized, loaded and dispatched from the base area of the base depots. The base area is seldom moved; however, an advanced base may be interposed when the line of communications is long or liable to interruption. The forward terminal of a line of communications is the point where the units transfer their supplies to the divisions transport regiments. The forward terminal is kept as close as possible to the front line and may be either the Division Maintenance Center (the more normal) or the Field Maintenance Center, whichever is the more accessible.

(2) *Maintenance terminals on the line of communications.* (a) *Advanced base* (see figures 150 and 152). The establishment of an advanced base will depend on the maintenance requirements

KEY TO ABBREVIATIONS

Amn	Ammunition
Bn	Battalion
CW	Chemical Warfare
Div	Division
DP	Delivery Point
FAD	Field Ammunition Depot
F	Field
FMSD	Field Medical Stores Depot
FMTD	Field Motor Transport Depot
FOD	Field Ordnance Depot
FSD	Field Supply Depot
FVD	Field Veterinary Depot
Hosp	Hospital
LC	Line of Communication
MT	Motor Transport
Ord	Ordnance
POL	Fuel, Oil, and Lubricants
Regt	Regiment
Regtl	Regimental
Sup	Supply
Vet	Veterinary
——	Normal Supply Route
– – –	Alternate Supply Route

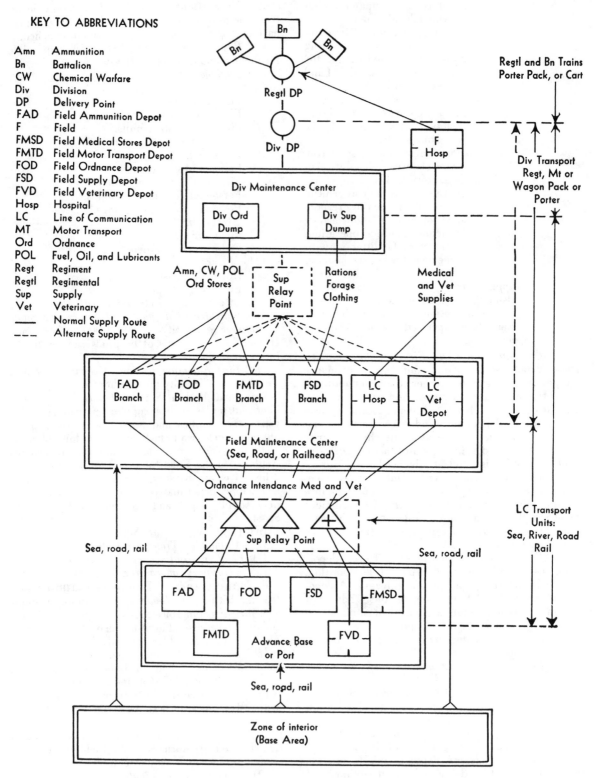

Figure 150. Japanese supply system and layout of lines of communications.

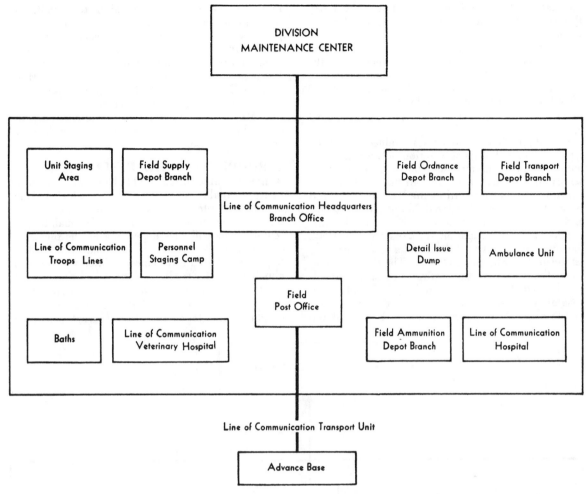

DIVISION
MAINTENANCE CENTER

Unit Staging
Area

Field Supply
Depot Branch

Field Ordnance
Depot Branch

Field Transport
Depot Branch

Line of Communication Headquarters
Branch Office

Line of Communication
Troops Lines

Personnel
Staging Camp

Detail Issue
Dump

Ambulance Unit

Field
Post Office

Baths

Line of Communication
Veterinary Hospital

Field Ammunition
Depot Branch

Line of Communication
Hospital

Line of Communication Transport Unit

Advance Base

Figure 151. Field Maintenance Center (sea-. road-, or rail-head).

of the supported force; the length of the line of communications, the possibility of enemy interference, and climatic conditions. Advanced depots of the base installations are usually represented at the advanced base.

(*b*) *Supply Relay Points* (see figures 150 and 152). These points are established on the line of communications as required. The organization of each will depend on its location on the line of communications and the weight of traffic to be handled. Relay points are maintained for reloading and dumping supplies, as staging points for transients, and as terminals and technical maintenance points for transport echelons.

(*c*) *Field Maintenance Centers* (see figures 151 and 153). These are also referred to as either Sea, Road or Railheads. Their size and organization will depend upon the size of the force being maintained, and the extent to which reserve stocks must be held in the area. Main service depots will be normally represented here by their branch depots or their advanced sections.

(*d*) *Division Maintenance Centers* (see figure

150). With the division administrative area are located ordnance and supply depots under the control of the division administrative staff.

e. Operation of line-of-communications supply system (see figure 150). Supplies are shuttled between Relay Points, Division Maintenance Center and from the Field Maintenance Center in one of three ways, depending on the distance between each.

(1) A loaded supply column moves forward from the supply Relay Point next closest to the Division Maintenance Center, unloads its supplies, and returns empty to the Relay Point for reloading.

(2) A Supply Column moves empty from one Relay Point to the Relay Point nearest to the Field Maintenance Center (assuming more than one Relay Point is established between the Divisional Maintenance Center and the Field Maintenance Center) loads and returns to its original Relay Point for unloading.

(3) (*a*) A loaded supply column moves from the Field Maintenance Center directly to the Di-

visional Maintenance Center, by-passing the Relay Points, if any. This method is considered to be the most expeditious.

(*b*) When the rate of advance of the force being supplied necessitates a forward movement of the depots, this is generally done by pushing forward a branch or advanced section of the main depot and after the forward branch has been established and functioning, the balance of the depot will be moved up.

(*c*) Supply Relay Points are introduced when the type and method of transportation between delivery points or terminals must be changed, or when reserves must be held in the rear of the Field Maintenance Center but forward of the Base or Advanced Base and between Divisional Maintenance Center and Field Maintenance Center. For example, during the Japanese occupation of Guadalcanal, in 1942, the advanced base was Rabaul and a relay point was established on Shortland Island. The Field Maintenance Center was on the northwest coast of Guadalcanal. Supplies were delivered from the advanced base or direct from Japan to either the relay point or the Field Maintenance Center. The size of the force, the nature of the campaign, the quantity of stores to be held in reserve, and the extent to which permanent maintenance has replaced temporary maintenance will modify the layout of the line of communications. Thus at one stage the Division Maintenance Center may operate at the Field Maintenance Center, supplied direct from base or advanced base. Then as the force advances, the Division Maintenance Center may move forward, and the Field Maintenance Center may be developed as an advanced base.

2. SUPPLY IN THE FIELD. a. Maintenance requirements.
(1) There are few or no figures available (except on rations) which indicate the exact maintenance requirements of the Japanese soldier in the field. As in all Armies, maintenance requirements will vary depending on the theater of operations. It is generally accepted that the daily requirements of the Japanese soldier are considerably less than for soldiers of the Allied Forces.

(2) Ration and ammunition may be considered the principal items of daily requirements. The weight of the Japanese ration (except emergency

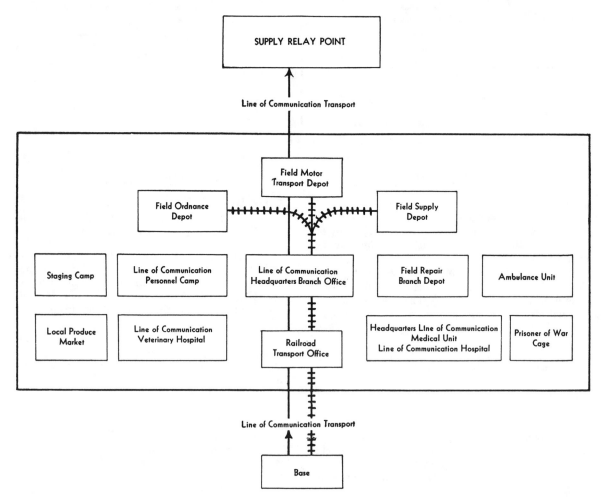

Figure 152. Japanese advanced base served by a railway system.

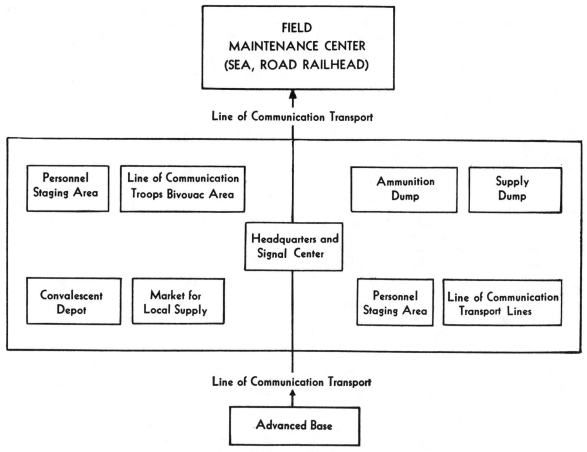

Figure 153. Supply Relay Point.

ration) is approximately two-thirds that of the American ration, or slightly above 4 pounds. Ammunition requirement is also smaller due to less employment of artillery by the Japanese, however, it is worthy of note, that the Japanese estimate as high as 4.2 pounds a day per man for active operation, compared with 5.17 pounds for United States forces. In the southwest Pacific Area, the daily ammunition requirement of the Japanese has been estimated by Allied Forces to be as low as 1 pound a day.

(3) As to other items of maintenance requirements, there is no agreement as to the exact amounts required. In the absence of detailed information no definite amount can be stated, but in making an estimate it is well to keep in mind that there is no substitute for many of the daily requirements and in the absence thereof, the ability to fight is considerably curtailed. For example, without fuel the Japanese cannot operate. The item of fuel is given as an illustration to show that while the individual soldier may be able to live for awhile on emergency rations, he cannot survive unless other necessary supplies are brought. Any estimate which leaves out fuel is therefore likely to be erroneous. While allowing for variation in need, it should be remembered that there are many irreducible requirements in operation. Roads cannot be used, ordinarily,

without repair and the poorer the road the greater the need for repair. Likewise medical attention cannot be neglected if health is to be maintained. The Japanese realize the necessity of meeting daily requirements and their doctrine states that it is well to establish Advanced Supply Bases wherever possible.

(4) To summarize while no definite figures can be given at this time for daily requirements, due consideration should be given to all essential items when an estimate is attempted. The daily maintenance requirements have been roughly estimated from 10 lbs. to over 30 lbs. a day per man, depending on the operation and availability of local supplies.

b. Rations and forage. (1) *Garrison.* In garrison the Japanese ration consists of about 1.25 pounds of rice and a certain amount of barley plus a cash allowance which is made for each soldier to be spent on the purchases of meat, fish, and vegetables. This ration is both varied and adequate. On maneuvers rations are somewhat increased. The following are common constituents of the purchased ration:

(*a*) *Cereals and staples.* Rice, wheat, barley, canned rice cakes, canned powdered rice dumplings, canned rice boiled together with red beans, biscuits, hardtack, vitamin biscuits, sugar. soy bean flour.

(*b*) *Canned meat and seafood.* Beef, salmon, sardines, mackerel, seaweed, clams. trout, tuna fish, cod livers, seaweed and beans packed in layers, crab meat.

(*c*) *Dried meat and fish.* Flounder, salmon, bonito, squid, cuttlefish. laver meat.

(*d*) *Canned fruits and vegetables.* Tangerines, pineapples, bamboo sprouts, bean and burdock, boiled lotus root, sprouted beans, arum root paste, spinach, mushrooms, beanflower, mixed vegetables, carrots.

(*e*) *Vegetables and fish in barrels.* Pickled salted plums, pickled radishes, sea cucumbers in curry powder, smelts in oil.

(*f*) *Dried fruit and vegetables.* Apples, carrots. Chinese greens, red beans, onions, potato chips. mushrooms, squash, kelp.

(*g*) *Seasonings, etc.* Soy bean sauce, dehydrated soy bean sauce, soy bean paste, vinegar, curry powder, salt, ginger.

(*h*) *Beverages.* Tea, *sake*, condensed milk.

(2) *Field.* (*a*) Rations and forage supplies in the field may be both "imported" or "local." The former are manufactured and purchased by base supply depots operated by the Intendance Bureau in Japan. The latter are obtained by purchase, requisition, or confiscation. The field ration in the Japanese Army is fixed by regulation as consisting of the following:

1. Standard, or normal field ration (total. about 4⅛ pounds), consisting largely of rice and barley, fresh meat and fish, fresh vegetables, and various condiments and flavorings.

2. Special field ration (total, 3 pounds), consisting largely of rice, dried, canned, or pickled items. This ration is the one most likely issued in combat.

3. Reserve (emergency) ration: Class A (total, 2¼ pounds) consisting of rice. canned meat, and salt; Class B (total. 1¾ pounds) consisting of rice or hardtack, canned meat, and salt.

4. Iron rations, weighing about one-half pound for one meal, include special Japanese biscuits and extracts that have been successfully tried out in various climates.

5. Nutritious rations, consisting of extra amounts of all kinds of food are allowed to men who need them.

6. Substitute items according to a regular system.

7. Supplementary articles, to be issued as available, consisting of cigarettes, either *sake* or sweets.

(*b*) There are indications that the average ration in active theaters is about 3½ pounds, and that

because of failure of supply, this ration has often been reduced to a half or third of the normal amount. The Japanese use local provisions whenever possible and encourage the local cultivation of vegetables by units. Vitamin pills are a part of the regular issue, and delicacies, especially canned fruits, are issued occasionally.

Type	Item	Standard ration	Special ration	Reserve emergency ration
Cereal	Rice	23.3	20.5	30.7(A)
	Barley	7.4		
	Hardtack		8.1	24.4(B)
Meat	Fresh	7.4		
	Canned	(5.3)	(5.3)	(5.3)
	Dried	(2.1)	2.1	2.1
Vegetable	Fresh	21.2		
	Dried		4.2	
Pickles	Vegetables, etc.	2.1	1.8	
Condiments	Salt	.18	.18	.18
	Sugar	.7	.7	.35
Flavoring	Soy	1.4	1.1	1.1
	Bean paste	(2.6)	1.1	
Extras	Tea	.11	.11	
	Sweets		(4.2)	
	Sake		² .4	
	Cigarettes	¹ 20	¹ 20	
Total		³ 64/69	³ 40/45	(⁴)(⁵)

Fuel: 2.8 oz per man.
Water (drinking and cooking) 4–6 liters (4.2 to 6.3 quarts U. S.) per man.
¹ Pieces. ² Quarts. ³ Ounces. ⁴ 34/38 Ounces (A). ⁵ 28/31 Ounces(B.)

Figure 154. Table of ration scales. All weights are in ounces. Items in parentheses are alternatives in the same type of commodity.

(*c*) The calorie content of the above Japanese rations has been calculated as being as follows:

Calories

Standard ration _____ 3,470
Special ration _____ 3,540
Reserve ration (A) _____ 3,140
Reserve ration (B) _____ 3,000

1. *Method of supply of rations.* The system forward of the base area is shown in figure 150, page 174. From the field supply depots the line-of-communications transport units carry provisions to the division maintenance area. where the division transport regiment picks them up and carries them to supply points, usually in regimental headquarters areas. Here supplies are broken into unit lots and issued to units under the supervision of the Intendance personnel. The unit trains carry them to forward delivery points, which may be unit or company kitchens.

2. In peacetime under normal conditions 5-days rations were carried at one time: 2-days on the man, 1-day by the unit train, and 2-days by the division transport regiment. In active theaters the amount of rations carried by forward troops is apparently ordered

for each operation, and is a combination of special field and emergency scales varying from 3 to 10-days rations. The method of transportation varies locally, but supplies are packed for ease of handling in bags or packages no heavier than 88 pounds or larger than 9 cubic feet. In the southwest Pacific Area, provisions have been floated ashore from barges or destroyers in drums and in rubber bags holding 132 pounds.

(3) *Forage.* The standard amount of forage per horse per day is approximately 10–12 pounds of grain, 9 pounds of hay, and 8 pounds of straw, but normally only the grain is taken into the field.

c. Ammunition. Provision and handling of ammunition is an Ordnance service responsibility. The system of supply is shown in figure 150, page 174. Bulk ammunition is stocked and issued in the base area by ammunition depots; in the forward line-of-communications through the Ordnance Depots. Distribution on the forward line-of-communications is much the same as for rations. The line-of-communications transport units carry from field ammunition depot or field ammunition branch to the division maintenance area where an ammunition column of the division transport regiment picks up regimental bulk supplies and transports them to the ammunition point. Here, unit requirements are issued under supervision of the regimental ordnance staff to unit or regimental ammunition parties, who in turn hand over to battalion ammunition parties, again under supervision.

d. Fuel, oil and lubricants. These are Ordnance issues, handled through ordnance depots, field motor-transport depots and field motor transport branch depots, to the division maintenance area. Fuel is transported in the Southwest Pacific Area by tanker or cargo vessel in either bulk or in drums up to 50-gallon capacity. Storage and filling is done in advanced base areas.

e. Ordnance. Engineer stores are supplied through their respective service depots.

f. Medical and veterinary supplies. Medical stores, which include medical supplies and patients' clothing, are handled through field medical supply depots and branch depots to the line-of-communications medical units or to the division maintenance center for forward medical units. Veterinary supplies are similarly handled through field veterinary supply depots to veterinary units.

g. Army Air Force maintenance. Army Air Force supplies of all kinds, excluding rations, are handled by the Army Air service personnel and are provided from an Army Air service maintenance or branch depot in the base area. In the advanced base area are located army air service arsenals (or air maintenance stores) which include a workshop section. These issue to field air supply parks and field air depots on the forward line-of-communications, which in turn issue to the air force units.

Field air repair depots are also established on the forward line-of-communications for technical maintenance, assembly, and repair of aircraft stores.

Section II. MOVEMENTS

1. SEA TRANSPORTATION. a. General. Various means of sea transportation, depending upon existing conditions and circumstances, are employed by the Japanese Army for troop movements. Cargo and passenger vessels, some converted to troop carriers, from 3,000 to 10,000 tons, are used for basic transportation; frequently, ships of less than 3,000 tons are employed. In one theater of operations "sea trucks" and various types of barges have been used for short runs. In extreme cases and under adverse combat conditions, reinforcement, maintenance, and evacuation are accomplished by means of warships such as cruisers, destroyers, and submarines.

b. Regular transport and cargo vessels. (1) *Shipping Measurements.* Several types of tonnage are used to denote the size of a ship or its cargo carrying capacity, namely, gross registered, net, deadweight, displacement, and measurement tonnage. An explanation of these measurements is given below:

(a) Gross registered tonnage (GRT), or simply gross tonnage is the entire inclosed space of a ship expressed in units or "tons" of 100 cubic feet.

(b) Net tonnage is the ship's volume of useful cargo space in units of 100 cubic feet.

(c) Displacement tonnage is the weight of the water displaced by the ship in tons of 2,240 pounds (long tons). Displacement loaded is the weight of the water displaced by a fully loaded ship including cargo, passengers, fuel, water, stores, dunnage, and other items necessary for use on a voyage. Displacement light is the weight of the water displaced by the ship minus the items listed above. Displacement tonnage usually is used to designate the size of naval vessels and only rarely that of cargo or passenger ships.

(d) Deadweight tonnage is the ship's total carrying capacity, expressed in long tons, and represents the difference between displacement loaded and displacement light. The effective pay load of an average cargo vessel is 80 percent of its deadweight tonnage.

(e) The shipping or measurement ton is a volume of 40 cubic feet. The size of Japanese ships usually is given in gross tons. There is no absolute relationship between the gross tonnage of a ship and its cargo carrying capacity. However, as an approximation, it may be assumed that for an average cargo ship the effective deadweight tonnage is equal to its gross tonnage multiplied by a factor of 1.5.

(2) *Tonnage requirements.* The amount of tonnage required to transport troops will depend upon the type of units transported; the amount of cargo; and the type of loading used; i. e., commercial, com-

bat, organizational, or convoy. The following figures may be used as a guide:

Classification	Tonnage
1 man_____	3.
1 horse_____	9 (equals 3 men).
1 field gun_____	18 (equals 6 men).

In moving large bodies of troops and their usual impedimenta, over long distances where proper loading facilities are available and cargo can be stowed with the least loss of space, an estimated average of 5 gross tons per man will be required. Such conditions will prevail in moving troops from home ports to theaters of operation. The following table gives the amount of estimated tonnage required to transport various units:

Unit	Tonnage
Army headquarters_____	3, 400
Divisional headquarters_____	2, 800
Infantry regiment_____	14, 000
Field artillery regiment_____	24, 000
Engineer battalion_____	3, 000
Division signal unit_____	1, 000
Transport company_____	5, 500
Division medical unit_____	5, 000
Field hospital _____	1, 400

Figure 155.

A division with a proportion of Army Troops is estimated to require 125,000 tons when making a long haul. In moving troops within the theaters of operations, particularly where opposed debarkation may be expected, or where rapid unloading is of paramount importance, light loading is employed. Thus in Rabaul-Guadalcanal movements tonnage figures averaged about 9.0 gross tons per man. The following chart is an example of this latter type of loading for various ships in a convoy:

Gross tonnage of ships	Personnel	Horses	Items of freight	Gross tons/man
5, 823	699	167	990	8. 4
4, 130	477	--------	975	8. 8
5, 467	457	165	2, 202	12. 0
5, 425	491	9	595	10. 9
5, 859	803	309	2, 127	7. 3
7, 006	816	166	1, 698	8. 6
6, 498	688	113	2, 230	9. 5
40, 208	4, 431	929	10, 817	9. 0

Figure 156.

(3) *Convoys.* Ships carrying troops usually assemble at a predetermined point, where convoys consisting of at least five ships are formed. These then proceed under a naval escort directly to their final destination, or to a staging area for transshipment to the theaters of operation. For illustration of convoy, see figure 158.

(4) *Speed of convoys.* The speed of convoys depends on the speed of the slowest ship in the convoy

and on the extent of zigzagging. Average speed is estimated at 200 nautical miles per 24 hours; small convoys of fast ships may average a speed as high as 15 knots.

(5) *Escort of convoys.* Convoys are escorted most frequently by destroyers or smaller escort vessels. A convoy of 10 ships usually is accompanied by 3–4 destroyers, but larger or more important convoys may have heavier protection. Convoying distances will vary according to the safety of the passage. Changes of escorts may take place at intermediate points, particularly where a convoy passes from one patrolling area to another.

(6) *Loading and discharging.* Japanese are expert at handling ships and have achieved a considerable degree of efficiency in loading and discharging military cargo. The rate of loading and discharging will depend on many factors, such as availability of piers, cranes, trained stevedores, etc. It is estimated that in well equipped ports loading and unloading of a ship combat-loaded averaging 5,000 gross tons, using shore or ship's gear, could be accomplished in 3 days (operating 24 hours a day). Where piers are not available, but an adequate number of Motor Barges (MLC) can be utilized, the same rate could be achieved for combat-loaded ships. Where lighters have to be used, as many as 6 days may be required to unload a ship. Harbor congestion or lack of an adequate number of lighters and stevedoring crews may extend the required time to several weeks. General cargo can be unloaded at an average rate of 1,500 long tons per 24-hour day at piers or with MLC, and at 800 long tons per 24-hour day by lighters.

c. **Transport by small craft, "sea trucks", and barges.** (1) *Sea trucks.* These are small coastal cargo boats, luggers, and the like, generally stack aft, and varying in size from 120 to 1,000 gross tons. To these may be added latest types of wooden craft (100–300 gross tons) now being built by the Japanese on a large scale. These vessels are chiefly employed in combat zones and for coastal and inter-island transport. They can navigate in shoal waters, can be easily concealed along the coast, and generally are well adapted for the transport of small bodies of troops.

(2) *Barges.* In view of the danger of attack on large vessels in close waters, the Japanese Army has used landing barges extensively in the Southwest Pacific area for the transport of troops and supplies. They travel by night over set routes and hide during the day in small coves or along a stretch of coast overhung by trees. Figure 157 shows the characteristics and capacities of the barges and small transport craft used in a supply and replacement role.

d. **Transport by naval vessels.** (1) Cruisers may carry an average of 300 to 400 troops on long runs, and perhaps as many as 1,500 or more on short ones, but few instances of the latter type have been noted.

(2) Destroyers have been used extensively in the Southwest Pacific Area for reinforcement, evacua-

Table 1 — Loads:

Types	Draft (feet)	Length	Beam	Equipped men	Horses	Supplies (tons)	Field artillery gun carriage	Field artillery store wagon	Field artillery ammunition wagon	Field artillery car (observation)	Guns (75 mm AA)	Guns (105 mm)	Guns (Howitzers 15 cm)	Howitzers (70 mm)	Guns (37 mm TK/A)	Tanks	Motors	Provision wagon	Bicycles with personnel
Tokubetsu Daihatsu Special large MLC.		69	14.8	170	20	22	6	3	4	3		2	3			2 light or 1 medium tank.	2		
Daihatsu, Army type, "A" large MLC.	3/4	49.3	11.5	70/90	10	10/15	3	3	4	3	2 or 1; 40 men	2	3	2; 40 men	2; 28 men	1 light tank and 10 men; 2 light armored cars.		36	36
Daihatsu, Navy type, "A" large MLC	3/4	45.5	10.8	80	10/15	9.8	3				2 or 1; 40 men			2; 40 men	2; 28 men	..do..			
Shohatsu Types "B" and "C" small MLC.	2/3; 2.7	30/35	6.5; 8.7	30/40		3.5												15	14
Barge, type "C"		49	13	50															
Barge, type "D"		38.5	11	60															
Yanunasen or sampan, Barge type "E".		63.2	8.9	60															
Barge, type "F".		21	7	20															
Barge, type "G"		52	13.2	50	10	15	3	3	4	3	2	2	3					30	
Large lighters		41.2	9.9	70	6	3/4	2	2	3	2	1	1	2					15	
Small lighters		30.8	7.9	40															

Table 2 — Characteristics:

Types	Draft (feet)	Length	Beam	Crew	Endurance (hours)	Speed Full (m.p.h.)	Speed Empty (m.p.h.)	Armament	Uses	Remarks
Tokubetsu Daihatsu Special large MLC.		69	14.8	8/10	13	9.5	10.5	20 mm gun; 2 LMG fwd; 2 LMGs aft.	Special large landing barge.	Often used to carry tanks, heavy guns and other big eqpt.
Daihatsu, Army type, "A" large MLC.	3/4	49.3	11.5	5/7	9.5	6.2	10	One or more 13, 20, or 37 mm guns and HMGs or LMG.	Transport of troops and supplies.	After section compartmentation capable conveying 100/120 on short runs. Will also carry 1 armored car and 15 men.
Daihatsu, Navy type, "A" large MLC	3/4	45.5	10.8	7/9	9.5	6.2	10	..do..	..do..	Do.
Shohatsu Types "B" and "C" small MLC.	2/3; 2.7	30/35	6.5; 8.7	3/5	10	8		7.7 mm HMG	Principally for landing tps in face of the enemy, or landing light stores.	Loading figures for short runs only for sea journey 1 week 10 equipped men and supplies.
Barge, type "C"		49	13			25		2 MG fwd 1 MG aft	Reconnaissance, fire support for landing operations	
Barge, type "D"		38.5	11			8		Nil	Lighter work in harbors.	
Yanunasen or sampan, Barge type "E".		63.2	8.9			10		1 or 2 MG	To penetrate shallow waters.	Flat bottom, airscrew propulsion.
Barge, type "F".		21	7	2		8/10		Nil	Used as MLO at Guadalcanal.	Two section collapsible wooden boat.
Barge, type "G"		52	13.2							
Large lighters		41.2	9.9	2		8				
Small lighters		30.8	7.9	2						

698462—44

Figure 157. Japanese small transport craft.

Transport	No. I 5,493	No. II 6,493	No. III 6,869	No. IV 3,793	No. V 2,746	No. VI 2,883	Sea truck 953	29,230 total
Speed (knots)	10	10	10	8.5	9	10		
Unit and personnel:								
Army Hq	2	56	21	2	2			83
2d mixed Arty Brigade	97	100	99	50				346
AA Bn (less 2 coys)	96	90	96	80				362
Army Sigs	18	20	32					70
Ind. Eng. Regt		50						50
Ship. Eng. Regt	70	150	150	50	50	100		570
Debarkation unit	150	150	176	50	50	100		676
Div. Hq	27	67	71	7				172
Inf. Regt	500	389	828	488				2,205
Fd. Arty. Regt	81	159	134					374
Eng. Regt (less 1 coy)	50		206	225				481
Div. Sig		38	30					68
Fd. hospital	102	50						152
Unassigned troops	10	5	55	100	150			320
Water purifying unit			25					25
Total	1,203	1,324	1,923	1,052	252	200		5,954
Equipment:								
AA	3	3	3	3				12
Bn gun	2	1	2	2				7
Regt. gun			1	1				2
Anti-tank gun		1		1				2
Mt. gun	2	2						4
Light mortar	4	1	2	2				9
Machine guns	6	7	8	7				28
105 mm How			2	1				3
150 mm How	2	2						4
Rapid fire guns			3					3
Gun limbers	4	4	4	2				14
Vehicles:								
Wagons	26	23	23	5				77
Trucks	4	14	8	2				28
Tractors	2	4	2	1				9
Passenger cars			1	1				2
Rear cars				1				1
Landing craft:								
Collapsible boats	10	1	15	15				40
Large MLC	4	8	6	4	5	11		38
Outboard motors	8		6	6				20
Unsinkable drums	500	300	500			200		1,500
Logs	25	25		25				75
Planks	125	125		125				375
Various freight:								
Munitions (cu. m.)	2,000	2,000	1,500	200	300	1,000		7,000
Provisions and cargo (cu. m.)				500	500			1,000
Aircraft ammunition (cu. m.)				120	120			240
Belly tanks (cu. m.)				100	100			200
Aviation gasoline (drums)				540	540		1,500	2,580
Boat fuel oil (drums)				150	250		500	900
Motor gasoline (drums)							150	150
Unit baggage (pcs.)	1,911	1,678	2,559	1,191				7,339

NOTES

1. Additional 958 personnel, 14 small MLC, 48 collapsible boats and 420 unsinkable drums carried on 8 destroyers.
2. Horses were not included in this transport.

Figure 158. Example of sea transportation in convoy.

tion, and supply. Their employment as carriers usually is limited to extremely urgent cases. Such trips are short and usually made at night with loads varying according to circumstances. An average load for a 1,500-ton ship may be assumed to be 200–300 troops with some equipment or stores. On some occasions destroyers were known to have towed barges loaded with troops.

(3) Submarines are constantly employed to carry supplies and small parties of troops. Average capacity of submarines is 10 to 15 men plus stores, in addition to their crew. I-class submarines are reputed to be able to carry 50 troops and 20–40 tons of cargo, depending on whether deck cargo is carried and large submarines were reported to have carried as many as 100 troops. For transport by naval vessels, see figure 159, page 182.

LIGHT CRUISERS

Class	Dis-placement (tons)	Dimensions		At maximum speed		At economical speed		Draft	Example of loads	
		Over-all length	Beam	Knots	Range	Knots	Range		Troops	Cargo
		Ft. *In.*	*Ft.* *In.*		*Miles*		*Miles*	*Ft.*		
Yubari_____	2,890	463	40	33	1,400	10	5,500	11.8	360	Plus 42 tons, equipment and for supplies.

DESTROYERS

Fubuki_____	1,700	379	6	34	34	1,100	15	4,700	10	280
Asashio_____	1,500	361	6	33	34	960	15	5,700	9	270
Mutsuki_____	1,315	336		30	34	960	15	4,350	9–10	250
Shigure_____	1,368	341	3	31	9	34	1,020	15	6,000	9–10	250
Hatsuharu_____	1,368	344		32	6	34	1,020	15	6,000	9–10	250
Kamikaze_____	1,315	336		30	34	960	15	4,350	9–10	240
Momo and Kuri__	770	287		26	6	31	800	15	3,000	8	_____

Cargo column (Destroyers): 3 vehicles; 2 bn guns, 2–105 mm hows; 29 boxes amm.: 20 collapsible boats, 2 MLC; 10 outboard motors. Averaged 250 men, plus 60–70 tons of equipment and/or supplies.

SUBMARINES

Class	Displacement	Speed on surface (Knots)	Speed, submerged (Knots)	Personnel carried	Cargo carried (tons)	Remarks
New type, I class___	1,150/2,200	14/20	9	Up to 40 (largest types reported to be able to carry up to 100).	350	Unconfirmed. Latest I class reportedly carry an aircraft in a deck hangar and have fittings to secure midget submarines and Daihatsu (type A MLC).
RO class_____	650/1,000	13/17	10	_____	_____	

Figure 159. Japanese warship classes used for transportation in Southwest Pacific Area.

2. RAIL TRANSPORTATION. a. General.

(1) *Japan, proper.* The Japanese have considerable experience in rail transportation, both in Japan proper and on the Asiatic continent. Their railroad system is well managed, and their rolling stock is normally in good repair. Honshu, the main island, is encircled by the principal trunk lines, and the interior is well traversed with branch lines and a few trunk lines. The other prominent islands of Japan proper, Hokkaido, Shikoku, and Kyushu are also well served with railroad transportation. The rolling stock of Japan proper is estimated to consist of 6,300 locomotives, 120,000 freight cars, and 16,000 passenger cars.

(2) *Korea.* The railroads on the Korean peninsula run in a generally north-south direction and link the chief Korean ports with the Manchurian railroad net. There are several east-west connecting lines. The rolling stock in Korea is estimated at 600 locomotives, 7,500 freight cars, and 1,500 passenger cars, exclusive of rolling stock used on approximately 670 miles of narrow gauge railroads.

(3) *Manchuria.* The Manchurian railroad system, which is characterized by a series of parallel and inter-linked north-south and east-west lines, is built mainly around the South Manchurian Railways' double-tracked Dairen-Harbin line. The Manchurian rail net connects with the Korean system at five points and with the North China system at three points, while numerous strategic lines have been built to the Manchurian-Russian border.

(4) *Gauge.* The gauge in Japan proper is 3 feet 6 inches, while in Manchuria and Korea, except for a few narrow gauge lines in the latter, it is standard (4 feet 8½ inches).

(5) *Capacity.* The average load capacity of freight cars in Japan proper is 13 tons, in Manchuria 35 tons, and in Korea 30 tons. In actual movement of freight, it generally may be assumed that the Japanese freight car capacity is half that of freight cars used in the United States. In Manchuria and Korea the capacity would be the same as for similar American freight cars. Third class passenger cars have a seating capacity of 64 passengers in Japan, while in Manchuria and Korea they accommodate from 80 to 100 passengers.

b. **Troop trains.** (1) *Composition of trains.* In Japan proper, military trains on the main trunk lines may consist of as many as 35 cars, while smaller trains which must be used on branch lines reduce the number of cars to as low as 20. In Manchuria and Korea military trains average 27–30 cars each. So far as it is practicable, complete units travel as such in separate trains; the composition of the train will vary depending on the type of material belonging to the unit. Officers usually travel in first or second class passenger cars (coaches); other troops travel in third class passenger cars (coaches) or freight cars used temporarily for troop movement. Livestock cars are used for horses; box cars for supplies; and flat cars for vehicles, tanks, and guns.

(2) *Dispatch and speed.* Troop trains can be dispatched at the rate of one every hour on the main trunk lines in Japan and Manchuria; on the branch lines the rate of dispatch will vary between 10 and 15 trains a day, depending on siding facilities. About 15 miles an hour is the average estimated speed of troop trains on the principal trunk lines in Japan, while in Manchuria it is about 20 miles

an hour. On branch lines, the average speed is reduced to 10 to 12 miles an hour.

(3) *Loading.* In Japan proper, a flat car will carry one 75-mm gun and two caissons; a gun tractor, limber, and gun; two large vehicles; or a large vehicle and two motorcycles. In Manchuria and Korea, the loading may differ only slightly from practices in the United States, since much of the rolling stock was purchased in the United States or followed American standard of construction. The box cars used for troop movements will accommodate between 50 and 60 men. Equipment, when loaded, is secured by blocks and ropes and usually covered by canvas. End, as well as side, ramps are used in loadings and if necessary, ramps are carried by the unit moving by rail. In Japan, entraining ordinarily can be accomplished in 1–1.5 hours, while detraining may be done in less than an hour. For movements in Manchuria or Korea, the time required would be about the same as elsewhere where standard railroad equipment is used.

(4) *Illustrations.* Troop movements in Japan and Manchuria are shown in individual tables below, followed by comparative figures of the estimated number of cars required for rail movements in these two regions.

Train	1	2	3
Troops	510 officers and men belonging to Infantry and Artillery units.	760 officers and men belonging to Infantry.	500 officers and men belonging to Infantry.
Horses	70	40	90.
Material	1 gun carriage, 14 vehicles, machine guns.	Infantry guns, machine guns.	4 gun carriages, 3 vehicles, machine guns.
Cars	1 passenger coach, 24 closed freight cars.	1 passenger coach, 24 closed freight cars, 3 open freight cars.	1 passenger coach, 25 closed freight cars, 4 open freight cars.

Figure 160. Troop trains in Japan proper.

Trains	A total of 41 trains: average length 27.5 cars.
Troops	1,019 officers and warrant officers: 22,679 other troops. This force consisted of a regular infantry division with several units attached including 1 Bn. Mt. How.; 1 Tk. Bn; 4 AA units, etc.
Horses	5,100.
Material	As required by the force.
Cars	29 first and second class passenger coaches; 26 third class coaches; 315 temporary coaches (covered freight cars); 60 partly covered boxcars; 467 livestock cars; 115 boxcars; 115 flat cars; total, 1,127.

Figure 161. Troop trains in Manchuria.

Unit	Trunk lines in Japan	South Manchuria railways (main lines)
Army headquarters	54	26
Division headquarters	45	22
Infantry regiment	153	82
Field artillery regiment	452	242
Engineer company	15	8
Transport company	94	42
Field hospital (1)	23	11
A division with a proportion of Army troops is estimated to require	1,500–1,700	750–860

Figure 162. Estimated number of cars needed for Japanese troop movements by rail.

3. MOTOR TRANSPORTATION. a. General. The Japanese have several types of trucks, varying in carrying capacity from ¾ ton to 3 tons. The most common type called the Nissan, is of 1½ tons carrying capacity. In most data on motor transport movements it will be found that calculations usually are based on the employment of the

Material	1½-ton truck	1-ton truck	¾-ton truck
Soldiers, equipped	18	12	9.
LMG	3 guns, 3 boxes of amm., 16 men.	2 guns, 2 boxes of amm., 11 men.	1 or 2 guns, 1 or 2 boxes of amm., 8 men.
HMG, Model 92	1 gun, 3 boxes of amm., 15 men.	1 gun, 4 boxes of amm., 10 men.	1 gun, 4 boxes of amm., 7 men.
Howitzer (70 mm.) Model 92	1 gun, 6 boxes of amm., 15 men.	1 gun, 3 boxes of amm., 10 men.	1 gun, 6 boxes of amm., 6 men.
Mortar (50 mm.) Model 98	1 gun, 20 boxes of amm., 11 men.	1 gun, 8 boxes of amm., 9 men.	1 gun, 6 boxes of amm., 5 men.
Field artillery gun (75 mm.), Model 38.	1 gun, carriage or limber, 7 men.	1 gun, carriage or limber, 1 man.	
Mountain (Infantry) gun, Model 41.	1 gun, 10 men	1 gun, 3 men	1 gun.
Rifle ammunition, Model 38	32 boxes	22 boxes	16 boxes.
HMG ammunition, Model 92	60 boxes	40 boxes	30 boxes.
Mortar ammunition, Model 98	57 boxes	38 boxes	28 boxes.
Hand grenades	42 boxes	28 boxes	21 boxes.
Field artillery Gun amm. (75 mm.) Model 38.	38 boxes	26 boxes	19 boxes.
Provision, forage, clothing, etc.	1½ tons	1 ton	¾ ton.
Gasoline	100 cans (5 U. S. gals.)	66 cans (5 U. S. gals.)	50 cans (5 U. S. gals.).

Remarks: Trucks are loaded at full capacity. A fully equipped soldier's estimated weight is 150 pounds.

Figure 163. Standard chart showing transportation capacity of motor trucks.

Force classification	Speed of march in kilometers per hour (figures in parentheses are miles per hour)				1 day's march	
	Daytime		Nighttime		Km.	Miles
A force composed of all arms	4	(2.48)	3 to 4	(1.87 to 2.5)	24 to 40	(14.9 to 24.84).
Mounted cavalry force	6 to 10	(3.73) to 6.21	4 to 5	(2.5 to 3.11)	40 to 60	(24.84 to 37.26).
Fast march of horse-drawn artillery force.	10	(6.21)	8	(4.97)		
Motorized artillery force (field artillery).	10 to 20	(6.21 to 12.42)	Dimmed lights; 6 (3.73)	No lights; 4 (2.48)	} 100 to 120	(62 to 74.52)
Motor-car company	12 to 20	7.45 to 12.42	Dimmed lights; 6 to 10 (3.73 to 6.2).	No lights; 4 (2.48)		
Tank company:						
Medium tanks	12	(7.45)	Dimmed lights; 6(3.73)	No lights; 4 (2.48)	80	(49.7)
Light tanks	16	(9.94)	Dimmed lights; 8 (4.97).	No lights; 4 (2.48)	} 100	(62.1)
Tankettes	16	(9.94)	Dimmed lights; 8 (4.97).	No lights; 8 (2.48)		

NOTES
1. A short rest every hour was included in determining average speeds.
2. The length of march is the average distance covered per day in marching lasting a number of days.
3. The roads are considered to be average ones in level country.

Figure 164. Chart of the standard rates and length of march.

1½ ton truck. For capacity of trucks, see figure 163.

b. Requirements. Motor transport required for moving of troops is as follows:

Unit (personnel with combat equipment)	Number of trucks
Infantry company	16
Infantry battalion	100
Regimental gun company	25
Infantry regiment	375
FA battalion (75-mm)	80
Engineer battalion (105-mm)	120
Engineer company	16
Division signal unit	22
Division, total	3,000

(1) Estimate based on 1½-ton capacity trucks.

(2) Unit combat and field trains included.

(3) Horses and vehicles excluded.

(4) For moving horses and vehicles, it is estimated that, generally, the additional number of trucks required would be equal to the number needed for moving troops and combat equipment.

4. MARCH TABLES AND ROAD SPACES.
a. General. The Japanese Army, in its training, has for years stressed marching, and the ability to make long marches. This has resulted in the marching ability shown in Malaya, Burma, and the Pacific islands where Japanese columns have made 10–12 miles per day through heavy jungle and over terrain considered impassable. In New Guinea, a Japanese column, burdened by its heavy weapons, averaged 8–9 miles a day along jungle trails. Jungle marches are ordinarily made on a basis of 20 minutes marching and 20 minutes rest.

b. Marching ability of the various arms.
See figures 164 and 165.

Section III. EVACUATION

1. GENERAL. The Division Medical Service consists of a Headquarters, three to five Field Hospitals with a capacity of 500 patients each, a Medical Unit, and Regimental and Battalion medical personnel. The Medical Unit is divided into Headquarters; Stretcher; and Ambulance Companies, whose duty is to collect the wounded, bear them to Advance Dressing Stations, give them first aid treatment, and transport them, ordinarily by horse-drawn or motor ambulance, to the Field Hospitals in the rear. The medical officer of the Regimental Headquarters supervises the medical personnel within the Regiment. Each Battalion, supervised by a Battalion medical officer, has certain medical personnel assigned to companies and platoons at the rate of one medical orderly to each platoon.

2. DETAILED ACTION. When a soldier is wounded in action he is attended by the medical orderly of his platoon who renders first aid. If necessary, the medical orderly directs the companion of the wounded soldier to help move the wounded to a place where he can be found by the stretcher bearers of the platoons of the collecting companies. The stretcher bearers carry the casualties to the First Aid Station (or Dressing Station) where supplemental first aid is rendered, and a tag attached to the patient giving details of injury and treatment. Thereafter the patient is taken to a Casualty Clearing Station (Transfer Station) and evacuated, probably by ambulance, to a Field Hospital. If seriously wounded, the patient may be transported by the Patient Evacuation Section of the Line of Communications to the Line of Communications Hospital. A variation of the above may occur if the division advances and moves up its Field Hospital. In such event, the Reserve Field Hospital of the Line of Communications moves in and takes over the serious cases of the Division Field Hospital and continues the treatment of the patient until evacuated to the Line of Communications Base Hospital.

3. EVACUATION SYSTEM. See figure 166.

Name of units	Length of column for combat units	Length of column for unit trains	Intervals between units
Army headquarters	200	200	
Infantry:			
Division headquarters	150	150	
Infantry rifle company	75		8
Machine gun company	110		8
Battalion (less train)	440	95	20
Battalion (with train)	580	(135)	20
Regimental gun company	170	(35) 25	
Regiment (total)	2,100	(500) 370	20
Cavalry:			
Cavalry company:			
In column of 2	210		15
In column of 4	120		15
Cavalry regiment:			
In column of 2	400–670	(320)	20
In column of 4	260–440	200	20
Horse artillery unit	1,000		
Machine gun unit	550		
Cavalry brigade (less trains)	3,500	800	
Cavalry brigade (with trains)	1,900	800	
Field artillery:			
Company (less train)	220		20
Company (with train)	300		
Battalion (less train)	1,050	270	30
Battalion (with train)	1,230	270	30
Regiment (less train)	4,000	1,000	
Regiment (with train)	4,500	1,000	
Mountain artillery:			
Company (less unit train)	220		
Company (with unit train)	330		
Battalion (less unit train)	1,230	(390)	30
Battalion (with unit train)	1,400	(390)	30
Regiment (less unit train)	4,400	(1500)	30
Regiment (with unit trains)	5,400	(1500)	30
105-mm gun regiment	4,000		
150-mm howitzers:			
Company (less train)	320		20
Company (with train)	480		20
Battalion (less train)	1,550	400	30
Battalion (with train)	2,000	400	30
Regiment (less train)	4,100	1,050	30
Regiment (with train)	4,950	1,050	30
Heavy arty brig tnpt unit	5,000		
Field AA arty unit	300		
Engineers:			
Company (less train)	120	50	8
Company (with train)	190	(60)	8
Regiment (less train)	260	120	15
Regiment (with train)	400	(150)	
Bridge building company	(6,200)		
Transport:			
Company (draft)	1,600		
Company (pack)	(1,610)		
Company (MT)	1,200		
Horse depot	(160) 130		
Signals: Signal unit	(230) 200		
Medical unit	(240) 800		
Field hospital	(440) 375		

NOTES

1. Figures in parentheses indicate pack formations.
2. Foot units are calculated as marching columns of four.
3. All distances are in meters.

Figure 165. Road space table.

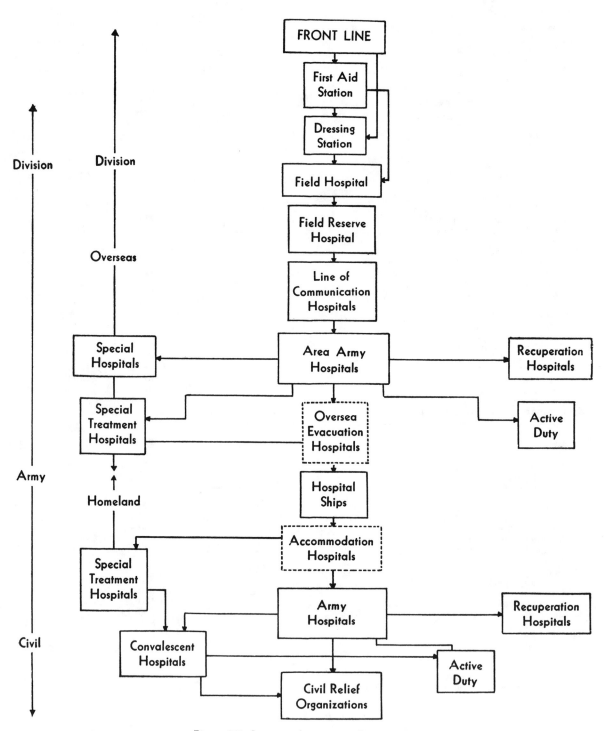

Figure 166. Japanese Army evacuation system.

CHAPTER IX

WEONS

Section I. INTRODUCTION

1. In general, the development of Japanese weapons may be divided into periods, each of which follows a war.

2. The progenitors of current Japanese weapons, as well as some of the weapons still in use, were designed between 1905 and 1912. A few models were modified in 1914–1915. Developments of the First World War were noticeable in a group of weapons developed in 1921 and 1922. Then in 1925 began a great program of redesign which finally included all Japanese weapons of every description.

3. All categories of artillery were redesigned between 1925 and 1936. Infantry mortars were redesigned between 1929 and 1939, and automatic weapons, with many new weapons added, between 1932 and 1939.

4. Although no weapon designed in 1940 is known, a modern, efficient 47-mm gun was produced in 1941, and it is possible that the design of this weapon was influenced by the Nomonhan Incident when Japanese and Russian border forces fought for 24 days in 1939. It is believed that other new designs, especially anti-aircraft artillery, have made their appearance, but up to this writing these have not been encountered.

5. As a result of early Japanese successes in the present war, various United States, Dutch, and British weapons are found in use by the Japanese. In one or two cases the Japanese have copied captured weapons exactly. In others, they have manufactured ammunition to use in the captured artillery.

Section II. INFANTRY WEAPONS

1. PISTOLS, REVOLVERS, AND RIFLES.
a. General. (1) All known Japanese rifles and carbines are of Arisaka design. Immediately after the Russo-Japanese War, Model 38 (1905) 6.5-mm Rifle was introduced and all subsequent rifles and carbines have adhered to this design. Later models have a folding monopod attached to the lower band. The design closely follows the Mauser and is simple and sturdy. The safety mechanism is an unusual feature.

(2) The only known Japanese military revolver is a very clumsy copy of a Smith and Wesson top-break revolver. This weapon was introduced in 1893.

(3) The first Japanese military magazine pistol was designed by General Nambu. Despite its superficial resemblance to the German Luger, the action of the Nambu pistol is unique. The original design was improved in the Model 14 (1925) pistol.

(4) The Model 94 (1934) pistol is a crude attempt to make a small pistol along general Browning lines.

b. Nambu 8-mm pistol. (1) *General description.* This is a semiautomatic, recoil-operated, magazine-fed hand weapon (fig. 167). It is equipped with a grip safety below the trigger guard.

Figure 167. Nambu 8-mm. pistol.

The markings 南部式 on the right side of the receiver read "Nambu model". In addition to the markings, the weapon is easily identified by the recoil-spring housing (a bulge on the left side of the receiver) and the adjustable rear sight. This is a leaf with an open V notch sliding on a ramp and is graduated from 100 to 500 meters. The weapon may be equipped with a wooden holster, also designed to be used as a shoulder stock when attached to the heel of the butt.

(2) *Characteristics.*

Caliber	8-mm (.315 inch).
Capacity of magazine	8 rounds.
Weight (empty)	31 ounces.
Muzzle velocity	950 feet per second.

(3) *Ammunition.* Rimless ball cartridges are provided and are interchangeable in the model 14 and the model 94 pistols described on the following pages.

c. Model 14 (1925) 8-mm pistol. (1) *General description.* The model 14 (1925) 8-mm pistol is a semiautomatic, recoil-operated, magazine-fed hand weapon (fig. 168). It is a development of the Nambu 8-mm pistol. Markings 十四年式 on the left side of the receiver read "14th year model". The front sight is a blade type sight and the rear

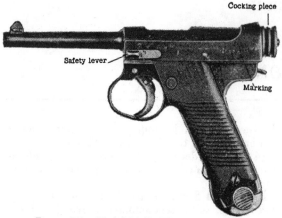

Figure 168. Model 14 (1925) 8-mm pistol.

sight is a non-adjustable open **V** notch. The safety lever is moved to the forward position for "fire" and rearward for "safe." An unusually large trigger guard permits firing with a gloved hand.

(2) *Characteristics.*

Caliber_____ 8-mm (.315 inch).
Magazine capacity____ 8 rounds.
Weight (empty)_____ 2 pounds.
Muzzle velocity_____ 950 feet per second.

(3) *Ammunition.* Rimless ball cartridges are provided and are interchangeable in the Nambu and the model 94 pistols.

d. Model 94 (1934) 8-mm pistol. (1) *General description.* The model 94 (1934) 8-mm pistol (fig. 169) is the latest design of semiautomatic pistol manufactured by the Japanese. It is believed to be inferior to the Nambu and the model 14 pistols because of poor design and manufacture. It is a semiautomatic, recoil-operated, magazine-fed hand weapon. Markings 九四式 on the left side of the receiver read "Model 94". The front sight is a blade type sight and the rear sight is a non-adjustable open **V** notch type. A safety catch on the left rear of the receiver is moved upwards for "safe" and downwards for "fire".

(2) *Characteristics.*

Caliber_____ 8-mm (.315 inch).
Magazine capacity____ 6 rounds.
Weight (empty)_____ 1 pound 11 ounces.
Muzzle velocity_____ 900 feet per second.

(3) *Ammunition.* Rimless ball cartridges are provided and are interchangeable in the Nambu and the model 14 pistols.

e. Model 26 (1893) 9-mm revolver. (1) *General description.* This revolver is solely a double action weapon with a cylinder having six chambers (fig. 170). It is a copy of the old Smith and Wesson top-break type. The weapon is equipped with blade type front sight and notch type rear sight. There is no positive safety device and owing to the extremely heavy trigger pull it has a comparatively

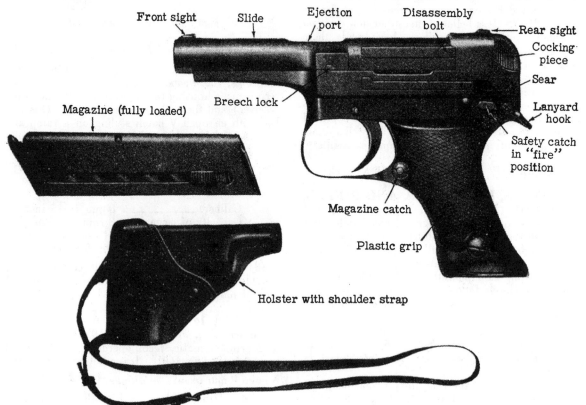

Figure 169. Model 94 (1934) 8-mm pistol, showing holster and magazine.

TM–E 30–480
1 OCT 44

RESTRICTED

Figure 170. Model 26 (1893) 9-mm revolver.

low rate of fire. Moreover crude construction prohibits positive alignment of barrel and cylinder making its accuracy questionable. The markings 二十六年式 on the right side of the frame read "26th year model."

(2) *Characteristics.*

Caliber_____ 9-mm (.354 inch).
Weight (empty) _____ 2¼ pounds.
Over-all length_____ 8.5 inches.

(3) *Ammunition.* This weapon fires 9-mm rimmed ball ammunition.

f. Model 38 (1905) 6.5-mm rifle. (1) *General description.* This rifle is a manually operated, clip loaded, magazine-fed weapon, with the Mauser type bolt action which is found in most military rifles. It is commonly referred to as the Arisaka rifle. The rifle is manufactured in 3 standard lengths as shown in figure 171; the longest of which is the standard infantry weapon. The shorter rifles are issued to other arms. The "safety" is locked by pressing the knob at the end of the bolt and turning it to the right. It has a blade type front sight and a leaf rear sight graduated from 100 to 2,400 meters. There is no windage or drift adjustment. The small caliber, long barrel, and medium muzzle velocity of this piece results in relatively no recoil and comparatively little muzzle flash. The markings 三八式 on top of the receiver read "Model 38."

(2) *Characteristics.*
Caliber_____ 6.5-mm (0.256 inch).
Muzzle velocity____ 2,400 feet per second.
Magazine capacity__ 5 rounds.

(3) *Ammunition.* The cartridges are semi-rimmed. Ball ammunition and tracer ammunition have been recovered.

g. Model 44 (1911) cavalry carbine. (1) *General description.* This carbine (fig. 172) is substantially the same as the model 38 (1905) short rifle. The action, operation, and sights are similar on all Arisaka rifles. This model, however, has a permanently attached spike type bayonet, that folds under and rests in a slot in the stock while being carried. This rifle has a blade front sight and a leaf rear sight graduated from 300 to 2000 meters. There is no windage or drift adjustment.

(2) *Characteristics.*
Caliber_____ 6.5-mm (0.256 inch).
Length over-all
  (bayonet fold-
  ed). 38¼ inches.
Weight_____ 8.75 pounds.
Muzzle velocity____ 2,400 feet per second.
Magazine capacity__ 5 rounds.

(3) *Ammunition.* The weapon uses the same ammunition as the model 38 rifle, and the cartridges are semirimmed. Both ball and tracer ammunition have been recovered.

RESTRICTED

189

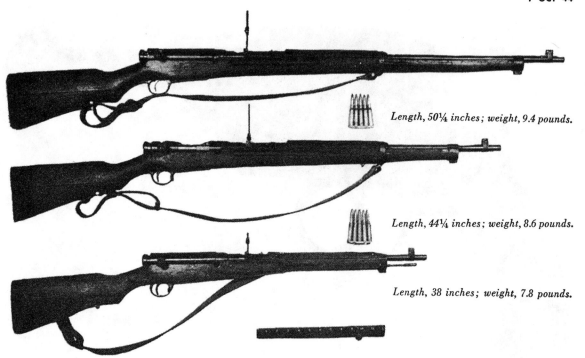

Length, 50¼ inches; weight, 9.4 pounds.

Length, 44¼ inches; weight, 8.6 pounds.

Length, 38 inches; weight, 7.8 pounds.

Figure 171. Model 38 (1905) 6.5-mm rifles.

Figure 172. Model 44 (1911) 6.5-mm cavalry carbine (showing bayonet folded and open).

h. Model 99 (1939) 7.7-mm rifle. (1) *General description.* The Japanese are replacing their 6.5-mm weapons with this shorter, heavier caliber weapon (fig. 173). This rifle is an improved version of model 38 (1905) Arisaka rifle. The rifle has a blade front sight and a leaf rear sight graduated from 300 to 1500 meters. Modifications, other than the larger caliber which also help to identify this piece, are as follows: Monopod under fore end; anti-aircraft sight arms attached to rear sight leaf; magazine floor plate hinged to forward part of trigger guard; sling swivels attached to side instead of under part of rifle. The markings 九九式 on the top of

the receiver read "Model 99." Reports have been received that a short model (38 inches overall) is being issued to service troops.

(2) *Characteristics.*

Caliber	7.7-mm (0.303 inch).
Length over-all (without bayonet).	44 inches.
Muzzle velocity	2,300 feet per second.
Weight	8.8 pounds.

(3) *Ammunition.* This is supplied in 5 round clips, 3 clips to a package. It is a rimless type sup-

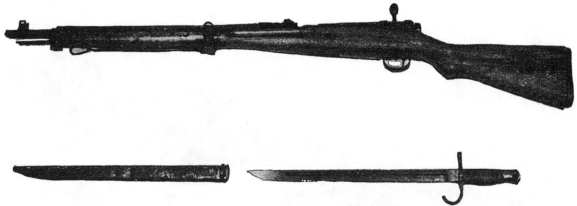

Figure 173. Model 99 (1939) 7.7-mm rifle and bayonet.

plied in ball, tracer, and armor piercing varieties, and has standard markings. This ammunition can be used in the 7.7-mm model 92 (1932) machine gun, but the model 92 ammunition is semirimmed and cannot be used in the rifle.

i. Sniper's rifle. (1) *General description.* This particular piece of equipment is found in two models, model 97 (1937) 6.5-mm and model 99 (1939) 7.7-mm (fig. 174). The two rifles are the same length as the long model 38 (1905) 6.5-mm and can be identified by the fact that, in addition to standard sights, the sniper's model has a telescope mounted on the left of the receiver, a turned down bolt handle, and a monopod under fore end. It is believed that these rifles are manufactured more carefully than the standard rifles.

(2) *Characteristics.*

Model 97 caliber_____ 6.5-mm (0.256 inch).
Model 99 caliber_____ 7.7-mm (0.303 inch).
Weight (with scope; both 9¾ pounds.
　models).
Length over-all (both models) _ 50¼ inches.
Sights:
　　Front_____ Blade type.
　　Rear_____ Sliding leaf, graduated
　　　　　　　　　　　　　　　　　from 300 to 1,500
　　　　　　　　　　　　　　　　　meters.
Telescope sight:
　　Type_____ Fixed focus.
　　Magnification_____ 2.5x.
　　Field of vision_____ 10°.
　　Weight_____ 17 ounces.

(3) *Ammunition.* The model 97 (1937) 6.5-mm fires standard 6.5-mm semirimmed ammunition. Model 99 (1939) 7.7-mm fires standard 7.7-mm rimless ammunition.

j. Rifle grenade launchers (dischargers).
(1) *Spigot type launcher.* This attachment (fig. 175) is placed over the rifle muzzle and locked into place, behind the front sight. Two types of grenades are known to be fired from this launcher. Both types are projected by a special cartridge (fitted with a wooden bullet) which is normally packed in the grenade fin assembly.

(*a*) *Fragmentation grenade Model 91 (1931).* This grenade has been adopted for use as a rifle grenade by replacing the propellant charge normally found screwed into the base of this grenade, with a fin assembly. Prior to firing, the safety pin must be removed from the fuze. When projected, the fuze action will be started by the shock of the explosion upon the base of the grenade. Grenade will detonate in 7–8 seconds (approx.) after firing.

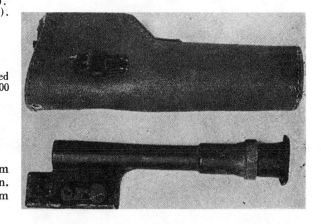

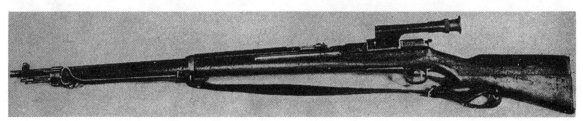

Figure 174. Model 97 (1937) 6.5-mm Sniper's Rifle (with telescope and carrying case).

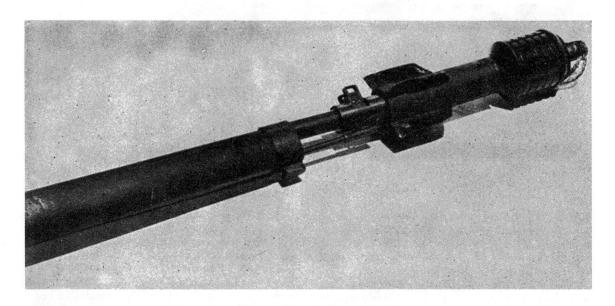

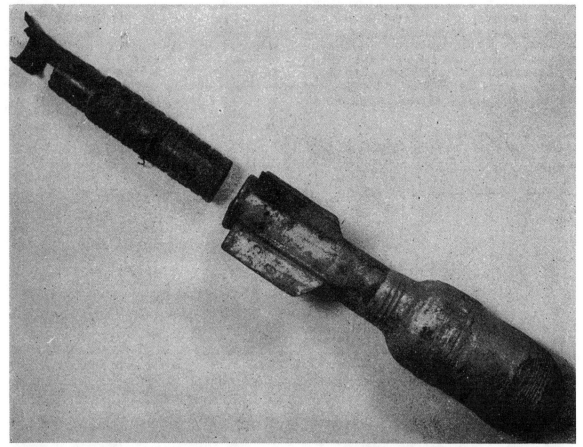

Figure 175. Spigot type grenade launcher and ammunition (at the top is shown the fragmentation grenade in position for firing, at bottom, the smoke grenade and launcher).

(*b*) *Rifle smoke grenade.* The rifle smoke grenade weighs 1.3 pounds and is painted silver. It contains approximately 0.6 pounds of an HC white smoke mixture. No fuze is used, the action being started by the flash of the propelling charge.

(2) *Rifled type launcher.* This launcher (fig. 176) is designed for projecting the hollow charge

(3) *Cup type launcher Model 100.* This launcher is used for projecting the Model 99 (1939) fragmentation grenade. The launcher is attached to the muzzle of the rifle, and the grenade, with safety pin removed, placed inside the cup. Standard ball ammunition is used for projecting the grenade, which has a range of approximately 100 yards when using

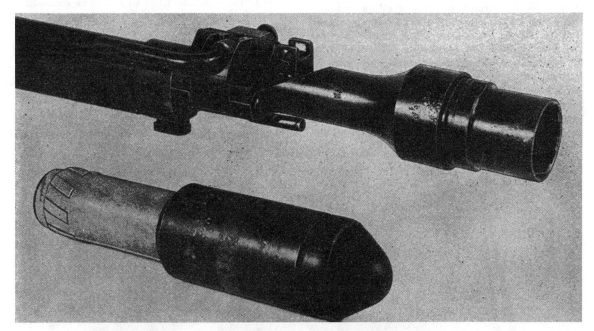

Figure 176. Rifled-type grenade launcher with armor piercing (hollow charge) rifle grenade.

Figure 177. Cup type launcher Model 100 fitted on muzzle of rifle.

high explosive AP grenade. When fired, the action of the discharger cup rifling on the lugs (prerifled rotating band) of the grenade forces the projectile to rotate, giving stability in flight. It is reported that this grenade is projected by a special cartridge fitted with a wooden bullet.

any standard Japanese rifle. The grenade time fuze is started when the weapon is fired, detonating in approximately 4–5 seconds.

2. MACHINE GUNS. a. (1) The basic machine gun is the "Nambu," Model 11 (1922) 6.5-mm light machine gun, which is a modification of the French Hotchkiss. Other types that have been directly copied are the Lewis, the Vickers, and in one instance the Oerlikon. These weapons will be found listed in the following pages. A matter of note is that Japanese machine guns generally do not employ slow initial extraction and therefore stoppages are frequent. The Japanese, in order to overcome this, have employed various methods of oiling ammunition either by automatic or gravity oilers, built directly on to the weapon, or oiling ammunition before loading into box magazines. To complicate the ammunition picture even further, they have indicated that their 6.5-mm machine guns normally use a reduced charge, possibly to overcome stoppage and to avoid pre-oiling. Also their 7.7-mm light and heavy machine guns are built to use either a rimmed, semirimmed or rimless ammunition,

(2) *Characteristics.*

Caliber	6.5-mm (0.256 inch).
Hopper capacity	6–5 round clips.
Weight	22½ pounds.
Muzzle velocity	2,440 feet per second.
Sight graduations	300 to 1,500 meters.
Cyclic rate of fire	500 rounds per minute.

(3) *Ammunition.* Clips of 5 rounds standard or reduced charge 6.5-mm ball rifle ammunition are used.

c. Model 96 (1936) 6.5-mm light machine gun. (1) *General description.* This is a gas-operated, magazine-fed, air-cooled, full automatic light machine gun (fig. 179). Its appearance is somewhat similar to that of the British Bren. The markings 九六式 read "Model 96" and are stamped on the top of the receiver. This weapon has a blade

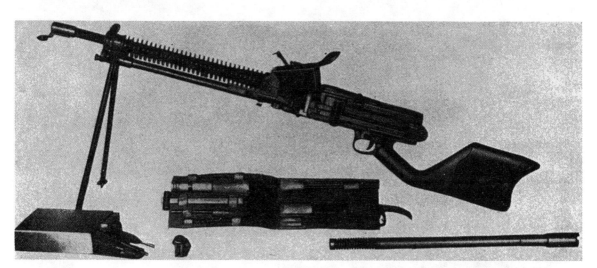

Figure 178. Model 11 (1922) 6.5-mm light machine gun.

which, with one exception noted in the following pages, is not interchangeable.

(2) *Submachine guns.* No submachine gun of Japanese manufacture, comparable to the Thompson, M3 or Reising has been found, although several German Solothurn 7.63-mm (.30 cal.) and 9-mm (.35 cal.) SMGs and Schmeisser MP 28¹¹, SMGs have been recovered.

b. Model 11 (1922) 6.5-mm light machine gun. (1) *General description.* This is a gas operated, air-cooled, machine gun with hopper feed which holds 6–5 round clips of ammunition (fig. 178). Positive identification can be made from the following markings which appear on the top of the receiver 十一年式 and read "11th year model." It is equipped with a blade front-sight and a **V** notched rear leaf-sight sliding on a ramp. There is no windage or drift adjustment. The safety lever (see fig. 178) is turned down to a vertical position to make the weapon safe.

front sight and a leaf rear sight controlled by a "click" drum. The graduations are from 200 to 1,500 meters and there is a windage adjustment. There is also a telescopic sight with a 10° field of view and a 2½ x magnification. A safety lever is located on the left side of the trigger housing and is set at horizontal to "fire," and vertical for "safe."

(2) *Characteristics.*

Caliber	6.5-mm	(0.256 inch).
Weight (without bayonet or magazine).	20 pounds.	
Magazine capacity	30 rounds.	
Muzzle velocity	2410 feet per second.	
Rate of fire (cyclic)	550 rounds per minute.	

(3) *Ammunition.* 6.5-mm semirimmed cartridges in boxes marked Ⓖ are provided for this weapon. These have the same dimensions as the

standard 6.5-mm cartridge although the Japanese have indicated that these have a reduced propelling charge. The regular rifle ammunition may cause stoppages, but can safely be used.

d. Model 99 (1939) 7.7-mm light machine gun. (1) *General description.* This is a gas-operated, magazine-fed, air-cooled, light machine gun (fig. 180).

Its appearance is almost identical to model 96 with the two exceptions, that it has an adjustable rear monopod and a barrel locking nut instead of a barrel catch. It can further be identified by the markings on the top of the receiver 九九式 meaning "99 Model". It has a blade front sight and a rear peep sight controlled by a "click" drum graduated from 200 to 1,500 meters. There is a windage adjustment. A telescopic sight 10° field of view and 2½× magnification is also provided. The safety lever on the right side of the trigger housing is set at horizontal to "fire", and vertical for "safe".

Figure 179. Model 96 (1936) 6.5-mm light machine gun (showing magazine, magazine filler and telescopic sight).

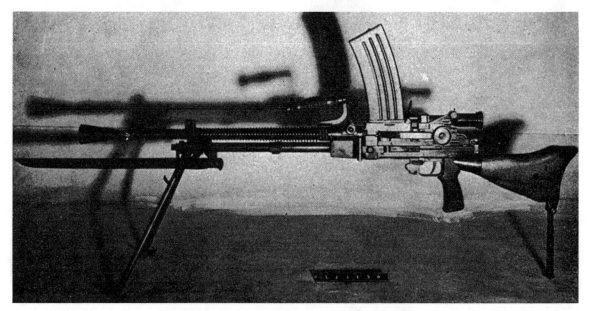

Figure 180. Model 99 (1939) 7.7-mm light machine gun.

(2) *Characteristics.*

Caliber _ _ _ _ _ _ _ _ _ _ _ _ _ 7.7-mm (0.303 inch).

Length over-all _ _ _ _ _ _ _ _ 42 inches.

Weight (without magazine or bayonet). 20 pounds.

Magazine capacity _ _ _ _ _ 30 rounds.

Muzzle velocity _ _ _ _ _ _ _ 2,300 feet per second.

Rate of fire (cyclic) _ _ _ 800 rounds per minute.

(3) *Ammunition.* The weapon uses 7.7-mm rimless ammunition *only*. This ammunition can be used in model 92 heavy machine gun, but the semi-rimmed ammunition for model 92 *cannot* be used in this gun.

e. Model 92 (1932) 7.7-mm Lewis type MG.
(1) *General description.* This weapon is an air-cooled, gas operated, drum-fed, full automatic gun. (See fig. 181.) With the exception that the cocking handle is on the left and that there is no provision allowing it to be changed to the right side of

Figure 181. Model 92 (1932) 7.7-mm Lewis type machine gun.

the gun, if so desired, this weapon is a duplicate of the British Lewis. It can easily be recognized by its similarity to the latter weapon. The markings 九二式 meaning "92 Model" are stamped on the receiver. Without removing the gun from its mount, the main portion of the tripod head can be moved from a horizontal to a vertical position, making a satisfactory AA mount. This can be done in approximately 15 seconds.

(2) *Characteristics.*

Caliber	7.7-mm (0.303 inch).
Length over-all	56 inches.
Weight (without tripod)	26 pounds.
Traverse	360°.
Elevation (with mount in AA position).	85°.
Magazine capacity	47 rounds.*
Muzzle velocity	2,400 feet per second (approximately).
Rate of fire (cyclic)	600 rounds per minute.
Sight:	
Front	Blade type.
Rear	Folding leaf peep-sight graduated from 0 to 1,700 meters.

(3) *Ammunition.* 7.7-mm rimmed ammunition, Japanese copy of British 0.303, and British MK VII .303 in. ball ammunition.

f. Model 92 (1932) 7.7-mm heavy machine gun. (1) *General description.* This is the standard Japanese heavy machine gun. It is a gas-operated, strip-fed, full automatic, air-cooled, modified Hotchkiss-type weapon (fig. 182).

Its forerunner, which may still be used, was the Model 3 (1914) which fired 6.5-mm ammunition.

Markings which appear on the receiver 九二式 read "92 Model." The standard sights consist of a blade front sight and a rear peep sight mounted on a post adjustable for windage and range (300 to 2,700 meters). Special antiaircraft front and rear sights are provided, and there are 3 variations of optical rear sights which are often used. The weapon is set on safety by turning the trigger thumb piece.

*Magazines having 97 round capacity also have been found.

(2) *Characteristics.*

Caliber	7.7-mm. (0.303 inch).
Weight (including tripod).	122 pounds.
Strip capacity	30 rounds.
Rate of fire (cyclic)	450 rounds per minute.
Muzzle velocity	2,400 feet per second.

(3) *Ammunition.* This gun uses 7.7-mm semi-rimmed ammunition (Ball, tracer, AP and incendiary). It can also use the 7.7 rimless ammunition if loaded on strips.

g. Model 93 (1933) 13-mm machine gun. (1) *General description.* This is a gas-operated, air-cooled, magazine-fed, full automatic, Hotchkiss type weapon (fig. 183). While it is primarily an antiaircraft gun, it can be used for ground purposes. This weapon has been found in single and twin mounts (see sec. III, par. 3). The markings 九三式 meaning "93 Model" appear on the receiver. The antiaircraft sights on dual mounts are of the calculating type graduated for ranges from 200 to 3,000 meters, with provision for corrections based on plane speeds varying up to 500 kilometers per hour. For

Figure 182. Model 92 (1932) 7.7-mm heavy machine gun—showing carrying handles and ammunition strip.

ground use there is a blade front sight and a leaf rear sight graduated from 200 to 3,600 meters.

(2) *Characteristics.*

Caliber	13.2-mm (0.52 inch).	
Length over-all (including flash hider).	89 inches.	
Weight (without mount or magazine).	87 pounds.	
Magazine capacity	30 rounds.	
Muzzle velocity	2,250 feet per second.	
Elevation	0° to +85°.	
Traverse	360°.	
Sights:		
A/A—(dual mount only).		Calculating type graduated from 200 to 3,000 meters range and an estimated speed of from 0 to 500 kilometers per hour.
A/T—Front		Blade.
Rear		Folding leaf graduated from 300 to 3,600 meters.

Figure 183. Model 93 (1933) 13-mm machine gun.

(3) *Ammunition*. Ball, armor piercing, and tracer cartridges are provided.

3. MORTARS AND GRENADE DISCHARGERS. a. General. Although all known types of both mortars and grenade dischargers are dealt with here, there are indications that the Japanese Army has mortars heavier than 90-mm and at least up to 150-mm.

b. Model 10 (1921) 50-mm grenade discharger. (1) *General description*. This is a smooth-bore, muzzle-loaded weapon (fig. 184). It has the special feature of a range control device in the form of a graduated thimble by which a gas port at the base of the tube can be varied in size. For shorter ranges, part of the propellant gases escape to the side. It is believed that this weapon is used primarily for discharging flares and that the heavier model 89 grenade discharger is used for firing high explosive and other projectiles.

(2) *Characteristics*.

Caliber _____ 50-mm (1.97 inch).
Length of barrel _____ 9½ inches.
Over-all length _____ 20 inches.
Weight _____ 5½ pounds.
Range for M 91 65-175 yards.
(grenade).

(3) *Operation*. There is no safety device on this weapon. To operate, first remove the safety pin from projectile. The grenade or signal projectile is placed in the barrel. The weapon is fired by a trigger attached to the pedestal.

(4) *Ammunition*. This weapon fires Model 91 grenade, Model 11 smoke shell, Model 10 flare shell, Model 10 signal shell, Model 91 pyrotechnic grenade and Model 10 blank.

c. Model 89 (1929) 50-mm grenade discharger. (1) *General description*. This is a muzzle-fed, rifled weapon which is widely used in the Japanese Army (fig. 185). The standard projec-

Figure 184. Model 10 (1921) 50-mm grenade discharger (at bottom is the discharger prepared for carrying).

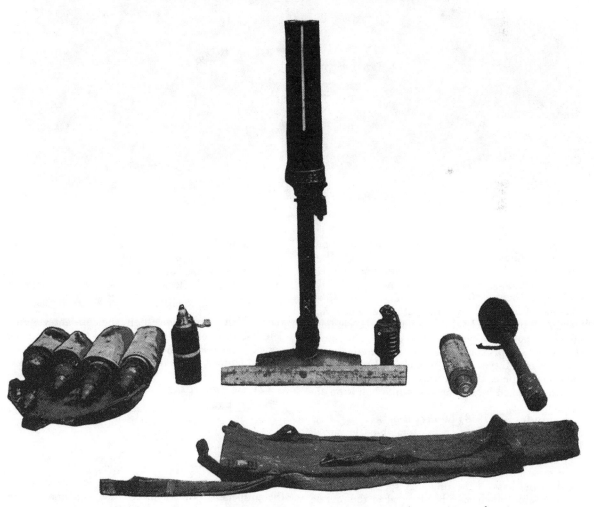

Figure 185. Model 89 (1929) 50-mm grenade discharger with various types of ammunition and equipment.

tile is a high explosive shell which contains the propellant charge in its base. Ranges are controlled by rotation of the knurled range knob. Rotation of the projectile is obtained because the rotating band is expanded against the rifling when the weapon is fired. The weapon is trigger fired. A recent modification of the discharger is fitted with a device to indicate the correct firing angle (45°). There are two range scales. One gives the ranges (120 to 670 meters) governing the use of the Model 89 HE shell and the other (50 to 170 meters) is used for firing Model 91 grenade.

(2) *Characteristics.*

Caliber_____	50-mm (1.97 inch).
Weight_____	10¼ pounds.
Range (Model 89 shells).	120 meters (131 yards) to 670 meters (737 yards).

the stick extends into the barrel, the greater the range.

(2) *Characteristics.*

Length of barrel_____	25 inches.
Total weight (complete with base).	48 pounds.
Elevation_____	40°.
Traverse_____	7°.
Weight of ammunition_	10 pounds.
Fuse_____	Time (activated by friction igniter).

(3) *Ammunition.* The weapon fires a stick bomb weighing approximately 10 pounds and containing 7 pounds of picric acid in blocks. A smaller bomb containing 5 pounds of picric is also used. A finned bangalore torpedo may also be fired. No other ammunition has been recovered to date.

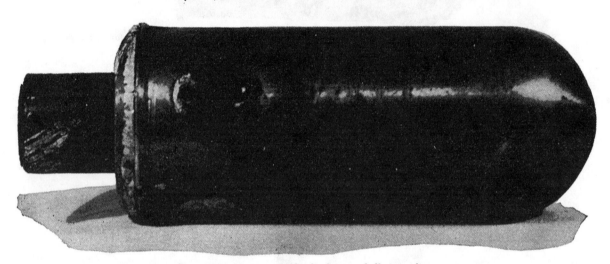

Figure 186. 50-mm grenade discharger shell, incendiary.

(3) *Ammunition.* The following types of ammunition are known to be provided: Model 89 High explosive shell, model 91 grenade, smoke shell, model 94 practice shell, pyrotechnic signals (described in chapter 10), and incendiary (fig. 186). The incendiary shell has a light metal body and weighs approximately 1.25 pounds. It contains about 0.7 pound of incendiary mixture. The smoke shell weighs approximately 2 pounds, contains about 4 ounces of HC type smoke mixture. The body has the same shape as the high explosive shell, but may be distinguished by having two white bands on the body.

d. Model 98 (1938) 50-mm mortar. (1) *General description.* This is a smooth-bore muzzle loaded weapon with fixed elevation of approximately 40° and limited traverse (fig. 187). It is fired by a lanyard attached to a friction primer affixed to the base of the tube. A special feature is a range slide which may be clamped to the muzzle. This regulates the length of the stick (spigot) extending into the barrel. The greater the distance

e. Model 11 (1922) 70-mm mortar. (1) *General description.* This is an obsolescent muzzle-loaded, rifle-bore weapon (fig. 188). The barrel is supported by a single elevating screw. The markings on the breech end of the barrel 十一年式曲射歩兵砲 read "11th year model high angle infantry gun." The latch pin on the breech end of the barrel must be set in to release the safety device. The weapon is fired by means of a lanyard attached to the striker arm.

(2) *Characteristics.*

Caliber_____	70-mm (2.76 inch).
Total weight (including base-plate).	133.75 pounds.
Elevation_____	37° to 77°.
Traverse_____	23°.

(3) *Ammunition.* The high explosive shell has the propellant powder in its base and operates in the same manner as the model 89 grenade discharger shell previously described.

f. 70-mm barrage mortar. This is a smoothbore, muzzle-loaded weapon of very simple construction (fig. 189). It fires a shell probably designed for use against low flying aircraft (fig. 189), or firing over the heads of ground troops. When fired, the projectile reaches a range of 3000 to 4000 feet when it expels parachute-supported high explosive charges $11/16$ inch in diameter and 3 inches long which in turn explode in the air. If an unexploded shell be found on the ground, it should be marked "Dangerous" and left for disposal by trained personnel.

(2) *Characteristics.*

Caliber_____ 81-mm (3.19-inch).
Maximum range (light 3,100 yards (approximately).
 shell).
Length of barrel_____ 49½ inches.
Total weight_____ 145 pounds.
Weight of shell_____ 6.93 pounds (1 pound of TNT).

(3) *Ammunition.* This weapon fires high explosive shells which are interchangeable with the United States M43 81-mm light shell. Heavier

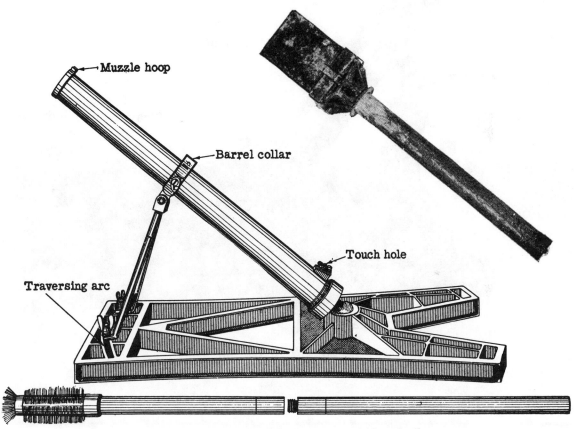

Figure 187. Model 98 (1938) 50-mm mortar with projectile.

g. Model 97 (1937) 81-mm mortar. (1) *General description.* This weapon is very similar to United States 81-mm mortar M1. It is a smoothbore, muzzle-loading, high-angle fire weapon, (fig. 191) which breaks down into 3 sections for transport. The markings 九七式 小迫撃砲 which appear on the base of the barrel read "97 model small trench mortar." The mortar is provided with a collimator sight which is heavier and more complex than the U. S. M1 sight.

shells have been reported but no specimens have been recovered. The fuzes can be adjusted to give instantaneous or delay action detonations.

h. Model 99 (1939) 81-mm mortar. (1) *General description.* Model 99 is similar to model 97 except that it has a much shorter barrel and is equipped for trigger firing with a mechanism at base of the barrel (fig. 192).

The weapon is fired by hitting the protruding end of the firing pin cam shaft with a wooden mallet.

Figure 188. Model 11 (1922) 70-mm mortar.

Figure 189. 70-mm barrage mortar showing spike and block used as base.

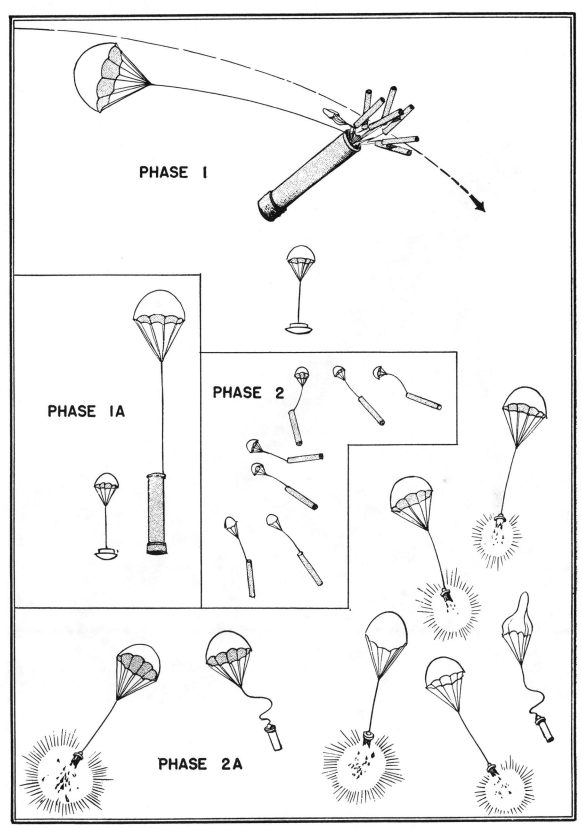

PHASE I

PHASE IA

PHASE 2

PHASE 2A

Figure 190. Shell used in 70-mm barrage mortar and its method of functioning.

Figure 191. Model 97 (1937) 81-mm mortar.

Figure 192. Model 99 (1939) 81-mm mortar and standard projectile.

For transport, this mortar breaks down into three sections, each weighing approximately 17 pounds. It may be fired with United States M43 81-mm mortar shells, in which case a maximum range of 2,500 yards may be obtained.

(2) *Characteristics.*

Caliber_____ 81-mm (3.19-inch).
Maximum range_____ 2,200 yards.
Length of barrel_____ 25¼ inches.
Total weight_____ 52 pounds.

(3) *Ammunition.* HE and smoke or chemical shells have been recovered. The fuse may be adjusted for instantaneous or delay detonation.

i. Model 94 (1934) 90-mm mortar. (1) *General description.* This is a smooth-bore, muzzle-loading weapon with a fixed firing pin (fig. 193). A special feature is the recoil system, consisting of two recoil cylinders on a one piece U-shaped frame with cylinders located on each side of the barrel. The Japanese markings on the base of the barrel 九四式 輕迫擊砲 read "94 model light trench mortar."

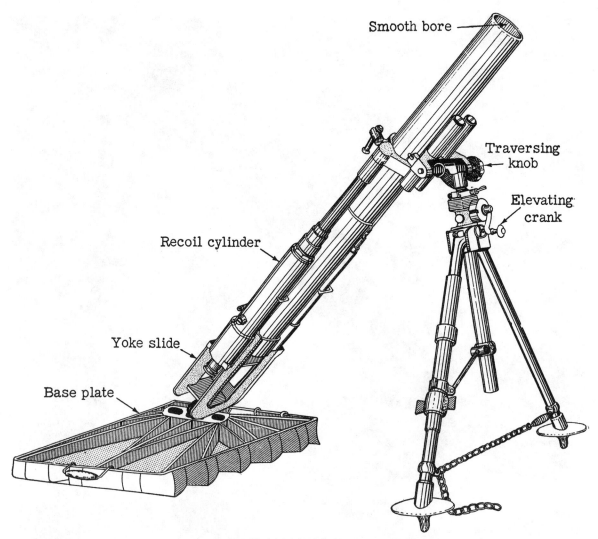

Figure 193. Model 94 (1934) 90-mm mortar.

(2) *Characteristics.*

Caliber_____ 90-mm (3.54-inch).
Maximum range_____ 4,150 yards.
Length of barrel_____ 52 inches (approximately).
Total weight_____ 340 pounds.
Sight_____ Panoramic telescope sight.

(3) *Ammunition.* Model 94 mortar fires HE and incendiary ammunition. The incendiary shell is 16 inches long, weighs 11.5 pounds. The mixture is white phosphorus, carbon disulphide and 40 impregnated rubber pellets. This shell can be identified by a red band below the fuse, a blue band between the fuze and bourrelet, a yellow band between the bourrelet and fin, and a white band at the junction of the shell body and the fin. The fuze may be

adjusted to give either instantaneous or delayed detonation.

j. Model 93 (1933) 150-mm mortar. (1) The photograph (fig. 194) shown is believed to be that of the model 93 (1933) 150-mm mortar, a smooth-bore, muzzle-loaded, lanyard fired weapon.

(2) *Characteristics reported.*

Caliber_____	150-mm (5.9 inch).
Maximum range_____	2,100 meters (2,300 yards).
Length of tube_____	59 inches (approximately).
Weight of tube_____	220 pounds (approximately).
Elevation _____	43° to 80°.
Traverse_____	7°.
Sights_____	Telescopic.

(3) *Ammunition.* Projectile reported as weighing (total) 56 pounds and containing approximately 14 pounds of explosive.

4. GRENADES, LAND MINES, AND BOOBY TRAPS. a. General. The following pages give a general picture of Japanese grenades and land mines. Certain of these can be and have been used as booby traps.

b. Booby traps. Although the Japanese use of booby traps has been limited as compared to the German, it is to be expected that these traps will be more and more frequently encountered as Allied Forces push the Japanese from prepared positions. As many types of Japanese ammunition are suitable for employment as booby traps only the most common are listed. The model 23 pull type fragmentation grenade is particularly suitable for this purpose when attached to doors, window frames, and general items of abandoned equipment. In addition numerous reports have been received of captured allied grenades (i. e. British No. 36 and United States MK 2) being similarly employed. Although there is no evidence to date that the stick grenade, the bangalore torpedo, or the explosive cannister from the barrage mortar shell have been used as booby traps, the fact that all have pull igniters and accidents have occurred to troops handling them, prove that they are most suitable as such. The 3 types of fragmentation grenade models 91, 97, and 99 ("Kiska") grenade are equipped with percussion ignited fuses. They have been used with a suspension wire device which can be tripped. The grenade is placed bottom-up inside an improvised tube thus ensuring that the grenade will fall head first so as to detonate the fuse, when a wire is tripped (see fig. 195). A piece of bamboo or empty cartridge case is sometimes used in lieu of a tube.

Figure 194. A probable Model 93 (1933) 150-mm mortar in action.

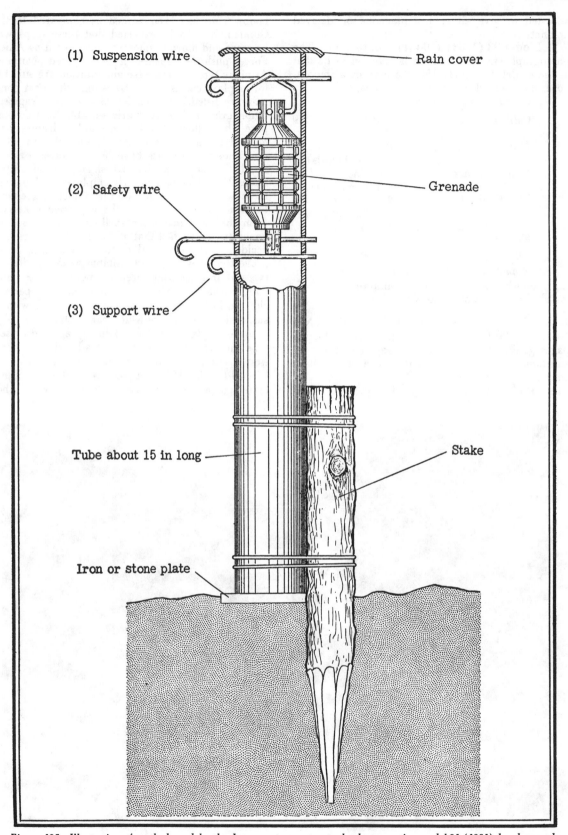

(1) Suspension wire

Rain cover

Grenade

(2) Safety wire

(3) Support wire

Tube about 15 in long

Stake

Iron or stone plate

Figure 195. Illustration of method used by the Japanese to construct a booby trap using model 91 (1931) hand grenade.

Another and less elaborate variation is found in the use of the above listed grenades under a foot board. The delay powder train may be first removed. The weight of the foot fires the detonator instantaneously. Many of the land mines have been used as booby traps and work on the same principle, model 93 being equipped so that it can be activated by pressures from 7 to 200 pounds. Only one or two electrically operated booby traps have been encountered so far. They operate on a low voltage and are generally attached to equipment such as radios and vehicle ignition switches. It can be expected that booby trap fuzes of more advanced design, will probably appear in the near future, as the Japanese are driven back.

c. Model 91 (1931) hand grenade. (1) *General description.* Model 91 (1931) fragmentation grenade (fig. 196) can be thrown by hand, fired either from models 10 or 89 grenade dischargers, or fired from a rifle grenade launcher (discharger) with tail assembly added. The base contains a primer and propelling charge for use when firing from a grenade discharger.

(2) *Characteristics.*

Over-all length_____ 4.95 inches.
Fuze delay_____ 7 to 8 seconds (approximately).
Diameter_____ 1.97 inches.
Weight with
propellant charge__ 18.8 ounces.

(3) *Operation.* (*a*) *To arm.* With safety pin in position, screw firing pin down into firing pin holder, with screw driver or knife blade, as far as it will go.

(*b*) *To use as hand grenade.* Hold grenade with fuze pointing downward, remove safety pin, being sure that safety cover does not fall off. Strike head of fuze against solid object such as helmet keeping hand clear of gas vent hole. Throw immediately *since action of fuze is sometimes erratic.*

(*c*) *To use in grenade discharger.* Remove safety pin and drop into discharger.

d. Model 97 (1937) hand grenade. (1) *General description.* The model 97 (1937) fragmentation hand grenade, (fig. 197) is carried by all front line troops and is almost identical with model 91, except that it has no provision for a base propellant attachment and has a shorter fuze delay time. It cannot be fired from a grenade discharger.

(2) *Characteristics.*

Over-all length___ 3.75 inches.
Diameter_____ 1.97 inches.
Weight_____ 1 pound (approximately).
Fuze delay_____ 4 to 5 seconds (approximately).

(3) *Operation.* (*a*) *To arm.* With safety pin in position, screw firing pin down into firing pin holder as far as it will go.

(*b*) *To throw.* Hold grenade with fuze pointing downward. Remove safety pin, being sure that safety cover does not fall off. Strike head of fuse

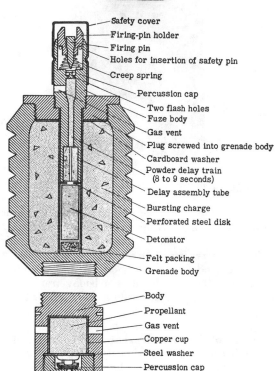

Safety cover
Firing-pin holder
Firing pin
Holes for insertion of safety pin
Creep spring
Percussion cap
Two flash holes
Fuze body
Gas vent
Plug screwed into grenade body
Cardboard washer
Powder delay train (8 to 9 seconds)
Delay assembly tube
Bursting charge
Perforated steel disk
Detonator
Felt packing
Grenade body

Body
Propellant
Gas vent
Copper cup
Steel washer
Percussion cap

Figure 196. Model 91 (1931) hand grenade (including propellant charge for use in grenade discharge).

against solid object such as helmet, keeping hand clear of gas vent hole. Throw immediately *since time of fuze is sometimes erratic.*

e. Model 99 (1939) hand grenade. (1) *General description.* This grenade has been identified as model 99 (fig. 198). It is smaller than the model 97 and 91 fragmentation grenades and unlike these, it has a smooth, cylindrical body with a flange at either end. It may be launched from a special launcher mentioned previously under "Rifle grenade launchers" (figures 176 and 177).

(2) *Characteristics.*

Over-all length____ 3½ inches.
Diameter_____ 1⅝ inches.
Weight_____ 10 ounces (approximately).
Fuze delay_____ 4 to 5 seconds (approximately).

(3) *Operation.* (*a*) *To arm.* Remove safety pin which is held in place by a cord.

Figure 197. Model 97 (1937) hand grenade.

(*b*) *To use as a hand grenade.* Strike the head of the fuze on a hard object and throw immediately. Since the firing pin is integral with firing pin holder no screwing or unscrewing is necessary, as with the model 91 and model 97 fragmentation grenades. It can be used as a booby trap by removing the safety pin and setting under a floor board or chair.

(4) *Alternative fuze.* It is believed that there is a variation of this grenade, known as the model 99B, which is activated by a friction igniter fuze.

f. Model 23 grenade. (1) *General description.* This grenade (fig. 199) appears to have been designed for use either as a hand grenade or a booby trap. It has a pull type friction igniter fuze with a time delay reported as approximately 5 seconds. Because a pull (from 2½ pounds to 5 pounds) on the fuze cord ignites the time fuze, it could easily be

adapted for use as a booby trap by tying the cord to a trip wire. The lugs and rings on the side are convenient for anchoring the grenade in place when

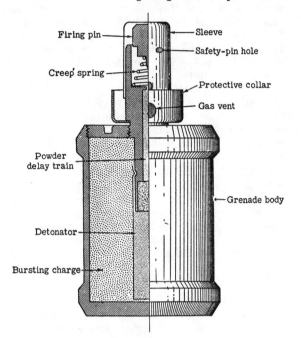

Figure 198. Model 99 (1939) hand grenade ("Kiska").

so used. It has also been found in a booby trap with a high explosive artillery shell tied to it for augmenting the power of the explosion.

(2) *Characteristics.*

Over-all length____ 3¾ inches.
Diameter of body_ 2 inches.
Weight_____ 1 pound (approxi-
mately).
Filler_____ Granular TNT.

g. ½ kg. incendiary grenade. 5.3 inches long
and weighing 1.1 pounds (approximately), it may
be thrown by hand or projected from the grenade
discharger model 89. Incendiary filling is white
phosphorus.

h. Incendiary stick grenade. (1) *General
description.* The body of this grenade (fig. 200)
is filled with impregnated rubber pellets in a phosphorus carbon disulphide solution. There are some
40 pellets in each grenade, which are scattered by a
central bursting charge. It is also possible that this
grenade is sometimes filled with phosphorus smoke
filling. The grenade is 13.2 inches long and the body
has a diameter of 2.1 inches.

(2) *Operation.* (*a*) To arm. Make sure that
the safety pin is in position and that the firing pin
is threaded down into the firing pin holder.

(*b*) *To throw.* With the fuze pointing downward,
withdraw the safety pin. Making sure that the
safety cover does not fall off, strike the head of the
fuze against some hard object, such as the heel of
your shoe or the top of your helmet. There should
be no delay in throwing the grenade, since actual
fuze delay time is not known.

i. High-explosive stick hand grenade. (1)
General description. This is the well known "potato
masher" type of grenade with a pressed metal cap
at the end of the handle (fig. 201). It has a smooth
cylindrical body.

Figure 199. *Model 23 hand grenade.*

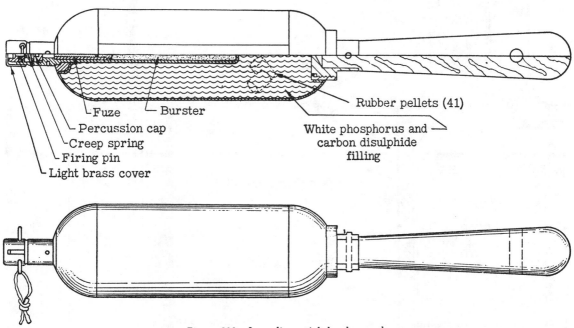

Figure 200. *Incendiary stick hand grenade.*

(2) *Characteristics.*

Over-all length_____ 7⅞ inches.
Diameter of grenade
   body_____ 2 inches.
Weight of bursting
   charge (lyddite)__ 2¾ ounces.
Total weight_____ 19½ ounces.
Fuze delay_____ 4 to 5 seconds (ap-
              proximately).

(3) *Operation.* Remove the metal cap. A ring with a string attached will be found. This ring is slipped on the finger and the grenade thrown. The string pulls away from the grenade and starts the time fuze burning. This grenade can be used as a booby trap by attaching one end of a trip wire to the ring and the other end to a moveable object such as a door, helmet, etc.

j. Molotov cocktail incendiary grenade. (1) *General description.* This is a Japanese version of

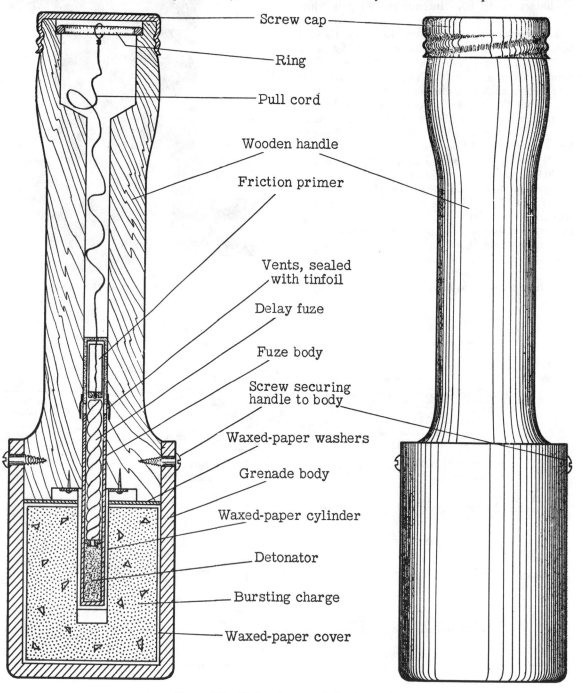

Screw cap

Ring

Pull cord

Wooden handle

Friction primer

Vents, sealed
with tinfoil

Delay fuze

Fuze body

Screw securing
handle to body

Waxed-paper washers

Grenade body

Waxed-paper cylinder

Detonator

Bursting charge

Waxed-paper cover

Figure 201.   High-explosive stick hand grenade.

the "Molotov cocktail." It consists of a standard bottle (fig. 202) filled with a mixture of oil and gasoline. (The bottle illustrated in figure 202 is a Japanese beer bottle.) The fuze is an "all-ways" type that will ignite when the grenade is thrown no matter in what position the bottle lands, for the impact drives the firing pin down into the detonator which ignites the contents of the bottle.

(2) *Operation.* Remove safety pin, then throw.

k. Frangible Smoke Grenade, white. Spherical, flat bottomed glass flask 3 inches in diameter and filled with a yellowish liquid varying from 100

Figure 202. Molotov cocktail incendiary grenade with fuze.

percent titanium tetrachloride to a mixture of approximately 60 percent titanium tetrachloride and 40 percent silicon tetrachloride. The grenade (fig. 203) is packed in sawdust in a cylindrical sheet metal container.

Figure 203. Frangible smoke grenade.

l. Frangible Hydrocyanic Acid (AC) Grenades. Two different types exist. One is stabilized with copper powder and is packed in a sheet metal outer container, the other is stabilized with arsenic trichloride and packed in a cardboard container. The grenade (fig. 204) consists of a spherical glass flask about 3½ inches in diameter containing approximately 1 pint of hydrocyanic acid. The flask is packed in a mixture of sawdust and a neutralizing agent. The outer container is approximately 5¼

inches high and 5½ inches in diameter, it is painted khaki and banded in brown.

m. Bangalore torpedo. (1) *General description.* This is the standard bangalore torpedo (fig. 205) for the Japanese Army. It has a pull type delay fuze and is threaded at each end to permit an indefinite number of tubes to be attached end to end. Because of the type of fuze, it may be used in a booby trap, with the igniter string tied to a trip wire.

(2) *Characteristics.*

Over-all length (one tube).	46 inches (approximately).
Diameter	2 inches.
Weight (one tube).	10 pounds.
Fuze delay	6 to 7 seconds (approximately).
Charge composition.	TNT 36 percent. Cyclonite 64 percent.

(3) *Operation.* (*a*) Remove plugs, screw together the selected number of tubes, remove the bullet shaped cap from fuze and place on one end. Screw fuze in place. When ready to detonate the bangalore torpedo, pull out the safety pin, and pull the lanyard (requires about a 13-pound pull). The fuze delay will be approximately 6 to 7 seconds.

Note. Another bangalore type land mine which may be an antitank mine has been found. Its characteristics are as follows:

Length	36 inches.
Width	3.5 inches.
Height	2 inches.
Charge	6 pounds picric acid.
Form	Oval cross section.
Color	Olive drab.
Fuze	4 pressure type shear wire fuzes inside base—pressure about 300 pounds.

Figure 204. Frangible hydrocyanic acid grenade, arsenic trichloride stabilized type.

Figure 205. Bangalore torpedo.

(*b*) For additional information concerning Japanese bangalore torpedoes see chapter 10, section V, paragraph 5b.

n. Model 93 (1933) mine. *General.* This mine (fig. 206) is exploded by pressure applied anywhere on its upper surface. It is used either for antipersonnel or antitank purposes. Fuzes are provided

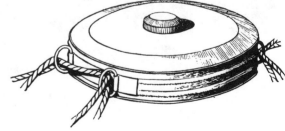

Figure 206. Model 93 (1933) mine.

with shear wires of various strengths, so the fuzes may function under pressures of from 20 pounds* to as much as 250 pounds depending on the fuze selected. Additional explosive may be placed beneath the mine to give it greater force.

o. Model 99 (1939) armor piercing mine (grenade). (1) *General description.* This mine (fig. 207) is issued to infantry units and is carried by the individual soldier. It is sometimes referred to as the "magnetic antitank bomb" or "armor piercing grenade." The magnets serve to hold the mine against a metal surface such as a tank (or iron pill box door) until it explodes.

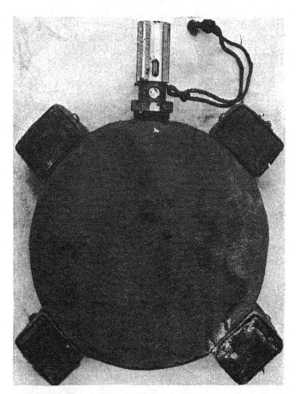

Figure 207. Model 99 (1939) armor piercing mine, with fuze.

(2) *Characteristics.*

Diameter------------ 4¾ inches.
Thickness----------- 1½ inches.
Total weight-------- 2 pounds, 11 ounces.
Length of fuze------ 5¼ inches.
Charge------------- 1½ pounds TNT.

(3) *Operation.* Screw fuze into fuze hole. Remove safety pin. Place by hand against object to be destroyed. Give the fuze cap a sharp blow. A time delay of approximately 5 to 6 seconds gives a man time to withdraw. It has been claimed that

---

*Mines have been reported which function with a pressure as low as 7 pounds.

the mine can be thrown against the target rather than having to be placed there by hand.

p. Model 96 (1936) mine. (1) *General description.* This is a large, very powerful mine (fig. 208) adapted for use either on land or under water.

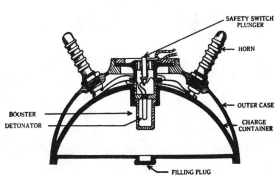

Figure 208. Model 96 (1936) mine.

The two lead alloy horns enclose glass vials containing an electrolytic fluid. Pressure on either of these horns will crush the vial, releasing its contents. This activates the chemical electric fuze thus detonating the mine. Several sizes of this mine are believed to exist.

(2) *Characteristics*.

Height of mine____ 10½ inches (approximately).
Diameter at base__ 20 inches (approximately).
Total weight_____ 106.5 pounds (approximately).
Charge_____ 46 pounds.

NOTE. Another type of underwater mine, is an 8½-inch by 8-inch canister, total weight 20 pounds, containing 8 pounds of perchlorate explosive.

5. ANTITANK AND INFANTRY GUNS. a. General.

(1) The Japanese infantry is comparatively well armed. The first effort to give heavy weapons to the infantry was in 1921–1922, when the model 10 (1921) 50-mm grenade discharger, the model 10 (1921) 70-mm mortar, and the model 11 (1922) 37-mm gun were introduced. These three weapons were later replaced by the model 89 (1929)

Japanese antitank weapons take on a much more serious aspect.

(6) The fact that model 41 (1908) 75-mm infantry gun is provided with armor-piercing, high-explosive and hollow charge AP ammunition must be borne in mind, because this gun is so widely distributed in the Japanese Army.

(7) Japanese infantry must be considered well supplied with heavy weapons; the Army is primarily an infantry army, and the weapons of the infantry have always been the first consideration of the military.

b. Model 97 (1937) 20-mm antitank rifle.
(1) *General description*. This is actually a single purpose, selective full or semi-automatic gas operated, antitank automatic cannon (fig. 209). Infantry can maneuver it in any sort of terrain. Two men can carry it, since it weighs but 150 pounds complete with shield and carrying handles, and it is easy to hide because of its low silhouette (16½ inches

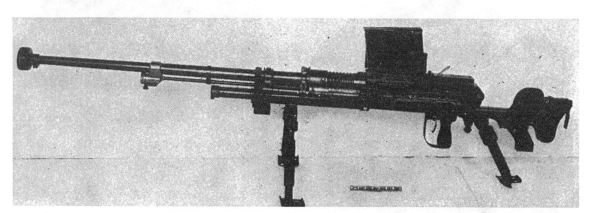

Figure 209. Model 97 (1937) 20-mm antitank rifle.

50-mm grenade discharger, the model 92 (1932) 70-mm battalion howitzer, and the model 94 (1934) 37-mm gun. However, in some areas the older weapons are still in use.

(2) In 1936, the model 41 (1908) 75-mm mountain gun was replaced by a newer weapon in the mountain (pack) artillery units. The model 41 gun then was issued four to each infantry regiment and is known as the regimental gun. This move gave the infantry a lightweight 75-mm weapon of its own.

(3) When first issued, model 11 (1922) 37-mm gun was no doubt intended in part for an antitank role, although it could not be considered a threat today. Its successor, model 94 (1934) 37-mm gun, has a much higher velocity.

(4) It was not until 1937, however, that the Japanese produced a purely antitank weapon. Model 97 (1937) 20-mm antitank rifle is a hard-hitting mobile weapon. Model 98 (1938) 20-mm antiaircraft antitank machine cannon can also be used against tanks.

(5) With the appearance of model 1 (1941) 47-mm gun, a modern, mobile, high-velocity weapon,

without the shield). However, its sights do not permit accurate laying for the longer ranges, and tracking is difficult because traversing must be accomplished by shoulder control. In addition, the weapon has a very violent recoil. The Japanese markings 九七式 which mean "97 Model" appear on the top of the receiver.

(2) *Characteristics*.

Caliber_____ 20-mm (0.79 inch).
Muzzle velocity____ 2,500 feet per second.
Weight_____ {Gun itself—120 pounds.
With shield and carrying handles—150 pounds.
Length (without handles)_____ 82.5 inches.
Traverse (total)____ 1,600 mils (90°).
Sights:
Front_____ Blade type.
Rear_____ Peep-sight controlled by "click" drum graduated from 0 to 1,000 meters in 100 meter graduation.
Type feed_____ 7 round box magazine.
Rate of fire_____ 12 rounds per minute (semi-automatic).

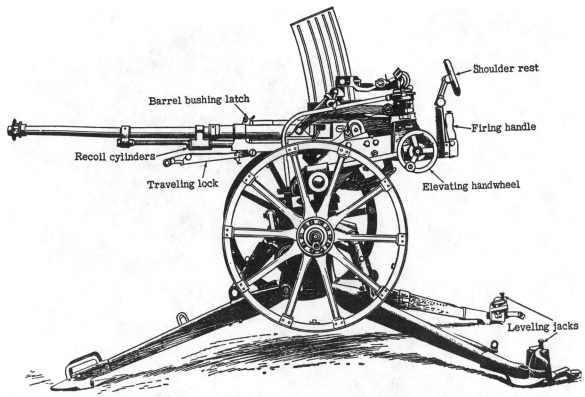

Figure 210. Model 98 (1938) 20-mm antiaircraft antitank automatic cannon.

(3) *Ammunition.* Armor piercing tracer and high explosive tracer ammunition has been recovered.

c. Model 98 (1938) 20-mm antiaircraft antitank automatic cannon. (1) *General description.* This is a gas-operated, semi- or full-automatic, all purpose weapon (fig. 210), similar in mechanism, but larger and heavier than the model 97, 20-mm antitank rifle. The ammunition is not interchangeable. The carriage permits firing from its wheels. Supported on outriggers with wheels removed it has a fast 360° traverse.

(2) *Characteristics.*

Caliber	20-mm (0.79 inch).
Type feed	20 round box magazine.
Weight	836 pounds (without wheels).
Maximum range—horizontal	5,450 yards.
Maximum range—vertical	12,000 feet.
Muzzle velocity	2,720 feet per second.
Rate of fire	120 rounds per minute.
Traverse	6,400 mils (360°).
Principle of operation.	Gas-operated, semi-or full automatic.

(3) *Ammunition.* High explosive tracer and armor piercing tracer have been recovered.

d. Model 11 (1922) 37-mm gun. (1) *General description.* This weapon (fig. 211) is still in use in some areas, although its place in the infantry organization has been taken by model 94 (1934) 37-mm gun and other antitank weapons. It resembles the U. S. 37-mm infantry gun, M 1916. The gun

is carried by four men. This weapon is listed by the Japanese as 十一年式平射歩兵砲 which is translated "11th year model low trajectory infantry gun".

Figure 211. Model 11 (1922) 37-mm gun.

(2) *Characteristics.*

Caliber	37-mm (1.46 inch).
Weight in action	205.75 pounds.
Length (with trails folded)	90 inches.
Over-all width (in firing position)	49.25 inches.
Breechblock	Vertical sliding wedge, which may be operated semiautomatically.
Traverse	584 mils (33°) by handwheel.
Elevation	248 mils (14°) by handwheel.
Depression	85 mils (−4.8°).
Sight	Telescopic, used for direct laying.

e. Model 94 (1934) 37-mm gun. (1) *General description.* This weapon (fig. 212) is referred to by the Japanese as the "Infantry rapid fire gun." It

Figure 212. Model 94 (1934) 37-mm gun.

is an infantry close support weapon firing both high explosive and armor piercing high explosive ammunition. It has a semiautomatic, horizontal, sliding type breechblock. When the shell is loaded, the rear of the cartridge case trips a catch that closes the breechblock. Recoil action of firing opens the breech and extracts the cartridge case. Sighting is by a straight telescopic sight. This weapon has marked on the barrel the following 九四式三十七粍砲 which reads "94 model 37-mm gun."

(2) *Characteristics.*

Caliber	37-mm (1.46 inch).
Length (over-all in travelling position)	114 inches.
Width (over-all in travelling position)	47 inches.
Weight	714 pounds.
Traverse	1,062 mils (60°).
Elevation	+480 mils (27°).
Maximum range	5,000 yards.
Muzzle velocity (armor piercing ammunition)	2,300 feet per second.

NOTE. This piece may be found mounted on wooden spoke wheels or with perforated steel disc wheels as illustrated in figure 212.

f. Model 1 (1941) 47-mm gun. (1) *General description.* This is an antitank weapon of modern design (fig. 213). The wheels are independently sprung, and a lock is provided on each wheel for locking the springs out of action. It has a semiautomatic, horizontal, sliding wedge breech mechanism. The low silhouette, wide tread, and long split trails give this gun excellent stability. Preliminary tests indicate a muzzle velocity of 2,700 feet per second. The steel disc wheels are fitted with sponge rubber filled tires. This weapon has marked on its breech the following symbols 一式機動四十七粍砲 which mean "Model 1 47-mm mobile gun."

(2) *Characteristics.*

Caliber	47-mm (1.85 inch).
Weight	1,600 pounds.
Traverse	60°.
Elevation	+19°
Depression	−11°
Muzzle velocity	2,700 feet per second.

(3) *Ammunition.* Armor piercing high explosive and standard high explosive shells have been recovered.

Figure 213. Model 1 (1941) 47-mm gun.

g. Model 92 (1932) 70-mm howitzer (Battalion gun). (1) *General description.* This weapon (fig. 214), despite its unusual appearance, has proved to be effective as an infantry support howitzer. It has an interrupted thread type, drop breech-block mechanism. Light in weight and maneuverable, it fires a projectile of relatively large weight, and can deliver fire at ranges varying from 110 yards to 3,000 yards. The Japanese markings 九二式歩兵砲 which read "92 model infantry gun", appear on the barrel.

(2) *Characteristics.*

Caliber	70-mm (2.76 inch).
Total weight in action	468 pounds.
Thickness of armor shield	0.156 inch.
Traverse	800 mils (45° total).
Elevation	+50°
Depression	−10°
Range	3,075 yards.
Danger area of burst	40 yards (approximately).

(3) *Ammunition.* The ammunition is semifixed, the propelling charge being divided into four incre-

Figure 214. Photograph of model 92 (1932) 70-mm howitzer (Bn. gun) showing gunner and sights.

Figure 215. Side view of model 41 (1908) 75-mm infantry gun, showing unusual trail construction.

ments. High explosive, armor piercing, and smoke shells are fired. The standard model 88 delay and instantaneous fuzes are used.

h. Model 41 (1908) 75-mm infantry gun. (1) *General description.* This weapon (fig. 215) was originally the standard pack artillery weapon, but when it was largely superseded by the Model 94 (1934) 75-mm mountain (pack) gun, it was then used as an infantry "regimental" gun. It is widely distributed throughout the Japanese Army. It has an interrupted screw type breechblock and a hydrospring recoil mechanism. There are no equalizers or equilibrators. The markings 四一式山砲 which appear on the barrel, mean "41 model mountain gun." This weapon may be easily and quickly disassembled for pack into loads, the maximum weight of each being approximately 200 pounds. Actual firing of the weapon at a range of 3,200 yards resulted in 75 percent of the rounds falling in a rectangle 20 by 30 yards. At maximum range (7,800 yards) 75 percent of the rounds fell within a rectangle 100 yards wide and 200 yards long.

(2) *Characteristics.*

Caliber	75-mm (2.95 inch).
Length (over-all)	170 inches.
Width (over-all)	48 inches.
Weight	1,200 pounds.
Traverse (total)	106 mils (6°).
Elevation	+650 mils (+40°).
Depression	−319 mils (−18°).
Maximum range	7,800 yards.

(3) *Ammunition.* Ammunition recovered included common high explosive, armor piercing, high explosive, shrapnel, hollow charge AP and incendiary. For description of incendiary shell see chapter 9, section V.

Section III. ARTILLERY

1. GENERAL. Between 1925 and 1936, all Japanese artillery pieces were either redesigned or replaced by newer designs. An examination of a majority of the designs known to exist leads to the belief that the following features will be incorporated in any newer designs produced since 1936, although no weapons over 47-mm in size and bearing a model date later than 1936 as yet have been reported:

Hydropneumatic recoil systems.
Use of equilibrators.
Muzzle brakes.
Increased muzzle velocities.
Improved high speed mounts on all medium and heavy pieces (using either pneumatic tires or tires filled with sponge rubber).

Since Japan has had access to German weapon designs for some years, it may be assumed that Japanese weapons embodying the following features may be encountered:

Hollow charge projectiles.
New incendiary projectiles.
Self-propelled mounts of various kinds.
Rockets.

2. FIELD ARTILLERY. a. Model 94 (1934) 75-mm mountain (pack) gun. (1) *General description.* This is the standard Japanese pack artillery piece (fig. 216) which replaced the model 41 mountain gun. Designed for rapid assembly and dismantling, it breaks down into 11 units, the heaviest of which weighs 210 pounds. The weapon is normally transported by 6 pack horses. It is characterized by a comparatively long split-trail, hydropneumatic recoil mechanism, and a horizontal sliding breechblock. The shield is ⅛-inch armor plate.

(2) *Characteristics.*

Caliber_____ 75-mm (2.95 inch).
Maximum range_____ 8,000 meters (8,750 yards).
Maximum elevation____ +45°.
Maximum depression___ —9°.
Traverse_____ 40°.
Weight in firing po-
sition_____ 1,200 pounds.
Sight_____ Panoramic.
Barrel length_____ 5 feet 1½ inches.
Muzzle velocity_____ 1,300 feet per second.
Maximum rate of fire___ 10 to 12 rounds per minute.
Weight of high explo-
sive projectile_____ 13 pounds.

(3) *Ammunition.* HE, AP, shrapnel, chemical, star, and incendiary.

b. Model 38 (1905) 75-mm gun. (1) *General description.* One of the early weapons of the Japanese division artillery, this weapon (fig. 217) has been subject to considerable modification, and several versions are known to exist. There is no evidence that this parent model has been employed in recent operation; probably now it is regarded as obsolete. It may be readily identified by the single

box trail which, by its design, considerably limits the elevation of the piece. Other characteristics are a hydrospring recoil system, interrupted screw type breechblock, and 1/16-inch shield.

(2) *Characteristics.*

Caliber_____ 75-mm (2.95 inch).
Maximum range_____ 8,350 meters (9,025 yards).
Maximum elevation____ +16° 30 minutes.
Maximum depression___ —8°.
Traverse (total)_____ 7°.
Weight in firing posi-
tion_____ 947 kg (2,083 pounds).
Sight_____ Panoramic.
Barrel length_____ 7 feet 6 inches.
Maximum rate of fire___ 8 to 10 rounds per minute.
Weight of high explo-
sive projectile_____ 13 pounds.

(3) *Ammunition.* HE, AP.

c. Model 38 (1905) gun improved (possibly 4th year model). (1) *General description.* This is an improved version of the 75-mm model 38 (1905) field gun, which appears to have been entirely replaced. Modifications on the present model (fig. 218) consist of trunnioning the barrel further to the rear; the addition of two spring and cable equilibrators to compensate for muzzle overhang;

Figure 216. Model 94 (1934) mountain (pack) gun.

Figure 217. Model 38 (1905) 75-mm gun with ammunition.

Figure 218. Model 38 (1905) gun improved (inset shows breech mechanism).

replacement of the old box trail by a longer open-box type through which the barrel can recoil at high elevations; change of the breech to a horizontal sliding wedge mechanism. The most significant results of the above modifications are a much longer range and an increased rate of fire. Although reports have indicated that this weapon was to be replaced by model 90, the fact that the newer gun has not been encountered in any combat areas indicates that this plan has not yet been consummated.

(2) *Characteristics.*

Caliber	75-mm (2.95 inch).
Maximum range	11,600 meters (12,565 yards).
Maximum elevation	+43°.
Maximum depression	—8°.
Traverse (total)	7°.
Weight in firing position	1,113 kg. (2448.6 pounds).

Maximum rate of fire	10 to 12 rounds per minute.
Sight	Panoramic.
Barrel length	9.2 feet.

(3) *Ammunition.* HE, AP, shrapnel, smoke, star shell, and chemical.

d. Model 90 (1930) 75-mm gun. (1) *General description.* Surrounded with considerable secrecy by the Japanese, this gun (fig. 219) has been reported as the modern weapon of the division artillery. In 1936 it was believed to have been in process of issue to organizations, but to date it has not been encountered in any theater of war. The gun is equipped with either pneumatic tires for motorized towing or large, steel-rimmed wheels for horse draft. It is characterized by a split trail, a horizontal sliding breechblock. and a hydropneumatic recoil system. An unusual feature is the muzzle brake, which so far has not been found on any other Japanese artillery weapon.

(2) *Characteristics.*

Caliber_____ 75-mm (2.95 inch).
Maximum range_____ 15,000 meters (16,250 yards).
Maximum elevation____ +43°.
Maximum depression___ —8°.
Traverse (total)_____ 43°.
Weight in firing posi-
tion_____ 3,300 pounds.
Sight_____ Panoramic.
Muzzle velocity_____ 2,230 feet per second.
Maximum rate of fire_ 10 to 12 rounds per minute.

(3) *Ammunition.* HE, AP, shrapnel, incendiary, smoke, star shell.

e. Model 95 (1935) 75-mm gun. (1) *General description.* The 75-mm model 95 gun is horse-drawn (fig. 220) with split trails, hydropneumatic recoil mechanism, and horizontal, sliding-wedge type breechblock. A comparison with the Model 90, designed five years earlier, reveals that this later weapon has only the apparent advantage of reduced weight. On the other hand, it suffers from loss of range and lower muzzle velocity. It is seemingly more rugged in construction than the model 94 mountain gun and yet gives a lower performance

than the model 90 field gun. The possibility therefore suggests itself that the model 95 was not designed to replace either of these guns, but was to be used by some unit other than the field or pack artillery. It is possible therefore that it may be the new weapon of the horse artillery, replacing the old adaptation of the model 38 with which such units previously had been equipped.

(2) *Characteristics.*

Caliber_____ 75-mm. (2.95 inch).
Maximum range_____ 11,000 m e t e r s (12,000 yards).*
Maximum elevation____ +43°.
Maximum depression___ —8°.
Traverse (total)_____ 50°.
Muzzle velocity_____ 500 meters per second (1,640 feet per second).
Weight_____ 2,438 pounds.
Sight_____ Panoramic.
Maximum rate of fire___ 10 to 12 rounds per minute.

*Also reported as 9,000 meters (9,850 yards).

(3) *Ammunition.* HE. AP, shrapnel, smoke star and chemical.

f. Model 14 (1925) 105-mm gun. (1) *General description.* The 105-mm model 14 (1925) gun (fig. 221) is used for long-range fire. There is no

Figure 219. Model 90 (1930) 75-mm gun (inset shows the weapon on a high-speed carriage with pneumatic type tires).

Figure 220. Model 95 (1935) 75-mm gun.

Figure 221. Model 14 (1925) 105-mm gun.

information to show that this gun is still in production, and it is felt that in all probability it has been superseded by the more modern model 92 (1932). Mounted on heavy wooden wheels, the weapon is normally tractor drawn, and is capable of being moved at a maximum speed of 8 miles per hour. As an alternative it may be drawn by 8 horses. The weapon possesses an interrupted screw breechblock, a hydropneumatic recoil mechanism, and a split trail.

(2) *Characteristics.*

Caliber_____ 105-mm. (4.13 inch).
Maximum range (with long pointed projectile)_____ 14,500 yards (also reported as 15,000 meters (16,500 yards)).
Maximum elevation____ +43°.
Maximum depression__ −5°.
Traverse (total)_____ 30°.
Weight in firing position_____ 6,850 pounds.
Muzzle velocity_____ 2,040 feet per second.
Sight_____ Panoramic.
Tube length_____ 11 feet 9 inches.
Maximum rate of fire___ 6 to 8 rounds per minute.
Weight of HE projectile (long pointed shells) _____ 33 pounds.

(3) *Ammunition.* Ammunition is semifixed. The following types of projectiles have been reported: High explosive (long pointed shell); high explosive; shrapnel; chemical; and armor piercing. Time fuzes are provided for the smoke, incendiary, and shrapnel projectiles. The standard model 88 point detonating (instantaneous or delay) fuzes are used with the HE and chemical shells.

g. Model 91 (1931) 105-mm howitzer. (1) *General description.* A light weight modern field piece (fig. 222) possessing a hydropneumatic recoil mechanism, split trail, and interrupted screw breech mechanism. The weapon can be readily identified by the short barrel and long sleigh. Normally it is towed by six horses.

(2) *Characteristics.*

Caliber_____ 105-mm (4.13 inch).
Maximum range_____ 11,500 yards.
Maximum elevation____ +45° (also reported as +65°).
Maximum depression__ −7°.
Traverse (total)_____ 45° (also reported as 56°).
Weight in firing position.
4,250 pounds.
Muzzle velocity_____ 1,790 feet per second.
Sight_____ Panoramic.
Tube length_____ 8 feet 4 inches.
Maximum rate of fire___ 6 to 8 rounds per minute.
Weight of HE projectile. 33 pounds.

(3) *Ammunition.* Ammunition is semifixed. The following types of projectiles have been reported; high explosive (long pointed shell); high explosive; armor piercing; shrapnel; and chemical.

h. Model 92 (1932) 105-mm gun. (1) *General description.* It is considered that this weapon (fig. 223) has superseded the model 14 (1925) 105-mm gun. Readily recognized by its long slender barrel and trail, it has been designed particularly for long-range fire. Other distinctive features are the pronounced length of the sleigh and the three step interrupted thread breechblock. The recoil system is hydropneumatic. Mounted on heavily constructed wooden wheels with solid rub-

Figure 222. Model 91 (1931) 105-mm howitzer.

ber tires, the weapon is normally tractor drawn, but may be drawn by a 5-ton truck.

(2) *Characteristics.*

Caliber_____	105-mm (4.13 inches).
Maximum range (with long pointed shell).	18,700 meters (20,100 yards) (also reported as 16,400 yards).
Maximum elevation___	+48°.
Maximum depression_	−10°.
Traverse (total)_____	30°.
Weight in firing position.	6,600 pounds.
Muzzle velocity_____	2,500 feet per second.
Sight_____	Panoramic.
Tube length_____	15 feet 6 inches.
Maximum rate of fire__	6 to 8 rounds per minute.
Weight of HE projectile (long pointed shell).	33 pounds.

(3) *Ammunition.* Ammunition is semifixed. The following types of projectiles have been recovered: High explosive (Long pointed shell); high explosive; chemical; armor piercing. Time fuzes are provided for the smoke, incendiary, and chemical shells. The standard model 88 point detonating (Instantaneous or delay) fuzes are used with the HE and chemical shells.

i. Model 4 (1915) 150-mm howitzer. (1) *General description.* One of the older type horse-drawn weapons (fig. 224) which nevertheless is still in service. For purposes of transportation the trail breaks in the middle. The barrel is removed from the cradle and placed on the rear portion of the trail, to which has been attached an extra pair of wheels. A limber is attached to each section, and each load

may then be towed by six horses. The weapon possesses a vertical sliding breechblock, a hydropneumatic recoil mechanism, and a box type trail.

(2) *Characteristics.*

Caliber_____	150-mm (5.9 inch).
Maximum range_____	7,000 meters (7,560 yards) (also reported 10,500 yards).
Maximum elevation____	+65°.
Maximum depression___	−5°.
Traverse (total)_____	6°.
Weight in firing position_	6,100 pounds.
Muzzle velocity_____	1,350 feet per second.
Sight_____	Panoramic.
Tube length_____	7 feet 3 inches.
Maximum rate of fire___	3 to 4 rounds per minute.
Weight of HE projectile_	80 pounds.

(3) *Ammunition.* Ammunition is semifixed. The following types of projectiles have been reported: High explosive; armor piercing; shrapnel; and chemical. Time fuzes are provided for the smoke, incendiary, and shrapnel projectiles. The standard point detonating (Instantaneous and delay) fuzes are used with the HE and chemical shells.

j. Model 89 (1929) 150-mm gun. (1) *General description.* A tractor-drawn weapon (fig. 225) of improved design employed for long range fire. It is designated by the Japanese Army as a heavy field artillery piece. Although manufacture was commenced in 1929, it is believed that issue was not completed until 1937. For purposes of transportation the barrel is removed from the cradle and placed on a separate carriage. The weapon has a split trail, hydropneumatic recoil mechanism, and an interrupted thread block.

Figure 223. Model 92 (1932) 105-mm gun.

Figure 224. Two views of model 4 (1915) 150-mm howitzer.

Figure 225. Two views of Model 89 (1929) 150-mm gun in action.

(2) *Characteristics.*

Caliber_____ 150-mm (5.9 inch).
Maximum range_____ 22,000 yards (also reported as 27,000 yards).
Maximum traverse____ 47°.
Weight in firing posi- 7,500 kg (16,500 pounds).
tion.
Maximum rate of fire__ 1 to 2 rounds per minute.

(3) *Ammunition.* AP, HE, shrapnel, HE (long pointed shell).

k. Model 96 (1936) 150-mm howitzer. (1) *General description.* A well designed and effective weapon (fig. 226) which is, to date, the most modern of its type known to be possessed by the Japanese. It is reported that three modifications exist. Variations, however, are believed to be extremely slight. Mounted on sturdy, rubber-shod, wooden wheels, the weapon is normally tractor drawn. One of the outstanding characteristics is the extreme elevation of 75° which can be obtained. This, however, can be used only when a deep loading pit is dug beneath the breech. It is probable that the weapon could not be fired at an elevation greater than 45° without construction of such a pit. Other features are a long split trail, interrupted thread breechblock, and a hydropneumatic recoil mechanism.

(2) *Characteristics.*

Caliber_____ 150-mm (5.9 inch).
Maximum range_____ 10,000 meters (11,000 yards) (also reported 15,000 yards).
Maximum elevation___ +75°.
Maximum depression_ −7°.
Traverse (total)_____ 30°.
Weight in firing posi- 8,765 pounds.
tion.
Sight _____·_____ Panoramic.
Tube length_____ 11.57 feet.
Rate of fire_____ 6 to 8 rounds per minute.
Weight of HE projec- 80 pounds.
tile.

(3) *Ammunition.* Semifixed; HE, AP, shrapnel, smoke, incendiary tracer.

l. Model 45 (1912) 240-mm howitzer. It is reported that this piece has a maximum range of 11,000 yards, firing a semifixed round weighing approximately 400 pounds. It is broken down and transported on 10 vehicles.

m. Miscellaneous heavy artillery. In recent years the Japanese have bought 17-cm, 21-cm and

Figure 226. Model 96 (1936) 150-mm howitzer at maximum elevation.

24-cm weapons from Germany and therefore Japanese copies of these may be expected. In addition to the above, the following heavy artillery pieces have been reported, but none have been captured, therefore the characteristics given below have not been confirmed.

Caliber	Type	Length of bore (inches)	Muzzle velocity (feet per second)	Type of shell	Weight of shell (pounds)	Maximum range (yards)	Elevation	Weight in action (tons)	Remarks
24-cm	Railway gun		3, 560	HE	440	54, 500		35	Several types reported.
30-cm	Howitzer M 18	196	1, 310	HE	880	12, 750	46°	14. 72	Unconfirmed.
30-cm	Howitzer M 18	324	1, 140	HE	1, 100	16, 600	48°	19. 76	Do.
41-cm	Howitzer (seige)	538	1, 760	HE	2, 200	21, 200	45°	80	Do.

Figure 227. A possible 240-mm howitzer (model number unknown).

3. ANTIAIRCRAFT ARTILLERY. a. Introduction. It has been emphasized to the Japanese soldier that effective antiaircraft defense depends on the use of all arms. Many of the weapons primarily designed for ground action and previously described under infantry armament also are designed to perform an antiaircraft role.

(1) The new basic infantry weapon model 99 (1939) 7.7-mm rifle (fig. 228) has a rear sight, with arms calculated to give the rifleman the approximate lead required to hit a low flying plane.

(2) The model 92 (1932) 7.7-mm heavy machine gun (fig. 229) is provided with an antiaircraft adapter as illustrated in figure 229, and standard antiaircraft ring sights.

(3) The Lewis type model 92 (1932) 7.7-mm machine gun (fig. 230) has a standard mount which can be adapted for antiaircraft defense (see fig. 230).

(4) The model 93 (1933) 13-mm machine gun is shown in figure 231 in a dual mount for antiaircraft fire.

(5) The model 98 (1938) 20-mm AA/AT automatic cannon and probably the 70-mm barrage mortar (Chap. 9, Sec. II) have been designed principally for an antiaircraft role.

(6) In addition to the more common antiaircraft weapons described in detail on the following pages, 120-mm and 127-mm naval antiaircraft guns have been encountered. The latter were in dual mounts.

(7) There are indications that Japanese heavy AA artillery is possibly more modern and of larger caliber than the standard 75-mm model 88, which is the only heavy antiaircraft weapon captured in quantity to date.

(8) Tabulated below are the estimated capabilities of Japanese antiaircraft weapons.

Caliber	Weapons	Approximate maximum rate of fire	Estimated maximum vertical range (feet)
7.7-mm	Model 92 Heavy machine gun.	450	4,000
7.7-mm	Model 92 (Lewis) machine gun.	600	4,000
13.2-mm	Model 93 machine gun	450	13,000
20-mm	Model 98 automatic cannon.	200	12,000
25-mm	Model 96 naval automatic cannon.	300	14,000
40-mm	Vickers type		14,000
75-mm	Model 88 gun	15	30,000
105-mm	Model 14 gun	10	36,000
127-mm	Model 89 gun	10	40,000

gets. Traverse and elevation are controlled by hand wheels.

(2) *Characteristics.*

Caliber	25-mm (.984 inch).
Estimated vertical range	14,000 feet.
Maximum elevation	+80°.
Maximum depression	−10°.
Traverse	360°.
Magazine capacity	15 rounds.
Weight (single gun without mount).	246 pounds.
Weight (three guns triple mount).	5,330 pounds.
Sight	Calculating.
Cyclic rate of fire (per barrel)	300 rounds per minute.
Muzzle velocity	2,978 feet per second.

(3) *Ammunition.* The weapon is furnished with high explosive tracer, high explosive, and armor piercing tracer ammunition.

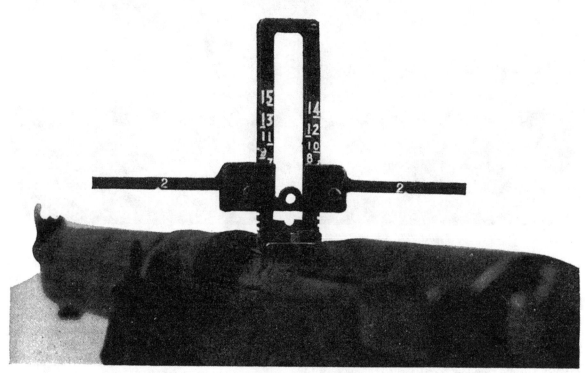

Figure 228. Rear sight on model 99 (1939) 7.7-mm rifle.

Information concerning fire control equipment used with some of the weapons listed will be found in Chapter 10.

b. Model 96 (1936) type 2, 25-mm antiaircraft-antitank automatic cannon. (1) *General description.* This (fig. 232) is a gas-operated, air-cooled, magazine-fed, full automatic, or semiautomatic machine cannon. It has been found in dual and triple fixed mounts, emplaced customarily around air strips for antiaircraft defense. However, it is capable of a 10 degree depression which makes it effective for direct fire against ground tar-

c. 40-mm single and dual antiaircraft and antitank automatic cannon. (1) *General description.* This weapon (fig. 233) is a Vickers type recoil-operated, water-cooled, link belt-fed, automatic or semiautomatic machine cannon. Several of these have been captured. Single mounted guns were marked "Vickers-Armstrongs 1931," but the dual mounted guns were Japanese-manufactured copies. Elevation and traverse are obtained by hand. The weapon is fitted with a telescopic calculating sight and an automatic fuze setter.

Figure 229. Model 92 (1932) 7.7-mm HMG with AA adapter.

Figure 230. Model 92 (1932) 7.7-mm machine gun (Lewis type) in position for AA fire.

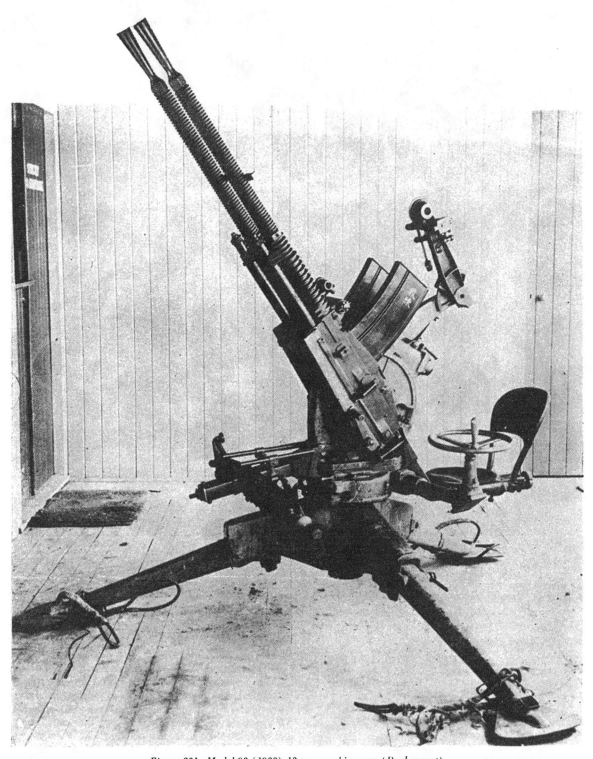

Figure 231. Model 93 (1933) 13-mm machine gun (Dual mount).

Figure 232. Rear view of model 96 (1936) type 2, 25-mm AA/AT automatic cannon, triple mount.

(2) *Characteristics.*

Caliber	40-mm (1.57 inch).
Maximum vertical range	14,000 feet (approximately).
Maximum elevation	+85°.
Maximum depression	—5°.
Traverse	360°.
Weight in firing position (dual mounted gun).	2,500 pounds (approximately).
Sight	Calculating.
Length of barrel	5 feet 2 inches.

(3) *Ammunition.* Armor piercing high explosive, high explosive with time fuze, high explosive with point detonating fuze, and tracer.

d. Model 88 (1928) 75-mm antiaircraft gun.
(1) *General description.* This has been the standard Japanese mobile heavy antiaircraft weapon (fig. 234). Specimens have been found on all airfields captured from the Japanese. It is a truck drawn weapon. For firing, the wheels are removed, and the gun is supported by five outriggers. During transit, the barrel is dropped back on a cradle extension and secured to the ends of two outriggers. The gun has a hydropneumatic variable recoil system and a semiautomatic horizontal, sliding wedge breech mechanism. Fire control instruments captured indicate that the older system of transmitting

corrections to the gun pointers vocally is still in use. However, evidence is on hand that an electrical data transmission system and operation by the "Matched Pointers" method is used sometimes. This gun has been used against ground targets.

(2) *Characteristics.*

Caliber	75-mm (2.95 inch).
Maximum range:	
Vertical	30,000 feet.
Horizontal	15,000 yards.
Maximum elevation	+85°.
Maximum depression	0°.
Traverse	360°.
Weight, overall	5,830 pounds.
Muzzle velocity	2,360 feet per second.

(3) *Ammunition.* High explosive, shrapnel, and incendiary.

e. Model 14 (1925) 105-mm antiaircraft gun. (1) *General description.* This is the heaviest mobile Japanese antiaircraft weapon (fig. 235) in use at present. As originally designed, it was not satisfactory, and probably has been redesigned by this time. It has a pedestal mount, horizontal sliding breechblock, and a hydropneumatic recoil system. In firing position the wheels are detached and the gun rests on six outriggers. Thirty to 45 minutes are required to prepare the gun for action. The fuze setter is continuous and automatic.

Figure 233. Dual mounted 40-mm Vickers type 40-mm AA/AT automatic cannon.

598462°—44——16

Figure 234. Model 88 (1928) 75-mm antiaircraft gun.

Figure 235. Model 14 (1925) 105-mm antiaircraft gun showing detachable wheels used for transport of piece.

(2) *Characteristics.*

Caliber	105-mm (4.13 inch).
Maximum range:	
Vertical*	36,000 feet.
Horizontal*	20,000 yards.
Maximum elevation	+85°.
Maximum depression	0°.
Traverse	360°.
Weight in firing position	7 tons.
Muzzle velocity	2,300 feet per second.

   *Unconfirmed.

(3) *Ammunition.* High explosive.

4. N A V A L WEAPONS. a. General. In all areas captured from the Japanese, naval guns have been found installed for coastal and antiaircraft defense. These weapons have been of standard naval design, and in many cases appear to have been removed complete (including turret, mounting, etc.) from the decks of ships. It is known that the Japanese have recovered the armament from beached

ships and transferred them to land positions. Since they are on pedestal mounts with wide traverse, they not only are used for coastal defense but also may be brought to bear against inland targets. On the following pages are found examples of the naval guns which are most likely to be encountered. Of these weapons the model 10 (1921) 3-inch gun has been most frequently installed. In addition to those weapons described, guns of 127-mm (5 inch) and 8 inch calibers have been captured. The 127-mm guns have been found mounted in pairs in turrets which permit antiaircraft fire.

b. Model 10 (1921) 3-inch gun. (1) *General description.* The Japanese refer to this weapon (fig. 236) as the "8-cm, 40 caliber, high angle gun." Actual measurement shows it to be 76.2-mm (3 inch). A dual purpose piece on a pedestal mount, it is used for antiaircraft as well as coastal defense. To compensate for muzzle preponderance, an equiliberator is mounted in the pedestal. The recoil sys-

Figure 236. Model 10 (1921) 3-inch gun.

Figure 237. Model 3 (1914) 12-cm naval gun.

tem is hydropneumatic, and the breechblock is the sliding wedge type. A noticeable feature is the unusually long recoil cylinder on the top of the tube.

(2) *Characteristics.*

Caliber	76.2-mm (3 inches).
Maximum vertical range	26,000 feet.
Maximum elevation	+75°.
Maximum depression	—5°.
Maximum traverse	360°.
Muzzle velocity	2,240 feet per second.
Sight	Computing type.
Tube length	10 feet 8½ inches.
Rate of fire	10 to 12 rounds per minute.
Weight of HE projectile	12.7 pounds.

(3) *Ammunition.* High explosive.

c. Model 3 (1914) 12-cm naval gun. (1) *General description.* Guns of this type (fig. 237) have been encountered on a number of islands in the Pacific Area. No provision has been made on the gun illustrated in figure 237 to provide for use as an antiaircraft weapon, but other weapons of this caliber allegedly are mounted for such purposes. It has a hydropneumatic recoil system and an interrupted thread breechblock.

(2) *Characteristics.*

Caliber	120-mm (4.72 inch).
Length of tube	17 feet 8 inches.
Muzzle velocity	2,700 feet per second.
Maximum elevation	+55°.
Maximum depression	—5°.
Maximum traverse	360°.
Maximum range	16,000 meters (17,500 yards).

(3) *Ammunition.* Separate loading high explosive with a cartridge case used for obturation.

d. Model 3 (1914) 14-cm naval gun. (1) *General description.* An orthodox type of naval gun and pedestal mount (fig. 238) which has been used as a coastal defense weapon. It has been found both with a shield and mounted in a hand operated turret (casemate). It has a hydropneumatic recoil system and a truncated cone, interrupted thread breechblock.

(2) *Characteristics.*

Caliber	14-cm (5.5 inch).
Length (tube and breech)	23 feet 8 inches.
Muzzle velocity	2,780 feet per second.
Maximum elevation	+30°.
Maximum depression	—7°.
Maximum traverse	360°.
Maximum range	17,000 meters (18,700 yards).

(3) *Ammunition.* Separate loading ammunition is used. The projectiles recovered were high explosive, with fuzes designed for use against vessels.

Section IV. TANKS AND ARMORED CARS

1. GENERAL. Until 1929 Japan did not produce any tanks (Sensha) of her own. As usual, her ideas were borrowed from the West, particularly from the British and French, and her first tanks were versions of early Renault, Vickers, and Carden-Lloyd models. Later she turned to Russia for new developments.

Prior to 1941 the Japanese had every opportunity to study the experience of the Allies in war, and it is also reasonable to assume that they are still borrowing freely from other nations. What influence German design will have on future Japanese tank production is still to be seen. During 1935–37 the Japanese apparently were concentrating on tankettes, light tanks, and medium tanks, perfecting one model in each class. It is probable that a few heavy tanks also were produced. Their tanks fall into four main types, divided according to weight. These are:

Classification	Short tons (2,000 pounds)	Metric tons (2,204 pounds)
Tankette, Chōkei Sensha.	Less than 5½	5
Light tanks, Kei Sensha.	Less than 5½–11	5–10
Medium tanks, Chu Sensha.	Less than 11–22	10–20
Heavy tanks, Ju Sensha.	Over 22	Over 20

a. Tank nomenclature. For purposes of general information, annotated photographs illustrating various items of tank nomenclature, are reproduced in figure 239.

b. Horsepower. Horsepowers indicated throughout the following text are all Japanese rat-

ings. In each instance, where engines have been examined (e. g., M 2595 Light Tank and M 2597 Medium Tank) it had been clearly shown that they are capable of developing a considerably greater degree of power than that reported. Consequently, wherever possible, theoretically indicated horsepowers, derived from computations based on engine specifications, have been shown.

c. Crews. Crew compartments so far examined are limited in size, and little attention has been given to comfort. The turret and hulls, however, have been found to be well insulated with material such as asbestos.

d. Armament. In the light and medium tanks, relatively low velocity 37- and 57-mm guns are used. There is also evidence that a 47-mm gun is used in medium tanks. Although a machine gun is normally mounted in the rear of the turret, and is of some tactical use, it is doubtful if the main turret weapon and rear machine gun can be fought at the same time. The use of armored sheaths is standard for all machine gun barrels. All machine guns are ball mounted, and the main turret armament has a limited traverse, independent of that of the turret. In both the light and medium tanks a hull machine gun is mounted.

e. Armor. Japanese tanks, so far examined, have been lightly armored, but the plates tested have been of good quality. In the arrangement of armor, use

Figure 238. Model 3 (1914) 14-cm naval gun.

CUPOLA

MANTLET

TURRET

PRIMARY ARMAMENT

BALL MOUNTED MG

ENGINE LOUVRE

VISOR

PISTOL PORT

EXHAUST
MUFFLER

BALL MOUNTED MG

GLACIS PLATE

IDLER

NOSE PLATE

BOGEY WHEEL

SPROCKET

RETURN ROLLERS

BELL CRANK

ARMORED COMPRESSION
SPRINGS

TRANSVERSE EVEN LEVER

Figure 239. Above—Model 95 light tank, illustrating various items of tank nomenclature referred to in this section.
Below—A ditching tail (shown at right of photograph).

has been made of deflection angles, but not to any considerable degree. In many cases reentrant angles have been formed, but no steps have been noted to protect turret rings or mantlets against jamming or splash.

f. Engines. Diesels are mainly used.

g. Suspension. In all these models the same basic suspension is used. This consists of bell-crank arms carrying rocking pairs of wheels. These arms are sprung by horizontal suspension springs, protected by armored casings.

h. Vision. Little use has been made of periscopes, etc., vision being dependent on slits, occasionally backed by a glass block.

i. Doors. The question of escape in case of fire or other emergency has received little attention.

j. Communication. As far as known, radio is used only on the basis of 1 set per platoon in the medium tanks, and probably not at all in light tanks and tankettes.

k. Insignia. Army tanks have a 5 point star mounted on the front, while navy tanks have the anchor insignia. Many tanks either fly or carry the national flag as an identification sign. Naval tanks usually have the small naval insignia painted on the sides.

l. Future developments. (1) *General.* It would be dangerous to measure Japanese tanks by models now known to exist. Evidence exists that Japan is in close touch with German development, and it may well prove that Japanese tanks will show considerable German influence. That Japanese tank design is not stagnant is clearly indicated by the recently captured new type amphibious tank described in this section. In this particular tank the coaxially mounted machine gun is considered of significance. Hitherto, there has been no evidence that the Japanese have mounted weapons in this manner, so it must be considered indicative of a new trend.

(2) *Armament.* High velocity antitank guns, of at least 75-mm caliber, and modern high performance armor piercing high explosive ammunition, as well as hollow charge types, may be expected. As a temporary measure, earlier model tanks, such as the medium which mounts a 57-mm gun, could be given a new lease of life in a tank vs tank role by providing hollow charge ammunition.

(3) *Armor.* Early model tanks may be fitted with additional plates at vulnerable points; modern tanks can be expected to have heavier armor. Armor angles can be expected to receive more attention.

(4) *Performance.* So far Japan has used high power weight ratios. If these are maintained, high speeds and good cross country mobility will result. Suitable preparations, depending on tactical roles, may be undertaken to increase fording ability.

(5) *Communication.* Radio may be introduced down to individual tanks.

(6) *Other improvements.* Special items, like vision aids, escape facilities, and gun fume extraction may be developed. As an illustration of the

trend in tank improvements, in the new type amphibious tank, many of the objectionable features of the older designs have been overcome. Reentrant angles have been eliminated, while the hull design has been simplified and welded construction used throughout. In addition, firepower has been improved by the substitution of a higher velocity 37-mm weapon and the coaxial mounting of a machine gun.

(7) *Heavy tanks.* The Japanese are capable of designing an efficient, modern, heavy tank, but it is thought that they may have difficulty in its quantity production. In the past the Japanese have produced a number of heavy tanks which must now be considered obsolete.

m. Miscellaneous types. Reports suggest that Crane, Repair, and Supply tanks may exist. These are believed to consist basically of a tank chassis, less the turret, and fitted out according to requirements.

2. TANKETTES. a. Tankette model 92 (1932). Development of the tankette has been progressive. In China it was used on a wide scale by Japan in a cavalry and reconnaissance role. In addition it is employed for towing tracked trailers carrying supplies and ammunition. Both welded and riveted construction are used throughout the hull (fig. 240). The suspension is an early Japanese development. Four point suspension of the hull is achieved by use of bell cranks, resisted by armored compression springs on each side. Four rubber tired bogie wheels, two return rollers, and outside center guide tracks are used. Front sprocket drive and left rear mounted engine are employed.

Approximate specifications

Weight	3 tons.
Length	10 feet 3 inches.
Width	5 feet 3 inches.
Height	5 feet 4 inches.
Clearance	13½ inches.
Crew	2 men.
Armor	6 to 14 mm (0.24 to 0.55 inch).
Armament	1—7.7 MG ball mounted.
Ammunition	1,980 rounds.
Engine, 4 cylinder	32 horsepower, gasoline.
Transmission	4 forward, 1 reverse.
Ground contact	6 feet.
Width of track	5 inches.
Track pitch	3 inches.
Diam. sprocket	21 inches.
Diam. bogie wheel	15 inches.
Diam. rear idler	15 inches.
Height to center of sprocket	25 inches.

Approximate maximum performance

Speed	25 miles per hour.
Range of action	100 miles.
Gradient	27°.
Obstacles:	
Trench	4 feet 6 inches wide.
Step	2 feet 1 inch high.
Ford	2 feet deep.

Figure 240. Model 92 (1932) tankette.

b. Tankette model 94 (1934). This tank embodies the general design of the original tankette (fig. 241). The rear idler has been replaced by a trailing idler, while the drive sprocket has been lowered accordingly. Suspension: bell crank, with armored compression springs. Rubber tired bogie wheels, and two return rollers are used. The engine is reported to be a four cylinder in line Ford tractor motor of 32 hp. Steering is the clutch brake principle.

Figure 241. Model 94 (1934) tankette.

Approximate specifications

Weight_____ 3.4 tons.
Length_____ 11 feet.
Width_____ 5 feet 3 inches.
Height_____ 5 feet 4 inches.
Clearance_____ 12 inches.
Crew_____ 2 men.
Armor_____ 4- to 12-mm (0.16 to 0.47 inches).
Armament_____ 1–7.7 MG.
Traverse_____ 360°.
Ammunition_____ 1,980 rounds.
Fuel capacity_____ 23.3 gallons.

Approximate maximum performance

Speed_____ 26 miles per hour.
Range of action_____ 100 miles (estimated).
Gradient_____ 27° (also reported as 30°).
Obstacles:
    Trench_____ 4 feet 6 inches wide.
    Step_____ No details.
    Ford_____ 2 feet deep.

Approximate specifications

Weight_____ 4.5 tons.
Length_____ 12 feet.
Width_____ 6 feet.
Height_____ 6 feet.
Clearance_____ 14 inches.
Crew_____ 2 men.
Armor_____ 4 to 12-mm (0.16 to 0.47 inches).
Armament_____ 1–37-mm gun.
Ammunition_____ 96 rounds.
Transmission_____ 4 forward 1 reverse.
Steering_____ Drive shaft brake.
Fuel capacity_____ 20 gallons (also reported 24 gallons).

Approximate maximum performance

Speed_____ 28 miles per hour.
Gradient_____ 30° (also reported as 34°).
Obstacles:
    Trench_____ 5 feet 3 inches wide.
    Step_____ No details.
    Ford_____ 2 feet 6 inches deep.

Figure 242. Model 97 (1937) tankette.

c. Tankette model 97 (1937). Various specifications have been reported for a tank of this size (fig. 242). It is not certain if these refer to several different models of the M2597 or whether they relate to an even later model, the M2598 (1938). The suspension of this tank remains unchanged from that of the M2594 tankette. The hull, however, has been completely redesigned. More room has been provided in the turret to accommodate the 37-mm tank gun. As an alternative, a machine gun sometimes is mounted in place of the 37-mm weapon. Particular attention has been paid to a more simple design of the front plate and improved deflection angles. This tank is powered by a 4 cylinder, in line, air-cooled Diesel engine of 48 horsepower. Engine specifications indicate, however, that this engine would theoretically develop 105 hp at 2000 rpm.

3. LIGHT TANKS. a. Light tank model 93 (1933). This tank (fig. 243) represents the early development of the light tank series. The box type hull is divided into three compartments. The center portion is the fighting compartment, the superstructure of which overhangs the tracks. The right hand side at the front of the fighting compartment is extended forward to form a sponson for the ball mounted machine gun. The driver sits left, while the hull gunner sits right, in the forward compartment. The 6 cylinder gasoline engine is mounted to the rear of the hull. The suspension consists of six small, rubber-tired bogie wheels mounted on three semielliptic springs on each side. There are three return rollers. Front sprocket drive and center guide track are employed. The turret mounts one machine gun to the front, while some photo-

Figure 243. Model 93 (1933) light tank.

graphs show another mounted in the rear.   Traverse 360°.

Approximate specifications

Weight_____ 7.8 tons.
Length_____ 14 feet 8 inches.
Width_____ 5 feet 11 inches.
Height_____ 6 feet.
Clearance_____ 15 inches.
Crew_____ 3 men.
Armor_____ Up to 22-mm (0.87 inch) (reported).
Armament_____ 1 light mg (Hull), 1 light mg (turret).
Steering_____ Clutch brake.
Ground contact_____ 10 feet.
Engine_____ 6 cylinder 85 horsepower Mitsubishi.
Cooling_____ Air.

Width of track_____ 7½ inches.
Pitch of track_____ 3½ inches.
Diam. of sprocket_____ 1 foot 6 inches.
Diam. of rear idler____ 1 foot 3 inches.
Height of sprocket center. 1 foot 8 inches.

Approximate maximum performance

Speed_____ 28 miles per hour.
Obstacles:
    Trench_____ 5 feet 8 inches wide.
    Step_____ 1 foot 6 inches high.
    Ford_____ 2 feet 8 inches deep.

b. Light tank model 93 (1933) improved. Probably produced in 1933–34, this tank is an improved model of the M2593 in that the suspension has 4 bogie wheels coupled together in pairs via transverse even lever.   It is not clear whether the apex is mounted to the hull by means of a bell crank or a stub shaft. Likewise it is not clear whether the armored compression spring is used at this stage of development. Two return rollers are used, as well as front sprocket drive. The hull of this vehicle is almost identical with that of the previous model.

Approximate specifications

Weight	7.8 tons.
Length	14 feet 8 inches.
Width	5 feet 11 inches.
Height	6 feet.
Clearance	15 inches.
Crew	3 men.
Armor	up to 22-mm (0.87 inch) (reported).
Armament	1–37-mm tank gun, 1 turret machine gun.
Engine	6 cylinder, 85 horsepower air-cooled (Mitsubishi).
Ground contact	9 feet 6 inches.
Width of track	7½ inches.
Track pitch	3½ inches.
Diam. bogie wheel	15 inches.
Steering	Clutch brake.
Fuel	Gasoline.

Approximate maximum performance

Speed	28 miles per hour.
Range of action	120 miles.
Obstacles:	
Trench	5 feet 8 inches wide.
Step	1 foot 6 inches high.
Ford	2 feet 10 inches deep.

c. Light tank model 95 (1935). In production from 1935 to at least 1942, there is a great deal of evidence to show that Japanese light tank design

was frozen in 1935 to produce large numbers of these tanks (fig. 244). The hull has been completely redesigned. The suspension has been improved to utilize the bell crank and armored compression spring. The tank is powered by a 6 cylinder in-line air-cooled Diesel engine. The hull is constructed over an angle iron frame, with backing plates at the corners; insulation is provided by layers of woven asbestos. Ammunition for the 37-mm tank gun is carried stored in clips and racks in the fighting compartment. Two types are known. Model 94 shell—presumably HE of 1934 model, and model 94 AP shell—presumably APHE of 1934 model. 1170 rounds of 7.7-mm ammunition are stored in magazines just below the hull machine gun. 1800 rounds are carried in the fighting compartment for turret machine gun.

Specifications from actual examination

Weight	10 tons (laden).
Length	14 feet 4 inches.
Width	6 feet 9 inches.
Height	7 feet.
Clearance	15½ inches.
Crew	3 men.
Armor	6 to 12-mm (0.24 to 0.47 inches).
Armament	1–37-mm model 94 tank gun, 1 7.7-mm rear turret mg, 1 7.7-mm hull mg.
Ammunition:	
37-mm	130 rounds.
MG	2,970 rounds.
Engine	110 horsepower at 1,400 rpm (240 theoretically indicated h.p. at 2,000 rpm based on reported engine specifications).

Figure 244. Model 95 (1935) light tank.

Specifications from actual examination—Continued

Transmission_____ 4 speeds forward, 1 reverse.
Steering_____ Clutch brake.
Ground contact_____ 7 feet 8 inches.
Width of track_____ 9⅞ inches.
Track pitch_____ 3¾ inches.
Diameter sprocket_____ 21 inches.
Diameter bogie wheel__ 22¼ inches.
Diameter rear idler____ 21 inches.
Height to center of 32 inches.
    sprocket.

Approximate maximum performance

Speed_____ 28 miles per hour.
Range of action_____ 100 miles.
Gradient_____ 40°. 30° for long climb.
Obstacles:
    Trench_____ 6 feet wide.
    Step_____ 2 feet 8 inches high.
    Ford_____ 3 feet 3 inches deep.

d. Light tank, "Keni." It is considered that this tank is not an obsolete model; it probably has been produced subsequent to the M2595 light tank. The 47-mm gun is a significant feature.

Approximate specifications

Weight_____ 7.7 tons.
Length_____ 13 feet 6 inches.
Width_____ 7 feet.
Height_____ 5 feet 11 inches.

Ground clearance_____. 14 inches.
Crew_____ 3 men.
Armament_____ 1 47-mm gun and 1 MG.
Armor_____ 6 to 16-mm (0.24 to 0.63
                          inches).
Engine_____ 140 horsepower.

Approximate maximum performance

Speed_____ 31 miles per hour.
Gradient_____. 34°.
Obstacles:
    Trench_____ 6 feet 7 inches wide.
    Ford_____ 2 feet 3 inches deep.

4. MEDIUM TANKS. a. Medium tank model 89 A (1929). This tank (fig. 245) is characterized by its box type hull, short front plate with door to the right, vertical front plate above this with hull machine gun mounted to the right, and small cupola hinged to top of turret. Five small return rollers are mounted along a girder. There are 9 small bogie wheels. The leading bogie wheel is independently mounted, while protective skirting all but covers the suspension. This tank is rear sprocket driven and powered by a gasoline engine. There is a rear turret machine gun, while the main armament is a 57-mm low velocity gun. Traverse 360°.

Figure 245. Model 89 A (1929) medium tank.

Figure 246. Model 89 B (1929) medium tank.

Approximate specifications

Weight	13 tons.
Length	19 feet 3 inches.
Width	7 feet 1 inch.
Height	8 feet 6 inches.
Clearance	19 inches.
Crew	4 men.
Armor	6 to 17 mm (0.24 to 0.67 inches), also reported as 17 to 25 mm (0.67 to 1 inch).
Armament	1–57-mm, 1 Hull mg, 1 Rear turret MG.
Ammunition	57-mm 100 rounds, SAA 2,745 rounds.
Engine	136 brake horsepower.
Ground contact	12 feet.
Width of track	12 inches.
Track pitch	6 inches.
Diam. rear sprocket	30 inches.
Diam. bogie wheel	9 inches.
Diam. front idler	36 inches.
Height to center of idler.	33 inches.
Fuel	Gasoline.

Approximate maximum performance

Speed	15 miles per hour.
Range of action	100 miles.
Gradient	34°.
Obstacles:	
Trench	8 feet 3 inches wide.
Step	2 feet 9 inches high.
Ford	3 feet 3 inches deep.

b. Medium tank model 89 B (1929). Also reported as the M2592 (1932), this tank (fig. 246) differs from the M 89 A in that it has a long front which combines with the driver's front plate. The turret has been completely redesigned to include a new type of cupola and a more practical aperture for mounting the 57-mm gun. The gasoline engine has been replaced by a Diesel engine, but the armament and the armor thickness remain the same.

Approximate specifications

Weight	13 tons.
Length	19 feet 3 inches.
Width	7 feet 1 inch.
Height	8 feet 6 inches.
Clearance	19 inches.
Crew	4 men.
Armor	6- to 17-mm (0.24 to 0.67 inches), also reported as 17- to 25-mm (0.67 to 0.98 inches).
Armament	1–57-mm, 1 Hull mg, 1 rear turret mg.
Ammunition	57-mm, 100 rounds, SAA 2745 rounds.
Engine	120 brake horsepower.
Ground contact	12 feet.
Width of track	12 inches.
Track pitch	6 inches.
Diameter rear sprocket.	30 inches.
Diameter bogie wheel	9 inches.
Height to center of idler	33 inches.

Approximate maximum performance

Speed_____ 15 miles per hour.
Range of action_____ 100 miles.
Gradient_____ 34°.
Obstacles:
   Trench_____ 8 feet 3 inches wide.
   Step_____ 2 feet 9 inches high.
   Ford_____ 3 feet 3 inches deep.

c. Medium tank model 94 (1934). Probably produced in 1934 in quantity, this tank (fig. 247) has been extensively used in China. Comparison with the M 2589 models A and B shows that the return rollers have been reduced to four, the girder has been removed, and the skirting redesigned. The long front plate has a door on the left, above which is mounted the hull machine gun. The driver sits to the right. The Diesel engine has been increased to 160 brake horsepower. With the above exceptions the M 2594 is practically identical with the M2589 B. This tank is often seen with a ditching tail.

Specifications

Weight_____ 15 tons.
Length (including 23 feet.
  ditching tail).
Width_____ 7 feet 1 inch.
Height_____ 8 feet 6 inches.
Clearance_____ 19 inches.
Crew_____ 4 men.
Armor_____ 6- to 17-mm (0.24 to 0.67 inches).
Armament:
   Main_____ 1–57-mm gun.
   MG_____ 1 Hull MG.
               1 Rear turret MG.

Ammunition_____ 57-mm 100 rounds, SAA 2,750 rounds.
Engine_____ 160 brake horsepower air-aircooled Diesel.
Ground contact_____ 12 feet.
Width of track_____ 12 inches.
Track pitch_____ 6 inches.
Diam. rear sprocket___ 30 inches.
Diam. front idler_____ 36 inches.
Diam. bogie wheel____ 9 inches.
Height to center of 33 inches.
  front idler.

Approximate maximum performance

Speed_____ 20 miles per hour.
Range of action_____ 100 miles.
Gradient_____ 34°.
Obstacles:
   Trench_____ 9 feet wide.
   Step_____ 2 feet 9 inches high.
   Ford_____ 3 feet 3 inches deep.

d. Medium tank model 97 (1937). Probably produced in 1937–1940. Some of the design features of this tank (fig. 248) are directly due to lessons learned from tankette and light tank construction. The four central bogie wheels are paired and mounted on bell cranks resisted by armored compression springs. Each end bogie wheel is independently bell crank mounted to the hull in a similar manner. There are three return rollers, the center one carrying the inside half of the track only. Backing plates are used to reinforce hull joints and corners. Numbers of these tanks are known to have been used in Burma. Other specimens were encountered on Guadalcanal.

Figure 247. Model 94 (1934) medium tank.

Figure 248. Model 97 (1937) medium tank.

Specifications by examination

Weight_____ 15 tons.
Length_____ 18 feet.
Width_____ 7 feet 8 inches.
Height_____ 7 feet 8 inches.
Clearance_____ 16 inches.
Crew_____ 4 men.
Armor_____ 8- to 25-mm (0.32 to 0.98 inch).
Armament:
    Main_____ 1–57-mm model 97 gun.
    Hull_____ 1–7.7-mm model 97 mg.
Rear turret_____ 1–7.7-mm model 97 mg.
Ammunition_____ 57-mm 80 rounds HE—40 rounds APHE, MG 2350 rounds Ball, 1350 rounds AP.
Engine_____ 12 Cylinder Diesel.
Horsepower_____ 150 (365 theoretically indicated hp at 2,000 rpm based on reported engine specifications).
Transmission_____ 4 speeds forward, 1 reverse—high low range.
Steering_____ Clutch brake.
Ground contact_____ 12 feet 8 inches.
Width of track_____ 13 inches.
Track pitch_____ 5 inches.
Diameter front sprocket_ 23 inches.
Diameter rear idler____ 23 inches.
Diameter bogie wheel__ 21 inches.

Height to center of 32½ inches.
  sprocket.
Fuel consumption_____ 4 gallons per hour.

Approximate maximum performance

Speed_____ 25 miles per hour.
Radius of action_____ 100 miles.
Gradient_____ 34°.
Obstacles:
    Trench_____ 8 feet 3 inches.
    Step_____ 2 feet 6 inches high.
    Ford_____ 3 feet 3 inches deep.

e. Medium tank (unidentified). Probably produced in 1939, this tank is believed to have been employed on Corregidor. Its identity (fig. 249) has not been confirmed. With the exception of the turret and main armament, it is basically the same in design as the model 2597 medium tank. The turret has been improved to accommodate a modern high velocity gun, believed to be of 47-mm caliber. As usual there is a rear turret machine gun. The long overhanging rear portion of the turret would therefore provide more room for the simultaneous firing of both these weapons. With the exception of the turret and armament, specifications are believed the same as those for the model 2597 (1937) medium tank.

5. HEAVY TANKS. a. Little is known of Japanese heavy tanks. As far as can be ascertained, they have been produced only in limited numbers, and those seen have been reported as being clumsy, lightly armored, and of poor performance. In addition, some years prior to the war, a limited number of "heavies" were bought by Japan. The majority of these (including the "Vickers Independent," weight 32 tons) are obsolete.

b. In 1939, the battle of Nomonhan clearly demonstrated the inadequacy of Japanese tanks. At the conclusion of this conflict considerable reorganization took place within the Japanese Army. It is reasonable to assume, therefore, that Japan is now in possession of a modern heavy tank.

6. AMPHIBIOUS TANKS. a. General. Little specific information is available concerning the Japanese development of this type of tank. Similar to the ground tanks, the first amphibians were purchased from foreign countries, a specific instance being the 3 to 4 ton "Vickers amphibious light tank." Several modifications of this are believed to have been produced by the Japanese.

b. Model 2594 (1934) light amphibious tank. An unconfirmed report indicates the existence of a tank, tentatively identified as the model 2594 (1934) light amphibious tank, possessing the following specifications:

Weight	4 tons.
Length	14 feet 10 inches.
Width	7 feet 11 inches.
Height	8 feet 10 inches.
Armament	1–37-mm, 1 MG.
Armor	Up to 20-mm (0.79 inch).

It is considered that the armor and armament, coupled with the dimensions, are hardly compatible with a weight of only 4 tons.

c. New type amphibious tank. The photograph illustrated in figure 250 shows the most modern trend yet encountered in Japanese tank design. No information is available to indicate the model number or date of production. The system of flotation is extremely interesting and is achieved by attachment of a bow and stern pontoon. Pontoons conform to the shape of the hull, and are attached by a series of pincer clamps, which are controlled by a handwheel situated inside the tank, enabling their quick release if so desired. The volume of the bow pontoon is estimated at 220 cubic feet, and that of the stern pontoon at 105 cubic feet. Two rudders are situated in the stern pontoons and are operated from within the hull. Two propellers are fitted to the rear of the tank. With exception of the suspension, this tank is an entirely new Japanese design, the hull being simplified, reentrant angles eliminated, and welding used throughout. In addition, the round turret is of a new type, characterized by its considerably increased diameter, giving the impression of greatly reduced height. To prevent water entering, rubber seals are fitted around all openings up to and including the turret ring. The tank hull is not divided into individual compartments. Suspension closely resembles that of the M 2594 and M 2597 tankettes, excepting that the compression springs are mounted within the vehicle. No specific details are available, but there are definite indications that the primary armament of this vehicle shows improvement. Of particular significance is the coaxial mounting of the turret machine gun. As no Japanese tank has been encountered in the past with its weapons so mounted, this fact must be regarded as a radical departure in their tank

Figure 249. Unidentified medium tank (basically the same design as the model 97 medium tank).

Figure 250. New type amphibious tank.

design. The following data have been obtained from a preliminary examination:

Specifications

Weight:
    Tank (only) ____ 13 tons (estimated).
    Pontoons (only) . 3 tons (estimated).
Length:
    Tank (only) ____ 15 feet 8 inches.
    With pontoons_ 24 feet 7 inches.
Width _____ 9 feet 2 inches.
Height _____ 7 feet 6 inches.
Ground clearance_____ 14 inches.
Crew _____ 5 men.
Armor:
    Turret:
        Sides ____ 13.2-mm (0.52 inch).
        Top _____ 6-mm (0.24 inch).
    Hull:
        Front ____ 12-mm (0.47 inch).
        Sides ____ 9-mm (0.35 inch).
        Rear _____ 8-mm (0.32 inch).
        Top _____ 6-mm (0.24 inch).
        Bottom___ 8.5-mm (0.334 inch).
Armament _____ 1–37-mm model 1 (1941) in turret, 1–7.7-mm MG coaxially mounted, 1–7.7-mm MG in hull forward.
Engine _____ 6 cylinder air-cooled Diesel (reported to be identical with that in the model 2595 Light Tank).
Fuel capacity _____ 66 gallons (2 tanks).
Suspension _____ 2 bogies on each side of vehicle. Bogies consist of 2 wheels mounted on a transverse even lever. Rear trailing idler serves as an additional bogie.
Track:
    Length, overall_. 32 feet 1 inch.
    Ground contact_ 11 feet 1 inch.
    Width _____ 1 foot.
    Angle of approach. 56¼°.
Vision apertures and pistol ports.:
    Hull _____ 1–4 x 1 inch slit for driver; 1–4 x ⅛ inch slit for hull gunner; 4 pistol ports, one on each quarter of the hull.

Turret _____ 2–3.75 inch diameter vision ports, one on each side of 37-mm gun. 2–4 x ⅛ inch slits, one on each side of turret. 3 pistol ports, one at each side and one at the rear.
Safety glass_____ Shatter proof blocks are clamped over all vision slits to prevent "bullet splash" or entrance of water. Vision ports are protected by 3-inch safety glass windows.

7. ARMORED CARS. a. Armored car model 25 (?) "Vickers Crossley." This armored car (fig. 251) may be classified as obsolete and is readily identified by its hemispherical turret. A small domed cupola, in two hinged halves, surmounts the turret. Traverse 360°, the turret mounts only two machine guns, although there is provision for four. Each of the weapon openings is covered with a small flap, which is closed when the gun is removed. All machine guns are of the Vickers type. Guns are ball mounted and have a limited traverse independent of that of the turret. The front wheels are single, while the rear wheels are dual. The chassis is believed to be a standard commercial type weighing 2.8 tons. In the past, this armored car was incorrectly classified as the "OSAKA" model 2592 (1932).

Approximate specifications

Weight _____ 5.4 tons.
Length _____ 16 feet 6 inches.
Width _____ 6 feet 2 inches.
Height _____ 8 feet 6 inches.
Ground clearance__ 10 inches.
Crew _____ 4 men.
Armament _____ 2 Vickers' MGs.
Armor _____ 5.5-mm (0.217 inches).
Ammunition _____ 3,500 rounds.
Engine _____ 4 cylinder, 50 horsepower "Crossley."
Fuel _____ Gasoline.
Fuel capacity _____ 26 gallons.
Cooling _____ Water.
Drive _____ Rear axle.

Figure 251. Model 25 (?) "Vickers Crossley" armored car.

Approximate maximum performance

Speed_____ 40 miles per hour.
Range of action____ 124 miles.

b. Armored car model 92 (1932) naval type.

This probably was produced in 1932. The insignia indicates that it (fig. 252) is a naval vehicle. In addition to the machine gun in the front and rear, one is mounted on each side of the hull. One is also mounted in the turret. Semielliptic springs provide the suspension for the 6-disc wheel chassis. Wheels are fitted with pneumatic tires. To prevent bellying, when crossing rough terrain, auxiliary wheels are mounted on the frame to the rear of the front wheels. The radiator is provided with armored shutters. Reconnaissance and guard duties constitute the chief role for this vehicle.

Approximate specifications

Weight_____ 7 tons.
Length_____ 15 feet 9 inches.
Width_____ 5 feet 11 inches.
Height_____ 7 feet 6 inches.
Ground clearance_____ 16 inches.
Crew_____ 4 men.
Armament_____ 5 MGs.
Armor_____ 8 to 11 mm (0.32 to 0.43 inch).
Engine_____ 6 cylinder, 85 brake horse-power.
Cooling_____ Water.

Approximate maximum performance

Speed_____ 50 miles per hour.

c. Armored car model 92 (1932) "OSAKA."

Until recently, considerable confusion has existed between this armored car and the model 25(?) "Vickers Crossley," specifications of the "Osaka" being attributed to the latter vehicle. While no details are available, it is believed that the "Osaka" is of Japanese origin, a standard commercial chassis being used for its manufacture. Wheels are fitted with pneumatic tires, the front single and the rear dual mounted. Machine guns are of the Vickers type; one is mounted in the front of the turret. As an extensive free traverse has been allowed to this gun, it is considered possible that the turret is fixed and cannot be traversed. As the design of the driver's front plate gives no indication that the second machine gun is mounted in the front of the hull, it is probable that this weapon is mounted at the rear of the vehicle.

Approximate specifications

Weight_____ 6.4 tons.
Length_____ 16 feet 5 inches.
Width_____ 6 feet.
Height_____ 8 feet 8 inches.
Ground clearance___ 11 inches.
Crew_____ 4 to 5 men.
Armament_____ 2 MGs.
Armor_____ 8 to 11 mm (0.32 to 0.43 inches).
Engine_____ 4 cylinder, 35 horsepower.
Fuel_____ Gasoline.
Cooling_____ Water.

Figure 252. Model 92 (1932) naval type armored car.

Approximate maximum performance

Speed_____ 37 miles per hour.
Range of action_____ 150 miles.

d. Armored car model 93 (1933) "Sumida".
This vehicle (fig. 253) has been used extensively in China and was specially designed to run either on railway lines or hard roads. To effect the change from rails to road, the vehicle is raised up by 4 built-in jacks. Solid rubber tires then are placed over the 6 flanged steel wheels, and the vehicle can be driven off the rails onto the road. This operation

Figure 253. Model 93 (1933) "Sumida" armored car.

Figure 254. Model 91 (1931) 6.5-mm tank machine gun. Hopper and butt are missing.

is said to take 10 minutes. When traveling on rails, 3 solid rubber tires are attached on each side of the hull.

Approximate specifications

Weight	7.5 tons.
Length	21 feet 6 inches.
Width	6 feet 3 inches.
Height	9 feet 8 inches.
Ground clearance	16 inches.
Crew	6 men.
Armament	1 MG mounted in turret. Slits for rifles or LMGs.
Armor	Up to 16-mm (0.63 inch).
Engine	40 horsepower.
Fuel	Gasoline.
Vision	Drivers visor slits and gun ports.

Approximate maximum performance

Speed:

On rails	37 miles per hour.
On road	25 miles per hour.

8. ARMAMENT OF JAPANESE ARMORED UNITS. The following weapons are known to be used in Japanese tanks and armored cars:

a. Model 91 (1931) 6.5-mm MG. This weapon (fig. 254) is merely the infantry machine gun, model 11 (1922) adapted to tank requirements by the removal of the bipod. It is considered possible that it has now been replaced largely by the better designed and heavier calibered model 97 (1937) 7.7-mm machine gun. For detailed characteristics of the model 11, see chap. 9, sec. II.

b. Model 97 (1937) 7.7-mm MG. This is the standard MG (fig. 255) at present used in Japanese tanks. A shoulder controlled weapon, it is fitted with conventional sights. It may readily be identified by the specially designed modified stock. When used for tank purposes, a fixed focus telescopic sight of 1½ power x 30° field of view is usually fitted. To prevent injury to the gunner, a heavy rubber eye pad is attached to the rear of the telescope. By the addition of a bipod, this weapon may be converted to ground purposes.

Characteristics

Caliber	7.7-mm (.303 inch).
Principle of operation	Gas operated, full automatic only.
Type of feed	Vertical box.
Magazine capacity	30 rounds.
Length of barrel	28 inches.
Over-all length	46 inches.
Weight	34 pounds.
Cyclic rate of fire	500 rounds per minute.
Ammunition	Fires special model 99 rimless.

c. Model 94 (1934) 37-mm tank gun. Although bearing the same type number as the field piece of similar caliber, these two weapons must in no way be confused, for each has been designed for its own specific purpose. In addition, ammunition is NOT interchangeable, as the chamber of the tank gun (fig. 256) is considerably smaller than that of the antitank gun. This gun appears to constitute the primary armament of Japanese light tanks. In addition, there is evidence that one model of tankette is similarly equipped. It is considered that this weapon has neither the performance nor armor piercing qualities of the U. S. 37-mm tank gun. Mounted in the turret, the Japanese weapon is carried by two sets of trunnions, one set allowing the gun a limited "free" traverse, while the other permits the gun to be elevated or depressed. Traverse and elevation/depression are manually applied by means of an adjustable shoulder rest attached to the left side of the cradle. The main traverse is obtained by rotating the turret. Telescopic sight, pistol type grip, and trigger are mounted to the left of the gun.

Characteristics

Caliber	37-mm (1.46 inch).
Muzzle velocity	2,100 feet per second (estimated).
Maximum elevation	+24°.
Maximum depression	—20°.
Traverse	10° right, 10° left, without rotating the turret.
Breech mechanism	Vertical sliding, semiautomatic in action.
Recoil system	Hydrospring.
Ammunition	APHE and HE.

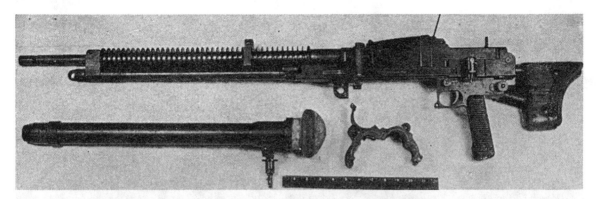

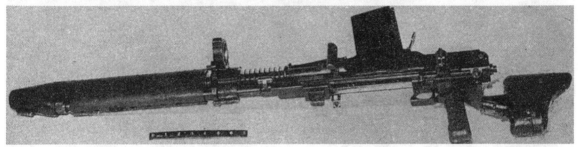

Figure 255. Model 97 (1937) 7.7-mm tank machine gun. (The lower figure illustrates the armor shield normally used when this machine gun is mounted in a tank.)

d. Model 1 (1941) 37-mm tank gun. This gun has been recovered, but detailed examination has not yet been made. However, from the length of the barrel and the size of the chamber, a muzzle velocity much higher than that of Model 94 (1934) 37-mm tank gun may be expected, and it is believed that this gun will have good armor-piercing qualities.

e. Model 97 (1937) 57-mm tank gun. It is believed that this weapon (fig. 257) is the standard heavy armament of Japanese medium tanks. The gun is mounted in the turret and is manually controlled. Elevation and depression are free. The weapon may be traversed also approximately 10 degrees to left and right, independently of the turret.

Although several specimens have been captured, the condition of the guns has prevented a detailed examination. Sufficient information is available, however, to indicate that it is a short barrelled, medium velocity weapon that would be more suitable for employment against ground troops. This would appear to conform to the Japanese past policy of using mainly tanks for the close support of infantry, rather than for tank vs. tank action. No information is available to indicate if this policy is still being adhered to, or whether the future trend will be to substitute a high velocity weapon similar to the model 1 (1941) 47-mm antitank gun (for characteristics see ch. 9, sec. II).

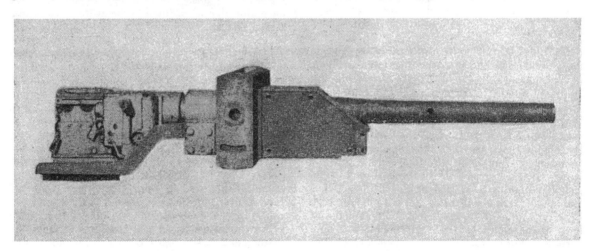

Figure 256. Model 94 (1934) 37-mm tank gun.

Figure 257. Model 97 (1937) 57-mm tank gun (showing its appearance from the outside of the turret).

Characteristics

Caliber	57-mm (2.24 inches).
Weight	283 pounds.
Length of tube	3 feet 1.6 inches.
Length of chamber	5.1 inches.
Number of lands and grooves.	20.
Maximum length of recoil.	11 inches.
Maximum elevation	+45°.
Traverse	10° right, 10° left, without rotating the turret.
Type of beechblock	Vertical sliding.
Ammunition	Only high explosive rounds have been recovered to date. They are characterized by a rather short cartridge case.

f. Model 90 (1930) 57-mm tank gun. No information is available concerning this weapon. Photographs of early Japanese tanks suggest that this gun is a short barrelled piece resembling the model 97. It is probable that the model 90 was the forerunner of the latter weapon.

g. 47-mm tank gun. While no details are available, indications are that the Japanese are now mounting a 47-mm gun in certain of their medium tanks. It is also reported that a model of the light tank is mounting a weapon of this caliber. It is reasonable to assume that this gun is a modern, high velocity antitank piece, in all probability, a modified form of the model 1 (1941) gun adapted to tank purposes. For characteristics of the model 1 (1941) 47-mm antitank gun, see section II, chapter 9.

Section V. CHEMICAL WARFARE

Part I

PROTECTIVE EQUIPMENT

1. GAS MASKS. a. General. All the known models of gas masks used by Japanese military forces are of the air hose and separate canister type. Rubber stoppers are provided to permit sealing of the canister when not in use to protect the contents against moisture. In general the Japanese gas masks afford good protection against the common types of war gases; their facepieces, however, are uncomfortable when fitted to the average occidental face. The American canisters can be fitted to these masks for better protection against hydrocyanic acid (AC) and cyanogen chloride (CC) gas than the Japanese canister gives. The existence of horse gas masks of the damp mask type has been reported.

b. Army gas mask "model 95". It has a khaki stockinette covered facepiece (fig. 258) with molded tissot tube and circular eyepieces with removable threaded rims. The khaki-colored canister is approximately 6 inches high, 5 inches wide and 2¾ inches thick. The carrier is a rectangular canvas bag. A rubberized hood is sometimes attached to this mask to protect head and shoulders.

c. Army gas mask "model 99". Similar in appearance to "model 95" (fig. 259), it is fitted with a rubber nosepiece held inside the facepiece by a stud, and has a short canister only about 4½ inches high.

Figure 258. Army gas mask "model 95".

Figure 259. Army gas mask "model 99".

Figure 260. Civilian gas mask type 1, model A (Improved).

Figure 261. Navy gas mask model 93, No. 2.

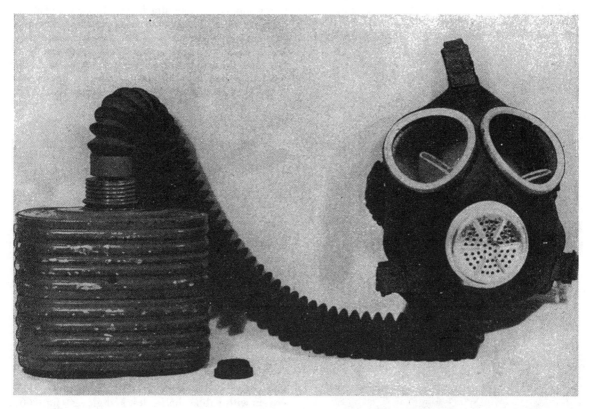

Figure 262. Navy gas mask model 93, No. 3.

d. Civilian gas mask type 1, model A (improved). This gas mask (fig. 260), although originally designed for civilian use, also is issued to Army personnel. The facepiece is tan colored with molded tissot tube and circular eyepieces with fixed rims. The tan colored canister is approximately 4¾ inches high, 5¼ inches wide and 2¾ inches thick. The carrier is a small rectangular canvas bag with a 1½ inch diameter hole in the bottom.

e. Navy gas mask model 93, No. 2. Gray colored facepiece, with aluminum rimmed eyepieces, (fig. 261) and a tissot tube held by two metal studs. The grey canister is approximately 5½ inches high, 6½ inches wide and 3 inches thick. An auxiliary canister, approximately 2 inches high, can be attached to the base of the main canister to give protection against carbon monoxide. A fabric carrier bag is provided for the facepiece only; the canister is carried on the back held in a fabric harness.

f. Navy gas mask model 93 No. 3. The facepiece (fig. 262) is practically identical with that of No. 2. However, the valve housing may be made of brown plastic instead of aluminum. The canister is approximately 4½ inches high, 5¾ inches wide and 3 inches thick. The carrier is a canvas bag tapered toward the bottom which is provided with 2½-inch diameter hole. This model may be used with the auxiliary carbon monoxide canister provided for the No. 2 model.

2. GAS MASK ACCESSORIES. The carriers of most Army gas masks are provided with a packet of antifog discs (fig. 263), a container for antifreeze liquid (fig. 264), a hinged metal clamp for closing the air hose, and a cleaning rag. In addi-

Figure 263. Package of antifog discs.

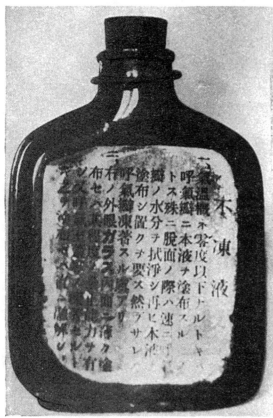

Figure 264. Metal flask for antifreeze liquid.

tion a small cloth bag attached to the carrying straps contains a can of decontaminant powder. The antifog discs are carried in a thin, black, plastic box. These discs are used to cover the eyepieces when the temperature is below the freezing point. The antifreeze liquid co'tainer is either a flat square metal flask or a black cylindrical syringe (fig. 265)

Figure 265. Syringe for antifreeze liquid.

made of plastic material. The antifreeze liquid is applied to the inlet valve of the gas mask when the temperature is below the freezing point. Navy gas mask carriers contain an antifog compound in a small cylindrical sheet metal container and a cleaning rag.

3. PROTECTIVE CLOTHING. a. Light protective clothing. Two types of light weight impermeable protective clothing designed to be worn over regular clothing exist:

(1) *"Cellophane type" light protective clothing.* Comprises jacket with fixed hood, trousers, boot covers with rubber half soles, and gloves (fig. 266). The garments are made of rubberized silk with a cellophane interlining.

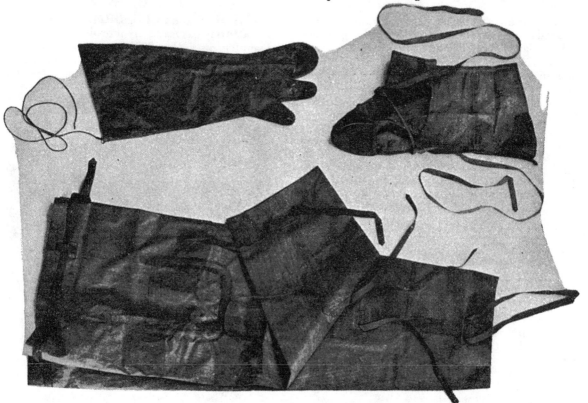

Figure 266. "Cellophane type" light protective clothing.

Figure 267. "Casein type" light protective clothing.

(2) *"Casein type" light protective clothing.* The set (fig. 267) consists of trousers, overboots, gloves, and a carrier pouch. All items are made of casein-coated, rubberized silk.

b. Heavy protective clothing. Is made of heavy red brown rubberized fabric and comprises an over-all suit with fixed boots and hood (fig. 269) and a pair of gloves. This suit weighs approximately 21 pounds.

c. Protective cover and leggings for horses. The existence of these items has been definitely established. The cover is made of cotton fabric, rubberized on both sides, and has semispherical, plastic eyepieces. No details are available concerning the leggings.

4. DECONTAMINANTS. a. Individual decontamination kit. This kit (fig. 268) is intended for use by the individual soldier in neutralizing liquid blister gas that may have come in contact with the skin. The kit consists of a fabric carrying pouch, with a tiestring containing a roll of absorbent cotton, and a green metal can (approximately 3 inches by 2¼ inches) with a small screw cap lid. The decontaminant in the metal can is a powder containing chloramine-T as the active ingredient. Decontamination is accomplished by mixing the powder with water to form a paste and applying the mixture to the skin. It is effective against both mustard gas (H) and lewisite (L).

Figure 268. Can of individual decontaminant.

Figure 269.   Heavy protective clothing.

inches square (see fig. 271) with two blue bands around the casing, contains approximately 2.25 pounds of flaked sodium hydroxide.

e. Decontaminating agent, No. 3. A rectangular sheet metal box, 13¼ inches high, 7¾ inches wide and 5¾ inches thick, with three green bands around the casing (see fig. 271) contains approximately 15 pounds of chloride of lime.

f. Decontaminating agent, No. 4. A cylindrical sheet metal can, 2¾ inches high, 2⁷⁄₁₆ inches in diameter, with four blue bands around the casing (see fig. 271) contains a spherical glass ampule wrapped in cotton gauze. The ampule holds approximately 1.8 ounces of a yellow liquid consisting of a 20 percent solution of chlorine in carbon tetrachloride.

g. Uses. These decontamination agents are used as follows:

Nos. 1 and 2. For decontamination of tear gases and vomiting gases.
No. 3. For decontamination of blister gases. Probably used to refill the pouch.
No. 4. For decontamination of blister and vomiting gases.

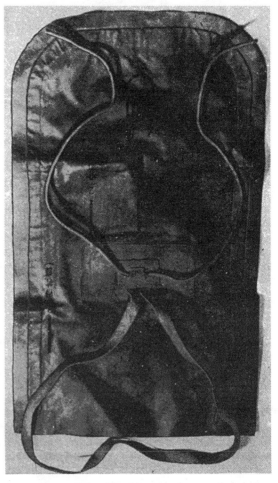

Figure 270.   Bleaching powder pouch.

b. Bleaching powder pouch. The pouch (fig. 270), measuring approximately 12 inches by 7 inches, is made of rubberized fabric and is provided with a tiestring, carrying strap, and a pocket containing several pieces of cotton gauze. The pouch holds approximately 5 ounces of bleaching powder, presumably for use in the decontamination of articles of individual equipment.

c. Decontaminating agent, No. 1. A cylindrical sheet metal container, 2½ inches high and 2½ inches diameter, with one blue band around the casing (fig. 271) contains approximately 0.33 pounds crystalline potassium permanganate.

d. Decontaminating agent, No. 2. A rectangular sheet metal box, 4½ inches high and 4³⁄₁₆

Figure 271. Decontaminating agents, (1) No. 1, (2) No. 2, (3) No. 3, and (4) No. 4.

The effectiveness of these agents is not known, but is considered comparable with similar Allied agents.

5. GAS DETECTORS. a. Blister gas detection satchel. The square satchel, 6 inches x 6 inches, with a carrying strap, contains detector papers, a small box of calcium hypochlorite, a box containing 16 glass ampules of detector material, and a supply of small flags for marking contaminated areas. The white detector material contained in the ampules turns red in contact with blister gases.

b. Gas detector kit. The kit (fig. 272) comprises a light metal cylindrical barrel, 10¼ inches

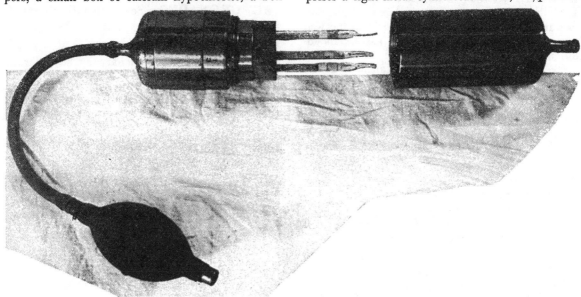

Figure 272. Gas detector.

long and 2½ inches in diameter; a rubber bulb and tubing; and a set of five detector tubes. When testing for war gases the five detector tubes are placed inside the barrel and held in the holes of a rubber stopper provided for this purpose. Air is then drawn through the tubes by means of the rubber bulb. The kit is contained in a wooden carrying case.

c. Gas detector kit (Navy model). The kit (fig. 273) comprises a rubber, bulb-actuated, metal

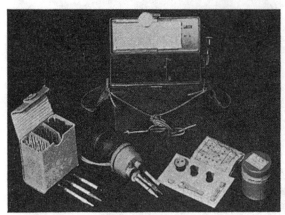

Figure 273. Gas detector kit (Navy model).

air pump and a set of three detector tubes. Air is drawn through the detector tubes. It is said that the presence of blister gases, choking gases, and carbon monoxide can be determined by color changes of the indicator materials contained in the detector tubes. The kit is carried in a grey metal case.

Part II

OFFENSIVE EQUIPMENT

1. MARKING OF CHEMICAL MUNITIONS. Indications are that the Japanese attention to war gases has been confined largely to the well known blister, tear, vomiting, etc., gases. In addition, agents for the production of screening smokes are manufactured. The Japanese distinguish between ordinary smoke and toxic, or tear, clouds by referring to the latter as "special smoke." The type of agent contained in a chemical munition is usually identified by a color band according to the following scheme:

	Color of band
Choking gases	Blue.
Tear gases	Green.
Blister gases	Yellow.
Vomiting gases	Red.
Blood and nerve poisons	Brown.
Screening smoked	White.

Chemical projectiles and most chemical aerial bombs are generally grey in color. Filled shells have a red band at the nose, followed by a blue band to indicate special handling because of the chemical filling. According to the best evidence available, the type of war gas filling is indicated by a colored band in accordance with the above scheme. This band is about twice as wide as any other band on the shell. A narrow yellow band is believed to indicate a HE burster change, while a white band indicates that the projectile is constructed of steel.

2. GAS SHELLS AND BOMBS. a. General. The 90-mm mortar and the 81-mm mortar are believed to have chemical munitions, as is a reported 150-mm mortar, but shells containing these fillings have not been captured. Likewise, the 105-mm gun and 150-mm howitzer shells probably have a chemical filling. The following shells and bomb are definitely known to be filled with war gases.

b. 50 kg aerial gas bomb. Over-all length 45 inches, body diameter 7.5 inches. Total weight 110 pounds. Filling 50 : 50 lewisite mustard mixture. Grey colored with one yellow and one white band between nose and lug and one yellow band between tail and lug.

c. 75-mm blister gas shell. Weight 12.5 pounds. Filling 1.4 pounds 50:50 lewisite mustard mixture. Markings; red band followed by blue band (indicating CW filling) on nose, one white and one *wide* yellow band on body, which indicates blister gas filling.

d. 75-mm vomiting gas shell. Weight 13.25 pounds. Filling 0.4 pounds diphenylcyanarsine. Markings, red band followed by blue band on nose. Yellow band below burrelet indicating HE filling, then a *wide* red band indicating vomiting gas and finally a white band indicating a steel shell.

3. FRANGIBLE HYDROCYANIC ACID (AC) GRENADES. See section II, chapter 9, for description.

4. GAS CANDLES. Most Japanese gas and smoke candles of the stationary or hand thrown type are fired by means of a matchhead fuze and scratcher block. All Japanese self projecting gas and smoke candles (figs. 274, 275, 276, and table) are composed of an outer container equipped with a

Figure 274. Small vomiting gas candle.

sliding metal spike. Before firing the candle this spike is driven into the ground to maintain the candle at the desired angle. A matchhead fuze at the lower end of the candle is ignited with a scratcher block and sets off the propellant charge which expels the inner container (projectile) carrying the main charge. The main charge is then set off by a delay fuze ignited by the propellant charge.

Figure 275. Medium vomiting gas candle.

Figure 276. Self projecting vomiting gas candle.

Tear gas candles

Description	Approximate dimensions (inches)		Body color	Markings	Approximate total weight (pounds)	Filling	Notes
	Length	Diameter					
Tear gas candle_____	7. 2	2. 2	Grey_____	Green band__	0. 5	CN mixture_	Main filling nitrocellulose wafers containing CN.
Small tear gas candle___	5. 5	2. 5	___do_____	_____do_____	. 4	_____do_____	Believed obsolete.

Vomiting gas candles

Light vomiting gas candle.	7. 2	2. 2	Grey_____	Red band____	0. 6	DC_____	Metal ring handle at bottom.
Heavy vomiting gas candle.	9. 8	4. 4	Brown___	_____do_____	4. 4	_____do_____	Metal ring handle at bottom. Under cover 16 taped vent holes. Separate compartments for fuel mixture under smoke charge.
Medium vomiting gas candle.	8. 8	4. 4	___do_____	_____do_____	3. 3	_____do_____	Metal ring handle at bottom. Fixed hinged metal prong at side.
Light self projecting vomiting gas candle.	7. 9	2. 0	___do_____	_____do_____	1. 5	_____do_____	Projectile has cardboard casing.
Heavy self projecting vomiting gas candle.	8. 2	2. 0	___do_____	_____do_____	2. 2 2. 6	_____do_____	Projectile has sheet metal casing and wooden bottom.

Considerable variation has been found in dimensions and weights of the above candles.

5. SMOKE GRENADES. a. 50-mm smoke shell for grenade discharger type 89. See section II, chapter 9, for description.

b. Rifle smoke grenade. See section II, chapter 9, for description.

c. Frangible smoke grenade, white. See section II, chapter 9, for description.

6. SMOKE CANDLES.

Figure 277. "Type 94" small smoke candle (White label).

Figure 278. "Type 99" self projecting smoke candle.

Figure 279. Type 94, model B, floating smoke candle.

Figure 280. 10 kg smoke candle and igniters.

Figure 281. Type 94, smoke candle, white band.

Designation	Approximate dimensions (inches)		Body color	Markings	Approximate total weight (pounds)	Smoke mixture	Notes
	Length	Diameter					
Type 94 small smoke candle A.	6.9	2.2	Grey	White label	2.2	Berger type	Metal ring handle at bottom. Probably an early model.
Do	6.9	2.2	Green or brown	do	2.2	do	No handle. May be wrapped in paper with printed instructions. Probably a later model.
Type 94 large smoke candle A.	18	6	Grey	do	44	do	Hinged wooden handle at top, attached to metal band around casing. Small screw cap lid.
Type 94 floating smoke candle B.	31.2	3.1	Grey or brown	White label or white band.	15.4	HC type	Metal ring bracket for float around upper part. "10 year pattern" hand grenade time fuze fits opening on top closed by wing screw plug.
1 kilogram smoke candle "Revision 4."	8.3	2.1	Tinplate	White labels top and side.	*2.2	Berger type	Naval smoke candle.
1 kilogram smoke candle "Revision 7".	8.3	2.1	do	White labels top and side.	*2.2	HC type	Naval smoke candle. Igniter removable.
10 kilogram smoke candle.	9.5	6	Grey	Labels on top and side.	*22	Berger type	Naval smoke candle. Igniter well fitted with wooden plug. Igniters packed separately.
30 kilogram smoke candle.	9.5	10.5	do	do	*64	do	Naval smoke candle. Igniter well closed by wooden plug. Igniters are packed separately. The candle may be fitted with a float.
Experimental self-projecting smoke candle.	8.2	2.1	Grey or brown	May have white band.	1.5	HC type	Sometimes wrapped in paper. Projectile has cardboard casing and short igniter tube.
Type 99 self-projecting smoke candle.	8.2	2.1	do	White Japanese characters on side.	2.9	do	Projectile has sheet metal casing. Igniter tube extends whole length of projectile. Under bottom cover match head exposed through slot.

* As weight varies considerably, figures shown are merely the conversion of the indicated kilogram weight to pounds.

7. AERIAL INCENDIARY BOMBS. Army type incendiary bombs are painted grey whereas the HE bombs are black. Navy type bombs, both HE and incendiary, are painted grey. Red and silver tail struts designate an incendiary filling.

a. 1 kg smoke incendiary/antipersonnel bomb, Army type. Characteristics are as follows:

Over-all length	10.25 inches.
Body diameter	3 inches.
Color and markings	White rubber nose, black body, white tail cone and fins.
Main charge	Red phosphorus.

Used in conjunction with demolition bombs as a marker. On explosion antipersonnel effect by fragmentation of cast iron body.

b. 32 kilogram incendiary bomb. Characteristics are as follows:

Over-all length	24.4 inches.
Body diameter	5.75 inches.
Total weight (approximately).	70 pounds.
Filling	Phosphorus filled steel pellets.
Color	Grey.
Markings	Silver band on nose and silver tail fin tips.

c. 50 kilogram incendiary bomb. Characteristics are as follows:

Over-all length	3 feet 9 inches.
Body diameter	7.75 inches.
Weight (approximately).	101 pounds.
Filling	Rubber pellets and phosphorus in carbon disulfide.
Color	Grey.
Markings	One yellow and one white band.

d. 50 kilogram incendiary bomb, Army type 100. Characteristics are as follows:

Over-all length	3 feet 4 inches.
Body diameter	7 inches.
Filling	Rubber pellets and phosphorus in carbon disulfide.
Color and markings	Grey body and tail, yellow and white bands just forward of suspension lug.

This bomb is differentiated from the 50 kg incendiary bomb described in c above by a longer tail cone with a rounded apex.

e. 60 kilogram solid oil bomb, Navy type. Characteristics are as follows:

Over-all length	3 feet 6½ inches.
Filling	Normal filling mixture of paraffin wax and kerosene but a filling consisting of pellets made of rubber-like incendiary material also exists.
Color and markings	Grey body and tail, red tail struts.

f. 60 kilogram incendiary thermite bomb, Navy type. Characteristics are as follows:

Over-all length	3 feet 4 inches.
Body diameter	8 inches.
Filling	Electron containers filled with thermite.
Color and markings	Grey body and tail, red tail struts.

g. 250 kilogram HE/incendiary bomb. Characteristics are as follows:

Over-all length	5 feet 9 inches.
Body diameter	12 inches.
Weight (approximately).	550 pounds.
Filling	HE and about 750 small metal cylinders filled with incendiary substance.
Color and markings	Painted grey with a red band on tail and a silver band on end of nose.

8. OTHER INCENDIARIES. a. One-half kilogram incendiary grenade. See section II, chapter 9, for description.

b. Incendiary grenade "Molotov cocktail". See section II, chapter 6 for illustration and complete description.

c. 90-mm mortar projectile. Characteristics are as follows:

Weight (approximate).	11.5 pounds.
Filling (approximate).	2.2 pounds phosphorus in carbon disulfide and rubber pellets.
Markings	Red band followed by blue band on nose, one yellow and one white band on body.

d. 50-mm grenade discharger projectile, incendiary. See section II, chapter 9, for description.

e. 75-mm Incendiary Shell, for model 41 (1908) infantry gun.

Weight (approximate).	14.5 pounds.
Filling (approximate).	22 oz., rubber pellets impregnated with a solution of phosphorus in carbon disulfide.
Markings	Blue—grey projectile, red band below fuze.

f. Incendiary stick grenade. See section II, chapter 9, for description.

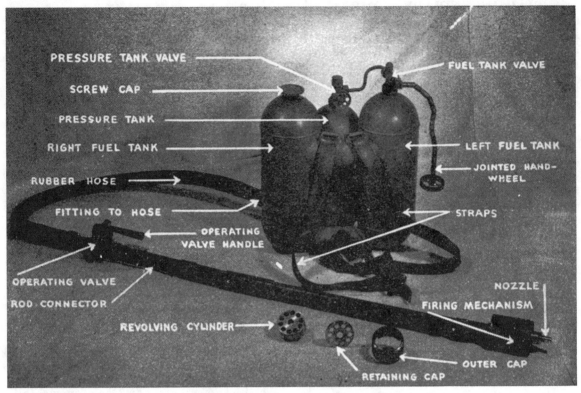

Figure 282. Flame thrower, type 93.

9. FLAME THROWERS. a. Flame throwers, type 93. The fuel unit comprises 2 fuel tanks and a nitrogen pressure cylinder. Ignition of fuel jet is effected by flash from a blank cartridge, ten of which are loaded in the revolving cylinder located at nozzle end of flame gun (fig. 282). The firing mechanism is actuated by operating handle which controls fuel ejection valve. Characteristics are as follows:

Maximum range_____ 25 to 30 yards.
Duration of continuous 10 to 12 seconds.
  discharge.
Fuel capacity_____ 3.25 gallons.
Total weight, charged____ About 55 pounds.

b. Flame thrower, type 100. Very similar to type 93 flame thrower. The fuel units of the two types are identical as are range and duration of flame. The differences are found in the flame guns as follows:

	Type 93	Type 100
Over-all length_____	47⅛ inches	35½ inches.
Weight_____	10 pounds	8½ pounds.
Nozzle outlet tip_____	Fixed	Removable.
Diameter of cartridge____	0.44 inch	0.484 inch.
Chambers of revolving cylinder.	10	10.

c. Pyrotechnics. See chapter 10.

CHAPTER X

EQUIPMENT

Section I. INTRODUCTION

1. GENERAL. a. M o s t Japanese equipment shows evidence of careful thought to adapt it to the needs of the soldier. The Japanese Army expects to fight, mostly on foot, in all the varied climates and terrains of Asia, where roads often are lacking. The equipment therefore is made as light in weight as is practicable, and, when possible, is arranged to pack on horses or to be carried by men. The Japanese have given much attention to animal pack, and there are a great variety of pack saddles for specialized purposes. All of the organic heavy infantry weapons are designed for animal pack and can be manhandled when necessary.

b. The two-wheeled military cart is the most common vehicle. This cart, of which four types are known, is built almost entirely of wood. The smallest has a capacity of about 400 pounds. It is strong and light and is pulled by one horse which the driver leads. A larger type, of greater capacity, is pulled by two horses. A heavier military vehicle also has been developed which often is designed to carry artillery spare parts or other heavy equipment. This vehicle is pulled by either 2 or 4 horses.

c. Most of the Japanese Army's automotive equipment is of foreign design and construction. However, Japanese models have been designed and constructed. These are of two general types: a 4-wheeled commercial design of about 2 tons capacity, and a 6-wheeled military vehicle of larger size, made in several capacities but according to the same general design. Originally, these heavier vehicles were equipped with 6-cylinder, heavy-duty, gasoline engines, but later types have Diesel engines. This trend toward Diesel power no doubt will be intensified.

d. Japanese engineering equipment is fairly complete, and includes a wide variety of amphibious, construction, maintenance, and demolition equipment. Heavier equipment, however, does not appear to have been developed on a scale comparable with the American standard. The following types

of Japanese equipment are described in the chapters indicated below:

Type of equipment	Chapter
Air corps equipment	4
Chemical equipment	9
Armored unit equipment	9
Personal equipment	11

Definite information concerning ordnance and other mobile maintenance equipment has been omitted because of lack of available data. There is sufficient evidence, however, to conclude that such equipment exists in the Japanese Army.

Section II. INFANTRY EQUIPMENT

1. GENERAL. Details of infantry equipment have not been shown in this section when it has been possible to place them under specific headings. For example, personal items issued to the individual soldier have been described, where possible, under chapter 11, while weapons are treated in chapter 9.

2. OBSERVATION EQUIPMENT. All reported specimens of Japanese optical instruments have been of good quality and have been found to resemble German designs. A particularly wide range of patterns has been developed, and specimens examined have been characterized by sturdy construction. In all cases definition in the central part of the field of view was good. There are no indications that the Japanese have attempted to tropicproof these instruments.

a. Binoculars. Details of binoculars, having a magnification in excess of 8 X, are shown in the Artillery Equipment section of this chapter. Tabulated below are the characteristics of some Japanese binoculars, of 8 X magnification or less.

Magnification	Field of view	Size of objective lens
	°	mm
8 X	6. 25	56
7 X	7. 1	50
6 X	9. 3	24

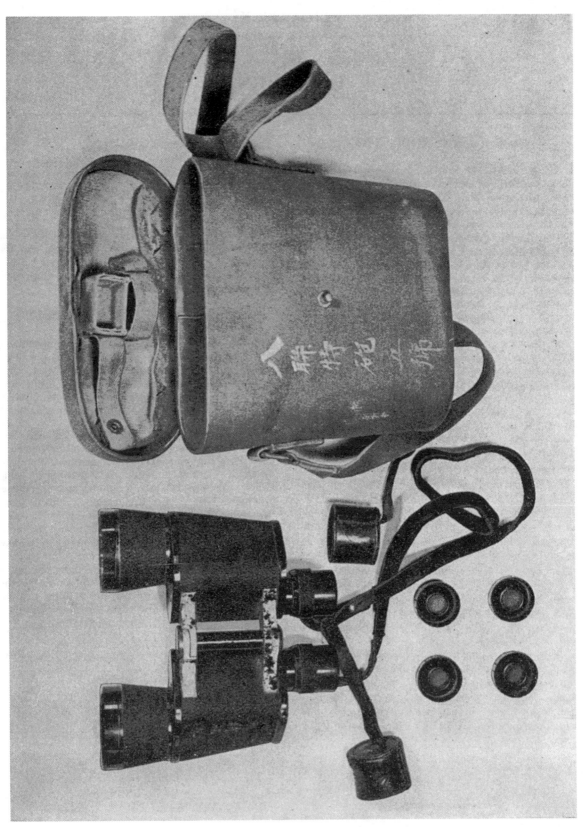

Figure 283. Japanese binoculars, filters, and carrying case. These binoculars have a 7 × magnification and a 7.1° field of view. Special color filters may be fitted over the eyepieces.

b. Periscopes.

Figure 284. Periscope binocular, weighing 1.9 pounds, has a 10 × magnification and a 3° field of view.

Figure 285. The hand held periscope, weighing 2.3 pounds, has a 5 × magnification and 10° field of view.

3. INFANTRY FIRE CONTROL EQUIPMENT. a. Range finders.

Figure 286. Model 92 (1932) 40-cm base range finder is calibrated for measuring ranges up to 1,500 meters (1,640 yards). It is a coincidence type of range finder with a 4 × magnification.

b. Aiming and laying devices.

Figure 288. Panoramic sight for model 94 (1934) mortar has a 3 × magnification and a 13° field of view. Micrometer drums enable readings to be made to the nearest mil.

Figure 287. Collimator sight for model 97 (1937) infantry mortar.

Figure 289. Telescopic sight for model 96 (1936) 6.5-mm light machine gun. The magnification is 2.5 ×, the field of view is 13°, and the weight is 20 oz. The reticle (Graticule) pattern provides for drift and windage, and is calibrated for a maximum range of 1,500 meters (1,640 yards).

(*Above*) *Figure 290. Telescopic sight for model 92 (1932) 7.7-mm machine gun has a 4 × magnification, a 10° field of view, and a weight of 3 lbs., 6 ozs.*

(*Left*) *Figure 291. Telescopic sight for the model 94 (1934) 37-mm gun.*

4. PERSONAL ARMOR. a. Model 99 (1939) armor shields, portable.

Figure 292. Model 99 (1939) armor shield, size 12 in. x 16 in., with the model 96 (1936) 6.5-mm light machine gun.

(1) *General.* While these shields are suitable for use in the open, specimens, constructed from what appears to be face-hardened plate, have been found built into the weapon ports of pillboxes. Two sizes have been recovered, the larger measuring 14 by 20 by ¼ inches (fig. 293) and the smaller 12 by 16 by ¼ inches.

(2) *Penetration.* Tests have shown that these shields will resist penetration by .30 caliber ball ammunition at 100 feet. However, some damage may be caused by flaking (chipping). These shields have been penetrated readily by .30 caliber AP ammunition as indicated below:

Range (yards)	Angle of impact from normal	Results
33	10°–15°	Clean penetration and heavy flaking.
100	30°	Do.
200	Normal	Clean penetration.
500	Normal	No penetration.

b. Body armor. (1) *Bullet-proof vest.* The vest (fig. 294) is made from olive-green drill cloth, with 3 pockets on each side to accommodate armor plates arranged in fish-scale fashion. Characteristics are as follows:

Weight complete	9 pounds.
Thickness of plates	0.08 inch.
Plate overlap	0.05 inch.

It is believed that the weight of this vest would preclude its general use by infantry and probably would tend to confine its use to special troops. Tests have shown that the plates are penetrated easily by .303 ball ammunition at 100 yards range, with a 30° angle of impact from normal.

(2) *Body protector.* No details are available concerning this body protector (fig. 295), but it is reasonable to assume that it is made from an armor plate of thickness approximating that of the bullet-proof vest. It is possible that the armor plate is in 3 sections for purposes of flexibility.

c. Steel helmets. See chapter 11.

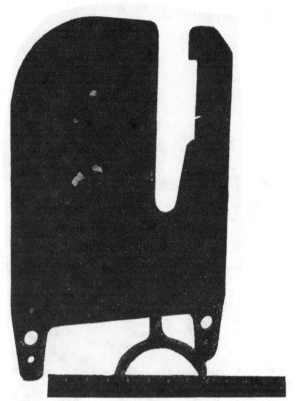

Figure 293. *Rear of armor shield, size 14 in. x 20 in., showing penetration made with .30 cal. AP ammunition at 100 yards range and 30° angle of impact from normal.*

Figure 295. *Unidentified body protector.*

Figure 294. *Bullet-proof vest.*

Section III. ARTILLERY EQUIPMENT

1. GENERAL. a. Optical instruments are outstanding among specimens of Japanese artillery equipment. Examination of them shows good, versatile design, sturdy construction, and satisfactory definition. Knowledge of antiaircraft fire-control equipment is limited; specimens examined to date are obsolescent, although it is entirely possible that much improved designs exist, but have not yet been encountered.

b. Artillery communication equipment is described in the Signal Equipment section of this chapter. Trucks and other automotive equipment are described in the Automotive and Land Transport section.

c. Although the Japanese Army is provided with a variety of prime movers, few types of these have been encountered in forward areas. These have been older models; more modern types, with improved specifications, well may exist.

2. ARTILLERY FIRE CONTROL INSTRUMENTS. a. General. Illustrated and described on the following pages are various examples of artillery fire control equipment used by the Japanese. Their optical equipment is well made, sturdy, and versatile, but none examined differs from standard optical design. Panoramic sights for artillery weapons have not been recovered, but sights for infantry guns and mortars (described in sec. II) suggest that the Japanese have suitable sights for use on artillery pieces.

b. Off-carriage fire-control instruments.

Figure 296. The 75-cm. base range finder is an inverted coincidence-type range finder with a 12 × magnification, a vertical field of view 2°, and a 3° horizontal field of view. It is calibrated to measure ranges up to 10,000 meters.

Figure 297. One meter base stereoscopic range finder. The reticle of this instrument is graduated from 250 to 6,000 (presumed to be meters). Markings indicate an 8° × magnification, a 4.5° vertical and 5° horizontal field of view.

Figure 299. This battery commander's telescope has an 8 × magnification and a 6° field of view. It is constructed so that the telescopic arms may be placed in a horizontal position for better stereoscopic vision.

Figure 298. The model 93 battery commander's telescope permits measurement of angle of site from −300 to +300 mils, as well as measurement of azimuth. An unusual feature is that the telescopes cannot be placed in a horizontal plane for better stereoscopic vision. It has an 8 × magnification and a 6° field of view.

Figure 300. Battery commander's telescope. Although giving a high magnification and wide field of view, the individual telescopes cannot be placed in a horizontal position to improve stereoscopic vision.

Figure 301. This artillery spotting telescope may be used with three different eyepieces, each of which gives a different magnification—the maximum being 33 power. Provision is made to measure azimuth, and elevation (from −30° to +30°).

c. Aiming and laying devices.

Figure 302. This panoramic sight appears to have been designed for use on more than one artillery piece. It is shown above mounted on the model 41 (1908) infantry gun. The sight has a 3 × magnification and a 13° field of view.

Figure 303. This aiming circle has a 4 × magnification and a 10° field of view. Similar to the American aiming circle, it is used by artillery units for measuring angles in azimuth and site, and for general topographical work.

Figure 304. This gunner's quadrant is calibrated from 0 to 90°, with a vernier reading to 1/16 of a degree.

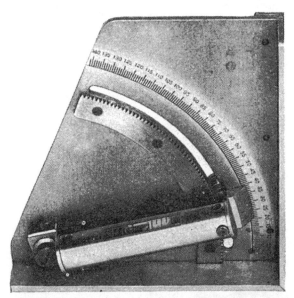

Figure 305. *This gunner's quadrant is calibrated in units of 10 mils, extending from 0 to 1,410 mils (79°). A vernier scale enables adjustment to the nearest mil. It is considered possible that this quadrant has been designed primarily for use with the model 41 (1908) 75-mm infantry gun.*

3. ANTIAIRCRAFT FIRE CONTROL EQUIPMENT. a. Automatic weapons. The model 92 (1932) 7.7-mm and the single mounted model 93 (1933) 13-mm machine guns, described in chapter 9, are provided with antiaircraft ring sights. The latest type ring sight recovered, illustrated in figure 306, is rotated automatically around its horizontal axis as the gun is elevated. It is believed that the purpose of this design is to correct automatically for the angle of approach. The fol-

Figure 306. *Front and rear antiaircraft sights mounted on the model 92 (1932) 7.7-mm machine gun.*

lowing automatic weapons are provided with more complex sights than the ring sights.

(1) *Dual-mounted model 93 (1933) 13-mm machine gun.* To date only incomplete sights (fig. 307) have been examined on dual mounts. They are constructed in such a manner that estimates of target course and speed are fed into the instrument, which then applies the appropriate deflection to the sighting telescope. The sight would appear to require 3 men for its operation.

(2) *Model 98 (1938) 20-mm automatic cannon.* Complete antiaircraft sights for this weapon have not yet been recovered. It is known that some form of computing sight is used.

(3) *Model 96 (1936) 25-mm automatic cannon.* A computing sight, similar to the one described in a (2) for the 13-mm machine gun, is provided for this weapon (fig. 308).

(4) *Vickers type 40-mm automatic cannon.* This weapon also has a computing sight for use in antiaircraft fire. In addition, an automatic fuze setting mechanism is provided. The time setting given to each fuze is adjusted, thru a complex series of gears and linkages, by the manipulation of the gun in elevation and depression.

b. Heavy antiaircraft weapons. According to modern standards the Japanese heavy antiaircraft fire control equipment seen to date has been outmoded and designed for use with the Model 88 (1928) 75-mm antiaircraft gun. Off-carriage fire-control instruments and computing mechanisms used with these guns are as follows:

(1) *2-meter-base height and range finder.* This instrument (fig. 309) is of good optical construction and standard, but most specimens recovered had no provision for electrical data transmission. It supplies the "present altitude" to the guns.

(2) *Target-speed and course-angle calculator.* This instrument (fig. 310) is mounted on a tripod for use. The illustration in figure 310 does not include an elbow telescope, which must be mounted on its top in order to operate the instrument. The calculator supplies the angle of approach (course angle) of the target at the present position and ground speed of the target.

(3) *Corrector scale.* This is a metal board (fig. 311) on which may be read mechanically the correction angles required for wind direction and powder temperature.

(4) *Spotting binoculars.* These are used to obtain spot corrections, and have 15 × magnification and 4° field of view (fig. 312).

Data from each of the instruments shown in figures 309, 310, 311, and 312, are shouted to the gun crew, certain individuals of which operate the "on carriage" components. This procedure theoretically results in the gun being correctly aimed and the time fuzes being so adjusted that the projectiles burst on the target. The "on carriage" components are:

(*a*) Elevation computing apparatus.
(*b*) Azimuth computing apparatus.

Figure 307. Computing head for AA sight used on dual mounted model 93 (1933) 13-mm machine gun.

Figure 308. Computing sight for Japanese model 96 (1936) 25-mm automatic cannon.

Figure 309. 2-meter-base height and range finder.

*(Left) Figure 310. Target speed and course angle calcu-
lator with carrying box.*

Figure 311. Powder-charge temperature and wind correction scale.

Figure 312. Model 89 (1929) 10-cm AA spotting binoculars.

(*c*) Auxiliary elevation and lead correction disc.

(*d*) Fuze setter.

c. Computing director. A few data computing directors have been captured, and provision for electrical data transmission has been seen on height finders. Mounting surfaces for data receivers have been found on some model 88 (1928) 75-mm antiaircraft guns. There is evidence of more general use of electrical data transmission and computing directors than would be indicated by the equipment captured to date.

d. Searchlights. Japanese searchlights include the following sizes:

> 60-cm (23.6 inches).
> 90-cm (35.4 inches).
> 98-cm (38.6 inches).
> 100-cm (39.4 inches).
> 110-cm (43.3 inches).
> 150-cm (59.1 inches) (fig. 313).

The following equipment is used by Japanese searchlight units:

(1) *Generator truck (standard 2-ton truck chassis)*.

(2) *Searchlight comparator.* The searchlight comparator illustrated in figure 314 is an instrument with which an observer, by keeping a plane in the crosslines of the telescope, automatically directs the searchlight on the plane. It was found satisfactory for operation of U. S. searchlights.

(3) *Sound locator.* Several varieties of Japanese sound locators are known to exist. One of the small models is illustrated in figure 315.

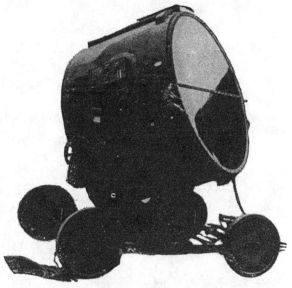

Figure 313. 150-cm searchlight.

Figure 314. Searchlight comparator.

Figure 315. Small sound locator.

Figure 316. Komatsu tractor.

4. PRIME MOVERS AND TRACTORS. a. Komatsu tractor. This small, full-tracked vehicle (fig. 316) is designed solely for towing purposes. Steering is of the clutch-brake type, with hand levers operating the clutches. Two foot brakes are located on the right side, and are so placed that either or both brakes may be operated by the right foot. The gear box allows 3 forward and 2 reverse speeds. The vehicle is supported by 4 small bogie wheels on each side. Examination of a specimen revealed that a number of the bearings were of Swedish manufacture. Characteristics are as follows:

Weight	3 tons (estimated).
Length	8 feet 2 inches.
Width	4 feet 4 inches.
Engine	4 cylinder, gasoline.
Cooling	Water.
Ignition	Bosch magneto.
Length of track in contact with ground.	5 feet 7 inches.
Width of track	10 inches.

b. Light prime mover. The model number and date of manufacture of this vehicle (fig. 317) are not known.

In the case of a specimen examined, the word "seventy" was found marked in English on the side of the radiator, probably indicating the engine horsepower. A name plate on the power unit shows it to be a "Kato engine model K 3." Suspension consists of 2 bogies mounted on each·side of the vehicle. Each bogie has 3 small wheels, and the sprocket is at the rear. Details are reported to be as follows:

Approximate characteristics

Weight	4 tons (estimated).
Length, width, height	No details.
Engine	4 cylinder, gasoline.
Cooling	Water.
Length of track in contact with ground.	7 feet 5 inches.
Diam. of sprocket	2 feet 2 inches.

Figure 317. Light prime mover.

c. Model 92 (1932) 5-ton prime mover. It is reported that there are 2 variations of this vehicle. Model A is powered by a 6-cylinder in-line "L" head "Sumida" gasoline engine, and model B by a 6-cylinder in-line, air-cooled "Isuzu" Diesel. As far as may be ascertained, with exception of a modification in radiator design, the general appearance and suspension of these 2 models are similar. Both vehicles are reported to be identical in the following respects:

Common characteristics

Length	11 feet 8 inches.
Width	5 feet 11 inches.
Height	7 feet 8 inches.
Ground clearance	11¾ inches.
Fording depth	1 foot 7½ inches.
Grade	30°.
Turning radius	Can pivot.
Winch capacity	2¾ tons.

(1) *5-ton prime mover (model A)* (fig. 318).

Characteristics

Weight	5⅛ tons.
Engine	6 cylinder, "Sumida."
Cooling	Water.
Cylinder bore	110-mm (4.3 inch).
Piston stroke	135-mm (5.3 inch).
Horsepower	64 to 98 (160 theoretically indicated hp at 2,800 rpm—based on reported engine specifications).
Ignition	Bosch magneto.
Generator	Bosch 12 volts.
Storage batteries	2–12 volts, 60 amperes.
Fuel tank capacity	Main 27.5 gallons, auxilliary 12.1 gallons.

NOTE. The model A is believed to be similar to, if not identical with, a recently examined prime mover. This vehicle was found to be well constructed and capable of

Figure 318. 5-ton prime mover (model A).

operating over most types of terrain. The present gasoline engine is estimated to be of approximately 140 horsepower, considerably more powerful that the standard unit. It is believed that this particular engine is a replacement of the unit originally installed.

(2) *5-ton prime mover (model B)* (fig. 319).

Characteristics

Weight_____ 5.5 tons.
Engine_____ 6 cylinder, Diesel.
Cooling_____ Air.
Cylinder bore_____ 110-mm (4.3 inch).
Piston stroke_____ 140-mm (5.5 inch).
Horsepower_____ 65 to 90 (135 theoretically indicated hp at 2,000 rpm—based on reported engine specifications).
Ignition_____ Compression.
Generator_____ 12 volts, 300 watts.
Storage batteries_____ 2–12 volts, 120 amperes.
Fuel tank capacity_____ Main 22 gallons, auxiliary 13.2 gallons.

d. Model 92 (1932) 8-ton prime mover. It is reported that 2 versions exist of this vehicle; the model A is powered by a 6-cylinder in-line, water-cooled gasoline engine, and the model B by a 6-

cylinder in-line water-cooled Diesel. The following data are believed to be common to both models A and B:

Common characteristics

Length_____ 14 feet 1 inch.
Width_____ 6 feet 6 inches.
Height_____ 8 feet 6 inches.
Grade_____ 15°.
Winch capacity_____ 5 tons.
Cylinder bore_____ 130-mm (5.1 inches).

Characteristics of model A

Weight_____ 8.4 tons.
Ground clearance_____ 11½ inches..
Engine_____ 6-cylinder, gasoline.
Cooling_____ Water.
Piston stroke_____ 5.6 inches.
Horsepower_____ 80 to 130 (230 theoretically indicated hp at 2,800 rpm— based on reported engine specifications).
Ignition_____ Bosch magneto.
Generator_____ 12 volts, 100 watts.
Storage batteries_____ 2–12 volts, 100 amperes.
Fuel tank capacity_____ Main 39½ gallons, auxiliary 9 gallons.

Figure 319. 5-ton prime mover (model B).

Characteristics of model B

Weight	9.3 tons.
Ground clearance	12 inches.
Engine	6 cylinder, Diesel.
Cooling	Water.
Piston stroke	6.4 inches.
Horsepower	105 to 120 (215 theoretically indicated hp at 2,000 rpm—based on reported engine specifications).
Generator	12 volts, 500 watts.
Storage batteries	4–12 volts, 140 amperes.
Fuel tank capacity	Main 39½ gallons, auxiliary 9 gallons.

e. Model 98 (1938) 4-ton prime mover. It is believed that this prime mover, powered by an 8-cylinder **V**-type air-cooled gasoline engine, is capable of hauling a load at 25 miles per hour, and that it can travel a distance of 125 miles in a period of 10 hours. Steering is of the clutch brake type, with foot and hand operated brakes. A central selector type gear box allows 4 forward speeds and 1 reverse.

Although no 4-ton model has been encountered as yet, it is believed that the following data apply:

Characteristics

Weight	4 tons.
Length	12 feet 5 inches.
Width	6 feet 1 inch.
Height	7 feet 3 inches.
Ground clearance	11½ inches.
Tread	No details.
Fording depth	20 inches.
Grade	30°.
Turning radius	Can pivot.
Winch capacity	Over 2 tons.
Engine	8 cylinder **V**-type, gasoline.
Cooling	Sirocco type fan.
Cylinder bore	90-mm (3.5 inch).
Piston stroke	125-mm (4.9 inch).
Horsepower	73 to 88 (130 theoretically indicated hp at 2,800 rpm—based on reported engine specifications).
Ignition	Bosch magneto.
Generator	Bosch, 75 watts.
Storage batteries	12 volts, 80 amperes.
Fuel tank capacity	Main 22 gallons, auxiliary 13 gallons.

f. Model 98 (1938) 6-ton prime mover. Examination of this prime mover (fig. 320) indi-

Figure 320. Model 98 (1938) 6 ton prime mover.

cates that it is an unarmed artillery tractor, suitable for the additional roles of reconnaissance vehicle and ammunition carrier. Suspension follows the pattern of the model 2597 medium tank. Since steering is of the clutch-brake type, the vehicle is capable of turning within its own length. It is reported that this vehicle is used as a prime mover for the 105- and 150-mm howitzers and the 105-mm gun. Details are believed to be as follows:

Weight	7.75 tons.
Length	14 feet 1 inch.
Width	6 feet 9 inches.
Height	6 feet 3 inches.
Ground clearance	13½ inches.
Grade	15° pulling field gun.
Turning radius	19 feet.
Winch capacity	5.5 tons.
Engine	6 cylinder, Diesel.
Cooling	Water.
Cylinder bore	120-mm (4.7 inch).
Piston stroke	155-mm (6.1 inch).
Horsepower	88 to 110 (175 theoretically indicated hp at 2,000 rpm—based on reported engine specifications).
Generator	24 volts, 100 watts.
Storage batteries	2–12 volts, 180 amperes.
Fuel tank capacity	Main 17.6 gallons, 1st auxiliary 18.7 gallons, 2d auxiliary 6.6 gallons.

g. Model 95 (1935) 13-ton prime mover. This heavy prime mover is reported to be produced in two models: the model A is powered with a 6-cylinder in-line, water-cooled, gasoline engine; the model B with a 6-cylinder, water-cooled Diesel. Both models are believed to be equipped with multiple disc, clutch type steering, with hand and foot operated brakes. The following data is reported to be common to both types:

Length	16 feet.
Width	7 feet 6 inches.
Height	9 feet 3 inches.
Ground clearance	12 inches.
Grade	13 tons, 15°—29 tons, 7½°.
Turning radius	65 feet.
Winch capacity	11¼ tons.

Characteristics of Model A

Weight	14.3 tons.
Engine	6 cylinder, gasoline.
Cooling	Water.
Cylinder bore	5.4 inches.
Piston stroke	6 inches.
Horsepower	130 to 160 (265 theoretically indicated hp at 2,800 rpm—based on reported engine specifications).
Ignition	Magneto.
Storage batteries	2–120 volts, 80 amperes.
Fuel tank capacity	Main 61.6 gallons, auxiliary 9½ gallons.

Characteristics of Model B

Weight	15 tons.
Engine	6 cylinder, Diesel.
Cooling	Water.
Cylinder bore	5.6 inches.
Piston stroke	7.6 inches.

Characteristics of Model B—Continued

Horsepower_____ 145 to 165 (295 theoretically
indicated hp at 2,000
rpm—based on reported
engine specifications).
Generator_____ 300 watts.
Storage batteries_____ 2–12 volts, 80 amperes.
Fuel tank capacity_____ 60 gallons.

5. CAISSONS, LIMBERS, AND OTHER ARTILLERY VEHICLES. a. Caissons and limbers.

(1) *Horse-drawn caisson and limber.* Figure 321 depicts a typical Japanese horse-drawn caisson and limber, for use with the 75-mm field gun. Mounted on standard artillery, iron shod, wooden wheels, the two units are drawn by six horses. Characteristics are reported as follows:

Total weight (empty)____ 2,130 pounds (approximately).
Weight (loaded):
    Limber only_____ 1,750 pounds.
    Caisson only_____ 2,080 pounds.

Capacity:
    Limber_____ 40 rounds.
    Caisson_____ 60 rounds.
Diameter of wheels_____ 55 inches.

Caissons and limbers of design similar to figure 321, but carrying fewer rounds, are provided for field guns of heavier caliber.

(2) *Alternative type caisson and limber.* The caisson and limber illustrated in figure 322 is an alternative type for use with the 105-mm field gun. Primarily designed to be towed by a tractor, it also may be drawn by six horses. The heavy artillery-type wheels have solid rubber tires. Characteristics are reported as follows:

Total weight (empty)_____ 2,530 pounds.
Total weight (loaded)_____ 5,040 pounds.
Total capacity_____ 48 rounds.
Diameter of wheels_____ 55 inches.

(3) *High-speed caisson.* The photographs illustrated in figure 323 show the most modern type of

Figure 321. Typical horse-drawn caisson and limber.

Figure 322. Alternative type caisson and limber for 105-mm field gun.

Figure 323. High speed caisson for 75-mm ammunition.

Japanese caisson seen to date. Constructed of metal, it is mounted on steel disc wheels, of comparatively small diameter, fitted with solid rubber tires. The probable capacity of the caisson is 48 complete rounds of 75-mm ammunition. Units of similar appearance carry a smaller quantity of 105-mm ammunition.

b. Battery wagons. (1) *Battery wagon for antiaircraft gun.* The trailer (fig. 324) apparently is constructed for high-speed transportation of communication equipment, miscellaneous spare parts, and bulk ammunition. The body is made from lightweight metal plate, which is not considered to be proof against small-arms fire. Compartments are provided for the stowage of the various items of equipment carried. This vehicle is mounted on metal disc wheels fitted with pneumatic tires. For antiaircraft defense, a tripod, apparently designed for the model 92 (1932) 7.7-mm heavy machine gun, is mounted on the roof. Characteristics of the vehicle are as follows:

    Over-all length of frame 11 feet 10 inches.
    Width_____ 6 feet 3 inches.
    Wheel base_____ 7 feet 7 inches.
    Ground clearance_____ 12 inches.

(2) *Battery wagons for field artillery.* These units are similar to the horse-drawn limber and caisson in construction (fig. 325). They are used for the transportation of general artillery equipment, such as range finder, binoculars, battery commander's telescopes, communication materials, tools, etc. Characteristics are reported to be as follows:

    Total weight loaded (limber 4,318 pounds.
      and caisson).
    Diameter of wheels_____ 55 inches.

c. Spare parts wagons. These are used for the transportation of spare parts, tools, and maintenance and repair materials (fig. 326).
Characteristics are believed to be as follows:

    Total   weight loaded 3,770 pounds.
      (limber and wagon).
    Diameter of wheels____ 55 inches.

The two units are normally drawn by 6 horses.

6. PACK EQUIPMENT. a. General. Great attention has been paid to the development of pack transportation of infantry support guns, namely, models 41 (1908) and 94 (1934) 75-mm mountain pack guns (sec. II, chap. 9), as well as of machine guns, ammunition, supplies, etc. Illustra-

Figure 324. Battery wagon for model 88 (1928) 75-mm antiaircraft gun.

Figure 325. Battery wagons for use with field artillery.

Figure 326. Spare parts wagon for 150-mm howitzer.

tions on the following pages show in detail pack saddles, draught harness, and an infantry support gun, broken down into loads averaging 200 pounds per load and packed for horse transportation.

b. Pack saddles. Two standard pack saddles are illustrated in figure 327. The saddle is adjustable so that it comfortably fits the back and girth of the horse. Saddle A carries the weapon (such as a heavy machine gun); Saddle B is fitted to hold ammunition or spare-parts chests. (See also figs. 328–334.)

c. Draught horses. Extensive use of draught horses is made by the Japanese. Figure 336 shows a typical 4-horse harness hookup, with the type of saddle (which differs from the cavalry saddle) used by artillery and infantry gun crews.

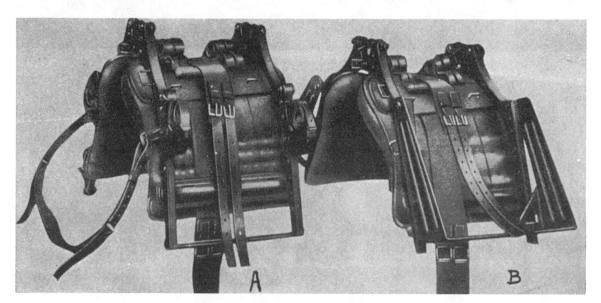

Figure 327. Standard pack saddles.

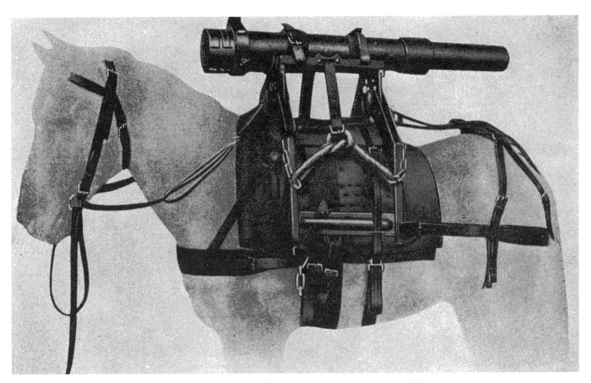

Figure 328. Tube of model 41 (1908) 75-mm infantry (mountain) gun fastened to pack saddle.

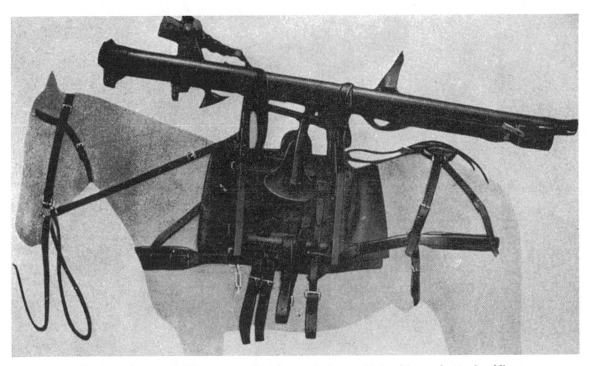

Figure 329. Trail of 75-mm infantry (mountain) gun disassembled and fastened to pack saddle.

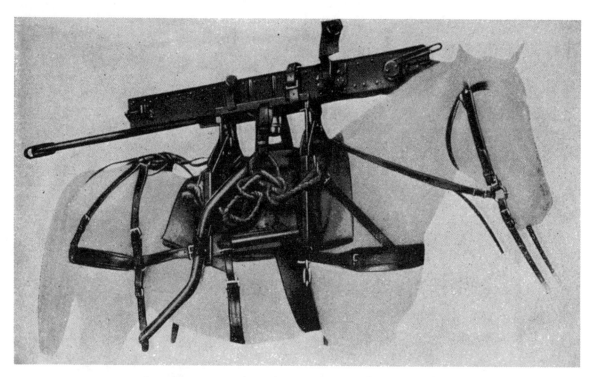

Figure 330. 75-mm infantry (mountain) gun cradle on pack saddle.

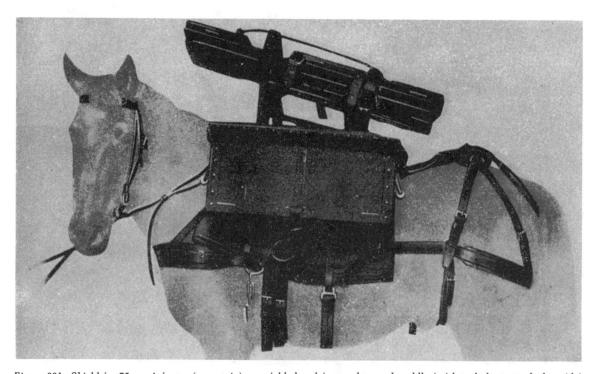

Figure 331. Shield for 75-mm infantry (mountain) gun folded and fastened to pack saddle (with tool chest attached to side).

Figure 332. Breech mechanism and tray for 75-mm infantry (mountain) gun.

Figure 333. Wheels and axle attached to pack saddle.

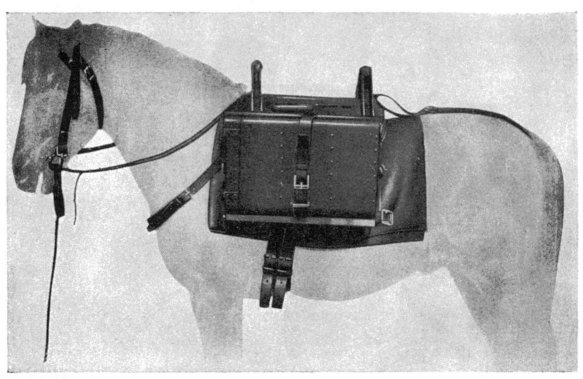

(*Above*) Figure 334. *Method of fastening ammunition
chest to pack saddle.*

(*Left*) Figure 335. *Standard ammunition chest for 75-mm
infantry (mountain) gun. The chest, made of steel plate,
carries 6 rounds. It weighs 29 pounds empty and 118
pounds with ammunition. Two chests can be carried on
one pack saddle.*

(*Below*) Figure 336. *4 draught horse harness with saddles.*

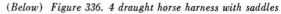

Section IV. SIGNAL EQUIPMENT

1. GENERAL. The following data have been derived from the examination of Japanese signal equipment.

2. RADIO EQUIPMENT. a. Ground. (1) The Japanese place most emphasis on wire communication. However, radio is used initially where communications must be established rapidly or where other means are not practicable. After wire communications have been established, radio assumes a secondary role as a stand-by communication link except where other means cannot be employed.

(2) Apparatus, to date, is of obsolescent design. Circuits and components are comparable with those used by the Allied Nations between 1935 and 1937. Transmitters and receivers almost invariably have wide frequency ranges and use plug-in coils to cover the various bands. In regiments or smaller units, transmitters generally vary from approximately 1 to 50 watts. High-powered sets (500 watts and above) are used primarily for Army administrative traffic and air/ground liaison. Simple Hartley oscillator circuits, connected directly to the antenna, are used. The smaller receivers employ regenerative detectors without radio frequency amplification. While such arrangements are simple to service and maintain, the frequency stability suffers greatly. It therefore would be difficult to "net" these radio sets and keep them on frequency.

(3) A great variety of small transceivers and transmitter-receiver combinations of 1 to 2 watts power are in operation. Such sets are usually man-pack. The transceivers are contained in one case which is carried on the chest; the batteries are carried in another case on the back. In the small transmitter-receiver models, the transmitter, receiver, batteries, and the hand generator for transmitter power, are all carried in separate cases, making it necessary for two to three men to pack and operate a set. Sets of from 10 to 50 watts power are usually of the portable type, and are carried in 4 or 5 separate cases. Power connections are made by means of plugs and cables. The sets, in general, have a complexity of control which does not permit ease of operation. The many controls of the Direction Finder and Intercept Receiver, Model 94 (1934), Type 1, indicate that a comparatively long time is necessary to obtain an accurate "fix" on a transmitter. It must be borne in mind, however, that Japanese operators are well trained and capable of making good use of their equipment.

(4) Most of the transmitters have provision for crystal operation, and, although few crystals have been found, it is reasonable to assume that crystal operation is used extensively. All crystal operated Army ground sets also can be employed as master oscillators.

(5) Since many ammeters, both for antenna and power, are supplied with separate shunts, the same meter movement can be used for many different sets.

(6) Examination of equipment shows that there is little indication of moisture- or fungus-proofing.

(7) All phone transmitters are amplitude modulated, and there is no evidence of frequency modulation.

(8) Technical characteristics and photographs of sets used by Japanese ground forces are illustrated in figures 337 to 354.

Figure 337. Model TE–MU Type 2. Transmitter. Front view.

Figure 338. Model TE–MU Type 2. Transmitter. Rear view. Tube shown is Japanese Type UV812, Mfgd. by Tokyo Electric Co.

Figure 339. Model 94 Type 1. Transmitter. Front view.
140–15000 KC. MOPA. 275 watts.

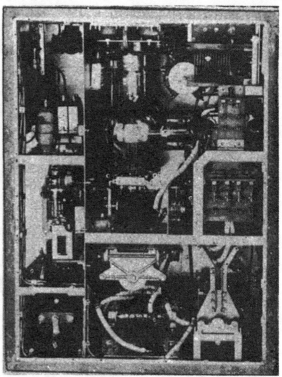

Figure 340. Model 94 Type 1. Transmitter. Rear view.
140–15000 KC. MOPA. 275 watts. Tube at left of photo
is Japanese Type UY511–B master oscillator. Two screen
grid tubes in center are parallel connected PA Tubes,
Japanese Type UV812.

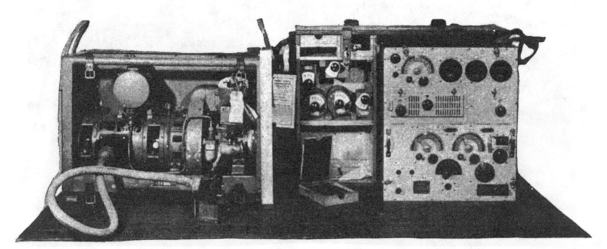

Figure 341. Model 94 Type 2B. Transmitter-receiver. No. 55–D Transmitter. 950–6675 KC. 200 watts. Shown with power
supply. Gas driven motor generator delivers 1300 volts DC.

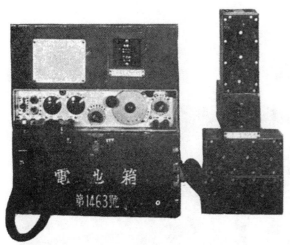

Figure 343. Model 94 Type 5. Transmitter-receiver Model 32. Transmitter. Operates CW or phone. Used with receiver shown below.

Figure 342. Model 94 Type 2B. Transmitter-receiver. No. 27 receiver. 140–15000 KC. 7 plug-in coils. Power supply—batteries.

Figure 344. Model 94 Type 5. Transmitter-receiver Model 32. Receiver. Used with transmitter shown above.

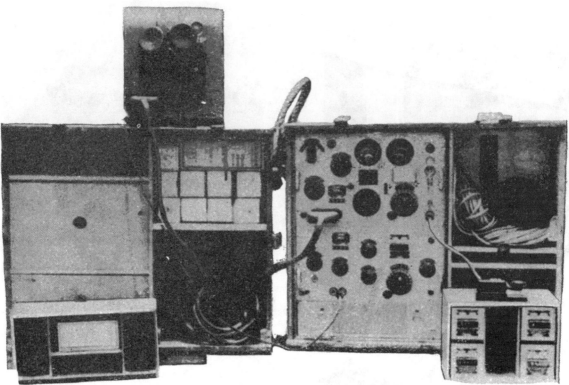

Figure 345. Model 94 3A No. 36. Transmitter-receiver. Transmitter, 400–5700 KC. 15 watts. CW only. Power supply—hand generator. Receiver; 350–600 KC. Power supply—batteries.

Figure 346. Model 94 Type 6. Transceiver. No. 23 Model H. Date: April 1940.

Figure 347. "Walkie Talkie" Type 66. Transceiver. Model A. 2500–4500 KC. Power supply—batteries.

Figure 348. Model 97 Type 3. Transceiver, with hand generator. Pack type. Dipole elements of antenna fasten to wing nuts
at ends of case.

Figure 349. Model TM Type 2. Transceiver, 4000–12000 KC. CW only. Power output about 1 watt. (Also reported as 2.5 watts.)

Figure 350. Model 92 Revision 3. 7 Tube, combination TRF and superheterodyne, all-wave receiver. 200–2000 KC. Shown with AC power supply. Delivers 75 and 200 volts DC.

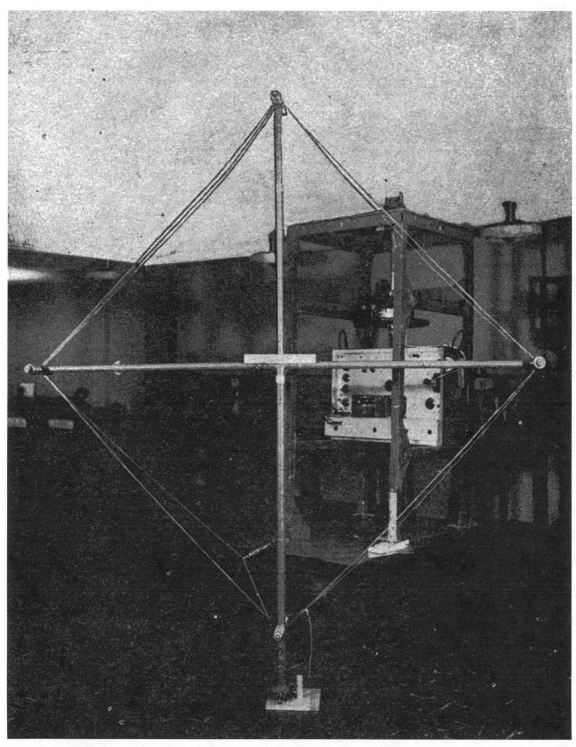

Figure 351. Model 94 Type 1. Direction finding and intercept receiver. 100–2000 KC. Loop shown dismounted from frame.

Figure 352. Model 94 Type 3–A. Receiver only. Pack type.

b. Airborne. (1) Japanese airborne transmitters and receivers, sturdily and compactly constructed, are of excellent workmanship and material. More attention appears to have been given to compactness of design than to ease of maintenance. In many instances, the equipment is so constructed that it is difficult, or even impossible, to service. To some extent, sets are designed to fit a particular type of aircraft, rather than standardized for general use. It has been noted that some tubes (valves) are equipped with leather handles to facilitate removal. Japanese equipment uses a large amount of aluminum, so that even bulky pieces are unusually light in weight. Although no precautions have been taken against corrosion and fungus control, reports indicate that equipment later than 1940 is far superior to that of earlier design. Electrically and mechanically, new radio equipment appears to approach Allied standards.

(2) It has been noted that not all Japanese planes have radio equipment. While radio direction finders are standard equipment on medium and heavy bombers, there have been no reports indicating that they are normally fitted to fighters.

(3) Radio equipment that was made in America, either in whole or in part, has been found on several Japanese (0) Zero fighters (Zekes). Most parts are of Japanese manufacture, but components of German and English manufacture have been noted. Exact imitations of American and German designs also have been reported. There is no evidence of quantity production; indeed, all equipment noted is hand-made and of good construction. Good quality crystals are used in the majority of radios to control the frequencies of transmitters and receivers.

(4) Technical characteristics and photographs of airborne equipment are shown in figures 355 to 363.

Classification	Transmitter output (watts)	Form	Model	Type No.	Date of original model	Function	Type transmission	Range (miles)
Transmitters	100	Portable	TE–MU	3		Used on some islands in local radio net.	Unknown CW, phone, or both.	15–20
	50 or 250	Fixed station	TE–MU	2	1942	Ground to air.	CW, phone.	50
	275	Semiportable. Fixed station.	94	1	1934	Hq–Army Div	CW, MCW, phone.	
	300	Semi-fixed station	Not known	Not known		Marine ground unit.	CW only	
	500	Fixed station	95	4	1935, modified 1941.	High power, island to island.	Phone	Long distance
	1,000	do	92	3	1932, modified 1941.	do	CW	do
	1,000	do	95	Not known	1935	do	Unknown if CW, phone, or both.	do
	1,000	do	94	1	1934	Army Div Hq	CW phone	150
	2,000	do	87	1	1927	Comm. GHQ		300
	1–2	Man pack	94	5	1934	Limited range. Comm. between Inf. units.	CW phone	5–CW, 1–2–phone
Transmitter-receiver.	4.5–C W. 3 phone.	Portable	Not known	Not known		Portable field set	do	
	10	Pack	94	do	1934	Field equipment in div.	CW only	
	15	3-Man pack	94	SP–3A–36	1934	Comm. in Inf. Cav. and F. A. from brigade down to Inf.	do	Approximate 25
	20		87	2	1927	Field, ground, and air.		Field–25 G/A190.
	80–C W. 200 phone.	2-Man pack	94	2–B	1934	Commd. set in Inf. div.	do	
		2–3 man pack	94	3–A–36D	1934		Receives C W, MCW, phone.	
			99	3	1939		CW, MCW, phone	
	0.5	Man pack	94	6	1934	Walkie-talkie type. In Inf.	CW, MCW, phone	1–2
	1	2–3 man pack	TM	2	Revis. 1942		CW only	1–2
Transceivers	1–2	Walkie-talkie	97	3	1937	Walkie-talkie, also air Gnd.	CW, phone	2–8
		do	Not known	66		Infantry squads, platoons.	do	1
	2		do	Not known			CW only	
	2.5	Portable	do	do		Infantry ground; portable.		Several
Receivers		Fixed sta	92	do	1932	Comm. bet. Corps and Div.		
		Direction finder and intercept receiver.	94	1	1934	Direction finder and intercept receiver.		

RF coverage in MC	Frequency shifting capabilities	Present frequency	Antenna system	Tuning—MO or crystal (number of crystals)	Selectivity receiver	Sensitivity receiver	Receiving circuit
1.5–15.0 (plug-in-coils)		Unknown (At least 1).	Wire	MO or crystal. (Number of crystals unknown.)			
3.38–10.4; 12.2–14.0 (4 bands, tapped coils and switches.)	Good. Continuous coverage.		Wire-link coupling from PA to ant. coupler. Coupling adjusted from transmitter panel.	MO			
0.14–15.0 shift bands by plug-in coils. No. of bands and coils unknown.	Good	Unknown	Wire–2 ant. ckts. in transmitter—Series resonant for high freq., Parallel resonant for low freq.	Crystal. (Number of crystals unknown.)			
3.0–10.0.							
3.7–18.2			Wire				
0.05–0.6			Wire–Uses loading coils in antenna system.				
3.7–8.0 (plug-in coils)		Unknown (at least 1).	Wire	MO or crystal (number of crystals unknown).			
0.02–0.5. 0.1–(?). *Transmitter:* 0.779–3.061 (3 bands) tapped coil and switch. *Receiver:* 0.779–7.0 (4 bands) tapped coil and switch.	Continuous coverage on MO.	10	Wire—Same ant. for both Xmtr. and Rec. connected by Send-receive switch. Counterpoise wires incl.	MO or XTAL (number of XTALS–10).	Fair	Poor	1 Stage RF. Regen. Det. 1 Stage AF.
0.9–5.3 (3 bands)		1		Crystal			4 Tube TRF Regn. Det.
0.4–6.0 (5 bands) plug-in coils. Both Xmtr. and receiver.	Continuous coverage on band used.	Unknown (at least 1).	Wire	MO or Crystal (number of crystals unknown.			
XMTR. 0.4–5.7 Rec.—0.35–6.0 (5 plug-in coils).	Continuous coverage for band used on MO.	1	do	Crystal or MO (number of XTALS, 1).	Fair	Very sensitive.	5 Tube Superhet. Regen. 2d Det.
0.33–0.60.							
Rec.: 0.14–15.0 (7 plug-in coils) XMTR: 0.95–6.675.	Continuous coverage on band used.	Adjustable presets on dials.	Wire "L" type. Total length 29.7 yds. Counterpoise wires 22′ long.	Crystal or MO (Number of XTALS 1).			5 Tube Superhet.
0.4–5.75 (5 plug-in coils)	Continuous coverage for band used.		Wire-rubber covered lead in 6 feet long. Gnd. wire same length.		do	Good	4 tubes, 1 stage RF., Regen Det. 2 stages AF.
Rec. 1.5–6.7 (3 plug-in trays of coils).	do	3		MO–Crystal (Number of Crystals 3).			do
24. 2–49, 3 (3 bands)			Rod, 5 feet	MO			Super-regen. Det and one stage AF.
4.0–12.0	Continuously variable.		Wire with reel—to vary length, and tune ant. ckt.	do	Poor-except when on verge of Osc.	Extremely poor	Regen. Det. one stage AF.
25. 5–31 (tapped coil and switch).	Continuous coverage.		Dipole— each half 23 inches long. Elements fasten to case.	do	Poor	Poor	Super-regen. Det. and One stage AF.
2.5–4.5	Continuous cover on MO	1	Either long or short antenna. Ant. tune system.	Crystal or MO. (No. of XTALS–1).			3 Tube. Regen. Det
0.1–2.0; 4.0–5.0.	5 crystals	1	Rod 6 feet long	Crystal			
4.5–11.0.			Wire				
0.2–20.0 (Use total of 7 plug-in coils at one time.)	Continuously var. for coils used.	None	do		Fair	Fair	7 Tube comb. TRF and Superhet. No AVC.
0.1–2.0 (In 5 bands) switches and taps on coils.	Continuously variable for range of coils used.	None	Square loop—ea. side, 4 foot long. 6 turns, unshielded rotation—400° to stops.		Very selective	Poor	6 tube TRF, 3 stages RF., Regen. Det., 2 stages AF.

Classification	Transmitter output (watts)	Transmitter/circuit	Frequency stability	Meters used	Power source	Remarks
Transmitters	100	MOPA. Tubes used–UV202A, UX814, and UV812.	Good		220 volts, 3 phase, 50–60 cycle A.C. Half wave rect. Uses 3 X968 tubes.	Medium power. Short wave portable station. Used primarily in local radio nets on island.
	50 or 250	3 stages–Osc., Buffer, PA. No freq. multiplication. Keyed in buffer and PA.	Fair	Osc. indicator. Osc. plate current. Buffer plate current. PA plate current. Ant. ammeter.	Rectified AC; low power 1,000 v; high power–2,000 v.	Used with rectifier unit. Carried in 2 cases, slung on poles. Fixed station operation. Buffer and PA tubes, screen grid type. No neutralization used. Capable of low or high power operation by switching arrangement.
	275	MOPA-Hartley Osc. MO-UY511B. PA–two UV812 in parallel screen grid voltage keyed for CW. Grid modulation for MCW and phone.	do	Ant. ammeter. PA plate current. PA grid current. Osc. plate current. Fil. voltmeter.	Motor generator: 2,000 volts DC; 1,000 volts DC; 400 volts DC; 100 volts DC; 12 volts DC.	Semiportable. Fixed station operation. Weight with Mot. gen. approx. 500 pounds. 2 cases and Mot. Gen. Each case carried by 2 men. Has neon osc. indicator. Various voltages go through power distribution panel.
	300					
	500	Grid modulated tubes–UV202, UV865, UV–814, UV860, UV861.	Good		220 volts, 3 phase 50–60 cycle AC, output voltages 3,000 volts—2,000 volts—500 volts—300 volts. Fil. 16V rect. tubes used 9–H 830, 6–X968.	Transmitter modification No. 1: High-power, short wave fixed station. Used island to island over long distances. Has emergency power supply gas-driven generator. All filaments on DC. Tubes replicas of American types. Uses speech amplifier and modulator–4 tubes in all; 1-58, 1-56, 2-2A3. Legend on name plate for mod. unit "Modulator for type 95 Short Wave No. 4 transmitter modification No. 1".
	1,000	MOPA. Final tube SN 146.	do		220 volts, 2 phase, 50–60 cycle AC output voltages 2100 volts–1000 volts and 16 volts. 6 Rect tubes. Type H–836.	Transmitter modification No. 1: high power, long wave, long distance. Fixed stations. Used island to island. All filaments on DC. Final tube Japanese type; all others replicas of American tubes.
	1,000	MOPA. Tubes used–202, 865, 814, 812. Final–SN146.	do		220 volts, 3 phase, 50–60 cycle AC. Output voltages 3,000 volts–2,000 volts–500 volts–300 volts and 16 volts. Uses 9–H830 and 6–X968 rect. tubes.	High power, short wave, fixed station. Used over long distances. Not known if used on phone or CW or both.
	1,000					Transmitter.
	2,000					
Transmitter-receiver.	1–2	XTAL or MO control (Hartley ckt.) Osc. connected to antenna.	XTAL – Fair MO–Poor.	Ant. current 0–200 Ma.	Transmitter: Hand generator in separate case. Fil.–6 volts. Plate–150 volts. (Model F) receiver: batteries. In case with receiver. Fil.–1.65 volts. Plate–90 volts.	Stationary use. One twin triode tube. Triodes in parallel for CW operation. For phone, one triode becomes mod. Two man pack and operation. Throat mike used. Model 32 transmitter; Model 32 receiver.
	4.5 – CW. 3 phone.					Transmitter-receiver.
	10	Hartley Oscillator		Ant. Ammeter, Plate current.	Hand generator: 7 volts filament, 500 volts plate.	Pack transmitter-receiver.
	15	1 Tube Hartley oscillator.	Poor	Plate voltmeter. Ant. ammeter.	Transmitter, hand generator receiver; batteries.	Pack animal or 3 man pack. Carried in 2 wooden cases. Transmitter keyed in high volt. Neg. ckt. Transmitter-receiver type.
	20					
	80 – CW. 200 phone.	1 Tube Hartley oscillator.	Fair		Rec.—Batteries; Xmtr.—Gasoline; driven motor generator; 12V–Fil. 1,300V-plate.	Receiver can be used for intercept. Transport by 2 man pack or car; No. 55 D transmitter; No. 27 receiver.
			do		Batteries: 1.5V-Filament; 22.5V-Plate; 1.5V-Bias.	Receiver only. Dials marked with luminous paint and have clamps for locking. Straps provided for carrying on back. Not a "Walkie-Talkie."
Transceivers	0.5	2 Beam Type Tubes. Osc.-Plate Mod. Oscillator and Mod	do	Antenna Ammeter	Batteries-separate case. Fil. 6V; plate 135V.	Transceiver. One coil with 3 taps and switch, 2 to 3 men to pack and operate. No. 23 Model H.
	1	2 tubes in parallel. Hartley osc.	Poor-Freq. shift when keyed.	Fil. voltmeter Ant. ammeter.	Rectified AC. DC voltages—150 and 180 V.	Transceiver. Portable 2 or 3 man pack, cycle, or car. Revision 2. Transmitter output also reported as 2½ Watts, and R. F. coverage as 4.5–11 M. C.
	1–2	Master Osc. (Hartley) and modulator.	Poor	Antenna ammeter	Hand generator: Fil.—3 volts, Plate—135 volts.	Transceiver—Uses one twin triode, UX 19, for all functions. Dipole elements of ant. fasten to each end of case. Case intended to be strapped to back; Generator to chest.
		3 tube Hartley oscillator.	do	Plate current Ant. ammeter.	Batteries: 1.5V filament; 135V plate	One man pack. Transmitter carried on chest, and batteries on back, by means of straps. Model A.
	2					Transceiver.
	2.5					Do.
Receivers					Rectified AC	Used in conjunction with transmitter Model 94 Type 2B. Fixed station Receiver. Total of 25 plug-in coils used.
			Freq. calibration not good.	No visual bearing indicator used.	Batteries—1.5V filament; 4.5V bias; 135V Plate.	Receiver only. 4 wooden chests. Weighs 350 pounds complete. Numerous controls. Slow and difficult to get a "fix." Set installed under shelter over which loop is mounted.

Figures 353–354. Japanese radio equipment—ground.

*Figure 355. Model 96 (1936) Type 3. Transmitter-receiver. From Type 1 medium bomber (Betty). Top of unit: receiver.
Bottom of unit: transmitter.*

Figure 357. *Dynamotor power supply for transmitter of model 96 Type 3 airborne radio set. Used in Type 1 medium bomber (Betty).*

Figure 356. *Radio Homing and D/F loop antenna used with some types of Japanese airborne equipment.*

Figure 358. *Vibrator power supply for receiver of model 96 Type 3 airborne radio set. Used in Type 1 medium bomber (Betty).*

POWER UNIT

RECEIVER

A.E. TUNER

CONTROL UNIT

TRANSMITTER

Figure 359. *Model 99 (1939) Type 3. Transmitter-receiver. Used in single-seater fighter (Oscar). Transmitter: 2500–5000 KC. Receiver:1500–6700 KC. Transmitter and receiver crystal controlled. Photo shows complete complements of equipment.*

Classification	Transmitter output (watts)	Model	Type No.	Date of original model	Function	Type trans.	Range miles	RF coverage in MC
	10	98	4	1938	V. H. F.			44.0–50.4
	10	96	1	1936	Used in plane type (Zeke).	CW, phone	30	Exact coverage unknown.
	10–CW, 8.6–phone.	96	1	1936	Communicate between naval fighters.	do		3.8–5.8.
	10	97	Not known	1937	Bomber, RCN	do		5.0–7.0.
	10–CW, 6–phone.	99	9	1939	Used in (Oscar)	CW, MCW, phone.		XMTR — unknown, Rec. — 1.5–6.7 (3 bands) Plug-in tray of coils.
	10–CW, 6–phone.	99	8	1939	Used in single seat fighter. Type 01 MK II (Oscar).	do	CW–200, phone 100.	XMTR: 2.5–5.0 Fixed coils—Receiver 1.5–6.7 (Two sets of plug-in coils).
	12	Not known	4		Used in Jap type 88 2EB (Lily)—Air to air and Air to gnd. VHF.	Phone only	Purposely limited. Used for short range work only.	Xmtr and receiver. 44.0–50.0.
	20	99	4	1939	Bomber command	CW only		0.45–16.5.
	20	NA	3			CW, MCW		Xmtr—5.0–6.93, Rec. 0.3–2.5, 1.5–15.0.
	20	Not known	3		Fighter command	CW, phone	20	2.0–6.0.
Transmitter-receiver.	20	96	3	1936	Air to air, and to ground. In (Betty) medium Bomber.	CW, MCW, phone.	200 miles from 10,000 feet on CW.	0.22–0.5, 5.0–10.0.
	25	98	4	1938	Air to ground on medium bombers.	do	5–60	29.5–52.5.
	25–30	96	HI No. 2	1936	Air to air and air to ground.	do		Xmtr—1.5–7.5 (3 bands). Rec. 1.48–7.3 (6 bands). Receiver uses plug-in coil assemblies.
	26–CW 9–phone.	96	1	1936	Air to air and air to ground in Mitsubishi bomber.	CW phone	300	XMTR — 7.6–10.6, Rec.—7.5–10.8.
	30	96	2	1936	Naval air	do	9	4.0–5.0.
	50	96	1	1936		Phone only	30	Xmtr—4.2–5.0; Rec.—4.2–5.0.
	50	97	3	1937	General—Air-Naval Air-Gnd.	CW phone		0.3–0.5; 5.0–10.0.
	150	96	2	1936	Air and Ground in RCN bombers	do	450	Xmtr — 0.3–0.5; 5.0–10.0; Rec.—5.0–10.0.
	150	94	Not known	1934	Naval air and bombers.	do	150	0.1–0.5; 5.0–10.0.
	300	94	1	1934	Naval air	do		Xmtr—5.0–10.0; Rec—5.0–10.0.
	Not known	Not known	Not known		In dive bomber	CW, only		7.635 and 0.458 (see remarks.)
	do	96	3	1936	Used in type 97 single seat fighter (Nate).	Phone only		Exact coverage unknown. Had 2 XTALS for 4.810 and 4.835 MC.
	do	EI	Not known				1,250	Xmtr—2.5–15.0; Rec—2.5–18.0.
	do	1			D/F naval			1.76–7.5.
	do	2			D/F and homing			0.14–0.41; 0.55–1.5; 2.8–7.7.
Receivers	PY	3N			do	Aural and visual		0.165–1.0 (2 bands).
	RO	4			do	do		0.17–0.46; 0.45–1.2.
	ADF	6			do	do		0.18–2.8 (3 bands).

Classification	Transmitter output (watts)	Model	Type No.	Date of original model	Frequency shifting capabilities	Present frequency	Antenna system	Tuning MO or crystal (Number of crystals)	Selectivity of receiver
	10	98	4	1938	→	Unknown		XTAL (number of XTALS unknown).	
	10	96	1	1936	One preset freq. cannot be changed in flight.	1	Mast behind pilot's cockpit. (See remarks).	Crystal (number of crystals—1).	
	10-CW, 8.6-phone.	96	1	1936	Preset—Not changeable in flight.	Number unknown.	30-foot mast	Crystal (number of crystals unknown).	
	10	97	Not known	1937					
	10-CW, 6-phone.	99	9	1939	One preset freq. cannot be changed in flight.	1 — Both XMTR and receiver.	Wire—Variometer used to tune Ant. to Sets frequency.	XMTR—crystal receiver—crystal controlled. (1 crystal for each).	Fair
	10-CW, 6-phone.	99	8	1939	...do...	1	Has Ant. tuning unit so set may operate on any length Ant. Probably mast used. Could use trail wire also.	Crystal (number of crystals—2).	Good
	12	Not known	4		Instantaneous shift to any of many preset frequencies.	Many preset frequencies.	Variable—vertical on some planes, horizontal on others.	Crystal (number of crystals Xmtr — 3 Rec.—3).	Fair
Transmitter-receiver.	20	99	4	1939		Number unknown.		Crystal (number of crystals unknown).	
	20	NA	3			...do...	Fixed inverted "L". 22.9 ft. long.	...do...	
	20	Not known	3		Preset—Not changeable in flight.	1			
	20	96	3	1936			Fixed red and trailing wire.	Crystal (number of crystals—2).	
	25	98	4	1938	Preset—Not changeable in flight.	Unknown		MO or XTAL (number of crystals unknown).	
	25–30	96	III No. 2	1936	Preset Freq. by plug-in XTALS.		Ant. lead coils for vertical "T" and inverted "L" Ant Coils—1.5-7.5 MC. Trail wire Ant. may also be used.	MO or XTAL (MO operation by removing XTALS) (number of XTALS unknown).	Good
	26-CW 9-phone.	96	1	1936	Plug-in crystals enable change to 2 frequencies quickly.	2 preset freq., both Xmtr. and Receiver.	Trail or double wire.	Crystal (number of crystals—2).	
	30	96	2	1936					
	50	96	1	1936					
	50	97	3	1937	Preset	Number unknown.		Crystal (number of crystals unknown).	
	150	96	2	1936					
	150	94	Not known	1934	Separate XTAL for each frequency used.	1		Crystal (number of crystals unknown).	
	300	94	1	1934					
	Not known	Not known	Not known		4 plug-in crystals.	2		Crystal (number of crystals—4).	
	...do...	96	3	1936	Plug-in XTALS.	1		Crystal (number of crystals—1).	
	...do...	EI	Not known			Unknown		Crystal (number of crystals unknown).	
		...do...	1						
		...do...	2						
Receivers.		PY	3N					MO only	
		RO	4						
		ADF	6						

Sensitivity of receiver	Receiving circuit	Transmitter circuit	Frequency stability	Meters used	Power source	Remarks
---------	7 tube superhet. IF-1500KC.	3 tube.........				Very good construction.
---------	Operates on 1 preset frequency XTAL controlled.	Operates on 1 preset frequency XTAL controlled·			Two motor generator. For Xmtr and receiver. Use 12-volt plane batteries for power.	Provides 2 way communication from plane—Same Antenna used on transmission and reception; connections made by "Send-receive" switch. Side-tone provided—Components cramped and inaccessible for servicing. Appeared on planes early in 1942.
---------	5 tube superhet. IF-500KC.					
---------	5 tube superhet.........	4 tubes.........				Transmitter and Receiver on 1 frame. Reported that phone output can be scrambled.
Fair......	5 tube superhet. RF, convertor, IF, Det. and AF. HF osc. XTAL controlled. Tubes used—1-US-657A 4—KC804A.	Hartley osc. Osc.-807, plate mod. by 807. No speech Amp.	Poor......			Set can be remotely controlled on CW, MCW, or phone. Receiver tuned manually. 1 set captured used ceramic insulation thruout. Another used bakelite and is believed to be of later manufacture. Easier to machine.
Good......	4 tube superhet. 6F7A triode-pent. RF, Convertor, IF, Det. and AF. Local Osc. either MO or XTAL controlled.	Hartley osc., UY-807A, choke Mod. by a UY807A.	Xmtr—Poor. Receiver fair.		Motor generator Hi voltage—600V. Tube Filaments supplied from separate 8V winding on motor generator.	Main components of complete set are transmitter, receiver, power unit, control unit, and antenna tuning unit. Antenna disconnected from receiver by keying relay. Can "Listen through" while sending.
Fair......	XTAL control—4 tube superhet. Uses 6F7. HF Osc. Frequency is fixed by XTAL, and IF is variable by tuning cond.	XTAL control only. 3 tubes used, type 807.	Good......	Volt- milliammeter which can be switched into various circuits for metering.	Dynamotor: Supplies Hi and Lo voltage for xmtr and receiver—HiV-500V LoV-13V.	Manufactured in December 1942. Entire set shows great improvement over older equipment. Simple to operate and maintain. Design especially of Receiver very modern. High grade bakelite and ceramic insulating material used throughout. On receiver, a chart shows dial setting of variable IF and proper XTAL to use to receive on certain frequency. Termed "Flying Mark 4".
---------	5 tube double superhet. 2—IF Frequency.					
---------	4 tube.........				Dynamotor. Supplies Hi voltage for Xmtr and receiver—700v. Low voltage from planes battery—24 V.	Positive lead to PA stage keyed for CW. PA grid modulated for MCW. Plane engine has ignition shielding.
---------	Crystal controlled superhet.					
---------	6 tube.........				Dynamotor............	Not D/F type. Used in med. bomber. (Betty).
---------	6 tube superhet. IF-2400 KC.	MOPA............				Transmitter and Receiver mounted separately.
Good......	5 tube superhet. RF-77, Mixer-6A7, IF-78, Det. and BFO-6F7, AF Output 41. IF Freq.—400KC.	4 tube MOPA. Osc. UZ47GRF Amp.—UY510B AF Amp.—UY76 Mod.—UZ-47D Supressor Grid mod.	Good.........		Dynamotor. Provision also made for use of generator.	Sidetone provided for monitoring on CW—800 cycle modulation on MCW. No remote control.
Poor......	Superhet. IF—628KC.	MOPA. XTAL controlled.	Fair.........	Ant. meter provided with separate shunts on back. Same meter can be used on other Transmitters.	Xmtr—1000V—DC dynamotor from 100V DC source. Receiver –250V from 12VDC source. Vibropac can power receiver if dynamotor fails.	Transmitter and receiver clamped together on rack. Neon tuning indicator in transmitter antenna circuit. Provision for sidetone. No shock mounting used. Susceptible to damage by humidity and extremes of temperature. Many parts of German manufacture. Model 13.
---------	2 tube.........					Aviation 3.
---------	5 tube superhet.........	MOPA; 1-UX 476; 3-UV816D; 1-UV 56B.				
---------	.....do.........	MOPA 4 tubes......				No intercommunication system provided for plane crew.
---------	6 tube.........				Dynamotor	Transmitter and Receiver mounted together on brass frame. Design sound, but not advanced. Components well made but inaccessible for servicing.
-----						Can be set up for operations as shown in "RF coverage." Alternate set of 2 crystals provided for operation on 7.435 and 16.580 MC.
---------	Pretuned. Cannot be adjusted in flight.				See remarks............	Other parts consist of combined generator and supply voltage regulator, smoothing choke assembly, remote control box, antenna selector box, and separate low frequency receiver. Parts very inaccessible for servicing. Workmanship good altho quality of parts poor. Aviation Radio No. 2.
---------	7 Stages. 2 RF, Mixer 2 IF, Det.-AVC.—BFO and Push-pull AF, Has IF XTAL Filter.	MOPA Tri-tet osc. and RF Amp.				Very modern, good construction.
---------	6 tube TRF Has 2 RF Amp. BFO and neon peak limiter.					
---------	12 tube superhet......					Installed in fighters and large aircraft.
---------	5 tube superhet......					Installed in RCN or light bomber.

Figure 360. Model 99 (1939) Type 3. Transmitter-receiver. Close up of transmitter and receiver. Receiver at left, transmitter at right.

Figure 361. Model 96 (1936) Type 1. Transmitter-receiver model 13. From Mitsubishi bomber. Transmitter: 7600–10600 KC. Receiver: 7500–10800 KC.

Figure 364. Model 92 field telephone.

3. TELEPHONES. a. Model 92 (1932) telephone (fig. 364). This telephone is of conventional design and normally is used on a ground return circuit, although it may be used also on a metallic circuit. It is equipped with a buzzer and key arrangement for sending code. The complete unit is encased in a metal-reinforced, wooden box, approximately 12 inches long, 5 inches wide, and 7 inches high. Directly beneath the aluminum cover is a transmitter, handset receiver, extra single earphone, and the buzzer key. Permanent lead-in wires are fitted to the telephone to which the field wire is attached. Current is supplied by a hand-cranked

Figure 365. Model 2 trench telephone.

generator which generates ringing current rated at 55 volts A. C. It is not advisable, therefore, to use this set with U. S. Army generators which deliver up to 90 volts A. C. It will, however, receive and transmit clearly over U. S. Army circuits, being equipped with two 1½ volt dry cell batteries which furnish 3 volts when connected in series. These batteries normally are connected in parallel and are stored on a metal rack inside the cabinet. Compared with Allied standards, the general mechanical construction of the set is inferior. It has been found that the hand-switch on the handset receiver causes frequent cut-outs as well as noise during operation. The set is contained in a heavy leather carrying case and may be carried easily by one man. A new carrying case, composed of layers of rubberized canvas, also has been observed. This material will withstand tropical climate much better than leather. The complete set weighs approximately 12 pounds.

b. Model 2 (1942) trench telephone (fig. 365). This telephone normally is used with a ground-return circuit, although it may be employed with a metallic circuit. The unit is contained in a wooden cabinet, with metal-reinforced corners. The handset; batteries; and generator, bell, condenser, and induction coil are housed in three compartments. The set may be operated on local or common battery circuits, while magneto signaling facilities also are included. The generator hand crank folds up and fits within the generator armature shaft. A fiber driving gear on the generator eliminates noise to some extent during cranking.

c. Sound-powered telephone (fig. 366). The microphone of the sound-powered telephone, deriving its energy directly from the sound waves, is a reversion to the original principle of the telephone in that the receiver unit is used also as a microphone. The instrument consists of a handset, with a single dual-purpose operating unit and an additional unit

Figure 366. Complete assembly of sound-powered telephone.

as an extra receiver. It is used to provide inter-communication within vehicles, or over short lines when circumstances require rapid and simple set-ting-up and disconnection.

d. Lip microphone. This carbon type micro-phone is attached to a leather and elastic strap. Total weight is approximately $3\frac{1}{2}$ ounces. Other than the fact that it is used with head receivers, there is nothing to indicate for what purpose it was intended. However, since the output of this micro-phone is low, it is possible that it may be used in connection with radio equipment in armored ve-hicles.

4. SWITCHBOARDS. The Japanese have field switchboards, but in place of these they frequently connect field telephones together to form a party line system. At higher headquarters and large air-fields commercial switchboards and pole lines of open wire construction have been used.

5. TELEGRAPH SETS. Figure 367 illustrates the Model 95 set which can be used in conjunction with Model 92 telephone. The set has a built in key arrangement. It probably is used by lower units for administrative traffic.

6. SIGNAL LAMPS. a. Portable signal lamp. This lamp, provided with universal adjust-ment, is mounted on a tripod and powered by a hand generator. At the front, a hinged cover, equipped with a shutter adjustable to 6°, controls the intensity of light. A reflector and 6-volt lamp, rated ap-

proximately 32 candlepower, are contained inside the housing. Usually 3 different-colored filters—green, amber, and red—are provided with each lamp. A metal-reinforced wooden cabinet, $10\frac{3}{4}$ inches long, $5\frac{3}{8}$ inches high, and $8\frac{3}{8}$ inches wide, is provided for the equipment with the exception of the generator.

b. Hand signal lamp. This small pocket lamp measures $3\frac{1}{2}$ inches long. While resembling a cylindrical flashlight, it contains no batteries; in-

Figure 367. Model 95 telegraph set with sound and buzzer.

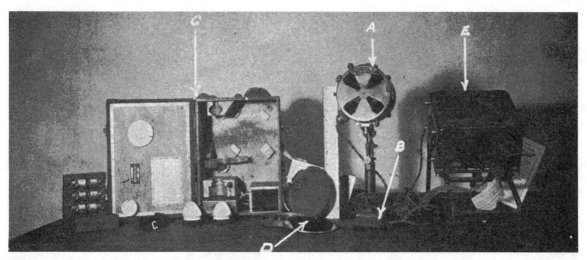

Figure 368. Portable signal lamp. (a) Signal lamp, (b) Key with lock device, (c) Carrying case with spare lamp, eyepieces, filters, etc., (d) Filters; red, amber and green, (e) Hand generator.

stead, a cord, connected to an external battery, passes through the hollow wooden handle. The 3.5-volt bulb and reflector are of conventional design. Installed in front of the bulb is a glass filter, divided into red, blue, amber, and clear sectors. A cover, in front of the filter, can be revolved so that its opening will disclose a lighted segment of the desired color. Signaling is accomplished by a combination push button and slide switch on the side of the case. This lamp should be useful at short range, but the degree of security would be limited by the fact that its beam is not highly directional.

7. FIELD WIRE. The three principal types of field wire in general use are as follows:

a. Assault wire. Assault wire is very small in diameter. It consists of a single conductor and is composed of 8 strands (1 copper and 7 steel) with an outer covering of yellow-colored braid. This wire is for ground-return circuits and is used between regiments and forward units.

b. Seven-strand wire. This single conductor, 7-strand wire (3 copper and 4 steel) is larger in diameter than assault wire. The wire is rubber insulated, and tests have shown that the insulation resistance can remain high throughout a 14-day immersion period. It has an outer covering of yellow colored braid. Tensile strength of the wire is high, but its abrasion resistance is low, and its electrical characteristics are not as good as indicated by its construction. This wire is for ground-return circuits and is used between regimental and battalion headquarters.

c. Heavy wire. Heavy wire, consisting of two rubber-insulated, solid conductors (one black, the other red), is used for metallic circuits, probably between division and higher headquarters as well as at the larger airfields. It has an outer covering of green-colored braid.

8. CABLE. Different types of cables are used by the Japanese for various purposes. Figures 369 and 370 show types used and their characteristics.

9. WIRE REEL UNITS. The Japanese use various types of hand wire reel units, most of which appear to be designed primarily for handling single conductor wire.

a. Hand wire reel unit. The reel is carried on the shoulders, or to one side of the body, by means of a broomstick handle and it will hold approximately 1,600 feet of the larger diameter, yellow-braided, field wire. No crank is provided for convenient recovery of the wire. Perforations on the head and splines of the drum tend to damage the insulation if the wire is stored on the reel for any length of time. This unit, which is light in weight and not very rugged, can readily be dismantled without the use of tools. (See fig. 371.)

b. Head wire reel. The unit (see fig. 372) is solidly made of pressed metal, with leather straps for carrying on the chest or back. This reel evidently is designed for use by troops in forward areas and normally is carried on the back to allow free use of the hands. (See fig. 372.) When recovering wire, for which purpose a handle is provided, the reel normally is carried on the chest. The reel may be folded up when not in use.

10. AIRPLANE PANELS. Cloth air-ground panels are usually 1½ to 3 feet wide and 6½ to 13 feet long. Some shorter panels, and some triangular panels 3 to 6½ feet on each side, have been used. In most cases panels are white, but other colors, contrasting to the terrain, also may be used. When regular panels are not available, rags, maps, or pieces of paper may be substituted. On occasion, Japanese soldiers have been observed to lie on the ground to form panel signals.

Outside Diameter (inch)	Cross section of cable	1	2	3	4	5	6	7	8	9	Remarks
7/16	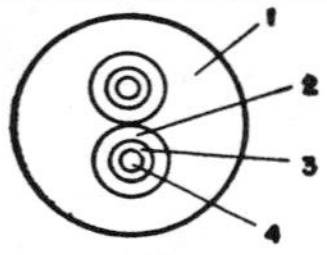	Rubber insulation.	Rubber insulation.	Cotton string wrapping	No. 14 Stranded wire.						This was taken from the power cord of a test lamp. It corresponds to ordinary rubber covered lamp cord.
7/16	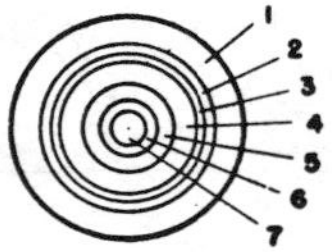	Woven steel wire sheath (lead).	Impregnated cloth.	Impregnated paper.	Lead sheath.	Cotton cloth wrapping.	Rubber insulation.	Copper wire core.			The conductor of this cable consists of 19 strands of No. 20 copper wire. Probably used as buried underground cable.
7/16	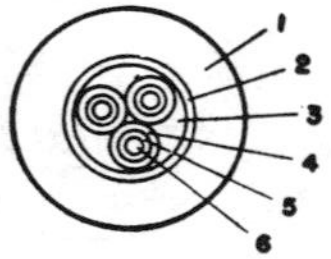	Lead sheath.	Cotton cloth.	Jute or hemp cord filler.	Silk cloth.	Rubber insulation.	Solid copper wire.				Each of the three conductors is composed of No. 17 solid copper wire.
7/16	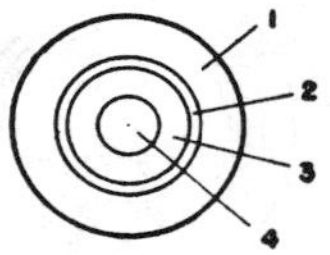	Lead sheath.	Cotton cloth.	Rubber insulation.	Stranded copper wire.						This was taken from a Japanese radar transmitter and was used to carry power to the tube filaments. The single conductor core consists of 30 strands of No. 20 copper wire.
3/8	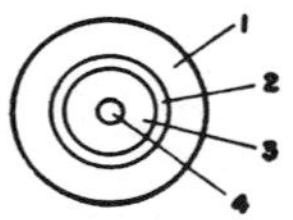	Lead sheath.	Cotton cloth.	Rubber insulation.	Solid copper conductor						This was used to carry 600 volts to a radar transmitter. The solid copper conductor is size No. 14.
9/32	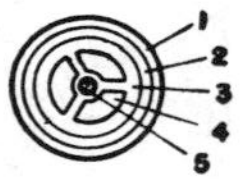	Black cotton cloth.	Woven steel wire sheath.	Rubber insulation.	Air holes in rubber.	Solid copper conductor, size No. 23.					The cloth covered coaxial line is used to carry radar video and pulse signals between the various units of a radar. The estimated impedance of the line is 100 OHMS. The capacitance of the cable has been decreased by extruding three holes in the otherwise solid rubber dielectric. These holes are in a symmetrical position around the center conductor.

Figure 369. Various types of Japanese cables.

Outside Diameter (inch)	Cross section of cable	1	2	3	4	5	6	7	8	9	Remarks
1¼	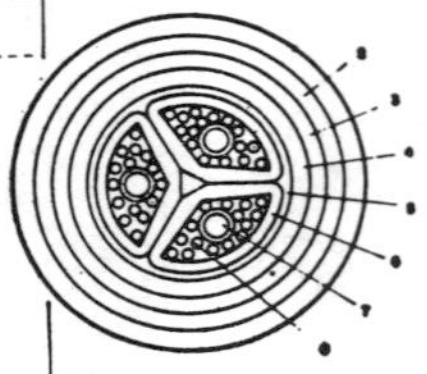	Tar coated hemp.	Spiral wound steel sheath.	Impregnated filler.	Lead sheath.	Impregnated paper.	Impregnated paper.	No. 10 solid copper wire.	15 conductors of No. 17 solid copper wire.		This cable is probably used as underground power cable.
1 1/16	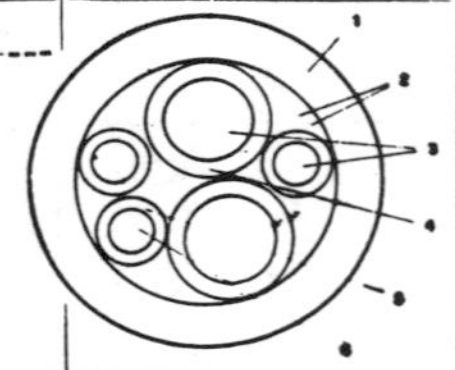	White rubber insulation.	Cotton string filler.	(⁵⁄₁₆" diam. stranded from No. 31 tinned copper wire.)	Rubber insulation.	Rubber insulation for H.V.	No. 9 stranded wire from No. 30 tinned copper wire.				This cable is probably used to carry power from a power supply unit to a communications transmitter. The large wires are for the filament power and the small are for B plus and bias voltages.
29/32	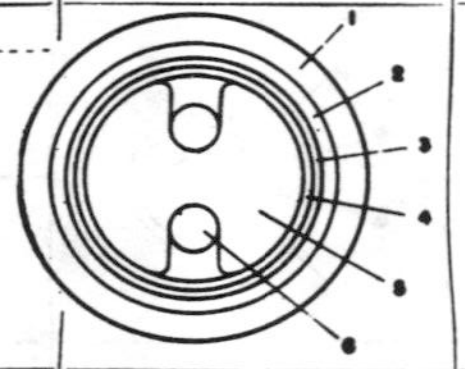	Lead sheath.	Brown paper.	Copper sheath.	Brown paper.	Polystyrene spacers every inch.	Copper No. 9 wire (solid).				The shielded balanced wire line is used to carry r-f power to the antenna of a Japanese Radio Navigation Aid. The characteristic impedance of the line is approximately 115 OHMS.
1 1/16	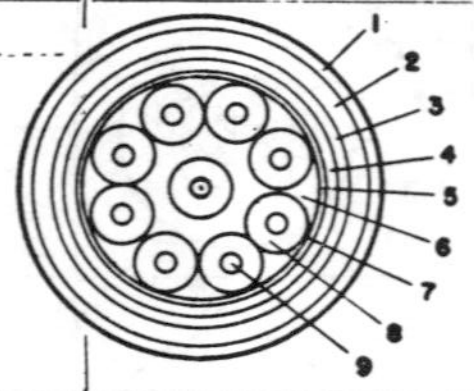	Woven steel wire sheath (white).	Impregnated cloth.	Impregnated paper.	Lead sheath.	Cotton cloth.	Jute or hemp cord filler.	Silk cloth winding.	Rubber insulation.	Solid copper conductor.	This is a nine conductor cable. Probably multi-conductor remote control cable. All the conductors are size No. 17.
½	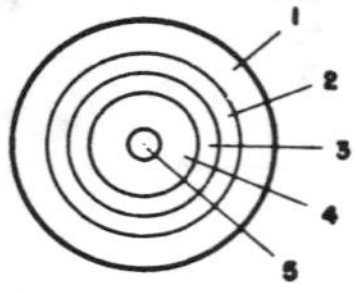	Lead sheath.	Cotton cloth.	Black rubber insulation.	White rubber insulation.	Stranded copper.					This high voltage cable was used on a radar transmitter to carry plate voltage at a potential of 6 KV. The stranded core, which is size No. 11, is made up of seven strands of No. 20 copper wire.
7/16	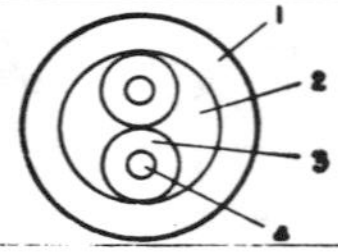	Rubber insulation.	Cotton string filler.	Rubber insulation.	No. 16 stranded copper wire.						This is probably ordinary power cable.

Figure 370. Various types of Japanese cables.

Figure 371. Hand wire reel unit with broomstick handle.

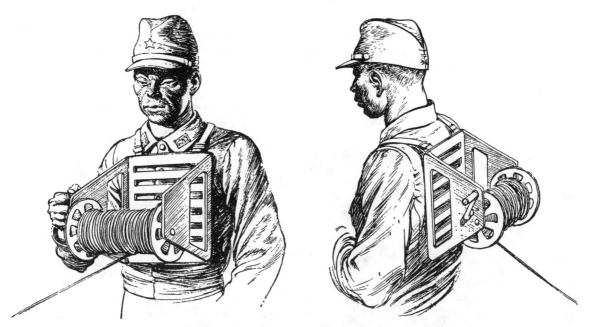

Figure 372. Head wire reel—used by field artillery. At left: Recovering wire. At right: Reeling out wire.

11. SIGNAL FLAGS. Two small hand flags, one red and the other white, are used for semaphore. For signaling Morse Code a large red and white flag, on a bamboo shaft about 5 feet long, is utilized.

12. MILITARY DOGS. Trained dogs, used to some extent for carrying messages, are cared for and trained by the division signal unit.

13. PIGEONS. Pigeons, also, are used for carrying messages.

14. HAND GENERATORS. a. Model "F". This simple and compact hand-driven generator, which weighs only 16 pounds, delivers 24 watts. It serves as a source of filament voltage (3 volts) and of plate voltage (125 volts). The mechanical transmission between driving handle and armature consists of 4 geared wheels, 2 of which are fiber, the others steel. According to the name plate, the normal rate of turning is 70 revolutions per minute, giving an armature speed of 5,200 revolutions per minute. Harness is provided for carrying the generator and for fastening it to a support. It is possible for a man to work the generator when the straps are slipped

over his shoulders, with the base resting against his chest.

Figure 373. Model "F" hand generator right side view— showing crank handle in place.

15. BATTERY CHARGER. Two charging circuits are provided. One uses a Tungar, half-wave rectifier, delivering 14 volts at 6 amperes. The other circuit uses a type 83, mercury-vapor, full-wave rectifier, delivering 130 to 160 volts at 0.1 ampere. Component parts are mounted on an angle-iron framework which fits into a metal carrying case. The case is provided with ventilating apertures, 3 weatherproof receptacles, a door at the rear, and a leather carrying handle. The charger is capable of charging one 12-volt storage battery and one storage "B" battery at an average efficiency of 30 percent. This efficiency compares favorably with that of half-wave Tungar chargers of American manufacture. The switching arrangement controlling the active turns in the transformer primaries allows operation of the charger from three different line voltages.

Figure 374. Battery charger, front view, showing controls.

16. POWER UNITS—DUAL VOLTAGE DC(1300V/12V). This is a completely self-contained, rope-starting, power unit, consisting of a single cylinder of 1.977-inch bore x 2.0-inch stroke. The air-cooled gasoline engine is coupled directly to a straight-shunt, 2-pole-field, dual-voltage 1300-V/12V generator, inclosed in an aluminum housing. Engine and generator are ruggedly con-

structed and supported, indicating long-life operation. This unit can be used to furnish plate voltage to U. S. Army SCR 177.

17. PYROTECHNIC SIGNALS. The Japanese make much use of pyrotechnic signals. Projection is achieved by means of Models 10 and 89 Grenade Dischargers, both of which are common infantry weapons.

Listed below are some of the pyrotechnic signals which can be used in grenade dischargers. They frequently have been referred to by the Japanese as dragons. The nature of the signal may be ascertained by two methods: (a) by color bands painted on the body, (b) by designs embossed on the cover (for use in the dark).

Signal	*Color bands on body*
Black smoke, parachute	One wide black band.
White star, parachute	One wide white band.
White star	One narrow white band.
White star, double	Two narrow white bands.
White star, triple	Three narrow white bands.
Orange smoke, parachute	One wide yellow band.
Green star, parachute	One wide green band.
Green star, single	One narrow green band.
Green star, double	Two narrow green bands.
Red star, parachute	One wide red band.
Red star, triple	Three narrow red bands.

Signal pistol, 35-mm (1.38-inch) parachute and cluster "stars" in red, white, or green colors, with a burning time of from 4 to 15 seconds, are reported to exist. The cartridge closely resembles a shotgun shell. Model 97 (1937) signal pistol: One and three barrel models of this newer type signal pistol have been reported. The pistol is well made of a good grade of steel with an excellent finish; its overall length is $9\frac{13}{16}$ inches, and its weight is 1 pound 13 ounces.

Section V

ENGINEER EQUIPMENT

1. GENERAL. a. Japanese engineers are well-equipped and are armed as infantry. They have shown outstanding ability in both the construction and demolition of bridges. On the other hand, airfields and roads so far encountered have not been up to Allied standards in speed of construction or serviceability. This may be attributable to the fact that the Japanese have depended more on manual labor than on heavy equipment, which they have not taken into forward areas in any quantity.

b. The construction of field fortifications has been very highly developed, and even at remote points Japanese engineers have been successful in constructing first class defense positions from material immediately available. (For detailed descriptions of various kinds of Japanese defensive constructions, see part 2, secs. III and IV, chapter 7).

c. Engineers are also well-equipped with a wide variety of explosive charges and other material for assault and demolition tasks.

d. The shipping engineers (Sempaku Kohei) are specially trained and equipped to operate a large

Figure 375. Dual voltage (1300V/12V) DC power unit.

Figure 376. Pyrotechnic signal for use in grenade dischargers.

Figure 377. 35-mm (1.38-inch) signal pistol.

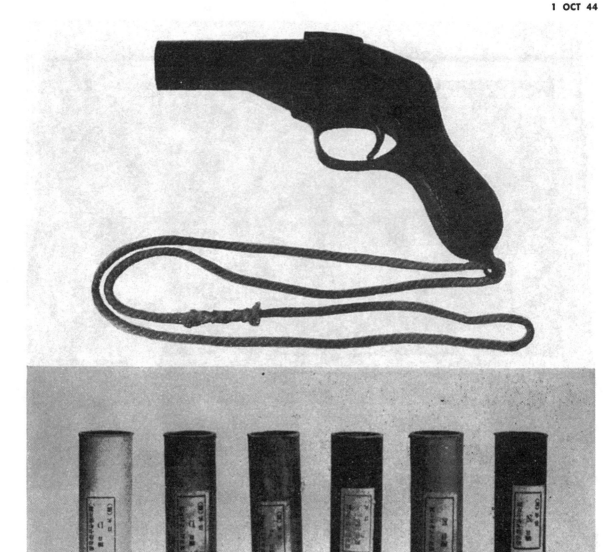

Figure 378. Model 97 signal pistol with various types of signal cartridges.

variety of transport craft, including landing barges. (For a chart showing specifications of all known types of Japanese landing craft, see chapter 8, fig. 157).

e. Pictures and detailed descriptions of certain items of engineer equipment will be found on the following pages.

2. AMPHIBIOUS EQUIPMENT.
a. Bridges. (1) *Assault bridges.* Several different models have been developed and standardized. Two types are illustrated in figures 379 and 380. One type is made of lengths of steel tubing, supported by bags filled with kapok. The sections are joined together and afterwards locked. They are light enough to be carried easily by foot soldiers. Crossings of streams 100 feet and more in width are reported possible with this type of bridge.

The foot bridge illustrated in figure 380 is supported by floats, each of which can be carried by one foot soldier. This type is for infantry only.

(2) *Ponton bridges.* The heavier bridge is suitable for artillery and heavy equipment. The boats which support it are of standard sizes, especially developed for this work. One type, designed for transport by wagon, has 2 bow sections, each 8.7

Figure 379. Assault bridges for infantry.

Figure 380. Small ponton bridge.

feet long, and 2 center sections, each 7.1 feet long. This boat weighs 1,650 pounds complete. An even larger boat of this type, which also comes in 4 sections, is 45 feet long and weighs 6,800 pounds complete. Another type is designed for packing by horses; it has 2 bow sections, each 4.4 feet long, and 3 center sections, each 4 feet long. The complete boat weighs 921 pounds, and is slightly over 20 feet in length. An even lighter version also exists.

(3) *Improvised trestle bridges.* The Japanese are skilled in the construction of wooden trestle bridges (fig. 381) which they erect with great rapidity from materials prepared beforehand or available locally. Joints usually are lashed with straw rope, and occasionally are strengthened with iron pins. Such trestles are found serving as approaches to ponton bridges in wide river beds; in shallow rivers they may be several hundred feet in length. Despite their flimsy appearance they are capable of supporting artillery and other heavy equipment.

(4) *Sectionalized steel bridges.* Prefabricated steel bridges are used by the Japanese, but not as widely as by some other Armies. One truss-construction, portable, steel bridge is 48 feet long and weighs 820 pounds.

b. Assault boats. (1) *Collapsible boats.* Several types of collapsible boats have been developed. One of these, model F (fig. 382) is an outstanding example of assault boat design, and is very widely utilized. The boat, divided into two sections, each of which collapses flat on itself, (fig. 383) is individually floatable. Each section is 13.6 feet long, 4.75 feet wide, and 2.18 feet high. The wooden frame is braced, and all joints are bonded with rubber. The boat will hold 20 men, and it is estimated that 9 such boats could be loaded flat on a 2 ton truck. Light outboard motors have been used to propel this boat. Three types of rubber (pneumatic) boats, of from 1- to 10-man capacity, are in use. These are similar in construction to the rubber boats used by other Armies.

(2) *Demountable boats.* Japanese engineers also operate a variety of demountable motor boats, fitted with outboard and inboard motors of various kinds. One small, 30-foot boat breaks into 4 sections and is propelled by an outboard motor. Some of the outboard motors are arranged for animal pack. Another larger type breaks into only 2 sections; the stern section is fitted with a 4-cylinder, inboard gasoline engine of 30 horsepower. It is

Figure 381. Improvised trestle bridge.

not believed that any of these demountable boats permanently mount any weapons.

c. Landing barges. (1) Japanese engineers operate a large variety of landing barges, which have been employed extensively in various theaters. Since Allied air superiority has seriously interfered with Japanese use of transports in many theaters, landing barges generally have been employed for the supply and evacuation of their forward areas. As many as 500 of these craft have been found congregated in one port.

(2) Some of the design features of these small vessels are of interest. The landing-barge screw shown in figure 384 is designated for operation in shallow waters and affords maximum protection to the screw. The Japanese generally are credited with the development of the folding ramp, which now is used so extensively.

(3) A typical landing barge is the Daihatsu Model A (Army). This Daihatsu is probably in wider use than any other type; the picture in figure 385 gives a general idea of it.

Figure 382. Model F, collapsible assault boat.

Figure 383. Half of collapsible assault boat, model F, completely folded.

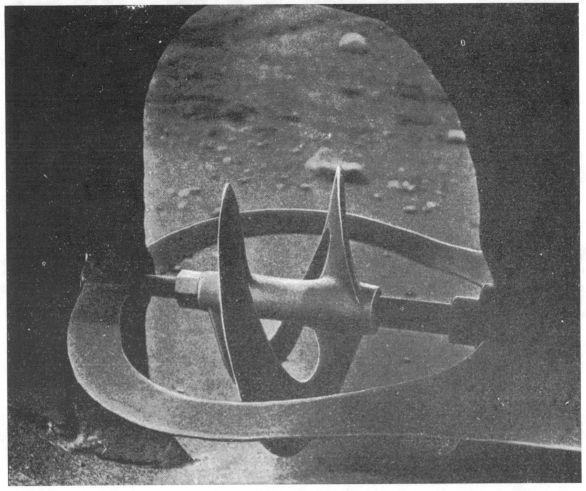

Figure 384. Landing barge screw.

Figure 385. Daihatsu model A (Army) landing barge.

Figure 386. Daihatsu model A landing barge, showing armor plate protecting controls.

(4) The specifications of the Daihatsu illustrated in figure 385 are as follows:

Length _____	49 feet (approximately).
Beam _____	11 to 12 feet.
Height _____	6.5 feet (approximately).
Draft _____	3 to 4 feet.
Freeboard _____	1.5 to 2 feet amidships.
Speed _____	6 knots (cruising (10 knots maximum) empty).
Engine _____	Diesel, 6 cylinder, 60 to 80 horsepower, preferred. Some may have heavy oil, electric ignition, or gasoline engines.
Capacity _____	100 to 120 men (short hauls only) 40 to 50 men on longer trips, or 10 to 15 tons, or 1 light tank (7 to 9 tons), or 1 150-mm howitzer (6 to 7 tons, complete).
Crew _____	5 to 7 men.
Armament _____	Not standardized. However, at least two machine guns, or one or two 13-mm heavy machine guns. Fire from 20-mm guns has been encountered from this type, and on several occasions 37-mm guns have been found.
Armor _____	A vertical shield of steel, .12 to .36 inch thick, usually protects the coxswain and control gear from frontal fire. Occasionally this type has steel plates, 15 inches by 12 inches, .36 inch thick, hooked to the gunwales.
Construction ____	Based on standard Japanese fishing boat design, this landing barge has been developed over a long period of years. The metal hull, about .2 inch thick, is of welded steel plate, supported by heavy wooden braces. The twin keels at the bow are of heavier steel and are riveted. The bow ramp is of wood, and the sides above the waterline are covered with timber. The Daihatsu has an open cockpit in the middle, with

a watertight compartment at each end. The engine room at the rear is steel decked.

This clumsy looking vessel is surprisingly versatile, and will stand a great deal of abuse. Its heavy, double-keeled bow and protected screw make it very serviceable in shoaly, rock-infested waters.

3. CONSTRUCTION EQUIPMENT. a. Rollers. Various types of road rollers, of small, medium, and large sizes, have been encountered. All are of simple and sturdy design. The small roller shown in figure 388 weighs about 9 tons and is powered with a Ford model B, 4-cylinder, gasoline engine. The medium roller shown in figure 389, about 18 tons in weight, is Diesel powered. Larger rollers also have been captured.

b. Prime movers. For detailed specifications, see section III of this chapter.

c. Power rock crushers. Power rock crushers of rather small capacity, but of good construction, have been seen. Power is furnished by small Diesel motors. These rock crushers are found mounted in pairs, usually on a platform.

d. Concrete mixers. Portable concrete mixers (fig. 390) of various types have been developed by Japanese engineers. The mixers, some of which are Diesel-powered, can be moved easily from one job to another and erected on a platform to facilitate pouring. Some army types are mounted permanently on trucks.

e. Portable railroads. Japanese engineers make extensive use of portable railroads of various kinds. One standardized type has a gauge of two feet. Rails are small in section, weighing about 10 pounds per foot, and are 18 feet in length. They usually are laid for temporary use. Switch sections are prefabricated. Light flatcars, 4 feet wide and 6

Figure 387. Yamasen model E flat-bottom landing barge.

Figure 388. Small gasoline roller.

feet long, are used on this type of portable railroad. Racks or sideboards can be fitted to give increased capacity to the flatcars. Such light cars can be pushed by manpower, or pulled by small, gasoline-powered locomotives.

f. Mobile power driven saw. The power saw is another piece of Japanese construction equipment used in forward areas, where defenses must be constructed of heavy logs. Power is furnished by a small gasoline motor. In rear areas, larger circular saws, permanently installed and driven by belt from Diesel motors, will be found.

g. Mobile well driller. The heavy, mobile, power-operated well driller is used in favorable terrain. Power is furnished by the truck engine, which drives an air compressor connected with a large compressed air tank.

h. Miscellaneous construction equipment. A wide variety of miscellaneous equipment for construction of bridges, defense works, roads, and air-

fields has been developed by Japanese engineers. In the forward areas so far overrun, however, main reliance has been placed on labor troops rather than on mobile equipment. Moreover, it is felt that Japanese engineers have not developed prime movers and earth-moving equipment of the heaviest variety, although medium-weight equipment of these categories has been identified.

4. MAINTENANCE EQUIPMENT. a. Electric power units. Electric generating units, both mobile and heavy, usually Diesel powered, are in wide use. They usually are of standard design and are utilized to supply light and power for a variety of purposes. On one island fortress, Diesel-powered generator units ranged from 20 to 100 KVA, all 2,300 volts, 3-phase, 50-cycle. Underground cables led to intermediate transformer vaults, where the current was stepped down to 110/220 volts for consumption by gun-turret mo-

Figure 389. Medium Diesel-powered roller.

Figure 390. Diesel-powered concrete mixer.

Figure 391. Field ice plant.

tors and communications equipment. Searchlights were DC arc type, with motor generator converters. A large number of battery-charging panels served to charge batteries for communication equipment.

b. Ice plants. Ice plants of varying capacities have been found on several islands occupied by the Japanese. These are well-constructed (fig. 391), and some of them have been used by our troops for long periods.

5. DEMOLITION EQUIPMENT. Japanese demolition equipment is similar to that of other Armies, but unusual attention has been given to small demolition charges employed in assault tasks. Much use is made of picric acid, and serious efforts have been made to preserve this compound from moisture. Plastic explosives also have been used by the Japanese for some time. Although electric detonators have been well developed, the Japanese take a very practical view of equipment of this nature, and therefore have retained friction-type igniters in many instances because of their simplicity.

a. Small charges. In addition to those described in section I, chapter 9, a variety of small charges, in either block or cylindrical form, are available. Picric acid, TNT, and toluol cheddite*

————————
*Ammonium perchlorate 76 percent.

are used in these charges, some typical specifications of which are as follows:

(1) *Block charges.*

Length	2.8 inches.
Width	1.6 inches.
Thickness	2 inches.
Weight	Picric acid and TNT .44 pound. Toluol cheddite* .42 pound.

(2) *Cylindrical charges.*

Length	4.6 inches.
Diameter	1.2 inches.
Weight	Picric acid and TNT .22 pound. Toluol cheddite* .20 pound.

There are several containers for these small charges. One zinc can, wired for an electric detonator, has the following specifications:

Length	8.2 inches.
Width	2.2 inches.
Thickness	3 inches.

This can contains three of the block charges mentioned in (1) above and is very widely used.

b. Large charges. In addition to the bangalore torpedo described in section IV, much larger demolition charges in this form are used by engineers. One large bangalore torpedo consists of 4 sections and a detonator. Each section contains 10 of the cylindrical charges described in a(2) above. The assembled torpedo is 34 feet long and weighs 225 pounds. Other large charges are assembled in various forms, as needed, with the addition of plastic explosive when necessary.

c. Plastic explosive. This explosive has the following composition:

Cyclonite_____ 80 percent.
Vegetable oil binder_____ 20 percent.

It is issued in rolls, 4 inches by 1.12 inches, each roll weighing .25 pound. These rolls are individually wrapped in parchment and in turn wrapped in a paper package.

d. Detonators. (1) *Nonelectric.* Several types have been recovered. One very large, non-electric detonator has the following specifications:

Length_____ 2.7 inches.
Diameter_____ 0.3 inch.
Contents_____ Fulminate of mercury—88 grams
                     PETN—4 grams.

This detonator is made of brass.

(2) *Electric.* There are a number of types and sizes. Model 97 (1937) electric detonator has outer and inner cases, both of brass, and has the following specifications:

Length_____ 3.25 inches.
Diameter_____ 0.27 inch.
Contents_____ Fulminate of mercury — 3.93
                     grams, fulminate of mercury
                     plus a deadening agent—0.28
                     grams, PETN—1.98 grams.

These detonators, each individually wrapped, are packed 10 in a waxed cardboard box, inside a metal container. Such detonators may be used with electric blasting machines, of which a variety are available.

(3) *Pull igniters.* These are very widely employed. One type consists of a brass body, with a red plastic outer sleeve. One end of the screw cap is fitted with an eye for attaching a trip cord. Attached to the inside of the cover is a short pull string which projects through a small pellet of friction ignition composition. When the sanded end of the string is drawn through the pellet, it ignites and flashes through the igniter body. The assembled igniter is 2.75 inches long, and .30 inch in diameter.

(4) Several types of slow burning and instantaneous fuzes have been developed. The instantaneous type (Primacord) is protected by a rubber-impregnated, hemp thread cover.

6. SURVEYING, MAP-MAKING, AND RE-PRODUCING EQUIPMENT. Japanese transits, theodolites, map-scribers, and reproducers are of good quality and workmanship. In design and development the Japanese have closely followed or even duplicated European or American patterns, and calibrations and markings usually are in Arabic numerals. Allied engineers have no difficulty in making good use of these instruments in the field.

Section VI. CAVALRY AND RECONNAISSANCE

1. GENERAL. The Japanese have given much thought to the cavalry arm, which is particularly useful in Manchuria and North China. Their specially bred cavalry horses, the get of Anglo-Arabian sires and native mares, average about 14.3 hands (approx. 57 inches). They have proved satisfactory, since they are sturdy, enduring, and relatively speedy.

2. SADDLES. The saddle (weight about 46 pounds with saddle bags, etc.) shows evidence of both English and American design (fig. 392).

3. SABER. The saber is a combination of a European type hilt with a Japanese cutting blade. It is 40 inches in length and weighs 3.13 pounds (fig. 393).

4. OTHER EQUIPMENT. a. The individual trooper carries model 44 (1911) 6.5-mm cavalry carbine. (See sec. II, chap. 9.) The horse artillery of the cavalry brigade is armed with a 75-mm field gun, which is a variation of model 38. It is possible that model 95 (1935) 75-mm field gun also is used by these units. Light and heavy machine guns are standard equipment of cavalry brigades.

b. The Japanese have formed reconnaissance units which contain both mounted troops and motorized units. In these latter units, tankettes, and possibly armored cars (see sec. IV, chap. 9), will be found. Personnel of such units are armed like the horse troops, except that the saber may be omitted.

Section VII. AUTOMOTIVE AND LAND TRANSPORT EQUIPMENT

1. G E N E R A L. a. Although the automotive manufacturing industry was comparatively new in Japan, considerable progress had been made by the end of 1941. Both Ford and General Motors had maintained large assembly plants in Japan proper for many years, and very large numbers of the trucks produced by these plants naturally are used now by the Japanese Army. In addition, very large numbers of European and American motor vehicles were captured by the Japanese in their advance southward.

b. All motor vehicles manufactured in Japan are right-hand drive. They have comparatively high ground clearance and small turning radii. The Diesel is the preferred power unit for heavy vehicles, and many are so fitted. Power-weight ratios generally are not good, and tires often are overloaded. Power take-off systems of various kinds often are

Figure 392. Standard cavalry saddle.

found. Hydraulic foot brakes were not installed until recent years; many vehicles still are equipped with mechanical brakes. Because of local regulations, the emergency, or handbrake, is always entirely separate from the main braking system and is mechanically actuated.

c. Because of gasoline shortages, charcoal and wood gas producers began to be installed in 1937. By 1942, all non-military vehicles had been converted to their use, and it seems probable that many military vehicles now operating in Japan proper are using self-generating fuel systems.

2. PASSENGER CARS. a. Japanese model 95 (1935) 4 x 4 scout car. This lightweight, unarmed, reconnaissance vehicle (fig. 394) was developed after the Manchurian Incident, when the need for an all-purpose scout car became pressing. Its air-cooled engine offers many advantages for operations in Manchuria and North China, where very low temperatures often are experienced. Initial difficulties with the four-wheel drive, particularly with the front universal joints, are believed to have been overcome. Special tires, with heavy rubber lugs, are provided for exceptionally difficult terrain.

Specifications

General:

Weight	2,310 pounds, complete.
Length	134 inches.
Width	60 inches.
Height	66 inches.
Clearance	9 inches.
Tread	50 inches.
Wheelbase	79 inches.

Engine:

Type	4 cycle, gasoline, air-cooled.
Number of cylinders.	2, set at 45 degree angle.
Horsepower	Maximum, 33 at 3,300 r. p. m.
Compression ratio.	5 to 1.
Fuel capacity	13 gallons.

Chassis:

Final drive reduction.	6.83 to 1.
Transmission	Selective, standard, 3 forward and 1 reverse.
Brakes	Mechanical; service, external contracting; emergency, internal expanding on driveshaft.

b. Standard Nissan 5 passenger sedan. First produced in 1937, the Nissan (fig. 395) has

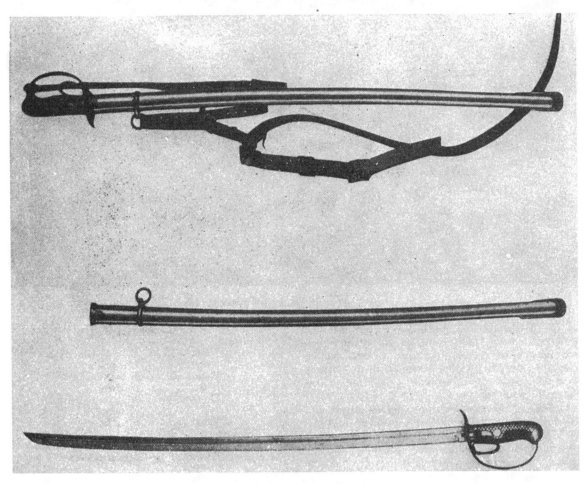

Figure 393. Standard cavalry saber.

Figure 394. Japanese model 95 (1935) 4 x 4 scout car.

had several modifications, but no major improvements. The design, and the tools to make it, were purchased from the Graham-Paige Co., which designed and tooled up for this model in 1935, but never went into production. The design is not remarkable in any way; from modern standards the power-weight ratio is poor.

Specifications

General:
Weight_____ 3,108 pounds.
Length (over-
all)_____ 186 inches.
Width_____ 67.5 inches.
Height_____ 69 inches.
Wheelbase_____ 110 inches.
Clearance_____ 8 inches.
Tread_____ 56.5 inches.
Engine:
Type_____ 4 cycle, gasoline, 6 cylinder, "L" head (Side valve). This possibly might be replaced by the Toyoda engine, an overhead valve type which is an exact copy of 1939 Chevrolet.
Horsepower_____ 85 maximum.
Bore_____ 82-mm (3.23 inches).
Stroke_____ 114-mm (4.49 inches).
Displacement___ 3,670-cc (224 cubic inches).
Compression
ratio_____ 6.5 to 1.
Electric system_ 6 volts.
Chassis:
Final drive re-
duction_____ 4.09 to 1.
Transmission___ Selective, standard shift, 3 forward, 1 reverse.
Brakes_____ Hydraulic; emergency is mechanical, internal-expanding on driveshaft.

c. Model 93 (1933) Staff car. This 6-wheeled staff car (fig. 396) was developed over a period of years. Originally, Hudson and Studebaker chassis were used, but a Japanese chassis ultimately was developed. Available specifications indicate a poor power-weight ratio, and a performance not comparable with that of any U. S. command car. How-

ever, this vehicle has not yet been reported from the field, and improved models may exist.

Specifications

General:
Weight_____ 5,720 pounds.
Length (over-all) 17 feet 8 inches.
Width (over-all) 6 feet 4 inches.
Height (over-all) 6 feet 6 inches.
Wheelbase_____ 8 feet 11 inches.
Clearance_____ 11 inches.
Tread_____ 5 feet 1 inch.
Engine:
Type_____ Gasoline, 6 cylinder, "L" head (side valve) water-cooled.
Horsepower_____ 68 maximum.
Bore_____ 90-mm (3.54 inches).
Stroke_____ 115-mm (4.53 inch).
Displacement___ 4,790-cc (292 cubic inches).
Compression ra-
tio.
Electrical sys-
tem. 12 volts.
Chassis:
Final drive re-
duction. 5.25 to 1.
Transmission___ Standard, 4 forward 1 reverse.
Brakes:
Foot_____ Mechanical, expanding type.
Emergency___ Mechanical, contracting type.

3. TRUCKS. a. Model 94 (1934) 6 x 4 truck. The development of this chassis (fig. 397), in which the rear 4 wheels drive and the 2 front wheels only steer, has been progressing for more than 15 years. In recent years an attempt has been made to distribute this vehicle to commercial users, and prior to 1941 a substantial subsidy was paid to private purchasers. Initial difficulties with the final drive now have been overcome, and the vehicle is reliable, although the power-weight ratio is not good. Ground clearance is unusually high, and one or more auxiliary transmissions can be fitted. More powerful Diesel engines than those mentioned in the specifications now may be in use. The chassis of the Model 94 is the basic one for the Japanese Army's armored car.

Specifications

General:	Type A (gasoline)	Type B (Diesel)
Weight	7,500 pounds.	8,170 pounds.
Length	17 feet 8 inches*	17 feet 8 inches.
Width	6 feet 2 inches	6 feet 2 inches.
Height	7 feet 4 inches	7 feet 4 inches.
Wheelbase	9 feet 2 inches	9 feet 2 inches.
Clearance	11 inches	11 inches.
Tread	4 feet 11 inches	4 feet 11 inches.
Engine:		
Type	Gasoline, 6 cylinder "L" head (side valve) water-cooled.	Diesel, 4 cylinder. Overhead valve, water-cooled.
Horsepower	68 maximum	70 maximum.
Bore	90-mm (3.54 inches)	105-mm (4.13 inches).
Stroke	115-mm (4.53 inches)	140-mm (5.51 inches).
Displacement	4390-cc (268 cubic inches)	4850-cc (296 cubic inches).
Compression ratio	5.25 to 1	17 to 1.
Electrical system	12 volts	12 volts.
Chassis:		
Final drive reduction	8.33 to 1	6.75 to 1.
Transmission	Standard, 4 forward, 1 reverse	Standard, 4 forward, 1 reverse.
Brakes:		
Foot	Mechanical, expanding	Mechanical, expanding.
Hand	Mechanical, contracting	Mechanical, contracting.

*Truck shown in figure 397 measures 16 feet 3 inches long.

Figure 395. Standard Nissan 5-passenger sedan.

Figure 396. Model 93 (1933) staff car.

Figure 397. Model 94 (1934) 6 x 4 truck.

b. Model 97 (1937) Nissan 4 x 2 cab-over-engine truck. The original model, produced in 1937, was a combination of Graham-Paige and Japanese designs. The cab-over-engine design was adopted because of the narrowness of Japanese roads. The whole front axle assembly proved to be too light, however, and great difficulty was encountered in maintaining the alignment of the front wheels to prevent excessive tire wear. An improved model of more conventional design was finally developed, but a very large number of the original models still are being used by the Japanese Army. The power-weight ratio of the Model 97 is not good.

Specifications (104 inch wheelbase model)

General:
    Weight_____ 2,880 pounds.
    Length (chassis) 169.5 inches.
    Width_____ 80 inches.
    Height_____
    Wheelbase_____ 104 inches.
    Clearance_____ 9½ inches.
    Tread_____ 54.7 inches.
    Maximum speed_ 50 miles per hour.
Engine:
    Type_____ Gasoline, 6 cylinder, "L" head (side valve) water-cooled.
    Horsepower_____ 85 maximum.
    Bore_____ 82-mm (3.23 inches).
    Stroke_____ 114-mm (4.49 inches).
    Displacement____ 3670-cc (224 cubic inches).
    Compression ratio_____ 6.5 to 1.
    Electrical system_____ 6 volts.
Chassis:
    Final drive reduction_____ 6.19 to 1.
    Transmission____ Standard, 4 forward 1 reverse.
Brakes:
    Foot_____ Hydraulic.
    Hand____ Mechanical.

c. Model 1 (1941) 4 x 2 Toyoda truck. After disastrous experiments with a truck of their own design, the Toyoda Company finally produced this model (fig. 398), almost an exact copy of the 1939 Chevrolet.
Some manufacturing difficulties have been encountered, and the present power-weight ratio is not considered satisfactory.

Specifications

General:
    Weight_____ 5,500 pounds.
    Length_____ 18 feet 10 inches.
    Width_____ 6 feet 4 inches.
    Height_____ 7 feet 5 inches.
    Wheelbase_____ 15 feet 6 inches.
    Clearance_____ 9 inches.
    Tread_____ 6 feet 1 inch.
Engine:
    Type_____ Gasoline, 6 cylinder, "L" head (side valve) water-cooled.
    Horsepower_____ 78 maximum.
    Bore_____ 3.31 inches.
    Stroke_____ 4.00 inches.
    Displacement___ 206 cubic inches.
    Compression ratio_____ 6 to 1.
    Electrical system_____ 6 volts.
Chassis:
    Final drive reduction_____ 6.167 to 1.
    Transmission____ Standard, 4 forward 1 reverse.
Brakes:
    Foot_____ Hydraulic.
    Hand____ Mechanical.

4. TRAILERS. a. Model 94 (1934) ¾ ton tracked trailer. This trailer (fig. 399) has been designed especially for towing behind the various model tankettes. In China, it has been used extensively for transportation of supplies and ammunition. The body of the trailer appears to be of pressed steel construction, and the suspension con-

Figure 398. Possible Model 1 (1941) 4 x 2 Toyoda truck.

Figure 399. Model 94 (1934) ¾-ton tracked trailer.

sists of 2 bogie wheels with front and rear idlers. Track is similar to that used on the tankette.

b. 2-wheel trailer. This 2-wheel trailer (fig. 400) is designed especially for high-speed transport. It is of metal construction and is equipped with pneumatic-type tires.

5. MOTORCYCLES. a. M o d e l 97 (1937) motorcycle. Japanese military motorcycles (fig. 401) are adaptations of Harley-Davidson designs. Several models, between 1,000-cc and 1,500-cc displacement, have been produced, but it is believed that model 97 is generally in use. Extra large wheels can be fitted to obtain maximum ground

clearance. The design of all types includes provision for a sidecar, which can be fitted with a light machine gun for which at least two different mounts are available. Only minor changes have been made in the original Harley-Davidson designs, and performance is generally satisfactory.

Specifications

General:
Weight_____ 1,100 pounds.
Length_____ 8 feet 6 inches.
Width w/sidecar 5 feet 11 inches.
Height_____ 3 feet 10 inches.
Wheelbase_____ 5 feet 3 inches.
Clearance_____ 8 inches.
Tread_____ 4 feet 1 inch.

Figure 400. 2-wheel trailer.

Specifications—Continued

Engine:
    Type_____ Gasoline, air-cooled, 4 cycle.
    Cylinders_____ 2, set at 45 degree angle.
    Horsepower_____ 25 maximum.
    Bore_____ 90-mm (3.54 inches).
    Stroke_____ 94-mm (3.70 inches).
    Displacement___ 1196-cc (73.0 cubic inches).
    Compression   4.8 to 1.
      ratio.
    Electrical sys- 6 volts.
      tem.
Chassis:
    Transmission___ 3 forward, 1 reverse.
    Brakes_____ Mechanical.

b. Motor tricycles (Sanrinsha). The motor tricycle (fig. 402) has been developed as a commercial freight carrier in Japan since 1930. Many commercial versions exist, with engines ranging from 350 cc to 1,000 cc in displacement. Lighter types have single-chain drive without differentials, whereas heavier types may have shaft or double chain drive, with differentials. Load capacities vary from 300 to 1,000 pounds. A standard three-speed transmission, and reverse, is used. It is believed that the Army adopted whatever types were available, and that no standard army model exists.

Figure 401. Model 97 (1937) motorcycle.

Lighter motor tricycles may have 2-cycle engines, and some 2-cylinder types have been encountered. The usual design, however, is chain driven, with a slow-speed, single-cylinder, 4-cycle engine of about 750-cc displacement.

Specifications

Length_____ 9 feet 6 inches.
Width_____ 4 feet 1 inch.
Wheelbase_____ 6 feet 2 inches.

Figure 402. Motor tricycle.

6. BICYCLES. Japan is one of the world's largest producers of bicycles; in 1940 there were 1,000,000 in Tokyo alone. There is a standard army type, designed along English lines, with front and rear wheel brakes and large wheels. It has been used extensively in the present war.

7. TRANSPORT CARTS. The Japanese Army employs a variety of hand- and horse-drawn carts. Several of these are shown in figures 403, 404, 405.

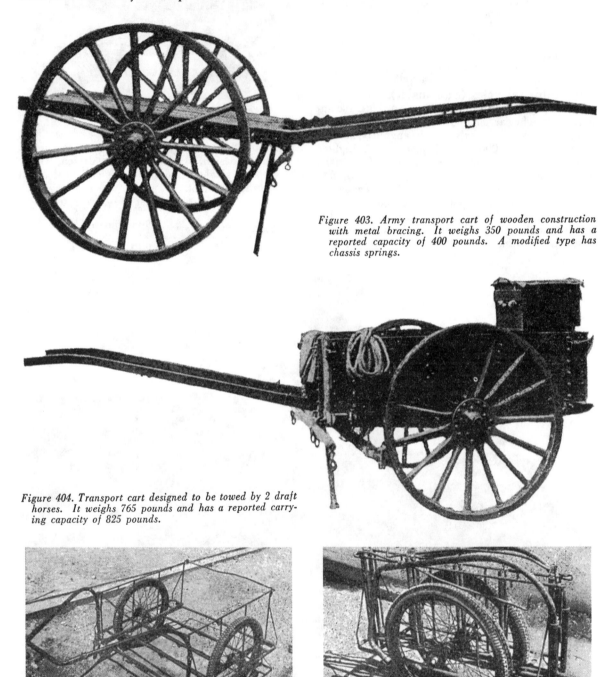

Figure 403. Army transport cart of wooden construction with metal bracing. It weighs 350 pounds and has a reported capacity of 400 pounds. A modified type has chassis springs.

Figure 404. Transport cart designed to be towed by 2 draft horses. It weighs 765 pounds and has a reported carrying capacity of 825 pounds.

Figure 405. Collapsible hand cart of metal construction weighing 100 pounds. It may be pulled by hand or towed by bicycle.

Section VIII. TENTAGE

1. GENERAL. Although the Japanese have excellent octagonal tents, very little use is made of tentage in training or in the field, aside from shelter-half tents. Tents are considered necessary only for medical units and field hospitals, or for troops in regions where other shelter is not available. In inhabited regions, troops are billeted in houses or other buildings; in jungles, native huts frequently are built as soon as the situation becomes sufficiently stabilized. The Japanese are unable to improvise shelters in cold barren regions and therefore house large numbers of men in tents. Even there, every effort is made to bring forward building materials in order to get the men from under canvas as soon as possible.

a. Octagonal tent. The octagonal tent ordinarily houses from 15 to 20 men, although the manual states that 40 can be accommodated in the tropics and 36 in cold regions (fig. 406).
Pyramidal in shape, it is made of comparatively lightweight, closely-woven duck. It is about 24 feet in diameter and uses a 12 foot 9 inch center pole.

b. Use of the octagonal tent in cold climates. (1) In cold regions a second tent of closely-woven, strong, white cotton is suspended inside the main tent and held in place by tie-tapes. The 6 to 8 inches of air space between the tent and tent liner gives good insulation against the cold, elimi-

nates drafts, and provides a second shelter against moisture. Such a tent may be heated efficiently and economically because of these double walls which also permit the use of dim lights at night without danger of violation of blackout discipline.

(2) Two types of stoves are used in these tents, both with grates for burning coal or charcoal. One is a drum stove, 20 to 22 inches in diameter and 24 inches high, with a 6 inch opening in the center of the top for the stovepipe. The second type of stove is cast iron, about 2 feet high, 18 inches deep, and 14 inches wide. Both types can be broken down to save shipping space.

c. Use of the octagonal tent in the tropics. The same tent also is used in the tropics, though to a very limited extent, because native type thatch huts usually are considered superior. A mosquito netting takes the place of the inner liner in tropical climates.

Section IX. MEDICAL EQUIPMENT

1. GENERAL. Japanese military medical equipment is practical, and civilian medical practices have been considered relatively modern.

2. FIELD EQUIPMENT. a. Drugs. Many of the drugs dispensed have been discarded in European and American medical circles, and some preventatives examined have been found to be without effect. Very extensive use is made of drugs

Figure 406. Japanese octagonal tent. (This complete tent weighs 118 pounds, without pegs and poles.)

that have to be injected, and field kits (fig. 407) contain ampoules of a wide variety of sizes and shapes, with no standardization for shipping and packaging. Much use is made of proprietary (patent) medicines, and standard drugs such as quinine, aspirin, and iodine are of course employed. Antimalarials, besides quinine, apparently are being used in increasing quantity. Vaccines and serums are comparable with those in use in other Armies, although there are indications that some of them are not very effective. Vitamin products are used extensively, in the form of powders or tablets (both vitamin B and C) as well as in solutions for injec-

tion. Even medical kits contain such vitamin tablets.

b. Instruments. A very great variety of instruments are in use. Most of these appear to be only fair in quality, of nickel-plated carbon steel instead of stainless steel. The case shown in figure 408 is heavy, lined with nickel-plated copper, and equipped with aluminum instrument racks. The tray can be removed with the instruments in it and used as a sterilizer—a very convenient feature. Blood transfusion kits examined are bulky and fragile, usable only with a system of transfusion discarded some years ago by other Armies. No evidence of the use of blood plasma has been found.

Figure 407. First-aid kit and contents.

1 OCT 44

RESTRICTED

Figure 408. Field instrument case, showing sterilizer tray.

347

598462°—44——23

Chapter XI

UNIFORMS, PERSONAL EQUIPMENT, AND INSIGNIA

1. STANDARD UNIFORMS. a. Types.
Aside from obsolete undress and special officer's
summer dress uniforms, there are 2 distinct types
of regular Japanese uniforms used in temperate
regions: the model 90 (1930) and the model 98
(1938). Both types have woolen winter and cotton
summer versions. There are no government issue
officer's uniforms; therefore, even within each type,
these vary considerably from each other in cut,
color, and material. Various types of Japanese
uniforms, together with items of personal equipment, are illustrated in figure 409 and plates I–VIII.

b. M–1930 coat. The older type M–1930 uniform, still worn by some Japanese soldiers, is made
of heavy, mustard-colored, woolen cloth. The coat
is not unlike the American coat of World War I.
It has a high stand-up collar, to which the insignia
of arm and unit are attached except when in the
field.

c. M–1938 coat. The newer type M–1938 uniform is olive drab in color and is made either of
cotton or wool, depending on the season. The coat
has a turn-down collar and four pockets with flaps.

d. Trousers. In the field the Japanese now ordinarily wear semibreeches, cut high in the waist and
held up by two webbing straps. Wrapped spiral
puttees usually are worn by dismounted enlisted
men. Officers wear puttees, boots, or leather leggings, with either breeches or semibreeches. Long
trousers without cuffs were worn with the M–1930
coat, but were covered with puttees, boots, or leggings in the field.

e. Headgear. (1) *Field cap.* The field cap is
made of olive-drab woolen cloth and is generally
the shape of the head, with a narrow visor of the
same material and a brown leather chin strap. It
has a star along the vertical front seam. This cap
may be worn under the helmet.

(2) *Steel helmet.* Steel helmets are generally
worn during combat. Webbing tapes tie under the
chin or at the back of the neck. The star insignia
also are worn on metal helmets. The steel is of
inferior quality and the helmets are easily pierced
or shattered.

(3) *Service cap.* The service cap is olive drab
in color and similar in shape to that of the United
States Army, but it has a smaller crown and shorter
visor. A red piping is inserted at the outer edge
of the crown and the headband is encircled with a
strip of red felt about 1½ inches wide. At the front
of the headband is a gold star. For officers and
men of the Imperial Guards a semicircular wreath

of leaves is fastened just below the star. The visor
and chin strap are of black leather in standard
military design.

f. Footgear. The dismounted enlisted man
wears russet service shoes of pigskin or cowhide.
The shoes are hobnailed and have a metal rimmed
heel. Men of the mounted services wear russet
riding boots or leather leggings and shoes. Officers'
boots and shoes are similar in design, but are usually
black. Rubber soled black canvas tabi often are
carried as a second pair of shoes, especially in warm
weather. Most, although not all, tabi have split
toes, which serve no special purpose but are characteristic of many Japanese shoes. The soles have
ridge-like cleats under the ball of the foot for better
traction. Japanese socks are typically heelless.
Both woolen and cotton socks are used.

g. Overcoat and cape. The M–1938 overcoat
for enlisted men is made of olive drab woolen material. It is single breasted and has a turn-down
collar. For marching the lower corners of the coat
buttons back behind the side pockets. Equipment
is worn outside over the coat. An older type of
overcoat is double breasted. Officers wear overcoats of similar design, but have sleeve insignia,
consisting of 1, 2, or 3 stripes of dark-brown braid
on or above the cuff to indicate company, field, or
general officers' grades respectively. Sometimes
service dress capes also are worn by officers. All
overcoats and capes are equipped with detachable
hoods which button on. The throat piece, which
gives good closure across the neck, carries 1, 2, or
3 strips as an indication of company, field, or general officer ranks.

h. Raincoats. Cotton raincoats with hoods are
issued to Japanese troops, but in most theaters they
prefer to use the shelter half as rain protection.

i. Clothing worn under the uniform. The
Japanese often wear a breech clout, cotton or cotton
and wool underwear, and cotton or cotton and wool
shirts. Usually only the officers' shirts have collars. In hot climates, the breech clout sometimes
is worn alone.

j. Senninbari (1000-stitch good luck belt).
This is a red sash, made with 1000 stitches and sometimes worn by Japanese soldiers around the waist
under the uniform. It is supposed to confer luck,
courage, and possible immunity from enemy fire.

**2. UNIFORMS FOR SPECIAL ARMS. a.
Tank personnel.** Tank troops wear coveralls of a
material similar to that used in the summer cotton

Figure 409. Japanese captain in winter service uniform.

uniform. The suit which buttons up the front has a turn-down collar and a left breast pocket.

b. Paratroops. The sleeveless cotton paratroop coverall is worn over the uniform and field equipment. It reaches to the knees and snaps tightly around the legs.

c. Individual camouflage. The Japanese rely to a great extent on the individual to improvise his own camouflage methods. Troops are taught how to attach leaves, wisps of grass, and foliage to helmet and body camouflage nets. The body nets, some of which have mottled patterns, are used especially as a drape to conceal the outline of the body. In other cases soldiers sew loops of thread over their clothing to use for attaching foliage.

3. SPECIAL COLD AND HOT WEATHER CLOTHING.

Japanese soldiers have been well trained in the use of cold weather clothing, and the different requirements of each individual are taken into consideration. They are well aware of the "layering" principle, adding or removing a layer of clothing as needed. The Japanese jungle soldier is issued a minimum of clothing and equipment. Open throat cotton shirts, with either short or long sleeves, and cotton trousers, worn with spiral puttees, are the usual clothing. In some areas shorts are worn, but rarely in combat areas.

4. INDIVIDUAL EQUIPMENT. a. Field equipment.

Generally speaking field equipment consists of the following items:

(1) *Pack.* The Japanese have several types of pack, the commonest now is a sack of heavy duck about 13 inches square and 5 inches deep. This is believed to supersede the older pack which was made of cowhide with the hair on. The noncommissioned officers' pack is slightly smaller; a type of officers' pack, with a leather backing is even smaller. Inside, the pack ordinarily contains extra shoes (frequently tabi), a shelter half with poles and pins, extra socks, a towel, soap, toilet articles, sewing kit, first aid dressings, an extra breech clout, and rations for several days. Outside, a blanket or the overcoat is rolled in a horseshoe shape around the pack; a raincoat or the shelter half is attached across the top, and the mess kit is strapped to the back of the pack. The hold-all is frequently used in place of the pack. This is merely a piece of light canvas with cords at both ends for tying it into a roll. It is carried on the back or slung over one shoulder. Aside from regular packs, there are numerous sacks, pouches, and bags which are used for carrying grenades, ammunition, and special equipment. Some of these are made of heavy duck. Others were formerly made of leather or a combination of duck and leather, but now a rubberized fabric, not unlike the material used in belting, is being substituted for leather in all field equipment. This new fabric actually has certain advantages, especially in wet tropical regions where leather deteriorates rapidly. Aside from these special bags, many boxes or bags

used by the Japanese soldier are designed for ease in carrying.

(2) *Mess kit.* The Japanese have the type of mess kit used by the Germans, Russians, and Italians. It consists of an aluminum container, with one or two tray-like dishes nested beneath the cover. In temperate and cold regions enough food for several meals is cooked and carried in the mess kit, ready to eat.

(3) *Shelter half.* Although small by American or British standards, the shelter half is very serviceable. As a raincape it provides excellent protection against wetness and is preferred by many Japanese soldiers to the issue raincoat. A cord is attached to the middle of one end so that the shelter half can be suspended from the shoulders and tied

Figure 410. Japanese soldier with full pack.

under the chin. Loops through the eyelets on one of the sides then may be slipped through the eyelets on the opposite side to close it securely in front. Two of the corners rest approximately elbow high, allowing the arms freedom of movement. The shelter half also is used as a ground sheet, or to roll up in for protection in a foxhole. It can be pitched as a tent, either alone or in combination with varying numbers of others. A standard method of pitching requires 28 shelter halves.

(4) *Canteen.* The canteen, which hangs from a shoulder strap and rests on the right hip in a network of webbing straps, is made of aluminum and painted brown. There are 1 pint and 2½ pint sizes.

(5) *Ammunition belt and pouches.* Ammunition pouches are worn on a belt around the waist, two smaller pouches in front and a larger one in the rear below the pack. On the side of the larger pouch there is a small metal or plastic can with

gun grease. The bayonet frog is also worn on the ammunition belt. Formerly all this equipment was made of leather, but recently it has been made of rubberized fabric.

(6) *Entrenching tool.* Entrenching shovels and picks carried by the Japanese are in the ratio of 2 shovels to 1 pick. The shovel has a short wooden handle which is removed from the blade when it is attached to the pack. A rope is attached from the upper end of the handle to a hole in one of the upper corners of the blade so that when the shovel is assembled it can be slung over the shoulder.

b. Cold weather equipment. (1) *Sleeping gear.* Even in cold climates the Japanese are unacquainted with the sleeping bag. Instead, woolen blankets which have an exceedingly high percentage of cotton are used. The inefficiency of this sleeping gear is clearly demonstrated by the fact that seven blankets were issued to each Japanese soldier after the landings on Attu. The Japanese also use a cotton filled sleeping pad about 3 x 5 feet in size when sleeping in barracks or tents. This does not, however, appear to be part of field equipment. In the field Japanese soldiers ordinarily take shelter in foxholes, covering themselves merely with their shelter halves.

(2) *Mess kit and canteen covers.* Most field equipment used in cold climates is the same as that used elsewhere. However, because of the possibility of food or liquids freezing, snug fitting mess kit and canteen insulation covers, made of insulating material such as kapok or pile, are provided.

(3) *Skis.* The Japanese use two types of skis, the standard normal length ski and the short glacial ski. Although the standard skis are of orthodox construction, the quality is generally quite poor. The short glacial skis, averaging about 4½ feet in length, are of fairly heavy construction; they are inflexible but easy to carry. Experienced skiers generally use the long skis, while novices are given the shorter one. A simple, but rather inefficient, metal and leather binding is used with both types of skis. The Japanese do not issue a special ski boot but simply adopt a standard service shoe by putting steel protectors on the edges of the sole and a special plate on the heel to hold the heel-strap in place. Such improvisation probably gives the skier only limited control over his skis. Ski poles are made of light cane. Plain web straps serve as ski climbers for uphill traction.

(4) *Snowshoes.* The snowshoes used by the Japanese are of standard European type, oval and smaller than the usual American bearpaw snowshoe.

(5) *Ice creepers.* Although it is believed that the Japanese do not have specific mountaineering equipment, such as used by German, Italian, British, or American mountain troops, they do have ice creepers which are strapped to the sole of boots for better traction. These are T-shaped with a spike at each of the three ends.

c. Special tropical and jungle equipment.
(1) *Tree climbers.* Extremely light weight tree climbers (fig. 411) are used by snipers. These consist of a framework of metal rods tied under the instep by means of a long cord. There are two sets of spikes which always point straight down from the sole of the foot. The two spikes on the outside of the foot are about an inch long, while the inner ones are only about ½ inch long.

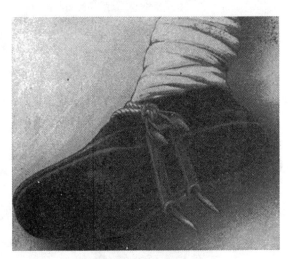

Figure 411. Tree climber.

(2) *Water purification.* (*a*) *Water filter-purifier.* This item is issued to Japanese troops in the field for purifying drinking water. It is not considered safe enough for use by Allied troops. The use is illustrated in figure 412. Two chemically treated wads, one either green or blue and the other white, are located on the inside of the plastic body. The end of the rubber tube is placed in the mouth, and untreated water is sucked past the chemically treated wads. When the water begins to flow, the tube is placed into a canteen or other receptacle and allowed to siphon. The cotton wadding must be replaced after 5 canteens have been filled.

(*b*) *Water purification kit.* Phials of water purification chemicals and a measuring spoon, contained in a flat tin, are provided as additional equipment for use in an emergency or when large quantities of impurities are found in the water.

(3) *Protection against insects.* (*a*) *Mosquito headnet.* The Japanese headnet usually has spring wires at the top and bottom, connected by a third piece of spring wire in the form of a spiral. This frame keeps the rather coarse green netting off the face when it is being worn, but permits it to be collapsed flat for easy carrying. The net also is used to camouflage the head and neck.

(*b*) *Mosquito gloves.* Lightweight cotton mittens are used by the Japanese to protect the hands from mosquito bites. They have slits in the palms so that the fingers can be freed to fire a rifle.

Figure 412. (Above) Japanese troops using the water filter purifier, (Below) illustrations showing components and methods of operation.

(c) *Insect repellent.* The Japanese insect repellent consists of a cream the essential constituent of which is citronella.

(d) *Mosquito bars.* The mosquito bar is used in rear areas.

5. INSIGNIA, DECORATIONS, AND AWARDS. a. Insignia.
Insignia of grade are worn on the collars of coats when coats are worn, or on the collars of shirts when no coats are worn. When wearing heavy cold weather clothing, insignia of rank generally are worn on either sleeve. Insignia of branch or service usually are worn on the right breast of either coats or shirts. However, in combat areas, neither officers nor men ordinarily will wear any insignia of rank or branch of service. Commanders of infantry often will wear some special insignia, such as crossed sashes of dark color, to enable their men to distinguish them. Recruits wear a white patch, sewed or pinned on the left breast of coat or shirt, on which is written their name and unit. In combat areas, all enlisted men may wear such a patch, containing general information and occasionally, some mark of rank.

b. Decorations and awards. Orders of merit and decorations were created in 1875 and supplemented in later years for the purpose of recognizing and rewarding persons who render distinguished and meritorious services to the state. The principal decorations available to military personnel are as follows:

(1) *The Order of the Golden Kite.* This decoration is purely military and is awarded for conspicuous service in operations against a foreign country. There are seven classes of this order, each carrying a life annuity. Enlisted personnel may be advanced only to the sixth order.

(2) *The Order of Rising Sun.* This decoration is not limited to the military, and is awarded to those who have rendered meritorious services. There are eight classes of this order, of which two are available to enlisted personnel. Foreigners occasionally are awarded this decoration.

(3) *The Order of the Sacred Treasure.* This decoration is awarded in both peace and war and is not limited to the military. It is awarded for long service with good conduct and does not carry a life annuity. There are eight classes, of which two are for enlisted men.

(4) In addition to these three principal decorations, medals for distinguished service (Kunkō Shō), meritorious service (Kunrō Shō), and ex-ceptional service (Korō Shō) are issued. For those whose services are "not inconsiderable," but are not qualified for these three medals, a monetary award may be granted. Campaign medals, good conduct medals, and badges for proficiency in different branches of the service also are awarded.

(5) The following awards are made:

(*a*) Diploma of merit. This may be awarded to either a unit as a whole or to individuals for distinguished service in front of the enemy.

(*b*) Wound badge. This is granted to anyone who, as the result of being wounded in action, thereby is entitled to an increase in pension in accordance with pension regulations.

(*c*) Medal for next of kin of those killed in action. This is also issued to the next of kin of anyone who has died within three years after contracting an illness resulting from active service.

(*d*) Other awards available to noncommissioned officers and privates are:

> Good conduct badge (Kinkō Shō).
> Good conduct certificate (Zenkō Shōsho).
> Diligence badge (Seikin Shō).
> Victory medal (Senshō Kishō).

CHAPTER XII

CONVENTIONAL SIGNS AND ABBREVIATIONS

Section I. INTRODUCTION

1. SOURCES. a. The geographic signs included under paragraph 1 of the next section are selected from those appearing on maps of the Japanese Empire prepared by the Imperial Land Survey Department. Variant or supplementary signs used by the Japanese Hydrographic Office are listed in paragraph 2.

b. The military signs and abbreviations included under sections III and IV have been selected from Supplement No. 1 of Japanese Field Service Regulations (Military Signs), August 1940 (*Sakusen Yomurei Furoku Sono Ichi, Guntai Fugo*), and are supplemented by information from other sources. The grouping of the Army signs follows that adopted by the Japanese; the Navy and Special Naval Landing Force signs are arranged arbitrarily. The abbreviations are arranged alphabetically.

2. GENERAL PRINCIPLES. a. Military signs. (1) *General.* A study of the lists of Japanese military signs will reveal certain basic signs and principles, a knowledge of which will aid in the interpretation of the signs. It is emphasized, however, that the Japanese do not exhibit a great degree of consistency in the formation of their signs. Furthermore certain signs considered obsolete may recur, and individual initiative in the drawing of extemporary signs, with explanatory notes if considered necessary, is condoned by the Japanese.

(2) *Basic signs.* Examples of basic signs follow: ⊬, field artillery; ⌐, cavalry; ⋀, engineers; ⋈, air (Army); ⌣, air (Navy); ◇ or ◊, tank; ⌂, shipping; ⌐, signal; ⌁, radio; ⌒, gas; ⋀ (placed over the rest of the sign), established depot.

(3) *Headquarters.* Headquarters, down to the battalion level inclusive, usually are distinguished by flags and/or circles. Brigade or group headquarters, however, are indicated by six-pointed stars ✡. The appropriate basic sign may be added to indicate the arm. For example: ⊕, area army headquarters; ⊙, division headquarters; ✡, cavalry brigade headquarters; ⊡, infantry battalion headquarters; ⊕, field artillery regimental headquarters.

(4) *Units.* The normal method of designating units is by adding a rectangle below the sign (in full or abbreviated) of the particular arm or weapon. For example: ⊥, medium mortar. ⊤, medium mortar unit; ⋀, engineer (basic sign), ⌂ engineer unit. (An exception to this principle should be noted: ⊬, field artillery, ⊞, field artillery ammunition train.)

(5) *Motorization.* In order to show that a unit is motorized, two rings (representing wheels) are added either below or at the side of the particular sign. For example: ⊞, field artillery ammunition train, ⊞, field artillery ammunition train, motorized.

(6) *Compound signs.* Basic signs such as those described above may be combined into compound signs. For example: ⋈ antiaircraft artillery regimental headquarters.

(7) *Classification.* An appropriate symbol, number, or abbreviation (either English letters, "kana", or characters) may be added to a sign when it is necessary further to classify the unit or equipment indicated by the sign. For example: ⌁, mobile ground radio station, ⌁₃, No. 3 type mobile ground radio station; ⌂, ship (general), ⌂水 water supply ship (the character included

means "water"), , armed ship; motor truck, repair truck, truck loaded with machine guns; , tank , light tank. The most common of such examples are noted in the list of signs.

(8) *Boundaries, directions.* Boundaries of districts or limits of fortified areas are shown by lines; directions of shooting, points of attack, and changes of direction of troops are shown by arrows.

b. Military abbreviations. (1) English letters, both capital and small, normally are used in military abbreviations.

(2) The basic army abbreviations appear in most cases to be derived from German words and, in the case of most recent additions, romanized forms of Japanese words. For example: BA (Bergartillerie), mountain artillery; SeE (*Sempaku eiseitai hombu*), shipping medical unit headquarters.

(3) Naval abbreviations are derived largely from English words and less frequently from romanized forms of Japanese words. For example: BC, battlecruiser; cdg, combined destroyer group; AtB (Attached "butai"), attached force.

c. Numbers. The numbers of units and weapons are shown by placing the appropriate figure, either Arabic or Japanese, with necessary additions, in parentheses after the particular sign or abbreviation. For example (2), two airplanes; A (三大) three battalions of field artillery (the two characters in the parentheses are, respectively, "three" and the first character of the Japanese word for "battalion").

d. Identification. (1) When it is necessary to distinguish between enemy and friendly forces, the Japanese show signs for the former in red, for the latter in blue.

(2) In indicating the organizational numbers of units, Arabic numerals usually are used for all units except battalions, for which Roman numerals are used. The number of the lower unit precedes that of the higher organization of which it is a part, the two being separated by a slanting line. For example: 18 P, the 18th Engineers; III/2i, 3d Battalion of the 2d Infantry Regiment. II St/1A, 2d Battalion Ammunition Train of the 1st Field Artillery Regiment.

(3) Platoons and sections usually are shown as fractions of a company. For example: 1/4 2/1P, 1 platoon of the 2d Company of the 1st Engineer Regiment; 1/16 2/5i, 1 section of the 2d Company of the 5th Infantry Regiment.

(4) Missing units of an organization are indicated by numerals, preceded by a minus sign, in parentheses. Units attached to an organization are shown similarly with a plus instead of a minus sign. For example: 2i (−7.8), 2d Infantry Regiment less the 7th and 8th Companies; 1(+iP)/2i, 1st Company, plus a labor unit, of the 2d Infantry Regiment.

Section II. GEOGRAPHIC SIGNS

1. IMPERIAL LAND SURVEY DEPARTMENT SIGNS.

Density of Construction in Urban Areas

Dense	Moderate	Sparse

Sign	Description	Sign	Description
	Navy Lookout Tower		Stumps
	Factory		Isolated Trees
	Bank		Chimney.
	Powder Magazine	96,1	Triangulation Point
	Water Wheel or Mill	365,37	Secondary Control Point
	Generating Plant	423,42	Bench Mark
	Masonry Wall	32,5	Spot Elevation
	Fences		Old Battlefield
	Bamboo Fences		Spring
	Stone Wall		Tomb
	Earthen Wall		Castle Site
	Hedge		Volcano
	Cemetery		Mineral Spring
	Ditches		Material Dump
	Shrine Gate.		Mine
	Stone Lantern		Boundary Marker
	Monument		Shrine
	Statue		Temple
	Signpost		Grave
	Stone Steps		Pagoda
	Crane		Church
	Oil Well		Japanese Government Building
	Mileage Marker		Foreign Government Building
			Military Reservation
			Naval Reservation

(All above Sea Level)

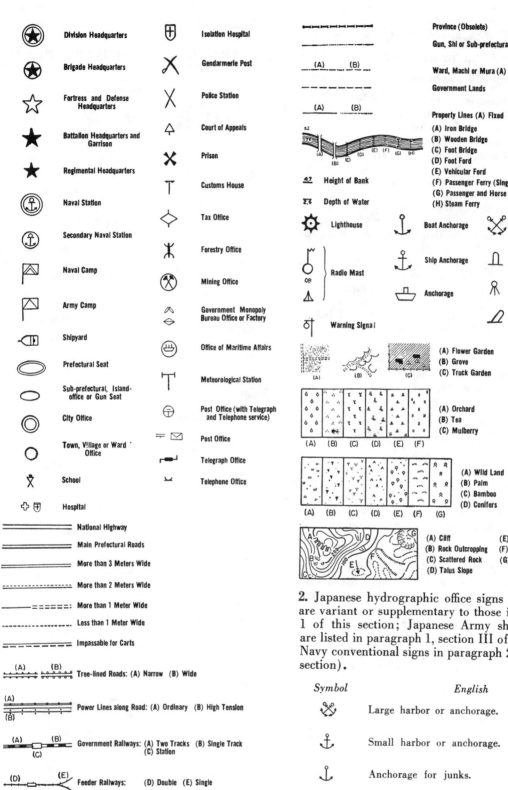

Symbol		English
	Division Headquarters	

2. Japanese hydrographic office signs (signs listed are variant or supplementary to those in paragraph 1 of this section; Japanese Army shipping signs are listed in paragraph 1, section III of this chapter, Navy conventional signs in paragraph 2 of the same section).

Symbol	English
	Large harbor or anchorage.
	Small harbor or anchorage.
	Anchorage for junks.
	Ship entrance.
	Ship anchorage with facilities.

Symbol	English	Symbol	English
⚓	Ship anchorage.		Beacons, flashing—*Continued*.
⚓	Possible anchorage.		Submarine cable.
⚓	Emergency anchorage.		Radio station.
⚓	Possible emergency anchorage.		Radio broadcasting station.
⊛ ★ ●	Lighthouse.		Obstruction.
	Lightship.	○	Tank (oil, gas, or water).
	Lightbuoy.		Race track.
	Mooring buoy.		Golf links.
	Buoys (in general drawn to represent the actual shape of the buoy).		Temple, shrine.
★ ★	Light beacon, fixed.		Imperial palace, garden, shrine, or mausoleum.
Beacons, flashing:			Coast line.
☆w	White.		Drying coast line.
★r	Red.		Sand beach.
★g	Green.		Steep coast line.
★a	Amber.		Reef.
	Lighting facilities.		10-fathom line (1 dot).
◎	Government landing field.		20-fathom line (2 dots).
○	Commercial landing field.		50-fathom line (5 dots).
⊤	Emergency landing field.		100-fathom line (10 dots).
	Seaplane anchorage with facilities.		Flood tide.
	Seaplane anchorage.	→	Ebb tide.
	Possible seaplane anchorage.	3–4 Kt	Ocean current (direction and speed).
	Emergency seaplane anchorage.		River and stream.
○	Marine bureau.		Bridge.
⊙	Coast guard station.		Ferry.
◓	Lifeboat station.		Waterfall.
⊕	Observation point.		Lake.
			Swamp and marsh.
			Fortified and aviation prohibited zone.
			Civil air line.
			High voltage transmission line.

Section III. MILITARY SIGNS

NOTE. The arrangement of the Army signs follows that adopted by the Japanese, and is outlined below. The arrangement of the Navy and Special Naval Landing Force signs is arbitrary.

1. ARMY SIGNS. a. Common to all arms—Continued.

Symbol	Japanese	English
	Butai no shudan	Group (mass) of troops.
	Fuzokutai	Attached unit.
	Butai no shudan chiiki	Area containing groups (masses) of troops.
	Tekidanto / Tekidanju	Grenade discharger. / Grenade rifle.
	Keikikanju	Light machine gun.
	Kikanju	Machine gun (heavy).
	Kikanjutai	Machine gun unit.
	Kikanho	Machine cannon.
	Kikanhotai	Machine cannon unit.
	Jidoho	Automatic gun.
	Jidohotai	Automatic gun unit.
	Sokushaho	Antitank gun.
	Sokushahotai	Antitank gun unit.
	Keihakugekiho	Light trench mortar.
	Keihakugekihotai	Light trench mortar unit.
	Chuhakugekiho	Medium trench mortar.
	Chuhakugekihotai	Medium trench mortar unit.

1. ARMY SIGNS. a. Common to all arms.

Symbol	Japanese	English
	Daihon-ei	Imperial Headquarters.
	Sogun shireibu	General Headquarters.
	Homengun shireibu	Area army headquarters.
	Gun shireibu	Army headquarters.
	Gundan shireibu	Corps headquarters (not part of the Japanese Army organization.)
	Shidan shireibu	Division headquarters.

NOTE. If in the above signs △ and △ are used instead of ⊙ and ○ respectively, the headquarters concerned are engaged in active operations and the signs represent the positions of command posts (shireijo).

Symbol	Japanese	English
	Johojo	Information (message) center.
	Chutaicho	Company commander.
	Shoko / Shotaicho	Commissioned officer—platoon commander.
	Kashikan / Buntaicho	Noncommissioned officer. Section leader.
	Hei	Private soldier.

NOTE. NCO's and privates may be classified by the addition of appropriate "kana," numbers, or signs, e. g.: ⊕, liaison NCO; ⊕, runner; ♩, bugler; ③, No. 3 man in section; ○, private in charge of grenade discharger.

Symbol	Japanese	English
	Kihei no hei	Cavalry private.

1. ARMY SIGNS. a. Common to all arms—Continued.

Symbol	Japanese	English
	Gasu kumo	Gas cloud.
	Dokuen	Toxic or poison smoke.
	Shukuei butai	Quartered or billeted troops: 2d Bn of the 4th Inf Regt.
	Chugun butai	Troops stationed for a period; garrison troops: 2d Co of the 1st Inf Regt, 2d Bn of the 1st Field Arty Regt.
		NOTE. The boundary of a billeting area is shown by a thick continuous line. The symbols of the units are written inside or outside.
	Keikyu shugojo	Alarm post.
	Keikyu daishugojo	Grand alarm post.
	Mizu kofujo	Water distributing center.
	Imbajo	Place for watering animals.
	Bakeijo	Horse lines.
	Kikanjusho	Machine gun depot.
	Hosho (yaho)	Gun depot (field artillery).
		NOTE: Depots for other types of artillery are shown by the appropriate symbol within a rectangle.
	Shasho	Vehicle depot.
	Jidoshasho	Motor transport depot.
	Bunsho / Kashisho	Sentry group (infantry or cavalry) with noncommissioned officer in charge.
	Sanninsho	Sentry group of 3 men.

1. ARMY SIGNS. a. Common to all arms—Continued.

Symbol	Japanese	English
	Juhakugekiho	Heavy trench mortar.
	Juhakugekihotai	Heavy trench mortar unit.
	Shomeito	Searchlight (general); groundflare (aero).
	Yasen shomeitai	Field searchlight unit.
	Kamo	Fire net; area covered by fire.
	Karyoku jumbi no ichi-rei	Examples of fire preparation: 2 Fld Arty Cos, 1 Med Arty Co; 2 MG Cos, 1 Regt Gun Co, 1 Bn Gun Co.
	Kogeki no juten	Main point of attack.
	Shageki no hoko (mokuhyo)	Direction of fire (target, objective).
	Zenshin hoko nado	Direction of advance, etc.
	Gasu butai hombu	Chemical warfare unit headquarters.
	Gasu butai	Gas unit.
		NOTE. Sandoku (poison spreading), shodoku (disinfecting), and jodoku (deontaminating) units are shown respectively by
	Gasu-gakari shoko	Officer in charge of gas.
	Gasu-gakari kashikan	NCO in charge of gas.
	Gasu-gakari hei	Private in charge of gas.
	Sandoku chiiki	Contaminated area.
	Emmaku	Smoke screen.

1. ARMY SIGNS. a. Common to all arms—Continued.

Symbol	Japanese	English
	Nininsho	Sentry group of 2 men.
	Tansho	Single sentry.
	Kashikan wo cho to seru sekko	Patrol with noncommissioned officer in charge.
	Tembosho	Observation group.
	Kotsu seirihan	Traffic control section.

b. Infantry.

Symbol	Japanese	English
	Hohei ryodan shireibu	Infantry brigade headquarters.
	Hohei rentai hombu	Infantry regimental headquarters.
	Hohei daitai hombu	Infantry battalion headquarters.
	Hohei butai	Infantry unit.
	Hohei butai (kogun taikei)	Infantry unit (in march formation.).
	Hohei butai no sokai	Deployment of an infantry unit.
	Dai-issen	Front line.
	Rentaiho	Regimental infantry gun.
	Rentaihotai	Regimental infantry gun unit.
	Daitaiho	Battalion infantry gun.

1. ARMY SIGNS. b. Infantry—Continued.

Symbol	Japanese	English
	Daitaihotai	Battalion infantry gun unit.
	Heisha hoheiho	Infantry gun.
	Kyokusha hoheiho	Infantry mortar.
	Sagyotai	Working party; pioneer unit.
	Hohei rentai (ryodan) tsushintai (han)	Infantry regiment (brigade) signal unit (section).
	Senryo chiiki	Occupied area.

c. Cavalry.

Symbol	Japanese	English
	Kihei shudan (shidan) shireibu	Cavalry group (division) headquarters.
	Kihei ryodan shireibu	Cavalry brigade headquarters.
	Kihei rentai hombu	Cavalry regimental headquarters.
	Kihei butai	Cavalry unit.
	Kihei butai no sokai	Deployment of a cavalry unit.
	Dai-issen	Front line (cavalry).
	Joba sankai butai	Deployment of mounted cavalry.
	Toho sampei	Dismounted skirmishers.
	Tohobutai	Dismounted unit.

1. ARMY SIGNS. c. Cavalry—Continued.

Symbol	Japanese	English
	Teuma	Led horses.
	Kihei rentai (ryodan) (shudan) tsushintai (han).	Cavalry regiment (brigade) (group) signal unit (section).

d. Artillery.

Symbol	Japanese	English
	Hohei shireibu	Artillery headquarters.
	Hoheidan (hoheiryodan) shireibu.	Artillery group (brigade) headquarters.
	Yahohei rentai hombu	Field artillery regimental headquarters.
	Yahohei daitai hombu	Field artillery battalion headquarters.
	Yahohei butai	Field artillery unit.
	Yahohei no danretsu	Field artillery ammunition train.
	Yahohei no horetsu	Line of guns (field artillery).
	Yahohei no renrakuhan	Field artillery liaison section.

NOTE. Horse, mountain, medium, and heavy artillery are represented by the signs ⊬, ⊬, ⊬, ⊬ respectively, instead of ⊬.

Guns and howitzers are represented by the addition of ∧ and ● respectively to the top of the appropriate sign.

Symbol	Japanese	English
	Choshatei yaho	Long-range field gun.
	Juryu	10-cm (105-mm) howitzer.
	Juka	10-cm (105-mm) gun.
	Jugoryu	15-cm (150-mm) howitzer.
	Kikyutai	Balloon unit.

1. ARMY SIGNS. d. Artillery—Continued.

Symbol	Japanese	English
	Kikyu jinchi	Balloon position.
	Kikyu shoto ichi	Balloon ascension point.
	Shikihan (shiki shotai)	Command section (platoon).
	Hoheidan (ryodan) kansokujo (hojo kansokujo).	Artillery group (brigade) observation post (auxiliary observation post).
	Rentai kansokujo (hojo kansokujo).	Regimental observation post (auxiliary observation post).
	Daitai kansokujo (hojo kansokujo).	Battalion observation post (auxiliary observation post).
	Chutai kansokujo (hojo kansokujo).	Company observation post (auxiliary observation post).

NOTE. Observation posts in general are represented by a blank triangle △.

Symbol	Japanese	English
	Hyotei no tame no hojo kansokujo.	Auxiliary observation post for plotting.
	Hyotei shikijo	Plotting control post.
	Hohei johotai honbu	Artillery intelligence unit headquarters.
	Hohei johotai	Artillery intelligence unit.
	Hyoteitai	Plotting unit.
	Hyoteisho	Plotting station.
	Shotai hyoteisho	Platoon plotting station.
	Chutai hyoteisho	Company plotting station.
	Ongentai	Sound locator unit.

1. ARMY SIGNS. d. Artillery—Continued.

Symbol	Japanese	English
	Cho-onsho	Listening post.
	Cho-on shusho	Main listening post.
	Cho-on zenshinsho	Forward listening post.
	Sokuchitai	Land survey unit.
	Kisosokuchi no kijunten	Base point of a primary survey.
	Jinchi oyobi zenchi no sokuchi no kijunten.	Base point of a military survey (position and advanced position).
	Kisen	Base line.
	Hoko kisen	Directional base line.

e. Engineers.

Symbol	Japanese	English
	Kohei shireibu	Engineer headquarters.
	Kohei rentai hombu	Engineer regimental headquarters.
	Kohei butai	Engineer unit. NOTE. The denomination of a unit is shown within the rectangle, e. g. [symbol] "A" unit, [symbol] "B" unit, [symbol] battalion, [symbol] company.
	Gakyo zairyo chutai	Bridging matériel company.
	Toka zairyo chutai	River crossing matériel company.
	Yasen sokuryotai	Field survey unit.
	(?) Shuteicho	Boat (landing craft) commander.
	(?) Shutei kohei	Boat (landing craft) engineer.
	(?) Rikujo kohei	Land engineer.

1. ARMY SIGNS. f. Air, antiaircraft, and meteorological.

Symbol	Japanese	English
	Kokugun shireibu	Air army headquarters.
	Hikoshidan shireibu	Air division headquarters.
	Hiko(ryo)dan shireibu	Air brigade headquarters.
	Hikosentai hombu. / Hikorentai hombu.	Air regimental headquarters.
		NOTE. If necessary the type of aircraft is shown. [symbol] represents a fighter regimental headquarters.
	Hikochutaicho	Air company commander.
		NOTE. If necessary the type of aircraft is shown.
	Hiko(bu)tai	Air unit.
		NOTE. If necessary the type of aircraft is shown.
	Hikoki	Aircraft.
		NOTE. Short horizontal lines on the tail represent the number of seats, for example [symbol] 2-seater aircraft.
	Teisatsuki (shireibu)	Reconnaissance aircraft (headquarters).
	Teisatsuki (gun)	Reconnaissance aircraft (Army).
	Teisatsuki (chokkyo)	Reconnaissance aircraft (direct cooperation).
	Sentoki	Fighter aircraft.
	Bakugekiki (Keibaku)	Light bomber.
	Bakugekiki (Jubaku)	Heavy bomber.
	Bakugekiki (Embaku)	Long-range bomber.
	Hikosentai ijo no kuchutaikei	Formations (tactical) of air regiment and above.

1. ARMY SIGNS. f. Air, antiaircraft, and meteorological—Con.

Symbol	Japanese	English
	Kohoyo hoko tanchiki	Navigation direction finder.
	Yakan koro hyoshiki	Night beacon.
	Musen koro hyoshiki	Radio beacon.
	Hikojo	Airfield.
	NOTE. The type of airfield and the type of aircraft for which it is suitable is shown by the appropriate sign or abbreviation.	
	Chakurikujo	Landing field.
	Chakuriku shi uru chiiki	Area within which landings can be made (by fighters).
	Yasen koku hokyusho	Field air supply depot.
	Yasen koku hokyu shisho mata wa shutchojo	Field air supply branch depot.
	Yasen koku shurisho	Field air repair depot.
	Yasen koku shuribusho mata wa shutchojo	Field air repair branch depot.
	Bokubutai shireibu	Antiaircraft defense unit headquarters.
	Koshaho rentai hombu	Antiaircraft artillery regimental headquarters.
	Koshaho daitai hombu	Antiaircraft artillery battalion headquarters.
	Koshahotai	Antiaircraft artillery unit.

1. ARMY SIGNS. f. Air, antiaircraft, and meteorological—Con.

NOTE. To show the type of aircraft the appropriate symbol is included. Thus △ represents formations of air regiment and above, comprising light bombers.

Symbol	Japanese	English
	Hikochutai no kuchutaikei	Formations (tactical) of air companies.
	Hikohentai no heimenzu	Formation of aircraft in a horizontal plane.
	Hikohentai no sokumenzu	Formation of aircraft in a vertical plane.
	Kodo san zen metoru ni okeru keibakugekiki no sanki hentai.	Formation of 3 light bombers at a height of 3,000 meters.
	Koku chiku shireibu	Air sector headquarters.
	Hikojo daitai hombu	Airfield battalion headquarters.
	Hikojo chutaicho	Airfield company commander.
	Koku chiku butai	Air sector unit.
	Koku tsushin hombu	Air signal headquarters.
	Koku tsushintai hombu	Air signal unit headquarters.
	Koku tsushintai	Air signal unit.
	Koku johotai hombu	Air intelligence unit headquarters.
	Koku johotai	Air intelligence unit.
	Koku johohan	Air intelligence section.
	Kosokutai	Direction finder unit.

1. ARMY SIGNS. f. Air, antiaircraft, and meteorological—Con.

Symbol	Japanese	English
	Koshahotai jinchi	Antiaircraft artillery position.
	Shoku butai hombu	Searchlight unit headquarters.
	Shokutai	Searchlight unit.
	Shokuto	Searchlight.
	Kuchu cho-onki	Sound locator.
	Dempa tanshingi	Radar.
	Boku kikyu	Barrage balloon.
	Kosha kikanju	Antiaircraft machine gun.
	Kosha kikanho	Antiaircraft machine cannon.

NOTE. In connection with antiaircraft defense if it be necessary to distinguish between field troops and troops protecting important strategic points, the latter are represented by a stroke under the appropriate sign, e. g.

Symbol	Japanese	English
	Yasen kisho tokatsu kikan	Field meteorological control organization.
	Yasen kisho butai	Field meteorological unit.
	Kisho hosojo	Meteorological broadcasting station.
	Kisho chutai	Meteorological company.
	Kisho kansokuhan	Meteorological observation section.

1. ARMY SIGNS. f. Air, antiaircraft, and meteorological—Con.

Symbol	Japanese	English
	Kisho hojokansokujo	Auxiliary meteorological observation post.
	Koso kisho kansokuhan	High-altitude meteorological observation section.
	Koso kisho hojokansokujo	High altitude auxiliary meteorological observation post.
	Taiku kanshisho	Antiaircraft observation post.

g. Armored Forces.

Symbol	Japanese	English
	Kikogun shireibu	Mechanized army headquarters.
	Sensha shidan shireibu	Armored division headquarters.
	Kido shidan shireibu	Motorized division headquarters.
	Sensha ryodan shireibu	Tank brigade headquarters.
	Sensha rentai hombu	Tank regimental headquarters.
	Sensha (tai)	Tank (unit).
	Sensha kogun taikei	Tank march formation.
	Sensha sokai taikei	Tank deployment formation (arrow indicates direction of advance).
	Sensha sento taikei	Tank battle formation.
	Sensha chutaicho	Tank company commander.

1. ARMY SIGNS. g. Armored Forces—Continued.

Symbol	Japanese	English
	Sensha shotaicho	Tank platoon commander.
	Keisensha (tai)	Light tank (unit).
	Chusensha (tai)	Medium tank (unit).
	Jusensha (tai)	Heavy tank (unit).

NOTE. The equipment of individual vehicles is shown by the addition of appropriate signs, e. g., represents a tank equipped with radio.

To indicate a cavalry unit is added to the top portion of the sign, e. g.

Symbol	Japanese	English
	Jisoho (tai)	Self-propelled artillery (unit).
	Hosensha (tai)	Tank destroyer (unit).
	Keninho (tai)	Truck or tractor-drawn artillery (unit).
	Sokosha (tai)	Armored car (unit).
	Suiriku ryoyo sensha (tai)	Amphibian tank (unit).
	Soko sagyo sensha (tai)	Armored construction tank (unit).
	Rikisakusha (tai)	Generator car (unit).
	Soko heisha (tai)	Armored troop carrier (unit).
	Sokiteisha (tai)	Half-track reconnaissance car (unit).
	Senshatai no danretsu	Tank unit ammunition train.
	Senshatai no seibi	Tank unit maintenance.

1. ARMY SIGNS. g. Armored Forces—Continued.

Symbol	Japanese	English
	Jidoteisha	Scout car.
	Shuri jidosha	Maintenance car.

NOTE. When it is necessary to differentiate between light and heavy, is used for the heavy.

Symbol	Japanese	English
	Joyosha	Passenger car.
	Kogata joyosha	Small model passenger car.
	Shikisha	Command car.
	Sokusha	Side-car.
	Jidokasha	Motortruck.

NOTE. The type of truck or the load carried may be shown by appropriate characters or signs, e. g. , repair truck; , truck loaded with machine guns.

Symbol	Japanese	English
	Jidokasha kusha	Empty motortruck.
	Sokikasha	Caterpillar truck or tractor.
	Sosakutai	Reconnaissance unit.
	Sosakutai hombu	Reconnaissance unit headquarters.
	Soko tsushintai	Armored signal unit.
	Soko tsushintai hombu	Armored signal unit headquarters.

h. Field works.

Symbol	Japanese	English
	Sampeigo, kotsugo	Firing trench, communication trench.

NOTE. Portions of the communication trench defended by fire are shown by a thick line.

1. ARMY SIGNS. i. Railway.

Symbol	Japanese	English
	Tetsudo yuso shireibu	Railway transport headquarters.
	Tetsudo yuso shireibu shibu	Railway transport headquarters, branch office.
	Teishajo shireibu	Railway station headquarters.
	Teishajo shireibu shibu	Railway station headquarters, branch office.
	Yasen tetsudo shireibu	Field railway headquarters.
	Yasen tetsudo shireibu shibu	Field railway headquarters, branch office.
	Tetsudo kambu	Railway inspectorate.
	Tetsudo rentai hombu	Railway regimental headquarters.
	Tetsudo daitai hombu	Railway battalion headquarters.
	Tetsudotai	Railway unit.
	Soko resshatai	Armored train unit.
	Tetsudo zairyosho	Railway supply depot.
	Tetsudo rentai zairyosho	Railway regiment supply depot.
	Teoshi keiben tetsudotai	Hand-car unit.

1. ARMY SIGNS. h. Field works—Continued.

Symbol	Japanese	English
	Keikikanjuza	Light machine gun emplacement.
	Kikanjuza	Machine gun (heavy) emplacement.

NOTE. The presence of weapons in the emplacement is shown by the appropriate symbol, e. g.

Symbol	Japanese	English
	Yasenhohei no entai	Field artillery shelter.
	Juhohei no entai	Heavy artillery shelter.
	Tetsujomo	Wire entanglements.
	Ido tetsujomo	Movable wire entanglements.
	Rokusai	Abatis.
	Jirai	Land mines.
	Taisenshago	Antitank ditch.
	Jukkobutsu no hakaibu	Artificial obstacles which have been demolished.
	Shinrin no bassaibu	Cleared area in woods, forest, etc.
	Doro, kyoryo, nado no sozetsubu	Barricade across road, bridge, etc.
	Shogaibutsu no hakaiko oyobi sandoku chiiki ni mokuru tsuro	Breach made in obstacles or passage opened through an area contaminated with gas.
	Empeibu	Dug-out; shelter.
	Engai	Cover; shelter.
	Konkuritosei engai	Concrete shelter.

NOTE. The type of fire-arm within a shelter is shown by the appropriate sign, e. g.

Symbol	Japanese	English
	Jinchi no zensen wo senryo seru butai	Unit in occupation of front line of position.
	Jinchi wo senryo seru butai	Unit in occupation of position.

NOTE. Dummy works and dummy positions are indicated by dotted lines.

1. ARMY SIGNS. i. Railway—Continued.

Symbol	Japanese	English
	Yasen tetsudosho	Field railway depot.
	Fukusen	Double track.
	Teishaba	Station.
	Tansen	Single track.

j. Shipping.

Symbol	Japanese	English
	Sempaku shireibu	Shipping headquarters.
	Sempaku heidan shireibu	Shipping group (main) headquarters.
	Sempaku yuso shireibu	Shipping transport headquarters.
	Sempaku dan shireibu	Shipping group headquarters.
	Sempaku yuso chikutai shireibu	Shipping transport sector unit headquarters.
	Sempaku yuso shibu	Shipping transport branch office.
	Suijo shireibu	Headquarters at sea.
	Teihakujo kambu	Anchorage inspectorate.
	Teihakujo shireibu	Anchorage headquarters.
	Teihakujo shireibu shibu	Anchorage headquarters, branch office.
	Sempaku kohei rentai	Shipping engineers regiment.

1. ARMY SIGNS. j. Shipping—Continued.

Symbol	Japanese	English
	Sempaku tsushin rentai	Shipping signal regiment.
	Sempaku hohei rentai	Shipping artillery regiment.
	Sempaku eiseitai hombu	Shipping medical unit headquarters.
	Byoinsen eiseihan	Hospital ship medical section.
	Kaijo yuso daita' hombu	Sea transport battalion headquarters.
	Kaijo yuso daitai butai	Sea transport battalion unit.
	Yorikutai	Disembarkation unit.
	Hansui sagyotai	Boat launching unit.
	Sempaku kosakusho	Shipping repair depot.
	Yasen sempakusho	Field shipping depot.
	Sempaku heikisho	Shipping ordnance depot.
	Yusoson	Transport (ship).
	Yuso sentai	Convoy.

NOTE. The type of ship is shown by the inclusion of an appropriate character or sign. Examples follow:

1. ARMY SIGNS. j. Shipping—Continued.

Symbol	Japanese	English
	Guntai yusosen	Army transport.
	Boku kikansen	Antiaircraft defense control ship.
	Gunjuhin yusosen	Munitions transport.
	Byoinsen	Hospital ship.
	Kyusuisen	Water supply ship.
	Kyutansen	Collier.
	Tsushinsen	Signal ship.
	Yusosen	Oil tanker.
	Boraigu fuzoku yusosen	Transport equipped with anti-mine apparatus.
	Senkai sokaigu fuzoku yusosen	Transport equipped with shallow water sweeping apparatus.
	Heiso jisshisen	Armed vessel.
	Suichu cho-onki tosaisen	Ship equipped with sound locator or equipment.
	Chigo (?) tosaisen	Ship presumably equipped with degaussing equipment.
	Chuhakugekiho tosaisen	Ship equipped with medium mortars.
	Juhakugekiho tosaisen	Ship equipped with heavy mortars.
	Kikyu tosaisen	Ship equipped with barrage balloons.

1. ARMY SIGNS. j. Shipping—Continued.

Symbol	Japanese	English
	Hakuyo musenki	Marine radio.

NOTE. Strength and wave-length (frequency) may be shown; e.g. 500 w, 500-watt, medium and short-wave set.

Symbol	Japanese	English
	Soshikitei	Control boat.
	Kijuntei	Pivot boat.
	Shutei	Small boat.

NOTE. The type of boat is shown by adding an appropriate sign or character. Examples follow:

Symbol	Japanese	English
	Kaijo torakku	"Sea truck."
	Kihosen	Motor sailboat.
	Gyosen	Fishing boat.
	Tokudaihatsu	Special large motorized craft.
	Daihatsu	Large motorized craft.
	Shohatsu	Small motorized craft.
	Kifu fushu	Motor-powered lighter.
	Sokotei	Armored boat.
	Kosokutei ko	Type "A" high-speed boat.
	Kosokutei otsu	Type "B" high-speed boat.

1. ARMY SIGNS. j. Shipping—Continued.

Symbol	Japanese	English
	Kosokutei hei	Type "C" high-speed boat.
	Kosakutei	Repair boat.
	Fushu	Lighter.
	Suifu	Water boat.
	Shojokisen	Small steamboat.
	Dampeisen	Barge.
	Umabune	Boat for horses.
	Denreitei	Messenger boat.
	(?) Shuteicho	Boat (landing craft) commander.
	(?) Shutei kohei	Boat (landing craft) engineer.
	(?) Rikujo kohei	Land engineer.
	Kai-un kichi	Sea transport base.
	Kai-un shuchi	Secondary sea transport base.
	Kai-un hojochi	Subsidiary sea transport base.
	Yusosen no byochi	Transport anchorage.

NOTE. Within a sea transport base the configuration of the anchorage is marked. Ship names or abbreviations are shown.

Symbol	Japanese	English
	Fuhyo	Buoy.

NOTE. When necessary the actual shape is sketched.

1. ARMY SIGNS. j. Shipping—Continued.

Symbol	Japanese	English
	Kaichu toka	Light buoy.

NOTE. If possible represented by the same color as the light.

Symbol	Japanese	English
	Kirai fusetsusen	Mined area boundary line.
	Fuyu shogaibutsu	Floating obstacles.
	Bozai aruiwa bogyomo	Boom or defensive net.
	Sambashi	Pier; jetty.
	Guntai shugojo	Place of assembly for troops.
	Gunjuhin shusekijo	Munitions dump.
	Teihakujo shireibu kojo	Anchorage headquarters workshop.
	Funairi-ba	Ship entrance.
	Shingosho; miharijo	Signal or lookout station.

k. Signal.

Symbol	Japanese	English
	Tsushintai hombu	Signal unit headquarters.
	Tsushintai	Signal unit.
	Tsushin chutai mata wa yusentai	Signal company or wire unit.
	Heitan tsushintai hombu	Line of communications signal unit headquarters.
	Heitan tsushin chutai	Line of communications signal company.

1. ARMY SIGNS. k. Signal—Continued.

Symbol	Japanese	English
	Soko tsushintai hombu	Armored signal unit headquarters.
	Soko tsushintai	Armored signal unit.
	Musentai	Radio unit.
	Idoshiki musentai	Mobile (ground) radio unit.
	Kotei musentai	Fixed radio unit.
	Musen johotai (tokushu musentai) hombu.	Radio intelligence (special radio) unit headquarters.
	Musen johotai (tokushu musentai).	Radio intelligence (special radio) unit.
	Shidan tsushintai	Division signal unit.
	Hohei rentai (ryodan) tsushintai (han).	Infantry regiment (brigade) signal unit (section).
	Kihei rentai (ryodan) (shudan) tsushintai (han).	Cavalry regiment (brigade) (group) signal unit (section).
	Denshin tsushinjo	Telegraph signal station.
	Denwaki	Telephone instrument.
	Denwa kokanki	Telephone switchboard.
	Tenkanki	Change-over switch; switch.
	Denshinki	Telegraph instrument (one-way buzzer).
	Taju denshinki	Multiplex telegraph instrument (duplex buzzer).

NOTE. ⊠, telephone with bell, when it is necessary to distinguish.

1. ARMY SIGNS. k. Signal—Continued.

Symbol	Japanese	English
	Taju denshinki	Multiplex telegraph instrument (quadruplex buzzer).
	Gempaki	Modulator.
	Jidoki	Automatic instrument.
	Jido teisoki	Automatic relay instrument.
	Insatsu denshinki	Teleprinter; teletype.
	Insatsu denshinki (musen)	Radio teleprinter or teletype.
	Shashin densoki (yusen)	Telephoto instrument (by line).
	Shashin densoki (musen)	Telephoto instrument (radio).
	Rensetsu tsushinjo	Relay signal station.
	Tsushinsen (denwa)	Signal line (telephone).
	Kisetsu tsushinsen	Existing signal line.
	Ofukusen	Duplex circuit.
	Fukusen	Twisted (or parallel) pair.
	Tenkasen	Supplementary line.
	Hansosen	Carrier circuit.
	Denshin denwa soshimpo	Line using both telegraph and telephone (simplexed).
	Idoshiki chijo musen tsushinjo	Mobile ground radio station.

NOTE. When necessary, insulated and submarine cables are represented by a wavy line, thus: ~

NOTE. For a telegraph line ○ is used instead of △.

NOTE. 1. A control station is represented by ⌐⊙.

NOTE. 2. The type of radio set may be indicated by inclosing within the circle the appropriate figure or symbol. Examples follow:

1. ARMY SIGNS. k. Signal—Continued.

Symbol	Japanese	English
	Musen denwaki (tsushinjo)----	Radio telephone (station).
	Idoshiki taiku musen denshinjo.	Mobile air-ground radio station.

NOTE. Different types may be shown as follows:

Symbol	Japanese	English
	Model 87 (1927), Type 1.	
	Model 87 (1927), Type 2.	
	Model 87 (1927), Type 6.	
	Model 94 (1934), Type 1.	
	Model 94 (1934), Type 2.	
	Model 94 (1934), Type 3C.	

Symbol	Japanese	English
	Hikoki ni sobi seru musenki	Aircraft radio.

NOTE. Different types may be shown as follows:

Symbol	Japanese	English
	Model 87 (1927), Type 1.	
	Model 87 (1927), Type 2.	
	Model 88 (1928), Type 3.	
	Model 94 (1934), Type 1.	
	Model 94 (1934), Type 2.	
	Model 94 (1934), Type 3.	

1. ARMY SIGNS. k. Signal—Continued.

Symbol	Japanese	English
	Model 87 (1927), Type 1.	
	Model 87 (1927), Type 2.	
	Model 0 (1940), Type 3.	
	Model 0 (1940), Type 4.	
	Model 0 (1940), Type 5.	

(Type 6, radio telephone, is represented by [symbol].)

Symbol	Japanese	English
	Model 94 (1934), Type 1.	
	Model 94 (1934), Type 2A.	
	Model 94 (1934), Type 2B.	
	Model 94 (1934), Type 3A.	
	Model 94 (1934), Type 3B.	
	Model 94 (1934), Type 4.	
	Model 94 (1934), Type 5.	

NOTE. The method of transportation used is shown as follows:

Symbol	Japanese	English
	Model 94 (1934), Type 1, by motorcar.	
	Model 94 (1934), Type 2B, by cart.	
	Model 94 (1934), Type 2B, by packhorse.	

1. ARMY SIGNS. k. Signal—Continued.

Symbol	Japanese	English
[symbol]	Kotei musen tsushinjo	Fixed radio station.
[symbol]	Kotei musen denshinjo	Fixed radio telegraph station.
[symbol]	Kaigun kotei musen denshinjo	Fixed naval radio telegraph station.
[symbol]	Kotei taiku musen denshinjo	Fixed air-ground radio telegraph station.
[symbol]	Kaigun kotei musen denshinjo	Fixed naval air-ground radio telegraph station.

NOTE. The strength in kilowatts of fixed stations may be shown by the requisite numbers (with or without KW). For example: [symbols]

Alternate forms:

Symbol		English
[symbol]		5-kilowatt fixed radio telegraph station.
[symbol]		1.5-kilowatt fixed radio telegraph station.
[symbol]		1-kilowatt fixed radio telegraph station.
[symbol]		0.5-kilowatt fixed radio telegraph station.
[symbol]	Musen jushinki	Radio receiving set.
[symbol]	Idoshiki hyoteiki	Mobile direction finder.
[symbol]	Koteishiki hyoteiki	Fixed direction finder.
[symbol]	Idoshiki chochiki	Portable sound detector.
[symbol]	Koteishiki chochiki	Fixed sound detector.
[symbol]	Dempa tanshingi	Radar.

1. ARMY SIGNS. k. Signal—Continued.

Symbol	Japanese	English
[symbol]	Dentambo	Radar defense.
[symbol]	Ensoki	Instrument operated by remote control.
[symbol]	Shikosei musen soshinki	Directional radio transmitter.
[symbol]	Hakujo musenki	Marine (shipboard) radio.
[symbol]	Musenki wo sobi seru shutei	Boat equipped with radio.
[symbol]	Musen tsushinkei	Radio signal network.
[symbol]	Shigo tsushinkei	Visual signal network.

NOTE.—The various means of signaling are represented by [symbol] for semaphore, etc. for heliograph, [symbol] for signal panels, [symbol]

Symbol	Japanese	English
[symbol]	Hatotai hombu	Carrier pigeon unit headquarters.
[symbol]	Hatotai	Carrier pigeon unit.
[symbol]	Hato tsushinjo	Carrier pigeon station.
[symbol]	Kyusho	Carrier pigeon post.
[symbol]	Hato tsushimmo	Carrier pigeon network.
[symbol]	Teidensho	Runner relay post.
[symbol]	Joba teidensho	Mounted relay post.

1. ARMY SIGNS. k. Signal—Continued.

Symbol	Japanese	English
	Jitensha teidensho	Bicycle relay post.
	Inu no renrakuro	Dog messenger route.
	Fuban shingosho	Panel signal station.
	Yubin ukewatashijo	Postal clearing house.
	Yasen yubinkyoku (tai)	Field post office (unit).
	Yasen yubinkyoku (teisokyo-ku)	Field post office (relay station).

l. Transport, Supply, and Medical Services.

Symbol	Japanese	English
	Danyakuhan (shotai)	Ammunition section (platoon).
	Kori	Baggage train.
	Shichohei rentai hombu	Transport regimental headquarters.
	Shichohei daitai hombu	Transport battalion headquarters.
	Shichohei dokuritsu daitai hombu.	Independent transport battalion headquarters.
	Bamba hensei shichohei butai	Horse-drawn transport unit.
	Daba hensei shichohei butai	Pack horse transport unit.
	Jidosha hensei shichohei butai	Motor transport unit.

1. ARMY SIGNS. l. Transport, Supply, and Med. Services—Con.

Symbol	Japanese	English
	Heiki kimmutai	Ordnance service unit.
	Keiri kimmuhan	Intendance service section.
	Boeki kyusuibu	Water supply and purification unit.
	Eiseitai hombu	Medical unit headquarters.
	Yasen byoin	Field hospital.
	Shidan byobasho	Division veterinary depot.

NOTE. Established field hospitals and veterinary depots are distinguished by the addition of ∧ to the top of the sign.

Symbol	Japanese	English
	Kanja shuyotai	March casualties collecting unit.
	Eiseitai tanga chutai	Medical unit stretcher company.
	Hotaijo	Dressing station.
	Byoba shugojo	Veterinary collecting station.
	Byoba kyugosho	Veterinary first-aid station.
	Yasen soko	Field warehouse.
	Ryomatsu kofujo	Rations and forage distributing point.
	Danyaku kofujo	Ammunition distributing point.
	Nenryo kofujo	Fuel distributing point.

1. ARMY SIGNS. l. Transport, Supply, and Med. Services—Con.

Symbol	Japanese	English
	Kagakusen shizai kofujo	Distributing point for chemical warfare material.
	Heiki, hifuku nado no shurijo	Repair depot for ordnance, clothing, etc.
	Gunjuhin no sekisae	Loading war material.
	Gunjuhin no shaka	Unloading war material.
	Gunjuhin no tsumikae	Trans-shipping war material.

m. Line of Communications.

Symbol	Japanese	English
	Heitan shuchi	Line of communications main base.
	Heitan chiku shireibu	Line of communications sector headquarters.
	Heitanchi	Line of communications intermediate base.
	Yotei heitanchi	Projected line of communications intermediate base.
	Heitanchi igai no hokyuten	Supply point other than a line of communications intermediate base.
	Yasen heiki honsho	Main field ordnance depot.
	Yasen heikisho	Field ordnance depot.
	Yasen heiki shisho	Branch field ordnance depot.
	NOTE. Subbranch (forward) depots and mobile repair sections are shown respectively by [symbol] and [symbol].	
	Yasen koku honsho	Main field air depot.
	Yasen kokusho	Field air depot.

1. ARMY SIGNS. m. Line of Communications—Continued.

Symbol	Japanese	English
	Yasen koku shisho	Branch field air depot.
	Yasen jidosha honsho	Main field motor transport depot.
	Yasen jidosha sho	Field motor transport depot.
	Yasen jidosha shisho	Branch field motor transport depot.
	NOTE. Subbranch (forward) depots and mobile repair sections are shown respectively by [symbol] and [symbol].	
	Yasen kamotsu honsho	Main field freight depot.
	Yasen kamotsu sho	Field freight depot.
	Yasen kamotsu shisho	Branch field freight depot.
	NOTE. Subbranch (forward) depots and mobile repair sections are shown respectively by [symbol] and [symbol].	
	The nature of the material in a depot or dump is shown by the proper abbreviation, e. g. [symbol] AM represents an artillery ammunition depot.	
	Yasen yusotai shireibu	Field transport unit headquarters.
	Jidosha daitai hombu	Motor transport battalion headquarters.
	Heitan shichohei butai	Line of communications transport unit.
	NOTE. Details of the organization are shown by appropriate lettering.	
	Ken-in jidoshatai	Tractor unit.
	Yuso kanshitai	Transport escort unit.
	Yasen hoju basho	Field remount depot.

1. ARMY SIGNS. m. Line of Communications—Continued.

Symbol	Japanese	English
	Rikujo kimmu chutai	Land service company.

NOTE. Similar companies may be represented by inserting the appropriate kana symbol within the rectangle. For example:

		Water service company.
		Road service company.
		Barge service company.

Symbol	Japanese	English
	Heitan tsushintai hombu	Line of communications signal unit headquarters.
	Heitan tsushin chutai	Line of communications signal company.
	Yubin ukewatashijo	Postal clearing office.
	Yasen yubinkyoku (tai)	Field post office (unit).
	Yasen yubinkyoku (teisokyoku)	Field post office (relay station).

NOTE. A branch office is represented by $\frac{\top}{(支)}$

n. Siege and fortress defense.

Symbol	Japanese	English
	Yosai shireibu	Fortress headquarters.
	Yosai juhohei rentai hombu	Fortress heavy artillery regimental headquarters.
	Yosai hohei shikikan	Fortress artillery commander.
	Yosai juhohei daitai hombu mata wa chikutai hombu.	Fortress heavy artillery battalion headquarters or sector unit headquarters.
	Yosai byoin	Fortress hospital.
	Yosai bun-in	Branch fortress hospital.
	Yosai tanshoto	Fortress searchlight.

1. ARMY SIGNS. m. Line of Communications—Continued.

Symbol	Japanese	English
	Heitan byohasho	Line of communications veterinary hospital.

NOTE. Established depots are distinguished by the addition of $\wedge$ to the top of the sign.

Symbol	Japanese	English
	Gumba boekisho	Veterinary quarantine hospital.
	Heitan eiseitai hombu	Line of communications medical unit headquarters.
	Heitan byoin	Line of communications hospital.

NOTE. Established depots are distinguished by the addition of $\diagup$ to the top of the sign.

Symbol	Japanese	English
	Heitan eiseitai ido chiryohan	Mobile treatment section of line of communications medical unit.
	Yasen bocki kyusuibu	Field water supply and purification section.
	Kanja yusotai	Sick transport unit.

NOTE. The position of headquarters is represented by the addition of ⊓ to the top of the sign.

Symbol	Japanese	English
	Kanja ryoyojo	Convalescent station.
	Kanja shugojo	Collecting station for sick and wounded.
	Yasen sakuseitai hombu	Field well-construction unit headquarters.
	Yasen sakuseitai	Field well-construction unit.
	Yasen kimmutai hombu	Field service unit headquarters.
	Yasen kenchikutai hombu	Field construction unit headquarters.

NOTE. Headquarters of similar units are represented by inserting the appropriate kana symbol within the rectangle.

1. ARMY SIGNS.   n. Siege and fortress defense—Continued.

Symbol	Japanese	English
	Suichu chosokuki	Under-water sound locator.
	Kyuryu yaho	Field gun under shelter.
	Eikyu horui	Permanent fort.
	Haneikyu horui	Semipermanent fort.
	Rinji horui	Temporary (improvised) fort. NOTE. Forts are drawn according to actual shape.
	Heisha eikyu hodai	Permanent gun emplacement.
	Heisha haneikyu hodai	Semipermanent gun emplacement.
	Heisha rinji hodai	Temporary (improvised) gun emplacement.
	Kyokusha eikyu hodai	Permanent mortar emplacement.
	Kyokusha haneikyu hodai	Semipermanent mortar emplacement.
	Kyokusha rinji hodai	Temporary (improvised) mortar emplacement.
	Hoto	Turret.
	Eikyu kyosha	Permanent block-house.
	Rinji kyosha	Temporary (improvised) block-house.
	Heisha	Barracks.
	Shosha, makuei	Barracks, tents.
	Kodo	Gallery, underground passage.
	Koro	Approach trenches, saps.
	Dangansho, dangan honko	Main shell magazine.

1. ARMY SIGNS.   n. Siege and fortress defense—Continued.

Symbol	Japanese	English
	Dansho	Shell magazine.
	Kayakusho, kayaku honko	Main powder magazine.
	Kayaku shisho	Branch powder magazine.
	Danyakusho, danyaku honko	Main ammunition depot.
	Danyaku chukansho; danyaku shiko	Intermediate ammunition depot, branch ammunition depot.
	Kohei kizai kofujo	Distributing center for engineer equipment and matériel.
	Yuso zairyosho	Transport supply depot.
	Heiki shuri kojo	Ordnance main repair shop.
	Heiki shurijo	Ordnance repair shop.
	Kanon	Gun.
	Ryudampo	Howitzer.
	Kyuho	Mortar.

NOTE. The caliber in centimeters of guns, etc., is shown by figures, the number of guns by short cross strokes, e. g. represents four 15-cm guns.

Example: Fortress with 4 12-cm guns, 2 7.5-cm guns, 2 15-cm guns, and 4 15-cm howitzers.

Sanjuka shi-mon no dai ichi eikyu hodai. Four 30-cm guns in No. 1 permanent battery.

1. ARMY SIGNS. n. Siege and fortress defense—Continued.

Symbol	Japanese	English
	Nijushiryu shi-mon no dai ni rinji hodai.	Four 24-cm howitzers in No. 2 temporary battery.
	Shijuka ni-mon no hoto	Two 40-cm guns in a turret.

2. NAVY SIGNS.

NOTE. For Army air and shipping signs see paragraph 1 of this section. Navy hydrographic signs are listed in section I, paragraph 2, of this chapter.

a. Bases, anchorages.

Symbol	Japanese	English
	Gunko; kaigunku shireibu shozaichi.	Naval port; naval station; naval district headquarters.
	Yoko	Minor naval station.
	Sensuikan haibichi	Submarine base.
	Kaigun bobitai mata wa shubitai.	Naval defense unit or garrison.
	Daikantai no teihaku ni tekisuru kowan.	Harbor suitable for large fleet anchorage.
	Kantai no teihaku ni tekisuru kowan.	Harbor suitable for fleet anchorage.
	Kansen no teihaku ni tekisuru kowan.	Harbor suitable for warship anchorage.
	Tobyo no eru hakuchi	Anchorage.
	Shoko	Commercial port.

2. NAVY SIGNS. a. Bases, anchorages—Continued.

Symbol	Japanese	English
	Joriku sambashi	Landing pier.
OR	Joriku ni tekisuru kaigan	Shore suitable for landings.
	Kansenkyo aru zosenjo mata wa shusenjo.	Construction and repair yard with drydock.
	Fusenkyo aru zosenjo mata wa shusenjo.	Construction and repair yard with floating dock.
	Hikagesendai wo yusuru kansen shurijo.	Warship repair yard equipped with marine railroad.
	Senkyo oyobi hikagesendai wo yusezaru kansen shurijo.	Warship repair yard without docks or marine railroad.
	Kaigun chotanjo	Naval coaling station.
	Sekitan wo kyokyu shiuru chiten.	Place able to supply coal.
	Kaigun choyujo	Naval oil fueling station.
	Juyu wo kyokyu shiuru chiten	Place able to supply fuel oil.

b. Ships, personnel.

Symbol	Japanese	English
	Kansen	Warship.
B	NOTE. The type of ship is shown by the addition of the appropriate abbreviation or sign, e. g., battleship. Other examples follow.	
OR d	Kuchikukan	Destroyer.

2. NAVY SIGNS. c. Air—Continued.

Symbol	Japanese	English
	Hikoki	Airplane (general).
	Rikugunki	Army plane.
	Rikujoki	Landplane.
	Ogata suijoki	Seaplane (large type).
	Kogata suijoki	Seaplane (small type).
	Kanjoki	Shipboard airplane.
	Hikotei	Flying boat.
	Koku kichi	Military air base (general).

NOTE.—The classification of the base is shown by the inclusion of the appropriate aircraft sign. e. g. [symbol], seaplane base; landplane base: [symbol], Army air base. Further examples follow.

Symbol	Japanese	English
	Ogataki hatchaku kanochi	Base suitable for heavy landplanes.
	Keihikoki hatchaku kanochi	Base suitable for light landplanes.
	Suiriku ryoyo hikojo	Land and seaplane base.
	Fujichakujo	Emergency landing field.
	Yotei kokuki kichi	Projected airbase.

NOTE. To indicate commercial airfields, substitute circles for the rectangles in the above examples, e. g. [symbol] commercial airfield suitable for heavy landplanes. Exception: the sign [symbol] is used for Army air base.

2. NAVY SIGNS. b. Ships, personnel—Continued.

Symbol	Japanese	English
	Koku bokan	Aircraft carrier.
	Suijoki bokan	Seaplane tender.
	Sensui bokan	Submarine tender.
	Kaijo sensuikan	Submarine (on surface).
	Suichu sensuikan	Submarine (submerged).
	Tai (shuryokukan)	Naval force including capital ships.
	Tai (shuryokukan igai)	Naval force not including capital ships.

NOTE. The type of unit is shown by the addition of the appropriate abbreviation or sign.

Symbol	Japanese	English
	Rengo kantai shirei chokan	Combined fleet commander-in-chief.
	Shirei chokan	Fleet commander.
	Shireikan	Division (squadron) commander.
	Shirei	Commandant; ship commander.
	Shirei	Ship commander.

c. Air

Symbol	Japanese	English
	Koku daitai	Air wing.

2. NAVY SIGNS   d. Fortifications, miscellaneous installations.

Symbol	Japanese	English
	Shomen koji aru yosaichi	Fortified zone with forward defenses.
	Eikyu hodai	Permanent battery.
	Kasetsu hodai	Temporary battery.
	Jissun ijo no kotei hodai	Fixed batteries for guns of 10 inches and over.
	Jissun miman no kotei hodai	Fixed batteries for guns of less than 10 inches.
	Kokaku hodai	Dual purpose gun battery.
	NOTE. The number of guns is shown by cross lines, and the caliber in centimeters is indicated by the appropriate number, e. g., [symbol], 2 8-cm guns; [symbol] 3 12-cm dual purpose guns.	
	Resshaho mata wo keninho	Railway or tractor-drawn gun.
	Koshaho	High-angle gun.
	Kikanju	Machine gun.
	Kiju tochika	Machine-gun pill box.
	Danyakuko mata wo dokugasu chozojo.	Ammunition or poison gas storage.
	Gyorai soko	Torpedo magazine.
	Bosenmo chozosho	Storage for anti-submarine nets.

2. NAVY SIGNS.   d. Fortifications, misc. installations—Con.

Symbol	Japanese	English
	Heisha	Barracks.
	Rikugun heiryoku shozaichi (omune shotai ijo).	Location of military troops (in general platoon or more).
	Junkeitai chuzaichi (50 mei ijo).	Location of patrol unit (50 men or more).
	Shinsui wo kyokyu shiuru chiten.	Fresh water supply point.
	Kijunten	Base point.
	Tanshoto	Searchlight.
	NOTE. The number is indicated by horizontal lines within the circle, the size by the appropriate number, e. g., [symbol] 80cm, 2 150-cm searchlights.	
	Miharijo; shingosho	Lookout station; signal station.
	Boro	Coastal signal station.
	Keiryu kikyu	Captive balloon.
	Todai	Lighthouse.
	Musen denshinjo	Fixed radio station (general).
	Idoshiki musen denshinjo	Mobile (ship) radio.
	Kaigun musen denshinjo	Navy radiotelegraph station.

3. SPECIAL NAVAL LANDING FORCE SIGNS—Continued.

Symbol	Japanese	English
	Shotaicho	Platoon commander.
	Kashikan	Noncommissioned officer.
	Hei	Private.
	Sempeicho	Advance or rear guard leader.
	Sempei	Advance or rear guard.
	Shoko sekko	Officer patrol.
	Sekko	Patrol.
	Shiki shotai	Command platoon.
	Butai	Unit.
	Fuzokutai	Attached unit.
	Kogunjutai	Column on the march.
	Hontai	Main unit.
	Yobitai	Reserve unit.
	Tsujo kogun	Ordinary march.

2. NAVY SIGNS. d. Fortifications, misc. installations—Con.

Symbol	Japanese	English
	Rikugun musen denshinjo	Army radiotelegraph station.
	Sono ta no musen denshinjo	Radiotelegraph station (other than Army or Navy).
	Musen denwasho	Radiotelephone station.
	Suichu choonki	Underwater listening device (hydrophone).
	Dempa tanshingi	Radar.
	Suirai fusetsu chitai	Mine field.
	Dempatsu suirai fusetsu chitai	Electrically fired mine fields.

3. SPECIAL NAVAL LANDING FORCE SIGNS.

NOTE. The following signs have been compiled from various sources, and are not considered complete or necessarily standard for all special naval landing forces. Although Navy signs are used wherever appropriate (e. g., the basic sign for aircraft), most of the signs are identical or similar to the corresponding Army signs because the functions and equipment of naval landing forces resemble more closely those of the Army than of the Navy.

Symbol	Japanese	English
	Rikusentai hombu; rikusentai shikikan.	Special naval landing force headquarters; Special naval landing force commander.
	Daitai hombu; daitaicho	Battalion headquarters; battalion commander.
	Chutaicho	Company commander.

3. SPECIAL NAVAL LANDING FORCE SIGNS—Continued.

Symbol	Japanese	English
	Jidokaki	Automatic weapon.
	Ho	Gun.
	Sampo	Mountain gun.
	Hotai fuzoku danyakutai	Ammunition unit attached to artillery unit.
	Sokushaho (koguntaikei)	Antitank gun (march formation).
	Jinchi ni tsukitaru sokushasho	Antitank gun in position.
	Jutekidanto	Heavy grenade discharger.
	Kyokushaho	High-angle gun (mortar).
	Hakugekiho	Trench mortar.
	Kaen hasshaki	Flame thrower.
	Hikoki	Airplane.
	Kokutai	Air unit.
	Hikojo	Airfield.
	Koshaho	Antiaircraft gun.

3. SPECIAL NAVAL LANDING FORCE SIGNS—Continued.

Symbol	Japanese	English
	Keikai kogun	March on the alert.
	Sampei	Skirmishers.
	Shukogeki hoko	Direction of main attack.
	Zenshin hoko	Direction of advance.
	Shageki hoko	Direction of fire.
	Keikai zenshin	Advance on the alert.
	Keikai zokko	Bringing up the rear on the alert.
	Koei sempei	Rear party of rear guard.
	Keikikanju	Light machine gun.
	Kikanju	Machine gun.
	Jinchi ni tsukitaru kikanju nicho.	2 machine guns in position.
	Kikanjutai	Machine gun unit.
	Kikanjutai no jutai	Machine gun unit in column formation.

3. SPECIAL NAVAL LANDING FORCE SIGNS—Continued.

Symbol	Japanese	English
	Jinchi ni tsukitaru koshaho	Antiaircraft guns in position.
	Tanshoto	Searchlight (land).
	Shingosho	Signal station.
	Musen denshinjo	Radiotelegraph station.
	Denwaki oyobi denwasen	Telephone instruments and line.
	Tsushintai	Signal unit.
	Sensha	Tank.
	Kogata sensha	Small type tank (tankette).
	Jidosha	Motor car.
	Sokosha	Armored car.
	Joyosha	Passenger car.
	Keninsha Kamotsusha.	Tractor; truck.
	Sokusha	Sidecar.
	Kijusha	Machine-gun carrier.

3. SPECIAL NAVAL LANDING FORCE SIGNS—Continued.

Symbol	Japanese	English
	Jitensha	Bicycle.
	Yobi danyakutai	Reserve ammunition unit.
	Kosakutai	Construction unit.
	Shukeitai	Intendance unit.
	Suijio	Field kitchen.
	Imutai	Medical unit.
	Tangatai	Stretcher unit.
	Chiryojo	Medical treatment station.
	Hotaijo	Dressing station.
	Jinchi	Position.
	Tetsujomo	Wire entanglements.
	Kyuba (ido tetsujomo)	Movable wire entanglement.
	Sandoku chitai	Gas contaminated area.
	Senshago	Tank trap.

3. SPECIAL NAVAL LANDING FORCE SIGNS—Continued.

Symbol	Japanese	English
(symbol)	Sozetsu shitaru hashi	Barricaded bridge.
(symbol)	Hakai shitaru hashi	Destroyed bridge.

Section IV.—MILITARY ABBREVIATIONS

NOTE. The abbreviations are arranged alphabetically.

1. ARMY ABBREVIATIONS.

Abbreviation	Japanese	English
A	Gun	Army.
A	Yahohei	Field artillery.
AA	Koshahotai; koshaho jinchi.	Antiaircraft artillery unit; antiaircraft artillery position.
AAS	Dokuritsu koshahotai	Independent AA unit.
ab	Hikojo daitai	Airfield battalion.
ac	Hikojo chutai	Airfield company.
AE	Yasen kisho butai	Field meteorological unit.
AL	Hyoteitai	Plotting unit (artillery).
AM	Hohei danyaku	Artillery ammunition.

NOTE. The kind of ammunition is represented as follows:
BAM, Mountain artillery ammunition.
SAM, Medium artillery ammunition.

Abbreviation	Japanese	English
AMT	Hohei danyaku chutai	Artillery ammunition company.
AN	Hohei johotai	Artillery intelligence unit.
AP	Keikyu shugojo	Alarm post.
AQ	Shokutai	Searchlight unit.
AQS	Dokuritsu shokutai	Independent searchlight unit.
AS	Ongentai	Sound locator unit (artillery).
AT	Sokuchitai	Land survey unit (artillery).
ATK	Tosensha (tai)	Tank destroyer (unit).
ATL	Tsushintai hombu	Army signal unit headquarters.
B	Ryodan, mata wa kore ni junzuru mono.	Brigade, or its equivalent.
b	Daitai	Battalion.
BA	Sampohei	Mountain artillery.
BAS	Dokuritsu sampohei	Independent mountain artillery.
BAM	Sampohei danyaku	(See AM above).
BG	Yasen sakuseitai	Field well-construction unit
biA	Daitaihotai	Infantry battalion gun unit.
BiZ	Hohei ryodan gasu butai	Infantry brigade gas unit.
BK	Gakyo zairyo chutai	Bridging matériel company.

1. ARMY ABBREVIATIONS—Continued.

Abbreviation	Japanese	English
BM	Ryodan danyakuhan	Brigade ammunition section.
Bo (BO)	Boeki kyusuibu	Water supply and purification unit.
BS	Dokuritsu konsei ryodan	Independent mixed brigade.
BSAA	Dokuritsu konsei ryodan koshahotai.	Independent mixed brigade AA unit.
BSP	Dokuritsu konsei ryodan kohei.	Independent mixed brigade engineer unit.
BTL	Hohei ryodan tsushintai (han).	Infantry brigade signal unit (section).
C	Gundan	Corps (not part of the Japanese Army organization).
c	Chutai	Company.
D	Shidan	Division.
DK	Shidan kihei	Division cavalry.
DO	Yasen dorotai	Field road unit.
DP	Shidan kohei	Division engineers.
DT	Shidan shicho	Division transport.
DTL	Shidan tsushintai	Division signal unit.
E	Tetsudotai	Railway unit.
EB	Tetsudo ryodan	Railway brigade.
F	Teki	Enemy.
FA	Kokugun (formerly kokuheidan).	Air army.
FA	Yosai hohei	Fortress artillery.
FB	Hiko (ryo) dan	Air brigade.
Fc	Hikochutai	Air company.
FD	Hikoshidan	Air division.
FeA	Juhohei	Heavy artillery.
FeAS	Dokuritsu juhohei	Independent heavy artillery.
FIS	Dokuritsu koku chikutai	Independent air sector unit.
FL	Yasen byoin	Field hospital.
FM	Hikobutai	Air unit.
FN	Koku johotai	Air intelligence unit.
FP	Yosai kohei	Fortress engineers.
FR	Hikosentai (rentai)	Air regiment.

NOTE. Reconnaissance, fighter, or bomber aircraft are shown by putting O, C, or B respectively on the lower right side of the abbreviation. Similarly light, heavy, or long-range aircraft are shown by L, S, or T, respectively.
Examples:
FRo, Air regiment (reconnaissance aircraft).
FRsc, Air regiment (heavy fighter aircraft).
FRLB, Air regiment (light bomber aircraft).

Abbreviation	Japanese	English
FS	Yasen kanja shuyotai	Field casualty collecting unit.
FTL	Koku tsushintai	Air signal unit.
FW	Hikojo setteitai	Airdrome construction unit.
G	Konoe	Imperial Guards.
GAP	Keikyu daishugojo	Grand alarm post.
Gr	Jidosha (hikoki) nenryo	Automobile (aviation) fuel.
H	Ryudampo	Howitzer.

ARMY ABBREVIATIONS—Continued.

Abbreviation	Japanese	English
HA	Koshaho	AA gun.
HeF	Hansui sagyotai	Boat launching unit.
HFI	Heitan byoin	Line of communications hospital.
HMA	Kosha kikanho	Antiaircraft machine cannon.
HMG	Kosha kikanju	Antiaircraft machine gun.
Hr	Eisei zairyo	Medical supply.
iA	Hohei	Infantry.
iB	Hohei hotai	Infantry gun unit.
iB	Hohei ryodan	Infantry brigade.
iH	Kyokusha hoheiho	Infantry mortar.
iK	Heisha hoheiho	Infantry cannon (gun).
iM	Hohei danyaku	Infantry ammunition.

NOTE.—The kind of ammunition is represented as follows:
iM (MG), Machine gun ammunition.
iM (TA), Antitank gun ammunition.

Abbreviation	Japanese	English
iMT	Hohei danyaku chutai	Infantry ammunition train.
iP	Sagyotai	Labor unit (infantry pioneers).
iR	Hohei rentai	Infantry regiment.
iRS	Dokuritsu hohei rentai	Independent infantry regiment.
iS	Dokuritsu hohei	Independent infantry.
iTL	Hohei rentai tsushintai (han)	Infantry regimental signal unit (section).
K	Kanon	Cannon (gun).
K	Kihei	Cavalry.
KA	Kihohei	Cavalry (Horse) artillery.
KaY	Kaijo yuso daitai hombu	Sea transport battalion headquarters.
KB	Kihei ryodan	Cavalry brigade.
KBAA	Kihei ryodan hotai	Cavalry brigade artillery unit.
KBAA	Kihei ryodan koshahotai	Cavalry brigade AA unit.
KBT	Kihei ryodan shicho	Cavalry brigade transport.
KBTAS	Kihei ryodan dokuritsu sokushahotai	Cavalry brigade independent antitank unit.
KBTK	Kihei ryodan senshatai	Cavalry brigade tank unit.
KBTL	Kihei ryodan tsushinhan (tai)	Cavalry brigade signal section (unit).
KD	Kihei shidan	Cavalry division.
Kg	Shubitai	Guard detachment, garrison.
KgS	Dokuritsu shubitai	Independent garrison.
Ki	Kikyutai	Balloon unit.
Kk	Kihei shudan	Cavalry group.
KKTL	Kihei shudan tsushinhan	Cavalry group signal section.
KS	Dokuritsu kihei	Independent cavalry.
KTK		(See TK below.)
KTL	Kihei rentai tsushinhan (tai)	Cavalry regimental signal section (unit).
LBK	Toka zairyo chutai	River crossing matériel company.
LG	Keikikanju	Light machine gun.
LM	Keihakugekihotai	Light trench mortar unit.

1. ARMY ABBREVIATIONS Continued.

Abbreviation	Japanese	English
LTK	Kyuho	(See TK below.)
M	Danyakuhan (shotai)	Mortar.
M		Ammunition section (platoon).
MA	Kikanhotai	Machine cannon unit.
MD	Kido shidan	Motorized division.
MG	Kikanjutai	Machine gun unit.
MM	Chuhakugekihotai	Medium trench mortar unit.
MS	Dokuritsu hakugekihotai	Independent mortar unit.
MTK		(See TK below.)
MW	Tekidanto, tekidanju	Grenade discharger, grenaderifle.
N	Kori	Baggage or train.
N	Johotai	Army intelligence unit.
NA	Kaigunho	Naval gun.
NSF	Kotei musentai	Fixed radio (wireless) unit.
P	Kohei	Engineers.
PA	Kikogun	Mechanized army.
PD	Shidan byobasho	Division veterinary hospital.
Pr	Ryomatsu	Provisions and forage.
PrT	Ryoshoku chutai	Provision train.
PS	Dokuritsu kohei	Independent engineers.
PT	Hatotai; shikyutai	Carrier pigeon unit.
PW	Sokoshatai	Tankette unit.
PWS	Dokuritsu sokoshatai	Independent tankette unit.
R	Rentai	Regiment.
RD	Tokushu musentai	Special radio unit.
RiA	Rentai hotai	Infantry regimental gun unit.
RSt	Rentai danretsu	Regimental ammunition train.
S	Dokuritsu	Independent.

NOTE.—Added at the end of the unit abbreviation.

Abbreviation	Japanese	English
S	Kanja shuyotai	March casualties collecting unit.
SA	Yasen juhohei	Medium artillery.
SAM	Yasen juho danyaku	(See AM above.)
SAS	Dokuritsu yasen juhohei	Independent medium artillery.
SeA	Sempaku hohei rentai	Shipping artillery regiment.
SeAA	Sempaku koshahotai	Shipping antiaircraft unit.
SeC	Sempaku shireibu	Shipping headquarters.
SeD	Sempaku dan shireibu	Shipping group headquarters.
SeE	Sempaku eiseitai hombu	Shipping medical unit headquarters.
SeH	Sempaku heidan shireibu	Large shipping group headquarters.
SeK	Sempaku kosakusho	Shipping repair depot.
SeP	Sempaku kohei rentai	Shipping engineers regiment.
SeS	Byoinsen eiseihan	Hospital ship medical section.
SeT	Teihakujo shireibu	Anchorage headquarters.
SeTi	Sempaku yuso chikutai shireibu	Shipping transportation area unit headquarters.
SeTL	Sempaku tsushin rentai	Shipping signal regiment.
SeU	Sempaku yuso shireibu	Shipping transportation headquarters.
SeUb	Kaijo yuso daitai	Sea transport battalion.

1. ARMY ABBREVIATIONS—Continued.

Abbreviation	Japanese	English
SeY	Yorikutai	Disembarkation unit.
SF	Musentai	Radio unit.
sM	Juhakugekihotai	Heavy trench mortar unit.
SO	Sosakutai	Reconnaissance unit.
STK		(See TK below.)
St	Danretsu	Ammunition train.
SuB	Suijo shireibu	Headquarters at sea.
SW	Yasen shomeitai	Field searchlight unit.
T	Shicho	Transport.
TA	Sokushahotai	Antitank gun unit.
TAS	Dokuritsu sokushahotai	Independent antitank gun unit.
TD	Sensha shidan	Armored division.
TG	Yusosentai	Group of transport; convoy.
TG		Tommy gun.
TK	Sensha (tai)	Tank (unit).

NOTE. Light medium, or heavy tanks are represented by putting L, M, or S, respectively, in front of the abbreviation. For example, STK represents a heavy tank unit. A tank unit employed as cavalry is represented by KTK.

TKP	Senshatai kohei	Tank unit engineers.
TKS	Dokuritsu senshatai	Independent tank unit.
TKTL	Senshatai tsushintai	Tank unit signal unit.
TL	Tsushin chutai, mata wa yusentai	Signal company; wire unit.
TLS	Dokuritsu tsushin chutai	Independent signal company.
TP	Kikaika butai	Mechanized unit.
TZ	Senshatai no seibi butai	Tank unit maintenance unit.
V	Yasen sokuryotai	Field surveying unit (engineers).
Vr	Jui zairyo	Veterinary supply.
Z	Gasu butai	Gas unit.
Zid	Jidohotai	Automatic gun unit.
Zr	Kagakusen shizai	Chemical warfare.
ZS	Dokuritsu gasu butai	Independent gas unit.

2. NAVY ABBREVIATIONS.

Abbreviation	Japanese	English
A	Koku bokan	Aircraft carrier.
a	Suijo hikoki	Seaplane.
Aa (A^a)	Hikotei (hikosen ?)	Flying boat (dirigible ?).
AB	Kushu butai	Air attack force.
aBg	Tokubetsu konkyochitai	Special base unit.
AdB	Zenshin butai	Advancing force.
AF	Koku kantai	Air fleet.
AG	Tokusetsu hokan	Auxiliary gunboat.
As or A^s	Suijoki bokan	Seaplane tender.
AtB	Fuzoku butai	Attached force.
B	Sentokan; senkan	Battleship.
BC	Junyo senkan	Battle-cruiser.
BG	Bobitai	Naval defense force.
Bg	Konkyochitai	Base unit.

2. NAVY ABBREVIATIONS—Continued.

Abbreviation	Japanese	English
bg	Keibitai	Guard unit.
BS	Senkan sentai	Battleship division.
C	C¹ (?)	Cruiser.
CA or C^A	Itto junyokan	Heavy cruiser.
CAS or C^{AS}	Itto junyokan; kojunyokan.	Heavy cruiser.
CB or C^B	Sentai	Heavy cruiser division.
CB	Otsu junyokan	Light cruiser (2d class cruiser).
CD	Tsushin butai	Communication unit.
cdg	Kaibokan	Coast defence vessel.
CF	Kuchiku rentai	Combined destroyer group.
cfg	Kenshi kantai	China Expeditionary Fleet.
Cg	Koku rentai	Combined air unit.
ch	Tsushintai	Communication unit.
chg	Kusentei	Sub-chaser.
Cl or CI.	Kusentai	Sub-chaser group.
CM	Denran fusetsusen	Cable layer.
CS	Kirai fusetsusen	Minelayer.
CsF	Junyokan sentai	Cruiser division.
	Shina homen kantai	China Area Fleet.
cwg	Sokai rentai	Combined mine-sweeper group.
D	Shotai	Division.
d	Kuchikukan	Destroyer.
Df	Koku bokan; kobo (abbr.)	Aircraft carrier.
dg	Kuchikutai; kuchi or ku (abbr)	Destroyer group.
Dp	Bokan	Depot ship.
Dpd	Suirai bokan	Destroyer (mine) depot ship.
Dpf	Koku bokan	Aircraft tender or depot ship.
Dps	Sensui bokan	Submarine tender.
Dpw	Sokai bokan	Mine-sweeper depot ship.
EB	Senken butai	Advance force.
EF	Goei kantai	Escorting fleet.
Eg	Goei tai	Escort unit.
EV	Gosokan	Escort vessel.
F	Kantai	Fleet.
f	Hikoki; ki (abbr)	Aircraft.
fB	Koku butai	Naval Air Force.
fb (f^b)	Bakugekiki: kogekiki	Bomber aircraft.
fb (f^b)	Kanjoki	Ship-borne plane.
fc (f^c)	Sentoki	Fighter aircraft.
fd (f^d)	Hikotei	Flying boat.
f^d 大	Ogata hikotei	Large flying boat.
fg BG	Kokutai	Air unit.
fg BG	Kichi kokutai	Base air unit.
fl (f^l)	Rikujo hikoki (rikujoki)	Land-based aircraft.
flo (f^{lo})	Rikujo kogekiki	Land-based attack plane.
f^{lo} 中	Chugata rikujo kogekiki	Land-based attack plane, medium.
fo (f^o)	Kogekiki	Attack plane.
fR	Renshuki	Training aircraft.

2. NAVY ABBREVIATIONS—Continued.

Abbreviation	Japanese	English
fr (fr)	Kansokuki; ka (abbr); teisatsuki	Reconnaissance or observation aircraft.
fs (fs)	Suijo hikoki (suijoki)	Seaplane.
fsr	Suijo teisatsuki	Reconnaissance seaplane.
fsr	Nizo suijo teisatsuki	2-seater reconnaissance seaplane
ft (ft)	Raigekiki	Torpedo plane.
ftb (ftb)	Raigekiki	Torpedo bomber (carrier type).
fT	Yusoki	Transport plane.
fTg	Yusokitai	Transport plane unit.
fvb	Kyukoka bakugekiki	Dive bomber (carrier type?).
fw	Suijo hikoki	Seaplane.
G	Hokan	Gunboat.
g	Tai	Unit, group.
GB	Keikai butai	Screening force.
GCg	Rengo tsushintai	Combined communications unit.
GF	Rengo kantai	Combined fleet.
Gfg	Rengo kokutai	Combined air unit.
Gg	Hokantai	Gunboat group.
GKF	Nansei homen kantai	Southwest Area Fleet.
GLg	Rengo tokubetsu rikusentai	Combined special naval landing force.

E. g., K6Lg: Kure 6th Special Naval Landing Force.

Abbreviation	Japanese	English
H	Byoinsen	Hospital ship.
HB	Hokuho butai	Northern Force.
HG	Juho	Heavy guns.
Hr	Kochotei	Harbor master's craft.
J	Saihyosen	Ice-breaker.
KCS	Koku chiku shireibu	Air sector (headquarters).
KdB	Kido butai	Striking force.
KEg	Kaijo goeitai	Surface escort unit.
KF	Nanken kantai	Southern Expeditionary Fleet.
Lg	Tokubetsu rikusentai	Special naval landing force.
M	Fusetsukan	Minelayer.
m	Shosen	Merchant ship.
MB	Shuryoku butai	Main force.
MC	Jishinro	Magnetic course.
mg	Shosentai	Merchant ship group.
MTB	Kosoku gyoraitei	Motor torpedo boat.
N		Number ——— unit.
n	Mosen	Net tender.
NA	Kaigunho	Naval gun.
NB	Yasen butai	Night combat force.
Ng	Yasentai	Night combat unit.
NPB	Nampo butai	Southern Force.
NTF	Nanto homen kantai	Southeast Area Fleet.
P	Kirai sentai	Mine squadron.

2. NAVY ABBREVIATIONS—Continued.

Abbreviation	Japanese	English
P	Shokaitei	Patrol boat.
PB	Shokai butai	Patrol force.
Pg	Shokaitai	Patrol unit.
R	Kosakusen	Repair ship.
RG	Kayo hokan	River gunboat.
S	Sentai	Squadron, division.

NOTE. Used as a prefix.

Abbreviation	Japanese	English
s	Sensuikan	Submarine.
SB	Sakuteki butai	Searching force.
sB	Sensui butai	Submarine force.
SCg	Tanshi sototai	Search and mopping-up unit.
Sd	Suirai sentai; suisen (abbr)	Destroyer squadron.
Sf	Koku sentai; kosen (abbr)	Air wing or carrier division.
sg	Sensuitai	Submarine group.
sM	Fusetsu sensuikan	Mine-laying submarine.
SNB	Gai nanyo butai	Outer South Seas Force.
SO	Sokaitai	Minesweeper group.

NOTE. See also wg.

Abbreviation	Japanese	English
Ss	Sensui sentai	Submarine squadron.
Sf	Koku sentai	Air division.
Sv	Kyunansen	Salvage ship.
Sy	Sokuryokan	Surveying ship.
T or Tv	Unsosen	Transport ship.
t	Suiraitei	Torpedo boat.
Ta or Tva	Kyuheisen	Munitions carrier.
Ta	Rikugun yusosen	Army transport ship.
TB	Hokyu butai	Supply (replenishment) force.
TC	Shin hoi	True course; true bearing.
Tc	Kyutansen	Coaler.
Tco	Kyutan oyobi kyuyusen	Coal and oil supplying ship.
Tg	Unsosentai	Transport ship group (convoy).
tg	Suiraiteitai	Torpedo-boat group.
Tm	Tsushinsen	Communications ship.
To	Kyuyusen	Tanker.
Tp	Kyuryosen	Provisions ship.
Tv	Unsosen	Transport ship.
Tva	Kyuheisen	Ammunition ship.
Tw	Kyusuisen	Water supply ship.
V	Chutai	Squadron.
va	Taiki sokudo	Air speed.
vb	Domokuhyo sokudo	Speed of moving target.
vg	Taichi sokudo	Ground speed.
vw	Fusokudo	Wind speed.
w	Sokaitei; sokaisen	Mine-sweeper.
wg	Sokaitai	Mine-sweeper group.

CHAPTER XIII

MILITARY TERMS AND CHARACTERS

Following is a list of military terms and their Japanese equivalents in Romaji and characters which may be useful to unit intelligence officers:

1. ORGANIZATIONS AND UNITS.

Military term	Japanese equivalent	Character
Air	Hikō, kōkū	飛行, 航空
—army	Kōkugun	航空軍
—brigade	Hikōdan	飛行團
—division	Hikō shidan	飛行師團
—intelligence unit	Kōkū jōhōtai	航空情報隊
—regiment	Hikō sentai	飛行戰隊
—signal unit	Kōkū tsūshintai	航空通信隊
—company	Hikō chūtai	飛行中隊
—training brigade	Kyōdō hikōdan	教導飛行團
—training company	Kyōiku hikō chūtai	教育飛行中隊
—transport unit	Kōkū yusōtai	航空輸送隊
Direct cooperation unit	Chokkyō hikōtai	直協飛行隊
Field — replacement unit	Yasen hojū hikōtai	野戰補充飛行隊
Independent — company (unit)	Dokuritsu hikō chūtai (tai)	獨立飛行中隊 (隊)
Raiding—company	Teishin hikō chūtai	挺進飛行中隊
Airfield	Hikōjō	飛行場
—battalion (company)	Hikōjō daitai (chūtai)	飛行場大隊 (中隊)
—training battalion	Kyōdō hikōjō daitai	教導飛行場大隊

1. ORGANIZATIONS AND UNITS—Continued.

Military term	Japanese equivalent	Character
Airfield—Continued.		
Field — construction unit.	Yasen hikōjō setteitai	野戰飛行場設定隊
Amphibious battalion	Kaijō kidō daitai	海上機動大隊
Antiaircraft artillery	Kōshahō	高射砲
—regiment	Kōshahō rentai	高射砲聯隊
Cavalry brigade—unit	Kihei ryodan kōshahōtai	騎兵旅團高射砲隊
Field—battalion	Yasen kōshahō daitai	野戰高射砲大隊
Independent — battalion	Dokuritsu kōshahō daitai	獨立高射砲大隊
Independent field company.	Dokuritsu yasen kōshahō chūtai	獨立野戰高射砲中隊
Independent mixed brigade—unit	Dokuritsu konsei ryodan kōshahōtai	獨立混成旅團高射砲隊
Shipping—regiment	Sempaku kōshahō rentai	船舶高射砲聯隊
Antiaircraft defense	Bōkū	防空
—regiment	Bōkū rentai	防空聯隊
—balloon unit	Bōkū kikyūtai	防空氣球隊
—observation unit	Bōkū kanshitai	防空監視隊
Field—unit	Yasen bōkūtai	野戰防空隊
Independent—battalion	Dokuritsu bōku daitai	獨立防空大隊
Anti-tank gun	Sokushahō	速射砲
Cavalry brigade—unit	Kihei ryodan sokushahōtai	騎兵旅團速射砲隊

1. ORGANIZATIONS AND UNITS—Continued.

Military term	Japanese equivalent	Character
Anti-tank gun—Continued.		
Independent—battalion (company.)	Dokuritsu sokushahō daitai (chūtai.)	獨立速射砲大隊(中隊)
Armored car	Sōkōsha	裝甲車
Independent—company.	Dokuritsu sōkōsha chūtai.	獨立裝甲車中隊
Independent light company.	Dokuritsu keisōkōsha chūtai.	獨立輕裝甲車中隊
Infantry group—company.	Hoheidan sōkōsha chūtai.	步兵團裝甲車中隊
Armored train	Sōkō ressha	裝甲列車
—unit	Sōkō resshatai	裝甲列車隊
Army	Gun	軍
—commander	Gun shireikan	軍司令官
—district	Gunkanku	軍管區
—headquarters	Gun shireibu	軍司令部
Area	Hōnengun	方面軍
Artillery	Hōhei	砲兵
—command	Hōhei shireibu	砲兵司令部
—group	Hōheidan	砲兵團
—intelligence (observation) regiment.	Hōhei jōhō rentai	砲兵情報聯隊
—unit	Hōheitai	砲兵隊
Border garrison—unit.	Kokkyō shubitai hoheitai.	國境守備隊砲兵隊
Cavalry brigade—unit.	Kihei ryodan hōheitai	騎兵旅團砲兵隊
Fortress heavy—regiment.	Yōsai jūhōhei rentai	要塞重砲兵聯隊
Field—regiment	Yahōhei rentai	野砲兵聯隊
Heavy—regiment	Jūhōhei rentai	重砲兵聯隊
Horse—regiment	Kihōhei rentai	騎砲兵聯隊

1. ORGANIZATIONS AND UNITS—Continued.

Military term	Japanese equivalent	Character
Artillery—Continued.		
Independent field—battalion (regiment).	Dokuritsu yahōhei daitai (rentai).	獨立野砲兵大隊(聯隊)
Independent garrison unit.	Dokuritsu shubitai hōheitai.	獨立守備隊砲兵隊
Independent heavy—battalion (company).	Dokuritsu jūhōhei daitai (chūtai).	獨立重砲兵大隊(中隊)
Independent mixed brigade—unit.	Dokuritsu konsei ryodan hōheitai.	獨立混成旅團砲兵隊
Independent mountain (pack)—bn. (regt.).	Dokuritsu sampōhei daitai (rentai).	獨立山砲兵大隊(聯隊)
Medium—battalion (regiment).	Yasen jūhōhei daitai (rentai).	野戰重砲兵大隊(聯隊)
Mountain (pack)—regiment.	Sampōhei rentai.	山砲兵聯隊
Shipping—regiment training unit.	Senpaku hōhei rentai kyōikutai.	船舶砲兵聯隊教育隊
Balloon	Kikyū	氣球
—company (regiment)	Kikyū chūtai (rentai)	氣球中隊(聯隊)
Battalion	Daitai	大隊
—commander	Daitaichō	大隊長
—headquarters	Daitai hombu	大隊本部
Board of Field Marshals and Fleet Admirals.	Gensuifu	元帥府
Border garrison	Kokkyō shubitai	國境守備隊
Bridge building material company.	Gakyō zairyō chūtai	架橋材料中隊
Brigade	Ryodan	旅團
—commander	Ryodanchō	旅團長
—headquarters	Ryodan shireibu	旅團司令部
Casualty clearing station	Kanja yusōbu	患者輸送部
Cavalry	Kihei	騎兵
—battalion	Kihei daitai	騎兵大隊
—brigade	Kihei ryodan	騎兵旅團

1. ORGANIZATIONS AND UNITS—Continued.

Military term	Japanese equivalent	Character
Cavalry—Continued.		
—group	Kihei shūdan	騎兵集團
—regiment	Kihei rentai	騎兵聯隊
Company	Chūtai	中隊
—commander	Chūtaichō	中隊長
Construction duty company.	Kenchiku kimmu chūtai.	建築勤務中隊
Debarkation group (unit).	Yōrikudan (tai)	揚陸團 (隊)
Depot	Shō	廠
Field freight	Yasen kamotsushō	野戰貨物廠
Field motor transport	Yasen jidōshashō	野戰自動車廠
Field ordnance	Yasen heikishō	野戰兵器廠
Field remount	Yasen hojū bashō	野戰補充馬廠
Depot division	Rusu shidan	留守師團
Detail	Han	班
Division	Shidan	師團
—commander	Shidanchō	師團長
—district	Shikan	師管
—headquarters	Shidan shireibu	師團司令部
Depot	Rusu shidan	留守師團
Engineer	Kōhei	工兵
—regiment	Kōhei rentai	工兵聯隊
—unit	Kōheitai	工兵隊
Border garrison—unit	Kokkyō shubitai kōheitai.	國境守備隊工兵隊
Cavalry brigade—unit	Kihei ryodan kōheitai.	騎兵旅團工兵隊

1. ORGANIZATIONS AND UNITS—Continued.

Military term	Japanese equivalent	Character
Engineer—Continued.		
Division—unit	Shidan kōheitai	師團工兵隊
Fortress—unit	Yōsai kōheitai	要塞工兵隊
Independent—battalion (co., reg.)	Dokuritsu kōhei daitai (chūtai, rentai).	獨立工兵大隊 (中隊, 聯隊)
Independent mixed brigade—unit.	Dokuritsu konsei ryodan kōheitai	獨立混成旅團工兵隊
Shipping—regiment	Sempaku kōhei rentai	船舶工兵聯隊
Tank group—unit	Senshadan kōheitai	戰車團工兵隊
Field construction unit	Yasen kenchikutai	野戰建築隊
Field duty unit	Yasen kimmutai	野戰勤務隊
Field replacement unit	Yasen hojūtai	野戰補充隊
Field road unit	Yasen dōrotai	野戰道路隊
Field well-construction company.	Yasen sakusei chūtai.	野戰鑿井中隊
Fortress	Yōsai	要塞
—headquarters	Yōsai shireibu	要塞司令部
Garrison	Shubitai	守備隊
Border	Kokkyō shubitai	國境守備隊
Independent	Dokuritsu shubitai	獨立守備隊
Gas	Gasu	瓦斯
—battalion	Gasu daitai	瓦斯大隊
Field—company	Yasen gasu chūtai	野戰瓦斯中隊
Independent—company	Dokuritsu gasu chūta	獨立瓦斯中隊
General Defense Headquarters.	Bōei Sōshireibu	防衞總司令部
General Staff	Sambō Hombu	參謀本部
Hospital	Byōin	病院

1. ORGANIZATIONS AND UNITS—Continued.

Military term	Japanese equivalent	Character
Hospital—Continued.		
Army	Rikugun byōin	陸軍病院
Field	Yasen byōin	野戰病院
Line of communication.	Heitan byōin	兵站病院
Line of communication veterinary.	Heitan byōbashō	兵站病馬廠
Veterinary quarantine	Gumba bōekishō	軍馬防疫廠
Imperial Headquarters	Daihonei	大本營
Independent mixed brigade.	Dokuritsu konsei ryodan.	獨立混成旅團
Independent mixed regiment.	Dokuritsu konsei rentai.	獨立混成聯隊
Infantry	Hohei	步兵
—brigade	Hohei ryodan	步兵旅團
—group	Hoheidan	步兵團
—mortar battalion (regiment).	Hakugeki daitai (rentai, tai).	迫擊大隊 (聯隊)
—regiment	Hohei rentai	步兵聯隊
Border garrison—unit.	Kokkyō shubitai hoheitai.	國境守備隊步兵隊
Fortress—unit	Yōsai hoheitai	要塞步兵隊
Independent—battalion (regiment, unit).	Dokuritsu hohei daitai (rentai, tai).	獨立步兵大隊 (聯隊 隊)
Independent garrison—battalion.	Dokuritsu shubitai hohei daitai.	獨立守備隊步兵大隊
Inspectorate General of Aviation.	Rikugun Kōkū Sōkambu.	陸軍航空總監部
Inspectorate General of Military Training.	Kyōiku Sōkambu.	教育總監部
Land duty company.	Rikujō kimmu chūtai.	陸上勤務中隊
Launching unit (boat).	Hansui sagyōtai.	泛水作業隊
Line of communication garrison.	Heitan shubitai.	兵站守備隊

1. ORGANIZATIONS AND UNITS—Continued.

Military term	Japanese equivalent	Character
Machine cannon	Kikanhō	機關砲
Field—company	Yasen kikanhō chūtai	野戰機關砲中隊
Medical	Eisei	衛生
—unit	Eiseitai	衛生隊
Division—unit	Shidan eiseitai	師團衛生隊
Independent mixed brigade—unit.	Dokuritsu konsei ryodan eiseitai.	獨立混成旅團衛生隊
Line of communication—unit.	Heitan eiseitai	兵站衛生隊
Meteorological	Kishō	氣象
—company (regiment, unit).	Kishō chūtai (rentai, tai).	氣象中隊 (聯隊 隊)
Field—battalion (unit).	Yasenkishō daitai (tai).	野戰氣象大隊 (隊)
Military affairs district.	Heijiku	兵事區
Mortar (artillery)	Kyūhō	臼砲
Independent—battalion (regiment).	Dokuritsu kyūhō daitai (rentai).	獨立臼砲大隊 (聯隊)
Motor transport.	(See transport).	
Platoon	Shōtai	小隊
—commander	Shōtaichō	小隊長
Radio	Musen	無線
Fixed—unit	Kotei musentai	固定無線隊
Special—location unit.	Tokushu musen hyōteitai.	特種無線標定隊
Special—unit	Tokushu musentai	特種無線隊
Raiding	Teishin	挺進
—group	Teishindan	挺進團
—regiment	Teishin rentai	挺進聯隊
—training regiment	Kyōdō teishin rentai	教導挺進聯隊

1. ORGANIZATIONS AND UNITS—Continued.

Military term	Japanese equivalent	Character
Railway	Tetsudō	鐵道
—inspectorate	Tetsudō kambu	鐵道監部
—regiment	Tetsudō rentai	鐵道隊
—transport command	Tetsudō yusō shireibu	鐵道輸送司令部
Field—command	Yasen tetsudō shireibu	野戰鐵道司令部
Special—command	Tokusetsu tetsudō shireibu.	特設鐵道司令部
Reconnaissance	Sōsaku	搜索
—regiment	Sōsaku rentai	搜索聯隊
—unit	Sōsakutai	搜索隊
Regiment	Rentai	聯隊
—commander	Rentaichō	聯隊長
—district	Rentaiku	聯隊區
—headquarters	Rentai hombu	聯隊本部
Independent mixed	Dokuritsu konsei rentai.	獨立混成聯隊
Replacement unit	Hojūtai	補充隊
Field	Yasen hojūtai	野戰補充隊
River crossing material company.	Toka zairyō chūtai	渡河材料中隊
Sea transport observation unit.	Kaijō yusō kanshitai	海上輸送監視隊
Searchlight	Shōkū	照空
—battalion	Shōkū daitai	照空大隊
Field—battalion	Yasen shōkū daitai	野戰照空大隊
Independent field company.	Dokuritsu yasen shōkū chūtai.	獨立野戰照空中隊

1. ORGANIZATIONS AND UNITS—Continued.

Military term	Japanese equivalent	Character
Shipping	Sempaku	船舶
—antiaircraft artillery regiment.	Sempaku kōshahō rentai	船舶高射砲聯隊
—artillery regiment training unit.	Sempaku hōhei rentai kyōikutai.	船舶砲兵聯隊教育隊
—engineer regiment	Sempaku kōhei rentai	船舶工兵聯隊
—forces	Sempaku heidan	船舶兵團
—command	Sempaku shireibu	船舶司令部
—transport battalion	Sempaku yusō daitai	船舶輸送大隊
—transport command	Sempaku yusō shireibu	船舶輸送司令部
—transport sector unit	Sempaku yusō chikutai.	船舶輸送地區隊
Signal (see also radio, wire).	Tsūshin, denshin	通信 電信
—regiment	Denshin rentai	電信聯隊
—unit	Tsushintai, denshintai.	通信隊 電信隊
Cavalry brigade—unit	Kihei ryodan tsūshintai.	騎兵旅團通信隊
Division—unit	Shidan tsūshintai	師團通信隊
Field—company	Yasen denshin chūtai	野戰電信中隊
Fixed—unit	Kotei tsūshintai	固定電信隊
Independent—company.	Dokuritsu denshin chūtai.	獨立電信中隊
Independent mixed brigade—unit.	Dokuritsu konsei ryodan tsūshintai.	獨立混成旅團通信隊
Shipping—regiment	Sempaku tsūshin rentai.	船舶通信聯隊
Squad	Buntai	分隊
—leader	Buntaichō	分隊長
Supreme Military Council.	Gunji Sangiin	軍事參議院
Survey unit	Sokuryōtai	測量隊

1. ORGANIZATIONS AND UNITS—Continued.

Military term	Japanese equivalent	Character
Tank	Sensha	戰車
—group	Senshadan	戰車團
—regiment	Sensha rentai	戰車聯隊
Cavalry brigade—unit	Kihei ryodan sensha-tai	騎兵旅團戰車隊
Division—unit	Shidan senshatai	師團戰車隊
Independent mixed brigade—unit	Dokuritsu konsei ryodan senshatai	獨立混成旅團戰車隊
Tractor company	Keninsha chūtai	牽引車中隊
Transport	Shichōhei	輜重兵
—regiment	Shichōhei rentai	輜重兵聯隊
Cavalry brigade—unit	Kihei ryodan shichōheitai	騎兵旅團輜重兵隊
Division—unit	Shidan shichōheitai	師團輜重兵隊
Independent—battalion (company, regiment)	Dokuritsu shichōhei daitai (chūtai, rentai)	獨立輜重兵大隊 (中隊, 聯隊)
Motor—regiment	Jidōsha rentai	自動車聯隊
Field motor—depot	Yasen jidōshashō	野戰自動車廠
Independent motor battalion (company)	Dokuritsu jidōsha daitai (chūtai)	獨立自動車大隊 (中隊)
Independent mixed brigade motor—unit	Dokuritsu konsei ryodan jidōshatai	獨立混成旅團自動車隊
Line of communication motor—co. (unit)	Heitan jidōsha chūtai (tai)	兵站自動車中隊 (隊)
Special motor—regiment	Tokusetsu jidōsha rentai	特設自動車聯隊
War Ministry	Rikugunshō	陸軍省
Sea duty company	Suijō kimmu chūtai	水上勤務中隊
Water supply and purification department	Bōeki kyūsuibu	防疫給水部
Wire	Yūsen	有線
Independent — company	Dokuritsu yūsen chū-tai	獨立有線中隊

2. ARMS AND SERVICES.

Military term	Japanese equivalent	Character
Air*	Kōkū	航空兵
Air troops	Hikōhei	飛行兵
Balloon troops	Kikyūhei	氣球兵
Branch of service	Heishu	兵種
Cavalry	Kihei	騎兵
Chemical warfare service*	Kahei	化兵
Engineers	Kōhei	工兵
Field artillery	Yahōhei	野砲兵
Field and mountain artillery.*	Yasampō	野山砲
Heavy artillery	Jūhōhei	重砲兵
Horse artillery	Kihōhei	騎砲兵
Infantry	Hohei	步兵
Infantry mortar troops	Hakugekihei	迫擊兵
Intelligence (observation) troops.	Jōhōhei	情報兵
Intendance department	Keiribu	經理部
Construction technician.	Kengi	建技
Finance	Shukei	主計
Intendance technician	Keigi	經技
Judicial department	Hōmubu	法務部
Line branch	Heika	兵科
Mechanized*	Kikō	機甲
Medical department	Eiseibu	衛生部
Dental*	Shika	齒科

*Items marked with an asterisk apply to officer personnel only.

2. ARMS AND SERVICES—Continued.

Military term	Japanese equivalent	Character
Medical Department—Continued.		
Pharmacy*	Yakuzai	薬剤
Sanitary	Eisei	衛生
Surgeon*	Gun-i	軍醫
Ward master	Ryōkō	療工
Medium artillery	Yasen jūhōhei	野戰重砲兵
Meteorological troops	Kishōhei	氣象兵
Military band	Gungakubu	軍樂部
Military police	Kempei	憲兵
Mountain (pack) artillery troops.	Sampōhei	山砲兵
Railway troops	Tetsudōhei	鐵道兵
Services	Kakubu	各部
Shipping troops	Sempakuhei	船舶兵
Signal*	Denshin	電信
Signal troops	Tsūshinhei	通信兵
Special motor transport.*	Tokuji	特自
Tank troops	Senshahei	戰車兵
Technical department	Gijutsubu	技術部
Technician	Heigi	兵技
Air technician	Kōgi	航技
Transport troops	Shichōhei	輜重兵
Veterinary department	Jūibu	獣醫部
Veterinary	Jūi	獣醫
Veterinary duty	Jūimu	獣醫務

*Items marked with an asterisk apply to officer personnel only.

3. RANKS AND GRADES.

Military term	Japanese equivalent	Character
Field marshal	Gensui	元帥
General officer	Shōkan	將官
General	Taishō	大將
Lieutenant general	Chūjō	中將
Major general	Shōshō	少將
Field officer	Sakan	佐官
Colonel	Taisa	大佐
Lieutenant colonel	Chūsa	中佐
Major	Shōsa	少佐
Company officer	Ikan	尉官
Captain	Tai-i	大尉
First lieutenant	Chū-i	中尉
Second lieutenant	Shō-i	少尉
Warrant officer	Junshikan	准士官
Warrant officer	Jun-i	准尉
Noncommissioned officer	Kashikan	下士官
Sergeant major	Sōchō	曹長
Sergeant	Gunsō	軍曹
Corporal	Gochō	伍長
Private	Hei	兵
Lance corporal (leading private).	Heichō	兵長
Superior private	Jōtōhei	上等兵
First class private	Ittōhei	一等兵
Second class private	Nitōhei	二等兵

4. WEAPONS—Continued.

Military term	Japanese equivalent	Character
Mountain gun	Sampō	山砲
Pistol	Kenjū	拳銃
Regimental gun	Rentaihō	聯隊砲
Rifle	Shōjū	小銃

5. MISCELLANEOUS.

Military term	Japanese equivalent	Character
Adjutant	Fukkan	副官
Assistant chief of staff	Sambō fukuchō	参謀副長
Attached, army headquarters	Gun shireibu zuki	軍司令部附
Chief of General Staff	Sambō sōchō	参謀総長
A chief of staff	Sambōchō	参謀長
Combat train	Shōkōri	小行李
Conscription system	Chōhei seido	徴兵制度
Field train	Daikōri	大行李
Greater East Asia War	Dai Tōa Sen	大東亜戦
Imperial Reservists Association	Teikoku Zaigō Gunjinkai	帝国在郷軍人会
Military administrator	Gunseikan	軍政官
Military service	Hei-eki	兵役
Operational order	Sakusen meirei	作戦命令
Prisoner of war	Furyo	俘虜
Prisoner of war internment camp	Furyo shūyōjo	俘虜収容所
Probational officer	Minarai shikan	見習士官
Promotion	Shinkyū	進級

4. WEAPONS.

Military term	Japanese equipment	Character
Antiaircraft gun	Kōshahō	高射砲
Antiaircraft machine cannon	Kōsha kikanhō	高射機関砲
Antiaircraft machine gun	Kōsha kikanjū	高射機関銃
Antitank gun	Sokushahō	速射砲
Automatic gun	Jidōhō	自動砲
Battalion gun	Daitaihō	大隊砲
Bayonet	Jūken	銃剣
Cannon	Kanon	加農
Carbine	Kijū	騎銃
Field gun	Yahō	野砲
Grenade discharger	Tekidantō	擲弾筒
Heavy	Jūtekidantō	重擲弾筒
Hand grenade	Shuryūdan	手榴弾
Howitzer	Ryūdampō	榴弾砲
Infantry gun	Hoheihō	歩兵砲
Flat trajectory	Heisha hoheihō	平射歩兵砲
Curved fire	Kyokusha hoheihō	曲射歩兵砲
Infantry mortar	Hakugekihō	迫撃砲
Machine cannon	Kikanhō	機関砲
Machine gun	Kikanjū	機関銃
Heavy	Jūkikanjū	重機関銃
Light	Keikikanjū	軽機関銃
Mortar (artillery)	Kyūhō	臼砲

6. JAPANESE-ENGLISH—Continued.

Military term	English equivalent
Dokuritsu—Continued.	
—jidōsha daitai (chūtai)	Independent motor transport battalion (company).
—jūhōhei daitai (chūtai)	Independent heavy artillery battalion (company).
	Independent light armored car company.
—keisōkōsha chūtai	
—kōhei daitai (chūtai, rentai)	Independent engineer battalion (company, regiment).
—konsei rentai	Independent mixed regiment.
—konsei ryodan	Independent mixed brigade.
—kōshahō daitai	Independent antiaircraft artillery battalion.
—kyūhō daitai (rentai)	Independent mortar battalion (regiment).
—sampōhei daitai (rentai)	Independent mountain (pack) artillery battalion (regiment).
—shichōhei daitai (chūtai, rentai)	Independent transport battalion (company, regiment).
—shubitai	Independent garrison.
—sōkōsha chūtai	Independent armored car company.
—yahōhei daitai (rentai)	Independent field artillery battalion (regiment).
—yasen kōshaho chūtai	Independent field antiaircraft artillery company.
—yasen shōkū chūtai	Independent field searchlight company.
—yūsen chūtai	Independent wire company.
Eiseibu	Medical department.
Eiseitai	Medical unit.
Fukkan	Adjutant.
Furyo	Prisoner of war.
—shūyōjo	Prisoner of war internment camp.
Gakyō zairyō chūtai	Bridge building material company.
Gasu daitai	Gas battalion.
Gensui	Field marshal.
—fu	Board of Field Marshals and Fleet Admirals.
Gijutsubu	Technical department.
Gochō	Corporal.
Gumba bōekishō	Veterinary quarantine hospital.
Gun	Army.
—shireibu	Army headquarters.
—shireibu zuki	Attached, army headquarters.
—shireikan	Army commander.
Gun-i	Surgeon.
Gunji Sangiin	Supreme Military Council.
Gungakubu	Military band.
Gunkanku	Army district.
Gunseikan	Military administrator.
Gunsō	Sergeant.
Hakugeki daitai (rentai)	Infantry mortar battalion (regiment).
Hakugekihei	Infantry mortar troops.
Hakugekihō	Infantry mortar.

5. MISCELLANEOUS—Continued.

Military term	Japanese equivalent	Character	English equivalent
Reserve officer candidate	Kambu kōhosei	幹部候補生	
Routine order	Nichi nichi meirei	日日命令	
Special volunteer officer	Tokubetsu shigan shōkō.	特別志願将校	
Staff officer	Sambō	参謀	
Yasukuni Shrine	Yasukuni Jinja	靖國神社	

6. JAPANESE-ENGLISH.

Military term	English equivalent
Bōei Sōshireibu	General Defense Headquarters.
Bōeki kyūsuibu	Water supply and purification department.
Bōkū	Antiaircraft defense.
—kanshitai	Antiaircraft defense observation unit.
—kikyūtai	Antiaircraft defense ballon unit.
—rentai	Antiaircraft defense regiment.
Bōkūhei	Antiaircraft defense troops.
Buntai	Squad.
—chō	Squad leader.
Byōin	Hospital.
Chōhei seido	Conscription system.
Chokkyō hikōtai	Direct co-operation air unit.
Chū-i	First lieutenant.
Chūjō	Lieutenant general.
Chūsa	Lieutenant colonel.
Chūtai	Company.
—chō	Company commander.
Dai Tōa Sen	Greater East Asia War.
Daihonei	Imperial Headquarters.
Daikōri	Field train.
Daitai	Battalion.
—chō	Battalion commander.
—hō	Battalion gun.
—hombu	Battalion headquarters.
Denshin	Signal.
—rentai (tai)	Signal regiment (unit).
Dokuritsu	Independent.
—bōku daitai	Independent antiaircraft defense battalion.
—denshin chūtai	Independent signal company.
—gasu chūtai	Independent gas company.
—hikō chūtai (tai)	Independent air company (unit).
—hohei daitai (rentai, tai)	Independent infantry battalion (regiment, unit).

6. JAPANESE-ENGLISH—Continued.

Military term	English equivalent
Han	Detail.
Hansui sagyōtai	Launching unit (boat).
Hei	Private.
Heichō	Lance corporal (leading private).
Hei-eki	Military service.
Heigi	Technician.
Heijiku	Military affairs district.
Heika	Line branch.
Heisha hoheihō	Flat trajectory infantry gun.
Heishu	Branch of service.
Heitan	Line of communication.
—byōbashō	Line of communication veterinary hospital.
—byōin	Line of communication hospital.
—eiseitai	Line of communication medical unit.
—jidōsha chūtai (tai)	Line of communication motor transport company (unit.)
—shubitai	Line of communication garrison.
Hikō	Air.
—chūtai	Air company.
—dan	Air brigade.
—sentai	Air regiment.
—shidan	Air division.
Hikōhei	Air troops.
Hikōjō	Airfield.
—daitai (chūtai)	Airfield battalion (company).
Hohei	Infantry.
—daitai	Infantry battalion.
—dan	Infantry group.
—hō	Infantry gun.
—rentai	Infantry regiment.
—ryodan	Infantry brigade.
Hōhei	Artillery.
—dan	Artillery group.
—jōhō rentai	Artillery intelligence (observation) regiment.
—shireibu	Artillery command.
—tai	Artillery unit.
Hojūtai	Replacement unit.
Hōmengun	Area army.
Hōmubu	Judicial department.
Ikan	Company officer.
Ittōhei	First class private.
Jidōhō	Automatic gun.
Jidōsha rentai (tai)	Motor transport regiment (unit).
Jōhōhei	Intelligence (observation) troops.
Jōtōhei	Superior private.
Jūhōhei	Heavy artillery.
—rentai	Heavy artillery regiment.
Jūi	Veterinary.
Jūimu	Veterinary duty.
Jūibu	Veterinary department.

6. JAPANESE-ENGLISH—Continued.

Military term	English equivalent
Jūken	Bayonet.
Jūkikanjū	Heavy machine gun.
Jun-i	Warrant officer.
Junshikan	Warrant officer (grade).
Jūtekidantō	Heavy grenade discharger.
Kahei	Chemical warfare service.
Kaijō kidō daitai	Amphibious battalion.
Kaijō yusō kanshitai	Sea transport observation unit.
Kanja yusōbu	Casualty clearing station.
Kakubu	Services.
Kanon	Cannon.
Kashikan	Noncommissioned officer.
Keigi	Intendance technician.
Keikikanjū	Light machine gun.
Keiribu	Intendance department.
Kempei	Military police.
Kenchiku kimmu chūtai	Construction duty company.
Kengi	Construction technician.
Keninsha	Tractor.
—chūtai	Tractor company.
Kenjū	Pistol.
Kihei	Cavalry.
—daitai	Cavalry battalion.
—rentai	Cavalry regiment.
—ryodan	Cavalry brigade.
—shidan	Cavalry group.
Kihōhei	Horse artillery.
—rentai	Horse artillery regiment.
Kijū	Carbine.
Kikanhō	Machine cannon.
Kikanjū	Machine gun.
Kikō	Mechanized.
Kikyū	Balloon.
—chūtai	Balloon company.
Kikyūhei	Balloon troops.
Kishō chūtai (rentai, tai)	Meteorological company (regiment, unit).
Kishōhei	Meteorological troops.
Kōgi	Air technician.
Kōhei	Engineers.
—rentai	Engineer regiment.
—tai	Engineer unit.
Kokkyō shubitai	Border garrison.
Kōkū	Air.
—jōhōtai	Air intelligence unit.
—tsūshintai	Air signal unit.
—yusōtai	Air transport unit.
—gun	Air army.
Kōsha kikanhō	Antiaircraft machine cannon.
Kōsha kikanjū	Antiaircraft machine gun.
Kōshahō	Antiaircraft artillery.
—rentai (tai)	Antiaircraft artillery regiment (unit).
Kotei musentai	Fixed radio unit.

6. JAPANESE-ENGLISH—Continued.

Military term	English equivalent
Kotei tsūshintai	Fixed signal unit.
Kyōdō hikōdan	Air training brigade.
Kyōdō hikōjō daitai	Airfield training battalion.
Kyōdō teishin rentai	Raiding training regiment.
Kyōiku hikō chūtai	Air training company.
Kyōiku Sōkambu	Inspectorate General of Military Training.
Kyokusha hoheihō	Curved fire infantry gun.
Kyūhō	Mortar (artillery).
Minarai shikan	Probational officer.
Musen	Radio.
Nichi nichi meirei	Routine order.
Nitōhei	Second class private.
Rentai	Regiment.
—chō	Regimental commander.
—hō	Regimental gun.
—hombu	Regimental headquarters.
—ku	Regimental district.
Rikugun byōin	Army hospital.
Rikugun Kōkū Sōkambu	Inspectorate General of Aviation.
Rikugunshō	War Ministry.
Rikujō kimmu chūtai	Land duty company.
Rusu shidan	Depot division.
Ryodan	Brigade.
—chō	Brigade commander.
—shireibu	Brigade headquarters.
Ryōkō	Ward master.
Ryūdampō	Howitzer.
Sakan	Field officer.
Sakusen meirei	Operational order.
Sambō	Staff officer.
—chō	A chief of staff.
—fukuchō	Assistant chief of staff.
Sambō Hombu	General Staff.
Sambō Sōchō	Chief of General Staff.
Sampō	Mountain gun.
Sampōhei	Mountain (pack) artillery troops.
—rentai	Mountain (pack) artillery regiment.
Sempaku	Shipping.
—heidan	Shipping forces.
—hōhei rentai kyōikutai	Shipping artillery regiment training unit.
—kōhei rentai	Shipping engineer regiment.
—kōshahō rentai	Shipping antiaircraft artillery regiment.
—shireibu	Shipping command.
—tsūshin rentai	Shipping signal regiment.
—yusō chikutai	Shipping transport sector unit.
—yusō daitai	Shipping transport battalion.
—yusō shireibu	Shipping transport command.
Sempakuhei	Shipping troops.
Sensha	Tank.
—dan	Tank group.
—rentai	Tank regiment.

6. JAPANESE-ENGLISH—Continued.

Military term	English equivalent
Sensha—Continued.	
—tai	Tank unit.
Senshahei	Tank troops.
Shichōhei	Transport troops.
—rentai (tai)	Transport regiment (unit).
Shidan	Division.
—chō	Division commander.
—shireibu	Division headquarters.
Shika	Dental.
Shikan	Division district.
Shinkyū	Promotion.
Shō	Depot.
Shō-i	Second lieutenant.
Shōjū	Rifle.
Shōkan	General officer.
Shōkōri	Combat train.
Shōkū daitai	Searchlight battalion.
Shōsa	Major.
Shōshō	Major general.
Shōtai	Platoon.
—chō	Platoon commander.
Shubitai	Garrison.
Shukei	Finance.
Shuryūdan	Hand grenade.
Sōchō	Sergeant major.
Sōkō ressha	Armored train.
Sōkō resshatai	Armored train unit.
Sōkōsha	Armored car.
Sokuryōtai	Survey unit.
Sokushahō	Antitank gun.
—tai	Antitank gun unit.
Sōsaku	Reconnaissance.
—rentai (tai)	Reconnaissance regiment (unit).
Suijō kimmu chūtai	Sea duty company.
Tai-i	Captain.
Taisa	Colonel.
Taishō	General.
Teikoku Zaigō Gunjinkai	Imperial Reservists Association.
Teishin	Raiding.
—dan	Raiding group.
—hikō chūtai	Raiding air company.
—rentai	Raiding regiment.
Tekidantō	Grenade discharger.
Tetsudō	Railway.
—kambu	Railway inspectorate.
—rentai	Railway regiment.
—yusō shireibu	Railway transport command.
Tetsudōhei	Railway troops.
Toka zairyō chūtai	River crossing material company.
Tokubetsu shigan shōkō	Special volunteer officer.
Tokuji	Special motor transport.
Tokusetsu jidōsha rentai	Special motor transport regiment.

6. JAPANESE-ENGLISH—Continued.

Military term	English equivalent
Tokusetsu tetsudō shireibu	Special railway command.
Tokushu musen hyōteitai	Special radio location unit.
Tokushu musentai	Special radio unit.
Tsūshin	Signal.
—tai	Signal unit.
Tsūshinhei	Signal troops.
Yahō	Field gun.
Yahōhei	Field artillery.
—rentai	Field artillery regiment.
Yakuzai	Pharmacy.
Yasampō	Field and mountain artillery.
Yasen	Field.
—bōkūtai	Field antiaircraft defense unit.
—byōin	Field hospital.
—denshin chūtai	Field signal company.
—dōrotai	Field road unit.
gasu chūtai	Field gas company.
—heikishō	Field ordnance depot.
—hikōjō setteitai	Field airfield construction unit.
—hojū bashō	Field remount depot.

6. JAPANESE-ENGLISH—Continued.

Military term	English equivalent
Yasen—Continued.	
—hojū hikōtai	Field air replacement unit.
—hojūtai	Field replacement unit.
—jidōshashō	Field motor transport depot.
—jūhōhei	Medium artillery.
—kamotsushō	Field freight depot.
—kenchikutai	Field construction unit.
—kikanhō chūtai	Field machine cannon company.
—kimmutai	Field duty unit.
—kishō daitai (tai)	Field meteorological battalion (unit).
—kōshahō daitai	Field antiaircraft artillery battalion.
—sakusei chūtai	Field well-construction company.
—shōkū daitai	Field searchlight battalion.
—tetsudō shireibu	Field railway command.
Yasukuni Jinja	Yasukuni Shrine.
Yōrikudan (tai)	Debarkation group (unit).
Yōsai	Fortress.
—jūhōhei rentai	Fortress heavy artillery regiment.
—shireibu	Fortress headquarters.
Yūsen	Wire.

APPENDIX

Supplemental data

1. JAPANESE YEAR DATES.

Year of Meiji	Year of our Lord
1st	1868
2d	1869
3d	1870
4th	1871
5th	1872
6th	1873
7th	1874
8th	1875
9th	1876
10th	1877
11th	1878
12th	1879
13th	1880
14th	1881
15th	1882
16th	1883
17th	1884
18th	1885
19th	1886
20th	1887
21st	1888
22d	1889
23d	1890
24th	1891
25th	1892
26th	1893
27th	1894
28th	1895
29th	1896
30th	1897
31st	1898
32d	1899
33d	1900
34th	1901
35th	1902
36th	1903
37th	1904
38th	1905
39th	1906
40th	1907
41st	1908
42d	1909
43d	1910
44th	1911
45th	
Year of Taisho	1912
1st	
2d	1913
3d	1914
4th	1915
5th	1916
6th	1917
7th	1918
8th	1919
9th	1920
10th	1921
11th	1922
12th	1923
13th	1924
14th	1925
15th	
Year of Showa	1926
1st	
2d	1927
3d	1928
4th	1929
5th	1930
6th	1931

Year of Showa	Year of our Lord
7th	1932
8th	1933
9th	1934
10th	1935
11th	1936
12th	1937
13th	1938
14th	1939
15th	1940
16th	1941
17th	1942
18th	1943
19th	1944

NOTE. When Japanese year dates are given the year may be found as follows:

In the Meiji period, add the Japanese year date to 1867.
In the Taisho period, add the Japanese year date to 1911.
In the Showa (present) period, add the Japanese year date to 1925.

For example Meiji 13 is 1880, Taisho 13 is 1924, and Showa 13 is 1938.

2. JAPANESE WEIGHTS, MEASURES, AND MONEYS. a. Distance and Length.

Ri=36 chō=2,160 ken=2.4403 miles=3.92727 kilometers.

Ri (marine)=1 nautical mile=1.85319 kilometers.

Ken=6 shaku=60 sun=5.965163 feet=1.81818 meters.

Shaku=10 sun=100 bu=0.994194 feet=0.30303 meter.

Shaku (cloth measure)=1.25 shaku.

Tan (cloth measure)=a roll of about 25 shaku.

b. Land measure.

Square ri=1,296 square chō=5.95516 square miles=15.52345 square kilometers.

Chō (area)=10 tan=3,000 tsubo=2.45065 acres=99.17355 ares.

Tsubo or bu=3.95369 square yards=3.30579 centiares.

Ko (Formosa)=2,934 tsubo.

c. Quantity, capacity, and cubic measures.

$$Koku=10 \ to=100 \ sho= \begin{cases} 4.96005 & \text{bushels} \\ 47.65389 & \text{gallons} \\ & \text{(liquid) U. S. A.} \\ 5.11902 & \text{bushels} \\ & \text{(dry) U. S. A.} \end{cases} =1.80391 \text{ hectoliters.}$$

Go=10th of a sho.
Koku (capacity of vessels)=10th of a shipping ton.
Koku (timber)=about 1 by 1 by 10 feet.
Koku (fish)=40 kwan (in weight).
Shakujime (timber)=about 1 by 1 by 12 feet.
Taba (fagot, etc.)=about 3 by 6 by 6 feet.

d. Weights.

$$Kwan \ (kan)=1,000 \ momme= \begin{cases} 8.26733 & \text{pounds avoirdupois} \\ 10.04711 & \text{pounds troy} \end{cases} =3.75000 \text{ kilograms.}$$

$$Kin=160 \ momme= \begin{cases} 1.32277 & \text{pounds avoirdupois} \\ 1.60754 & \text{pounds troy} \end{cases} =0.60000 \text{ kilograms.}$$

$$Momme=10 \ fun= \begin{cases} 0.13228 & \text{ounce avoirdupois} \\ 0.12057 & \text{ounce troy} \end{cases} =3.75000 \text{ grams.}$$

e. Moneys.

Yen (¥) = 100 sen = 1,000 rin = $\begin{cases} 0.49846 \text{ U. S. dollars (at par).} \\ 0.23196 \text{ U. S. dollars (average rate of exchange, November 1941).} \end{cases}$

3. METHOD OF NUMBERING MODELS.

a. Before 1926 the model number of weapons and equipment was indicated by the year of the reign in which the model was adopted. Since 1926 the model has been numbered from what is assumed to be the date of the founding of the Japanese Empire. The last two digits of this number are used up to the year 1940. Models adopted in 1940 are simply designated as "0" (Zero). Models adopted in 1941 are designated "1" and so on.

b. A comparative table indicating the western year, the Japanese year, and the model number corresponding thereto follows:

Western year	Japanese year	Model No.	Western year	Japanese year	Model No.
1930	2590	90	1938	2598	98
1931	2591	91	1939	2599	99
1932	2592	92	1940	2600	0
1933	2593	93	1941	2601	1
1934	2594	94	1942	2602	2
1935	2595	95	1943	2603	3
1936	2596	96	1944	2604	4
1937	2597	97			

c. This method of marking equipment is in general use in both the Army and the Navy for numbering types of equipment, including airplanes, tanks, pieces of ordnance, etc.

○

AFTERWORD: THE PACIFIC AIR WAR

When Japan invaded China in July 1937 the American view of Asian technology was hopelessly jaundiced. The prevailing wisdom held that Japanese aircraft and engines were merely poor copies of U.S. designs, and therefore not worth considering as advanced weapons. In spite of the warnings sent back to the U.S. from men like Claire Chennault, the majority of American planners refused to believe reports of superior aircraft being available to this potential enemy.

The opening month of the war was a terrible shock to American aircrews and commanders. Not only had most of the Pacific Fleet been sunk by air power on December 7, 1941, but the Mitsubishi A6M Zero-Sen fighter and G4M bomber were complete surprises, in spite of the Zero entering combat over China in August 1940, followed by the G4M in May 1941. The British capital ships HMS *Repulse* and HMS *Prince of Wales* were sunk by G4Ms and G3Ms on December 10, 1941, after sailing with no air cover. The Allies not only thought the land-based bombers to be carrier-launched, but incredulous Western observers insisted that German pilots flew this 'special mission' for their Axis partners.

This attitude was compounded by the racially motivated perception of the Japanese pilot as a buck-toothed idiot with thick glasses and speaking hopelessly broken English. In reality, Japanese Naval aviators of 1941 were among the finest pilots in the world. Their training was so rigorous that only a very small percentage of hopefuls graduated from flying school with the cream going to fighter units.

The combination of the Zero and its pilot was close to unmatched for a full year after Pearl Harbor. U.S. Army P-39 and P-40, and Navy F4F pilots held the fort against desperate odds, finding the Zero's maneuverability stunning. Using Chennault's dive and slash attack method, and Jimmy Thatch's weave, Americans managed to break even with their adversaries by avoiding the close-in dogfight. The only Allied fighter capable of fighting the Zero on even terms was the Spitfire but there were far too few in the Pacific to make a difference.

With the introduction of the P-38 Lightning in December 1942, the F4U Corsair in February 1943 and the F6F Hellcat in August 1943, the tide of the air war rapidly turned. American technology and training caught up with a vengeance. Not only were the new fighters faster than the Zero, but they retained the virtues of heavy armor protection and withering firepower. Even so, though dogfighting was still not recommended, an experienced American could twist and turn with a good Zero pilot.

Though Japanese Army Air Force pilots flying Nakajima Ki-43 Hayabusa fighters were not as highly trained as their naval counterparts, they gave the Allies a rough time for the first part of the war as well. The small Ki-43 was extremely maneuverable and, as with the Zero, had little armor protection in order to keep the aircraft light. The Japanese, irrationally, expected their moral superiority and disciplined training would never allow the Emperor's pilots to get attacked from the rear . . . therefore, no need for protective armor or self-sealing fuel tanks.

Japanese aircraft industry had a number of excellent designs in testing, but the Zero and the Hayabusa remained the war's mainstays well into 1944, unable to meet increasing Allied superiority on even terms. In addition, as Japan lost its best pilots, the training pipeline could not maintain the previous level of quality and the tables reversed even more dramatically. Allied fighter pilots, flying the P-47 and P-51 as well, roamed China and the Pacific at will by the end of 1944.

The Japanese found their bomber force to be relatively ineffective as well, particularly compared to what the Americans were introducing. Though the Japanese Aichi D3A and American Douglas SBD carrier dive bombers entered the war basically obsolete, they were quite effective for the first year. After that newer types entered combat but nothing changed as far as vulnerability . . . the same held true for the newer torpedo bombers. Fighter cover was a necessity.

The twin engined G4M remained the major land-based Japanese bomber of the war, hopelessly outmoded by 1944. Though the Americans used the B-17 in the Pacific, the B-24, B-25 and B-29 brought the fury of air power to all corners of the theater, and eventually across the Japanese homeland itself. Nothing could be done to stop the Allied onslaught.

New Japanese fighters such as the Ki-84 Hayate, N1K1 Shiden, J2M Raiden, Ki-44 Shoki and Ki-61 Hien were excellent counterparts to their American adversaries, equal in most respects, but they had been given too little priority in replacing the Zero and Hayabusa until it was too late. By 1945 Allied pilots could choose combat at will, eagerly looking for prey, confident of victory. While Japanese pilots could still put on impressive displays of frantic aerobatics, they were poorly trained in fighter tactics and thus became so much cannon fodder in the famous American aces races that took place during the last two years of World War II.

Jeffrey L. Ethell
Front Royal, Va., 1991